FRENCH TRAGEDY

IN THE TIME OF
LOUIS XV AND VOLTAIRE

1715-1774

FRENCH TRAGEDY

IN THE TIME OF
LOUIS XV AND VOLTAIRE
1715—1774

BY

HENRY CARRINGTON LANCASTER

Professor of French Literature in The Johns Hopkins University

IN TWO VOLUMES

———

VOLUME I

———

THE JOHNS HOPKINS PRESS
BALTIMORE, MARYLAND

LONDON: GEOFFREY CUMBERLEGE
OXFORD UNIVERSITY PRESS

LES BELLES-LETTRES, PARIS

1950

PRINTED IN THE UNITED STATES OF AMERICA
BY J. H. FURST COMPANY, BALTIMORE, MARYLAND

22423

TO MY GRANDCHILDREN:

KATHLEEN LANDIS LANCASTER   CHARLES FREDERICK RAND

CINDY KEEHN LANCASTER

CONTENTS

VOLUME I

FOREWORD

This work is a sequel to my *History of French Dramatic Literature in the Seventeenth Century* and *Sunset, a History of Parisian Drama in the Last Years of Louis XIV*. As it was started before the war was over, at a time when it was uncertain how soon normal relations with French libraries and publishers would be reestablished, I selected tragedy, as the kind of play most readily accessible, and limited my study to that of tragedies acted at the Comédie Française, almost the only Parisian theater where they could be produced. The fact that I am concerned with only one *genre* made it possible to cover a longer period than I could have done if I had included comedy, farce, and *drame*. In the case of five tragedies I have slightly exceeded the time limit set, that of May, 1774, in order to include Voltaire's last two tragedies, acted in 1778-9, and tragedies by de Belloy, Lemierre, and Dorat, which, though written some time before 1774, were not acted at Paris until after the death of Louis XV.

After the first chapter, which concerns the circumstances under which plays were given, the material is divided largely in accordance with the time when the tragedies were acted. As Voltaire was composing plays throughout most of his long life, six chapters are devoted to him, four exclusively, two largely. A chapter is assigned almost entirely to La Motte; another to Lemierre. One is concerned exclusively with de Belloy, one with Marmontel and Saurin. As the other authors wrote little, the tragedies of three or more are discussed in each of the remaining chapters. At times the dates indicated in the chapter headings are exceeded in order to complete the study of an author. A chapter of conclusions, a list of tragedies discussed, supplemenetary notes on earlier books, and two indices complete the volumes.

My method of discussing authors and plays is the same as that employed in my other literary histories except that I have been able to cite a larger amount of criticism from contemporary or nearly contemporary writers than heretofore, for the reason that the material is much more abundant than it is in earlier periods; and that, in contrast with my work on the seventeenth century before 1689, I have been able to acquire extensive information about the actors and the production of plays. This last fact is due to my securing, thanks to the generosity of the Modern Language Association of America and the kindness of the Comédie Française, reproductions on film of the actors' business records.

These records are complete except for the year that runs from Easter, 1739, to Easter, 1740, and for the months of February and March, 1759. They tell what play or plays were given on each day, what was the number of persons paying admission, in most cases the author's share in the receipts, and they name the actors who performed.[1] They also make known from time to time other items of interest. Further information about the theater has been obtained from the publications of Bonnassies and from the *Almanach des Spectacles,* sometimes from contemporary journalists and critics.

For the actors we have, in addition to the works just mentioned, the *Dictionnaire* of Lyonnet, the writings of Georges Monval, Campardon, Jal, and J.-J. Olivier, the memoirs of Le Kain, Mlle Dumesnil, and Mlle Clairon, Young's life of Baron, three books devoted to Garrick and his French colleagues, and, of course, the *Biographie universelle* and the *Biographie générale.*

The tragedies given at the Comédie Française have been listed by Joannidès and recently by C. D. Brenner. Information about them was given in the eighteenth century by such writers as the frères Parfaict, Beauchamps, Léris, and the compilers of the *Bibliothèque du théâtre fran-çois,* subsequently by Quérard and by Paul Lacroix in his *Catalogue de la bibliothèque dramatique de M. de Soleinne.* The writers who flourished in the eighteenth century and expressed their opinions about the tragedies discussed below are chiefly Dangeau, Mathieu Marais, La Motte, Voltaire, Mauger, de Belloy, Diderot, Rousseau, Grimm, Raynal, the abbé Le Blanc, Van Swieten, Marmontel, Collé, Bachaumont, Fréron, and La Harpe. All of these have been quoted as well as the *Mercure,* the *Journal des Savants,* the *Journal Encyclopédique,* and the *Journal étranger.*

Among the contributions of contemporary authors that I have examined are Lanson's *Esquisse,* Gaiffe's work on *drame,* publications on parody by Van Roosbroeck, Grannis, and Lindsay, Brenner's essay on national themes in French tragedy, Alfreda Hill's *Tudors in French Drama,* works by

---

[1] When a new tragedy is given alone, the complete list of players can be determined. Unfortunately in January, 1722, the custom was adopted of having a short comedy follow a new tragedy, so that one cannot always tell whether an actor played in the tragedy or in the comedy. However, if his name reappears on five or six days when the tragedy was given, each time with a different comedy, it is highly probable that he played in the tragedy.

Louis Bourquin, M. M. Moffat, and others on the controversy over the morality of the stage, the books of Ferrari and Coe on adaptations and translations of French tragedies in Italy and Spain.

Though the work on tragedy as a whole in the time of Louis XV has been confined largely to hurried discussions in histories of literature, a good deal of work has been done on individual authors. I may mention for Voltaire the bibliography of M. M. Barr; the edition of *Zaïre* by Fontaine and others, the edition of *Sémiramis* by Fuchs; articles by Gaiffe, Pinot, Jordans, Krappe, P. G. Adams, Perkins, Constans, and others; for relations with English literature, the books or articles of Jusserand, Lounsbury, Dubedout, T. W. Russell, and especially the extensive study by Henri Lion, the bibliographical work of Bengesco, and the essential edition of Moland. Crébillon has been discussed by Dutrait; La Motte, by Dupont; La Grange-Chancel, by Nietzelt; Le Blanc, by Mme Monod-Cassidy; Marivaux, by Deschamps; Boissy, by Zeek; Piron, by Rigoley de Juvigny; Nivelle de la Chaussée, by Lanson; François Tronchin, by Henri Tronchin; La Place, by Lillian Cobb; Morand, by Paul d'Estrée; Mme Du Boccage, by Grace Gill-Mark; Marmontel, by Lenel; Palissot, by Delafarge; de Belloy, by Gaillard; Dorat, by Courtines; Sauvigny, by Wade and Chinard; Ducis, by Jusserand.

I would express my warmest thanks for assistance to the management of the Comédie Française and that of the Modern Language Association of America, and to the librarians of the Arsenal, Bibliothèque Nationale, the Folger Shakespeare Library, The Johns Hopkins University, the Library of Congress, New York University, the Peabody Library, Princeton University, and the University of Michigan; also, for financial assistance in the preparation of this work, to the Rockefeller Fund for Research in the Humanities.

Those who are interested in the question of why *genres*, like empires, decay may find in these volumes material for thought. How was the type of play established by Corneille and Racine carried on by their successors? Is there a steady decline, or are there ebbs and flows? Can a man of genius like Voltaire save the kind of play he cherished? What external influences were exerted to weaken the structure? What was the influence of Shakespeare and other English dramatists? What of Italians, Spaniards, Germans? What internal causes were there that led ultimately to the substitution of romantic for classical tragedy? To what extent was tragedy used for propaganda connected with the catastrophe that lay ahead for the Ancien Régime? Is there human interest in the productions of a society that was composed, like ours, of some who held desperately to tradition and of others who propagated ideas, while hoping for or fearing what might lie around the corner? These and other questions I will attempt to answer.[2]

[2] The following special abbreviations are employed below:

Beauchamps: *Recherches sur les théâtres de France*, 1735.

Bengesco: *Voltaire. Bibliographie de ses œuvres*, 1882-90.

Bib. du th. fr.: *Bibliothèque du théâtre françois*, 1768.

Cor.: *Correspondance littéraire, philosophique et critique par Grimm, Diderot, Raynal, Meister, etc.*, 1877-82.

History: Lancaster, *A History of French Dramatic Literature in the Seventeenth Century*, 1929-42.

Jal: Auguste Jal, *Dictionnaire critique de biographie et d'histoire*, 1867.

Léris: *Dictionnaire portatif*, 1763.

Moland: *Œuvres complètes de Voltaire*, 1883-5.

Parfaict, frères: *Histoire du théâtre françois*, 1734-49.

Quérard: *La France littéraire*, 1827-64.

Registres: the business records of the Comédie Française.

Soleinne: Paul Lacroix, *Catalogue de la Bibliothèque dramatique de M. de Soleinne*, 1843-4.

Sunset: Lancaster, *Sunset, a History of Parisian Drama in the Last Years of Louis XIV*, 1945.

CHAPTER I

PATRONS, CRITICS, AND ACTORS

If French tragedy did not rise in the eighteenth century to the heights it had attained in the seventeenth, it was not because of war, economic conditions, or lack of distinguished and well organized actors. The wars of Louis XV's reign offered no parallel to the Fronde, nor was Paris ever in danger of capture by the enemy. As in the preceding century, the theater entertained warriors during the winter season. To a certain extent with Voltaire, but chiefly with de Belloy, tragedy became a medium for recalling the heroic deeds of earlier Frenchmen. The loss of Canada and of India was followed by the production of *Hirza ou les Illinois* and *la Veuve du Malabar,* tragedies that gave examples of French courage in conflict with Indians, both American and Asiatic, while *le Siège de Calais* became in the hands of the government an instrument of propaganda.

Nor did the bursting of Law's bubble or other financial disasters close the theater. However many paupers there may have been, there were always persons who could afford to become spectators at the Comédie Française. Even when the troupe was in financial difficulties, individual members of it appear not to have been seriously affected. Some of the leaders were quite prosperous. Nor do we hear that the production of tragedies suffered to any appreciable extent from their authors' lack of funds.

A few months after Louis XIV died, the Regent moved the court to the Tuileries and had the actors come there, or to the Louvre, or give plays, usually on Wednesdays, or Thursdays, at the Palais Royal, which had been occupied since Molière's death by the troupe of the Opera. In 1722 the young king returned to Versailles and took up once more his great-grandfather's stately routine. The actors then gave performances there as they had done early in the century and in autumn, sometimes earlier in the year, followed the court to Fontainebleau.

Louis XV occasionally allowed a play to be dedicated to him. He continued the subsidy to the troupe, contributed to the expenses of certain tragedies, and honored court performances with his presence, sometimes favoring an actor or objecting to the performance of too gloomy a play. His illness at Metz found an echo in a tragedy. Damiens's attempt upon his life occasioned the temporary closing of the theater. Lemierre praised his rule in the *Veuve du Malabar*. But such tributes did not win him

1

altogether. He was unwilling to improve the status of actors when he was asked to do so,[1] and he maintained the censorship of plays that his predecessor had established.

This restraint was probably rendered less severe by the fact that several of the censors were dramatists,[2] but even so a number of tragedies had to be altered or their production postponed.[3] In one case [4] the censor went to the Bastille because he failed to catch a remark that might be interpreted as a slur upon Louis XV. In another the ecclesiastic who had examined the text was reproved, and the tragedy, though acted, could be published only in secret.[5]

What was more irritating than the censor was the constant domination of the troupe by the four Gentlemen of the Chamber. La Noue was locked up for venturing to criticize one of their decisions, and several prominent actors were incarcerated in the affair of Dubois and the *Siège de Calais*.[6] There was also interference from such great ladies as the duchesse de Berry and the Regent's mother. To the latter Voltaire dedicated his first tragedy. Years later he dedicated *l'Orphelin de la Chine* to Mme de Pompadour, as did Crébillon his *Catilina*. Nor were the queen, the Regent, and other Bourbons forgotten. Their influence must have tended to keep the authors from wandering far from the beaten track, unless they had the resourcefulness of Voltaire and a few other " philosophes."

But interest in tragedy as shown by the duchesse du Maine and later by Mme de Pompadour, both of whom promoted private theatricals, did much to encourage such entertainments in French society and to spread the popularity of this type of play. Tragedies introduced to the public by the actors of the Comédie Française were performed in such circles as well as by professional troupes in the provinces and abroad. French tragedies were translated or adapted in Italy, Holland, England, Spain, and Germany. They had their share in the domination by France of European culture.

The popularity of tragedy in upper strata of society may have been a cause of its deterioration. Since tragedies led to social preferment, many writers may have been inspired by this consideration rather than by the urge of the creative imagination. There was also a moralistic impulse. Despite the censor, certain tragedies became vehicles for the ideas of the

---

[1] Cf. M. M. Moffat, *la Controverse sur la moralité du théâtre*, Paris, Boccard, 1930, p. 229.

[2] Danchet, La Motte, Fontenelle, Cahusac, Crébillon.

[3] Notably the anonymous *Caliste*, Voltaire's *Mahomet*, Lemierre's *Barnevelt*, Sauvigny's *Mort de Socrate*, Dorat's *Adélaïde de Hongrie*, Fontanelle's *Ericie*.

[4] That of Dorat's *Théagène*.

[5] Le Blanc de Guillet's *Druides*.

[6] See below, the discussion of that tragedy.

"philosophes," sometimes at the expense of esthetic values. And these ideas helped to create a reaction on the part of those who considered the theater a corrupter of public morals.

The celebrated controversy between Bossuet and Caffaro late in the seventeenth century [7] by no means ended the discussion. Its history to the middle of the eighteenth was traced by Louis Bourquin.[8] It was brought down to the Revolution by Miss Moffat.[9] They show that a large number of documents were published for and against the theater. Voltaire, Marmontel, Diderot, Rousseau, d'Alembert, and many churchmen took part in the dispute. Actors were accused of immorality, tragedies of exciting the passions rather than purifying them, of holding up as models of valor evil men like Catiline. The chief publication was, of course, Rousseau's *Lettre à d'Alembert*, in which, as Miss Moffat shows, the charges against the theater are, in contrast with Bossuet's, made from a lay rather than an ecclesiastical point of view.

This controversy may have had some influence upon the composition of a few tragedies without love and upon the development of the *drame bourgeois* with its moral teachings, but the contestants ended about where they started. Tragedies continued to be written and acted. Pious dignitaries continued to attack the stage. The church that refused burial in consecrated ground to Adrienne Le Couvreur still insisted upon an actor's renouncing his profession before he could receive ecclesiastical assistance. "Notre clergé gallican," wrote Le Kain [10] on May 16, 1769, " damne les acteurs en prenant leur argent." It was only twenty years later that the actors, like other minorities, were given full civil and religious rights.

There is no evidence that the course of tragedy was seriously affected by theoretical treatises first published in the eighteenth century. The dramatists so thoroughly accepted the principles illustrated by Corneille and Racine and preached by d'Aubignac, a new edition of whose *Pratique du théâtre* appeared in 1715, that there was little advice for a classically minded critic to give them. The chief of such critics, the abbé Du Bos, objected to modern subjects and to the showing of ghosts on the stage, but modern subjects were sometimes selected by dramatists and ghosts were occasionally seen. La Motte argued for the substitution of prose for verse, for the unity of interest instead of the three classical unities, but

---

[7] Cf. my *History*, Part IV, pp. 7-8.

[8] He was killed in 1915, during the First World War. His articles were published in *RHL*, Vols. XXVI-XXVIII (1919-21).

[9] Cf. above, note 1. Cf. also M. Barras, *The Stage Controversy in France*, New York, 1933, and M. Fuchs's edition of Rousseau's *Lettre à d'Alembert*, Geneva, Droz, 1948.

[10] *Mémoires de Lekain*, Paris, 1825, p. 397.

as, in his four tragedies that were acted, what he preached was not practised, Voltaire easily won in his defense of conservative usage. Theoretical writings by Voltaire and by such minor dramatists as Mauger, Portelance, Saurin, and Dorat show thorough devotion to classical principles. The true reformers were either silenced, like Landois by the failure of his *Silvie* in one act and in prose, or they developed, like Diderot, Beaumarchais, and Mercier, a new *genre*. The one exception among plays called tragedies is furnished by *Béverlei,* an adaptation of an English play.

Departures from seventeenth-century usage are found chiefly in the development of sentimental tragedies at the expense of those that emphasized analysis of motives, in the increase of medieval and modern subjects, in minor alterations in technique, in the participation of tragedy in the propagation of ideas cherished by the "philosophes," and in growing emphasis upon appeal to the eye rather than to the ear. These changes were due partly to general eighteenth-century interest in ideas and in sentiment, partly to the increasing importance of France as a world power, partly to the clearing of spectators from the stage, partly to the character of the dramatists, who were eager to create effective scenes and careless in regard to the processes that brought them about. Such tendencies were leading, without the realization of dramatists or theorists, to the substitution of romantic for classical tragedies.

More important than the influence of theoretical writers was that of criticism aimed at individual plays. Such criticism was not infrequently found in parodies. It also appears in journals like the *Mercure, l'Année littéraire,* and the *Journal Encyclopédique.* It is reflected in the correspondence of the abbé Le Blanc, Voltaire, Diderot, Raynal, Grimm, etc. It sometimes took the form of noisy protests from groups in the audience. A young dramatist, obliged to face such attacks, often had difficulty in establishing a reputation, and many of them renounced the art after composing one or two tragedies. No one, not even Voltaire and Crébillon, was safe from wagging tongues.

The troupe of the Comédie Française played from August, 1689, to Easter, 1770, in the theater of the rue des Fossés-Saint-Germain-des-Prés.[11] It was a semi-circular hall with an ample stage on which until Easter, 1759, spectators sat, a parterre in which they stood, three tiers of boxes,[12] and, behind the parterre, an *amphithéâtre.* There were also *balcons* above the stage. The hall could hold about two thousand spectators. In

---

[11] For its acquisition cf. Bonnassies, *Comédie Française, histoire administrative,* Paris, 1874, pp. 86-102.

[12] As twenty-four lower boxes were rented on March 16, 1709, and twenty-three in the second tier on April 9, 1707, and March 21, 1711, there must have been at least twenty-four of the former and twenty-three of the latter that could be rented as units.

1756 the pasage "qui descend à l'Amphithéâtre" was narrowed to form on either side a "petite loge." The following year others were constructed above the second *balcons* and above the first two boxes of the second tier.[13] Bonnassies[14] cites a decision of Nov. 14, 1757, to reestablish six "petites loges" that had been torn down in 1751 by order of the Gentlemen of the Chamber,[15] and to create four more, each seating four persons, "au fond de l'amphithéâtre." There were certainly fifteen "petites loges," probably sixteen, for fifteen were rented on May 7, 1768. Additional *balcons*[16] were constructed when spectators ceased to appear upon the stage. In spite of poor lighting and worse ventilation, it was in this hall that nearly all tragedies of consequence were produced until the troupe removed to the theater of the Tuileries,[17] where they played until 1781, when the present Odéon was ready for dramatic productions.

Throughout the reign of Louis XV the troupe was, financially speaking, a stock company, with twenty-three shares at its disposal. There were usually from sixteen to twenty-one actors and actresses who had full shares and a smaller number who had part shares. An actor might start with a fourth of a share and gradually work his way up to full membership. Sometimes he began with a larger fraction or even with a full share. Admission might be proposed by the troupe, but it had to be approved by the four Gentlemen of the Chamber or the king. An actor might be retired by these authorities. In return the troupe received from the government an annual subsidy of about 12,000 francs.

The actors who played at Fontainebleau earned a pistole a day, "de la poudre, de la pommade, du rouge, des gants, des bas de soie, des rubans et des rafraîchissements."[18] For playing at Versailles they were entertained at supper and received, in 1734, six francs a day. According to Garrick,[19] each French actor, when he played at court, was given a bottle of wine each day, a pair of silk stockings, and coach hire. In 1763 the troupe received each day 650 francs both at Fontainebleau and at Versailles. The actors who remained behind, when their companions played

[13] *Almanach des Spectacles* for 1757.

[14] *Op. cit.*, p. 105.

[15] The actors had apparently constructed them a short time before without getting permission from the Gentlemen of the Chamber. On April 25, 1751, Collé (*Journal*, Paris, 1807, I, 380-1) refers to the destruction of boxes for four persons placed in the "enfoncement de la premiere coulisse."

[16] These are first mentioned immediately after Easter, 1759. Seven of them were rented on Jan. 7, 1760.

[17] The Palais Royal was burned in 1763. While it was being rebuilt, the opera troupe moved to the hall of the Tuileries. After this troupe had vacated it, the hall was occupied by the actors of the Comédie Française.

[18] Bonnassies, *op. cit.*, pp. 226-9.

[19] R. C. Alexander, *The Diary of David Garrick*, New York, Oxford University Press, 1928, p. 27.

at Fontainebleau, were compensated by a "préciput" of two francs, raised in 1725 to three francs, with back-payments for 1724, and in 1730 to five francs.

In addition to his share in the company and regardless of his rank, each actor was paid a franc every time that he performed. Such fees are indicated in the *Registres* as "feux."[20] Members of the troupe received three francs for attendance upon assemblies at which new plays were read, but they were fined for absence from such gatherings, from rehearsals, and from performances.

A new actor had to invest in the company above thirteen thousand francs, an amount reduced in 1757 to less than 9,000 francs. If he did not have this amount, it was paid gradually out of his earnings. When he retired, he withdrew it. He then received a pension, amounting ordinarily to 1000 francs for a full-share actor, but it might be increased by sums from the royal treasury. He could also give lessons in declamation and, if he trained an acceptable actor, he might be rewarded by the government for doing so. The financial situation of individual actors was consequently better than that of the troupe, which was often in debt. The company owed over 235,000 francs in 1750, over 430,000 in 1754, as much as 487,000 in 1757,[21] when the king, to help meet the deficit, presented it with 276,000 francs.[22]

These difficulties were not caused by new tragedies, the receipts from which were, so far as the records show, much larger than in the seventeenth century, even if we take into consideration the fall in the purchasing power of money.[23] The question as to whether they were caused by taxation is more difficult to answer.

In the last part of Louis XIV's reign the troupe had been taxed a sixth of the total receipts before expenses were deducted, but the actors had at first interpreted the "sixième en sus"[24] in their own way. They raised

---

[20] Littré cites Castil-Blaize, who thought that the word was first used in this sense at the end of the eighteenth century. I have found it in the *Registres* as early as April, 1701. On and after Dec. 1, 1757, the value of a "feu" was raised from one franc to two francs.

[21] Bonnassies, *op. cit.*, p. 254.

[22] Bonnassies, *Spectacles forains*, Paris, 1875, p. 180.

[23] For instance, the first ten performances of *Iphigénie en Tauride* brought in, before reductions for expenses and taxation, 35080 fr.; of *l'Orphelin de la Chine*, 33764 fr.; of *Denys le Tyran*, 33335 fr.; of *Catilina*, 31851 fr.; of *Mérope*, 30629 fr.; whereas the "machine" play of 1675, *Circé*, had produced from its first ten performances 25334 fr., 10 s.; *Tartuffe* (1669), 21185 fr., 10 s.; *Andronic* (1685), 13398 fr.; *Manlius Capitolinus* (1698), 11991 fr., 14 s. After 1757 I note similarly 29596 fr. from Lemierre's *Hypermnestre* and 34933 fr. from *le Siège de Calais*.

[24] Bonnassies (*op. cit.*, pp. 144, 151) takes this to mean one seventh of the total receipts and even calls the actors' reference to the sixth an "habileté oratoire," yet Littré explains the expression as one fifth of the original amount, one sixth of the amount as increased to pay the tax, and the *Registres* confirm the correctness of Littré's definition.

their charges one tenth in the three best parts of the house, one fifth in the worst part, and handed over this supplement, usually amounting to less than a tenth of the total receipts. Then the government became aware of this tax evasion and insisted upon a sixth of the total, which the actors began to pay on Sept. 4, 1701. But this was not all. On Feb. 5, 1716, the Regent ordered a ninth of the five-sixths that remained paid to the Hôtel Dieu. This edict took effect five days later. The "neuvième" was counted, however, as one tenth of the five-sixths, or one twelfth of the whole. As a sixth plus a twelfth is a fourth, the total tax came to be known on March 31, 1716, as the "quart des pauvres."

For over two years this "quart" was calculated as a fourth of the total receipts, but on July 15, 1718, the actors began to subtract 300 francs as expenses before the fourth was determined. On Aug. 24, 1720, they were obliged to return to the original method of calculation, which remained in force until Oct. 6, 1736, when they were again allowed to deduct 300 francs before calculating the tax. On Oct. 14 of that year they seem to have understood their tax as fifteen percent, which is all they paid until Dec. 1, but in that month they had to pay the "neuvième" for October 14-31 and for all the month of November. On Dec. 1 they deducted for the poor fifteen percent of the whole, then 300 francs from the eighty-five percent remaining before calculating the "neuvième," which, with some variations, was treated as a tenth. After Easter, 1737, the habit of counting the "neuvième" as a tenth was so well established that the tax was printed as a "dixième" in the *Registres* for 1737-8 [25] and later years. The method of paying taxes had consequently become the following: subtract fifteen percent, subtract from the remainder 300 francs, then calculate ten percent of what is left. This fifteen percent plus the ten percent constituted the "quart des pauvres." [26]

This taxation gave the actors an excuse for increasing their charges, but it is impossible to tell whether such increase did not diminish the size of their audiences to such an extent that lower charges would have been more remunerative. Before taxation began, the actors, when they gave old plays, had usually charged 3 fr. for a seat on the stage or in a lower box; 1 fr., 10 s. for a seat in the second tier of boxes; 1 fr. for a seat in the third; 15 s. for admission to the parterre. When a new play was "au double," the corresponding charges were usually 5 fr., 10 s.; 3 fr.; 1 fr.,

[25] This led Bonnassies into the error of believing that the "neuvième" was first counted as a "dixième" on April 1, 1737, instead of Feb. 10, 1716. The act of Oct. 6, 1736, permitting the deduction of 300 fr. was published by Campardon, *les Comédiens du roi*, Paris, 1879, pp. 315-6.

[26] If, for instance, the receipts were 2000 fr., the "quart" amounted to twenty-two percent; if they were 1000 fr., the "quart" was twenty and a half percent.

10 s.; 1 fr., 10 s. From Sept. 4, 1701, until the Regent's additional tax took effect in 1716, the usual charges were those introduced in March, 1699: 3 fr., 12 s.; 1 fr., 16 s.; 1 fr., 4 s.; 18 s. After this event they were ordinarily 4 fr.; 2 fr.; 1 fr., 10 s.; 1 fr. This represented an increase over the 1698 charges of a little more than was required to pay the " quart des pauvres." At performances of new plays usage varied. Sometimes a seat on the stage cost more than one in a lower box. Sometimes prices were not raised at all, or were raised only for seats on the stage. At the first performances of Voltaire's *Artémire* and *Mariamne* [27] the charges were 8 fr., 4 fr., 3 fr., 2 fr., which more than compensated the actors for the tax they had to pay. Subsequently, however, the usual charges for a new tragedy were 6 fr., 3 fr., 2 fr., 1 fr., which brought in less than had been earned from new plays before taxation began, but, thanks to the manner in which the tax was calculated in 1736 and subsequent years, there was probably little difference between the new method and the old. It is also true that, after Sept. 20, 1753, the regular charges were, for old plays as well as for new, 6 fr., 3 fr., 2 fr., 1 fr., except on Tuesdays and Fridays, days of the Opera, when they were usually 4 fr.; 2 fr.; 1 fr., 10 s.; 1 fr.

Moreover, the troupe was often slow in paying its taxes and sometimes devised methods of partly evading them. I have already pointed out some of these. For a while after the " petites loges " were constructed, they were rented by the year and paid no tax. Protests from the charitable agencies involved produced a compromise. The actors were allowed to keep what they had already earned by this method, but, starting on May 28, 1762, they were obliged to report the receipts from the " petites loges " with the rest. The entire tax for the poor and the Hôtel Dieu was, however, estimated at 60,000 francs a year, which was less than the actors had previously been supposed to pay.[28] The government must have come to realize that there was little point in overtaxing the actors if the king had to pay a large part of the deficit.[29]

The troupe's financial difficulties were caused primarily by the fact that there were long periods in which no new plays were given and the audiences were so small that the receipts were less than the expenses. On May 6, 1718, for instance, admission was paid by only twenty-six persons; on Aug. 26, Sept. 12 and 24 of that year, by only forty-five. This in spite of the

---

[27] At the first performance of his *Œdipe* the charge for a seat on the stage was 8 fr.; for one in a lower box, 4 fr.; for the other categories, 2 fr.; 1 fr., 10 s.; 1 fr. At the second performance seats on the stage were reduced to 6 fr.

[28] Bonnassies, *op. cit.*, pp. 172-83.

[29] In 1742 the king gave them 72000 fr. to make up for the losses incurred during the war. Most of this amount went towards paying their debts. Cf. Bonnassies, *op. cit.*, pp. 161-4. On pp. 229-30 of his *Comédie Française, histoire administrative* he gives a list of other examples of royal bounty.

fact that audiences at new plays were, as a rule, larger than they had been in the late seventeenth century.[30]

The leading actors and actresses assumed at times a haughty attitude in regard to authors. They had great consideration for Voltaire, whose plays were usually highly profitable and who had friends among the Gentlemen of the Chamber, but they showed little consideration for such authors as Le Franc de Pompignan, Clairfontaine, Bauvin, and Renou. When an author had ready the manuscript of a play, he submitted it to the "semainier," who decided whether it merited examination by the troupe. If he favored it, he appointed a day for the company to assemble and hear it read by the author, who retired after the reading. The actors then voted with beans, white for acceptance, "marbrées" for alteration, black for rejection. In the second case the author revised his play and again read it to the actors. If it was accepted, the approval of the police, the censor, and the Gentlemen of the Chamber still had to be secured. If all went well, the author named an actor or actress for each rôle and arranged with the troupe the date of first performance.[31]

The author of a five-act play received a ninth of the receipts, after the taxes and the expenses of production had been deducted, until these receipts fell two or three times below a certain amount, which varied with the season and with the period. He also received, as late as Easter, 1758, a supplement of six francs. In 1726 an author received nothing after his play had brought in less than 550 francs twice in succession during the winter season, or less than 350 francs during the summer season. A little later this was changed from two in succession to two at any time, then to two in succession *or* three at any time.[32] By 1757 the regulation had been altered to mean that the author lost his share of the receipts if in winter they fell below 1,200 francs, in summer below 800 francs, twice in succession or three times otherwise. The records, however, do not indicate that such rules were always followed. Special arrangements could, of course, be made with the authors. There are cases in which a play was given only

---

[30] Compare, for instance, the reception given Campistron's *Andronic* in 1685 with that accorded a play that remained a much shorter time in the repertory, Grave's *Varon* of 1751. The average number of persons who paid admission to the first sixteen performances of *Andronic* was 467.5; of *Varon*, 928.9. In 1681-1701 the largest number of persons who paid admission to a tragedy was 1356 at a performance, not of a new play, but of *Polyeucte* just before Easter, 1701, while at the first performance of Voltaire's *Brutus* in 1730, 1564 persons paid admission, and, after the move to the Tuileries, 1463 at a performance on April 24, 1771, of *Gaston et Bayard.*

[31] Cf. *Almanach des Spectacles* for 1760. If the author was unknown, the rôles were distributed in accordance with the desires of the Gentlemen of the Chamber; cf. Bonnassies, *op. cit.,* p. 138.

[32] Bonnassies, *Auteurs dramatiques et la Comédie-Française,* Paris, 1874, pp. 24-7, 38, 43.

once, or was withdrawn in the middle of what appears to have been financially a successful career, or continued to remunerate its author even after it had fallen " dans les règles."

A few plays were presented by the authors to the troupe. Some earned very little, but some brought their authors larger sums than had ever, so far as the records show, been earned by a tragedy before the reign of Louis XV.[33] The author also received a few tickets to the performances and, if he had written two tragedies that were accepted, free admission to the theater for the rest of his life.

In this last case his name was added to the list of those who entered free, a list that numbered 416 persons in 1768 according to Le Kain.[34] It included actors of the Théâtre Italien and the Opera, officers of the musketeers, and, after March 23, 1732, members of the Academy. In addition to those on the list, two persons could be invited every other day by each actor or actress, and the parents, children, and spouses of actors and actresses were given free admission, provided they did not deprive paying spectators of seats. In view of these facts, one may suppose that at any performance there may have been present several hundred more persons than those who paid admission.

At the time of Louis XIV's death the troupe was composed of sixteen full-share [35] and thirteen part-share [36] members. On Oct. 20, 1715, the duchesse de Berry eliminated Moligny, Durant, Clavareau, and la Morancourt in order to allow the return to the troupe of Paul and Philippe Poisson.[37] Other actors soon retired: Dumirail and Louise La Chaise in June, 1717; old Guérin after July; Beaubourg and his wife, Dancourt, and la Desbrosses at Easter, 1718. In these years the young hero was usually played by Beaubourg; the heroine, by Charlotte Desmares. Ponteuil came next in importance to Beaubourg; la Duclos, to la Desmares. When the troupe played *Athalie* for the first time, March 5, 1716, la Desmares took

---

[33] *Mérope* earned for its author 6146 fr., 18 s.; *Inès de Castro*, 5765 fr., 19 s.; *Iphigénie en Tauride*, 5281 fr., 19 s.; *Hypermnestre*, 4589 fr., 9 s.; *Œdipe*, 4445 fr., 17 s.; *Catilina*, 3997 fr.; *Zaïre*, 3754 fr., 12 s.; *Alzire*, 3635 fr.; *Denys le Tyran*, 3529 fr.

[34] Cited by Bonnassies, *Comédie Française, histoire administrative*, p. 336.

[35] Dancourt, Beaubourg, their wives, Guérin, La Thorillière, Lavoy, Ponteuil, Legrand, la Desbrosses, la Duclos, la Fonpré, la Champvallon, la Dangeville, Charlotte Desmares, and Mimy Deshayes (née Dancourt). For these and other actors cf. the *Registres*; Monval, *Liste alphabétique des sociétaires*, Paris, 1900; and Lyonnet, *Dictionnaire des Comédiens Français*, Paris, n. d.

[36] Three-quarters: Du Boccage, Dangeville, Maurice Quinault, la Sallé. Five-eighths: Quinault-Dufresne, usually called Dufresne. Half: his sister (la Quinault), la Morancourt, and Louise La Chaise. Three-eighths: Fontenay, Clavareau, Durant, Moligny, and Dumirail.

[37] They returned on the same financial basis as they had left in December, 1711, Paul with a full share, his son with half a share. The remaining eighth was used to help pay the pensions of the four persons who had just retired.

the part of Athalie, la Duclos that of Josabet. Beaubourg played Joad; Dancourt, Mathan; Philippe Poisson, Abner; Mimy Deshayes, Zacharie. Joas was played by the young son of Laurent, the stage decorator.

The retirement of so many members might have seriously injured the troupe, if it had not been for the arrival of the celebrated Adrienne Le Couvreur.[38] Daughter of a workman, she was born at Damery in Champagne on April 5, 1692. She is said to have played in a troupe of children, then in professional companies at Lille, Nancy, and Strasbourg. After she was admitted to the Comédie Française, the first author to recognize her talent for tragedy was Deschamps, who gave her one of the two leading rôles for women in *Antiochus et Cléopâtre,* but even a year later Voltaire preferred to have la Desmares play Jocasta. It was not, indeed, until after la Desmares retired in May, 1721, that she became the leading actress, playing the heroine in new tragedies by Voltaire, Danchet, and Crébillon. Though La Motte gave her a less important rôle in *Inès de Castro* than he gave to la Duclos, she soon, as Voltaire put it, buried this actress. She seems to have been distinguished especially by the naturalness of her acting. Voltaire praised her very highly, though he thought that in pathos she was surpassed by la Dumesnil. Collé [39] said that she was perfect in details, that she made one forget the actress for the person she was representing. He declares that she excelled where finesse was required rather than force and that, though less gifted by nature than Michel Baron, she was superior to him in her art. No one had ever equalled her as Phèdre or Monime.

She must have been a somewhat difficult member of the troupe. She once refused to play Junie in *Britannicus* if Mlle Aubert was to play Agrippine.[40] On another occasion there could be no performance because she had the " vapeurs." However disagreeable her sister may have been, she seems hardly justified in relegating her to a convent. On the other hand, she attracted men of great distinction, chief among whom were Voltaire and the maréchal de Saxe. Her fame was consecrated by the refusal of the church to allow her decent burial. The hasty removal of her body on the night of March 30, 1730, to an improvised grave near the Seine inspired Voltaire's lines:

[38] She made her début on May 14, 1717, playing in Crébillon's *Electre.* When Dumirail and Louise La Chaise retired on June 20, they were replaced by Adrienne and la Gautier, who had been playing in the troupe since Sept. 3, 1716, each with half a share. It is reasonable to suppose that Adrienne received a full share at Easter, 1718.

[39] *Op. cit.,* I, 172.

[40] Jal, p. 757. Mlle Aubert was a member of the troupe only from May 27, 1721, to May 19, 1722.

Ils privent de sépulture
Celle qui dans la Grèce aurait eu des autels.[41]

Beaubourg was succeeded as young hero by Dufresne, who in 1718 played such a rôle in *Artaxare* and in *Œdipe*. " Beau comme un dieu d'orient," he created the rôles of young hero in *Inès de Castro, Zaïre, Alzire,* and many lesser tragedies. He played Herod in *Hérode et Mariamne,* Vendôme in *Adélaïde du Guesclin,* the sultan in La Noue's *Mahomet II.* His brother, Maurice Quinault, took in tragedy the kind of rôle previously assigned to Ponteuil, who had died on Aug. 15, 1718. His youngest sister, Jeanne-Françoise Quinault,[42] joined the troupe on Dec. 22, 1718, making the fourth member of her family playing at that time in the company. She retired with Dufresne in 1741.

Other recruits were Duchemin,[43] who became a member on July 20, 1718; Jean-Baptiste Duclos, who entered the troupe on July 10, 1719; and Legrand's son, known as Legrand de Belleville,[44] who was admitted to membership on Jan. 15, 1720. The last of these was distinguished for his beautiful voice, one that made him shine in tragic *récits.* He and his father, Fontenay, and Philippe Poisson were given rôles of some importance in tragedy, but there was need for a genuinely distinguished actor. Moreover, the death of la Fonpré, née Clavel, on Dec. 3, 1719, had created a new vacancy.

Then an extraordinary event occurred. Michel Baron,[45] who had distinguished himself in Molière's troupe, then in that of the Hôtel de Bourgogne, and who had been a founder of the Comédie Française, only to retire in 1691, returned to the stage at the age of sixty-six. Announced by La Thorillière just before Easter, 1720, he made his début on April 10 in *Cinna,* then appeared in *Polyeucte, Horace, Britannicus,* the *Misanthrope,* the *Menteur, Pompée,* etc.[46] The receipts were at once greatly increased,

---

[41] Cf. the article on Adrienne Le Couvreur in Lyonnet's *op. cit.* It is based largely on G. Monval's *Lettres de Adrienne Lecouvreur,* Paris, Plon, 1892.

[42] Born at Strasbourg on Oct. 13, 1699, she was known as Mlle Dufresne until May, 1727, when her brother married an actress. She was subsequently called Mlle Quinault, as her sister had retired in 1722.

[43] Born in Brittany about 1674, he had acted in Sweden from 1699 to 1705 and had been a notary at Rennes.

[44] For him cf. Collé, *op. cit.,* I, 182, and Moland, IV, 482, 543.

[45] Cf. B. E. Young, *Michel Baron,* Grenoble, 1904, pp. 106-39. On pp. 110-1 he calls attention to the fact that La Thorillière, Paul Poisson, and la Dancourt, who had acted with Baron in 1691, were still members of the troupe when he returned. As part of his demonstration Young publishes a list of the actors and actresses playing in 1720. To this list should be added the names of four actresses: Dangeville, Sallé, Mimy Deshayes, and Dufresne.

[46] He really received two shares as his wife, who no longer acted, was given one. It must have been on his account that, from April 10, 1720, to Easter, 1721, there were 24 shares in the company instead of 23. For nearly six months after his arrival, admission charges were doubled on the days on which he acted.

though he started his new career in a dull season. He represented men of various ages, such as the boyish Horace of *l'Ecole des femmes,* Rodrigue in *le Cid,* and much older Créon of Racine's *Frères Ennemis.* He also took part in new plays, creating the rôle of youthful Misael in La Motte's *Machabées,* of Tatius in his *Romulus,* of King Alphonse in his *Inès de Castro,* of Polemon in his *Œdipe.* Voltaire gave him the rôle of Herod in his *Mariamne* of 1724, but he substituted Dufresne when he rewrote the tragedy the following year. Baron also played Cambyses in Danchet's *Nitétis* and Glaucias in Crébillon's *Pyrrhus.* He seems, indeed, after his first flush of excitement over his return to the stage, to have preferred less youthful rôles.

There were those who considered it absurd of him to come back to the stage at all, especially when he appeared as a young lover, but others, like the abbé Nadal, Marais, and Voltaire, praised his acting highly. Collé [47] said of him that, if he had had more warmth, he would have been the greatest actor who ever lived. He supposed that he had had such warmth in his youth. When he saw him act, Baron was over seventy and impressed him especially by his intelligence, nobility, and dignity. If he played a king, he had eight or ten supernumeraries precede him, yet he could be familiar without losing his tragic dignity. He never declaimed. When he acted, one forgot the actor. He used to break the measure of the verse for the sake of the situation and indulged in long pauses, so much so that a play in which he appeared lasted a half hour longer than if anyone else had his rôle.

In the latter part of his life he was often ill, but would not renounce the stage. After Easter, 1729, he played only six times: on May 10 and 13 in Thomas Corneille's *Essex* and on Aug. 27, 28, 31, and Sept. 3 as the old king in Rotrou's *Venceslas.* At the last performance he was unable to finish. Taken home, he continued to suffer, but he was able to converse brilliantly with his friends. He lasted until Dec. 22.

While he was in the troupe, a number of changes took place. Charlotte Desmares retired on May 21, 1721; Philippe Poisson, on April 14, 1722. Anne-Louise de Heydecamp, known as la Jouvenot, was admitted on May 26, 1721, was dismissed on June 2, 1722, but was again admitted on Sept. 1 of that year. She became well known as a confidant. La Thorillière's son, who took minor parts in tragedy, entered in 1722 and in 1731 received a full share. Collé says of him, " Je l'ai vu sifflé pendant quinze ans de suite." [48] Catherine-Marie-Jeanne Dupré, known before her marriage as de Seine, was admitted on Nov. 17, 1724. She married Dufresne in May,

[47] *Op. cit.,* I, 170-2. [48] *Op. cit.,* I, 179.

1727, but, apparently to save what he had left of her fortune, asked to be separated from him in 1730. She was absent from the troupe between Dec. 24, 1732, and May, 1733. Upon her return she took leading parts in tragedy, creating the rôles of heroine in *Didon, Marie Stuart*, and *Sabinus*. She left the troupe in April, 1736. Mlle Clairon, for whom she recited after her retirement, gave her high praise.

The changes just mentioned and others that concern comedy rather than tragedy had altered considerably the personnel of the troupe by Easter, 1727. There were then sixteen full-share members [49] and twelve who had parts of shares.[50] Baron and Adrienne Le Couvreur were, of course, the stars, but Dufresne was taking over the young lovers' rôles as Baron was limiting himself to those of older men. The second actress, la Duclos, fell upon evil days when she married in 1725 young Duchemin, a youth of seventeen, less than a third her age. The following year he was admitted to the troupe with half a share, raised to five-eighths in 1728, but his conduct was such that she made three complaints to the police [51] in 1727-30 and was finally separated from him. He left the troupe in 1730. She continued until 1736, but played little in the last part of the time.

The elder Legrand, who, though a prolific author of comedies, had taken fairly important rôles in tragedy, died on Jan. 7, 1728. Fontenay retired on June 3 of that year. As we have seen, the troupe lost Baron late in 1729, Adrienne Le Couvreur in March, 1730. There was great need for new actors. The troupe had already admitted with a full share, on Jan. 21, 1728, Mlle Balicourt, who took several leading parts in tragedy before her retirement on March 22, 1738. Piron preferred her to Adrienne for the one woman's rôle in his *Callisthène*. She played the mother in his *Gustave*, Queen Elizabeth in Tronchin's *Marie Stuart*, and the queen in Morand's *Téglis*. She appeared, too, in older plays, as the widowed queen in *Amasis* and the heroine of Longepierre's *Médée*. She never acquired, however, a great reputation. Mlle Clairon [52] once attempted to reproduce what she described as her stiff and chilly air.

In 1729-31 three important new actors came to fill the gaps in the troupe. The first of them, Pierre-Claude Sarrazin, born in Burgundy

[49] Baron, Dangeville, their wives, La Thorillière, Legrand, Quinault, Dufresne, Duchemin, Fontenay, la Duclos, la Deshayes, Adrienne Le Couvreur, la Dufresne (soon to be called la Quinault), la Jouvenot, la de Seine (soon to be called la Dufresne).

[50] Seven-eighths, Legrand de Belleville. Three-fourths, Armand. Five-eighths, the younger La Thorillière, Du Breuil, and his wife. A half: Poisson de Roinville, younger son of Paul Poisson; Dumirail, who had left in 1717, but was again a member in 1724-30; Duchemin's son; Du Boccage's daughter; Legrand's daughter; la La Motte; la Labatte, who had the title-rôle in La Grange-Chancel's *Erigone*.

[51] Cf. Campardon, *les Comédiens du roi de la troupe française*, Paris, 1879, pp. 93-6.

[52] *Mémoires de Mlle Clairon*, Paris, 1822, pp. 14-5.

on June 18, 1689, was admitted, on Dec. 23, 1729, to replace Baron in elderly rôles. He played Don Diègue, Burrhus, old Horace, and Simon in Baron's *Andrienne*. Grimm [53] declared that one has no idea of dramatic perfection unless one has seen Sarrazin in the last of these rôles. He praised him, too, for his interpretation of Lusignan in *Zaïre*. Besides this last rôle, among those he created were those of Alvarez in *Alzire*, of Zopire in *Mahomet*, of Worcester in *Edouard III*, and of Zamti in *l'Orphelin de la Chine*. Though he subsequently acted in a number of plays by Voltaire, the dramatist reproved him for lack of force when he played the title-rôle in *Brutus*.[54] Collé [55] held that he was excellent only in "morceaux de sentiment." With this verdict Le Kain agreed,[56] adding that Sarrazin could never play properly Mithridate or Auguste. He was a member of the troupe for almost thirty years, leaving it on April 1, 1759.

J.-B. Charles-François Nicolas Racot de Grandval, born at Paris in 1710, was the son of a musician who composed for the troupe and the nephew of Mme Dangeville. He was received on Dec. 23, 1729, retired on May 20, 1762, returned to the troupe on Feb. 1, 1764, and retired finally on April 1, 1768. He was at first an understudy for the Quinault brothers and ultimately yielded to Le Kain important tragic rôles, but in the forties he was often the leading male performer and he had at other times rôles of distinction. He created those of Nemours in *Adélaïde du Guesclin*, of Gusman in *Alzire,* of Egisthe in *Mérope,* of Arzace in *Sémiramis,* of César in *Rome sauvée,* and the title-rôles in *Mahomet, Edouard III, Oreste, Philoctète,* and *Titus.* Mlle Dumesnil found him charming, as did at first Mlle Clairon,[57] but the latter declared that, as he grew older, his *grasseyement* disgusted the public and forced him to retire. Collé [58] considered his voice unpleasant and stated in 1756 that he was becoming so fat that he would soon be ridiculous as a lover. To Garrick [59] he seemed affected, ill-dressed, and inattentive, though he liked him in the title-rôle of *Manlius Capitolinus.* He must have been a useful rather than a great actor, lacking the beauty of Dufresne and the genius of Le Kain.

The third recruit was Jeanne-Catherine Gaussem, known as la Gaussin. A year younger than Grandval, she played in a troupe at Lille before entering, on July 26, 1731, the Comédie Française. Endowed with great

---

[53] *Cor.*, V, 457, 214.
[54] Cf. Moland, XL, 525, and below, the discussion of *Brutus*.
[55] *Op. cit.*, I, 175.
[56] *Mémoires de Lekain*, Paris, 1801, p. 12.
[57] Cf. *Mémoires de Mlle Dumesnil*, Paris, 1823, pp. 47-9; *Mémoires de Mlle Clairon,* Paris, 1822, p. 232.
[58] *Op. cit.*, I, 175-6; II, 146.
[59] R. C. Alexander, *op. cit.*, pp. 27, 31.

beauty and an appealing voice, she shone in rôles that required a certain naïveté, but she showed little variety in her acting. Her greatest achievement was creating the title-rôle in *Zaïre*. She was also the first to play Atide in *Zulime*, Palmire in *Mahomet*, Irène in *Mahomet II*, Belvidéra in *Venise sauvée*, Andromaque in *les Troyennes*, and the title-rôles in *Adélaïde du Guesclin, Alzire, Téglis, Caliste* of 1750, and *Briséis*. Collé [60] reports that, when she was over forty, she still seemed sixteen. Voltaire [61] said of her that it was as difficult for her to keep a secret as it was for her to keep a lover.

By Easter, 1734, there had been so many promotions in rank that the troupe had twenty-one full-share actors [62] and only four with parts of shares.[63] A number of them soon departed: la Duclos and Dufresne's wife in 1736; la Balicourt in 1738; la Dangeville the elder in 1739; her husband in 1740; la Jouvenot, Duchemin, Dufresne, and his sister in 1741. There were several persons to replace them. Louise Baron,[64] daughter of Etienne, was a member of the troupe from Dec. 12, 1736, till her death on Dec. 16, 1742. Mlle Connell, admitted on Aug. 8, 1736, played confidants in tragedy until her death in 1750. Dubois,[65] who is remembered for creating one of the chief scandals in the annals of the eighteenth-century theater, entered the troupe on Nov. 29, 1736. Far more celebrated than any of these was la Dumesnil, who joined the company on Feb. 2, 1738.

Her name was Marie-Françoise Marchand. She was born on Jan. 2, 1713, in Paris, where her paternal grandfather was a " loueur de chevaux." In 1733 she was acting at Strasbourg. On October 8, 1737, she became

---

[60] *Op. cit.*, I, 173-4.

[61] Moland, XXXV, 381.

[62] Dangeville, his wife and his niece, Dufresne, his wife and his sister, Du Breuil and his wife, Duchemin, Legrand de Belleville, the younger La Thorillière, Armand, Poisson de Roinville, Sarrazin, Grandval, and the actresses: Duclos, Balicourt, Gaussin, Jouvenot, La Motte, Du Boccage.

[63] Montmény, son of Lesage, with seven-eighths of a share; Fleury with three-eighths; Fierville, then sixty-three, with a fourth of a share; Dangeville le jeune with half a share. This Dangeville and his sister were the children of A. F. Botot-Dangeville, a dancer, and Anne-Catherine Desmares, sister of Charlotte. They were first cousins of Grandval. They began to play as children. The boy never distinguished himself, but the girl acquired a fine reputation in comedy. Her only important rôle in a new tragedy was that of Tullie in Voltaire's *Brutus*. Both retired in 1763.

[64] Born in Paris on Feb. 18, 1701, she married Jean Desbrosses and was a member of the troupe from Dec. 31, 1729, just after her grandfather's death, until May 3 of the following year. She played the heroine in La Grange-Chancel's *Cassius et Victorinus*.

[65] Louis Blouin, known as Dubois, was born in 1706. Collé (*op. cit.*, I, 181) describes him as a fiery actor who declaimed rather well in a *récit*, but, on the whole, mediocre. He played Casca in *la Mort de César*, Sophronime in Lemierre's *Idoménée*, Mauni in *le Siège de Calais*, Lénox in *Cromwel*. For his expulsion from the troupe and his obtaining a pension thanks to his daughter's influence cf. below, the discussion of de Belloy's *Siège de Calais*. He died in 1775.

an understudy for la Balicourt in queens' rôles at 100 fr. a month. She was soon the leading actress for rôles of women no longer young, playing the title-rôles in *Athalie, Zulime, Mérope,* and *Sémiramis,* Clytemnestre in *Oreste,* Medea in *Médus,* Hecuba in *les Troyennes,* Marguerite in La Harpe's *Warwick,* Gertrude in Ducis's *Hamlet.* Garrick [66] admitted that her face expressed terror and despair, but he thought her at times too violent and held that she looked on the ground too much and made use of " little startings and twitchings that are visibly artificial." Goldoni,[67] on the other hand, declared that she represented nature in all her truth. Collé [68] said that she lacked dignity, expressed love badly, and had a " vilaine voix," but that in certain passages she made one forget all her shortcomings. He thought that in " morceaux vifs " she showed more warmth than Adrienne Le Couvreur. Voltaire [69] asserted that " pour le grand pathétique de l'action, nous le vîmes la première fois dans Mlle Dumesnil." Grimm [70] called her the " actrice par excellence." Diderot reported that she went on the stage without knowing what she would say, that three-fourths of the time she did not know what she was saying, but that " le reste est sublime." She must have trusted to the inspiration of the moment. When uninspired, she irritated certain critics, but when roused she could impersonate a passionate queen as no one else could do. Her greatest rôle was probably that of Mérope. Unfortunately she held on too long for her reputation, not retiring until March 31, 1776. Fourteen years before, Bachaumont [71] had said of her that, although she was more the born actress than Mlle Clairon, her powers were fading and she was suffering from the effects of excessive drinking. She made such an impression, however, that in 1779 her pension was raised to 3500 fr.[72] She lived through the Revolution and into the First Empire, dying on Feb. 20, 1803.[73]

In 1740-42 there were several new actors. Lavoy's daughter was received on Jan. 4, 1740, played confidants' rôles, was given a full share in 1743, and retired in 1759. Collé [74] says of Bonneval, who entered on Jan. 8, 1742, that he played confidants and that he was " froid et mauvais," though

---

[66] R. C. Alexander, *op. cit.,* p. 33; G. W. Stone, Jr., *The Journal of David Garrick,* New York, Modern Language Association, 1939, p. 7.

[67] Cited by Stone, *op. cit.,* p. 43.

[68] *Op. cit.,* I, 173.

[69] Moland, XXIV, 220.

[70] *Cor.,* II, 265.

[71] *Mémoires secrets,* I, 30.

[72] Cf. Campardon, *op. cit.,* pp. 100-1.

[73] For her cf. *Mémoires de Mlle Dumesnil,* Paris, 1823; J.-J. Olivier, *Voltaire et les comédiens,* Paris, 1900; Lyonnet, *op. cit.*

[74] *Op. cit.,* I, 181.

his voice was one of the best in the troupe. Le Kain [75] declared that he was " dénué de naturel," but he remained for over thirty years in the company, retiring on March 31, 1773. Paulin, born at Paris in 1711, was a dragoon, then an actor at Lyons and Besançon. At the Comédie, which he entered on May 20, 1742, he was assigned rôles of kings and peasants. Voltaire gave him that of the villain in *Mérope*. He played the doge in *Venise sauvée,* Cato in *Rome sauvée,* Ulysses in *les Troyennes,* Thoas in *Iphigénie en Tauride,* Amblétuse in *le Siège de Calais,* the title-rôles in *Amasis* and *Paros.* Collé [76] admitted that he had a fine and strong voice, but he insisted that he had no taste, grace, or intelligence and that he spoke to princesses, " le poing sous le nez." La Noue was more important. Named J.-B. Simon Sauvé, he was born at Meaux on Oct. 20, 1701, played at Lyons, Strasbourg, Rouen, and Lille, and was at one time preparing to lead a troupe to Berlin. It was while he was managing a company at Lille that he produced Voltaire's *Mahomet* before it was acted at Paris. It was partly on this account that he was admitted to the Comédie on May 15, 1742. He had already written a tragedy that will be discussed below. In 1751 he was imprisoned briefly for criticizing the Gentlemen of the Chamber. Voltaire [77] expressed the opinion that, despite his " physionomie de singe," he played Mahomet at Lille better than Dufresne could have done. At Paris he created the rôles of Séide in *Mahomet,* Jaffier in *Venise sauvée,* Assur in *Sémiramis,* Cicero in *Rome sauvée,* Thestor in *les Troyennes,* Ulysses in *Philoctète.* In 1756-7 he played Titus in *Bérénice* and the title-rôle in *Polyeucte.* Garrick [78] found him to be a very sensible man, " a just actor, but not excellent." He retired on March 26, 1757, and died on Nov. 12, 1760.

None of these can be compared with the great actress, Claire-Josèphe-Hippolyte Léris de la Tude, known as Mlle Clairon.[79] Born at Condé-sur-Escaut on Jan. 25, 1723, she made her début at the Théâtre Italien in 1736, acted at Rouen in La Noue's troupe, was at the Opera in March, 1743, and began to play at the Comédie Française on Sept. 19 of that year. She was admitted to membership on Oct. 22. At first an understudy for la Dumesnil, she soon became her rival. She created the heroine's rôle in many tragedies.[80] Van Loo painted her as Medea flying in her magic

[75] *Mémoires de Lekain,* Paris, 1825, p. 222.

[76] *Op. cit.,* I, 181; cf. Grimm in *Cor.,* VIII, 454.

[77] Moland, XXXVI, 53. For La Noue's imprisonment cf. Paul Berret's article in *RHL,* VIII (1901), 456-9.

[78] R. C. Alexander, *op. cit.,* pp. 21, 26.

[79] Cf. *Mémoires de Mlle Clairon,* Paris, 1822, J. J. Olivier, *op. cit.,* and Lyonnet, *op. cit.*

[80] Voltaire's *Oreste, Orphelin de la Chine, Tancrède, Olympie*; Saurin's *Spartacus* and *Blanche et Guiscard*; de Belloy's *Zelmire* and *Siège de Calais*; Marmontel's *Denys*

chariot. She was an actress of unusual intelligence who studied her rôles with great care. Collé [81] said that she was quite superior to la Gaussin and was better than la Dumesnil in expressing love, especially that of an abandoned princess such as Ariadne and Dido, but he considered her inferior to la Dumesnil in "morceaux de sentiment." He found her declamation "ampoulée, chantée, remplie de gémissements, celle de la vieille Duclos." By the time, however, that she had made him weep in *l'Orphelin de la Chine* he noted that she was getting rid of declamatory tendencies and was attaining a natural manner. He thought that, if she continued to improve, she would equal Adrienne Le Couvreur.

Grimm [82] at first found her vehemence at times misplaced, but in 1755 he applauded her as Idamé and thought, like Collé, that she had changed her manner. In 1776 he compared her and la Dumesnil to Racine and Shakespeare, one famed for "perfection toujours soutenue," the other for "beautés hardies et saillantes." Garrick,[83] who knew her well, said that she pleased him more than any actress he had seen, but he found her "outrée" where less violence was desirable, and tame in the finest passages. On the whole, however, he preferred her to la Dumesnil. About 1768 he wrote to a Danish friend [84] that she had

tout ce que l'Art et une bonne intelligence, joints à beaucoup de vivacité naturelle, peuvent donner, mais je crains que son cœur n'ait aucun de ces mouvements instantanés, de ce sang vital, de cette vive sensibilité qui éclate tout à coup du génie.

He calls her an excellent actress, but not a genius of the first order. Yet Bachaumont [85] had written of her in 1762 that, as soon as she appeared, she was applauded "à tout rompre." He said that for six years she struggled with her voice, as it was too loud and did not move the audience, but that by dint of constant practice she had succeeded in making it express passion and rise to the sublime. Though of less than medium height, she seemed on the stage to be tall.

She became a leader in the troupe, worked hard to secure for her profession full social and ecclesiastical privileges, joined with Le Kain, whom she disliked, in reforming costume, and took an active part with him in expelling Dubois from the troupe. For her refusal to act in a play with the culprit she was imprisoned. When she was released, she

---

le Tyran and *Cléopâtre*; La Place's *Adèle de Ponthieu*; La Touche's *Iphigénie en Tauride*; Lemierre's *Hypermnestre*; Colardeau's *Caliste*, etc.

[81] *Op. cit.*, I, 174; II, 116.

[82] *Cor.*, II, 265, III, 89, XI, 303.

[83] R. C. Alexander, *op. cit.*, pp. 28, 31.

[84] F. A. Hedgcock, *David Garrick et ses amis français*, Paris, Hachette, 1911, pp. 134-5.

[85] *Mémoires secrets*, I, 29, 30.

took the matter so much to heart that she retired from the troupe at
Easter, 1766. After this she occasionally played in private theatricals,
appeared at court as Athalie, trained Larive for the stage, and lived for
a number of years at the court of the Margrave of Anspach. Like la
Dumesnil, she died in 1803. Thirty-five years later her remains were
removed to Père Lachaise.

Though two minor players made no great impression on the troupe,
their departure from it opened the way for a most important actor.
Antoine-François Raisouche-Montet, called Rosély, was born at Paris in
1722 of a good family, but his guardian squandered his fortune, he became
an actor, and was admitted to membership on Dec. 26, 1742, with half a
share. He played secondary rôles in tragedy. Collé [86] credited him with
much gentleness and politeness, but found him lacking in physique, voice,
and ability to express emotion. On Jan. 14, 1748, Nicolas Ribou, who
belonged to the well-known family of printers, also joined the troupe.
Raynal [87] praised his looks and attributed to him a " jeu plein de naturel,"
but added that his voice did not carry far and that he lacked " le touchant
et le pathétique." Collé [88] reported that he took secondary rôles in tragedy,
that he was handsome, but that he was a wretched actor. He quarreled
with Rosély over the rôle of Télémaque in *Pénélope,* challenged him to a
duel, and, as Rosély knew nothing about swordsmanship, easily wounded
him. Rosély was able to return to the theater and brought no charge
against Ribou, but his wound soon proved fatal and his assailant fled
from Paris.

The vacancy thus created made possible the admission to the troupe of
Henri-Louis Caïn, known as Le Kain. The son of a goldsmith who made
surgical instruments, he was born at Paris on March 31, 1729. Early in
his career he took part in amateur theatricals and became acquainted with
Voltaire, at whose home he acted and with whose support he was allowed
to make his début at the Comédie in September, 1750, as Titus in *Brutus,*
but he was not received until after Ribou had killed Rosély. After making
a second début on Feb. 21, 1751, he entered the troupe on the second day
of the following November with three-eighths of a share. His remarkable
talents were not at first recognized. Raynal [89] thought him intelligent,
capable of expressing passion, noteworthy for his " jeu muet," and possessed
of fine arms, but he called his face " ignoble," his voice weak and affected.
He thought it advisable to let him go and play in Germany. Collé [90] made
a similar criticism, which in 1780 he revised, but even then he admitted

[86] *Op. cit.,* I, 180-1, 326.
[87] *Cor.,* I, 113-4.
[88] *Op. cit.,* I, 182.

[89] *Cor.,* I. 476-7.
[90] *Op. cit.,* I, 285-6.

that he still found his acting disagreeable. Garrick [91] said in 1751 that
Le Kain had feeling, but swallowed his words and had a face so ill made
that distorting it did not stir the spectators. It may have been the result
of similar criticism that prevented his receiving a full share until 1758.

Yet he had already appeared in leading rôles, such as those of Genghis
Khan in *l'Orphelin de la Chine* and Orestes in *Iphigénie en Tauride*. He
became Voltaire's leading interpreter, visiting him at Ferney, reviving his
Adélaïde du Guesclin, taking important parts in *Rome sauvée, Tancrède,*
Olympie, les Scythes, and *Sophonisbe.* He created the rôle of Guiscard in
Blanche et Guiscard, of Bayard in *Gaston et Bayard,* of Edward III in
le Siège de Calais, of Achilles in *Briséis,* etc. He also played principal
rôles in older tragedies, such as *Venceslas,* in which he took the part of
Ladislas, *Rhadamiste, Hérode et Mariamne,* and *Alzire.* Molé [92] refers
to his versatility in passing from the " ton prophétique et fastueux de
l'imposteur Mahomet " to the " franchise noble et passionnée de l'impétueux
Vendôme," from the " emportements de la jalousie terrible d'Orosmane,
au ton sévère et profondément pénétré de Manlius, trahi par l'amitié ! " [93]

He gradually won over his critics. Bachaumont,[94] who had declared in
1762 that he was an astonishing mixture " de grandeur & de bassesse, de
sublime & d'enflure," asserted nine years later that it was not possible to
show more perfect talent than Le Kain had exhibited as Nero in *Bri-*
tannicus. Grimm [95] wrote in 1754 that his superior talent made up for
what was lacking in face and voice, that he tried to cause all his verses
to be felt, even every word. In 1771 he said that, though Le Kain was
very ugly, he became on the stage " beau, noble, touchant, pathétique, et
dispose de notre âme à son gré." After Le Kain's death he declared that
no actor had ever understood more profoundly the genius of tragedy. No
other actor could animate the stage as he could do. He had corrected
his voice until its inflections became varied and sure. He had learned the
art of costume, of arranging his hair, of moving his eye-brows. He preserved the nobility of the language and at the same time could reproduce
the accents of nature, the energy of passion, the particular color of each
character he represented. Voltaire [96] became so enthusiastic about his
acting that he declared he had no idea of real tragedy until he witnessed
the playing of Le Kain.

---

[91] R. C. Alexander, *op. cit.,* p. 31.
[92] *Mémoires de Lekain,* Paris, 1825, p. 418.
[93] The tragedies alluded to are, of course, Voltaire's *Mahomet, Adélaïde,* and *Zaïre,*
and La Fosse's *Manlius Capitolinus.*
[94] *Mémoires secrets,* I, 34, V, 216.
[95] *Cor.,* II, 398, IX, 290.
[96] Moland, XLVIII, 17.

He was a student of drama and reformed costumes to make them more expressive of the period and the country represented. He took great interest in the business of the troupe, helped bring about the exclusion of spectators from the stage, went to prison as a result of the Dubois affair, projected a school for actors, and trained Mme Vestris for the stage. That he was quick in repartee is shown by his reply to an officer who asked him why a " vil histrion " should get 12,000 fr. a year while he, though risking his life for the king, would have a pension of only 1000 fr. " Eh! comptez-vous pour rien, Monsieur," retorted Le Kain, " la liberté de me parler ainsi? " [97]

In the latter part of his life he suffered from ill health and was obliged to absent himself from the troupe during long periods, but he was back at his post before his death and had agreed to create the rôle of Léonce in Voltaire's *Irène* when, shortly after playing Vendôme in *Adélaïde du Guesclin,* he died on Feb. 8, 1778.

In the reign of Louis XV acting seems to have reached its highest point between 1750 and 1765, when Le Kain, la Dumesnil, and la Clairon were all playing. In 1753 the troupe was composed of eighteen full-share actors,[98] three with three-quarters of a share,[99] four with half a share,[100] and, with three-eighths of a share each, Le Kain and Bellecour. The last of these was named Jean-Claude-Gilles Colson. He was born at Paris on Jan. 16, 1725, and, like Le Kain, made his début in 1750. He was received into the troupe on Jan. 24, 1752, two months later than Le Kain, and died in the same year as he, 1778. He had studied painting and had acted in the provinces before making his début as Achilles in *Iphigénie.* The *Mercure* states that his charming face attracted the public. Raynal [101] called him handsome, awkward, and without intelligence in tragedy. Collé [102] also admired his looks, but found that he lacked " entrailles " and had a " voix grasseyante," though he considered himself a Roscius or a Baron. Grimm [103] states that for ten years he took secondary rôles in tragedy,[104] but that he subsequently limited his efforts to comedy.

[97] *Mémoires secrets,* III, 172.

[98] Grandval and his wife, the younger Dangeville and his sister, Legrand de Belleville, the younger La Thorillière, Armand, Poisson de Roinville, Du Breuil, Sarrazin, François Baron (grandson of Michel), La Noue, and the actresses: La Motte, Gaussin, Dumesnil, Clairon, Drouin (née Gaultier), and Lavoy.

[99] Dubois, Bonneval, and Paulin.

[100] Drouin, Deschamps, la Beauménard, and la Brillant.

[101] *Cor.,* II, 19, 20.

[102] *Op. cit.,* I, 384, III, 369.

[103] *Cor.,* XII, 181.

[104] He played Noricus in *Spartacus,* Leuson in *Béverlei,* Osmont in *Blanche et Guiscard,* Pilades in *Iphigénie en Tauride,* Antigone in *Olympie.* Grimm's ten years is consequently too short a period. The *Mercure* of October, 1759, states that he composed ballets for the troupe.

On May 21, 1753, Adélaïde-Louise-Pauline Hus [105] joined the troupe.
She was a beautiful woman with little dramatic talent, a pupil of la
Clairon, whom she imitated. Blainville, chiefly known for the support
he gave Dubois in his efforts to cheat his physician, took minor parts in
tragedy between April 1, 1758, and his forced retirement seven years later.
A much more important acquisition was Brizard, received exactly a year
after Blainville as the successor of Sarrazin. A native of Orléans, he had
played in the provinces and was already almost thirty-eight. With hair
that was naturally white and a handsome face, he took for many years
such elderly rôles as those of Argire in *Tancrède*, Jarvis in *Béverlei*, Siffredi
in *Blanche et Guiscard*, Priam in *Briséis*, Hermodan in *les Scythes*. At
times he had the leading rôle in a tragedy, that of Saint-Pierre in *le Siège
de Calais*, Montaigu in Ducis's *Roméo et Juliette*, and the title-rôles in
Lemierre's *Idoménée*, Dorat's *Régulus*, and Ducis's *Roi Léar*. Voltaire
thought him cold. Grimm [106] mentioned d'Alembert's comparing him to
Samson, whose strength was in his hair, and regretted that so fine a
gentleman with so handsome a face was not the greatest actor in the world.
But Bachaumont [107] considered him a very great actor, one who united
" la force au pathétique, la chaleur au sentiment," and Le Kain [108] declared
that no one could equal him in the limited number of rôles [109] that he
played, for, " quand son âme donne de l'expression à sa belle figure, il est
supérieur à tout ce que j'ai vu."

François-René Molé was born at Paris on Nov. 24, 1734. His first
performance on any stage was in the rôle of Britannicus at the Comédie
in 1754. He played shortly afterwards Nérestan and Séide. He was
considered too inexperienced for the troupe until he had acted for nearly
six years in the provinces. Received on Jan. 28, 1760, he soon charmed
Paris by his grace and beauty. He triumphed especially in comedy, but
he played the young hero in such tragedies as *Brutus, Mahomet, Mérope,*
and *Inès de Castro,* and created the rôles of Indatire in *les Scythes,* young
Montréal in *Hirza,* Gaston in *Gaston et Bayard,* and the title-rôles in
Ducis's *Hamlet* and *Roméo et Juliette.* Collé [110] considered him too violent
in tragedy. Le Kain [111] thought him full of pride and ambition, eager
to take leading rôles and to protect talentless young authors who would

[105] Born at Rennes on March 31, 1734, she was married in 1774 to Lelièvre, from
whom she obtained a divorce in 1793. She retired in 1780 and died in 1805.

[106] *Cor.*, X, 139, VI, 445.

[107] *Mémoires secrets*, I, 35.

[108] *Mémoires de Lekain*, Paris, 1825, p. 221.

[109] Among them were those of Agamemnon in *Iphigénie*, Joad in *Athalie*, and the
high priest in *Sémiramis*.

[110] *Op. cit.*, II, 62-3, III, 436.

[111] *Mémoires de Lekain*, Paris, 1825, p. 221.

produce plays in which other rôles would be sacrificed to his. He often acted with Le Kain and, after his death, sought to replace him.

Shortly after Molé entered the troupe, the actors admitted Marie-Madeleine Blouin, daughter of Dubois. Trained by la Clairon, she had made her début in the title-rôle of Le Franc's *Didon.* There is no doubt about her beauty. Voltaire [112] preferred her to Mlle Hus, though he had heard that she was a "grande marionnette." Bachaumont [113] liked her looks and her voice, but he thought her gestures monotonous and said she had so little soul that she was called "de bois." He reported that in 1762 the audience waited for her until six o'clock, when their money was returned. She claimed to have been ill, but it was discovered that she had been at the opera, a diversion for which she was imprisoned and fined. She had, however, enough influence with the Gentlemen of the Chamber to procure a pension for her father after his dismissal from the troupe in 1765. She played the heroine in Dorat's *Théagène* and, when la Clairon had retired, in Lemierre's *Artaxerce,* Sauvigny's *Hirza,* Ducis's *Hamlet,* and de Belloy's *Pierre le Cruel,* but she soon had to make way for more talented actresses. She retired on March 31, 1773, and died in 1779.

The troupe admitted to membership in 1763-74 a number of actors, most of whom were better known for playing in comedies than in tragedies.[114] Dauberval, who was a member from 1762 to 1780, usually took in tragedy the part of confidants, but he had more important rôles in *Hirza, les Druides,* and *Sophonisbe.* Mlle Durancy, who made her début in 1759 and was at the Opera in 1762-66, returned to the troupe in 1767. She was there long enough to play the heroine in *les Scythes,* but went back to the Opera in October. Le Kain's brother-in-law, Dalainval, had minor rôles in tragedy from 1767 to 1776, among them those of Capulet in *Roméo et Juliette* and of a satrap in Lefèvre's *Cosroès.* He is not to be confused with Molé's brother, Dalainville, who had been a member in 1758-9 and returned to the troupe from July 3, 1769 to Feb. 15, 1770. Monvel [115] ultimately became a distinguished actor, but, as he joined the troupe as late as April, 1772, he took in tragedy only secondary rôles before the death of Louis XV, such as those of the Jeune Bramine in the *Veuve du Malabar* and of Manlius in Dorat's *Régulus.* Jean-Baptiste Triboullet, called Ponteuil, played Amilcar in *Régulus,* but did not become a member

---

[112] Moland, XLI, 478, XLII, 54.

[113] *Mémoires secrets,* VI, 57.

[114] 1763, Augé and Mlle d'Epinay, who married Molé; 1764, Bouret, la Doligny, la Luzy; 1766, Feulie and la Fanier; 1768, la Dugazon; 1769, Mlle La Chassaigne; 1772, Dugazon; 1773, Des Essarts.

[115] Born at Lunéville in 1745, he remained in the troupe till 1781, subsequently headed a company of actors in Sweden, but rejoined the Comédie Française in 1799. He was the father of Mlle Mars. He died in 1812.

of the troupe till 1779. Similarly la Saint-Val cadette took part in plays of 1772-3, but was not admitted until 1776. Of greater importance are three actresses regarded as successors of Mlle Clairon.

Mlle Saint-Val [116] was small and unprepossessing, but she seems to have had some talent. When she made her début as Ariadne in 1766, Bachaumont [117] said that she had " beaucoup de feu, des entrailles, un jeu naturel à la fois & raisonné." She played the heroine in *les Druides* and in *Roméo et Juliette,* but, unable to compete with Mme Vestris, she attacked her in a document to which Le Kain [118] replied. The result of the controversy was the retirement of la Saint-Val in 1779.

Françoise-Marie-Rosette Gourgaud was born at Marseilles on April 7, 1743. She studied with Le Kain and was received on Feb. 11, 1769. Her sister, la Dugazon, was already a member of the troupe, and her brother, le Dugazon, entered the company three years later. She married Angelo Vestris, a dancer. As la Clairon had retired and la Dumesnil was old, she soon became the leading actress, overshadowing her rivals, Dubois, Hus, and Saint-Val. She created the heroine's rôle in *les Chérusques, Florinde, Gaston et Bayard, la Veuve du Malabar, Régulus, Sophonisbe,* and *Irène.* She took the part of the priestess, the longest woman's rôle in Voltaire's last play, *Agathocle.* She inherited many of la Clairon's rôles, such as Ariadne, Aménaïde, and Idamé. Grimm [119] spoke of her beauty, but thought that her features were not sufficiently large or noble for tragedy. He considered her voice weak and noted her *grasseyement.* Voltaire had heard her praised, but he wondered whether the credit should not go to her teacher rather than to herself.

The third actress was Marie-Antoinette-Josèphe Saucerotte, known as la Raucourt. Born at Paris on March 3, 1756, she played at first with her father, an unsuccessful actor, then became a pupil of Brizard and made an extremely brilliant début on Dec. 23, 1772. Grimm [120] described her as tall and shapely, with a noble countenance and a beautiful voice. She played Dido, Emilie, Monime, Idamé, Hermione, and Pulchérie (*Héraclius*). She created the title-rôle in *Orphanis.* She pleased Louis XV and la Du Barry, but, as no share was available, she could not as yet become a member of the troupe. Though she received a modest salary of 1800 fr., she managed to live extravagantly and, heavily in debt, left

---

[116] Born at Roquefort in 1743, she played abroad before entering the Comédie Française and at other French theaters after she left it. She died in 1830.
[117] *Mémoires secrets,* III, 27.
[118] *Mémoires de Lekain,* Paris, 1825, pp. 206-20.
[119] *Cor.,* VIII, 72-4, 260-2.
[120] *Cor.,* X, 138-43, 396.

Paris in 1776. When she returned in 1779, she received a share in the company. Her fame as an actress was acquired chiefly after that date.[121]

The most distinguished actors in the later years of Louis XV were undoubtedly Le Kain, Molé, and Brizard. As for the actresses, Mlle Dumesnil had a great reputation, but she had largely outlived it. Mlle Clairon was not replaced. The actress who came nearest to succeeding her was Mme Vestris. The troupe realized the need for training actors of ability. It was as a result of their efforts that was established in 1786 the Ecole royale dramatique. This institution soon produced the great actor, Talma, who studied under Molé and Dugazon. By him and others the traditions of Le Kain and Mlle Clairon were carried on into the nineteenth century, when they continued to bear fruit even after the coming of romanticism.

---

[121] In 1799 she was a member of the reconstructed troupe. Napoleon put her in charge of a French company that played in Italy. She died in 1815 and was buried in Père Lachaise.

CHAPTER II

TRAGEDY BEFORE VOLTAIRE, 1715-1718

In the three years that separate the death of Louis XIV from Voltaire's début as a dramatist, seven tragedies were acted at the Comédie Française, all but one or two of them by authors who had previously composed for that theater. They showed little novelty in theme or structure and met with slight success. Their sources were chiefly ancient historians, the most popular of whom was Justin. Their authors avoided Greek mythology and events that took place in Europe. Indeed, the most distinctive characteristic of the group is the fact that the incidents dramatized are exclusively African or Asiatic.

Of the six tragedies that have survived four have plots that are fairly complex, while two, *Cléarque* and *Antiochus et Cléopâtre* are quite simple. Love is essential in all of them. Crébillon continued to exemplify his fondness for recognition and for danger of incest. In the first respect he was seconded by Caux and Mme de Gomez; in the second by the latter. Several tragedies give a touch of the *merveilleux* by their use of prophecy, a dream, or the *cri du sang*. The ideas expressed are in the main conservative and monarchical, but Crébillon suggests in a line the plebeian origin of kings, and Deschamps introduces an anticlerical theme that anticipates Voltaire. The proprieties are carefully observed. There is nothing noteworthy about the spectacle the plays present. Their only departures from rules of unity are found in the facts that the action of *Artaxare* slightly exceeds twenty-four hours and that there is some "unfinished business" at the end of *Cléarque*.

None of the plays had less than three or more than eight productions when it first appeared. *Marius* alone was subsequently revived. It was given in all twenty times and was republished in the nineteenth century, an honor paid to none of the others except Crébillon's *Sémiramis*. The chief title to fame of this last play is that it inspired the *Sémiramis* of Voltaire, who may owe to *Artaxare* the conclusion of his *Adélaïde du Guesclin*. From an historical point of view, however, the group has a certain interest in the fact that it shows the kind of tragedy that was being composed just before Voltaire brought out his first play. The lack of spectacle in these tragedies, of bold ideas, and of striking lines helps to explain the great success that awaited his first production. He could see that the public, which took little interest in these tragedies, had been delighted with *Athalie,* given for the first time at the Comédie Française on March 5, 1716, and acted thirteen times in that year. It will not be surprising if we find some effect upon *Œdipe* of the contrast between the reception accorded Racine's play and that granted to those that form the subject of this chapter.

In dedicating MARIUS,[1] Gilles de Caux calls the play the " prémices de ma plume." In his preface he speaks of it as if it were entirely his own work. It was attributed to him without question by his son in 1738, by Beauchamps, by the frères Parfaict, by the *Mercure* of 1755, and by the *Almanach des Spectacles* of 1769. Léris, however, declared that he had been assured that the tragedy was the work of Hénault. In support of this attribution Henri Lion [2] quoted a note by Hénault to the effect that he gave the tragedy to

un homme ignoré dont elle fit la fortune, parce que je le présentai à Mme la princesse de Conti, qui était dans le secret et qui lui donna sa protection par la suite.

On the strength of this statement Lion devoted ten pages to the play, crediting Caux only with minor alterations in the text. But Hénault does not claim the play in his *Mémoires,* though he mentions his *Cornélie* and *François II.* Petitot explains the attribution to Hénault by referring to Caux's modesty and his " liaisons avec le président." As this accords with Caux's own evidence, that of his contemporaries, and that of his son, it seems to me highly probable that Petitot is correct in attributing the play to Caux, who may have received suggestions from Hénault, exaggerated by the latter's memory until by the middle of the century he believed himself to have been the author of the play.

According to the frères Parfaict,[3] Gilles de Caux was a Norman, born in 1682 in the diocese of Séez. They add that he was descended through his mother from Pierre Corneille, but this statement does not accord with what we know of Corneille's descendants,[4] though it is possible that he was related to the first husband of Corneille's oldest daughter, a man who lived, like Caux, in what is now the department of Orne. He belonged to a noble family, was educated at Caen and Rouen, and added to his name

[1] Paris, Pierre Ribou, 1716, 12°. According to Beauchamps, Danchet's approbation was given on Dec. 2, 1715; the *privilège* on Jan. 17, 1716. Dedicated to the prince de Conti, the play was republished in the *Théâtre françois* of 1737; in the *Nouveau Théâtre françois,* 1734; by Petitot in 1803; in the *Auteurs du second ordre,* 1808; and in the *Répertoire* of 1823. It was published by Serieys as *Marius à Cyrte* in *Œuvres inédites de M. le Président Hénault,* Paris, Hubert, 1806.

[2] *Le Président Hénault,* Paris, 1903, p. 195. He took the note from Serieys's *Œuvres inédites de . . . Hénault.*

[3] XV, 209-16.

[4] Cf. Taschereau, *Histoire de la vie et des ouvrages de P. Corneille,* Paris, 1869, II, 197-8.

that of his wife, Montlebert, when he married her in 1717. Through the influence of the princesse de Conti he became " Controlleur Général des Fermes du Roy " at Châlons-sur-Saone. He subsequently lived at Besançon, Troyes, Coutances, and Bayeux, where he died in 1733. His honesty, kindliness, and pleasing companionship are praised by his biographers.

The main source of his first tragedy is Plutarch, as Caux indicates. His *Life of Marius* supplies the background of civil war, the detention of the younger Marius at the court of Hiempsal, and the fact that the king's concubine fell in love with the youth and enabled him to escape. Lion suggests that the subject may have been inspired by " l'Héroïde de Fontenelle: *Arisbe à Marius,*" but he does not show that this poem was written before the play. If it was not, it is probable that the tragedy inspired the poem. In any case Caux could have got from it nothing that he could not have found in Plutarch except the heroine's name, which the biographer does not mention. Her suicide may have been suggested by the story of Dido.

Influenced by his idea of the proprieties and of tragic dignity, Caux made his heroine, not the concubine, but the fiancée of Hiempsal and the niece of Jugurtha. Young Marius, who was probably the nephew of Caius, becomes his son—an alteration that finds some support in Appian—in order to strengthen their devotion to each other. The time selected is the eve of Caius's seventh consulate; the place, " Cirthe, capitale de Numidie, dans le palais du roi." [5]

[5] The younger Marius, a refugee at the court of Hiempsal, King of Numidia, has fallen in love with that monarch's fiancée, who returns his affection. He hears that his father, Caius Marius, has been murdered and that the assassin, sent by Sylla, has come to ask that he be surrendered to the Romans. Arisbe offers to persuade Hiempsal not to give him up. Soon Caius appears and informs a friend that he has slain Sylla's agent, taken his papers, and spread a report of his own death. He describes his flight from Rome, his hiding in a marsh, and his narrow escape from death. When he presents the papers and asks that young Marius be surrendered, Hiempsal refuses, partly for hatred of Rome, partly in order to please Arisbe. While Caius is threatening him with the wrath of the senate, his son appears, intending to slay his father's murderer, recognizes Caius, and is deeply moved. The father prevents his secret from becoming known and urges the youth to satisfy Rome. Hiempsal is more than ever determined to detain young Marius, but he is troubled by Caius's remark that Arisbe may have her reasons for defending the young man. Caius urges his son to escape with the aid of Arisbe, who is hurt by his desire to depart and refuses to help him until he tells her that the envoy is his father. Then, when Hiempsal accuses her of loving his rival, she pretends to be indignant and insists that young Marius be delivered to the envoy. But the king, whose suspicions have been aroused, gets from Caius the admission that he is Marius, and plans to put father and son to death. Then Arisbe, with the help of her guard, led by Amyntas, enables the Romans to escape. At first young Marius thinks he has been betrayed by Amyntas and asks Arisbe to lend him her dagger in order that he may kill himself, but Caius appears, assures his son that their boat is ready, and leads him away. A report is brought that, after a violent struggle, the young man has leaped with his father into the sea and succeeded in reaching the boat. Hiempsal accuses Arisbe, who admits her love for the young hero and commits suicide with her dagger.

The four leading characters are well delineated: forceful Caius Marius, longing to return to power, a man of great determination, knowledge of men, and presence of mind; his son, torn between devotion to his father and love of the African princess; the king, dominated by hatred of Rome, love of Arisbe, and jealousy of his rival; and the princess herself, who makes possible her lover's escape, though she is unwilling to accompany him, and kills herself like other celebrated women of Northern Africa, Dido, Sophonisba, and Cleopatra. The political background is presented from a purely personal point of view. The rivalry of Marius and Sylla is clearly indicated, but there is no suggestion that one headed the democratic, the other the aristocratic forces. Nor is much stress laid on African opposition to Roman encroachments. The supernatural is limited to the prediction that Marius will again be consul.

Much of the play's merit lies in the skillful arrangement of the scenes in Acts I-IV and in the absence of romantic machinery. The exposition is enlivened by the report of Caius's murder. His appearance at the beginning of Act II alters the situation, as does the return of Theseus, after his death has been reported, in *Phèdre*. His plan to get his son's help at first defeats itself by alarming Arisbe. The author brings about four scenes of recognition. The first is in II, 1: " Oui, tu vois Marius." In the second the actor has to show by his expression that the recognition has taken place (II, 3):

> Quel mortel avouant ce forfait odieux
> En ira demander le salaire?
> Caius: Moi.
> Marius fils: Dieux
>   Que vois-je? où suis-je enfin? . . .

In the third case Arisbe has declared that her guards will slay the envoy. She is shocked by young Marius's trembling and his assertion that he objects to crime. He is at last obliged to declare that the supposed assassin is his father himself, an admission that completely alters the situation. Finally (IV, 3) Hiempsal learns who the envoy is:

> Le jeune Marius vous est cher.
> Caius: Moi, je l'aime?
> Hiempsal: Vous défendez un fils.
> Caius: Moi, son pére?
> Hiempsal: Oüi, vous-même.
> Caius: Enfin de mes projets le Ciel veut se jouer:
>   Mais mon nom est trop beau pour le désavoüer.
>   Oüi, je suis Marius. Tremble. Tu vois un homme
>   Redouté de la terre & craint même de Rome.

The author adds to the emotional effect of his verses by his rather frequent use of *enjambement*. His last act is less effective than the others, though it gains variety by the fact that young Marius believes at first that he has been betrayed. Unfortunately the nature of the subject required the two leading characters to leave the stage before the end of the play. The heroine's suicide, moreover, does not seem inevitable, though preparation has been made for her having a dagger in her possession. It was this fifth act, according to the frères Parfaict, that limited the play's success.

First produced on Nov. 15, 1715, the tragedy was acted every other day, but only until Nov. 27, seven times in that year. Beaubourg, Ponteuil, la Duclos, Legrand, Du Boccage, Dangeville, Quinault, Fontenay, and la Sallé composed the cast. It is reasonably sure that la Duclos played the heroine; Ponteuil, Caius Marius; Beaubourg, his son. The author's share in the receipts was 526 fr., 18 s. Subsequently the play was revived. It was given three times in 1755, ten times in 1789.[6]

In the preface Caux boasts that he has chosen a familiar subject, altered chiefly by his making Marius disguise himself as the ambassador he has murdered. He claims that the events spring from one another and defends the account of Marius's misfortunes, the fact that he learns of his son's love before Cethegus does, the first scene of recognition, the meeting of father and son in Act IV, and the fifth act. He admits that he altered the final scene of Act III, so that now the king is warned that Caius lives and has been seen with his son. One gathers from his remarks that the play received considerable criticism and that Act V won " nulle grace," an admission that agrees with the judgment of the frères Parfaict and with their quotation of Du Sauzet's *Nouvelles littéraires,* though the latter finds in the play several fine passages. The *Bibliothéque Françoise,* also quoted by the frères Parfaict, speaks of the tragedy at greater length:

Il y a des vers dans cette Tragédie, dont nos plus grands Maîtres se feroient honneur. Tels sont ceux que dit Marius le pere, lorsque Hyemsal l'a découvert, . . . le caractére que Marius donne aux Numides, & l'adresse avec laquelle il démêle la politique de leur Roy, sont parfaitement développés. L'amour du jeune Marius pour Arisbe y est traité avec toute la bienséance convenable.

The critic objects to some of the verses, but he considers that the author deserves great credit for renouncing marvelous incidents and the desire to " fourer de l'esprit partout." The frères Parfaict add that the interest aroused by Act IV is lost in Act V. They admit that it was difficult to end the tragedy otherwise, but contend that Caux should have given up the subject if he was unable to overcome this difficulty.

---

[6] The *Mercure* of September, 1755, stated that Arisbe was played by la Clairon and found the character of Marius Cornelian. For *Arisbe et Marius* cf. below, my discussion of Le Franc de Pompignan's *Zoraïde.*

Petitot praises the characterization, though he regrets that young Marius is less heroic than the woman who loves him. Both he and Lion note minor imitations of Racine. Lion suggests that Marius's impersonating the man he has slain was suggested by La Grange-Chancel's *Amasis*. He considers the play among the best of its time and praises especially the rôle of the elder Marius. He holds, however, that he does not dominate sufficiently the other characters, that love is not warmly enough expressed, and that the scenes of recognition and the sudden changes of fortune recall La Grange-Chancel rather than Corneille and Racine. He would probably not have denied, however, that in both characterization and situation it is the most striking tragedy that appeared after Crébillon's *Rhadamiste* and before Voltaire's *Œdipe*.

It is impossible to date the composition of Caux's other tragedy, LYSIMACHUS,[7] more accurately than to put it between 1715 and 1733, the year of its author's death. His son speaks of it as an " Ouvrage posthûme de mon Pere," refers to the " foible part que j'ai en cet Ouvrage," and dedicates it to the prince de Conti because the elder Caux had dedicated *Marius* to the prince's father. As we have no other evidence, it is better to attribute the tragedy, as Quérard does, to the father than to consider it the product of collaboration, as do Joannidès and certain eighteenth-century bibliographers.

The choice of Alexander's successor had been a theme in La Calprenède's *Cassandre* and in plays derived from it by Magnon and Pradon,[8] but there is no evidence that Caux turned to them rather than to Justin and Quintus Curtius, from whom he could learn of the discussions that followed the hero's death, the prominence of Perdiccas, the question whether Alexander's empire was to be divided among his generals, or whether he was to be succeeded by Roxana's unborn child, his son by Barsine, or his half-brother, Aridaeus. Justin states that Alexander left his kingdom to " the most worthy," that Lysimachus had a wife named Arsinoé, a son named Agathocles, and a daughter named Euridice, that parts of the dominion were bestowed upon Perdiccas, Lysimachus, and Cassander, and that Aridaeus became nominal king under the name of Philip.

These facts Caux altered considerably. Agathocles becomes the son of Lysimachus by Arsinoé, sister of Alexander, but he has been substituted by her for her brother's dead son. He is now, like Aridaeus, called Philip and is in love with Euridice without knowing that she is his sister. The

---

[7] Paris, Le Breton, 1738, 8°. Petitot, *Répertoire*, 1803, II, 299-305, analyzes the play and quotes from it about 70 verses. Strangely enough he finds that Perdiccas has an equivocal character.

[8] Louvart's *Mort d'Alexandre*, played in 1684, is lost. In Brueys's *Lisimachus*, published in 1735, the action takes place before Alexander's death.

problem of the Macedonian succession is consequently overshadowed by the human situation resulting from the danger of incest and from the attitude of Lysimachus and his wife towards their son.[9]

The tragedy is based upon moral ideas. Do not heed oracles, for they make one forget that reason is for man " un Oracle éternel " (IV, 1). Failure to realize this brings disaster upon Lysimachus and his family. Confusion results from refusal to base the right of succession upon blood relationship.

> Sur les Enfans des Rois, jamais un bras perfide,
> Ne léve impunément un glaive parricide. (IV, 4)

At the same time there is a warning to kings, for Lysimachus suggests in the same scene that it is Alexander's attempt to make himself a god that has caused his death and visited upon his children their misfortunes.[10]

Perdiccas is represented as an upright warrior, ready to sacrifice his love and his ambition to the law of succession. Opposed to him is Cassander, who claims that the empire belongs to the victorious generals

[9] In Boyer's *Tyridate* a princess named Euridice and her brother are in love and discover their relationship in the course of the play, but as this tragedy, published in 1649, may well have been unknown to Caux, the resemblance is not sufficient to establish relationship.

[10] The scene is laid in Babylon just after the death of Alexander. The army has left the choice of a successor to its leaders, Lysimachus, Cassander, and Perdiccas. The first of these proposes to put on the throne Philippe, a supposed son of Alexander by a Greek woman to whom he had been secretly married and who is now dead. His chief motive is personal ambition, for he plans to marry the young man to his daughter, Euridice. Though Perdiccas loves this girl, he agrees to sacrifice himself and support Philippe's claim to the throne. Alexander's infant son by Roxane is set aside because his mother is neither Greek nor Macedonian. Cassander would divide the empire among Alexander's leading generals. His opposition seems at first to be the only obstacle to Lysimachus's plan, for Philippe and Euridice are in love, but Arsinoé, sister of Alexander and wife of Lysimachus, informs Philippe that, as Euridice is his sister, he must not marry her. Arsinoé had cared for her brother's infant son and, when he died, had substituted her own, whose real name is Agatocle. She will not allow her son to tell his father of their relationship, for an oracle has warned her that, if her husband learns the secret, he will kill the young man, who can be saved only by mounting the throne. Agatocle-Philippe obeys his mother and agrees to keep the secret. As he is Alexander's nephew, he feels justified in seeking the throne, but he angers Euridice and his father by his refusal to marry her. Lysimachus now listens to Cassander. When Agatocle complains to his mother that he is misunderstood, she tells him of a dream she has had in which Lysimachus killed him. When Agatocle refuses a last chance to marry and reign, his father seeks to bribe Perdiccas by offering him his daughter, but Perdiccas is incorruptible and nearly convinces Lysimachus that he should be loyal to Alexander's son. Cassander tells him, however, that, since Perdiccas knows of their plot, it is now too late to give it up. Euridice reproaches herself for endangering the life of the man she loves by her complaints to her father of his unwillingness to marry her. When Agatocle tells her that their love is criminal, she insists on knowing why and threatens to kill herself. Fearing for her life, he admits that he is her brother. He then goes to help Perdiccas control the camp, while she informs Lysimachus that he is sacrificing his son, but it is too late to save him. Perdiccas, captured by Cassander, had been released by Arsinoé, but, before he could save Agatocle, the young man had been fatally wounded. Perdiccas avenges him by killing Cassander. Agatocle, dying, attributes his death to Fate and asks that his sister marry Perdiccas.

rather than to an infant and a youth, even if they are the sons of Alexander. Lysimachus wavers between the two. He does not have Perdiccas's passionate loyalty to the family of his dead master, but, when he turns against the supposed Philippe, he feels some compunction about depriving him of the throne. Murder means little to him, but he would not have been a party to his son's death if he had known of their relationship.[11]

Caux did not introduce the possibility of an incestuous marriage, although the historical Arsinoé married her brother. The modern objection to incest is maintained, for Euridice and Agatocle renounce their love as soon as they learn of their kinship. The young man errs through obedience to his mother and respect for what he takes to be the warning of an oracle; Euridice, through jealousy of an imaginary rival; Arsinoé, through ambition and superstitious belief in an oracle and a dream.

In Act I Lysimachus forms a plan that is thwarted in Act II by Agatocle's apparent indifference to marriage. He then joins Cassander in his efforts to divide the empire, but in Act IV encounters the opposition of Perdiccas. As the final act of his earlier play had been criticized, Caux now goes to the opposite extreme, assigning to it a large portion of the action, including the revelation to Euridice and to Lysimachus of their kinship to Agatocle, the deaths of the latter and of Cassander. The play would have been more effective if its leading characters had not acted so largely in ignorance of important relationships. Nor is one impressed by the strength of a passion that is so easy to give up. Caux preferred to write a romantic tale of substitution and danger of incest rather than to describe the destruction of an empire through the conflict of personal ambitions.

The tragedy was acted only on Dec. 13, 14, 16, and 21, 1737. Fierville, then sixty years old, played Lysimachus; Legrand de Belleville, Cassander; Sarrazin, Perdiccas; Dubois, Agatocle; la Dumesnil, Arsinoé; la Connell, Euridice; Louise Baron[12] and the younger La Thorillière, confidants. The share paid to the author's son was only 222 fr., 12 s. Perhaps the age of Fierville and the fact that the troupe had but recently received Dubois and the two leading women helped to bring about the failure of the tragedy.

Unlike Caux, Mme de Gomez, daughter of Paul Poisson, had begun her career as a dramatist before the death of Louis XIV.[13] She had won in 1714 considerable success with her *Habis,* a romantic tragedy that has

---

[11] Corneille would have thought the play more tragic if the father had known who his son was; cf. his criticism of Ghirardelli in his *Discours de la tragédie.*

[12] As she was married to Desbrosses, she is given this name in the printed text, though she appears as Mlle Baron in the *Registres.*

[13] Cf. my *Sunset,* pp. 79, 80.

nothing historical about it. When she wrote her next play, SÉMIRAMIS,[14] she employed a few historical or legendary names and relationships, but her plot was almost as purely invented as was that of her earlier tragedy. Semiramis is represented neither as a powerful queen, nor as the cause of her huband's death, nor as having a passion for her son, but as an Arabian princess, carried off in infancy by Menon, Governor of Syria, and brought up as his daughter. The subject of the play is her identification and her marriage to Ninus, whereas the author's predecessors, Gilbert and Desfontaines, had dramatized her accession to power by the execution of Ninus, and later dramatists, Crébillon and Voltaire, were to take up her passion for her son.

The facts that Semiramis became the wife of Ninus, son of Belus, and that before her marriage she was dependent upon Menon could have been derived from Diodorus Siculus or from Moréri. Except for these details, the plot seems to have been invented by the author, who, after the manner of Crébillon, sought to create scenes of recognition, brought about by mistaken identity.[15] She introduced an abduction, caused the lost princess to be sought during many years by her father and her brother, both disguised, and arranged a meeting in a single day of father, son, and daughter at the court of Ninus, where the heroine is asked to marry her

---

[14] Published in her Œuvres mêlées, Paris, Pierre Prault, Saugrain, Leclerc, and Mazuel, 1724, 12°. Republished in the Nouveau Théâtre françois, 1737.

[15] Menon, appointed Governor of Syria by his cousin, Bélus, King of Assyria, had plotted to seize the throne and had inspired the revolt of his son, who, when defeated, had fled to Arabia, had been delivered to Bélus by Simma, the Arabian king, and had been put to death. In revenge Menon had sought to kill Arétas, Simma's son, but his emissaries had instead carried off his infant daughter, Semiramis, who has been brought up as Nitocris, daughter of Menon, and is now loved by Ninus, who has succeeded Bélus. She has acquired two other lovers: Menon himself and Arétas, who has disguised himself as Arius and gone in search of her. Simma, too, is looking for his daughter. He is disguised as the ambassador of the Bactrians. An oracle had told him that he would find her on the banks of the Euphrates. He was imprisoned for twenty years until his captor, Zoroastre, discovered his identity and sent him to ask for peace and to arrange a marriage between Zoroastre and Nitocris, who is supposed to be the daughter of Menon. Ninus refuses to give his consent as he wishes to marry Nitocris himself. Menon bids Nitocris decline to marry Ninus, though she admits to a confidant that she loves him. Arius, who has won great distinction in arms, declares his love for Nitocris and is rejected. He is told by a dying soldier that Semiramis had been placed in Menon's power and may have been murdered by him. Menon now offers him the hand of Nitocris if he will admit him to the palace at night and enable him to kill Ninus. Arius agrees to admit him, but he is resolved to warn Ninus of the plot. A conversation with Simma leads to the discovery that they are father and son. They seek to save Ninus. Meanwhile Menon tells Nitocris that she is not his daughter, but a girl of obscure birth whom he will make queen if she will marry him. When she refuses, she is put under guard. At night Menon is arrested by Ninus, who thanks the Arabians for saving his life and learns from Nitocris that she is not the daughter of Menon. When the latter is questioned, he fears torture and takes poison. Before he dies, he declares that Nitocris is Semiramis and predicts that she will bring disaster upon Ninus. She is reunited to her father and brother. Undisturbed by Menon's prediction, she will marry Ninus.

adopted father, her brother, and the Kings of Assyria and Bactria. Yet the absurdity of these circumstances does not prevent the various elements of the plot from being well fitted together. Each incident leads up to the identification of Semiramis and her marriage to Ninus. Even the love of the brother for his sister, which may have been introduced to give a suggestion of incest to a story dealing with Semiramis, has its place, as it induces Menon to reveal his plans to the supposed Arius.

Ninus is represented as an ideal young prince, willing to marry Semiramis, whatever her birth may prove to be. Simma, Arius, and Semiramis are equally virtuous, while Menon is the typical villain, ambitious, treacherous, and moved by an almost incestuous love of his adopted daughter.

The play is not remarkable for its ideas, but there is one conservative utterance that is worth quoting (III, 5):

> Les crimes des mortels firent naître les loix,
> Et c'est pour les punir que le Ciel fit les Rois.

In the same scene Simma and his son recognize each other. They first discover that both are seeking Semiramis and that each is unable to master his tears, then Simma asks Arius to give his real name and discovers that he is his son. They make themselves known to Ninus in V, 5. In the last scene of the tragedy Menon identifies Semiramis and explains his conduct as follows:

> Je me tairois encore, en ce fatal moment,
> Si par là je croyois augmenter ton tourment,
> Mais de l'ingrate ici, découvrant la naissance,
> J'assurerai bien mieux l'effet de ma vengeance,
> Et prevoyant enfin son destin plein d'horreur;
> Je la vois destinée à servir ma fureur;
> Et le Ciel par sa main, vengera ma famille.
> Voilà Sémiramis!

Ninus: Ciel . . .
Semiramis: Mon pere . . .
Simma: Ah! ma fille.

This final scene of recognition introduces a prophecy that is not in keeping with the rest of the play. If the spectators were ignorant of the heroine's reputation, it is pointless; if they were aware of it, the prophecy would tend to turn them against the heroine, whose conduct in the play had been too exemplary to prepare for her murdering her husband and falling in love with her son. The author may have added it merely to increase the supernatural element, already exemplified by an oracle and the cry of the blood, but it may have served to bewilder the spectators rather than to impress them.

Whether or not this was the cause, the play certainly failed, for it was acted only on Feb. 1, 3, and 5, 1716. La Duclos played the heroine; la Sallé, her confidant. Other members of the cast were Ponteuil, Beaubourg, Legrand, Maurice Quinault, Dufresne, Dangeville, Du Boccage, and Fontenay. The author's share in the receipts was pitifully small, only 129 fr., 2 s. The frères Parfaict [16] cite an article by Le Fèvre in the *Mercure* that accuses the heroine of being a " Princesse Logogrif " with adventures badly invented and worse related, though the published text hardly justifies the title assigned to Semiramis. The audience had not objected to the strange adventures described in *Habis*, but may have looked for a nearer approach to reality in what was supposed to be a tragedy based upon history.

Mme de Gomez seems to have understood the failure of her play in this sense, for in her next tragedy, CLÉARQUE TYRAN D'HÉRACLÉE,[17] she followed history in its general outline, abandoning disguise and efforts at producing scenes of recognition. Justin [18] had related the story of Clearchus, recalled from exile by the people of Heracleia in Asia Minor, making a tyrant of himself, putting sixty senators to death, and obliging their wives and daughters to marry freedmen. He had also told how Chion and Leonidas had gone to Clearchus as if to have him settle a dispute, and, while one of them conversed with him, the other had slain him. Reference is also made to the tyrant's relations with Mithridates, father of Mithridates the Great. Mme de Gomez added a love interest by imagining that one of the senators was saved by his daughter and that both Clearchus and Leonidas had fallen in love with her. She made of Chion the captain of the tyrant's guards, added the commander of the city troops, and caused both of them to conspire with Leonidas. She did not discuss the social questions that lay back of the revolt, but concentrated her efforts upon the palace revolution and the desperate efforts of a daughter to save her heroic father.[19]

---

[16] XV, 217-9.

[17] Paris, Ribou, 1717, 12°, and in the author's *Œuvres mêlées*, Paris, Pierre Prault, Saugrain, Leclerc, and Mazuel, 1724, 12°. Republished in the *Nouveau Théâtre françois*, 1738.

[18] XVI, 4, 5.

[19] Leonidas, who has left Heracleia to serve in the army of Mithridates, has so distinguished himself that he is entrusted by this king with the task of freeing Heracleia from the tyranny of Clearchus. Leonidas hopes also to rescue Senator Entigesne and his daughter, Aristophile, with whom he is in love. Entering the city as an ambassador, he secures the help of Stratocle, commandant of the city, and arranges to have the gates opened at night. He informs Aristophile and her father of his plan. Clearchus suspects Leonidas, but he hopes to use him to lure Mithridates into the city. He offers to make Entigesne the second man in the government if his daughter will marry him, but threatens to kill him if she refuses. Aristophile is willing to sacrifice herself, but her father makes her swear not to

Clearchus is represented as a tyrant who has killed many senators before the play begins and now orders the murder of Entigesne and plots that of Mithridates. He has reached the end of his career without realizing that he has alienated many of those in whom he trusts. He reflects that crime has put him in power and that it is by crime that he must keep his authority. The heroism of Leonidas, Entigesne, and Aristophile contrasts sharply with his selfishness.

The plot is very simple. Leonidas encounters little opposition in taking the city. The only real difficulty lies in saving the senator's life. His rescue is accomplished in a manner that creates considerable suspense. There is "unfinished business" in the fact that we never learn whether Mithridates will allow the city's liberty to be restored. We are assured, however, that in any event the inhabitants will be better off than they were under Clearchus, for one should obey a king by birth rather than one who has assumed power without the support of royal blood (III, 2). Mme de Gomez did not offend the Bourbons.

Apart from the incompleteness of the ending, the tragedy is thoroughly classical in structure. There are a few striking scenes, chiefly in Act IV, but too few to make the play succeed. It was acted on Nov. 26,[20] 28, 30, and Dec. 2, 6, 1717. The author selected as the heroine and her confidant la Desmares and la Champvallon, but she kept the male portion of the cast as it had been in *Sémiramis* except that she added her brother, Philippe Poisson, and omitted Beaubourg and Dufresne. She succeeded in earning only 142 fr., 10 s., little more than the earlier tragedy had brought her. The frères Parfaict held that so slight a subject could succeed only by the creation of forceful situations, striking characters, and poetic diction, none of which they found in the production. They might have praised the author, however, for trying to follow the example of Corneille and Racine rather than again trusting for her effects to disguise and recognition.

In 1716-1717 the two most celebrated tragic authors of the day attempted to lend distinction to the *genre* by selecting familiar subjects that were to be dramatized by Voltaire. Both tragedies failed and are remembered chiefly because of other plays composed by their authors.

La Grange-Chancel's SOPHONISBE was acted only four times, Nov. 10,

---

consent to the marriage. Angered by their resistance, Clearchus orders his faithful follower, Cleon, to put the senator to death. Leonidas informs Aristophile that his troops will soon enter the palace, but she insists that, as they will not be in time to save her father, Leonidas must act at once. He hesitates to assassinate Clearchus, but, yielding to her eloquence, gets the help of Torax, pretends to quarrel with him, and, while his companion engages the tyrant in conversation, succeeds in murdering him. Entigesne kills Cleon with the sword of Clearchus. The people acclaim Leonidas, who will have the support of Mithridates and will marry Aristophile.

[20] This first performance was overlooked by the frères Parfaict (XV, 270-1).

12, 14, 16, 1716. As it was never published and the manuscript is lost, one has to derive knowledge of it from the *Registres*, the *Mercure*, and the frères Parfaict.[21] The first of these gives the cast: la Desmares and la Sallé, who must have played the heroine and her confidant; old Guérin, who probably represented Hasdrubal; Ponteuil, Beaubourg, and Dufresne, who may well have interpreted the rôles of Scipio, Syphax, and Massinissa; Legrand, Du Boccage, Dangeville, and Philippe Poisson. The fact that there are only two women suggests that the author did not attempt, like Corneille, a subordinate plot. According to the *Mercure*, the play was well constructed, the characters well sustained, the verses fine, and the sentiments noble. Its only real defect was that the subject had already been dramatized by Corneille. This, however, is not a satisfactory explanation of its failure, for Corneille's *Sophonisbe* is certainly inferior to his *Œdipe*, the memory of which tragedy did not prevent the success of Voltaire's *Œdipe* two years later. The frères Parfaict note the addition of Hasdrubal, father of Sophonisba, a character omitted by Mairet and Corneille. They quote four lines from a speech he addressed to his daughter, all that is left of the play:

> Songez qu'il est des tems où tout est légitime;
> Et que si la Patrie avoit besoin d'un crime,
> Qui put seul relever son espoir abbattu,
> Il ne seroit plus crime, & deviendroit vertu.

Prospering momentarily from the success of speculation under the guidance of Law, Crébillon composed his SÉMIRAMIS,[22] the first tragedy he had written since the failure of his *Xercès* early in 1714. The subject was probably called to his attention by the recent tragedy of the same name by Mme de Gomez. It doubtlessly appealed to him because it gave him an opportunity for disguise, recognition, and danger of incest, themes that had characterized his successful plays and which he had avoided, unwisely as it must have seemed to him, in *Xercès*. From the legend as related by Justin, Diodorus Siculus, and Moréri he retained the facts that Semiramis, Queen of Babylon, killed and succeeded Ninus, her husband, and that she fell in love with her son, Ninyas. Crébillon prevented the incest from being accomplished and added the themes of children secretly married, of a lost prince appearing as a hero of unknown origin, and of a palace intrigue led by Bélus, now the queen's brother instead of being her father-in-law.[23]

Semiramis, though she lacks decision in regard to her brother and is ineffective when she orders the death of her rival, has a rôle that may well have been impressive when played by an accomplished actress. She is at first triumphant, then suspicious, eager to win Agénor, happy in the thought that she has succeeded, then doubting his loyalty, demanding the death of Mermécide, and suddenly discovering that Agénor is her son. She tries not to believe it and, even when she does, remains jealous enough to seek her rival's death. She softens only in her last couplet, when she expresses the hope that Ninias will not find a Semiramis in his bride.

Bélus is presented as a prince who longs for justice, but is forced by those around him to make use of crime in order to accomplish it (III, 3) :

[23] Semiramis has put to death Ninus, her husband, and is ruling victoriously despite revolts among her Assyrian subjects. Her brother, Bélus, who has a fine reputation and considerable power, strives to avenge his brother-in-law and to give the throne to Ninias, his sister's son. When his daughter, Ténésis, and this prince were about five years old, he had secretly married them in a wood near Sinope. Ninias was subsequently brought up by Mermécide, but had disappeared ten years before the action begins. Early one morning Bélus learns from Madate that Mégabise, whom they had informed of their plot against the queen, had betrayed them and that Madate had lured him into a forest and stabbed him. Mermécide brings word that he has been unable to find Ninias, but that he has run across Mégabise and heard him blame Madate and Bélus for his wound. The approach of soldiers made him leave. He now offers to kill Semiramis and make her brother king. The conversation is interrupted by the queen, now triumphant over the Assyrians. She expresses her doubts about her brother's loyalty and admits her love for a young hero called Agénor, whom she has just made King of Media. She asks Ténésis to win him for her by offering him her throne. When the queen has left her, Ténésis declares that she is herself in love with Agénor, but that, as she was married in childhood, she cannot be his wife. She delivers the queen's message, however, and rejects Agénor when he courts her. Bélus informs the young man that his supposedly humble birth makes it improper for him to marry a princess. Irritated, Agénor agrees to wed Semiramis. When Bélus learns of this projected marriage and feels sure that Mégabise has revealed his plot against the queen, he takes steps to save the situation. Though he refuses to allow Mermécide to kill Agénor, he has his followers placed around the palace and spreads a report that Ninias is returning in order to avenge his father. He then tells Agénor of his plot against the queen and seeks to win his aid by offering him his daughter. Agénor replies that he still loves Ténésis and that he has intended to leave Babylon without marrying the queen, but that now he must stay to defend her. Thereupon Bélus resolves to put him to death, but he first allows his daughter to speak with him. Their conversation leads to the discovery that they had been married to each other as children, but both now believe that Agénor is the son of Mermécide. The latter brings the young man a letter and starts to stab him while he reads it, but Agénor seizes his arm and they recognize each other. When Semiramis calls upon Agénor to slay Mermécide as a rebel, the youth declares that the old man is his father, a statement that Mermécide contradicts by asserting that Agénor is Ninias, son of Semiramis. The queen calls Mermécide an impostor and refuses to believe that the man she loves is her son, but she is soon convinced that he has spoken the truth. She refuses, however, to give up her throne, orders her rival killed, and proposes to burn herself up with her palace. Ninias wins over the soldiers and urges the queen to love him as a son and to allow him to marry Ténésis. She replies that he will have the girl " sans vie," but Ténésis is saved by Mermécide and shows her magnanimity by seeking to protect Semiramis, who, seeing herself powerless and disgraced, commits suicide.

> Telle est donc de ces lieux l'influence cruelle
> Que jusqu'à la vertu s'y rendra criminelle.

He would have been more effective if his position in the empire had been made clear and if we had some other evidence of his boasted virtue than his desire to avenge his brother-in-law by killing his sister. Agénor is meant to be a typical young warrior and lover, but his extravagant boasts of loyalty and prowess weaken the impression. Ténésis is so admirable that she seeks to save the queen who has just ordered her death. Mermécide is a faithful and elderly upholder of Ninias's right to the throne. Despite his age, he always arrives at the right moment, finding Mégabise in the forest, recognizing Ninias, making him known to his mother, saving the life of Ténésis. The other characters perform the functions of confidants.

The play is constructed in accordance with classical principles, all the events leading up to the heroine's suicide in the last few lines of the final scene, but the exposition is unnecessarily tedious and involved. Crébillon must have prided himself on his fourth act, in which there are no less than three scenes of recognition. In IV, 2, Agénor's description of the secret marriage in a wood near a cave and in the presence of two old men leads Ténésis to exclaim, " vous êtes mon époux." In IV, 4, the scene of recognition is of the Merope type, much admired by Aristotle, for it is at the moment when Mermécide is holding his dagger over Agénor that the prince recognizes in him his supposed father. In the following scene Semiramis questions Agénor about Mermécide:

> S.: Quel intérêt si grand prenez-vous à ses jours?
> Ag.: Est-il besoin encor d'éclaircir ce discours?
>   Voulez-vous qu'à vos coups j'abandonne mon père?
> M.: Non, je ne le suis pas; mais voilà votre mère.

After crowding three such situations into his fourth act, Crébillon had scarcely enough material left for his fifth, but he tried to hold the interest of his audience by suspense over the fate of Ténésis and the queen. In the earlier acts the most interesting scene is the interview between Bélus and Agénor (II, 3), in which are set forth the relative merits of birth and valor:

> Bélus: Seigneur, une couronne
>   N'est jamais bien à nous si le sang ne la donne:
>   La Reine, comme moi, sort de celui des Dieux,
>   Elle règne, est-ce assez pour oser autant qu'eux!
>   Imitons leur justice, & non pas leur puissance.
>   L'équité doit régler & peine & récompense.
>   Quoi qu'il en soit, parmi de peu dignes ayeux,
>   Ma fille n'ira point mêler le sang des Dieux: . . .

> Ag.: Un Guerrier généreux que la vertu couronne,
> Vaut bien un roi formé par le secours des loix;
> Le premier qui le fut, n'eut pour lui que sa voix: [24]
> Quiconque est élevé par un si beau suffrage,
> Ne croit pas du Destin deshonorer l'ouvrage.

It must not be supposed that Crébillon was attacking the dogma of divine right, for he put the words into the mouth of the heir to the throne. They reveal a trait of character, but have no effect upon the plot, which results in the triumph of legitimacy.

Announced in January, 1717, the tragedy was acted on April 10. According to the *Mercure*,[25] Semiramis was played by la Desmares; Agénor by Beaubourg; Bélus by Ponteuil; Ténésis by la Dangeville; other rôles by Guérin, Du Boccage, Fontenay, and la Sallé.[26] Though the acting of those who took the leading parts was praised, the tragedy was performed only seven times in April and once in July, on the 22nd.

Crébillon may have offended some of his audience, as he did La Harpe,[27] by representing a mother in love with her son. He erred, as Henri Lion points out,[28] by stifling his principal action under a palace intrigue carried on by persons in whom we take little interest. He gave Voltaire an opportunity to write a simpler, more spectacular, and more appealing tragedy on the same subject, and to display his own talents at the expense of his predecessor, to whom he owed his theme and certain suggestions for its presentation.[29]

Another dramatist who had made his début before the death of Louis XIV brought out, like La Grange-Chancel and Crébillon, one tragedy in this period. Though Deschamps's *Caton d'Utique* [30] had won for him some notoriety, he may well have thought that a simpler plot, with less improbable incidents, would be more rewarding, and that fewer objections would be raised to alterations in his source if he selected characters less well known to his public than Cato and Julius Caesar. He accordingly composed ANTIOCHUS ET CLÉOPÀTRE,[31] taking his plot from Justin and

---

[24] Dutrait compares with this line Voltaire's well-known verse (*Mérope*, I, 3):
Le premier qui fut roi fut un soldat heureux.

[25] Cited by the frères Parfaict, XV, 254-65. They also quote *l'Europe vivante*.

[26] Guérin, the oldest member of the troupe, must have played Mermécide; la Sallé, the queen's confidant, Phénice. According to the *Registres*, Dangeville also played. The author earned 617 fr., 12 s.

[27] *Cours de littérature*, 1825, XII, 78. He called the queen's love an "égarement odieux et indécent."

[28] *Les Tragédies et les théories dramatiques de Voltaire*, Paris, Hachette, 1895, p. 199.

[29] Cf. below, the study of Voltaire's *Sémiramis*.

[30] For this tragedy and its author cf. my *Sunset*, pp. 140-3.

[31] Paris, Jean Musnier, 1718, 12°. Approbation, signed by Danchet, Nov. 15. Dedicated to the duc de Noailles. The only copies of this play that I have been

changing the incidents related by him in such a way as to avoid the horror of the tale and to bring about what is for a tragedy a happy ending.

In his dedication Deschamps longs for the force of Sophocles and the charm of Euripides in order to reward Noailles for his protection. In his preface he declares that his source is found in the thirty-ninth book of Justin. He admits that he has altered the ending of the story, but he defends his doing so on the ground that such a change is allowed if the source of the plot is not very well known. As precedent he refers to Racine's presentation of Monime in *Mithridate*. "C'est lui qui nous a montré qu'une action simple & soûtenuë par des sentimens naturels, pouvoit attacher beaucoup, & plaire infiniment." But a play must justify itself. Happy are those who, "sans anatomiser une Piece de Théatre, s'abandonnent au plaisir qu'ils en reçoivent!"

Now, according to Justin, the Cleopatra who was to be made famous to French audiences by Corneille's *Rodogune* had been survived by Antiochus Grypus, her son by Demetrius Nicator, and by Cyzicenus, her son by Antiochus, brother of Demetrius. Grypus had married Tryphaena, whose sister, another Cleopatra, had married Cyzicenus and had encouraged him to make war upon his half-brother. When Grypus defeated Cyzicenus and captured Cleopatra, Tryphaena insisted upon her being put to death, partly because she suspected her husband of loving her. Despite his protests, she sent soldiers into the temple where Cleopatra had taken refuge, and, when this princess grasped the altar so tightly that they could not remove her, the soldiers cut off her hands. Her death, which soon followed, was avenged by Cyzicenus when he killed her sister.

In the same book Justin relates that this Cleopatra had first married her brother, an Egyptian prince who loved her, but who had been forced by his mother to marry her sister. This incident is combined by Deschamps with the events of his main source, so that his Antiochus, who corresponds to Grypus, had been engaged to Cleopatra, had loved her deeply, and had been forced to give her up and marry her sister, whom he detested. Deschamps took his four main characters from Justin, but he added a fifth, Clitus, in order that he might foil Tryphaena's plans in such a way that it is she who is murdered in the temple instead of her sister. He also invented the suicide of Cyzicenus, which makes possible the unhistorical union of Antiochus and Cleopatra. The struggle in the temple is, of course, kept behind the scenes, while horror is avoided, even in a *récit,* by the omission of any reference to the amputation of a suppliant's hands.[32]

---

able to locate are at the Arsenal. A reproduction of one of them on film is at The Johns Hopkins University.

[32] Cizicène, defeated by his half-brother, Antiochus, King of Syria, has taken

Cleopatra is the noble character of the play. Though she still loves Antiochus, she is offended by her husband's jealous suspicions, swears to remain faithful to him, and promises to accompany him into exile. She condemns divorce, although, as she admits, it is allowed in Syria, and she promises never to marry Antiochus, if he is the cause of her husband's death. Her sister, Triphène, is devoid of moral scruples. She is deeply in love with Antiochus, knows that he loves her sister, and consequently plans her death. To bring this about she cleverly deceives both Antiochus and Cleopatra with a pretense of reconciliation, but she makes the mistake of trusting Clitus, whose unwillingness to carry out her murderous orders she is unable to foresee.

Antiochus is meant to embody conflicting emotions. He is guided mainly by his love for Cleopatra, but he has some affection for his brother, some desire to be a just and forceful ruler. He is, however, quite ineffective, for the conduct of the action is taken out of his hands and placed in those of the queen and Clitus. His brother is also mainly influenced by love of Cleopatra, which had caused him to oppose successfully her marriage to his brother, to marry her himself, and to seek to place her on the throne. His defeat, he tells us, would have made him kill himself but for his desire to be with her again. For her sake he delays his own escape, and the belief that she has been murdered is the cause of his suicide. He is full of jealousy and suspicion, faults that he overcomes only when he is at the point of death.

The most striking scenes are those of Act II, when Cleopatra pleads for her husband to the king who loves her and when Cizicène interviews his brother. The interest weakens in the third act and the fourth, largely

refuge, with his wife, Cleopatra, in the royal palace at Antioch. He fears that his wife, whom he had kept by intrigue from marrying Antiochus, will now desert him for his conqueror, but she promises to remain faithful. Before the end of the first act Antiochus captures the city and plans to marry Cleopatra after a double divorce. In Act II his conscience troubles him and he is touched by Cleopatra's plea for her husband, but the latter's jealousy and his defiant attitude cause him to arrest his brother. He puts in charge of him Clitus, the general who has captured the city. He also has Clitus guard his queen, Triphène, when he discovers her dangerous hostility to Cleopatra. As Clitus is under obligations to the queen, she trusts him to the extent of asking him to lure Cleopatra to the temple of Apollo outside the city and there to put her to death. Clitus pretends to agree, but plans to substitute another woman and to enable Cizicène and Cleopatra to escape by a secret passage. He frees the prince and bids him meet Cleopatra at night in the temple. He urges the princess to wait until her absence from the palace will not be detected, but she goes too soon, is threatened by Triphène's soldiers, and takes refuge at the altar. When the soldiers, moved by her eloquence, refuse to kill her, the queen herself advances with a drawn dagger, but just then soldiers sent by Clitus to escort Cizicène and Cleopatra enter the temple, rescue the princess, and slay the queen. When her mangled body is seen by Cizicène, he concludes that it is Cleopatra's, reports the murder to Antiochus, and gives himself a fatal wound. Thereupon Cleopatra enters unharmed. Cizicène bids her live happily with Antiochus, forget Triphène, but speak sometimes of his misfortunes.

devoted to Triphène's conspiracy and the efforts of Clitus to outwit her. Much of the fifth act is taken up with accounts of what takes place behind the scenes, but the suicide of Cizicène is witnessed by the audience.

Deschamps was too obviously interested in getting rid of the queen and her brother-in-law without divorce and without making Antiochus or Cleopatra responsible for their deaths. To dispose of them he invented the arrival of friendly soldiers just as Cleopatra is about to be murdered, the queen's death in the fighting that follows, and her unexplained disfigurement, which leads Cizicène to mistake her corpse for her sister's. Such puerile devices are enough to account for the failure of the play.

Apart from these events of the last act the tragedy does not lack *vraisemblance*. In this respect, in the simplicity of the plot, the emphasis placed on love, and the absence of horror, disguise, and recognition, the tragedy seems to be an imitation of Racine, but Deschamps lacked the great dramatist's style and his ability to make his action depend upon the logical conflict of his main characters. He may, however, have won some appreciation from those who were soon to applaud Voltaire's *Œdipe* by the anticlerical suggestion contained in the assertion that, when Cizicène sought to prevent his brother's marriage, he roused the people against it by bribing the priests (I, 1):

> Par tout des Immortels je séduis les Ministres,
> Je leur fais publier des prodiges sinistres.

The play was acted only on Oct. 29, 31, Nov. 2, 4, 6, 1717. The two princesses were played by la Desmares and Adrienne Le Couvreur; the confidant, by la Sallé. The other rôles were taken by Dufresne, Quinault, Legrand, Dangeville, Du Boccage, and Fontenay. The author's share was 165 fr., 16 s. The frères Parfaict [33] hold that Acts I and II are not without merit, but that the others are defective, especially the last. Their judgment of the characters may have been affected by a curious historical blunder, for they assert that all the characters are "dans le genre de fureur" except Cleopatra, who is, nevertheless, the famous Cleopatra of *Rodogune*. If they had read the play with care, they would have found (II, 3) a reference to the Cleopatra immortalized by Corneille, but she was the heroine's aunt and mother-in-law and had died before the action of the tragedy begins.

The last tragedy to precede Voltaire's *Œdipe* was ARTAXARE,[34] attributed on the title-page of the first edition to "M. D. L. S."; on that of

---

[33] XV, 268-9.
[34] Paris, veuve Pissot, 1734, 8°. According to Beauchamps, de Maunoir's approbation was given on Jan. 16; the *privilège*, on Jan. 21. Republished in the *Nouveau Théâtre françois*, 1735.

the second and by Beauchamps to " Mr. de la Serre," that is, to Jean-Louis Ignace de la Serre, 1662-1756, known for his opera librettos, his gambling, and his friendship with the author, Mlle de Lussan.   There would be no doubt about the attribution, if the frères Parfaict had not declared that it was a matter of common knowledge that La Serre had loaned his name to the real author, the abbé Pellegrin.   As the play has little resemblance to the latter's early tragedies, all of which were derived from Hyginus, there is nothing to support the statement of the frères Parfaict, but as, on the other hand, title-pages are by no means infallible, the question of the play's authorship remains in doubt.

The tragedy derives its name from the founder of the Sassanian dynasty, called Ardishir, Ardshir and Artaxerxes, but, by Moréri and Voltaire, Artaxare.   He is known to have overthrown Artabanus IV, the last Parthian king, to have fought against the Romans, who were supported by Arsaces, brother of Artabanus, and to have been succeeded by his son, Sapor.   The dramatist kept the names of Artaxare, Artaban, Arsace, and Sapor, but he attributed the new king's success to an unhistorical Pharnabaze and invented a plot largely concerned with the revolt of Arsace, the love inspired by his daughter, and Artaxare's difficulties with members of his own family.   The scene is laid in the Parthian capital of Ecatompile.[35]

[35] Pharnabaze, a Persian prince, has dethroned Artaban, made Artaxare King of the Persians and the Parthians, forced the Romans to retreat across the Euphrates. This king has had two sons by Arsinoé, daughter of Tigranes, King of Armenia. The elder, moved by jealousy of Pharnabaze and, perhaps, prompted by his mother, has revolted and been put to death by his father.   The younger, Sapor, fearing for his mother's life, has recently enabled her to escape with the intention of taking refuge in Armenia.   In this rescue he has been aided by Arsace, a Parthian prince, with whose daughter, Aspasie, both Sapor and Pharnabaze are in love.   Arsace, who longs to be king, offers his daughter to Sapor, who refuses to betray his father, and to Pharnabaze, who reports the conspiracy to Artaxare.   A former conspirator, Artane, is brought in to strengthen the case against Arsace, but he asserts that the real culprit is Sapor, who is arrested.   Aspasie is told by her father that the only way she can save Sapor is by marrying Pharnabaze.   She passes this information on to Sapor, but assures him that she loves him and that she will kill herself at the altar.   Despite her protest, Sapor informs Pharnabaze of her plan.   Meanwhile Arsinoé, called back by Arsace, defends Sapor to Artaxare and accuses Pharnabaze, who urges her to induce her son to disavow his support of Arsace.   The latter sends her a note declaring that Sapor is not in the conspiracy, but that he will be deserted by the conspirators if he disavows them.   Overestimating the strength of Arsace, she urges her son to support him.   When the king questions Sapor, the prince denies that he has conspired, but begs not to be confronted with Arsace.   News is brought that the rebels have surrounded the palace and that Armenian forces are coming by sea.   Sapor is imprisoned and Pharnabaze is told by the king to kill him.   Early next morning Pharnabaze reports that this order has been carried out.   The rebels declare Arsace king, but, when Pharnabaze appears, the soldiers desert the Parthian, the Armenians retire to their ships, and Arsace wounds himself fatally, but lives long enough to tell Artaxare that Sapor was not in the conspiracy.   The king is finally convinced of his son's innocence when the queen shows him the letter she had received from Arsace.   Artaxare is deeply distressed till Pharnabaze reports that he had dared disobey and that Sapor lives.   In a final display of magnanimity Pharnabaze renounces his claims on Aspasie, who will marry Sapor.

Except for the author's use of history and for minor borrowings,[36] the source is unknown. Artaxare is presented as a king jealous of his power. He is dependent upon Pharnabaze and never doubts his loyalty, but he suspects his wife, has put one son to death, and orders the execution of the other. He recalls the Parthian king in Corneille's *Suréna*, though his suspicions are turned, not against the commander of his army, but against his family. Sapor has inherited his father's pride in his rank. He resents the fact that he is overshadowed by Pharnabaze, but he is honorable, deeply in love, and obedient to his father except when he rescues his mother. This queen has some importance in convincing her husband of their son's innocence, but it is not clear whether she was involved in her elder son's revolt, or why, after she has fled for her life, she is not arrested immediately upon her return.

The principal character is Pharnabaze, a great warrior, absolutely loyal to Artaxare. He keeps the king informed of the conspiracy and at the same time endeavors to save the lives of the conspirators. It is he who puts down the rebellion, saves the prince's life, and renounces in his behalf the princess they both love. In sharp contrast with him is Arsace, who, as the last of the Arsacides, longs for the throne and intrigues to win it, offering his daughter as a prize for collaboration. He is a weak and disappointed man, forming plans that he cannot carry out, childishly pleased by his momentary elevation to the throne by rebels. His daughter is a typical young heroine who has inherited none of her father's guile except in her plan to kill herself on the eve of her forced marriage.

Pellegrin once criticized Campistron for going, in *Tiridate*, too deeply into Parthian history, but, if he was the author of the play, he would have done better to follow his example, for the historical and geographical background of *Artaxare* is far from being clear. No attempt is made to depict the manners of Parthians and Persians in the period when they were battling with one another and with Romans and Armenians. The characters are insufficiently analyzed. Pharnabaze, the person who most clearly deserves our sympathy, is not given often enough the center of the stage. His method of saving the prince, which should have been thrown into relief, is allowed little space in comparison with the many

---

[36] Aspasie's plan of saving Sapor by promising to marry Pharnabaze and then killing herself at the altar closely resembles that of Andromache in *Andromaque.* "Toujours un moindre crime entraîne un plus grand " (II, 3) recalls *Phèdre*, v. 1093. Artaxare's proposal to leave his kingdom "au plus digne " (III, 7) is exactly that which Justin attributes to Alexander the Great. V. 282 of *le Cid* was probably imitated in the line (IV, 8):

Arsinoé: Il faut immoler . . .
Sapor: Qui?
Arsinoé: Le Pere d'Aspasie.

complications that precede it. The structure departs slightly from the technique of the time, as the action begins before dawn on one day and ends at a later hour the next morning.

The tragedy was acted six times, from May 3 to 18, 1718. Artaxare was played by Legrand; Sapor, by Dufresne; Pharnabaze, by Maurice Quinault; Arsène, by Fontenay; Eurylas, captain of guards, by Dangeville; Arbate, confidant of Arsace, by Du Boccage; Arsinoé, by la Dangeville; Aspasie, by la Desmares; Cléone, her confidant, by la Sallé.[37] When he published the tragedy sixteen years later, the author declared that the performances ceased because Ponteuil, who played Arsace, fell ill, and that his death prevented the actors from reviving the tragedy the following winter.

Charny, whom the frères Parfaict cite, discussed the play at length. He thought that the real subject was disguised after the manner of Campistron and that the plot was modeled in accordance with an " Histoire arrivée de notre tems." The frères Parfaict seem to doubt that this assertion can be justified. Possibly Charny was trying to compliment the Regent, accused of causing the death of two French princes, but remaining loyal to Louis XV. Charny declares that the play was criticized because the first act resembles a second or third, which means that the exposition was considered unsatisfactory; because there were too many incidents; because virtuous Pharnabaze should not be unfortunate in love; because the queen endangers her son's life by urging him to support Arsace; and because the letter " ne produit rien " and should be suppressed. The author could easily have answered that he was not obliged to reward all lovers, that the queen thinks the conspiracy will succeed, and that the letter establishes, more satisfactorily than Arsace's dying words, Sapor's innocence. But he could not so easily have disposed of the charges that he had failed in his exposition and had allowed an excess of incidents.

The frères Parfaict are more severe than the critic just cited. " Le plan en est fort embrouillé, la conduite mal arrangée, & la versification assez foible." Artaxare lacks dignity and intelligence. Sapor is an " étourdi." Arsace does not know how to conspire. Pharnabaze lacks skill in governing and ardor in love. Aspasie is a " sotte." The queen is useless and creates an unfortunate impression. It was not, however, the selection of such characters that should have been criticized, but the manner in which they were presented. The king, Arsace, or Pharnabaze might have been made the central figure of an effective tragedy, but we are

---

[37] Cf. the frères Parfaict, XV, 280. The *Registres* indicate that the receipts were so small that the author earned only 16 fr., 10 s., awarded him after the first performance.

not allowed to see deeply enough into any of them to make us follow their designs with interest. The actors were probably wise not to revive the play.

The frères Parfaict call attention to an article in the *Mercure* [38] in which the author stated that he published the tragedy because the resemblance between its last act and that of Voltaire's *Adélaïde du Guesclin* had been widely noted. He was willing to admit that Voltaire had not borrowed from him, but he did not want it to be supposed that he had borrowed from Voltaire. It is true that his tragedy was approved for publication three days before *Adélaïde* was first acted, but Voltaire had completed his play in 1733 and had shown it to friends, who may well have talked about it to the author of *Artaxare*. Similarly, it is quite possible that Voltaire had seen the manuscript of *Artaxare*, or had been told about the play by Quinault-Dufresne, who had important rôles in both tragedies. [39] The resemblance lies in the facts that Pharnabaze, like Coucy, is told to put to death a near relative of his commander, that he pretends to carry out the order, that, when his master shows remorse, he admits that he has disobeyed, that his commander is delighted, and that the supposed victim appears. Pharnabaze renounces the woman he loves, as Coucy does earlier in *Adélaïde*, and she will marry the man who had been condemned to death. Voltaire declares that he found the incident in the history of Brittany, which may have been a common source of the two plays as well as of Charny's reference to the " Histoire arrivée de notre tems," but it is quite possible that the dramatic value of the situation was shown to Voltaire by his humble predecessor. [40]

---

[38] March, 1734, pp. 512-24.

[39] Lion (*op. cit.*, pp. 94-5) overlooked this fact when he argued that Voltaire could not have known of *Artaxare*. He found the accusation of borrowing, not in the frères Parfaict or the *Mercure*, but in the *Journal de la Librairie* of Aug. 4, 1742.

[40] The only verbal resemblance I have found between the two tragedies is in the phrase " Frappe; voilà mon cœur" (*Artaxare*, IV, 1; *Adélaïde*, III, 3), but this hemistich could easily have presented itself independently to the two poets.

4

CHAPTER III

ENTER VOLTAIRE

Œdipe, Artémire, Mariamne, 1718-1725

The preceding chapter has shown that the efforts of dramatists had been unavailing. No new tragedy, indeed, since Crébillon's *Rhadamiste et Zénobie* had been well received for more than a few performances. The only tragedy that had won striking recognition from the public had been Racine's *Athalie,* with its religious subject, its majestic style, and its impressive decoration. A young writer, eager to succeed, might well take this fact into consideration when he entered upon his career.

It would have been strange if Voltaire, when he left school in 1710, had not turned his attention to dramatic composition. He had received a good knowledge of the ancient classics from his Jesuit teachers, one of whom, Father Porée, wrote plays himself. He may have acted in a school tragedy, as many of his comrades did, and he had composed while a boy *Amulius et Numitor,* most of which is now lost. Moreover, the society of the Temple, into which his godfather introduced him, helped to develop in him the kind of daring social criticism that demands an outlet, and, *arriviste* that he was, he knew what social advantages the drama had conferred upon Racine, Campistron, and Crébillon.

In the preface of *Alzire* he states that Crébillon, by his *Rhadamiste* and *Electre,* " m'inspira le premier le désir d'entrer quelque temps dans la même carrière." In the *Epître* he addressed to the duchesse du Maine and published with his *Oreste* he adds that Malezieu's adaptation of *Iphigeneia among the Taurians,*[1] acted in 1713 with the duchess in the cast and Voltaire in the audience, gave him the idea of making similar use of *Œdipus Tyrannus.* Corneille had selected for the subject of his first tragedy one that had been dramatized by Euripides and Seneca, why should not Voltaire select a subject already put on the stage by Sophocles and Corneille?

According to his own statement, he began his ŒDIPE[2] when he was nineteen, that is, in 1713. Two years later he refers to " ce que j'ai fait d'Œdipe."[3] When he presented it to the actors, two of them, Beaubourg

---

[1] For this play cf. my *Sunset,* p. 7.
[2] Paris, Ribou, Huet, Mazuel et Coustelier, 1719, 8°; approbation, Dec. 2, 1718; *privilège,* Jan. 19, 1719. Dedicated to " Madame," the Regent's mother. This dedication is signed " Arouet de Voltaire." For later editions cf. Bengesco and Moland. An Italian translation was published six times in 1771-1803. For a study of the play cf. Lion, *op. cit.*
[3] Moland, II, 11, XXXIII, 29.

and Ponteuil, accustomed to Corneille's *Œdipe,* refused to accept Voltaire's. It was not till the first of them had retired and the other had died that the tragedy could be given, as it was on Nov. 18, 1718. By that time the success of *Athalie* may have suggested to Voltaire his showing of a temple on the stage and may have encouraged him in his choice of a subject with religious implications.

Voltaire derived his main theme from Sophocles, whom he followed rather closely in parts of his play,[4] but he also imitated Corneille, even borrowing from him, word for word, as he admits, a couple of verses.[5] Like Corneille, he observed that the material supplied by Sophocles would not fill five acts and accordingly added a subordinate plot. In doing so he was probably encouraged by the actors, who had criticized the small amount of love [6] they found in the play. Voltaire's Philoctète assumes some of Creon's functions and is given love for Jocasta that may have been suggested by Sévère's love of Pauline in *Polyeucte*. Unfortunately this new love-interest has so little connection with the main plot that Philoctète disappears before the third act is completed.

Like Corneille, Voltaire offers a reason for Œdipus's delay in seeking the murderer of Laius, has Œdipus and Jocasta meet after it is discovered that he had slain Laius, has Jocasta stab herself, and lets his audience know at the end of the tragedy that the plague has ceased—all details that he could not have found in Sophocles.[7]

---

[4] III, 4, IV, 1, 2, V, 2, 3.

[5] Lines 235 and 1984 of Corneille's *Œdipe* reappear in Voltaire's, I, 1, and V, 6.

[6] Moland, XXXIII, 199. Voltaire says they objected also to his chorus, though he had not intended members of it to sing, and to the scene of mutual confidence between Œdipus and Jocasta, in which he had followed Sophocles closely.

[7] Philoctète, who had won Jocasta's love, had left Thebes after her father had forced her to marry King Laius. He had become the companion of Hercules, whose recent death has made possible his returning to Thebes in order to gratify his lingering interest in Jocasta. He learns from Dimas that Laius has been dead for four years, that Œdipus has guessed the riddle of the Sphinx, married Jocasta, and become king, and that many Thebans are dying of the plague. The door of the temple opens, the high priest assures the people that he will reveal the future, and he declares that the slayer of Laius must be discovered. Œdipus undertakes the investigation. He learns from Jocasta that the king's death at the hands of unknown men had been reported by his follower, Phorbas, and that this attendant, suspected of murdering Laius, has been hidden by her in a neighboring château. Œdipus orders that he be brought in for questioning and begs the gods to punish the killer. It is reported that Philoctète is suspected of having slain Laius. Jocasta does not believe that he is the murderer. Œdipus thinks he ought to investigate the charge. Philoctète is indignant that he does not accept at once his statement that he is innocent. Jocasta admits that she still has some feeling for Philoctète, that she never loved Laius, and that she has only " tendresse " for Œdipus, but, when she interviews Philoctète, she gives him no encouragement. The high priest indicates Œdipus as the murderer of Laius and is cursed by the king, who is none the less troubled by the accusation. When Jocasta describes Laius to him and tells him that she had abandoned her child because an oracle had predicted he would kill his father and marry his mother, Œdipus remembers that a similar prediction had been made to him at Corinth and recalls his killing an elderly man when on his way to Thebes.

Œdipus has retained the haughtiness, the sense of justice, the feeling of obligation in regard to the people, and the respect for the gods with which Sophocles endowed him, but Jocasta's character is altered, as she has for Philoctète an emotional attitude that nothing in the Greek play suggests and as she has become quite skeptical about the decrees of the gods. Voltaire argues that she need not be over thirty-five. Her son, if this is true, can scarcely be more than twenty-one, though the play gives us the impression of a much older man. The presentation of Philoctète is far from satisfactory. Why should he be accused of killing Laius if he was away from Thebes at the time of the king's death? Why, if he was there, does he now show surprise when he hears that Laius is dead? Neither his love for Jocasta nor the accusation that is brought against him has any effect upon the plot. We are told nothing about him after the third act in the first edition of the play. Subsequently Voltaire made Œdipus wish him to succeed to the throne, but we do not learn whether, contrary to the legend, this desire was fulfilled.

Influenced in all probability by *Athalie*, Voltaire added a spectacular element by having the action take place at the entrance of a temple. There the afflicted Thebans prostrate themselves while awaiting the pleasure of the god. Dacier had urged Voltaire to introduce choruses and to give them the importance they have in Greek tragedy, but the dramatist, knowing his public better than the Hellenist, had refrained from taking his advice. His chorus is merely a group of Thebans, of whom none sings and only two speak. Even these two were not appreciated, for the parterre, instead of weeping over their prayer to Death, burst into laughter at the way in which such inexperienced actors spoke their lines.[8]

While the most effective scenes are those derived from Sophocles, Voltaire's tragedy is remembered especially for the quotable verses that criticize courtiers, kings, and priests. In III, 1, Jocasta lashes out against courtiers:

> A leur malignité rien n'échape & ne fuit,
> Un seul mot, un regard, un coup d'œil nous trahit.

Phorbas now describes the circumstances of Laius's death in such detail that Œdipus is convinced of his guilt and asks Jocasta to put him to death. She replies that he is innocent as he was ignorant of his victim's identity. At this point Icare comes from Corinth to announce the death of King Polybe, whom Œdipus had supposed to be his father. Icare tells Œdipus that he had himself brought him to Corinth after receiving him on Mount Citheron from a Theban. When Phorbas returns to the stage, he is recognized as the Theban in question and admits that the child he gave to Icare was Jocasta's. Œdipus sees the Eumenides, tells Jocasta that he is her son, and goes off to blind himself with his sword and to become a wanderer. The high priest announces that the pestilence has ceased. His announcement is supported by thunder and lightning. Jocasta, though she insists that she is innocent of intentional wrongdoing, stabs herself.

[8] Cf. the *Discours* that Voltaire published with his *Brutus*.

While the play as a whole exalts the power of kings and the perspicacity of ecclesiastics, individual verses are critical of both (II, 4):

> Un Roi pour ses sujets est un Dieu qu'on revere;
> Pour Hercule & pour moi c'est un homme ordinaire.

When it is said that Laius traveled with only one companion because he thought himself guarded by "l'amour de son peuple," Œdipus comments (IV, 1):

> Des veritables Rois exemple auguste & rare.

Priests are criticized:

> Ne nous endormons point sur la foi de leurs Prêtres;
> Au pied du sanctuaire il est souvent des traîtres. (II, 5)

> Un Pontife est souvent terrible aux Souverains. (III, 5)

Still more striking is the celebrated couplet (IV, 1):

> Nos Prêtres ne sont point ce qu'un vain peuple pense,
> Notre credulité fait toute leur science.

Equally skeptical remarks had been made in French plays before, but they had usually been put into the mouths of villains,[9] whereas this last couplet is assigned to Jocasta, with whom we sympathize. Not only is she anticlerical, but she denounces the gods as the real villains of the tragedy (V, 6):

> J'ai fait rougir les Dieux qui m'ont forcée au crime.

The Regent, who gave Voltaire a pension of 1500 francs on account of Œdipe,[10] may have protected him against those who took exception to such remarks. Encouraged, he subsequently added to his text lines of a similar nature:

> Qu'eussé-je été sans lui? rien que le fils d'un roi. (I, 1)[11]

> Les dieux veulent du sang, et sont seuls écoutés. (II, 1)

> Un prêtre, quel qu'il soit, quelque dieu qui l'inspire,
> Doit prier pour ses rois, et non pas les maudire. (III, 4)

Such remarks, which probably expressed what many persons in the audience felt, but dared not utter, added to the impressiveness of the setting and the interest that Œdipus Tyrannus, however altered, always

---

[9] Cf., for instance, Du Ryer, Scévole, II, 4; Jobert, Balde, V, 4, 5; Cyrano, Agrippine, II, 4; Th. Corneille, Mort de Commode, V, 7; Crébillon, Xercès, I, 1: "La crainte fit les Dieux, l'audace a fait des Rois."

[10] Cf. Lion, op. cit., p. 22.

[11] Moland declares that this verse was greatly applauded at the first performance, but this statement is hard to believe as the line is not found in the first edition of the tragedy.

inspires, made the play extraordinarily successful. Dangeau noted on Nov. 18 that, despite the prejudice against " Arouet," the play " a fort bien réussi et a été fort louée." On the 28th he stated that the duchesse de Berry went to see it at the Comédie Française; two days later, when the same troupe acted it at the Palais Royal, that there was a " monde prodigieux " at the performance, given in the presence of the duc d'Orléans and his mother. He noted that the duke saw it again on Dec. 14 and that it was " fort applaudie " when acted before young Louis XV on Feb. 11, 1719. Œdipe was played thirty times from Nov. 18 to Jan. 21, then twice in March, twice in April, 1719, and eight times in August, 1720. During all this time the attendance remained so good that Voltaire continued to receive his share of the profits, amounting in all to 4445 fr., 17 s., more than any tragedy had previously earned for its author, so far as the records show. Nor had any tragedy of the eighteenth century been played so often in the first two years of its existence.

Some credit for this must be given to the troupe, especially to Quinault-Dufresne, who played Œdipus, to his brother, Maurice, who played Philoctète, and to la Desmares, who took the part of Jocasta,[12] but the tragedy continued to be well received long after they had ceased to act, and La Motte was generous enough to express the opinion that it would be as popular when read as when acted. In approving the publication he wrote:

Le Public à la representation de cette Piece s'est promis un digne successeur de Corneille & de Racine; & je crois qu'à la lecture il ne rabatra rien de ses esperances.

The *Mercure*[13] praised the tragedy when it first appeared, finding it " plus nette & moins chargée d'évenemens " than Corneille's *Œdipe*, and alluding to its great success. After it was published the same journal reproduced a long article[14] that took exception to several passages in the play. There is a contradiction in I, 2-3, between the priest's assertion that the fate of the king and his people will be settled on the day represented and his insistence that the murderer of Laius must be discovered. In II, 2, Jocasta should defend Philoctète, not by referring to the nobility of his character, but by the fact that Phorbas has not recognized him as the killer. It was unwise to make the priest refer in III, 4, to Œdipus's father, as his remark might well have rendered the last two acts useless. When Hydaspe criticizes priests, in III, 5, he is not acting in accordance

---

[12] Cf. frères Parfaict, XV, 304, and Moland, II, 60. La Sallé took the part of Egine, a confidant. Others who participated in the dialogue or the chorus were, according to the *Registres*, La Thorillière, Lavoy, Legrand, Du Boccage, Dangeville, Fontenay, Philippe Poisson, Duchemin, la Champvallon, la Fonpré, and la Gautier.

[13] November, 1718, pp. 165-6; December, pp. 137-8.

[14] March, 1719, pp. 104-23.

with his character. As the messenger from Corinth is announced at the end of Act IV, too much time elapses before Œdipus meets him. The anonymous author concludes by attributing to Voltaire a "génie riche & saillant," from which much may be expected provided it is always regulated by "la droite raison." [15]

J.-B. Rousseau, who was to become a severe critic of Voltaire, wrote him on March 25 that the Frenchman of twenty-four had triumphed in many passages over the Greek poet of eighty.[16] La Grange-Chancel, though he took exception to two of Voltaire's rimes and to the introduction into a Theban play of the Indian name, Hidaspe, declared that "L'un & l'autre Sophocle ont été surpassés." [17] Others were less flattering. A parody by Dominique, Œdipe travesti, was given at the Théâtre Italien on April 17, 1719, Philoctète appearing as a Gascon, Finebrette.[18] A large number of pamphlets attacked or defended the tragedy.[19] Voltaire was blamed for attempting to rival Corneille, for plagiarism,[20] for introducing Philoctète, for not separating sufficiently the third act from the fourth, and for certain faults in rimes and elsewhere.

When he published his play, Voltaire replied to his critics. Just as Philoctète had referred to "Thesée, Hercule & moy," so Voltaire offered a critique of Œdipus tragedies by Sophocles, Corneille, and himself. He claimed that certain mistakes were due to his youth and boasted of the applause he had received and of the Regent's gift. He dismissed as absurd the accusation that he had no religion because "Jocaste se défie des oracles d'Apollon." As the audience was less interested in the fate of Œdipus than Dacier had supposed they would be, Voltaire had omitted about forty verses from the account of his hero's final disaster. He admitted that he had not explained satisfactorily Œdipus's delay in investigating the

---

[15] Voltaire did not act upon these suggestions except that he gave Hydaspe's remarks about priests to Philoctète. He might have pointed out that Sophocles had already made Tiresias refer in the corresponding passage to the parents of Œdipus.

[16] Cf. Lion, op. cit., p. 10.

[17] Œuvres, 1758, V, 220. That the poem appeared shortly after the play is shown by the author's referring to himself as forty-three years old. Voltaire subsequently changed Hidaspe to Araspe.

[18] Cf. V. B. Grannis, Dramatic Parody in Eighteenth Century France, New York, 1931, pp. 247-50.

[19] For a list of these cf. the frères Parfaict, XV, 308-16, and Moland, II, 9, 10.

[20] Lion (op. cit., p. 19) notes that one of the pamphleteers accused Voltaire of borrowing from Corneille, Racine, La Fontaine, Molière, Boileau, and Genest. Moland notes similarities with Corneille's Œdipe, Racine's Esther, and Du Ryer's Scévole. To these may be added the following:

De pareils sentimens n'apartenoient qu'à nous (II, 3; cf. Horace, v. 449)

Seigneur, dissipés mon effroi,
Vos redoutables cris ont été jusqu'à moi. (V, 5; cf. Phèdre, vv. 1167-8)

. . . cette épée
Qui du sang de son pere avoit été trempée. (V, 6; cf. Cid, vv. 857-8)

manner of his predecessor's death; that Philoctète contributes little to the *nœud*, nothing to the dénouement; that he is unnecessarily boastful; but he defended the introduction of this character, as it helps fill five acts and adds interest to the rôle of Jocasta. He criticized himself for not separating satisfactorily Acts III and IV, as well as for assuming that Œdipus had for a time forgotten his encounter with Laius. He declared that Creon, in place of Philoctète, would have appeared "bien froid." He denied that he had borrowed other verses than the two he took from Corneille's *Œdipe*.[21]

The criticism of the play had some effect. Voltaire made a number of changes in order to improve the expression. He placed greater emphasis on the chorus by giving to its leader four lines in II, 1. He altered the rôle of Philoctète by having him give up the statement that he had returned to Thebes for love of Jocasta, an omission that makes it easier to understand why he renounces her so readily. Instead of having him leave in the middle of III, 4, he had him remain throughout that scene and the one that follows and had Œdipus refer to him in V, 1. He seems never to have been satisfied with the rôle and is said to have prepared by 1763 a version of the tragedy from which it was omitted.[22]

A favorable estimate of the play was offered by two eighteenth-century critics who usually differed in their opinion of Voltaire. Although they condemned the rôle of Philoctète and the introduction of love into the tragedy, both Collé and La Harpe admired the whole of Acts IV and V. Collé [23] also praised Jocasta's account of her feeling for Œdipus. La Harpe [24] examined the play in greater detail, excusing the errors he detected on the ground of Voltaire's youth and the tastes of the day, and proclaiming the last acts superior to those of Sophocles. For the first time since Racine's death, verses were heard on the stage "tournés avec cette élégance poétique, cette sage précision, cette harmonie variée."

The tragedy long remained popular, ousting Corneille's *Œdipe* as the standard adaptation of *Œdipus Tyrannus*. It was in the repertory of the Comédie Française as late as 1852. Its record there of 336 productions was unequalled by the first acted tragedy of any other French dramatist.

---

[21] La Grange-Chancel had criticized Voltaire for riming *char* and *rempart* (IV, 1); *frein* and *rien* (II, 1). Voltaire defended this last rime, but he ultimately omitted it. He said nothing about the other. He defended *héros: tombeaux* and *contagion: poison*.

[22] *Mémoires secrets*, London, 1784, I, 178.

[23] Irritated by Voltaire's commentary on Corneille, Collé prepared criticisms of *Œdipe*, *Zaïre*, and *Alzire*, fragments of which with the lines to which the comments refer were published by Honoré Bonhomme in *Correspondance inédite de Collé*, Paris, 1864, pp. 391-470. Collé quoted less than 200 lines of *Œdipe*. Fault is found chiefly with the use of certain terms and rimes and with certain repetitions.

[24] *Op. cit.*, XI, 1-42.

It was a good many years before such success was repeated. Though he had won his spurs with the help of Sophocles and Corneille, Voltaire seems to have believed that he could dispense with such guides and that he was free to select a subject that would not be indicated by the title of the play. Accordingly, in June, 1719, he went to work on ARTÉMIRE,[25] produced the following winter. He used ancient history only to the extent of selecting as a leading character Cassander, who ruled over Macedonia and Greece after Alexander's death and destroyed the family of his dead sovereign. He was to reappear in Voltaire's *Olympie*.

The plot resembles *Œdipe* in that the heroine of both plays has been forced into matrimony, is loyal to her husband, but cherishes the love of a rejected suitor who reappears after her marriage. The character of the heroine's jealous and brutal husband, who condemns her to death after slaying her father, may be taken from the story of Herod and Mariamne that he was soon to dramatize. The rôles of Pallante and Ménas may well have come from Mme de Fontaines's *Comtesse de Savoie*, a novel read to Voltaire in 1713 that he probably imitated in *Tancrède*. It tells of a courtier who, when foiled in his attempt to seduce the countess, takes his nephew into his confidence, pretends that the young man is the lover of the countess, and kills him in order to accuse the countess of adultery without fear of contradiction.[26]

As only about 650 lines, probably less than half the play, exist, it is difficult to criticize it, but one may derive from these verses a reasonably correct idea of the plot.[27] The queen is presented as thoroughly virtuous,

---

[25] Only portions of the play have survived. Voltaire's editors succeeded in preserving the heroine's rôle and a few lines spoken by others. The fourth scene of Act IV, published with *La Ligue* in 1724, was reproduced by the frères Parfaict, XV, 363-74. It supplies a line omitted by Moland (II, 123-53), the fifteenth verse of IV, 4, " N'etoi[t]-ce pas assez de me joindre à mon pere? " The other differences are insignificant. In the preface of his *Mariamne* Voltaire declared the 1724 edition to be full of errors.

[26] Voltaire's editors suggest the connection with Herod. Auger pointed out the resemblance to the *Comtesse de Savoie* in editing the *Œuvres complètes de Mesdames de La Fayette, de Tencin et de Fontaines*, Paris, Lepetit, 1820, IV, 181. Voltaire's editors think that he imitated Racine, but they point to no specific borrowing. Lion, *op. cit.*, p. 26, suggests the influence on *Artémire*, IV, 4, of Agrippina's long speech to Nero in *Britannicus*. I have discovered that a line (IV, 4), " La honte est dans le crime, et non dans le supplice," is lifted from La Chapelle's *Zaïde*, IV, 5; cf. my *History*, Part IV, p. 204.

[27] Artémire, daughter of Antinoüs, had been in love with a prince named Philotas, but she had been forced by her father to marry Cassandre, King of Macedonia, who had then put Antinoüs to death and is thought to have killed Philotas. When the play begins, the king is away, conquering the Locrians. His evil genius, Pallante, brings Artémire a letter from Cassandre that orders him to execute her. He offers to spare her life if she will agree to marry him. This she refuses to do. Instead she expresses her loyalty to the husband she hates and her contempt for Pallante, who continues to intrigue and takes Ménas into his confidence. Philotas now appears, reproaches Artémire for her marriage, and is advised to escape. He invites her to go with him, but, though she admits that she still loves him, she refuses to do so.

resisting the plea of the man she loves and the threats of one whom she hates. Her rôle is repetitious and undramatic. Of the three men in her life, one is noble and devoted, doubting the queen's virtue only for a moment; another is a thorough villain who betrays both his friend Ménas and his sovereign; while the third is a brute, repentant only at the end of his career. So far as one can judge, the play showed none of the spectacular element or of the attacks on church and state that had distinguished Œdipe.

The tragedy was first acted on Feb. 15, 1720. Dangeau declares that it was such a failure that Voltaire himself admitted the weakness of the play and withdrew it. But it was given again on Feb. 23 because, according to Dangeau, some " gens considérables ont souhaité de la revoir; il y a changé quelques vers et la pièce a mieux réussi." It is said [28] that the important persons who favored it included " Madame," the Regent's mother. She had it played at the Palais Royal on March 6, according to Dangeau. The fact that it was performed as many as eight times may have been due, not only to " Madame's " protection, but to the talent of the new actress, Adrienne Le Couvreur, who had the title-rôle. She was supported by Maurice Quinault as Philotas, Quinault-Dufresne as Pallante, Legrand as Cassandre. Ménas was played by Legrand de Belleville; the queen's confidant by la Sallé; Hipparque, a minister, by Fontenay.[29]

It was Voltaire, rather than the public, who was dissatisfied with the tragedy, for the receipts never fell below 2300 francs and the author earned from the eight productions 2094 fr., 18 s., much more than he had received from the first eight performances of Œdipe. The play made,

---

Pallante now bids her choose between a sword and poison. Selecting the sword, she is about to kill herself with it when she learns that Cassandre has revoked his order. Pallante now pretends that he has caught Ménas with the queen, accuses her of adultery, and puts Ménas to death. When Cassandre returns, Artémire begs him to kill her without disgracing her. She admits that she has never loved him, but she assures him that she has done her duty as his wife and has saved his life by refusing Pallante's offer. Cassandre refuses to believe her, but Philotas accepts her explanation, conceals himself when Pallante appears, then returns to defend the queen. Cries are heard. Cassandre enters, mortally wounded. Apparently he has been attacked by Pallante and has killed him. In his last words he confesses his crimes, pardons Philotas, and does justice to the queen, who will marry the man she loves. La Harpe (op. cit., XI, 46) and Lion (op. cit., p. 25) indicate a different ending. According to La Harpe, Pallante is killed fighting against Philotas, and Cassandre is wounded in this combat. Lion asserts that Cassandre is wounded in a fight with Philotas. Both must be wrong, for Philotas is talking with Artémire when the noise of the conflict is heard. I would restore to the text a few words that have disappeared in V, 9 :

L'Envoyé: [Pallante est mort, Madame,] et votre époux expire.
Artémire: Lui! mon époux!

[28] Cf. Moland, II, 122, and Lion, op. cit., p. 23.
[29] Cf. the frères Parfaict, XV, 364, and Moland, II, 124. According to the Registres, minor rôles were taken by Du Boccage, Dangeville, Duchemin, and la Dufresne.

moreover, enough impression to inspire a parody by Dominique that was played at the Théâtre Italien on March 10.[30] Voltaire did not consider his tragedy worth publishing, but he treasured some of its lines sufficiently to incorporate them in subsequent productions.

La Harpe[31] thought the play suffered from the obvious imitation of *Mithridate* when the king prevents the heroine from committing suicide. He held that Pallante's hopeless efforts to win the queen wearied the audience and that there was no proper preparation for the attempt to blacken her character. With so much of the text lost, it is now impossible to determine whether or not the critic was justified in these contentions.

Voltaire, as has been suggested, may have used the story of Mariamne in composing *Artémire*. The fate of that tragedy and the great success of *Œdipe* may have made him believe he would be better advised to select a familiar subject rather than to disguise one under completely altered names of persons and places. Instead of rewriting *Artémire,* he would bring out a new MARIAMNE,[32] dramatizing a tale already turned into a tragedy by Alexandre Hardy and rendered famous by Tristan l'Hermite, but accepting suggestions and even borrowing verses from *Artémire*.[33]

---

[30] Cf. Moland, II, 121. It was published in the *Parodies du nouveau théâtre italien* and briefly analyzed by V. B. Grannis, *op. cit.*, pp. 251-6. Cassandre and Pallante are replaced, respectively, by Pantalon and Trivelin. The former, mortally wounded in an effort to suppress an insurrection, has an edifying end. Dr. Grannis also calls attention to a comic citation of the first two verses of *Artémire* in Piron's *Arlequin-Deucalion* of 1722 and to a comic *Prologue d'Artémire*, which attacks Voltaire's play while parodying *Phèdre*, substituting for the heroine and Œnone the names of Artémire and Céphise. It was published by Van Roosbroeck in *PQ*, I (1922), 137-41. Strangely enough, he did not recognize the pamphlet as a parody of *Phèdre*.

[31] *Op. cit.*, XI, 42-8.

[32] First acted under this title and analyzed in the *Mercure* for March, 1724, but published by Voltaire as *Hérode et Mariamne*, Paris, Noel Pissot et François Flahault, 1725, 8°; *priv.*, July 21, 1724. Dedicated to the new queen. According to the preface, three unauthorized editions, including one of Amsterdam, Changuion, had already appeared. Another was probably that of Amsterdam, veuve Desbordes, 1725. For the other editions cf. Bengesco and Moland. For three Italian translations, one of them reprinted eight times between 1751 and 1803, cf. Luigi Ferrari, *Le traduzioni italiane del teatro tragico francese*, Paris, Champion, 1925, pp. 155-8. A German translation was published at Nuremberg in 1740. For a study of the play cf. Lion, *op. cit.*

[33] Cf. *Artémire*, II, 1:
    Céphise: Madame, jusque-là deviez-vous l'irriter?
and *Hérode et Mariamne*, II, 3:
    Elize: Ah! Madame, à ce point pouvez-vous l'irriter . . .
also *Artémire*, IV, 4:
    Art.: Où suis-je? où vais-je? ô dieux! je me meurs, je le voi.
    Céphise: Avançons. . . .
    Art.: Mais l'hymen dont le nœud nous unit l'un à l'autre,
        Tout malheureux qu'il est, joint mon honneur au vôtre:
        Pourquoi d'un tel affront voulez-vous vous couvrir?
        Laissez-moi chez les morts descendre sans rougir,

He consequently altered the story as related by Josephus and dramatized by Tristan, and gave his heroine a lover who urges her to escape under his guidance, as Philotas had urged Artémire. At first he even had Mariamne respond to his affection[34] as Artémire had responded to that of Philotas.

Voltaire was working on the play as early as June, 1723. In September he sent to Adrienne Le Couvreur " une ébauche imparfaite " of it. Before the end of the year he had read it to the actors, but it was still unfinished on Dec. 23.[35] It was acted on March 6, 1724, with so little success that Voltaire withdrew it in order to make very considerable changes in his text.

He states in his preface that he had been too faithful to history in depicting his chief characters. Herod roused indignation rather than pity, and Mariamne upbraided him so emphatically that there could be no hope of a reconciliation. The scene between Varus and Herod[36] humiliated the king. Mariamne died on the stage from the effect of poison, " une faute contre l'Histoire, faute qui peut-être n'étoit rachetée par aucune beauté." [37] To remedy these defects he must have softened to a certain extent the speeches of the king and queen. He prevented Herod and Varus from meeting on the stage, rewrote the scene that followed their interview in the original, had Mariamne executed in the manner indicated by Josephus, and, like Tristan, but " contre mon goût," had the scene of her death narrated.

In its new form the tragedy was acted on April 10, 1725. The old title was then retained, but Voltaire seems to have realized that it might cause confusion with Nadal's recent *Mariamne,* so that, when his play was presented on April 12, it was called *Hérode et Mariamne.* According to Voltaire, the alterations " m'ont tenu lieu du mérite qui m'a manqué."

and *Hérode et Mariamne,* IV, 4:

> Mar.:   Où suis-je? où vais-je? ô Dieu! je me meurs . . . je le voi . . .
> Elize: Avançons. . . .
> Mar.:   D'un si cruel affront cessez de me couvrir.
>   Laissez-moi, chez les Morts descendre sans rougir.
>   N'oubliez pas du moins, qu'attachez l'un à l'autre,
>   L'hymen qui nous unit, joint mon honneur au vôtre.

Other resemblances could probably be found if we had the original version of *Mariamne* and the complete text of *Artémire.*

[34] In a letter of 1723 Voltaire speaks of suppressing his heroine's love; cf. Moland, XXXIII, 98.

[35] Cf. Moland, XXXIII, 91, 97, 101.

[36] This scene (III, 3) and the following were preserved by Voltaire's editors; cf. Moland, II, 220-5.

[37] The *Mercure* for March, 1724, states that someone in the parterre cried " la Reine boit " and spoiled the pathos of the scene, but, as Voltaire mentions no such incident and as the jest would have little point except at Epiphany, the reliability of the anecdote may well be doubted. The mere fact of the heroine's dying of poison in the presence of the audience would not have injured the play, for a similar situation is found in two most successful tragedies, *Phèdre* and *Inès de Castro.*

In its first year the altered tragedy had no less than twenty-five productions, which had earned for its author, by Jan. 6, 1726, 3072 fr., 14 s.[38] The rôles were not all distributed as they had been in 1724. Whereas Adrienne Le Couvreur and Legrand played Mariamne and Mazaël in both years, Herod was acted at first by Baron, subsequently by Dufresne; Salome, by la Duclos, subsequently by la de Seine; Varus, by Dufresne, subsequently by Quinault; Nabal, by Fontenay, subsequently by Legrand de Belleville.[39]

Voltaire retained the general outline of Josephus's narrative, the main traits of Herod, Mariamne, and Salome, the references to Jewish customs. From Tristan he took the character he called Nabal [40] and suggestions for his last scene, but he emphasized much less than Tristan had done the personality of Herod, introduced the Roman Varus,[41] chiefly known for his unfortunate campaign in Germany, omitted the scene of the trial, and made his heroine attempt to escape,[42] possibly in imitation of La Motte's recent *Machabées*.

[38] At eight productions in August and January, it was acted with Voltaire's one-act *Indiscret*. I count two-thirds of the author's share on those days as earned by the tragedy. In addition to the sum indicated, Voltaire had received 424 fr. for the single production of *Mariamne* in 1724.
[39] Cf. the *Mercure* for March, 1724, and for April, 1725. The latter article indicates that la Jouvenot played Elise; the younger La Thorillière, Albin; Du Breuil, Idamas.
[40] Tristan's Narbal.
[41] Josephus (*Antiquities*, XVII, 5) mentions Varus as Governor of Syria before Herod's death, but after that of Mariamne.
[42] According to the edition of 1725, Herod, though he has killed Mariamne's father and brother, has married her, has had two sons by her, and, despite her ill-disguised hatred, loves her passionately. As Antony's friend, he has been disturbed by the victory of Augustus and has gone to Rome in the hope of having his authority confirmed, leaving his sister, Salome, in charge of his government. When a report had reached the Jews that Herod had not won the emperor's favor, they had talked of putting Mariamne on the throne, but Mazaël had calmed them by assuring them that Herod would soon return. Through her agent, Zarès, Salome had persuaded Herod to sign the warrant for Mariamne's execution. She now hopes that this order is about to be executed, as Zarès has returned. However, there is danger that Varus, the Roman governor of Syria, may protect the queen, but Salome believes that the favor her brother has won at Rome will prevent Varus from acting. The latter, however, warned by his confidant, Albin, has had Zarès arrested. He now admits that he loves Mariamne, though seduction is not his aim. Learning that Herod has revoked the death warrant, Salome seeks to win Mariamne's favor, but is rebuffed. Acting upon the advice of a loyal old officer, Nabal, Mariamne sends for Varus and begs him to enable her to escape to Rome with her mother and children. He offers to help her, but in so doing he admits that he loves her. She rebukes him, but continues to prepare for her flight. Idamas, a virtuous minister, warns Varus that Herod is being turned against his wife by Zarès, who has been released, by Salome, and by Mazaël. Varus avoids Herod, but plans to save the queen. The king now appears, remorseful over his crimes and fearing that he cannot win Mariamne's affections. Mazaël flatters him, but Idamas persuades him to strengthen his throne by kindness rather than cruelty. Herod begins his reform by ordering his evil sister into exile, but Salome retorts by accusing Mariamne of loving another man. At this point Mazaël brings word that Mariamne, her mother, and her sons are escaping with the help of Varus. Herod acts promptly enough to recapture them. Accused of adultery, Mariamne indignantly denies the charge and declares that her attempt to escape was inspired by Herod's crimes. She pleads for their children and says that she would have loved him if he had wished her to. Overcome by his

Herod is represented as morose, conscious of his crimes, realizing that he is surrounded by flatterers, anxious to reform and to win the love of Mariamne, but overcome by jealousy and unable to resist his passions or to free himself from evil influences. Even after he had condemned Mariamne, he might have pardoned her if the execution had not been hastened. His final anguish is presented somewhat in the manner of Tristan, but more succinctly. The rôle, though still effective, is less so than in the tragedy of his predecessor. Though it is the longest in Voltaire's tragedy, Herod is not seen on the stage till III, 4, he has only two scenes with Mariamne, and, in the published version, no scene with his rival.

Mariamne has less pride and hate than in Tristan's play, but the same lack of caution in regard to Salome. She is almost a flirt in her relations with the two men who love her, telling Herod that it is his fault if she has shown him no affection, reproaching Varus for talking love, yet agreeing to escape under his protection, then refusing to do so. Her character is weakened by her fear for her reputation, which prevents her escaping with Varus. She is less effective than Tristan's heroine. Salome's rôle, almost as long as hers, is that of an intriguer and slanderer, but it is not made clear just what she accomplishes after the fighting has begun.

Varus, whose rôle Voltaire must have ultimately considered flat,[43] has found only in the Orient that love can be a "noble feu." For him Mariamne's resistance adds to her charm. When the play was first acted, he showed considerable force in his interview with Herod, but, when this scene was amputated, he became merely what Lion calls a " pauvre prêteur amoureux." His defeat by Herod is neither historical nor in keeping with the king's respect for Roman power. It even leaves " unfinished business," for, though Idamas warns Herod that Varus's blood may bring upon him the wrath of Rome, we are never told what was the sequel to the encounter. The other characters are little more than names.

Voltaire avoided the structural awkwardness and the rhetorical exaggera-

feeling for her, he admits his errors and is begging, apparently with some success, for her love when word is brought that Varus, after overthrowing the scaffold erected by Salome for the queen's execution, is leading the people against the palace. Herod suspects his wife of complicity and goes to meet the rebels. Varus bursts into the palace and offers Mariamne a chance to escape, but she refuses to go with him, now that her honor is at stake, and begs him to spare Herod. Varus has already slain Mazaël, but, when he goes against the king, he is himself " percé de coups." Victorious Herod decides to put Mariamne to death, but, when he learns from Nabal that she has been executed and that she had urged Varus to spare her husband, he is deeply afflicted, becomes unbalanced, asks for Mariamne, then comes to his senses, mourns her, calls down destruction upon his palace and the Temple, hopes the Jews will be dispersed, and desires that they may transmit to other nations " l'horreur de mon nom, & la honte du leur."

[43] Moland, XLII, 181.

tions of Tristan's *Mariane,* but he produced few striking scenes and failed to compensate for their absence by lines of social protest like those he had introduced into *Œdipe.* Nor did he make any special appeal to the eye. Nevertheless, both Voltaire and the *Mercure* of April 10 testify to the success of the play in its second form.

That this was not just what Voltaire published is shown by the commentary of the abbé Nadal,[44] who apparently attended a performance in 1725 and heard much talk about the play. He quotes several verses that were omitted or decidedly altered in the 1725 edition of Voltaire's tragedy:

> Mazaël: Votre pouvoir n'est rien si Rome n'a parlé. (I, 1)
> Salome: Qu'on me venge, il suffit, le reste est peu de chose. (I, 1)
> Souvien-toi qu'il fut prêt d'exterminer enfin,
> Les restes odieux du sang Asmonéen.[45]
> Mar.: Vous voyez en ces lieux ma mere infortunée
> Presser de mon départ l'heure déterminée.[46]
> Her.: L'amour que j'ai pour vous vous tient lieu d'innocence.[47]
> Mar.: Un juste repentir produit-il tes transports?
> . . . tes remords? (IV, 4).[48]

As Nadal objected to the fact that Mazaël's intervention at the end of Act IV is too much like the part he plays at the end of Act III, Voltaire assigned to a guard a speech in IV, 5, that had originally been Mazaël's. Nadal's statement that Varus " se fait tuer comme un sot " suggests that the death of the Roman was originally more clearly indicated than by the words " percé de coups." His reproach that Voltaire made no use of Herod's prophetic remarks about the Jews at the end of Tristan's tragedy shows that the lines on this subject in the last scene of the 1725 edition were not in the tragedy before Nadal's criticism was made.

Nadal made various other criticisms of the play. It is not clear where the scene is laid in Act V. All the characters come into the same palace

---

[44] *Observations critiques sur la tragédie d'Hérode et Mariamne de M. de V. . . .,* Paris, veuve Ribou, 1725. Republished in Nadal's *Œuvres,* Paris, Briasson, 1738, I, 256-315.

[45] These two lines were probably also in I, 1, and were replaced by:
> Jurer d'exterminer les restes dangereux
> D'un Sang toûjours trop chers aux perfides Hébreux.

Nadal had objected to the rime *enfin: Asmonéen,* and Voltaire had apparently considered the criticism just.

[46] Nadal had asked, " Peut-on presser une heure déterminée? " Voltaire had then changed the lines to (II, 4):
> Vous avez vû ma Mere au desespoir réduite
> Me presser en pleurant d'accompagner sa fuite.

[47] Nadal approved of this line, but accused Voltaire of borrowing it from Chaulieu. It was changed to (IV, 4):
> Ma tendresse pour vous, vous tient lieu d'innocence.

[48] Nadal protested against Mariamne's using " tes " in speaking to Herod. Voltaire changed the word to " vos."

room. Herod and Varus should meet on the stage. They leave the battle merely to show themselves. The first meeting of Herod and Mariamne is not dramatized. The king's return makes no change in the queen's plan of escape. The account of her death is a " déclamation froide." Herod lacks dignity and owes too much to Racine's presentation of Nero and Theseus. He would not have condemned Mariamne while he was at Rome and would have been rendered less unhappy by his success with Augustus. Mariamne is coquettish and is impolite to her sister-in-law. Salome is " méchante sans esprit," is slow in thinking that Varus loves Mariamne, is inconsistent in refusing to act upon Mazaël's advice and in then acting upon it, as well as in dreading the sympathy of the Jews for the queen and then allowing them to be present at her execution. He declares that Voltaire blamed la de Seine for the way she interpreted the rôle of Salome, but holds that the fault lay, not with the actress, but with the rôle.

He also objected to Varus's claiming to have saved Mariamne; to his agreeing, though a high official, to help her escape; to his suppressing the crowning of Herod, ordered by the Roman senate; and to his using armed forces instead of demanding justice in the name of Rome. He found Nabal imprudent and objected to the suggestion that he may be in love with the queen. He thought Mazaël improperly motivated, noted that Zarès and Mariamne's mother are kept off the stage, and held that the children were too young to have appealed to their father in the manner described by Voltaire. Executioners, moreover, should not come to a scaffold without their victim.

Voltaire's play was also criticized in parodies, the most important of which is le Mauvais Ménage by Legrand and Dominique. These authors change the characters into French provincials, make the tone comic, and reconcile the husband and wife at the end of the play. Comment is made upon the fact that Herod and Varus are not allowed to meet. The latter, who has become a dragoon officer, is ridiculed for his virtuous conduct, as is the protagonist for his changes of purpose and the heroine for her sentimentality. In scene 20 she expresses herself as follows:

> Tandis que l'on se bat, et qu'un moment me reste,
> Composons quelques vers sur mon état funeste:
> Les stances n'étant plus à présent de saison,
> En vers alexandrins faisons notre oraison.[49]

The authors are parodying Hérode et Mariamne, V, 1, a scene in which the heroine sends her guards to the back of the stage and speaks a mono-

---

[49] Quoted by M. S. Burnet, Marc-Antoine Legrand, Paris, Droz, 1938, pp. 153-8. Cf. also V. B. Grannis, op. cit., pp. 263-7. According to the Mercure of March, 1724, Mariamne spoke in stances when the play was first acted.

logue. The passage calls attention to Voltaire's imitation of *Polyeucte*, in which under similar circumstances the martyr expresses himself in *stances*.

The *Mariamne* of 1724 and other plays on the same subject inspired Fuselier's *Quatre Mariamnes,* in which Voltaire's heroine appears as "Mariamne l'étourdie." This version as well as *Hérode et Mariamne* are in the cast of Piron's *Huit Mariamnes*, in which the heroine's admission that she might have loved Herod becomes:

> Que mon vilain époux, tout vieux qu'il est m'a plu;
> Que je l'aurois aimé, pour peu qu'il l'eût voulu.[50]

There was criticism from other quarters. In a comic opera, *Momus censeur des théâtres*, the tragedy was said to be, like Arlequin's costume, "faite de toutes pieces." [51] The play was attacked by J.-B. Rousseau, who held that the second version was not an improvement upon the first; that the play is badly constructed and lacks verisimilitude; that the characters act absurdly; that the account of Mariamne's death is too long; that the fate of Salome remains unknown; and that Herod's final anguish, so touching in Tristan's tragedy, is here expressed in a perfunctory manner. To show the superiority of Tristan's *Mariane,* J.-B. Rousseau prepared a modernized version of it, but it was not published until 1731.[52]

Mathieu Marais, on the contrary, was so much pleased with the tragedy that he called Voltaire "le plus grand poète que nous ayons." [53] After 1725 *Hérode et Mariamne* remained for nearly thirty years in the repertory, but it was never given more than five times in a year. In August, 1754, Grimm,[54] who had seen a performance in which Le Kain played Herod, la Gaussin the heroine, praised the subject and the verses, as well as the fact that Herod and Varus do not meet on the stage, but he found the early acts unnecessarily long, thought that more should have been made of Salome, and objected to the use of a *récit* in the dénouement. He regretted that the dead body of the heroine was not shown on the stage.

In 1762 Voltaire rewrote the play, giving it the form reproduced by Moland. He altered most of the first act, much of the second, and portions of the other three, giving greater variety to the dialogue and eliminating

---

[50] Cf. Grannis, *op. cit.*, pp. 258-63. This writer also mentions a play for marionettes by Carolet in which both *Mariamne* and *Inès de Castro* are ridiculed. For this lost parody cf. F. W. Lindsay, *Dramatic Parody by Marionettes in Eighteenth Century Paris*, New York, King's Crown Press, 1946, pp. 163-4.

[51] Cf. Olivier, *op. cit.*, p. 17.

[52] Rousseau's letter was reproduced in the *Anecdotes dramatiques*, Paris, 1775, I, 523-5. Cf. also Madeleine's edition of Tristan's *Mariane*, Paris, Hachette, 1917, p. xli.

[53] Lescure, *Journal et Mémoires de Mathieu Marais*, Paris, 1863-4, III, 174.

[54] *Cor.*, II, 397-8.

a number of passages for which he had been criticized. His principal change was the substitution for Varus of Sohême, a Jewish prince, related to Mariamne and governing Ascalon independently of Herod. He belongs to the strict sect of the Essenes and is called by Voltaire a sort of Jansenist. As he is not a Roman, he could not be criticized, as Varus had been, for failing to crown Herod, for starting an insurrection, or for creating international complications by his defeat. As Voltaire makes him break his engagement with Salome, he gives her a new reason to hate Mariamne.

Though Salome has been left in charge of Herod's dominions during his absence, as in the version of 1725, she has not, before her brother's return, secured the warrant for Mariamne's execution, she no longer counts upon Zarès, of whom little is said, and she suspects in the first act Sohême's love of Mariamne. There is no longer a hint that old Nabal, whose name has become Narbas, is in love with the queen. But Voltaire retained the killing of the executioners before Mariamne's arrival at the scaffold. While he has Herod demand that his palace fall in ruins, he eliminates the reference to the destruction of the Temple and the dispersion of the Jews that he had introduced into the edition of 1725 in accordance with Nadal's suggestion and in imitation of Tristan l'Hermite.

Voltaire undoubtedly improved his tragedy by these changes, but though, in its new form, Herod was played by Le Kain, Mariamne by la Clairon, the play was given only twice in 1763. It was performed only three times subsequently, in 1817. Bachaumont[55] reported that many spectators regretted the suppression of certain details, while Collé[56] claimed that the alterations accomplished nothing, as the tragedy was still merely "des tracasseries de ménage mises en action." La Harpe[57] condemned the subject on the ground that one is not interested in a jealous person who is not loved in return. He evidently forgot for the moment the long success of *Phèdre* and of Tristan's *Mariane*. He also claimed that the other leading persons failed to excite interest, that Mariamne maintains one attitude throughout the play, and that Herod's final decision to put her to death is insufficiently motivated. On the other hand, he praised the style, declaring that it put the play among the tragedies of Voltaire that come closest in elegance and harmony to those of Racine.

While in certain respects Voltaire's play suffers by comparison with Tristan's, it is quite superior to a contemporary tragedy on the same subject, the abbé Nadal's MARIAMNE,[58] played on Feb. 15, 1725, nearly

[55] *Mémoires secrets*, I, 274-5.
[56] *Journal*, 1807, III, 57.
[57] *Op. cit.*, XI, 48-82.
[58] Paris, veuve P. Ribou, 1725, 12° and 8°. Dedicated to the prince de Vendôme.

a year after the first performance of Voltaire's and nearly two months before the second. In the preface the author refers to Tristan's *Mariane,* but he mentions by name neither Voltaire nor his play. It is possible that he borrowed from the latter the idea of beginning his action while Herod's return from Rome is awaited and of giving Mariamne a lover who urges her to escape, though Nadal claims to have followed history, that is, Josephus, and not to have substituted for " des évenements consacrés . . . les égaremens d'une imagination qui court après la nouveauté & toûjours plus dereglée qu'elle n'est brillante "—a dig at Voltaire.

It is true that he derived his important characters and most of the circumstances, including Herod's relations with Antony and Augustus, from Josephus, but he drew from Tristan Herod's reference to the dispersion of the Jews and he regretted that, on account of the " nouvelles bienséances du Théatre," he was unable to introduce some of Tristan's characters, probably the eunuch and the concierge. Herod's seeking to make his wife take part in a sacrifice to Caesar may have been suggested by his own *Machabées,* or by that of La Motte. Mariamne's reference to " l'abomination " in the Temple must come from the Bible. The idea of having his heroine put in charge of the woman who seeks her life may well be derived from *Inès de Castro.* The spectacular scene in which the Temple is shown, with flags, Roman eagles, and an altar " dans l'enfoncement " must have been inspired by *Athalie* or Voltaire's *Œdipe.* There are, besides these borrowings and what he owed Voltaire's *Mariamne,* minor departures from Josephus as an analysis of the play will show.[59]

Republished in the author's *Œuvres,* Paris, Briasson, 1738. For Nadal cf. my *Sunset,* pp. 87-93.

[59] Soesme, put in charge of Mariamne by Herod during the king's absence in Rome, reports that Augustus has condemned Herod, indicates his desire to protect the queen, and begins to talk of his love for her. When he meets with disapproval, he reveals to Mariamne the fact that Herod had ordered him to put her to death if he did not return from Rome. Mariamne speaks of her sufferings to her son, Alexandre, and avoids Salome, who admits that she invented the report of Herod's condemnation. Tharès, who has been at Rome with Herod, describes the king's success with Augustus. When Herod returns, he orders a sacrifice to be prepared in honor of the emperor and inquires about Mariamne. Soesme advises him to trust her; Salome, to show that he is her master. Mariamne receives him coldly, but she declares that she always obeys him. Irritated by her attitude, Herod readily accepts Salome's suggestion that Mariamne be directed to take part in the sacrifice, so that her refusal will deprive her of the emperor's protection. The entrance to the Temple and the altar are shown. Herod replaces the high priest, who has refused to take part in an unorthodox ceremony. Prompted by Salome, Tharès pretends that Herod was to have been poisoned with the sacrificial cup. The king orders his wife to be tried. When Soesme urges her to escape to the Parthians, she refuses to go. She is condemned by the Council. An insurrection in her behalf is suppressed by Herod. He interviews Mariamne, agrees to spare Alexandre, and is on the point of pardoning her when she refers to the fatal order he had left when he went to Rome. He hastily infers that she has been told this secret by Soesme and that she loves him. He has Soesme tortured and hears that he has died insisting that Mariamne is innocent and that Tharès is guilty of bearing false witness. Herod accuses Tharès, notes his

Nadal assigns the longest rôle to Herod, introducing him in the second act. He attributes to him intelligence in his dealings with Augustus and surprising perspicacity in discovering Soesme's love of Mariamne, but he makes him a victim of his blind passion for the queen and his jealousy that prevents him from appreciating her virtue. He follows Josephus and others in presenting Mariamne as proud of her family, hating Herod and Salome, weeping over her wrongs, but refusing to defend herself. He makes her decline to escape, shows her love for her son and her loyalty to her religion. Alexandre, who is useless in the development of the plot, is described as a noble young prince. Salome's rôle is of considerable importance, as she devises the plot against Mariamne and helps to carry it out. Soesme loves Mariamne as Varus does in Voltaire's play, but, when he confesses to the queen, we are given little opportunity to see the effect upon either of them.

This is typical of the play. The situations are not properly developed. There is much plotting, narration, and comment, but Nadal fails to take advantage in his dialogue of opportunities he has himself created. In fifteen lines Mariamne refers to the danger she is in from Herod's love and the king leaps to the conclusion that Soesme has betrayed him because he loves Mariamne and that she responds to his affection. Twenty-two lines after Herod has cried out that Soesme must be sacrificed, it is reported that he has died under torture. Herod's forcing Tharès to confess is as rapid, though nothing has prepared us for the guilty man's behavior:

> Th.: Moi l'auteur . . . Quels témoins déposent contre moi?
> H.: Le sang de l'innocence élevé contre toi,
> La vérité sacrée.
> Th.:   Oui, du Ciel équitable
> Le bras vengeur . . .
> H.:   Poursuis.
> Th.:   Votre cri redoutable . . .
> H.: Il s'égare.
> Th.:   Salome . . . A qui j'avois promis . . .
> H.: Parle . . .
> Th.:   A conduit le crime, & moi je l'ai commis.[60]

When he published his play, Nadal praised the excellence of the principal actors, especially of la Duclos, " l'inimitable actrice," who must have played Mariamne. He insisted that his tragedy "a toutes ses

---

pallor, and draws from him a confession. After implicating Salome, Tharès kills himself. Herod declares that he will punish his sister, but it is too late to save his wife, for Alexandre reports that she has been put to death in the palace while the people were waiting at the scaffold to save her. Herod blames himself, blames the people for giving him the throne, predicts ruin for the Jews, sees Mariamne's ghost, mourns, and longs to die.

  [60] V, 8. The suspension points are in the text.

parties; que les mœurs & les caracteres y sont vrais; que tous les incidens naissent du sujet," so that it can be criticized only for "quelques expressions, ou répétitions de mots." Unfortunately the public had not been influenced by such considerations. There had been disorder, according to Nadal, at the first performance. He insinuated that it had been instigated by a cabal that had bribed the parterre.[61] Considering this an attack upon himself, Voltaire replied that there had been a cabal, but that it was composed of Nadal's friends, who had distributed free tickets of admission to the parterre. He ridiculed the tragedy, concluding that the author of *Saül, Hérode, les Machabées,* and *Mariamne* had "mis l'Ancien Testament en vers burlesques." [62] The public and the actors seem to have agreed with Voltaire, for *Mariamne* was acted only four times.[63] It must have been soon forgotten after *Hérode et Mariamne* appeared, though it was remembered long enough to form one of Fuselier's *Quatre Mariamnes* [64] and of Piron's *Huit Mariamnes.*

Nadal's tragedy must have given Voltaire the satisfaction of realizing that, while he had written a play that had surpassed in popularity one by Corneille on the same subject, a contemporary of average reputation had failed in his attempt to contend with him. It must have consoled him for J.-B. Rousseau's claim that Tristan's old tragedy was superior to his and for the failure of *Artémire.* If a Parisian had been asked at the end of 1725 who were the three leading authors of tragedy then living, he would probably have named Crébillon, Voltaire, and La Motte, but he would have added that Crébillon had produced nothing of importance since *Rhadamiste* had appeared fourteen years before and that La Motte was no such poet as the author of the *Henriade,* even if *Inès de Castro* had shown more originality than *Œdipe* and had surpassed it in success. This was the situation when Voltaire went off to England, where he was to undergo new influences. Let us see what claims La Motte had to be considered his rival.

---

[61] According to Marais, Voltaire was in the audience and the parterre called for his play; cf. Lescure, *op. cit.,* III, 293-4.

[62] Letter of March 20, 1725 (Moland, XXII, 13-6).

[63] Feb. 15, 17, 19, 21. Each time it was accompanied by a comedy in one act. Baron, Dufresne, Quinault, la Duclos, and la Dangeville are indicated by the *Registres* as being in the cast. It is probable that they played, respectively, Herod, Alexandre, Tharès, Mariamne, and Salome. The play earned for its author only 309 fr., 11 s.

[64] The heroine praises Alexandre's appearance, as she had done in I, 3 of Nadal's tragedy, and accuses Voltaire's friends of preventing her from appearing more than four times.

CHAPTER IV

HOUDAR DE LA MOTTE, 1721-1726

Born in Paris in 1672, La Motte[1] died there in 1731. Though, educated by the Jesuits, he studied law and was for a while at la Trappe, most of his energies were devoted to literary composition. It is possible that he wrote *les Originaux,* a farce of the Théâtre Italien, assigned in Gherardi's edition to " D. L. M." His first success was achieved with an opera called *l'Europe galante.* Other operas followed, as well as odes, eclogues, and fables. He was elected to the Academy in 1710, frequented the Café Gradot, took part as a Modern in the Quarrel of the Ancients and Moderns, sought to improve the *Iliad,* thereby bringing upon himself the wrath of Mme Dacier,[2] and, although he greatly admired Corneille and Racine, boldly criticized the methods of classical tragedy, even holding that it was unnecessary to write in verse or to preserve the sacred unities.

It was not until he was approaching fifty that he attempted tragedy. The delay was partly caused by the difficulty of finding a subject that appealed to him " par sa singularité & par sa grandeur " and could at the same time be properly dramatized. " Enfin je sentis un jour dans le sacrifice de la mere des Machabées, les conditions que je cherchois." [3] It was, perhaps, the success in 1716 of *Athalie* and the actors' decision to play *Esther* that encouraged him to dramatize a Biblical subject.

The one he chose for Les Machabées [4] is the account of the Jewess and her seven sons who were tortured and put to death for their refusal to eat pork.[5] La Motte kept the effort of the Syrian king, Antiochus Epiphanes, to win over the youngest son by offering to " raise him to a high

---

[1] Cf. especially Paul Dupont, *Un Poète-Philosophe au commencement du dix-huitième siècle, Houdar de La Motte (1672-1731),* Paris, Hachette, 1898. The name is also written Houdart de La Motte and La Motte-Houdar(t).

[2] Cf. my *Sunset,* p. 330.

[3] *Œuvres,* Paris, Prault aîné, 1754, IV, 25-6. Dupont (*op. cit.,* pp. 59-60) expresses the belief that La Motte proposed to be first sublime, then heroic, next pathetic, and finally to rouse horror, with the result that he wrote in turn *les Machabées, Romulus, Inès, Œdipe,* but there is no evidence that he planned all four in advance, or that he thought of these plays as representing four different types of tragedy.

[4] Paris, Grégoire Dupuis, 1722, 8°; *priv.* ceded to Dupuis, Jan. 19; approbation signed, Feb. 9, by Fontenelle, who refers to the great success of the play on the stage. Dedicated to Louis XV. Republished in editions of the author's works. Italian translations were published at Rome and Bologna in 1730, at Venice in 1751, at Siena in 1756; a Dutch translation appeared in 1771. The catalogue of the Bibliothèque Nationale indicates that La Motte had as a collaborator Duché de Vancy, who had been dead for many years when the tragedy was written!

[5] II Maccabees, Chap. VII.

estate if he would turn from the customs of his fathers," but he substituted for eating forbidden meat the offering of incense to Jupiter. He emphasized the mother, but left her alive and triumphant at the end of the play. In selecting for her the name Salmonée and in making her family Maccabees, he followed a tradition not given in the Bible, the Vulgate, or Josephus, but one that had been preserved in a French play of 1599.[6]

As the narrative gave him little material, La Motte added Antigone, daughter of Apollonius,[7] and represented her as loved both by King Antiochus and by Misael, youngest of the Jewish brethren. This invention enabled him to add love scenes, an *enlèvement,* and the account of a combat, as well as to give his hero a struggle between love and piety.[8]

La Motte refers to various persons and events mentioned in I and II Maccabees, as well as to Jacob, Gideon, Solomon, etc. The most effective of such references is found at the end of Act III, when Antigone, turned Israelite, assures Misael that " Rachel suivra Jacob sans emporter ses Dieux." He also reproduces the argument found in Maccabees that afflictions suffered by the Jews are sent by God to correct their errors and are not to be attributed to the valor of their enemies, or to the weakness of the God they worship. Reference to eternal life is not necessarily a Christian anachronism, as it is also mentioned in II Maccabees. Nevertheless, and despite Racine's example, La Motte seldom imitates Biblical phraseology. He followed instead the Cornelian tradition, writing in his *Discours*:

---

[6] *La Machabée,* published at Rouen. The heroine is called Salmone. Cf. *Bib. du th. fr.,* I, 329-30. No one who had read II Maccabees could suppose that the sons were Judas and his brothers, but the fact that the story is told just before a chapter devoted to Judas Maccabaeus may well have led to the supposition that the martyred youths were also Maccabees.

[7] Mentioned as a general of Antiochus Epiphanes in II Maccabees, Chap. V, one who slaughtered many Jews in Jerusalem.

[8] Antiochus, King of Syria, orders the Maccabees, sons of Salmonée, to be put to death. Misael brings his mother an account of his brothers' tortures. He has been temporarily spared through the intervention of Antigone, who after her father's death has been highly favored by the king. She has fallen in love with Misael, who has sought her help for his people. When he is tempted with rewards if he will offer incense to Greek gods, he refuses and begs Antiochus to follow the example of Cyrus and Alexander in his attitude towards the Jews. Antigone urges the king to be humane. In return he offers her marriage. Before she can reply, Salmonée comes in search of her son, who, she fears, may be led astray by this pagan princess. She is unmoved by efforts to induce her to renounce her religion. Antigone, on the contrary, gives up her religion for that of Misael, marries him informally, and escapes with him and her attendant, Barsès. Through the treachery of a friend sent to liberate Salmonée, they are pursued, Barsès is killed, Antigone is captured, and, after a brief fight, Misael surrenders in order not to be separated from his wife. Antiochus proposes to spare Misael and to allow him to live with Antigone if he will offer incense, but to burn her before his eyes if he refuses. When he hesitates, his mother bids him die. The death of the lovers is described. Salmonée predicts the triumph of the Maccabees, their return to Jerusalem, and the horrible death of Antiochus. The king wonders whether God is speaking to him through her mouth.

où trouveroit-on plus de grandeur que dans l'action de la Mere des Machabées?
elle surmonte les sentimens les plus naturels; elle immole plus que sa propre vie,
en exhortant son Fils à mépriser la sienne; elle se met au-dessus des pensées des
hommes, ce que les plus grands Héros ne sauroient faire indépendamment de la
religion: . . . Point de sacrifice plus douloureux, mais point aussi de plus raison-
nable, ni par conséquent de si propre à enlever toute notre admiration.[9]

It is only when she is alone with her confidant that she admits her
maternal suffering (I, 3) :

> Es-tu content, Seigneur? J'accepte mon martire.
> La mort de mes enfans me perce, me déchire:
> Ce que jamais pour eux j'ai ressenti d'amour,
> Je le sens redoubler, quand ils perdent le jour:
> Mais sans en murmurer, je subis ces allarmes;
> Et ma fidélité t'offre toutes mes larmes.

When her youngest son brings her tidings of his brothers' death, she is
not so much moved by the fact as by the thought that he may have escaped
by renouncing his religion (I, 4) :

> Ils sont morts! Pourquoi donc vous revois-je, mon fils?

When Antiochus informs her (IV, 4) that her son has eloped with
Antigone, her reaction is not that he may have saved his life, but that he
has betrayed his faith by union with a pagan:

> Tes malheurs sont les miens; plus que toi j'en frémis;
> Tu perds une Maîtresse; & moi je perds un fils.

When her son hestitates to cause the death of Antigone and hopes that
in time God may soften the king's heart, she turns upon him with (V, 2) :

> Ingrat! Ne peut-il pas aussi t'abandonner?
> Quand tu te plais toi-même à trahir ton courage,
> Tremble qu'il ne te laisse achever ton ouvrage.

He still hesitates:

> Dans les sombres horreurs de ce cruel martyre,
> Je ne décide rien, Madame: mais j'expire.
> Salmonée: Expire; mais, mon fils, expire pour ton Dieu. . . .
> Si le plus tendre amour a veillé sur tes jours,
> Va mourir.

At the end of the play she gloats over the impression her predictions
make upon Antiochus. She is obviously heroic, but so unswerving in her
devotion to her religion that she is less dramatic than her son, torn
between the demands of religion and love, won over in the end by the

---

[9] *Op. cit.*, IV, 29, 30.

eloquence of his terrible mother. La Motte quite properly cites the text of II Maccabees to show that, contrary to general belief, Misael was old enough to be a lover.[10] What the dramatist added, besides his love, was his hesitation. He claimed that the devoutness of Misael and his mother gave the tragedy " cette unité d'interêt qui est à mon avis la condition la plus essentielle d'une Tragédie." [11]

La Motte admits that Antiochus was justly criticized as " odieux et petit," but he explains that he could not depart from his source. This allowed him, however, to attribute the king's cruelty to pride rather than lust for blood, as it is stated in II Maccabees, Chap. IV, that Antiochus wept over the death of Onias. But he should have explained why his pride led him to desire the conversion of the Jews.

Antigone has looked into the history of the Hebrews, has been impressed by the dignity of their God and the demand for the believer's heart rather than sacrifice. She pities the Jews, has none of the fanaticism found in the other leading characters, and even finds some good in Antiochus. The latter (IV, 8) makes the accusation that " Ton Dieu c'est ton amour." Without love, there would probably have been no conversion. Dupont [12] calls her " une agréable amoureuse, ni trop fade, ni trop énergique." She is one of the few characters portrayed by La Mottte that he is willing to praise.

The play is thoroughly classical in form except that the first scene, though it has only four verses, contains an order for the execution of the Jews. La Motte was evidently trying to rouse the interest of his audience from the start rather than to prepare in the usual manner for so decided an utterance. This first act gives the exposition; the second is devoted chiefly to Antigone; the third leads up to the elopement; the fourth gives its results; in the fifth Salmonée convinces her son and triumphs over Antiochus after the death of the lovers has been described.

La Motte [13] asserts that he received " éloges outrés " for his versification, but he modestly attributes this fact to the nature of the subject, which " répand de soi-même un sublime dans le discours." Similarly Racine had been praised for the style of Athalie, though " il y a mis moins du sien que dans d'autres morceaux de ses Tragedies où la matiere l'a moins soutenu." II Maccabees, however, did not inspire such passages as these, which recall Corneille:

[10] In the original he is referred to as νεανίας; in the Vulgate, as adolescens. The latter word was misunderstood, as we shall see, by Nadal and probably by others.
[11] Op. cit., p. 37.
[12] Op. cit., p. 69.
[13] Op. cit., IV, 56-7.

> Antigone: Je t'aime & tu gémis!
> Misael:　Vous m'aimez & je meurs! (II, 3)
> Misael:　Que la vie avec vous m'eût été précieuse!
> Antigone: Que la mort avec toi me sera glorieuse! (IV, 8)

The tragedy was first acted on March 6, 1721. It was played fifteen times, until May 3, when it made way for *Esther,* acted on May 8. Other evidence of its success lies in the fact that, as it appeared anonymously, " plusieurs Connoisseurs " supposed that the first three acts had been written by Racine. This statement is made in the *Mercure,*[14] which refers to the popularity of the play and to the distribution of the main rôles. Old Baron, who had recently returned to the stage, took the youthful rôle of Misael. Antigone was played by la Desmares, replaced, when she retired, by Adrienne Le Couvreur. Philippe Poisson played Antiochus; la Duclos, Salmonée. The author's share of the receipts was 1162 fr., 14 s.

By the time the play was published, popular enthusiasm had died down. It was not revived at the Comédie Française except in 1745, when it was acted only twice. An anonymous critic published a letter quoted by the frères Parfaict in which admiration is expressed for La Motte's morals, for his portrayal of Salmonée, and for Act III, scenes 3 and 7, containing Antigone's conversations with Salmonée and with Misael, but the critic held that the material is badly arranged, for Misael's brothers die too soon, the second act should be the first, and the fifth act is largely superfluous. He also objected to the manner in which the play begins, to the lack of preparation, to Misael's kneeling before Antiochus, and to the portrayal of the king, whose motives remain obscure, who lacks " grandeur royale," who returns to the stage within an act, and who talks like a king in a school tragedy. The critic was obviously one who insisted upon strict observance of even minor classical rules. He was blind to the fact that the fifth act was needed to make Salmonée's rôle an essential part of the action.[15]

La Harpe [16] held that the subject was too exceptional to be well adapted to the stage. He regarded with suspicion the relations between Antiochus and Antigone, considered her love for a Jew unnatural, her decision to

---

[14] Cited by the frères Parfaict, XV, 415. Cf. also the preface of Nadal's *Antiochus,* in which reference is made to La Motte's tragedy and to Racine, " dont quelques-uns vouloient que cette Piece fût un ouvrage posthume."

[15] La Motte himself reports that, at the first performance, laughter that came near injuring the tragedy was excited by the word *séparément* in the lines:

> Gardes, conduisez-les dans cet appartement;
> Et qu'ils y soient tous deux gardés séparément.

In the published play the verses have been changed to (IV, 8):

> Dans cet apartement conduisez-les tous deux,
> Gardes; suivez mon ordre; & me répondez d'eux.

[16] *Op. cit.,* XIII, 153-5.

elope too sudden. He added that the attempt to revive the play in 1745 was a failure. Dupont [17] believed that La Motte did not have enough material for more than two or three acts and was consequently obliged to "modifier la donnée historique, fausser le caractère du personnage principal," and call to his aid love that is "ni vrai, ni vraisemblable." None of these critics notes what seems to me to be the chief fault in the tragedy: the essential incongruity between the love story, with the elopement and its attendant circumstances, and the solemn theme of heroic resistance to religious persecution. Even so, it is distinctly superior to a play on the same subject which I will discuss before returning to La Motte.

This is Nadal's ANTIOCHUS, OU LES MACHABÉES,[18] acted twenty-one months later. The public saw in it a duplicate of La Motte's tragedy, though Nadal assures us [19] that

> J'étois bien avancé dans ma Tragedie, lorsqu'il commençoit la sienne dans le secret. Je m'en ouvris dans le tems à lui-même; mais M. de la Motte fut plus modeste que moi; il ne se venta point de son travail.

There is here a hint that Nadal inspired La Motte, but the accusation is indirect and is brought by an unreliable person, for in his *Saül* Nadal had borrowed from Du Ryer, without acknowledgment and with the boast that the public was startled by the novelty of a scene he owed to the older dramatist.[20] There is, moreover, no evidence that La Motte saw Nadal's text, whereas Nadal could easily have had access to La Motte's before his own tragedy was acted. While most of the resemblances go back to the common source in II Maccabees, there is reason to believe that Nadal made some use of his predecessor.[21]

---

[17] *Op. cit.*, p. 64.

[18] Paris, veuve Ribou, 1723, 12°. Dedicated to "Mr de Sacy, de l'Academie Françoise," that is, to Louis de Sacy (1654-1727), translator of the Younger Pliny. Republished in the author's *Œuvres*, Paris, Briasson, 1738.

[19] Preface to the play.

[20] Cf. my *Sunset*, p. 88.

[21] In both plays Antiochus offers marriage to a girl loved by one of the martyrs, and the mother recalls Abraham's sacrifice of Isaac (La Motte, I, 3; Nadal, II, 4). In La Motte's play, Salmonée's last words to Misael are "Va mourir"; in Act IV of Nadal's, Zoraïde's last words to Machabée are "Va braver le trépas." In both tragedies, a member of the persecuted family predicts the wretched death of Antiochus.

> Ton corps n'est bien-tôt plus qu'une honteuse plaïe;
> Tes amis, tes flateurs, tout fuit, & tout s'effraye (La Motte, V, 5)

is echoed by

> Je vois dans les douleurs ton corps couvert de playes.
> Mais tu pâlis, barbare, & déja tu t'effrayes. (Nadal, V, 3).

Nadal also borrows from Corneille:

> Mon Pere massacré,
> De votre gloire ici fut le premier degré. (III, 5; cf. *Cinna*, vv. 11, 12)
> . . . Du sang de mon Pere encor toute baignée. (IV, 6; cf. *Cid*, v. 858).

His methods were, however, different from La Motte's. He introduced a larger number of persons and interests, with the result that he violated the unity of action, laid less stress upon the mother, and divided the interest of the spectators between two of her sons, only one of whom had been put on the stage by his rival. He piously claimed that, as he had followed the original more closely, he had the advantage of a larger share in divine inspiration:

> Si je n'avois pas les mêmes ressources, qu'il trouvoit dans son peu d'assujettisse-ment aux incidens que le sujet fournit, je pouvois au moins profiter des beautez qu'il m'avoit laissées, & qu'il auroit pû tenir de la premiere main, c'est-à-dire, de l'esprit de Dieu même.[22]

As borrowings from II Maccabees he may have had in mind the intro-duction of Menelaus, mention of the massacre at Jerusalem, including the murder of Eleazar, the description of Alexander's reception (II, 3), an allusion to Sennecharib (II, 5), reference to "sacrilége mets" and "chair immonde" (II, 5), but the love of Antiochus for Zoraïde, the intervention of Egyptians, and the expulsion of the king from Jerusalem are as distinct additions to the Biblical narrative as are those made by La Motte. Nadal thought he kept closer to the common source by making Azaël a boy and, to prove it, referred the reader to II Maccabees, Chap. VII, but he misunderstood the Latin *adolescens* or its Greek equivalent and is consequently in this respect farther than La Motte from the original.

The principal rôle is that of Antiochus, boastful and brutal, but willing to stoop to hypocrisy to gain his ends. He reminds the Jews of their

---

[22] Preface. At the beginning of the tragedy Antiochus has already occupied Jeru-salem and slaughtered many Jews, including Manassè, with whose daughter, Zoraïde, he has fallen in love. He orders the Jews to give up their religion and adopt his own. Prompted by a renegade Israelite, Menelaus, he decides to make an example of the Maccabees, the eldest of whom, called Machabée, loves Zoraïde, while the youngest, Azaël, is still a child. Salmone, their mother, advises prudence. Machabée suggests that she take Zoraïde to Memphis with the help of their friend, Phostime, the Egyptian ambassador. Antiochus proposes to Zoraïde and pretends to believe that her God is "l'arbitre du monde," but she refuses to marry him. He then threatens Salmone, arrests her older sons, and has Azaël brought to the palace. Zoraïde appears before Antiochus, has Machabée brought in, assures the Jew of her love, and bids him go to his death, but Antiochus convinces him that, if Zoraïde becomes queen, she may save her people. The Egyptian ambassador warns Antiochus that he must stop persecuting the Jews and is ordered out of the country. Five of Salmone's sons are now put to death, but she is especially moved by the thought that her youngest boy may lose his faith. When he is brought to the palace, he feels a strong aversion for Antiochus, though he does not know that he is the king, and asks to be taken away. Zoraïde pleads for him, but she again refuses to marry Antiochus, even when Machabée asks her to be another Esther. The Egyptian ambassador receives a letter from Asaph, leader of the Jewish "underground," expressing the hope that Machabée will be rescued before night. This hope is vain. Machabée is executed. Salmone encourages Azaël to remain faithful to his religion. After he has predicted the death of Antiochus, he and his mother are sent out to die. When it is too late to save them, Asaph and Phostime triumph, Menelaus is killed, and Antiochus is expelled from Jerusalem.

defeats, criticizes their pride, and orders them to abandon their religion. He puts to death Salmone and her sons. Yet he is not inhuman, for he loves Zoraïde, feels pity for Azaël, and in the end trembles before the God of Israel. Like La Motte, Nadal makes no attempt to attribute his attitude toward the Jews to a desire for religious and political unity among his subjects.

The rôle that La Motte had given to the mother becomes less effective, as it is divided between Salmone and Zoraïde. Both are so firm in their faith that they show no dramatic struggle. It is Salmone who refers especially to the past of her race, while it is Zoraïde who braves and even insults the tyrant. Her love for Machabée may be genuine, but it is expressed with little emotion.

Similarly the part assigned by La Motte to one brother is now divided among two, but neither now hesitates in his willingness to die rather than to abandon his religion. This fact reduces the importance of their mother. The chief originality in the treatment of the elder brother lies in his effort to persuade the woman he loves to marry his rival in order to save the Jews. The younger brother is said to be a child, but there is nothing in his speech that recalls a child's vocabulary.

The two chief minor characters are Menelaus, the Jew who has betrayed his people and fears that he will not be rewarded for his treachery, and the Egyptian ambassador, whose only functions are to defend the Jews and to join in their ultimate triumph. He is given lines on religious tolerance (III, 8) that anticipate Voltaire's in thought if not in style:

> Persuadez, Seigneur, mais ne tourmentez point.
> Servir ainsi les Dieux, c'est en souiller la gloire.
> Moderez vos transports; & sans vouloir vous croire,
> Employez sur des cœurs, rarement abbattus,
> Les conseils, la raison, l'exemple des vertus.
> C'est de ces mêmes Dieux imiter la clemence.
> Est-ce par la rigueur que le zéle commence?
> Laissez la verité seule se soutenir,
> Et confondez l'erreur au lieu de la punir.

The play is not well constructed. The importance assigned to Menelaus in the first act and the first scene of the second makes us expect to see him again, but instead we have only the news of his death. The Egyptian ambassador is equally ineffective so far as the main action is concerned. Young Azaël need not have been brought on the stage, except that his youth adds to our impression of the king's cruelty. The situations lack variety. The final victory of the Jews is brought about by forces external to the play. The style is inferior to La Motte's. It was probably for these reasons that the tragedy was less well received. Acted first on Dec. 16, 1722, with Baron, la Duclos, and la Le Couvreur in the cast, it was given only seven times until Dec. 30, and was not revived. Nadal, who received only 417 francs as his share, tried to explain the failure of his tragedy by asserting that it appeared in an unusual season for religious plays, that the public thought he was duplicating the work of La Motte, and that the retirement of la Desmares prevented her from interpreting the rôle he had wanted her to take.[23] He adds bitterly that soon no religious plays can be given, since respect for religion

doit necessairement réfroidir l'action de la Tragedie. On commence même à en violer dans les Pieces profanes les régles les plus essentielles. Tout y est créé, jusqu'aux évenemens; on n'observe plus ni mœurs, ni caracteres; . . . l'esprit s'y produit par tout, . . . c'est une espece de mascarade, qui s'est introduite sur la Scene.

La Motte's second tragedy is entitled ROMULUS.[24] He had read, in Livy's First Decade, about the founding of Rome, the seizure of the Sabin women, their intervening between their relatives and their husbands, and the union of the two states. He kept, in addition to these events, the report that Romulus was the son of Mars, his murder of Remus, the heterogeneous character of the early Romans, the creation of the senate, the names of Tatius and Hersilie, the entrance of the Sabins into Rome by the help of treachery, and the joint kingship of Romulus and Tatius. He made Hersilie the daughter of Tatius, supposed that she did not marry Romulus till a year after her capture, added Proculus and Murena, the priest, their intrigues, the capture of Tatius, Hersilie's note, and minor details. He preserved the general character of Livy's narrative, increased the importance of love, developed the theme of treachery, and introduced an antireligious motif. He sought to make his play more spectacular than most of his predecessors had made theirs, but he cannot be considered a reformer in this respect, for his altar makes less impression than the temples of *Athalie* and of Voltaire's *Œdipe*.[25]

[23] Moland (XXII, 14) states that in the edition of 1723 Nadal spoke of the " animosité effrénée des partisans de La Motte," but that he subsequently suppressed the remark. As Voltaire declares that the chief rôle in the play was taken by Adrienne Le Couvreur, the retirement of la Desmares cannot have seriously injured the interpretation of the tragedy.

[24] Published with the *Machabées*, Paris, Dupuis, 1722, 8°. Dedicated to the Regent. Republished in editions of the author's works. Dutch translations appeared in 1722 and 1754; Italian translations in 1730 and 1746.

[25] A year has passed since, in violation of hospitality, the Romans have seized the Sabin women. Romulus has been begging Hersilie to marry him and winning victories in order to impress her with his courage. Though she admits to her confidant that she loves him, she continues to reproach him with her capture. He has resolved to marry her by force. Meanwhile his friend, Proculus, who also loves Hersilie, plots to admit Tatius into the city, to murder Romulus, and to reign in his stead. He has won over Murena, the high priest, who holds that Romulus is

In the *Discours* that accompanies the 1754 edition of the tragedy La Motte tells us that he depicted Romulus as having both virtues and vices. His extreme valor is partly based on superstition. His brutality, shown in his threatening to marry Hersilie against her will, is tempered by his love and by his postponement of the marriage for a year. He is magnanimous to captured Tatius, but he lacks the perspicacity to realize that Hersilie loves him and that Proculus is plotting against him. The rival king resents his daughter's capture, but he is impressed by Romulus and warns Proculus that there is to be no further treachery. Some critics thought that as, when captured, he refused to give his daughter to his captor, he showed more courage than Romulus, but La Motte refused to accept this point of view.

Hersilie is torn between her love and her sense of honor. It is with some difficulty that she admits, even to her confidant, that she loves Romulus. The author has to arrange the circumstances of the tragedy in such a way that to admit her love is the only means by which she can prevent a duel between her father and her lover.

Opposed to this trio are the villains, Proculus and Murena. While posing as a friend of Romulus, Proculus had intrigued against him. His failure to kill him is due, according to La Motte, not to fear, but to the deep respect a Roman feels for valor. A certain " B." reminded him,[26] however, that Proculus had admitted the necessity of atoning for his " moment de surprise." Moreover, Proculus had admitted that he might have felt terror and Murena had accused him of lacking valor. La Motte, as a dramatist, had obviously made him less brave than Romulus and Tatius, but, as a critic, he was unwilling to admit the fact, preferring to adhere to the absurd convention that to be a Roman was to be brave.

encroaching upon spiritual authority. When Tatius enters Rome and fights with Romulus, his sword breaks, he is captured, and is urged to give his daughter to Romulus. This he refuses to do. Proculus enables him to escape and tells Hersilie that her lover will soon perish. She writes a note informing Romulus of the danger he is in, but the king, not suspecting that she has written it, accuses her of plotting against him. He then leads his forces against Tatius, but the women interfere, peace is made, and it is decided that Romulus and Tatius shall fight to determine which is to rule over the two peoples. When they are about to fight before an altar that has been brought into the palace, Hersilie declares that she loves Romulus, who then comes to an understanding with Tatius. They will rule together and will increase the number of Roman senators. Murena, however, warns that omens predict misfortune if the marriage takes place. Hersilie is afraid to disobey the priest, but Romulus offers a new sacrifice. While he is inspecting the victim's entrails, conspiring senators attack him, but Tatius and the new senators arrive in time to assist him, and the conspirators are killed. Murena then seeks to turn the people against Romulus by accusing him of sacrilege, but, as Tatius informs his daughter, Romulus strikes him dead, proves in this way that the gods support him, and wins over the people. Proculus kills himself. Romulus will marry Hersilie and rule with her father over the Romans and the Sabins.

[26] Cf. *Œuvres*, 1754, IV, 142-3.

But La Motte showed no such classical restraint in regard to priests. Voltaire had written anticlerical verses in *Œdipe*, but he had put no lying pontiff on the stage. La Motte's Murena plots against his king, makes a false report in regard to the auspices, and seeks to rouse the people against the government. His motive is to prevent the intrusion of secular authority upon his own domain (IV, 1):

> Car tu sçais, Proculus, avec quel désespoir
> Je le vois toûjours prêt d'usurper mon pouvoir;
> Que sans mettre de borne aux droits du Diadême,
> Il prétend à son trône asservir l'Autel même; . . .
> Qu'il périsse; sa mort ne peut être trop prompte.

When his plot fails and he is murdered, his fate excites no sympathy. The fact that he is a pagan might not have protected La Motte, if he had not had the approbation of the Regent, to whom he took the precaution of reading his play before he presented it to the public.

La Motte insists that the time represented is only that of performance plus a half-hour between certain acts. He admits that some of the off-stage events may have required more time than he allows them, but he declares that such usage is permitted, for the spectator does not count the moments, " pourvû qu'on le touche." In order to preserve the unity of place and at the same time to add a spectacular element, he had an altar brought into the palace before the beginning of the fourth act. He argues that the sight of the two kings swearing on this altar to abide by the result of their duel and the sight of Hersilie rushing in to tell of her love are far more effective than if mere *récits* had been employed.

La Motte admits that he did not succeed in giving his audience a clear idea of the conspiracy. " On sent moins la justesse des mesures de Proculus, que le besoin que j'en avois moi-même." This confession seems unnecessary when one reads the play, but the remarks of the conspirator may have seemed less clear when they were spoken on the stage, or La Motte may have improved his text before he published it. On the other hand, he is well pleased with his exposition, which, as he puts it, is in action, that is, it results from the argument in which Hersilie's confidant draws from her the admission that she loves Romulus. Unfortunately this is not all of the exposition. The part concerned with the conspiracy is revealed in a conventional narration, made by Proculus (I, 4) to a friend from whom he has been separated.

La Motte's usage in regard to his exposition and the use of spectacle are typical of his methods. Though he found classical regulations open to criticism, he respected them and wrote his play with due regard for the progress and unity of his action. At the same time, he began his tragedy with discussion rather than narrative and introduced the altar, but he soon returned to the *récit* and failed to show on the stage the Sabin women rushing between the two armies, or the attempt made upon his hero's life while he was peering into the entrails of the sacrificed bull, or the murder of Murena. He was certainly in practice a most cautious reformer.

When *Romulus* was first acted, Jan. 8, 1722, Baron, who is said to have played Tatius, Dufresne, and la Duclos were in the cast. La Motte took the precaution of having the tragedy followed by a short play, a proceeding previously adopted, as a rule, only after a tragedy had been acted several times and the receipts were in danger of falling low.[27] He tells us that he heard a "battement de mains général" when Tatius told his daughter that Romulus was still alive, another when the hero returned to the stage. The performances were well attended. The play was given twenty-one times, until Feb. 26. The author received from these performances 1725 fr., 18 s. The tragedy was acted again on Feb. 22, 1723, and five times in 1731-2.

The *Critique de Romulus*[28] found the character of Romulus defective, that of Proculus cold. The writer held that there were too many events and that the play, lacking verisimilitude, interested only in spots. On the other hand, a writer in the *Mercure*[29] reported that the play was popular with the public and at court, where it was acted on Jan. 24. He praised its structure, its style, and the thoughts it expressed. Mathieu Marais,[30] who attended a performance, admitted that the play was very well received. He discovered in it very interesting situations and verses that struck him as "assez faciles," but he considered the style undramatic, the events crowded, and Romulus the kind of romantic hero that Boileau had attacked. He added, however, that Baron spoke his verses so admirably that, though the play seemed to end with the fourth act, the fifth was appreciated and a sixth would have been if the old actor had continued to declaim. Marivaux,[31] on the other hand, had no reservations. He admired the "élévation sensée des idées" and the three leading characters.

Subsequently La Harpe[32] admired the scene at the altar, but he argued that Proculus should have justified his ambition to become head of the

---

[27] Attention was called to this fact in the *Almanach des Spectacles* of 1761, p. 153. There were precedents for it in the cases of Mlle Barbier's *Arrie et Pétus*, which was, however, first acted in summer, and of *Athalie* and *Esther*, which were old plays when they were first produced at the Comédie Française.

[28] Cited by the *Mercure* of April, 1722, pp. 84-5.

[29] For January, 1722, pp. 96-106.

[30] Lescure, *op. cit.*, II, 241.

[31] In the *Spectateur françois*, *Œuvres*, Paris, 1781, IX, 24-5.

[32] *Op. cit.*, XIII, 155-9.

6

state and that Romulus should have been presented more as a political leader and less as a lover. He held that the tragedy ended with the fourth act, though he must have known that preparation had been made for Murena's intervention in the fifth. It is true, however, that in the early part of the play the rôle of the priest had not been sufficiently stressed. In fact, we do not see him until we reach the first scene of Act IV.

Dupont thought that III, 1, in which Romulus consults Proculus, his would-be assassin, was suggested by *Cinna* and that the portrayal of Murena was inspired by that of the high priest in Voltaire's *Œdipe,* though the latter is neither dishonest nor treacherous. He is of the opinion that Hersilie goes too far in pretending to hate Romulus and that the founder of Rome is made into a seventeenth-century " héros de roman." The latter criticism, which overlooks Romulus's threat to force Hersilie to marry him, had been offered when the play first appeared, not only by Marais, but by a *chansonnier,* and by Lesage and Fuselier in their marionette parody entitled *Pierrot Romulus.*[33]

In his third tragedy La Motte achieved far more than temporary success. His INÈS DE CASTRO [34] became one of the best known plays of the century and did much to create the tragedy of sentiment. According to d'Alembert,[35] the author first conceived the plan of his play, then asked his friends to find him a subject in history that would lend itself to his ideas, and they found only the story of Inès. La Grange-Chancel [36] accused La Motte of borrowing from Corneille's *Théodore* the figures of the queen and her daughter. The frères Parfaict [37] suggested as a source Rotrou's *Laure persécutée.* All of these hypotheses may be justified, but one needs more than d'Alembert's " on dit " to make us sure of them.

It may be that knowledge of Rotrou's play led La Motte to seek in history the theme of a persecuted princess, that his friends suggested the story of Inès de Castro, and that, in order to give it greater unity, he modified it under the influence of *Théodore,* but it is equally possible that familiarity with the theme, which had been treated by Camoens [38] and by

[33] Cf. Dupont, *op. cit.*, pp. 67-73. For the parody cf. F. W. Lindsay, *op. cit.*, pp. 121-31.

[34] Paris, Dupuis, 1723, 8° (two editions). Republished, Amsterdam, Du Sauzet, 1723; Paris, Prault fils, 1751; la Compagnie, 1754 and 1762; veuve Duchesne, 1772; Fages, 1802; in the author's works; in the *Petite Bibliothèque,* 1786; by Petitot in 1803; in *Auteurs du second ordre,* 1808; in *Répertoires* of 1803, 1813, 1817, 1818, 1821, 1822, 1824, 1828, and 1834. Italian translations were published at Rome in 1728 and 1730; at Lucca in 1762; at Florence in 1766; at Venice in 1768 (reprinted in 1776, 1784, and 1796). A Dutch translation was published at Ghent without date.

[35] *Eloge de La Motte,* quoted by Dupont, *op. cit.*, p. 59.

[36] *Œuvres,* 1758, V, 107.

[37] XIII, 168.

[38] *Luciads,* III, cxx-cxxvi. Mr. Martin Nozick is at present writing a dissertation on the general theme of Inès de Castro.

Portuguese and Spanish dramatists, as well as by historians of Portugal, may have inspired the tragedy. As the visiting princess appears in the story of Inès as related by Vélez de Guevara in *Reinar después de morir,* La Motte had no need for suggestions in this respect from *Théodore* or *Andromaque,* though, as her character is utterly unlike that of Blanca in the Spanish play, he may have altered it under the influence of Campistron's *Tiridate,* where Talestris finds herself in a similar situation and reacts to it in much the same manner. The introduction of the children may have been suggested by Guevara's play, by de la Cerda's *Doña Inés de Castro,* or by history. It is only the character of the queen, who is not historical and does not appear in these Spanish plays, that may have come from *Théodore.* La Motte's tragedy, however, differs decidedly from all of these suggested sources.

In 1340 the Portuguese won the battle of Salado and drove back the Moors to Granada or to Africa. In the same year Pedro, son of King Alfonso, married Constance, daughter of the Duke of Penafiel, a Castilian nobleman. She was accompanied to Portugal by Inès de Castro, daughter of a nobleman who had distinguished himself at Salado. She attracted Pedro's attention, became his mistress, and, after the death of Constance, may have been secretly married to him. On her account he refused to marry anyone else, thus incurring his father's displeasure. While Pedro was away from home, Alfonso visited Inès with the intention of putting her to death, but, when she showed him her children, his own grandchildren, he was so much moved that he spared her. Jealous nobles, however, persuaded the king to allow them to murder her. Pedro, deeply angered, started a revolt, but he came to terms with his father and shared the rule with him until Alfonso's death. Subsequently he caught two of the three murderers and tortured them to death. He then had the body of Inès exhumed and crowned.[39]

In dramatizing this tale, La Motte altered it considerably. Alfonso remains king and is the father by his first wife of Pedro, but he has taken as a second wife the widowed Queen of Spain, who is the mother of Constance. To this queen he gave the part taken historically by the jealous noblemen. He made of Pedro's revolt a brief uprising, quelled by the presence of the king, as is a similar disturbance in *Romulus.* He retained the essential characteristics of the king and the heroine, while altering the prince, introduced the children and the prince's judges, and emphasized the pathos of the main events.[40]

[39] Cf. Fortunato de Almeida, *História de Portugal,* Coimbra, 1922, I, 272-4, and H. Morse Stephens, *The Story of Portugal,* New York, 1891, pp. 95-9.
[40] Pedro has been secretly married to Inès long enough to have had two children

The fact that he had found an Hispanic subject in which a young hero fights against the Moors must have recalled to La Motte the *Cid* and may have persuaded him to make an Infanta of the woman who sighs in vain for the hero. He even lifted a line from Corneille's play, though he does not admit that he did so. In the preface of the first edition he writes:

J'ai laissé dans ma Piece un vers de Corneille, que la force de mon Sujet m'avoit fait aussi; & quand on m'a fait appercevoir qu'il étoit du Cid, je n'ai pas crû me devoir donner la peine de l'affoiblir pour le déguiser.[41]

In other cases there is less verbal resemblance,[42] but similarity in spectacle or in thought. In both plays a drawn sword is displayed and there is doubt as to who has been slain by it. In both the idea is expressed

by her. His father, Alphonse, King of Portugal, has engaged him to Constance, daughter of the Queen of Spain, now Pedro's stepmother. Alphonse promises the Spanish ambassador that Pedro's marriage to the princess, delayed by his victorious campaign against the Moors, will take place immediately. The queen, troubled by the young man's indifference to her daughter, threatens Inès, whom she suspects of winning his affections. Inès tells Pedro of the danger they are in, reminds him that she had married him only because he had threatened to kill himself, but refuses to escape with the children. He promises to protect her, but agrees that they should avoid each other. Constance admits to the king that she loves his son and asks that her marriage be delayed until she has won him, but Alphonse orders his son to marry her as soon as possible. The queen denounces Inès and calls attention to the lovers' embarrassment. Pedro admits that they love each other, but he insists that Inès is blameless. Alphonse puts her in the queen's keeping and subsequently offers to marry her to Rodrigue, a nobleman of royal blood. When she refuses, the king warns her that he will not forgive her if she is secretly married to Pedro. The queen reports that the prince has revolted and forced the palace guard. While Alphonse goes to investigate, Pedro enters, armed, and seeks to take Inès to a place of safety, but she insists upon his saving his father while she remains in the palace as a hostage. Constance informs Pedro that his father's presence has quelled the revolt and urges him to escape, even if he takes Inès with him, but the king enters, obliges Pedro to surrender his sword, and has him guarded. The prince begs his father to save Inès·and swears to avenge her if she is murdered. After some hesitation the king offers to spare Pedro if he will marry Constance at once. When the prince refuses, Alphonse has him tried by Rodrigue, Henrique, and two other nobles. Though he is Pedro's rival in love, Rodrigue is for mercy, whereas Henrique, whose life Pedro had saved, is for justice. The other judges say nothing, but they show by their tears that they agree with Henrique. Consequently Alphonse condemns his son to death. Constance begs the queen to save him and consults Inès, who asks her to let her see the king. When she does so, she tells Alphonse that she had married Pedro to save his life, but begs that she be punished rather than the prince. As he refuses to hear her appeal, she has her two children brought in by their governess. Deeply touched, Alphonse pardons Pedro and agrees to his remaining the husband of Inès, but the heroine suddenly feels that her blood is aflame. She has obviously been poisoned by the queen. Pedro comes to thank his father, finds Inès dying, and seeks to kill himself, but he is prevented by the king from doing so.

[41] The line in question is pointed out, not by La Motte, but by the authors of the parody, *Agnès de Chaillot*, sc. 8:

> Le Bailli: *Vous parlez en soldat, je dois agir en roi.*
> Pierrot: A quoi bon me citer ce beau vers de Corneille,
>   Dont vous avez cent fois étourdi mon oreille?

The line is v. 600 of *le Cid*. It occurs in *Inès*, II, 2.

[42]   Vous êtes aujourd'hui ce qu'autrefois je fus. (*Cid*, v. 212)
          Je prévis qu'il feroit ce qu'autrefois je fis. (*Inès*, I, 3)

A king's final decision is expressed by " Je le veux " (*Cid*, v. 364: *Inès*, II, 2).

that great deeds absolve a subject from the crime of disobedience.[43] Don Diègue and his son discuss the relative claims of honor and love as do Alphonse and Pedro those of politics and love.[44] Both kings show a benevolent attitude towards their subjects, while in both plays the thought is expressed that a subject in doing his duty puts his sovereign under no obligation.[45]

On the other hand, there is an essential difference between the two plays. Whereas Corneille had built his plot round a struggle in the souls of his lovers, the only character in *Inès* that has a well developed mental conflict is the king, but his decision is made, not as a result of the struggle, but because he is affected by the sight of his grandchildren. No such importance had been given to children in any seventeenth-century tragedy except *Athalie*. This sentimental appeal, reenforced by the weeping of the judges and the pity roused by Inès herself, marks the tragedy as a distinct eighteenth-century production.

Alphonse is presented as a king with a high sense of responsibility towards his subjects (II, 2):

> Du sang de nos Sujets sages dépositaires,
> Nous ne sommes pas tant leurs maîtres que leurs Peres;
> Au péril de nos jours il faut les rendre heureux;
> Ne conclure ni paix, ni guerre que pour eux.
> Ne connoître d'honneur que dans leur avantage:
> Et quand dans ses excès notre aveugle courage
> Pour une gloire injuste expose leurs destins,
> Nous nous montrons leurs Rois moins que leurs assassins.

He loves his son and remembers his obligations to Inès's grandfather. He is slow to yield to his wife's urgings, is ready to forgive Pedro's rebellion if he will marry Constance. Even when the prince refuses, he submits the question to four judges. As they condemn Pedro, one would expect the king, in accordance with his character, to have him executed, especially as no preparation has been made for the influence exerted by the children upon their grandfather, but his sparing the prince doubtless met with such approval from the audience that even La Motte's critics must have been disarmed.

Pedro is thoroughly romantic. He has won Inès by repeatedly threatening suicide, has defeated the Moors, seeks to use force in order to save his wife from his stepmother, but he lacks the foresight required to carry out his plan. His military prowess is not supported by political sagacity. He proposes to attack Castile without considering the disaster a war might bring upon Portugal. La Motte retains only in part his historical capacity

---

[43] *Cid*, II, 1; *Inès*, IV, 3.   [44] *Cid*, III, 6; *Inès*, II, 2.   [45] *Cid*, II, 1; *Inès*, III, 3.

for vengeance. He swears (III, 8) to avenge Inès with torrents of blood and to spare no one except his father and Constance, clearly implying that the queen will not escape, yet at the end of the play, when he is sure that Inès has been poisoned, he thinks only of his misfortunes and of suicide. La Motte admits that he had been tempted to end his play with a " fureur de Dom Pedre " in order to show that he would deserve his nickname of " Cruel," but this would have left a disagreeable impression and would have changed " en terreur la pitié, qui est un sentiment beaucoup plus doux." He was well pleased with his ending, justified during the eighteenth century by the success of the tragedy, but his play might have had a longer life if he had thought less of pity and more of reproducing on the stage the impressive character of the prince as it was offered to him by Portuguese history.

Inès is the most pathetic character of the play, but she is by no means inactive. It is not explained how she has managed to marry the prince and have two children by him without disclosing her secret.[46] She is thoroughly loyal to the king, refuses to escape when she might have done so, insists upon Pedro's rescuing his father, and offers to remain as a hostage in order to convince the king of his son's good behavior.[47] She thinks of her husband's safety rather than of her own and devises the plan of showing the children to their grandfather, which, but for the queen, would have given the play a happy ending.

Almost equally pathetic is Constance, who has fallen hopelessly in love with Pedro and appeals to the king, to the queen, and even to Inès in her efforts to save him. She is essential to the action, as it is Pedro's refusal to marry her that gets him into trouble with his father and turns her mother against Inès. She also arranges for her rival her important interview with Alphonse. She is a magnanimous princess, willing for Pedro to escape with Inès if there is no other way to save him.

Her mother contrasts sharply with her. Intensely proud of her rank and deeply resenting Pedro's refusal to marry her daughter, she is the first person to suspect Inès and is largely responsible for the discovery that her marriage has taken place. She has no pity for Inès and almost as little for Pedro. Even the fact that the prince has been condemned is not enough for her. She must have, too, the life of her daughter's rival, though just how she manages to poison her is left to our imagination.[48]

---

[46] This fact impressed the authors of *Agnès de Chaillot*, who made their Bailli ask:

> Ont-ils pu parvenir à l'âge où les voilà
> Sans qu'aucun du logis ait rien su de cela?

[47] An idea probably suggested by Duché's *Absalon*, a tragedy that La Motte praises highly.

[48] One wonders whether, in depicting this character and that of her daughter, La

The children and their governess do not speak. Their introduction may have been justified in La Motte's eyes by the example of Euripides in *Alcestis,* of Longepierre in *Médée,* and of Racine in *Athalie,* though La Grange-Chancel had been afraid to show children on the stage in his own *Alceste.*[49] They were not the only speechless characters in the play, for two of the judges also have silent rôles. In reply to criticism of these judges and the suggestion made in *Agnès de Chaillot* (sc. 18) that they were introduced merely to "orner la scène," La Motte asserted that the importance of the question submitted required the presence of four judges, and that it would have been difficult to find four actors accustomed to "plaire dans le tragique." Moreover, three speeches for condemnation would have wearied the audience. Consequently he had two judges remain silent. He believed that their silence and their tears were as pathetic as the speech of the judge who argued for the prince's condemnation.

In regard to the two speaking judges La Motte admits that he was guilty of artificiality in making Pedro's rival vote for acquittal and the man whose life he had saved vote for condemnation. It is true that he won the approbation of those who "s'abandonnent naïvement à l'impression de la chose même," but not of more intelligent critics, who note the " affectation du contraste " and feel that " c'est moi qui m'arrange à plaisir pour étaler tout cet héroïsme."

As in the two earlier tragedies, La Motte devoted his first scenes to something more striking than the usual expository narrative. This time he chose the reception of an ambassador, in which the costumes would appeal to the eye. The scene of the judges and that of the children are also pictorially unusual, as is the entrance of Pedro holding a sword red with blood. He probably considered these scenes as spectacular as those in which the altar figures in *Romulus.*

The material is so carefully distributed among the acts that there are one or two striking scenes in each of them.[50] Each act is, as La Motte claims, a unit in itself. There is, however, a certain artificiality in the postponement of information about the marriage. This was noted in *Agnès de Chaillot* (sc. 22):

Motte foresaw the indignation of the Spanish people that would follow the rejection of the Infanta who had been brought to Paris to marry Louis XV. She was, on account of her extreme youth, sent back to Madrid the year after *Inès* was first acted. The Spaniards protested violently, but they did not attempt to poison Maria Lecsinska.

[49] He admitted in the 1758 edition of his plays that La Motte's boldness had succeeded.

[50] Act I: the ambassador's reception and a love scene. Act II: the interview between father and son and the scene in which Inès is accused. Act III: Alphonse's appeal to Inès and the scene in which Pedro enters with drawn sword. Act IV: the trial scene. Act V: the scene in which Inès admits she is Pedro's wife, the scene of the children, and that of the heroine's death.

> Mais pourquoi m'avouer si tard un tel forfait?
> Dès le commencement vous deviez l'avoir fait,
> Vous dire de mon fils épouse, et non maîtresse;
> Mais vous avez voulu faire durer la pièce,
> Pour étaler ici tous ces beaux sentimens
> Que j'ai lus et relus cent fois dans les romans.

Despite such criticism, the play achieved phenomenal success. Already in October, 1722, the *Mercure* had reported that it had been received by the actors with applause and tears. When it was first acted, April 6, 1723, after the Easter recess, Baron played Alphonse; Dufresne, Pedro; Adrienne Le Couvreur, Constance; la Duclos, Inès; la La Motte, the queen; Quinault and Fontenay, Rodrigue and Henrique; Legrand, the ambassador.[51] About 1100 people paid admission.[52] There was a second performance on April 8, but the illness of Baron prevented there being a third until May 15. Then the play was given almost every second or third day until Aug. 21. The following year it was played from Feb. 10 to 28, then on March 3, 8, and 10, 1725. During these forty-three productions, the attendance remained so satisfactory that the author continued to earn a share in the receipts. The amount paid him was 5765 fr., 19 s., more than Voltaire had received from *Œdipe* or, so far as the records show, any other author had ever received from a French tragedy.

La Motte claimed that there had been, perhaps, no such success since the *Cid* first appeared. Collé,[53] who had attended a performance when he was very young, asserted in 1765 that it was the only play he had ever seen approach in success the *Siège de Calais*. Marivaux[54] admired it greatly and noted the simplicity and sweetness of Constance, an impression partly due to the acting of Adrienne Le Couvreur. He thought, however, that the author was too clever in his presentation of the judges' opinions. Voltaire,[55] who saw the tragedy early in its career, reported that it was being given twice a week and that "tout y est plein jusqu'au cintre." After Baron recovered from his illness, Marais[56] wrote that all Paris was returning to the play. La Motte admitted that "la perfection des Acteurs lui a donné tout l'éclat qu'elle pouvoit recevoir," but he added that it was equally well received when it was acted in the provinces. Mme Du Deffand[57]

---

[51] *Mercure*, April, 1723, p. 778. It indicates that the silent judges were played by Du Boccage and Duchemin.

[52] 820 plus those in boxes, which were sold for 940 fr. If we assume that 20 lower boxes were sold at 32 fr. each and 15 upper boxes at 20 fr. each, this would mean that 280 persons were present in the boxes.

[53] *Journal*, 1807, III, 169.

[54] *Op. cit.*, IX, 233-45.

[55] Moland, XXXIII, 88.

[56] Lescure, *op. cit.*, II, 459.

[57] Mrs. Paget Toynbee, *Lettres de la marquise du Deffand à Horace Walpole*, London, Methuen, 1912, II, 37-8.

recalled that, when it was a novelty, everyone knew it by heart. Yet
Mathieu Marais [58] remarked that, though all Paris wept over it, he did
not. He criticized the verses severely and quoted with approval the verdict
of Desfontaines that the success of the play was due to the acting and that
La Motte would be wise not to publish it. Nevertheless, it remained in
the repertory till 1801, long after its original interpreters were dead. It
was acted at the Comédie Française 200 times, a record for eighteenth-
century tragedies surpassed only by *Rhadamiste,* Ducis's adaptation of
Hamlet, and seven plays by Voltaire.

Evidence of its success is also shown by the fact that it was parodied
several times [59] and that, according to La Motte, it received "un grand
nombre de Critiques." [60] He was himself amused by *Agnès de Chaillot,*
though he answered the charge contained in it that the silent judges were
useless. He defended his introduction of conjugal love by the examples
of *Manlius Capitolinus* and *Absalon.* He boasted of his play's structure,
overlooking the fact that he gave no hint as to Pedro's future relations
with his father and his stepmother. He admitted that he had exaggerated
Alphonse's anger in I, 3, and had consequently omitted eight of his verses
when he published the play. He defended himself against the charge of
inconsistency in having Pedro conceal his love in Act I and admit it in
Act II, by saying that the prince knew his love had been discovered and
wanted to make it clear that he would protect Inès. He argued that
Alphonse was right to yield when his grandchildren appeared, for he
realized that the heirs to his throne should not have their father's memory
blackened. To excuse some of his devices he referred to passages in
Corneille and Racine where probability is sacrificed to scenic effect.

Voltaire [61] claimed to have found in the tragedy two hundred "fautes
contre la langue," but he admitted that the fifth act made him weep and
that, if *Inès* had been well written, it would be "au rang des pièces de
Racine."

La Grange-Chancel [62] criticized the tragedy in a poem addressed to the

[58] Lescure, *op. cit.,* II, 477, 485-6.
[59] Cf. Grannis, *op. cit.,* pp. 228-44; M. S. Burnet, *Marc-Antoine Legrand,* Paris,
Droz, 1938, pp. 146-53; Lindsay, *op. cit.,* pp. 163-4. The best known parody, *Agnès
de Chaillot* by Legrand and Dominique, has already been mentioned. The king
becomes in it a bailiff, married to a baker's widow. His son's sweetheart is the
bailiff's cook. The judges are the beadle, the village teacher, the *marguiller,* and the
bell-ringer. Constance, though mentioned as the bailiff's stepdaughter, does not
appear. The plot is followed closely, though there is only one act. Agnès, instead
of dying from the effect of poison, has an attack of colic, from which she recovers.
The play ends with a "divertissement" furnished by peasants.
[60] For two of these cf. the *Mercure* for July and October, 1723.
[61] Moland, XXIII, 380-1, XX, 564-6, XXXIII, 493.
[62] *Œuvres,* 1758, V, 104-13.

author and in a *Lettre à M. le Baron de Walef*. He held that the rôle of Constance is as useless as that of the Infanta in the *Cid* and objected to Rodrigue's love, as it produces no effect. He found the presence of the children "nouvelle et touchante," but less effective than the absence of Astyanax from Racine's *Andromaque*.[63] He thought it strange that Euripides should be imitated by a persecuter of the Ancients. In his poem he tells La Motte that he would have omitted the judges, the children, their attendant, Constance, and the ambassador, but in the *Lettre* he says he would have developed the last of these, making him inspire the queen's suspicions of Inès, plot with her, and employ the poison, apparently in order to make the queen less odious.[64] In short, he would have deprived *Inès* of two effective rôles, substituting for them merely confidants, and he would have destroyed the variety, pathos, and appeal to the eye that La Motte was seeking to produce.

Mme Du Deffand [65] was sufficiently interested in the tragedy to write a parody "d'Inès en mirliton," which she sent in 1770 to Horace Walpole. Raynal [66] declared that it was one of the most interesting plays he knew and that its success had always been maintained. Fréron [67] thought a reader would be entranced by the subject, so that he would overlook stylistic weakness and lack of color. La Harpe [68] held that "si le talent de l'auteur eût répondu au sujet, Inès devait être un des chefs-d'œuvre de la scène française."

The play has historical importance as the first genuinely successful French tragedy to lay its chief emphasis upon sentiment. Its popularity may be compared to that of *la Dame aux camélias*. Both plays have obvious faults, but both have had great appeal for more than one generation of French audiences.

La Motte's last tragedy was ŒDIPE.[69] He had tried a Biblical, a Roman, and a medieval subject, but he had not previously selected one from Greek literature. In dramatizing the legend he chose he had been preceded by Corneille and Voltaire. His principal source was the *Œdipus Rex* of Sophocles, but he made a number of changes, some of which may well have

---

[63] Du Bos, on the contrary, had argued that the presence of Astyanax would have rendered Andromaque more pathetic; cf. his *Réflexions*, Paris, 1740, I, 418-9.

[64] Strange advice from the author of *Ino et Mélicerte*, but La Grange's long exile may have made him prudent in regard to the presentation of royalty.

[65] *Op. cit.*, II, 37-8, 48.

[66] *Cor.*, II, 161.

[67] *Année littéraire*, 1754(7), p. 132.

[68] *Op. cit.*, XI, 130; cf. also XIII, 160-73.

[69] Published in the author's *Œuvres*, Paris, Dupuis, 1730, 8°. Dedicated to the duchesse du Maine, who, according to La Motte, applauded when the tragedy was read to her. Republished in the author's *Œuvres* of 1754 and in *Pièces de théâtre*, Paris, veuve Duchesne, 1765.

been suggested by his French predecessors. Like them he explains, though in a different way, why nothing had been done about arresting the murderer of Laius. As in their tragedies we see Œdipus and Jocasta together after Œdipus has been identified as the slayer of Laius and before it is known that he is Jocasta's son; Jocasta stabs herself; and information is given about the cessation of the plague. The name Iphicrate is employed by both Corneille and La Motte. As in Corneille's tragedy there is confusion over the identity of the person who, according to an oracle, is to be sacrificed.[70] Like Voltaire, La Motte emphasizes the call of the blood when Laius is fatally wounded by his son.

La Motte probably borrowed from *Phèdre* the scene in which a queen denounces and orders from her presence a woman who has longed served her. The introduction of Eteocles and Polyneices seems to have been his own idea, but their hostility to each other and the fact that they are the sons of Œdipus and Jocasta came from Greek legend and had already been dramatized by Rotrou and Racine.

In his *Discours* La Motte gives us a good deal of information about his method of composing the tragedy. He objected to the fact that in Sophocles Œdipus and Jocasta are punished for crimes committed in ignorance. He consequently made them both disobey oracular pronouncements, he through excessive ambition, she through excessive love. Like Corneille and Voltaire, he found the Greek theme too slim for a five-act play, but he considered it artificial to add episodes, as they had done. Instead he introduced Eteocles and Polyneices, whose interests are so closely attached to their father's that their fortunes do not constitute an episode. To explain why no effort had been made to avenge Laius, he invented a false report that he had been destroyed by a lion.[71] He blamed his predecessors for not offering a similar explanation, overlooking the facts that in Corneille's tragedy Œdipus thinks he has himself killed the murderer of Laius, while in Voltaire's Œdipus declares that he has purposely avoided investigating the cause of Laius's death in order not to wound Jocasta's feelings. La Motte admits that the scene in Act III when Polémon first appears failed to hold the attention of the spectators. He attributes their indifference to the fact that Polémon speaks to Eteocles and Polyneices rather than to an unimportant person, and concludes that, when a scene is purely informative and does not affect the characters on the stage who receive the information, these last should not be persons from whom the audience may look for an expression of feeling. He hopes that it will not be thought

---

[70] For Corneille's " le sang de ma race," La Motte substitutes " un des Fils de la Reine."

[71] This invention was severely criticized by Nadal (*Œuvres*, II, 150-1). He excused the lack of explanation in Sophocles on the ground that Laius's death occurs before the play begins.

that he is attempting to rival Corneille, whom he considers the greatest of dramatists, but who wrote so much that he did not perfect all of his plays and consequently left room for other authors to dramatize anew some of his subjects.[72] About Voltaire he says nothing.

La Motte's alterations show considerable technical skill, but his play falls far short of its Greek model because he fails to center the interest, as Sophocles had done, upon Œdipus himself. Moreover, while we are told that the king had formerly erred by excessive ambition, we see no evidence of it in the play, where he appears as most self-sacrificing in regard to his people and as a devoted husband and father. He has none of the overbearing qualities attributed to him by Sophocles. He shares with Jocasta the task of discovering the truth about their relations. Similarly the queen admits that she had sinned through excessive love, disregarding an oracle that would have saved her if she had obeyed it, but her love, as represented in the dialogue, appears no greater than that of many other heroines of tragedy. Again, we are told that Eteocles and Polyneices hate each other, but little evidence of such hatred is given in the play.

As in his earlier tragedies, La Motte makes an initial effort to capture the attention of the audience. The opening lines are:

> Quels ordres! non Seigneur; ce seroit vous trahir.
> Non; l'horreur que je sens me défend d'obéïr.

The material is well distributed, with the first act chiefly devoted to the peril in which Œdipus finds himself; the second, to that of his sons; the

[72] Œdipus has had a vision of Apollo and learned from him that Thebes will continue to suffer from the plague unless his blood is shed. He consequently prepares to sacrifice himself in spite of protests from his wife and sons, but a report is brought from a priest to the effect that the god wishes one of Jocasta's sons to perish. Eteocles and Polyneices vie with each other in their efforts to be sacrificed, but Œdipus tells them that, before coming to a decision, he must seek the murderer of Laius. He learns from Jocasta that she has already sent for Iphicrate, who was with Laius when he lost his life. An old man named Polémon brings word that Iphicrate, who has just died of the plague that is afflicting Thebes, admitted that he lied when he asserted that a lion had killed Laius, and that the real murderer was a young man they had met in a road that separated the fields of Thebes from those of Corinth. When Jocasta gives this information to Œdipus, he realizes that he is himself the slayer of Laius. Jocasta forgives him, as his deed was in self-defense and he did not know who his opponents were. She feels sure that there will be no fulfillment of the oracle that had predicted Laius would be slain by his son, a boy whom she had sent to the bears on Mount Cytheron. Œdipus now recognizes Polémon as the shepherd who, he believes, is his father, but the old man informs him that he is not his son, but one whom he had rescued from a woman who intended to abandon him in the wilds. Jocasta confronts Polémon with her attendant, Phœdime, whom he recognizes as the woman who had given him the child. Jocasta learns in this way that Œdipus is her son, denounces Phœdime for disobeying her, and orders her away. She shudders when she meets her husband, but she agrees, upon his urging, to tell him what she has discovered, if he will allow her a few moments to herself. She then stabs herself, leaving a note confessing that the oracle she doubted has been fulfilled, for her son has killed his father and entered into her bed. Œdipus, understanding that he is the son in question, stabs himself. Before he dies, word is brought that Thebes is saved and that Apollo's priest guarantees the clemency of the god.

third, to the discovery that Œdipus killed Laius; the fourth, to Jocasta's
learning that her husband is her son; the fifth, to the suicide of the two
leading characters. Preparation is carefully made. The age of Œdipus
is given as thirty-five, doubtless in an effort to make it possible that his
sons are no longer children. The supernatural element is large. There
are several oracular pronouncements, Apollo appears to Œdipus, and the
plague ceases when he dies. When Laius attacked Œdipus, the young man
had a "mouvement secret" advising him that the person of his opponent
should be sacred (III, 6).

This is the first tragedy in which La Motte makes use of recognition.
It is also the first in which the only kind of sexual love he allows is
conjugal. However, he owes so much to his Greek and French predecessors
that *Œdipe* must be considered the least original of his tragedies. On the
other hand, it may be said to his credit that, by his omission of a subordinate plot, his tragedy resembles that of Sophocles more closely than
do the corresponding tragedies of Corneille and Voltaire.

Œdipe must have been completed before July 23, 1725, as on that day
Voltaire [73] wrote that La Motte was anxious to have it acted, but it was
not performed until March 18, 1726. Dufresne and la Duclos had the
leading rôles. Baron played Polémon; la Jouvenot, Phœdime. The boys
were represented by actresses, de Seine and Labatte. The tragedy was
given again on the 20, 23, 24, then, followed by La Motte's comedy, *le
Talisman,* on March 31 and April 3. Though the receipts never fell below
1200 francs, production then ceased for some unexplained reason. Voltaire
states that performances were interrupted in the midst of great success.
La Motte's share in the receipts was 505 fr., 2 s.

The tragedy was well enough known to inspire a parody by Legrand
called *le Chevalier errant*.[74] Collé,[75] though he considered the play "très-
mauvaise," admired the introduction of Eteocles and Polyneices. Voltaire [76]
admitted that La Motte had avoided errors he had himself committed, but
he condemned the play as cold and insipid on account of its "versification
lâche," the bringing on the stage of two "grands enfants d'Œdipe," and
the entire absence of terror and pity. La Harpe,[77] indignant with La Motte
for dramatizing a subject recently put on the stage by his hero, Voltaire,
declared that the tragedy was "la pièce la plus régulièrement glaciale qu'il
fût possible: le sujet demandait une force poétique dont il était absolument
dépourvu."

[73] Moland, XXXIII, 143.
[74] Cf. M. S. Burnet, *op. cit.*, pp. 158-9.
[75] *Correspondance inédite*, Paris, 1864, p. 413.
[76] Moland, II, 47; VIII, 564; XXXII, 171.
[77] *Op. cit.*, XIII, 159-60.

One might suppose from these criticisms that a prose version of the play would have been less severely criticized. One was composed by La Motte to illustrate his ideas on the possibility of employing prose in tragedy. He kept the characters and events as they had been. Indeed, with only very minor exceptions, the new version follows the old, scene by scene and speech by speech.[78] Nothing is gained in clarity or brevity in the change from verse to prose, but La Motte's verses are so prosaic that the test carried little weight. There is no evidence that this prose version was ever acted. It seems to have been ignored by the usual critics of theatrical productions.

Fréron [79] summed up La Motte's activities by saying that he had tried all kinds of tragedy, " le sublime dans les *Machabées,* l'héroïque dans *Romulus,* le pathétique dans *Inès,* & le simple dans *Œdipe,*" but that in all he lacked purity, clarity, force, and elegance. He had lifted up his voice against the tyranny of verse with the result that his own verse was heartily condemned by classical critics.

The question, however, is not whether La Motte was a poet—according to twentieth-century standards, there was none in France at the time,—but whether he was a tragic dramatist. In theory he was a forerunner of the Romanticists, restive under the glorification of the Ancients, insisting that in tragedy prose might be substituted for verse, demanding for dramatists the privilege of replacing the classical unities by the unity of interest. He was far, of course, from putting these theories into practice. Three of his four tragedies were derived from ancient history or legend. His only prose tragedy was the second version of *Œdipe,* which was never acted. The three unities he, in the main, preserved.

His chief reforms are in his manner of beginning his tragedies, in his occasional efforts to appeal to the eye—the altar in *Romulus,* the sword stained with blood in *Inès,*—his introduction of a malevolent and rebellious priest into *Romulus,* and the great emphasis he placed in *Inès* upon sentiment. His *Machabées* suffered by comparison with *Polyeucte*; his *Œdipe,* by comparison with Sophocles and, for his contemporaries, with Voltaire; his *Romulus,* through the modernization of the hero and heroine and of primitive Roman manners. *Inès,* however, may still appeal, even if La Motte's efforts to cause tears to flow are hardly in accord with modern taste. It is the most striking tragedy of the period between *Rhadamiste* and *Zaïre,* one that shows La Motte to have been more than a skillful technician or a timid reformer who did not dare put his theories into practice.

---

[78] Occasionally brief speeches are interjected or omitted. The change of seven " lustres " (IV, 5) to thirty years as the age of Œdipus would make children of his sons.

[79] *Année littéraire,* 1754 (7), p. 133.

CHAPTER V

TRAGEDY, 1719-1729. DANCHET, MARIVAUX, CRÉBILLON

Besides Voltaire, La Motte, and Nadal, ten authors contributed in these eleven years to the repertory of the Comédie Française, but none of the ten tragedies they produced rivaled the success of *Œdipe* or *Inès de Castro*. The most distinguished of them was Crébillon's *Pyrrhus*. Danchet's *Nitétis* was temporarily popular, but *Coriolan* and *Dom Ramir* had each only one production. Possibly under the influence of Voltaire, Greek mythology regained the popularity it had lost in the decade that preceded *Œdipe*. Events of ancient Europe were dramatized as well as those that took place in Asia and Africa. Ancient historians and dramatists, French dramatists, and a French novelist provided the sources of the tragedies. Only one play has, like *Inès de Castro*, a medieval subject.

Several tragedies introduce recognition and danger of incest; one of them real incest, as does *Œdipe*. Except for the "suite" of the Roman high priest in *Coriolan*, none of the authors followed Voltaire and La Motte in their efforts to provide a spectacular element. There are well-drawn characters in *Annibal* and *Pyrrhus*. The author of *Tibère* attempts to personify various political opinions of ancient Rome. The anticlericalism of Voltaire and La Motte is echoed in *Coriolan* and in *Admète et Alceste*. In the former it is associated with an attack upon imperialism; in Boissy's play it becomes the dominant idea and is given greater emphasis than in any earlier French tragedy. While classical usage in regard to form is usually respected, there are departures from it in the brevity of *Admète et Alceste*, which is about two-thirds the length of the usual tragedy, and in *Polixène*, which constitutes only one act of a play that has three acts and a prologue. In the last three years of the period performances of new tragedies became so rare that the public may have thought the *genre* was about to disappear, as tragi-comedy and pastoral had disappeared in the preceding century.

The first of these tragedies was composed by Antoine Danchet,[1] who had brought out two in 1706-7, but had since that time devoted his talents chiefly to writing opera librettos and to his duties as censor, which must have kept him well informed as to contemporary output in tragedy, with the result that, when he produced two new tragedies, they showed the

---

[1] Cf. my *Sunset*, pp. 130-4. Neither of his first two tragedies had been played since 1708.

influence, not only of Euripides and Herodotus, but of French dramatists still living or not long dead.

Before discussing the first of these I must say a word about a tragedy with the same title that is one of its two main sources. When I spoke of de Brie in 1940, I mentioned a manuscript of his *Héraclides* that I had been unable to locate.[2] In December, 1946, I discovered that it was in the Bibliothèque Nationale [3] and had a microfilm made of it. As the frères Parfaict had cited an article in the *Mercure* of 1715 to the effect that de Brie had been inspired by Dacier [4] with the belief that no genuine tragedy existed in French, and that he had written *les Héraclides* to supply the lack, I expected to find a radically different type of tragedy from that written by Corneille and Racine, whose plays he is said to have despised. But I found nothing of the sort except in departures from their usage due to de Brie's lack of talent as a dramatist and a poet. He proceeded as Corneille had done in *Œdipe* or Racine in *Iphigénie,* taking as his model a Greek tragedy, omitting its chorus, shortening its speeches, and adding characters and interests to make up for the omissions.

From the *Heraclides* of Euripides he derived the idea of the refuge accorded by Athens to the children of Hercules, the demands of Eurystheus, King of Argos, the sacrifice of a high-born maiden, required as the price of victory, the triumph of Athens, and the death of Eurystheus. He also took from the Greek tragedy the names of Démophon, Hillus, and Euristée, but he kept the last of these behind the scenes, while Hillus, whom Euripides had failed to bring on the stage, became one of his principal characters. From a bare mention by Euripides of Demophon's daughter he created the character of Ismène. He omitted Alkmena, changed the name of Makaria to Iole, gave her a confidant named Cléone, and substituted for Kopreus, the herald, an Argive ambassador. His scene is laid at Athens instead of Marathon. His most important alteration is the introduction of love, jealousy, and danger of incest.[5]

---

[2] Cf. my *History*, Part IV, pp. 400-1.

[3] Réserve, anc. f. fr., 25475, II, 117-54. The microfilm is at The Johns Hopkins University.

[4] The *Mercure* mentions his " Poëtique," apparently his translation of Aristotle's *Poetics*, published in 1692.

[5] Euristée has been besieging Athens for ten days. Hillus thinks that Démophon may have to surrender the city, but his relative, Iolas, knowing that Démophon wishes to marry his daughter, Ismène, to Hillus, believes that he will continue to fight. The Argive ambassador demands the surrender of Hercules's children and threatens Démophon with the destruction of Athens. In reply Iolas recalls the great deeds of Hercules, including his rescue from Hades of Démophon's father, Theseus. The king postpones his decision until he has consulted the Athenian people and senate. When alone with his confidant, Arsace, Démophon tells him of his desire to marry Iole, daughter of Hercules, a girl whom he has brought up and who has not been told who she is, as an oracle had predicted for her a cruel death if she acquired such information. Arsace advises the king to surrender Hillus in order to save

In altering the character of Hercules's daughter so that she kills herself partly through disappointed love, de Brie was probably influenced by Racine's *Iphigénie,* in which Eriphile is similarly motivated and in which her death also fulfills an oracle. He borrows from *Phèdre* his alteration of a reference in Euripides to Hades, so that it reads (I, 3), "Il força l'Acheron a relacher sa proye." Racine, however, would have made it clearer that Iole knew that she was the daughter of Hercules and that her death would satisfy the oracle.

While de Brie gave unity to the poorly organized Greek original, he did not improve it, for the love affairs, without being in themselves effective, confuse the main issue. Démophon seems more concerned with getting himself an unwilling wife than with saving his city or rescuing the children of his father's friend, the political interests involved are not set forth, and much that is important takes place behind the scenes.

The tragedy was given six times in 1695, from Feb. 5 to 19. The author's share of the receipts was 270 francs, 6 sous, less, according to Gâcon, than he spent on meals supplied the actors in order to induce them to accept the tragedy. The frères Parfaict[6] declare that he spent the money on tickets distributed among his friends in order that they might applaud the play.

However this may be, the tragedy attracted the attention of Danchet, to whom the manuscript may have been shown by an actor who was a member of the troupe both in 1695 and in 1719. The popularity of Voltaire's *Œdipe* may have made the actors think that the adaptation of another Greek tragedy would bring them success. It is true that Danchet

---

Iole, but Démophon replies that the young man knows she is his sister and may reveal the fact if he despairs of his life. He then tells his daughter that he is inclined to surrender Hillus, but would first consult the gods. Ismène admits to her confidant that she loves Hillus. In Act II Iole learns that the senate favors Hillus, but she fears that, if he remains in Athens, he will marry Ismène. Démophon now decides to dismiss the ambassador, to marry his daughter to Hillus, and to give battle next day. Iole is overcome, but she seeks to explain her tears as due to joy. Her refusal to marry Démophon turns the king against Hillus, but an oracle must first be consulted. Ismène, noting the change in her father, advises Hillus to escape from the city, but he refuses to do so. In Act III the oracle declares that to obtain a victory over Argos a girl belonging to the race of Hillus must be sacrificed. Hillus proposes to attack the enemy. Iole, though still ignorant of her birth, proposes to sacrifice herself and is still more determined to do so when she learns from Iolas that her love for Hillus is criminal. In Act IV Hillus, accused by Ismène of deserting her for Iole, declares that this girl is his sister. In Act V Iole, who has apparently solved the problem of her relationship to Hillus, decides to kill herself. She learns that he has penetrated to Euristée's tent, then goes behind the scenes to stab herself. Iolas reports that Hillus and his friends have slain the King of Argos. Démophon offers Hillus the hand of Ismène and the throne. Arsace tells them that he found Iole bleeding to death and insisting that she was pleased with her fate. Démophon points out that the result of the fighting had been uncertain until she sacrificed her life in order to win the victory.

6 XIII, 393-4.

had not previously made such an adaptation, but he had at least based one of his earlier tragedies on Greek mythology.

His own HÉRACLIDES [7] was derived partly from Euripides, partly from de Brie. In imitation of the former he called the King of Athens Démophoon, the son of Hercules Hylus, his daughter Macarie, the champion of the Heraclides Iolaus, and he preserved, as de Brie had not done, the old man's rejuvenation. Like de Brie, he brought Hylus on the stage and did not introduce Alkmena; laid his scene in Athens; gave Démophon a daughter who loves and is loved by Hylus; had the latter's sister fall in love with him while she is ignorant of their relationship; made Démophon desire to marry this girl, who fails to accept his proposal; gave her a confidant named Cléone; and had the dénouement brought about by disappointment in love. His first two acts even begin in the same manner as de Brie's, by a conversation between Hylus and Iolaus and by one between Cléone and the daughter of Hercules.

He made, however, a number of changes. The Argive ambassador does not appear. Iolaus becomes the " gouverneur " of Hylus. Ismène's name is changed to Laodice; Iole's to Astérie; Démophoon decides much more quickly to defend Hylus. The oracle demands the blood of Hercules, which might mean Hylus, whereas in de Brie's tragedy the victim had to be a girl. Démophoon does not know who Macarie is. The problem is solved by a letter. Astérie dies on the stage.[8]

---

[7] Published in Danchet's *Œuvres*, Paris, Grangé, 1751, 8°.

[8] Hylus, son of Hercules, and Iolaus have taken refuge at Athens, where they are protected by King Démophoon, son of Theseus, but their enemy, King Euristée of Argos, has led an army into Attica to demand the surrender of Hylus. While the matter is being discussed by the King of Athens and his advisers, Hylus admits that he loves Laodice, daughter of Démophoon, and that he is loved by Astérie, a girl of noble, but unidentified parents with whom Démophoon is in love. The latter decides to reject Euristée's demand and, with Hylus, to lead the Athenian forces against him. In Act II Astérie confides in Cléone that she loves Hylus, but with little hope of success. Informed by Laodice that there are sinister forewarnings, she hopes to have Hylus sent away. The king decides to consult an oracle. In Act III Démophoon approves of his daughter's marriage to Hylus. He tells Astérie he knows her blood to be illustrious, but he had been warned by Theseus that, if the secret of her birth were revealed, disaster would follow, and that a faithful friend would bring him at the proper time a statement in regard to her written by the hand of Theseus. He then proposes marriage, but Astérie warns him that she may be his sister. The god's answer is now received: Athens will be victorious, but the blood of Hercules will flow. Fearing that Hylus is indicated, Démophoon withholds his consent to the marriage. In Act IV Astérie threatens to commit suicide if Hylus weds Laodice. Démophoon is unwilling to send the young man into battle and Laodice begs him to make his escape, but he is urged by Iolaus to meet the enemy. In Act V we hear that the victory is being won, but that Hylus cannot be found. Then Iolaus brings word that his youth had been renewed, that he and Hylus had reached Euristée, and that Hylus had killed him. He produces the letter left by Theseus. Démophoon recognizes the handwriting and sends for Astérie, who comes upon the stage in a dying condition just when Hylus has announced a complete victory and his inability to understand the oracle. Démophoon explains that, according to Theseus's letter, Astérie is Macarie, daughter of Hercules, so that hers

There is some evidence of Racine's influence. The death of Astérie resembles that of Eriphile, but in this case Danchet may be following de Brie, who had already imitated *Iphigénie*. On the other hand, she resembles Phèdre in loving a man who does not respond to her affection, in struggling against her passion, in consoling herself with the thought that he loves no other woman, in the shock of her discovery that she has a rival, and in her subsequent efforts to oppose his interests. Hylus also recalls *Phèdre* when, like Hippolytus, he would imitate his father's virtues, but not his " foiblesse."

Danchet failed to express properly Astérie's jealousy and to arouse interest in the hesitant king and the conventional young lovers. While he makes it clear, as de Brie had failed to do, that dread of incest has nothing to do with the suicide of Hercules's daughter, he does not explain why Iolaus waits until after the battle to deliver Theseus's letter. As in de Brie's play, too many situations are reported instead of being directly presented. Both authors unified their plays, but they complicated their plots and failed to produce individual scenes as effective as those of the Greek original. The anonymous *Prologue d'Artémire* [9] referred to Danchet's tragedy as cold. The frères Parfaict [10] noted the weakness in the characters of the king and his daughter, the fact that we see Hylus chiefly as a lover, the unsatisfactory presentation of Astérie's jealousy, and the ineffectiveness of the final scene. They conclude with Alceste that it is " bon à mettre au Cabinet."

After reading these comments, one is surprised to find that the play, though it had only a brief career, was well attended. It was acted eight times, from Dec. 29, 1719, to Jan. 15, 1720. The cast was composed of Adrienne Le Couvreur, la Desmares, Quinault, and Dufresne, who probably took the leading rôles, and of Du Boccage, Dangeville, Fontenay, and Duchemin. The author's share of the receipts was 1137 fr., 8 s. The attendance far exceeded that attracted by de Brie's tragedy. Danchet may well have been encouraged by it to attempt the stage once more.

His last tragedy, NITÉTIS,[11] is much more interesting than *les Héraclides*. He tells us that he drew his plot from the third book of Herodotus, where

---

is the blood demanded by the god. Astérie is glad that her death brings victory to Athens. She hopes that Hylus will be happy with Laodice.

[9] *PQ*, I (1922), 139.

[10] XV, 358-61.

[11] Paris, Huet, Pissot, Morin et Flahault, 1724, 8°. Approbation, Oct. 23, 1723. Dedicated to Louis XV in an *épître* that praises tragedy, emphasizes its moral qualities, and suggests that, if the new king will favor drama as Louis XIV had done, " nous verrons encor, sur les pas des Corneilles, Des Rivaux accourir . . ." There is a copy of this edition at The Johns Hopkins University. The play was republished, The Hague, Van Dale, 1733, and in the author's *Œuvres*, Paris, Grangé, 1751.

he found the account of Nitétis, daughter of Apriès, sent to Cambyses by the usurper, Amasis, as his own daughter and revealing to him the fact that her father had been slain by Amasis; the rôle of Phanès, with the murder of his children and his escape from Egypt to advise Cambyses as to how to transport his troops across Arabia; and the story of the proud Ethiopian king who preferred arms to gold. Danchet prolonged the life of Amasis so that he could be captured by Cambyses and commit suicide after causing, in an effort to kill the Persian, the death of his own son Psamménite. He altered this last name from Psammétite in the same way that La Grange-Chancel had done in *Amasis,* made this young man twice save the life of Cambyses, and gave him love for Nitétis. He softened the account of the manner in which Phanès's children were put to death and brought the King of Ethiopia near enough to Memphis to be killed in battle by Cambyses. He introduced the widow of Apriès and supposed that she had been kept for years in prison. In making these changes he altered the characters of Cambyses and Psamménite, developed those of Phanès and Nitétis, and invented minor rôles. His treatment of Phanès may have been influenced by La Grange-Chancel, who had, in his *Amasis,* made this faithful minister even more prominent than Danchet made him. He gave his young hero a struggle against what he supposed to be incestuous love, then put him, when he discovers that the girl is not his sister, in a tragic situation, created by the hostility of their families.[12]

[12] At the beginning of the play Phanès releases his friend, Arsane, from prison in Memphis. Phanès had been a minister of Apriès, had been hostile to Amasis from the time that this usurper had murdered his master, but had bided his time until he knew that Cambyses was about to invade Egypt. He had then joined the Persian king and suggested his alliance with the Arabs, who had provided the water needed for the invasion. He tells Arsane that Cambyses has defeated Amasis, followed him into Memphis, and captured him. Before the battle Amasis had had Phanès's wife and children slaughtered in the space that separated the armies and had had his warriors dip their darts in their blood. Phanès seeks revenge, but Arsane would spare Nitétis, whose intervention has saved his life. Similarly Cambyses would spare Psamménite, son of Amasis, as he has saved his life in battle. He frees the young man, promises, at his request, to spare Nitétis, and even suggests that he may spare Amasis. When Cambyses sees Nitétis in the temple, he falls in love with her. Mérope, widow of Apriès, is freed from prison, is recognized by Phanès, and is honored by Cambyses. She asks that her husband's enemies be punished. Phanès has heard that her daughter still lives. Amasis, allowed to converse with his son, expresses his desire to kill Cambyses and proposes that Psamménite urge Nitétis to give herself to the Persian king in return for his restoration to the throne of Egypt. When Psamménite replies that she would be a slave, Amasis confides in him the secret that Nitétis is not the young man's sister, but the daughter of Apriès, substituted for a child he had lost. Psamménite is delighted to learn that his love for Nitétis is not incestuous, but he fears that she will never marry the son of Amasis. His fears are confirmed when the princess, though troubled by his love, asks him to leave her. Cambyses prepares to meet the King of Ethiopia, leader of the forces allied against him. Nitétis urges him to avenge her mother. When the allies attack at night, Cambyses defeats them and slays the King of Ethiopia. Amasis, unable to secure the services of his son, makes use of a secret passage in order to reach Cambyses when he returns from battle. He tries to kill Cambyses and fatally wounds Psamménite when the latter intervenes. Amasis then kills himself. The people rend

Cambyses is by no means the pathological brute that Herodotus depicts, but a generous conqueror, eager to reward those who have helped him, most respectful to the captive Nitétis and her mother, willing even to show kindness to Amasis. Psamménite is equally noble, quixotic enough to spare Cambyses when he meets him in battle, crossed in love, first by thought of incest, then by the knowledge that the princess who might have loved him is separated from him by his father's crime.[13] Nitétis, brave and beautiful, tells us so little of her feelings that we can hardly suppose she will long mourn Psamménite, or will remain unreconciled to her marriage to Cambyses. Her mother is introduced to add pathos, especially when she is reunited to the daughter she had supposed for fifteen years to be dead. Phanès is, as La Grange-Chancel had presented him, the intelligent and experienced supporter and avenger of a royal family.

Opposed to these characters who win our sympathy is the villain, Amasis. After rising to be a general in the army of Apriès, he had murdered the king and his son, had usurped the throne, and had oppressed his subjects. To avenge himself upon Phanès for his desertion, he has put to death his wife and children. In Herodotus the soldiers drink their blood, mixed with wine and water, but Danchet merely has them dip their darts in the mixture, an indication that he has renounced the type of horror he had aroused with his *Cyrus,* in which a father admits that he has been forced to eat his son. Amasis seeks to regain his throne by offering the daughter of his predecessor to Cambyses as a concubine and by urging his son to assassinate the conqueror. Failing in these endeavors, he seeks to murder him with his own hand, but accidentally kills Psamménite in the attempt and finds no other solution than suicide.

Danchet refers to altering his source in order to meet the requirements of time and place. To "enrichir" his play he added material from Herodotus, such as the conversation between the King of Ethiopia and Cambyses's envoy and the report of the way in which the family of Phanès perished. He brought in other superfluous material by introducing Mérope and Arsane. He evidently considered the unities of place and time more important than that of action.

He won his public, not by the strictness of his adherence to formal regulations, but by arranging pathetic situations and by presenting heroic characters in such a way as to lead the spectators to appreciate virtue and

his body. While Psamménite is dying, he expresses the hope that Cambyses will reign happily with Nitétis.

[13] Danchet says that he had profited by criticism to make certain changes in his text and that he would have made others except that he wished to spare the memories of the actors, especially that of old Baron, who played Cambyses and whom he compared to Roscius.

justice, to rejoice over the punishment of vice. He supplied scenes of
recognition, of rescue, of reunited relatives. He respected the manners of
the ancients to the extent of representing Cambyses as a worshipper of the
sun and of referring to Isis and the tombs of Egyptian kings. The
monarchical society for which he wrote may have liked such lines as these:

> Quiconque sur le Trône est une fois monté,
> Même des autres Rois doit être respecté. (I, 4)
> Connoissez d'un Tyran les amis mercenaires; . . .
> Aveuglement soûmis à son obéïssance,
> Ils étalent pour lui leur zele, leur constance;
> A ses seuls intêrets on les croiroit liez,
> Renversez leur Idole, ils la foulent aux pieds. (II, 4)

It was the most frequently acted of Danchet's tragedies. According to
the *Mercure* of March, 1723, Baron played Cambyses; la Duclos, Mérope;
Adrienne Le Couvreur, Nitétis; Dufresne, Psamménite; Legrand, Amasis;
Quinault, Phanès. It was given thirteen times, from Feb. 11 to March 12,
1723, and twelve times from Jan. 7 to Feb. 6, 1724. The author shared
in the receipts from all of these productions, his remuneration reaching
the sum of 2667 fr., 2 s. The tragedy was parodied by Piron in *Colombine-
Nitétis*,[14] acted on March 7, 1723.

None of Danchet's plays showed enough constructive imagination or
charm of style to remain long in the repertory. *Nitétis*, the best of them,
was called by the abbé Le Blanc " une bien mauvaise Tragédie." [15] Subsequently Raynal [16] declared that Danchet had composed four tragedies " sans
génie et sans caractère, faiblement et froidement écrites."

ANNIBAL [17] is Marivaux's only tragedy. In it he combined a thorough
understanding of classical technique with some of his gift at expressing
psychological nuances. The story of Hannibal's death had been told by
Livy, Nepos, Plutarch, and Justin. It had been dramatized by Thomas
Corneille, who, in *la Mort d'Annibal*, had introduced Prusias and Flaminius,
as his brother had done in *Nicomède*. Marivaux may have followed all of
these guides as well as *Polyeucte*, but he was the first to give Prusias a
daughter and to make her fall in love with Flaminius. He kept some of
the irony found in *la Mort d'Annibal* and *Nicomède*, but his plot is simpler
than that of either. It may have been this simplicity that caused it to be
unsuccessful.[18]

---

[14] Lindsay, *op. cit.*, pp. 131-7.
[15] Hélène Monod-Cassidy, *Un Voyageur philosophe au XVIIIᵉ siècle, l'abbé Jean
Bernard Le Blanc*, Cambridge, Harvard University Press, 1941, p. 209.
[16] *Cor.*, II, 104.
[17] Paris, N. Pissot, 1727, 12°. Republished, The Hague, Benjamin Gibert, 1738,
12°; Paris, Prault père, 1740 and 1755; and in collected editions of the author's
plays. For Marivaux cf. Gaston Deschamps, *Marivaux*, Paris, Hachette, 1897.
[18] Laodice loves Flaminius, the Roman ambassador, though her father, Prusias,

Prusias is a weak ruler, plotting desperately and ineffectively to save his state from the encroachments of Rome. He had invited Hannibal into his dominions and had offered him his daughter in the hope that his presence would make Rome respectful, but it has had the opposite effect. When he hears that Flaminius is coming, he wishes to placate him by going to meet him, but Hannibal opposes his doing so. When the ambassador arrives, Prusias humbles himself and protests but mildly against the Roman's insolence, though occasionally there is a flash of independence (II, 3):

> Les Rois, dans le haut rang où le Ciel les fait naître,
> Ont souvent des Vainqueurs, & n'ont jamais de Maître.

But soon he holds that " La menace n'est rien " (II, 4) and complains of "Impitoyable honneur " (III, 6). Like Félix in *Polyeucte*, he sees that he has selected the wrong son-in-law and reproaches himself for not having made of Flaminius a member of his family. Throughout the play his respect for his word weakens before his fear of Rome. He listens to the casuistry of Hiéron, who argues that, if Flaminius captures Hannibal while the latter is leaving Bithynia, Prusias is not responsible for the mistakes of fortune (V, 1). The king's punishment is to hear himself upbraided by Hannibal in prophetic words (V, 10):

> Prusias; car enfin je ne crois pas qu'un homme,
> Lâche assez pour n'oser désobéir à Rome,
> Infidèle à son rang, à sa parole, à moi,
> Espére qu'Annibal daigne en lui voir un Roi,
> Prusias, pensez-vous que ma mort vous délivre
> Des hazards, qu'avec moi vous avez craint de suivre?
> Quand même vous m'eussiez remis entre ses mains,
> Quel fruit en pouviez-vous attendre des Romains.
> La paix? Vous vous trompiez. Rome vous veut apprendre,
> Qu'il faut la mériter, pour oser y prétendre.
> Non, non de l'épouvante, esclave déclaré,
> A des malheurs sans fin vous vous êtes livré.

He is between Hannibal and Flaminius. The Carthaginian general had

King of Bithynia, has engaged her to Hannibal, who has taken refuge at his court. Flaminius comes, ostensibly to reprove Prusias for making war upon Artamène, a protégé of Rome, but really in order to get possession of Hannibal and to win the hand of Laodice. His suit is rejected by the princess, who feels that she is bound by her engagement. When Prusias releases her from this obligation, she tells Flaminius that she will marry him on condition that he save Hannibal's life. He cannot promise to do so, but he urges the Carthaginian to visit Rome under his protection. Meanwhile Prusias plans to persuade Hannibal to leave the country. The king's confidant, Hiéron, tells Flaminius that he will notify him as to the time of Hannibal's departure, so that he may capture him, but Hannibal, wearying of seeking to bolster up the courage of kings, tells Flaminius that, as his only places of refuge are Rome and death, he has chosen the latter and taken poison. The failure of Flaminius to save him makes Laodice refuse the ambassador's offer of marriage.

hoped to unite the eastern kings against Rome and had believed that they, supported by his military genius, could succeed, but now, " abattu sous le faix de l'âge & du malheur," he sees that neither his direct admonition, nor his ironical thrusts at Flaminius will deliver the king from his dread of Roman punishment. Convinced that it is impossible to rouse Prusias to resistance, he releases him from his promise and gives to Flaminius his final decision (V, 9):

> Il ne me restoit plus, persécuté du sort,
> D'autre azile à choisir que Rome, ou que la mort.
> Mais enfin c'en est fait, j'ai crû que la derniere
> Avec assez d'honneur finissoit ma carriere.

Flaminius understands that the kings, if led by Hannibal, may cause trouble it is well to avoid. He consequently threatens Prusias and demands Hannibal's surrender. When he argues with the enemy of his people about the danger Rome had been in during the Punic wars and her final victory, each seeking to impress Prusias, the debate recalls Corneille. The love Flaminius feels for Laodice is closely associated with his politics, for he serves his own interests as well as Rome's when he opposes the marriage of Hannibal and Laodice, but, when his love conflicts with Roman policy, he suppresses his emotions. All he can promise Laodice for Hannibal is an asylum at Rome, which, as he must have foreseen, the city's most formidable foe cannot accept.

There is only one important woman in the play. Her account of her falling in love recalls Marivaux's comedies. She had resented Flaminius's treatment of her father and had tried to express contempt in her glance (I, 1):

> Mes dédaigneux regards rencontrerent les siens,
> Et les siens, sans effort, confondirent les miens.
> Jusques au fond du cœur, je me sentis émûë:
> Je ne pouvois ni fuir, ni soutenir sa vûë.
> Je perdis, sans regret, un impuissant courroux;
> Mon propre abaissement, Egine, me fut doux.
> J'oubliai ces respects, qui m'avoient offensée:
> Mon pere même alors sortit de ma pensée;
> Je m'oubliai moi même; & ne m'occupai plus
> Qu'à voir, & n'oser voir, le seul Flaminius.

But she has too high a conception of her duty to yield to her emotions. Though released from her engagement, she insists that Hannibal must be saved. She cannot profit by his death and accept a Roman husband. She follows the example of Pauline in *Polyeucte,* though the religious question is not raised. Her last words to Flaminius are these:

Enfin Rome a vaincu.
Il meurt, & vous avez consommé l'injustice,
Barbare, & vous osiez demander Laodice.

The play is well written. Its failure may have been due, not only to the simplicity of the structure, but to the fact that it recalled too distinctly *Nicomède* and *Polyeucte*. First given on Dec. 16, 1720, it was acted only three times in that year and only five when it was revived in 1747, though the frères Parfaict, who quote it at length, assert that it was well received in the latter year and that, to do justice to all of its " morceaux saillans," almost all the scenes would have to be reproduced. According to them Prusias was played in 1720 by Legrand; Hannibal, by Michel Baron; Flaminius, by Quinault-Dufresne; Laodice, by la Desmares.[19] Subsequently La Harpe [20] called the play a " pitoyable tragédie," but he was probably influenced by Marivaux's hostility to Voltaire. The work deserved for its structure, presentation of character, and style greater appreciation than it received, though it by no means possesses the charm of Marivaux's comedies.

The winter season of 1721-2 produced three tragedies, but only one of them was published, La Motte's *Romulus*. The two others must soon have been forgotten. The first to appear was ÆGYSTE,[21] by Séguineau and Pralard. It was accepted by the actors on July 20, 1719, with the condition that the last scene, in which Atreus died on the stage of his wounds, should be omitted. Though this alteration could not have required much time, the tragedy was not acted until Nov. 18, 1721. It was acted subsequently only on Nov. 20, 22, 24, and 26.[22] Information about its contents comes from the *Mercure* of Nov. 18, 1721, and from the frères Parfaict, who based their account of the tragedy partly on this journal, partly on information they derived from one of the authors.

The plot [23] was taken primarily from Hyginus, Fable LXXXVIII, but

---

[19] These statements are not in disagreement with the *Registres*. Fontenay, Duchemin, Duclos, and la Gautier also acted. The average attendance of those who paid admission to the first three productions was 476; to the last five, 602. In 1720 Marivaux received only 200 fr., 12 s., but 325 francs in 1747. In the latter year la Clairon had a part in the cast, probably that of the heroine.

[20] *Op. cit.*, XV, 9.

[21] Cf. the frères Parfaict, XV, 454-65. According to them, Séguineau was the son of a secretary to a " Conseiller de la Grand'Chambre," lost his fortune in the speculation that Law inspired, obtained a position as clerk in the financial bureaux of the government, and died in 1722; while Pralard, whose father was a book-dealer, prepared for a legal career, failed to practise, and died in 1731.

[22] The authors' share of the receipts was 159 fr., 6 s.

[23] Tyndare, King of Sparta, seeks to make peace between the brothers, Atreus and Thyestes. He has sheltered the latter, driven from Argos by Atreus, and, in order to show favor to both sides, he now offers his daughter, Clytemnestra, in marriage to Agamemnon, son of Atreus. The brothers meet at Sparta after Atreus has sent Agamemnon to put down a revolt of Argives in favor of Thyestes. Atreus accuses Thyestes of inspiring this uprising. He tells us in a monologue that he has agreed

it may have owed certain details to the original text of Pellegrin's *Pélopée*,[24] where, as in *Ægyste,* we find an uprising in favor of Thyestes, and an oracle connected with the arrival of Pélopée at court. According to a note sent to the *Mercure* by one of the authors, Clytemnestra originally had a rôle in the play and Pélopée did not, but his colleague had "chassé la fille de la maison" and replaced her by a woman guilty of incest. Apparently the author of the note had tried to diminish the horror of the tale by keeping Pélopée behind the scenes, but his comrade had been less merciful, though he failed to follow Pellegrin in making Egisthus fall in love with his mother.

The failure of the tragedy cannot well be attributed to its interpreters, who included several distinguished actors. The *Mercure* states that Pélopée was played by Adrienne Le Couvreur; Thyestes, by Michel Baron; Egisthus, by Maurice Quinault; Agamemnon, by Quinault-Dufresne; Atreus, by Legrand; Tyndare, by Philippe Poisson.[25]

The other unpublished tragedy, CORIOLAN,[26] by the chevalier de Chaligny, or Chaligny de Plaine, was still less successful. The author followed Livy and Plutarch, or Dionysius of Halicarnassus,[27] but he altered the ancient legend through his respect for the unities and his desire to emphasize the importance of sexual love. He laid his scene in the camp of Coriolanus before the walls of Rome, had his events take place within a few hours,

to talk peace merely in order to secure an opportunity to bring about his brother's death. After suppressing the revolt, Agamemnon comes to Sparta with a hostage, Irène, who is supposed to be the daughter of the Argive governor, but who is in reality Pélopée, daughter of Thyestes. She tells a confidant that her father, frightened by an oracle, had banished her, that she had consecrated herself to Minerva, and that in the temple of the goddess she had been raped by an unknown man who had left his sword in her hands. This sword had shown her that the ravisher was her father. Her horror over this discovery had induced her to expose the son born of incest, but Egisthus had been rescued by shepherds and, after some years, restored to his mother. She had armed him with his father's sword and, obeying Minerva's order, had gone off in the hope of finding peace at the court of Tyndare. Agamemnon has fallen in love with her, but she sends him to Clytemnestra. Atreus promises Egisthus the throne of Sparta and the hand of Clytemnestra if he will kill Thyestes. The young man agrees, but the sword he draws induces Thyestes to question him and discover that he is his son. Realizing that Atreus has sought to make him murder his father, Egisthus takes revenge by killing his uncle, who remains motionless in the midst of his guards "par une espéce de miracle." When the tragedy was first given, Pélopée came upon the stage, stabbed herself, and made certain predictions, but she was subsequently kept behind the scenes at the end of the play.

[24] Cf. my *Sunset*, pp. 127-9. This tragedy was read at court in 1710, but it was not acted until 1733, after a good many changes in the text had been made. Its final version may owe to *Ægyste* the important rôle assigned in it to Tyndarus.

[25] According to the *Registres*, another rôle, probably that of a confidant, was taken by la Duchemin.

[26] The manuscript is at the Bibliothèque Nationale, anc. sup. fr. 9381. A microfilm of it is at The Johns Hopkins University. Permission to act the play was granted on Feb. 27, 1722. According to Beauchamps (II, 522), the author died the following year.

[27] Cf., below, the discussion of Mauger's *Coriolan.*

and added an important character of his own invention, Tullie, daughter of Tullus and second wife of Coriolanus. He held the Romans responsible for his hero's divorce and gave Tullie, as well as her husband, a mental struggle. He kept the Volscian leader off the stage, but he replaced him by a certain Titus, for whose important intervention in the plot there is insufficient preparation.[28]

We are told that Coriolanus is a warrior of great distinction, but we see little evidence of it in his conduct. It is not made clear why the Roman people had exiled him or on what terms Tullus had received him. His fortitude is shown only in his resisting the pleas of the high priest and those of his former wife. He weakens when he learns that he cannot induce his mother to leave Rome and that his capture of the city will mean her death. His mother retains the heroic and patriotic character that the ancient authors assigned to her. Volomnie is a mild person, so deeply moved by her talk with her former husband that she has to leave argument to her mother-in-law. Valérie could easily have been omitted, though she is given a certain importance by keeping the other Roman women in the camp. The most emotional rôle is that of Tullie. She is influenced by her love for her husband, her desire to save his life, and her jealousy of Volomnie. It is this last emotion, rather than the oath she has sworn, that induces her to give Titus her father's order, which brings about the death of Coriolanus.

The first act is well designed, as it not only gives the exposition, but

[28] A Roman senator, Appius, refuses as shameful the terms offered Rome by Coriolanus, but introduces the high priest, whose effort to win over the hero fails. Tullie informs her confidant that, though her father had entrusted Coriolanus with the command of the Volscian and Latin armies, he had feared that his former enemy might weaken and had consequently persuaded her to marry the Roman in order that, if she detected in him an inclination to spare his city, he might be put to death. She admits, however, that she loves her husband and that she would be unable to cause his punishment. Her hope lies in the continuance of his hostility to Rome. In Act II Valérie, Véturie, and Volomnie enter, but they are refused an interview with Coriolanus. Valérie persuades her companions to remain in the camp. In Act III Véturie, mother of Coriolanus, accuses Tullie of jealousy and in this way gets her to arrange an interview between Coriolanus and the Roman women. In Act IV Volomnie is received by her former husband, but, though they show that they still love each other, she is unable to make him give up his demands upon Rome. Then Véturie seeks to awaken her son's patriotism, warns him that, if he destroys Rome, he will cause her death and that of his sons, embraces his knees, and finally persuades him to grant the city honorable terms. In Act V Tullie expresses her desire for vengeance and gives Titus her father's order. Though Coriolanus admits that he loves Volomnie, he declares that he will remain faithful to Tullie and that he has carried out his obligations to the Volscians and Latins by saving them from Roman domination. When Tullie urges him to escape, he realizes that he has been condemned to death, but, as most of the soldiers sympathize with him, he might have led the army away had he not been attacked by Titus and a score of followers. Tullie's message ordering Titus to spare Coriolanus fails to be delivered. The hero is mortally wounded, though his attackers are killed. He comes in to accuse Tullie's father of perjury, to deny that he has betrayed him, and to declare that he dies "satisfait." Tullie ends the tragedy by predicting that her own death will soon follow.

contains the interviews between Coriolanus and the Roman senator and
between Coriolanus and the high priest, whose "suite" adds an element
of the picturesque; but the two acts that follow are dull and give little
progress to the action.   The two *scènes à faire,* the conversations between
Coriolanus, his mother, and his former wife, take place in Act IV, the
most dramatic portion of the play.   Act V, which brings the solution,
consists largely of reports concerned with action that takes place behind the
scenes.   It seems probable that by the end of Act III the spectators had
lost interest in the tragedy and showed their displeasure so clearly that
the actors did not venture upon a second performance.[29]

The most interesting passage in the play is one in which Coriolanus
accuses the Romans of concealing their imperialistic ambitions under a
pretense of divine guidance.   When the high priest claims that oracles
have given to Rome the right to possess the lands she has conquered, the
general comments (I, 4):

> Je connois ces mysteres
> Que pour leurs interêts ont inventé [sic] nos Peres,
> Et tout ce vain amas de superstitions
> Dont ils authorisent [sic] leurs usurpations.
> Les Dieux dont ils dictoient à leur gré les oracles
> Ont selon leurs besoins enfanté des Miracles
> Et le Peuple seduit par la voix des Devins
> A par religion dépoüillé ses Voisins.

Such lines may have been suggested by *Œdipe,* but Chaligny connected
religious trickery with conquest in a manner not as yet employed by
Voltaire.   The possibility that the verses might be regarded as a criticism
of French foreign policy was so deeply felt by the censor, Taschereau de
Baudry,[30] that he struck them out one by one and refused to allow them
to be recited by the actors.   They were written in, apparently by the
author, and were not removed by his nephew, the "chanoine de Verdun."
The failure of the tragedy on Feb. 28, 1722, induced this nephew to
admit that the play did not have the success for which the subject had
made the author hope.

In the three years that followed the unique performance of *Coriolan* the
only new tragedies to appear were written by dramatists who had recently
brought out others, Voltaire, La Motte, Nadal, and Danchet.   Then Crébillon, who had given the actors no new play for nine years, presented

---

[29] As the list of actors given in the *Registres* includes those who played in the
Comtesse d'Escarbagnas, which followed the tragedy, it is not certain who played in
each, but it is highly probable that Baron and Adrienne Le Couvreur, who are
mentioned, took leading rôles in *Coriolan.* Dufresne and Maurice Quinault played
in neither.   The author's share in the receipts was 112 fr., 4 s.

[30] According to Jal, he was a " conseiller d'Etat, intendant des finances."

them with PYRRHUS,[31] the best of his tragedies that followed *Rhadamiste*.
The subject had already been dramatized, with many complications, by
Thomas Corneille in his *Pyrrhus roy d'Epire*.[32] Crébillon may have owed
him the change of Androcleon's name to Androclide and the suggestion
for his hero's love of Néoptolémus's daughter, but his main source, like
Thomas Corneille's, was Plutarch's *Life of Pyrrhus*. He found there that
Neoptolemus had succeeded to the throne of Æacide, that Androcleon had
taken the young prince, Pyrrhus, to Glaucias, King of Illyria, who had
placed him on his father's throne, and that Pyrrhus, defeated by Neoptolemus, had eventually returned to share the rule with the usurper. Crébillon reduced the material to the events of a single day and located the
action in Byzantium, a neutral spot where the rivals had met in order to
see if they could come to terms.[33]

In composing the tragedy Crébillon avoided horror, incestuous relations,
and descriptive passages, but he retained his fondness for mistaken identity
and resulting scenes of recognition. In *Sémiramis* there are three of
these, but here there are four, of which three are more effective than those
of the earlier play because, as they are found in three different acts, there
is more room for preparation. Though the plot is simple, it introduces
various psychological problems. It is Cornelian in its emphasis upon
magnanimity and the effect of this quality in one person upon others.
The self-sacrifice of Glaucias and Illyrus leads to emulation on the part of

---

[31] Paris, veuve A.-U. Coustelier, 1726, 8°. Dedicated to "Mr Paris, garde du
Trésor Royal." Dutrait notes a second edition in October. It was republished in
Crébillon's *Œuvres*. An Italian translation appeared in 1757. For a study of the
play cf. Dutrait, *op. cit.*, pp. 49, 50, 193-4, 300-1, 338-43, 359-61, 417-21.

[32] Cf. my *History*, Part III, pp. 445-7.

[33] Néoptolémus had slain his cousin, Æacide, and usurped the throne of Epirus.
Androclide had taken the dead king's infant son to Glaucias, King of Illyria, who
had sworn to protect him and had brought him up as his own son under the name of
Hélénus. When the boy grew up, he developed into an extraordinary warrior and,
with the help of Glaucias, reconquered Epirus, but, as he was wounded while fighting
against Néoptolémus and Cassander, Glaucias was obliged to retreat after the
capture of his son, Illyrus. Néoptolémus now threatens to put this captured prince
to death unless Pyrrhus is surrendered to him. He rejects the proposal of Glaucias
to marry Illyrus to the usurper's daughter, Ericie, in lieu of putting Pyrrhus in
his power. Then he offers Ericie to Hélénus, whose prowess he admires, but this
prince, though he, like Illyrus, loves the girl, refuses to marry her, as a condition
of the union is the surrender of Pyrrhus. Illyrus suspects that his rival, Hélénus,
may be Pyrrhus, but he nobly refuses to make known his suspicions. Both Glaucias
and Ericie urge Néoptolémus to withdraw his demand, but without success. Glaucias
refuses to give up Pyrrhus, even though Néoptolémus informs him that his refusal
will mean the death of his son. Néoptolémus interprets his action as meaning that
Illyrus is the real Pyrrhus. He so informs Hélénus, who is assured by Glaucias
that Illyrus is his son. Then Hélénus threatens to save his adopted father by force
and induces Glaucias to inform him that he, Hélénus, is Pyrrhus. Resolving to
surpass in self-sacrifice both Glaucias and Illyrus, the prince promises to deliver
Pyrrhus to Néoptolémus, lays his sword at the usurper's feet, and makes himself
known to him. Néoptolémus is so deeply impressed that he not only spares him,
but offers him his daughter and his throne. Pyrrhus accepts Ericie, but refuses to
take the throne from the reformed usurper.

Pyrrhus, whose noble conduct solves the problem of the play by its effect upon Néoptolémus. The chief defects are the difficulty of accepting Glaucias's willingness to sacrifice his son's life in order to save that of a refugee, even if he has sworn to protect him, the fact that the conversion of Néoptolémus is insufficiently prepared, and the clumsiness of the exposition.

If, however, we can accept Glaucias's ethical standards, we must sympathize with his situation when he is torn between his affection for his real and his adopted son. Dutrait describes him as Crébillon's most appealing father. Ericie has to be loyal to Néoptolémus and at the same time to retain, if possible, the love of the supposed Hélénus. Illyrus, who is disappointed in love, whose life is threatened, and who sees himself abandoned by his father, nevertheless keeps the secret that, as he believes, might, if divulged, save his life. Hélénus, whose devotion to Glaucias obliges him to adopt the king's attitude towards Pyrrhus, sacrifices his love to his loyalty and, when he learns that he is himself Pyrrhus, gives himself up in order to save his adopted brother. It is the struggles of these persons with themselves, with one another, and with Néoptolémus that constitute the bulk of the play.

The nobility of Glaucias, the princes, and Ericie contrasts until the last scene of the play with the brutality of Néoptolémus. Though he is of royal blood, he has no right to the throne he has seized. His excuse for murdering his predecessor is that he was too suspicious. It is true that he feels some remorse and that he is weary of holding his position by force, but he continues to be relentless in his demand for Pyrrhus and in his insistence that only by this prince's death can he retain his power. He rejects in turn the appeals of his daughter, of Glaucias, and of Hélénus. Nevertheless, he is so deeply moved by Pyrrhus's act of self-sacrifice that he reforms as completely as does Félix in *Polyeucte*, but without his religious motivation. One suspects that Crébillon's chief interest in depicting him was not characterization, but the desire to create a surprising situation that would give his tragedy a happy ending.

The play begins with a monologue, followed by an informative conversation in which Glaucias makes known to Androclide that Hélénus is the prince he had saved. The audience is thus let into what remains a secret for the other characters. In Act II there are effective interviews between the usurper, Glaucias, and Hélénus. The action warms in Act III, leading to the discovery by Hélénus of his identity:

> H.:   Je commence, Seigneur, à ne me plus connoître.
> *Il embrasse avec violence les genoux de Glaucias.*
> Pour la dernière fois j'embrasse vos genoux.

G.:   Ah! quel emportement! c'en est trop, levez-vous,
      Reconnoissez Pyrrhus à ma douleur extrême.
H.:   Achevez . . .
G.:   Je me meurs . . . malheureux! c'est vous-même.

In the next act Ericie recognizes Pyrrhus through her knowledge of her lover's character:

> Vous allez, dites-vous, livrer un malheureux,
> Sans cesser d'être grand ni d'être généreux.
> Ah! je vous reconnois à cet effort suprême.
> Justes Dieux! c'est Pyrrhus qui se livre lui-même.

The last example of recognition is the most striking. Néoptolémus has just declared (V, 3) that, if Pyrrhus is delivered to him, he will be put to death. The prince retorts:

> S'il ne craignoit que toi, tyran, ta barbarie
> Te coûteroit bien-tôt & le trône & la vie. . . .
> Je vais te rassurer contre un fer redoutable
> Qui rendroit dans mes mains ta perte inévitable;
>   *Il jette son épée aux pieds de Néoptolème.*
> Frappes, voilà Pyrrhus.

A few lines later, when all the characters are on the stage, Crébillon gives us his final *coup de théâtre*:

N.:   Tu vois un ennemi qui se livre lui-même,
      Et qui loin d'essayer de fléchir ma rigueur,
      Ose par sa fierté défier ma fureur,
      Qui me brave, me hait, me méprise & m'offense.
G.:   De quoi va s'occuper ton injuste vengeance!
      Sont-ce les mouvemens qu'il te doit inspirer!
      Il se livre à tes coups, que veux-tu!
N.:   L'admirer.

These scenes captured the audiences of 1726. The play was first given on April 29, at the opening of the season after the Easter recess. Dufresne played Pyrrhus; Baron, Glaucias; Quinault, Illyrus; Legrand, Néoptolémus; Fontenay, Androclide; Adrienne Le Couvreur, Ericie.[34] Except on May 11, when it was played at Versailles, it was acted every other day at the Comédie Française until June 1. As no author's share is mentioned in the *Registres,* Crébillon must have presented his play to the troupe.

The *Mercure* and the abbé Bonady referred to the success of the tragedy, as did Crébillon in his dedication. The abbé Nadal,[35] who was present at the first performance, wrote next day to the author, praising the virtue of his characters and the final change of fortune with the resulting happy

---

[34] Cf. the *Mercure* for April, 1726, p. 1023.   [35] *Œuvres,* I, 207-9.

ending. He predicted that the tragedy would restore true taste, which had seemed to be threatened with speedy decay, would destroy " ce jargon de tendresse," and would bring back " ces bienseances Théatrales où tout est subordonné au devoir." With *Atrée et Thyeste* it ranks third among Crébillon's plays in popularity at the Comédie Française, where it was acted sixteen times in 1726, twenty-three in 1729-47, five in 1781.

Voltaire and La Harpe [36] were, however, far from agreeing with Nadal. They admitted that *Pyrrhus* was superior to Crébillon's *Sémiramis,* but condemned the style. Voltaire found the tragedy tedious, unnatural, and uninteresting. La Harpe went into greater detail. He considered the magnanimity of Glaucias forced, the scene in which Pyrrhus makes himself known to Néoptolémus long foreseen, the love intrigue cold, and the rivalry in magnanimity monotonous. The *Mercure* of 1781 seems to have been in agreement with this verdict, for it referred to *Pyrrhus* as a feeble production. However, the celebrated actor, Molé,[37] answered the *Mercure* by praising the " simplicité attachante du sujet," the energy of the style, and the " beauté mâle des caractères."

Of the two tragedies first acted in the winter season that followed, one appeared anonymously, while the other was written by a man chiefly known for his comedies. Before TIBÈRE [38] was published, the rumor started that it was the work of a Jesuit, Father Folard, to whom is attributed an unpublished tragedy called *Agrippa*.[39] To the accusation of plagiarism the author of *Tibère* replied in his preface:

> Je déclare hautement que je n'avois jamais ni lû, ni entendu lire la Tragedie d'Agrippa, quand j'ay fait celle de Tibere. Si l'on ne m'en croit pas sur ma foy, je prie l'Auteur de la premiere de vouloir bien la faire imprimer,[40] la difference sera sans doute à son avantage; mais du moins elle me rendra ma gloire, en me disculpant du larcin qu'on veut m'imputer.

Maupoint must have accepted this statement, for he indicates no author. Beauchamps wrote that the tragedy had been attributed to too many persons for him to express an opinion. By the middle of the century, however, an anecdote had developed in accordance with which Father Folard's manuscript had been stolen and had fallen into the hands of the président Dupuy, who entitled the play *Tibère,* instead of *Agrippa,* and had it acted

[36] Cf. Moland, XXIV, 359, and La Harpe, *op. cit.,* XIII, 105.

[37] *Mémoires de Molé,* Paris, 1825, p. 16.

[38] Paris, Flahault, 1727, 8°. Approbation, signed by Secousse, Jan. 4. Republished, The Hague, Van Dole, 1733. According to the *Mercure* of Feb., 1726, it had then been recently accepted by the actors and was called *Agrippa.*

[39] Cf. *Bib. du th. fr.,* III, 166: " L'Auteur prit la précaution d'en faire défendre la représentation."

[40] This request shows that the *Agrippa* in question was not that of Riupeirous, for he had long been dead.

under his own name after he had employed Pellegrin to make some changes in the text.[41] Léris, though he followed Maupoint in much of his wording, declared that the président Dupuis was the author of the tragedy and that Pellegrin "y eut grand part," as, indeed, he must have had, if he wrote the parts spoken by women, for they take up over two-fifths of the play, while many lines addressed to women could not well have appeared in the Jesuit tragedy.

Much more reliable evidence was tucked away in the *Registres,* where nobody thought of looking for it. On Jan. 24, 1727, this note was entered there: "la part d'auteur de Tibere oubliée le 19. decembre 1726 et payée a Mr L'abbé Pelegrain aujourdhuy." This makes it highly probable that Pellegrin wrote the play, and that the story of Dupuy or Dupuis should be rejected. Nor is there any reason to doubt the author's statement that, when he wrote *Tibère,* he had never heard of Folard's *Agrippa.* Whatever resemblance there may have been between the two tragedies may well be due, as the author of *Tibère* suggests, to their common source in the *Annals* of Tacitus.

He derived from this work his leading characters and certain events, but he altered history freely. From the fact that Augustus, shortly before his death, conversed with his exiled grandson and was much affected by the interview the dramatist inferred that the emperor named Agrippa his successor. Though he admitted that, according to Tacitus, Sextus Pompeius was one of the first to greet Tiberius as emperor, he presented this consul as striving desperately to restore the republic. He added the consul's daughter, Emilie, and had both Tiberius and Agrippa fall in love with her. He created a distinct difference between Livia's methods and those of her son. He brought all of these characters together at Nola and had the murder of Agrippa take place at the bedside of the dead emperor. By his changes he succeeded, without violating what he calls "le vray-semblable," in representing three classes of Romans: those who supported Tiberius, those who preferred to make the empire more strictly hereditary, and those who wished to restore the republic.[42]

[41] Cf. Collé, *Journal* (July, 1750), 1807, I, 251-2, and Raynal, *Cor.,* I, 349-50. The date the latter assigns to the theft, 1736, reduces the value of his evidence, as *Tibère* had been published nine years before that. In the *Anecdotes dramatiques* of 1775 the tale is repeated, though the authors are doubtful about its authenticity. They indicate that Pellegrin was employed to add feminine rôles, ordinarily lacking in Jesuit school plays. Collé says that Pellegrin received 10 écus for adding the rôle of a princess.

[42] Augustus is dying at Nola. The Empress Livia wishes him to be succeeded by the son of her former marriage, Tiberius, but, as the emperor has recalled from exile his grandson, Agrippa, it is thought that he may leave him his throne. Both Tiberius and Agrippa love Emilie, daughter of Pompée, a consul descended from Pompey the Great. Livia thinks that marriage with Emilie would strengthen her son's position, but the girl prefers Agrippa. Tiberius pretends to his mother that he

In the portion of the play that is not derived from Tacitus the author may well have been influenced by *Britannicus*, to which he may have turned because of the resemblance between the fate of Augustus's family and that of Claudius's. In both tragedies the prince who is excluded from the throne is preferred by the woman he loves to the man who is or is to be emperor. In both the rôle assigned to the mother of the hero's rival is emphasized. In both there is a certain amount of conflict between this mother and her son, ending in her realization of the fact that she cannot control him.[43]

Tiberius, like Racine's Nero, knows that he owes his position to his mother's marriage to the emperor and prefers to manage his affairs without her assistance, but their motives are different. Nero merely resents the restraint upon his actions that his mother attempts to exercise, whereas Tiberius fears that his mother's bold speech and actions will thwart his efforts to win the empire. Both men are unsuccessful in love, though each has his rival put to death, but Tiberius at times pretends that he does not wish to marry, as Nero does not do. Tiberius also wishes to make it appear, both to his mother and to his rival, that he is not interested in becoming emperor, whereas Nero is in *Britannicus* already on the throne. Tiberius is a thorough hypocrite, making his plans known only to his confidant, whom he hopes to put out of the way as soon as he can conveniently do so. There is no alteration in his character, as there is in Nero's. Tiberius is restrained only by lack of power. The portrait, though in keeping with Tacitus's, may have suffered by comparison with

does not wish to be emperor, but he has paid the augurs to make the gods speak in his favor and he is bringing an army to Nola. He hopes to reign when Augustus dies and the troops arrive, but he keeps his plans secret, even from his mother, of whose bold methods he disapproves. He tells Emilie that, though he loves her, he does not aspire to the honor of marrying her. Agrippa finds that he is loved by Emilie and that, if he will free Rome, her father will approve of his marrying her. Livia insists that Tiberius must reign and asks Pompée's approval of his marriage to Emilie. Pompée receives the emperor's will and learns that Agrippa is to succeed. He tells his daughter she may marry Agrippa, provided he restore the republic. She agrees to lay the proposition before Agrippa, who insists upon making her empress. He receives Tiberius haughtily when his rival comes to assure him of his submission. Livia has the Pretorian guards attack Agrippa, but he is rescued by Tiberius.   In return Agrippa pardons Livia. When Tiberius learns that Augustus has died while Agrippa was near him, he orders his confidant, Martian, to murder the prince, then tells his mother that for her sake he is willing to reign. Agrippa declares that he accepts power only to restore the republic. Shortly afterwards he is murdered by Martian, who, when fatally wounded, admits that he was carrying out the order of Tiberius. Emilie denounces the new emperor and refuses to marry him. Pompée looks to the gods for revenge. Livia predicts that both she and Rome will be mastered by Tiberius.

[43] Cf. with *Sertorius*, v. 1194, and *Tartuffe*, v. 966, a verse in III, 3:

Quoy pour être Romaine en suis-je moins Amante?

and with *le Cid*, v. 274, one in V, 2:

Ce n'est qu'avec le sang, qu'un tel crime s'efface.

Racine's portrayal of Nero, but it is by no means that of the usual protagonist of tragedy.

Livia, who has even a longer rôle than her son, contrasts with him in her lack of prudence, exhibited in her admitting to Agrippa that she has sought to have him killed and in her openly plotting against him before Augustus is safely out of the way. Like Agrippina she longs for power, but she misunderstands her son as Nero's mother does not do. She has made her contribution to his success before the play begins and is now more of an obstacle than an aid to his schemes.

The young lovers, Agrippa and Emilie, resemble closely Britannicus and Junie. According to Tacitus, Agrippa was "an uncultured youth with nothing but brute bodily strength to recommend him." [44] In *Tibère* he has become, like the French Britannicus, frank, gentlemanly, and appealing, the more so as he is unable to penetrate his enemy's designs. Emilie, who may have borrowed her name from *Cinna,* finds herself in a situation like that of Junie. She gives her love and her sympathy to the dispossessed prince and scorns his powerful rival. She differs from Junie in that she must defer to the wishes of her father, who is meant to represent "cette ancienne vigueur Romaine, que le grand Corneille a mis si heureusement sur la Scene." His character weakens at the end of the play. After boldly declaring in II, 6, that, if the Romans have no Brutus, "il leur reste un Pompée," he meekly leaves to the gods the task of avenging Agrippa. Perhaps the author meant to show in this character the tragic fate of Roman liberty, but, if he did, he did not make his thought sufficiently clear. The remaining characters are given few lines. Martian, though important in the plot, is no Narcisse. He is merely a tool of Tiberius.

It would seem that the conception of the five leading characters might have brought the play success if the author had had greater knowledge of the stage. In Acts I-III there is almost no action. We have to wait for Augustus to be in extremis before there is anything to excite us. It is not until IV, 3 that we are aroused by the report of the attack upon Agrippa. After this the action moves rapidly, but even an eighteenth-century audience could not wait so long without becoming bored.

The author claimed that the accusation of plagiarism caused his tragedy to be condemned before the verses were recited, as one of the actresses "le reprocha tout haut au Parterre." That was why the first performance, Dec. 13, 1726, failed,[45] though the two that followed were so well received that his play "se seroit sans doute relevée, sans l'indisposition d'une prin-

---

[44] *Annals,* I, 3 (p. 7 in G. G. Ramsay's translation, London, Murray, 1904).
[45] Collé, *loc. cit.,* supports the author's admission that the first performance was a failure and adds that he joined in the hissing.

cipale Actrice." [46]   He hoped that the publication of *Tibère* would rouse such interest in it that it would be played again, but the actors were not convinced that a fourth performance was advisable.

The tragedy that followed, six weeks after the failure of *Tibère,* was ADMÈTE ET ALCESTE [47] by Louis de Boissy. The *Alcestis* of Euripides had been put on the French stage by Alexandre Hardy and by La Grange-Chancel. The great difficulty presented by the theme was that of retaining the sympathy of the audience for the king when he accepts his wife's offer to sacrifice her life in order to save his. La Grange-Chancel had sought to solve the problem by having Admetus swoon at the proper moment, but this naïve device had brought his tragedy no success and could not well be attempted again. Boissy made a much more fundamental change in the legend by turning the divine command into the devilish invention of an ambitious priest. This alteration enabled him to arrange his material in such a way that the husband never accepts his wife's offer to sacrifice herself and that, though she is saved, as in the Greek tragedy, by the intervention of Hercules, her rescue takes place before Death has seized her. Boissy's tragedy depicts primarily a struggle between Hercules, who has our sympathy, and a high priest who invents oracles for his own purposes. If one chooses to substitute Christianity for paganism, one will find in the play a thorough criticism of priestly power in France, one that would certainly have locked up the author in the Bastille, if he had not disguised himself under the mantle of Euripides. [48]

[46] Yet, according to the *Registres,* though 756 tickets were bought for the first performance, 563 were bought for the second and only 287 for the third. The author's share in the receipts was 172 fr., 8 s. Baron, Adrienne Le Couvreur, la Duclos, and Maurice Quinault are among those playing in *Tibère* or in a comedy that followed.

[47] The Hague, Van Dole, 1738, 8°. Republished, Paris, Duchesne, 1758, and in the author's *Œuvres,* Amsterdam et Berlin, Jean Néaulme, 1758. For Boissy cf. C. F. Zeek, Jr., *Louis de Boissy, auteur comique (1694-1758),* Grenoble, 1914.

[48] The King of Thessaly had left his dominions to the one of his two sons that Alceste would elect to marry. She had chosen the younger, Admète, and had married him about two years before the play begins. He now rules at Yolcos, while his brother, Polidecte, has been forced to become high priest and renounce the woman he loves. Polidecte plots with her father, Adraste, to get the throne and has taken advantage of a plague that has swept through the country to make an oracle declare that Admète must die by high noon in order to save his people. He bids Adraste get ready an armed force so that, as soon as Admète is dead, he will be made the ruler rather than Alceste. He reveals to Adraste that he makes the gods speak and that he has poisoned the incense Admète will offer in the temple so that his death will be attributed to the gods. When, however, he learns that Hercules is returning, he fears that he will seize the throne and marry Admète's widow. He consequently invents a new oracle, one that offers life to Admète if another Greek will die in his stead. When Alceste learns that no substitute has come forward, she resolves to sacrifice herself in the temple, but she returns to say farewell to her husband. At this point Hercules arrives. His suspicions have been roused by the fact that the city of Larissa, anticipating the death of Admète, has declared Polidecte king. He insists upon consulting the gods and interviewing the priest before the sacrifice takes place. Polidecte tells him that he speaks for the gods and will rouse the

The *Dictionnaire dramatique* of La Porte and Chamfort declares that the high priest is a disfigured copy of Racine's Mathan [49] and compares his threats to those of the priest in Voltaire's *Œdipe*, but Mathan has changed his religion and does not invent oracles, while Voltaire's priest, like that of Sophocles, delivers a divine message, not one that he has invented for his own advantage. Polidecte resembles more closely the priest in La Motte's *Romulus*, who also puts messages into the mouth of a god, but he is a minor figure, whereas Boissy gives to his priest the longest rôle in his play.

It is true that " Notre crédulité fait toute leur science " is the notion on which Polidecte acts and may have given Boissy a hint,[50] but the plot of Voltaire's *Œdipe* does not support this statement, while that of Boissy does. His priest, more highly developed than those of Voltaire and La Motte, considers himself the lawful heir to his father's throne, is jealous of his brother, and plots to become king by employing both force and intrigue. He says to Adraste (I, 1), " Réponds-moi des soldats, je te réponds des Dieux." In his mind Admète, Alceste, and the people are the dupes of religion, to be controlled by skillfully invented oracles. He even regards Hercules as an adventurer, claiming to be the son of Jupiter, but capable of being frightened by imprecations. His valor and resourcefulness are such that, when he kills himself, even Hercules regrets that his great abilities were not employed to better purpose.

The second rôle in length and importance is that of Hercules. He shows his intelligence by suspecting Polidecte, promptly suppressing the insurrection, and wresting information from Adraste. By saving Alceste and denouncing Polidecte he becomes the most important agent in bringing about the dénouement. He is not the rollicking figure that Euripides presents, but a thoughtful warrior who sees even in his own trials an opportunity to distinguish himself. His love for Alceste, probably borrowed from La Grange-Chancel, has no function in the plot and would better have been omitted.

The king and queen are less interesting than in the Greek play. Admète

people. He threatens Hercules, who has him guarded while he and Admète go out to suppress an uprising, headed by Adraste. Alceste goes to the temple with the intention of killing herself in order to placate the gods, but Hercules mortally wouds Adraste, who confesses that Polidecte has invented the oracular pronouncements, and reaches the temple in time to save Alceste. He restores her to her husband and charges Polidecte with perjury and the intent to cause the death of his brother and sister-in-law. Polidecte kills himself in order to avoid condemnation.

[49] They would have done better to point out the resemblance of the opening scene to that of *Athalie*, as in both tragedies the speakers are a priest, who is preparing a change of rulers, and an army officer who does his bidding.

[50] Boissy, like Voltaire, introduces a " chœur du Peuple." Cf. *Œdipe*, II, 4, " Pour Hercule & pour moi, c'est un homme ordinaire," and *Admète et Alceste*, III, 6, " Mais Hercule à mes yeux est un homme ordinaire."

is an ideal monarch, who avoids war, is ready to die for his people, is devoted to his wife and son. Unfortunately he is too ready to boast of his virtues. He refuses to accept his wife's offer to sacrifice herself and even declares that, if the gods do not relent in their demands, he will disobey them. Dr. Zeek is not justified in saying that Alceste "ne s'offre qu'après avoir vu tous les autres sujets refuser de s'offrir," for she learns at the same time that substitution is allowed and that no one has offered to replace the king as the victim of the gods. She speedily decides to offer herself and would have carried out her purpose if Hercules had not intervened. Nor is she presented as "une ancienne maîtresse d'Hercule." There is nothing in the play to indicate that she knew he had ever loved her. She is less effective than in Euripides because little is made of her love for her child and because the problem she has to face is largely taken out of her hands.

When the play was first acted, Jan. 25, 1727, there were fifteen actors in the cast, including Baron, Dufresne, Maurice Quinault, and la Duclos,[51] and there was no afterpiece. It was given again on the 27, then on Feb. 14 and 16, and finally, with the title changed to *la Mort d'Alceste,* on Nov. 26 and 30.[52] All the performances were well attended, the receipts never falling below 1000 francs and the author earning 661 fr., 2 s. There was obviously no financial reason why it should not have been played again. When to this information, derived from the *Registres,* are added the facts that the published play has only ten rôles, less than 1200 verses, and that Acts II and V have each less than 200 lines, it seems clear that the author was obliged to eliminate a number of his verses. Beauchamps, indeed, writing only a few years after the play was acted, stated that on Nov. 26 it was "reprise avec des changemens," and Léris [53] declares that Boissy made alterations, especially in the title-rôles, and composed 600 new verses.

The censor would not have objected to remarks about the fickleness of the mob, or about educating a prince to control his desires, or to what appears to be intended as a compliment to Louis XV, who, like Admète, had recently married, had recently taken over the direction of public affairs, and had avoided war:

J'ai préféré la Paix aux horreurs de la Guerre,
Et jamais votre sang n'a rougi cette terre,
Ce sang pour l'exposer, m'étoit trop précieux;
J'ai beaucoup mieux aimé vous rendre tous heureux. (II, 1)

---

[51] The others were La Thorillière, father and son, Dangeville, Fontenay, Duchemin, the younger Legrand, Dumirail, Du Breuil, and the actresses, Jouvenot, Du Boccage, and Legrand.

[52] Zeek, following the *Dictionnaire dramatique* of 1776, declares that after the second performance further production was forbidden until the play had its new title.

[53] The evidence of Léris is weakened by the fact that he represents Boissy as adopting his new title after the second performance instead of the fourth.

If, as seems probable, there was governmental interference, it was rather on account of lines such as these that Boissy put into the mouth of the high priest, who says to Adraste (III, 6),

> Sous le voile sacré de la Religion,
> Va semer l'épouvante & la rebellion,

who pretends, like Tartuffe, that (IV, 4)

> L'intérêt des Autels est le seul qui m'attire,

and who is denounced by Hercules in words that might be applied to other priests in other lands (IV, 4) :

> Je sçai d'avec les Dieux distinguer leurs Ministres. . . .
> Votre ame ambitieuse, usurpe leur puissance,
> Partage leur encens, fait taire leur clémence;
> Et vous osez vous rendre, abusant de vos droits,
> Les Idoles du Peuple, & les Tyrans des Rois.

The original text may have been still more anticlerical, or Boissy, after trying a milder version in November, 1727, may have returned, when he published his play, more nearly to the original.   Note that the tragedy was first published in Holland and that the first French edition appeared as late as 1758, when the censorship may have become more liberal.   If the text that has been preserved is that of 1726, the work is, of all French tragedies written up to the time that it was acted, the one that makes the most devastating attack upon the priesthood.

Another tragedy attributed to Boissy differs from it in many respects. It is called DOM RAMIR ET ZAÏDE.[54]   According to Léris, Boissy denied that he had written it and indicated the author as a certain La Chazette. The name was written La Chassette on the manuscript, but it was so unfamiliar that some one sought to alter it to La Chaussée, with the result that the play is attributed to the latter in the catalogue of manuscripts at the Bibliothèque Nationale.   This means, however, only that the compiler of the catalogue was familiar with the name of Nivelle de La Chaussée and had never heard of La Chassette.

Léris asserts that the subject of the play had been made into a Latin tragedy by Father Porée, who not long before had had it acted at Louis le Grand, but no such production is mentioned by J. de La Servière.[55] Léris may have had in mind the fact that in *Brutus* (1708) and in a comedy, *Caecus amor patrum* (1717), two brothers of different character

---

[54] The manuscript is at the Bibliothèque Nationale, f. fr. 25474.   Mme Brodin located it for me in the summer of 1946.   A microfilm of it is at The Johns Hopkins University.

[55] *Un professeur d'ancien régime, le père Charles Porée, S. J.*, Paris, Oudin, 1899.

are presented as are two supposed brothers in *Dom Ramir,* but there is too little resemblance to justify the claim of influence.

La Chassette's point of departure may well have been Mme de La Fayette's novel, *Zaïde,* where he could have found the background of war between the Moors and the Kingdom of Leon, a heroine who is the daughter of an Arab, as La Chassette's heroine is for some time supposed to be, and the names, Zaïde, Ramire, and Alphonse. But in the novel there is no suggestion of the intrigue found in the tragedy, which resembles in certain respects several French plays. The labors of a clever minister to put his son on a throne result in the death of the son, as in Thomas Corneille's *Stilicon;* a boy and girl are exchanged with resulting danger of incest, as in Colonia's *Jovien;* [56] a girl is threatened with the death of the man she loves if she refuses to marry the man in whose power she is, as in Rotrou's *Hercule mourant.* But the young hero plays no part in bringing about his own destruction as he does in *Stilicon;* the lovers never believe, as they do in *Jovien,* that they are brother and sister; and the heroine's problem is taken away from her far sooner than in *Hercule mourant.* One must conclude that the author showed little originality, but that he did not necessarily imitate these tragedies. [57]

[56] Cf. my *History,* Part IV, p. 343. In both tragedies a man of importance in the state exchanges his child with the ruler's, without the latter's knowledge, but with the connivance of the ruler's wife. In both plays the children differ in sex. In *Jovien* a girl is substituted for a prince; in *Dom Ramir* a boy is substituted for a princess.

[57] Dom Fernand, King of Leon, has as his prime minister a Moor. After eight years of marriage the queen had become pregnant, but her husband, called away by war, was unable to be present at the birth of his heir. As this turned out to be a girl and as Almanzir's wife gave birth to a boy on the same day to a boy, an exchange was effected, so that Ramir grew up as heir to the throne, Zaïde as the daughter of Almanzir. Subsequently the queen gave birth to a son, Alphonse, and died at his birth. Fernand, Ramir, and Alphonse are now all in love with Zaïde, who loves Ramir. As Almanzir fears that Fernand may make Alphonse his successor, he tries to create trouble between the king and his son in order that Ramir may inherit the throne. To carry out his plans he makes use of Osmen, commander of the palace guard, and bribes Sanche, a military leader. He has to act quickly as Fernand insists upon marrying Zaïde before night. When Alphonse hears that his father has selected a husband for the woman he loves, he supposes that it is Ramir and challenges him to a duel, which is stopped by Sanche. The king reproves the young men, puts them under arrest, and, suspecting that Zaïde loves one of them, threatens that, if she continues to refuse to marry him, he will put them both to death in her presence. Zaïde yields in order to save Ramir, who learns from her confidant, Fatime, the story of the exchange, which had been told her by Almanzir's wife. He repeats it to Zaïde, who, fearing for his life, begs him not to tell the king. When he insists, she leaves him, apparently with the intention of committing suicide, but she is abducted by Alphonse and Osmen. When Ramir reproaches his father for putting Zaïde in danger of an incestuous marriage, Almanzir assures him that Osmen will take her to safety in Grenada. He has given him a letter to his brother there and claims to have the support of Sanche, whom the king has sent in pursuit of the fugitives. Ramir insists upon telling Fernand that he is not his son, but will wait until next day in order that his parents may escape. Meanwhile Sanche arrests Alphonse and Osmen, brings them home with Zaïde, accuses Almanzir to the king of attempting to bribe him, and produces the letter as evidence. Fernand has

Though the plot is built up with strict regard for the unities, the circumstances on which it is based are not satisfactorily explained. Why should the King of Leon accept as prime minister a Moor, especially one who, as far as we are told, has not been converted? How could the queen allow her daughter to be entrusted to this Moor? Why did the physical appearance of Zaïde and Ramir fail to betray their origin? Too much importance in the plot is left to Almanzir's wife, who does not appear on the stage, and to Sanche, who is given relatively few lines. Ramir and Zaïde, with whom we sympathize, accomplish nothing. Each is given a problem, but is not allowed to work it out. The king is a brute, who threatens with death his real and insolent son and his supposed and admirable son. We are not prepared, however, for his putting to death innocent Ramir merely to punish his father. Almanzir should have been the most dramatic character, but he is not allowed to appear in Acts II and III and, when we see him elsewhere, he is preparing for action or suffering from his errors rather than engaged in a dramatic conflict.

The play has few arresting situations. Moorish manners are not portrayed. The only idea of consequence that is expressed is found in V, 1, when Fernand declares that his fate should be a warning to kings not to entrust affairs of state to foreigners. In the time of Cardinal Mazarin such a remark might have aroused interest, but in the administration of Cardinal Fleury it was a platitude. Lacking appealing characters, dramatic situations, and ideas, and without striking verses, the tragedy was a complete failure. It was acted only once, Jan. 24, 1728.[58]

Yet it was the only new tragedy of the winter season, 1727-8, and in the winter season that followed there was none at all. The composition of tragedies had rarely sunk so low. All that was offered before 1730 was one act of tragedy in a hybrid play that appeared in the summer of 1729 under the title of LES TROIS SPECTACLES.[59] This work consists of a prologue in two scenes and of three acts, the first of which is a tragedy

---

Almanzir arrested and Osmen tortured. In a violent interview with Alphonse he warns him that he will put him to death if he does not renounce Zaïde. He now learns from Osmen's confession under torture that Zaïde is his daughter. Word is brought that Alphonse has snatched a sword from a guard and killed himself. The king reproaches Almanzir for causing his son's death and punishes him by poisoning Ramir, who comes on the stage in a dying condition. Zaïde renounces her father, gives Ramir her hand in marriage, and seeks to kill herself on his corpse. Fernand bids Sanche watch over her and exiles Almanzir to Africa in the belief that his sufferings will be worse than death.

[58] The author may have been comforted by the fact that he received from this unique production, 154 fr., 4 s.

[59] Paris, Tabarie, 1729, 8°; approbation, according to Beauchamps, July 28. Republished in the *Théâtre françois* of 1737. The author, Dumas d'Aigueberre (1692-1755), was a " conseiller au parlement de Toulouse"; cf. Quérard. He wrote one other play, a comedy called *le Prince de Noisy*, acted on Nov. 4, 1730.

entitled POLIXÈNE; the second, a comedy called *l'Avare amoureux*; and
the third, a miniature opera, *Pan et Doris,* "pastorale héroïque."

A similar experiment had been tried by Quinault in the middle of the
seventeenth century. His *Comédie sans comédie*[60] had consisted of a
preliminary discussion, a pastoral, a farce, a tragedy, and a tragi-comedy
with "machines," but by 1729 taste had changed to the point of making
the three kinds selected by Dumas d'Aigueberre the only ones of importance
to those who sought amusement at the Comédie Française and the Opera.

In the prologue the relative merits of tragedy, comedy, and opera are
briefly discussed by a group of aristocrats who are giving amateur performances at the country home of the Marquise. The Commandeur insists
that a one-act tragedy is a "monstre," but the Marquise holds that it may
succeed like a one-act comedy. She thinks that its novelty may be appreciated at the "Comédie Françoise." When the Commandeur insists that
there must be five acts in order that the author may "disposer les choses
pour remuer le cœur," and the Marquise replies that this brief tragedy
has moved her to tears, the Commandeur retorts that her tears were not
in accord with the rules. The young Chevalier prefers a comedy as
tragedies bore him, but the opinion of the Marquise is supported by a
"grand flandrin de Vicomte."[61] Another guest suggests a pastoral set to
music. Finally it is proposed to play all three kinds. The Commandeur
is allowed to walk in the garden while the "monstre" is being performed.

Polixène then follows. It is a simplified version of La Fosse's *Polyxène*[62]
with only four speaking characters: the heroine, her confidant, Pyrrhus,
and Thessandre, who serves to bring in accounts of Achilles's message and
the reaction of the Greeks.[63] From La Fosse's version of the Greek legend
the author took the love of Pyrrhus and Polyxena for each other, his offer
of marriage, her confession of love, and his overthrowing the altar. As he
allowed himself only one act, he eliminated Télèphe and Ulysses. He
added Pyrrhus's final threat of vengeance and showed on the stage Polyxena's suicide.

The heroine appears in scenes in which she struggles against her love,

---

[60] Cf. my *History*, Part III, pp. 98-101.
[61] Cf. *le Misanthrope*, V, last scene.
[62] Cf. my *History*, Part IV, pp. 385-8.
[63] The scene is laid "sur le débris de Troye." Polyxena has been allotted to
Pyrrhus, who has killed her father. She is ashamed of her love for him and dis-
courages his advances till she hears that the ghost of Achilles demands her death.
When Pyrrhus starts to fight in her defense, she shows such distress that he gets
from her a confession of love. He then quiets the people, overthrows the altar
that Calchas had set up, and casts suspicion upon the reported speech of the ghost,
but Polyxena, fearing for her lover, stabs herself. As she dies, she begs Pyrrhus
to protect her mother. He thinks of suicide, but decides to live in order to punish
the Greeks.

reveals it to Ægine, then to Pyrrhus himself, and kills herself, both to atone for her love and to protect Pyrrhus. The latter has the rôle of a conventional lover. His violence is shown in his account of what he has done off the stage and in his final threats. The other two characters are a confidant and a messenger.

The effective scenes are the fourth, in which Pyrrhus discovers that Polyxena loves him, and the ninth, in which she kills herself. An echo of the skepticism with which oracular statements had been greeted by characters in plays of Voltaire, La Motte, and Boissy is found in Pyrrhus's declaring that his father's message had been " dicté par l'artifice," but this interpretation of it has no effect upon the plot.[64] After reading the play, one must agree with the Commandeur that a French classical dramatist required more than one act in which to produce a tragedy.

It must have been the novelty of *les Trois Spectacles* rather than the attraction offered by *Polixène* that enabled the actors to produce the play twenty times in 1729, from July 6 to August 16.[65] It attracted enough attention for a parody of it, *Melpomène vengée,* to appear at the Théâtre Italien on Sept. 4 and for Dumas d'Aigueberre to compose a parody of his one-act tragedy called *Colinette.*[66] But those who desired to see new tragedies at the Comédie Française must have been deeply disappointed to find that *Polixène* was the only one produced there in two years. They must have thought that it was time for Voltaire to return from England.

---

[64] Certain persons, perhaps because they detected heresy in a suggested conflict between tombs and altars, objected to lines in scene 4:

Défendre contre lui les droits des immortels,
Et forcer les tombeaux de céder aux autels,

that is, Pyrrhus proposes to marry Polyxena in order to quiet his father's ghost. To oblige his critics the author changed the verses to the grandiloquent couplet:

N'obéïr qu'à ma flâme, & plein d'un feu si beau,
De l'Hymen sur sa tombe allumer le flambeau.

[65] It earned for the author 877 fr., 8 s., and would have earned more if there had not been special expenses of nearly 4000 fr. required by the performances.

[66] Cf. Léris. Beauchamps (II, 529-30) mentions two productions connected with the play, a *Lettre d'un Garçon de Caffé au Soufleur de la comedie de Roüen, sur la piece des trois Spectacles* (Paris, Tabarie, 1729) and a *Reponse du Soufleur* (Paris, 1730). The catalogue of the Bibliothèque Nationale lists these and a *Seconde Lettre*. It attributes all three pamphlets to Dumas d'Aigueberre.

CHAPTER VI

VOLTAIRE RETURNS FROM ENGLAND

Brutus, Eriphyle, Mort de César, Zaïre

Voltaire's visit to England is supposed to have had a profound effect upon his ideas of dramatic composition. Moland cites his remark that " un heureux et adroit mélange de l'action [1] qui règne sur le théâtre de Londres et de Madrid, avec la sagesse, l'élégance, la noblesse, la décence du nôtre, pourrait produire quelque chose de parfait." Let us see to what extent his tragedies give evidence that he attempted such a synthesis.

Not long after the successful run of *Hérode et Mariamne,* the dramatist, as a result of his quarrel with the chevalier de Rohan, sailed for England, where he sojourned most of the time from May, 1726, to the latter part of 1728, or early in 1729. He learned to speak and write English and acquired some familiarity with the English stage, but he retained as his chief guides the dramatic principles he had applied in composing *Œdipe* and *Hérode et Mariamne.*

It was in England that he began his Brutus.[2] According to his *Discours,* he wrote the first act in English prose " à peu près tel qu'il est aujourd'hui en vers français." By Oct. 15, 1729, the tragedy had taken on enough form to be read to the actors, who prepared to perform it,[3] but for some reason [4] Voltaire withheld it, perhaps in order to revise it, so that it was not acted until Dec. 11, 1730.

There is nothing in the choice of subject, the presentation of characters, or the structure that shows English influence.[5] The story, told by Livy,

---

[1] He means physical activity. Voltaire understood as well as anyone that there was abundant moral and psychological activity in Corneille and Racine.

[2] Paris, J.-Fr. Josse, 1731, 8°. Accompanied by a *Discours* addressed to Lord Bolingbroke, in which he defended the use of rime in French plays, the unities, the introduction of love, expressed his objection to certain restrictions, and criticized in some respects both Greek and English plays. Republished, Amsterdam, Ledet et Desbordes, 1731; Paris, Prault, 1736; Paris, Duchesne, 1764 (an edition criticized severely by Voltaire; cf. Moland, VI, 336). For other editions cf. Moland, L, 486, and Bengesco. For five Italian translations cf. Ferrari, *op. cit.,* pp. 61-4. For translations into Dutch and Spanish cf. J. A. Van Praag, *RLC,* XVI (1936), 173-180. For a study of the play cf. Lion, *op. cit.,* pp. 45-53.

[3] Cf. Destouches's letter of Dec. 16, 1729, in *RHL,* XIV (1907), 665, and the *Mercure* for October, 1729, p. 2264.

[4] Voltaire's explanation is that he had heard of an intrigue formed against the play by Crébillon and Chabot (Rohan). Desnoiresterres thought it unlikely that Crébillon was engaged in such an activity and ventured the suggestion that the actors did not at first approve of the play (cf. Moland, XXXIII, 195). The evidence of Destouches, however, destroys the hypothesis that the actors were unwilling to accept the play.

[5] T. R. Lounsbury, *Shakespeare and Voltaire,* New York, 1902, pp. 74-7, states that

had already been dramatized in France by the unknown author of *la Mort des enfans de Brute*,[6] by Mlle Bernard in her *Brutus,* acted at the Comédie Française in 1690, and by Father Porée in his Latin *Brutus,* played at Louis le Grand on Aug. 1, 1708, when Voltaire was a pupil in that school.[7] He seems to have drawn material from all of these, especially from Livy and Mlle Bernard.

Livy had written that, while Brutus and Valerius were consuls, ambassadors came to ask that the property of the exiled Tarquins be restored to them; that these ambassadors intrigued with young men who were dissatisfied with the republic, urged them to restore the Tarquins to power, and presented letters from exiled royalty; that Titus and Tiberius, sons of Brutus, were involved in the conspiracy, which was revealed by a slave; and that the young men, including Brutus's sons, were, with his approval, put to death. To this account a love theme was added in *la Mort des enfans de Brute,* a play that presents the two sons of Brutus as in love with Tullie, daughter of Tarquin. Mlle Bernard altered Livy's chronology in such a way that Tarquin, supported by Porsenna, is already at war with Rome. Titus becomes an important military leader, in charge of the Quirinal gate. Tiberius becomes Tiberinus and is now jealous of his brother. Both young men are in love with Aquilie, daughter of a conspirator. The ambassador addresses flattering remarks to the consul, while condemning the violence and the fickleness of the mob. The influences brought to bear upon Titus are emphasized. When he yields to them and his crime is detected, the senate leaves the decision to Brutus, who condemns his sons to death. Aquilie commits suicide.

Voltaire's tragedy resembles Mlle Bernard's more closely than his *Œdipe* resembles Corneille's, or his *Mariamne* Tristan's. He adopts all her changes mentioned in the last paragraph, except that he has Tiberinus, who does not appear on the stage, die while resisting arrest, and that he follows *la Mort des enfans de Brute* in selecting for his heroine Tullie, daughter of Tarquin.[8] He occasionally follows Mlle Bernard's wording.[9] He

---

there is no relationship between Voltaire's play and that of Nathaniel Lee on the same subject.

[6] Paris, Quinet, 1648. Moland attributes this play to La Calprenède, but there is no justification for his doing so.

[7] Moland and others have mentioned Voltaire's debt to these sources. For the last of them cf. J. de la Servière, *Un professeur d'ancien régime, le père Charles Porée, S. J. (1676-1741)*, Paris, Oudin, 1899, pp. 236-46. In comparing Porée's tragedy with Voltaire's, La Servière failed to consider what the latter owed to Mlle Bernard.

[8] He may also have derived from the anonymous tragedy the thought that the people should leave to the gods the judgment of kings.

[9]   Consuls, quelle est ma joie,
De parler devant vous pour le Roi qui m'envoie,
Et non devant un Peuple aveugle, audacieux. (B., I, 2)
Consuls, et vous, sénat, qu'il m'est doux d'être admis

simplified her plot by omitting the daughter of Valerius and her unrequited
love for Titus. He improved the structure and the style of her tragedy,
adding, like Father Porée, Tarquin's appreciation of Titus, the young man's
appeal, after his condemnation, for assurance of his father's love, and
Brutus's final reference to Rome.[10]

It was difficult to present the two leading characters, a traitor and one
who condemns his son to death, without their losing the sympathy of the
audience. Brutus is portrayed in his traditional rôle of patriot and
unbending enemy of kings. He argues that Tarquin's breaking his promise
to rule justly absolves the Roman people of their oath to obey him. His
own first duty is to represent those who have placed him in office, but he

> Dans ce conseil sacré de sages ennemis, . . .
> Loin des cris de ce peuple indocile et barbare. (V., I, 2)
>
> Br.:   S'il me demeure un Fils, ou si je n'en ai plus.
> T.:   Non, vous n'en avez point.   (B., IV, 6)
> Br.:   Parle: ai-je encore un fils?
> T.:   Non, vous n'en avez plus. (V., V, 7)
> T.:   Il faut servir d'exemple à qui peut m'imiter. (B., IV, 6)
> T.:   . . . il faut épouvanter
>   Les Romains, s'il en est qui puissent m'imiter. (V., V, 7)
> Br.:   Porte sur l'échafaut cette mâle assurance.
>   Ton Pere infortuné tremble à te condamner:
>   Va, ne l'imite pas, & meurs sans t'étonner. (B., V, 7)
> Br.:   Va, porte à ton supplice un plus mâle courage;
>   Va, ne t'attendris point, sois plus Romain que moi. (V., V, 7)

[10] Brutus and Valerius announce to the senate the mission of Arons, whom Valerius
would not receive while the enemy is at the gates of Rome, but whom Brutus would
admit in order that he may realize the city's power. After Arons and Brutus have
argued over the rights of the kings and of the people, and Brutus has offered a
prayer to Mars, the ambassador is allowed a day in order that he may collect
Tarquin's gold. He is allowed to talk with Tarquin's daughter, who, since her
father's exile, has been a guest in the home of the consuls. Arons takes advantage
of his visit to consult with Messala, who tells him that his friends will rebel if a
leader can be found who is important enough to make Tarquin remember them after
his restoration. Titus has attained such distinction by winning trophies from the
enemy. He may be persuaded, as he loves Tullie and is embittered by the senate's
refusal to make him a consul. Arons offers Tullie to Titus, but warns him that, if
he refuses to support Tarquin, the princess will marry the king of Liguria. Tibérinus
joins the conspiracy. Tullie shows Titus a letter in which Tarquin offers to let him
share the throne with Tullie, when she inherits it. Titus at first refuses, but he
weakens when his father orders Tullie to leave with Arons and the girl threatens to
die if he does not yield. He finally agrees to their terms, excusing himself with the
thought that his first allegiance had been to Tarquin. Brutus now tells him that an
attack on the city will be made at night and urges him to save Rome. When the
young man has left the stage, Valerius reveals the fact that there is a conspiracy,
and a slave requests an interview. Brutus announces to the senate that, after the
slave's revelations, he had arrested Messala, who has killed himself. He declares
that no pity must be shown to traitors. Arons and Tullie are forced to witness the
executions. Valerius brings the list of the guilty, including the name of Tibérinus,
who had been killed when he resisted arrest. Brutus continues to read the list till
he sees the name of Titus and falls into the arms of a tribune. The senate leaves
to him the decision in regard to his son. Valerius tells him that Tullie has killed
herself. Brutus gets from Titus the admission that in a moment of weakness he had
agreed to conspire and the request that he be put to death. Brutus embraces him,
but sends him out to be executed. His consolation is in the fact that Rome is free.

has a softer side, for he is kind to his enemy's daughter and is overcome when he discovers that Titus is a conspirator. Obliged to condemn him to death, he embraces him and hopes that he may himself soon die for his country. Titus is a distinguished warrior, impetuous and ambitious, but disappointed ambition was not enough to make the son of Brutus betray Rome. Consequently, like Mlle Bernard and unlike Porée, Voltaire added his love for Tullie, his jealousy at the thought of losing her to his brother or to the king of Liguria, his fear for her life. He made his weakness temporary, enough to make him guilty in his own eyes and his father's, but not enough to turn the audience against him.

To avoid duplication, Voltaire kept the other son behind the scenes. He gave Tullie a struggle between her love for Titus and her loyalty to her father. The solution she seeks would put Tarquin on the throne and, after his death, Titus. When her plan fails, suicide is inevitable. The leading minor rôles are those of prudent and energetic Valerius; the wily ambassador; and Messala, the collaborator.

The plot is unified. The first act is concerned with the exposition and the treacherous activities of Arons and Messala. Neither Titus nor Tullie appears in it. In Act II we see the first efforts to win Titus. Tullie was originally given a prominent part in two scenes for which conversations between Titus and Tarquin's male agents were substituted, with the result that the heroine is not seen before the middle of Act III. In the second and third acts Titus resists the appeals of Rome's enemies, but he is shaken by the fear of losing Tullie. In Act IV he joins Tarquin's party and news of the conspiracy is brought to Brutus. The fifth act is devoted to the rescue of the republic and the condemnation of Titus.

Voltaire paid more attention to the setting than he had previously done, even more than in Œdipe. It is here that English influence may show itself. The stage represents a part of the consular house on the Tarpeian rock:

Le temple du Capitole se voit dans le fond. Les sénateurs sont assemblés entre le temple et la maison, devant l'autel de Mars . . . les sénateurs sont rangés en demi-cercle. Des licteurs avec leurs faisceaux sont debout derrière les sénateurs.

In his Discours Voltaire states that the senators wore red robes. Though he found a precedent for unusual costuming and stage decoration in a lost tragedy, Ferrier's Montézume, he offered the spectacle to the public with some misgivings.[11] He would have allowed the senators to speak if he

---

[11] The spectacle was criticized by La Grange-Chancel in the preface to the 1758 edition of Amasis: " Je ne puis m'empécher aussi de combattre la fausse opinion de ceux qui voudroient corrompre la noble simplicité de la tragédie par des spectacles inutiles, ou qui du moins ne peuvent être reçus que dans les tragédies en machines.

had not remembered the unfortunate impression that untrained actors in *Œdipe* had made in a similar situation.   He ventured to have Arons, preceded by lictors, pass before the consuls and senators to a seat prepared for him at the front of the stage.   In IV, 5, "le fond du théâtre s'ouvre." The stage directions indicate that the interior of an apartment is shown as well as the place where the senate assembles.

Voltaire introduced a number of lines in praise of popular government and condemning the rule of kings:

> Destructeurs des tyrans, vous qui n'avez pour rois
> Que les dieux de Numa, vos vertus et nos lois. (I, 1)
>
> Et l'esclave d'un roi va voir enfin des hommes. (I, 1)
>
> Crois-moi, la liberté, . . .
> Donne à l'homme un courage, inspire une grandeur,
> Qu'il n'eût jamais trouvés dans le fond de son cœur. (I, 3)
>
> Qui naquit dans la pourpre en est rarement digne. (II, 4)
>
> Je connais trop les grands: dans le malheur amis,
> Ingrats dans la fortune, et bientôt ennemis:
> Nous sommes de leur gloire un instrument servile,
> Rejeté par dédain dès qu'il est inutile. (I, 4)

The priesthood is attacked but once:

> Esclaves de leurs rois, et même de leurs prêtres,
> Les Toscans semblent nés pour servir sous des maîtres. (I, 2)

Liberty brings responsibility in regard to the laws, for "Qui veut les violer n'aime point sa patrie" (II, 4), and limits the power of the police:

> Arrêter un Romain sur de simples soupçons,
> C'est agir en tyrans, nous qui les punissons.[12]

These last lines may have been suggested by Voltaire's contact with Englishmen, for in England one could be less easily arrested than in France, but the verses previously cited could have been devised as readily in one country as the other, for the English, too, were living under an hereditary monarchy.

The point of view of royalists is expressed by Arons and Messala:

On s'est fait une si grande idée du Sénat romain, que ce seroit le tourner en ridicule que de l'exposer sur notre théâtre, d'autant plus que les acteurs muets sont toujours représentés par les domestiques des comédiens, dont la figure est ordinairement choquante, & que la tragédie est assez majestueuse par elle-même pour n'avoir pas besoin de ces ornemens étrangers.   C'est un goût de l'enfance qu'on a pris dans les colleges."

[12] IV, 7. Moland quotes Villemain's statement that during the Terror the couplet was changed to

Arrêter un Romain sur un simple soupçon,
Ne peut être permis qu'en révolution.

Ils [les sénateurs] ont brisé le joug pour l'imposer eux-même. (I, 4).

Vos lois sont vos tyrans; leur barbare rigueur
Devient sourde au merite, au sang, à la faveur: . . .
Aimé du souverain, de ses rayons couvert,
Vous ne servez qu'un maître, et le reste vous sert. (II, 2)

De ces républicains la triste austérité
De son cœur généreux révolte la fierté. (III, 3)

Ce pouvoir souverain . . .
Est des gouvernements le meilleur ou le pire;
Affreux sous un tyran, divin sous un bon roi. (III, 7)

These lines may have persuaded Louis XV's censor to tolerate the tragedy. When it was first acted, three of the leading parts were taken, according to Moland, by new recruits: Brutus, by Sarrazin; [13] Valerius, by Grandval; Tullie, by Marie-Anne Dangeville, a girl not quite sixteen who was encouraged by Voltaire in a letter that has been preserved.[14] Titus, on the other hand, was played by Dufresne. At the first performance 1564 persons paid admission, and the receipts reached the unusually large sum of 5,065 francs. The play was acted fifteen times, until Jan. 17, 1731.[15] After this it was crowded off the stage for several years by other tragedies of Voltaire. On Jan. 2, 1738, he wrote to la Quinault that he had made considerable changes in Tullie's rôle and hoped that the tragedy might be revived, as it was, but not until after this actress had retired. Between 1742 and 1786 it was played sixty-nine times. Its greatest popularity came with the Revolution, when it was played twenty-three times in four years, 1790-93.[16] It was not presented at the Comédie Française after 1799. The total number of its productions there was 110.

Two parodies appeared, le Bolus and le Sénat académique. The play was discussed in a letter attributed to Pellegrin, in two pamphlets entitled Réflexions, and in a Jugement en dernier ressort.[17] Voltaire admitted that his tragedy was " très-défectueuse," [18] and abbé Le Blanc found it dull,[19]

---

[13] In the Mémoires de Lekain, Paris, 1801, pp. 11-2, it is said that Sarrazin was so mild when he recited Brutus's invocation to Mars that Voltaire cried, " Monsieur, songez que vous êtes Brutus . . . et qu'il ne faut point parler au dieu Mars, comme si vous disiez: Ah! bonne Vierge, faites-moi gagner un lot ce cent francs à la loterie."

[14] Moland, XXXIII, 202.

[15] It has been said that Mlle Bernard's Brutus was more successful when it first appeared than was Voltaire's. It is true that her tragedy was acted twenty-one times; his, fifteen; but the number of persons that paid admission to hers was 9,191; to his, 12,448; and Voltaire's share in the receipts was 1980 fr., 7 s., more than half again as much as Mlle Bernard's.

[16] For an account of tumultuous performances at this time cf. Moland, II, 305-6. La Harpe's statement that during the Terror it was considered counter-revolutionary is hard to believe. Cf. also K. N. McKee, MLN, LVI (1941), 100-6.

[17] Moland, II, 309. The Mercure for August, 1731, states that both Brutus and Bolus had just been played in a school attached to the University of Caen.

[18] Moland, XXXIII, 221.

[19] Monod-Cassidy, op. cit., p. 142.

but président Hénault [20] called it "une des pièces les plus raisonnables qu'il y ait au théâtre, c'est la mieux écrite de Voltaire et le cinquième acte me paraît très touchant." Condorcet claimed that it combined the force of Corneille with the elegance of Racine, and that the last act is a "chef-d'œuvre de pathétique." [21] La Harpe [22] admired especially the first and fifth acts, the rôle of Brutus, which he called a "modèle parfaict," and the style. He considered it the most "fortement écrit" of Voltaire's plays. But he condemned the rôle of Tullie, who appears too late and is merely a tool in the hands of Arons, and he held that the action does not progress from the third act to the fourth, and that in these acts the only scenes that interest are those in which Brutus appears. Lion adds that there are two actions in the tragedy, one centered around Titus, the other around Brutus, and that the resulting confusion was at first more serious, as Brutus did not then appear in the second act.

These criticisms seem to me to be justified. They may explain, along with the essential difficulty of winning sympathy for the two leading characters, why *Brutus* won no such success as *Œdipe* and *Zaïre*. The play shows, however, progress both in style and in structure over Voltaire's earlier tragedies, a fact that cannot be attributed to his acquaintance with English drama, but rather to his continued study of French tragedy. [23]

The next tragedy that Voltaire brought out after his return from England was ERIPHYLE, [24] sometimes regarded as a superficial imitation of *Hamlet*, though it owes much more to other sources. Whether he began with *Hamlet* and then looked for a Greek legend that resembled it, or whether he began with the legend and modified it under the influence of *Hamlet* cannot be determined.

A connection with the stories of Œdipus and Orestes was suggested in Boissy's *Triomphe de l'ignorance,* played on March 20, 1732. [25] Dr. A. H. Krappe [26] pointed out Voltaire's debt to the Greek legend related in the

---

[20] Quoted by Lion, *op. cit.*, p. 50.
[21] Moland, I, 203. Cf. also Grimm's praise, *Cor.*, V, 256-7.
[22] *Cours de littérature*, XI, 82-123.
[23] Moland notes passages in Act I influenced by *Cinna*, II, 1 and *Bajazet*, I, 1.
[24] First published in 1779 from a manuscript that had been in Le Kain's possession and had been shown to Voltaire in 1777 by Decroix (Moland, II, 456). Moland gave variants from this version, but he preferred to reproduce a manuscript "de Longchamp," looked upon by Decroix as the authentic text. It may, indeed, represent the final form that Voltaire gave to the play, but the Le Kain manuscript is nearer the version that was acted, for it contains the rôle of the high priest, which was suppressed after performances had ceased (Moland, XXXIII, 274), and passages in it correspond more closely than those of the other version to citations from the play in a letter that Voltaire wrote on May 8, 1732 (Moland, XXXIII, 261-3). An Italian translation appeared at Modena in 1784. For a study of the play cf. Lion, *op. cit.*, pp. 64-70.
[25] Cf. Antony Constans, *PMLA*, XXXVIII (1923), 859-68.
[26] *RR*, XVIII, 142-8.

Library of Apollodorus. The same tale is found in Hyginus, Fable LXXIII. According to these accounts, Amphiarius was persuaded by his wife, Eriphyle, to take part in the Theban war. He left an order that his sons, when old enough, should kill their mother. One of them, Alcmeon, obeyed and lost his mind in consequence. From this tale Voltaire undoubtedly derived three important names, the father's death, and the murder of the mother by her son. The mother's crime, her complicity in her lover's murder of her husband, may come either from the Electra story, or from *Hamlet,* but the son's disappearance and the effort of the lover to kill him make the play closer to the former, especially to the form of it found in Longepierre's *Electre,* where the mother is unintentionally slain by the son and a correct report of the killing is made by a person who sees the deed only in imagination. Eriphyle's account of her feeling for the prince—maternal instinct mistaken for sexual love—resembles closely Jocasta's statement about her attitude towards her son in Voltaire's own *Œdipe.*[27]

Voltaire may have thought that he was making an innovation by portraying violent passions in the English manner, but the text of the play indicates nothing of the sort. In *Eriphyle* there is only danger of incest,

[27] The high priest declares that the war in which Argos has been engaged has ended in the defeat of two kings by Alcméon, a youth of unknown origin, brought up as the son of old Théandre. As an oracle has declared that Queen Eriphyle, widow of Amphiaraüs, must select a husband on the day when two kings are defeated, it has been decided that the day has come. Gossip has it that Eriphyle has had a hand in the king's murder. She complains of a ghost, armed with a sword, who has haunted her, and admits that she did not intervene when Hermogide, whom she had loved before her marriage, killed her husband. Pursued by remorse, she now feels only hatred for Hermogide and relies upon Alcméon for help against him. This young man, who admits to Théandre that he loves the queen, promises to protect her. Hermogide insists that he should himself be chosen as the queen's mate, but Eriphyle declares that her son, though supposed to be dead, has been brought up in the temple and must succeed his father. The high priest must produce him in spite of a prediction that he will kill his mother. Thereupon Hermogide asserts that he killed the child in order to save his mother. He leads his followers out in order to start an insurrection. Alcméon asks permission to attack him. Eriphyle promises to marry him if he will avenge her. Théandre reports that the high priest has drawn a sword from the king's tomb and that Furies have appeared upon the altar. Alcméon repels Hermogide's attack and refuses to believe a report of the queen's guilt. Eriphyle brings Alcméon the crown and offers her hand in marriage, but the temple door opens, the ghost of Amphiaraüs appears in a threatening attitude, and Alcméon is ordered to avenge him by killing his mother on his tomb. Alcméon admits that he is the son of Phaon, a slave, but the queen remembers that she entrusted her child to this slave and tells Alcméon that she is his mother. The high priest gives Alcméon the sword that Hermogide had left in the boy's bosom when he thought he had killed him. When Hermogide invades the temple with his troops, Alcméon kills him with this sword on his father's tomb. Bewildered by the ghost, he also gives his mother a fatal wound. After pardoning her son and admitting that the gods are just, she dies on the stage. Alcméon seeks to commit suicide, but is prevented from doing so. In the later version the high priest does not appear, and in Act IV the sword is not brought on the stage. Hermogide admits at the beginning that he has killed Amphiaraüs and his children. In Act V Eriphyle goes to the tomb in order to save Alcméon from treachery on the part of Hermogide, who dies on the stage after crying to Alcméon, " Je suis vengé: tu viens d'assassiner ta mère."

whereas in his own *Œdipe,* as in those of Corneille and Sophocles, there had been actual incest, while a son's murder of his mother had been reported in the *Electre* of Longepierre and in that of Crébillon.   There remains the ghost.   Du Ryer had shown one in *Saül* some ninety years before, but early in the eighteenth century Nadal had kept the same ghost behind the scenes.   The showing of the ghost would consequently seem to be borrowed from Shakespeare, though the apparition is far less impressive than in *Hamlet,* and the request for vengeance made by a ghost we do not see had been employed in Voltaire's *Œdipe.*

Voltaire admitted that the queen is too constantly lugubrious.   La Harpe reproached him for her lack of decision.   Her son is a typical young hero; Hermogide, a typical villain.   None of the characters is given a moral conflict of any consequence.   The changes of fortune in Act III are crowded together in such a way as to be rendered ineffective.   As Voltaire himself put it: [28]

On assemblait le peuple, au troisième acte; on déclarait roi le fils d'Eriphyle; Hermogide donnait sur-le-champ un nouveau tour aux affaires en disant qu'il avait tué cet enfant.   La nomination d'Alcméon faisait, à l'instant, un nouveau coup de théâtre.   Théandre arrivait dans la minute, et faisait tout suspendre, en disant que les Dieux faisaient le diable à quatre.   Tant d'éclairs coup sur coup éblouissaient . . . et, quand l'ombre arrivait après tant de vacarme, ce n'était qu'un coup de massue sur Alcméon et Eriphyle.

Nor did the cries of Eriphyle from behind the scenes, where she was being murdered by her son, soften the impression.   Voltaire realized too late that he was startling the spectators rather than moving them.

Apart from the showing of the ghost, the tragedy is not more spectacular than *Œdipe,* for in both tragedies a temple is represented, people gather before it, and at the proper moment we see its interior.   The ideas expressed are less daring than those of the earlier tragedy.   They go no farther than defense of the humble and criticism of the court and of aristocratic notions, by no means new themes on the French stage:

> Les mortels sont égaux: ce n'est point la naissance,
> C'est la seule vertu qui fait leur différence.
> C'est elle qui met l'homme au rang des demi-dieux;
> Et qui sert son pays n'a pas besoin d'ayeux.[29]

As for courtiers,

> Si l'on croit de leurs yeux le regard pénétrant,
> Tout ministre est un traître, et tout prince un tyran: . . .

---

[28] Moland, XXXIII, 235.
[29] II, 1.   The last line reappears, almost word for word, in *Mérope,* I, 3.   For similar statements cf. the subject index of my *History, s. v.* democracy.

> Et sitôt qu'un grand roi penche vers son déclin,
> Ou son fils, ou sa femme, ont hâté son destin.[30]

In his later version Voltaire put into the mouth of his villain an attack upon priests that is much less impressive than what Jocasta had said about them and may be discounted as spoken by a man with whom we are not in sympathy:

> Mais la voix de ces dieux, ou plutôt de nos prêtres,
> M'a dépouillé vingt ans du rang de mes ancêtres.
> Il fallait succomber aux superstitions
> Qui sont bien plus que nous les rois des nations. (I, 1)

Voltaire's correspondence supplies a good deal of information about his play. On June 30, 1731, he speaks of having "fait *César* et *Eriphyle,* et achevé *Charles XII,* en trois mois." On Sept. 3 he declares that he is seriously occupied with correcting *Eriphyle,* which the actors are eager to produce, and that he is not satisfied with Androgide, as he first called Hermogide. He fears that the queen will appear to have been the mistress of this rascal. On Sept. 5 he is displeased with Théandre's lines in Acts III and IV. He also finds Act V unsatisfactory. In October he quotes twenty-two lines from the tragedy and states that he has improved Act I, altered Act II greatly, and worked hard over Act V, but is not yet satisfied. In November he writes that his tragedy will be acted after La Grange-Chancel's *Erigone.* On Feb. 3, 1732, he says that he has reworked his tragedy and has had it acted at the home of Mme de Fontaine-Martel, where tears were shed over it, but he still fears that it will fail on account of the fifth act. Nor can Dufresne and Sarrazin save it, for he has written it for himself, not for them.[31]

Eriphyle was acted at the Comédie Française on March 7, 1732. Alcméon was played by Dufresne; Hermogide, by Sarrazin, who had had the title-rôle in *Brutus*; Eriphyle, by la Balicourt; her confidant, by la Jouvenot.[32] Voltaire thought that the "assez belle assemblée" was not dissatisfied, though the fifth act received criticism.[33] The tragedy was played seven more times before Easter. Voltaire shared the receipts in all of these productions, the last of which was on March 26. Then he renounced further profit[34] and hoped that this fact and the protection of the comte de Clermont would induce the actors to give the tragedy after Easter. On

---

[30] IV, 1. Note the incorrect rime of the first two lines. La Harpe asserted that these verses attracted attention because in 1732 there was still talk about the mysterious deaths of two of Louis XIV's grandsons and of Charles II of Spain.
[31] Moland, XXXIII, 214-46.
[32] The *Registres* show that Legrand de Belleville, the younger La Thorillière, Montmény, and Bercy also played.
[33] Admission was paid by 1183 persons.
[34] The amount he received from the eight performances was 1098 fr., 7 s.

April 14 he promised Thieriot, in English, that he would send him "the new *Eriphyle,* with a compliment in rhyme,[35] which Dufresne will recite at the ouverture of the French theatre." He subsequently declared that three of his acts had been revised.

Thanks to these precautions, the tragedy reappeared on April 24, 26, 30, and on May 3, but, except on the first of these days, the audiences were much smaller than they had been before Easter. Voltaire began to prepare it for publication with a dedicatory epistle to the comte de Clermont, but he continued to alter his text, eliminating the high priest and, though keeping the ghost, seeking to substitute " le vrai au merveilleux." He was still at work on it in May, 1733. On the 15th he referred to it as " vêtue à la grecque, corrigée avec soin." Choruses had been added and a dedication to the abbé Franchini. But he never saw the play in print except in so far as lines from it were inserted into *la Mort de César, Mahomet,* and *Mérope,* and much of the plot reappeared in *Sémiramis,* where a ghost is seen and a queen is in love with her son. Except to make use of it in composing these tragedies, he lost interest in it so completely that, according to Decroix,[36] he possessed no manuscript of the play in 1777.

On March 11, 1732, the abbé Le Blanc [37] wrote that he had attended a performance, that the play had been badly received by the public, and that, though there were certain fine lines and passages, it was the worst tragedy he had ever seen. He objected to the ghost, suited only to an opera or a new *Festin de Pierre,* and considered the work a mixture of *Œdipe* and of Crébillon's *Sémiramis* and *Electre.* He attributed to Voltaire himself only the attacks on powerful persons and on superstition. Though in this same month an article in the *Mercure* praised the diction of the tragedy and the thoughts expressed in it, Boissy's contemporary *Triomphe de l'ignorance* took much the same attitude as Le Blanc in regard to Voltaire's borrowing and his introduction of the ghost, but added other criticisms in regard to the apparent youthfulness of Eriphyle, her willingness to pardon her son, the high priest's prediction of the dénouement, and the use of the tomb for a duel.[38]

When the play was published after Voltaire's death, it was analyzed in

---

[35] This is the *Discours* published with the play. He praises the judgment of the audience, compliments Destouches on his *Glorieux,* attributes the success of Pradon's *Régulus* to the acting of Baron, and that of a rôle in *Inès de Castro* to Adrienne Le Couvreur.

[36] Moland, II, 456.

[37] Monod-Cassidy, *op. cit.,* pp. 152-3.

[38] Cf. Moland, II, 456, Grannis, *op. cit.,* pp. 271-2, and especially Constans, *loc. cit.* In Boissy's farce Eriphyle explains her magnanimity as follows:

Je lui pardonne, hélas, de s'être ainsi mépris:
Dans la nuit, on sait trop que tous les chats sont gris.

l'Année littéraire.[39]   The writer protested, like Le Blanc and Boissy, against the introduction of the ghost and criticized unfavorably the structure of the tragedy, most of the characters, and the style.   La Harpe[40] considered the sentiments, situations, and characters only sketched.   He held that the heroine's remorse seems due to weakness, that she is not sufficiently concerned about the fate of her son, and that she lacks the strength and pomp of Semiramis.   He notes that about eighty verses were transferred by Voltaire to other tragedies.

In these lie the only value of the play, except that it has some historical importance as the first French tragedy to show the influence of *Hamlet* and as a forerunner of Voltaire's *Sémiramis*.   Except in certain moments when pride of authorship overcame his better judgment, Voltaire was never pleased with his own production.   He could not have expected his critics to look upon it more favorably than he did himself.

A third tragedy, LA MORT DE CÉSAR,[41] owes more to Shakespeare than does any other play by Voltaire.   It was outlined in England as early as 1726, but it did not near completion until 1731.   On June 30 of that year Voltaire wrote, " j'ai fait toute la tragédie de *César* depuis qu'*Eriphyle* est dans son cadre."   The new tragedy was acted at the Hôtel de Sassenage in 1733 ; at the collège d'Harcourt on Aug. 11, 1735 ; and, after the brilliant reception given *Mérope,* at the Comédie Française on Aug. 29, 1743.[42]

Although the subject had been dramatized in Muret's Latin play, in Grévin's imitation of it, and in tragedies by Georges de Scudéry and Mlle Barbier,[43] it was Shakespeare's *Julius Caesar* rather than these French authors that Voltaire imitated.   According to Lamare's *avertissement* of the 1736 edition, Voltaire began by translating from Shakespeare the scene containing Antony's speech over Caesar's body.   He was asked to translate the whole play, but he felt that he could not reproduce what he considered evidence of Shakespeare's lack of taste and disregard of the unities.   However, he determined to write a " *Jules César* qui, sans ressembler à celui de Shakespeare, fût pourtant tout entier dans le goût anglais." that is, I suppose, without love and with a more daring use of spectacle than

[39] 1779 (6), pp. 145-73.
[40] *Op. cit.*, XII, 64-71.
[41] An unauthorized edition appeared in 1735, with Amsterdam given as the place of publication.   The first authorized edition is that of Amsterdam, Desbordes, 1736. For other editions cf. Bengesco and Moland.   For five Italian translations, cf. Ferrari, *op. cit.*, pp. 173-8.   A Spanish translation was published in 1791; cf. Ada M. Coe, *Catálogo bibliográfico*, Baltimore, Johns Hopkins Press, 1935, p. 160.   For a study of *la Mort de César* cf. Lion, *op. cit.*, pp. 53-64.   For its relation to Shakespeare cf. M.-M. H. Barr, *A Bibliography of Voltaire's Writings*, New York, 1929, pp. 91-2.
[42] Cf. Beuchot's *avertissement* (Moland, III, 305) and Moland, XXXIII, 214.
[43] For Voltaire's contemptuous and inaccurate reference to her play cf. my *Sunset*, p. 78.   Lion, *op. cit.*, p. 61, refers to his statement without correcting it.

could be found in other French plays of the time. Voltaire himself, in
the preface of the 1736 edition, refers rather to "cet amour dominant de
la liberté, et ces hardiesses que les auteurs français ont rarement," but love
of liberty is no stronger than in his own *Brutus* or in that of Mlle Bernard,
nor is there greater "hardiesse," except in the display of the "robe
sanglante," than there is in Crébillon's *Atrée* and *Rhadamiste*.

Voltaire wished to incorporate in a play about Caesar's death the speech
he had translated, but he did not attempt to paint, as Shakespeare had
done, a large historical picture, or to show the tragic futility of patriotic
murder by following to the end the fortunes of the conspirators. Instead,
he turned to Suetonius and to Plutarch's *Caesar, Antony,* and *Brutus,* to
find there what Shakespeare had not utilized: Caesar's plan of invading
Asia, the character of Dolabella, Caesar's capture and pardon of Brutus,
and the report that the latter was his son by Servilia. He then sought
to make of his play a psychological tragedy built around Brutus, who is
called upon to sacrifice either his father or his country.

He seems originally to have ended the play with the unhistorical assassination of Brutus, for he wrote on October 24, 1735, that he had suppressed
this deed before the performance at the collège d'Harcourt.[44] He did not
restore it when the play was published, nor was he willing to have Brutus
rejoice in public over his father's murder. It is consequently Cassius,
instead of Brutus, who harangues the Romans in a speech suggested by
Shakespeare. Though there are eight scenes in the last act, Brutus disappears after the fourth; Caesar, after the fifth. The audience sees the
Roman people won over by Antony and hears him say, " Succédons à Cesar
en courant le venger," but whether he becomes a dictator, or fails, whether
Brutus and Cassius live or die, whether the republic is restored or the
empire replaces it are questions answered by history, not by Voltaire.[45]

[44] Moland, XXXIII, 544.

[45] Caesar tells Antony that he is planning an expedition against the Parthians and
that, as an oracle has predicted that only a king can conquer them, he wishes to be
crowned. He asks Antony to look after his children: Octave, whom he has adopted,
and Brutus, his son by a secret marriage to Servilie, daughter of Cato. He shows
him a note left by Brutus's mother, and hopes that, when his son learns from it who
his father is, he will give up his republican notions. Antony doubts that he will
do so, for Brutus is a Stoic. Dolabella, who supports Caesar, introduces several
senators: Brutus, Cassius, Cinna, Décime, and Casca. Caesar tells them about his
plan, indicates what provinces they and their friends shall rule in his absence, and
hints that he would like to be a king. They are unfavorable to the idea. Caesar
dismisses all except Brutus, who refuses to support him if he persists in his effort
to be crowned. Antony would have Caesar show severity in regard to his opponents,
but Caesar himself prefers to be lenient. In Act II Brutus finds at the base of
Pompey's statue notes calling on him to liberate Rome. Cimber tells of Antony's
placing a crown on Caesar's head and of the dictator's winning popular approval by
refusing it. It is thought that the senate may vote to make him king. Cassius
proposes suicide; Brutus, murder. They and their associates swear to get rid of
the tyrant. When Caesar finds Brutus alone, he shows him his mother's letter and

In composing his tragedy, Voltaire may have been influenced by Grévin to the extent of introducing Antony into his first act and of having him argue for force, while Caesar insists on milder measures, but the resemblance is not striking enough to make it certain that he imitated this rhetorical and undramatic tragedy of the sixteenth century.[46] I find no evidence that Voltaire used Scudéry or Mlle Barbier. The elimination of love and of women may be due to the fact that he had in mind a school performance when he wrote the tragedy, an idea realized by the production of the play at Harcourt. This intention may also explain why Voltaire wrote the tragedy in three acts instead of five and allowed himself a large cast, one, with its " Romains " and " licteurs," ample enough to provide rôles for the whole student body.

Cascar is presented as a ruler and a father. He is ambitious to be crowned king and to avenge upon the Parthians the defeat of Crassus. He is not purely selfish, for he feels that the old virtues on which the republic was based have disappeared and that new conditions call for a new form of government:

> Rome demande un maître . . .
> Nos mœurs changent, Brutus, il faut changer nos lois.
> La liberté n'est plus que le droit de se nuire:
> Rome, qui détruit tout, semble enfin se détruire. . . .
> Ce colosse effrayant, dont le monde est foulé,
> En pressant l'univers, est lui-même ébranlé.
> Il penche vers sa chute, et contre la tempête
> Il demande mon bras pour soutenir sa tête. (III, 4)

He is as brave and as free from superstition as in Shakespeare and is less easily influenced by others. He differs with Antony in regard to the

embraces him, but Brutus urges him to renounce his ambition, for he would save both his father and Rome. In Act III Brutus reveals to the conspirators the fact that he is Caesar's son, asks their advice, and is told that he must keep his promise. This Brutus decides to do, but he first renews his plea, even kneeling to Caesar and warning him that it is a matter of life or death. Caesar is unmoved. When Brutus has gone, Dolabella urges Caesar not to appear before the senate, for there have been terrible omens, but Caesar goes. Soon cries are heard, and Cassius, a dagger in his hand, announces that Caesar has been murdered. He addresses the Romans, who approve of the deed. Then Antony enters in tears, mounts the tribune, speaks of Caesar's virtues and his will. The back-stage opens to show Caesar's body, covered with a " robe sanglante." Antony kneels beside the corpse and describes the murder. The Romans, completely won over, demand revenge. Antony calls on them to burn the homes of the conspirators and suggests to Dolabella that they may, in avenging Caesar, succeed him.

[46] Cf. G.-A.-O. Collischonn, *Jacques Grévin's Tragödie " Caesar " in ihrem Verhältniss zu Muret, Voltaire und Shakespere*, Marburg, 1886. Lucien Pinvert (*Jacques Grévin*, Paris, Fontemoing, 1898, pp. 156-64) accepts Collischonn's conclusions that Voltaire used Grévin extensively, but, if one takes into consideration what Voltaire owed to Plutarch and Shakespeare and the facts that in Grévin's tragedy Brutus is not Caesar's son and that a large part of Acts III and IV is assigned to Calpurnia, one can find little in Voltaire's plot that he could have owed to Grévin, while the latter's ponderous style could certainly not have attracted him.

measures to be taken, is stern to the senators when they oppose him, and turns a deaf ear to his son in spite of his strong paternal feeling.

Brutus is said to be a Stoic and to have the ideas of Cato. He never wavers in his political views. He delays the plot against Caesar only so long as he thinks there is hope of persuading him to renounce his plan. Cassius is equally determined and gloats over Caesar, when he is dead, as Brutus does not do. In his speech he gives the Romans a warning against Antony that has no equivalent in the passage in Shakespeare's tragedy that he imitates. The other conspirators are not clearly differentiated except that Cimber gives the account (II, 4) of Antony's offering Caesar a crown that Shakespeare had assigned to Casca. Antony has the same devotion to Caesar that Shakespeare gives him, but he is much less subtle in the funeral oration (III, 8), even in verses directly inspired by the English play:

> Oui, je l'aimais, Romains;
> Oui, j'aurais de mes jours prolongé ses destins.
> Hélas! vous avez tous pensé comme moi-même;
> Et lorsque de son front ôtant le diadème,
> Ce héros à vos lois s'immolait aujourd'hui,
> Qui de vous, en effet, n'eût expiré pour lui?
> Hélas! je ne viens point célébrer sa mémoire;
> La voix du monde entier parle assez de sa gloire; . . .
> Contre ses meurtriers je n'ai rien à vous dire;
> C'est à servir l'état que leur grand cœur aspire.
> De votre dictateur ils ont percé le flanc:
> Comblés de ses bienfaits, ils sont teints de son sang.
> Pour forcer des Romains à ce coup détestable,
> Sans doute il fallait bien que César fût coupable;
> Je le crois. Mais enfin César a-t-il jamais
> De son pouvoir sur vous appesanti le faix?
> A-t-il gardé pour lui le fruit de ses conquêtes?
> Des dépouilles du monde il couronnait vos têtes. . . .
> Là, Cimber l'a frappé; là, sur le grand César
> Cassius et Décime enfonçaient leur poignard.
> Là, Brutus éperdu, Brutus l'âme égarée,
> A souillé dans ses flancs sa main dénaturée.
> César le regardant d'un œil tranquille et doux, . . .
> " O mon fils! " disait-il.
>
> Un Romain: O monstre que les dieux
> Devaient exterminer avant ce coup affreux!
> Autres Romains: Dieux! son sang coule encore.
> Antoine: Il demande vengeance,
> Il l'attend de vos mains et de votre vaillance.
> Entendez-vous sa voix? Réveillez-vous, Romains.

It is only this scene and its predecessor that violate the unity of action, for in Act I we learn of Caesar's relationship to Brutus and of the senators' opposition to his ambitious plan; in Act II the conspiracy is formed, and Brutus learns that he is Caesar's son; and in Act III Brutus seeks in vain to save his father, joins his fellows, and, behind the scenes, assists in the murder. After this it was necessary only to announce Caesar's death, or to show, as Shakespeare does, how it was avenged. Voltaire went half way and stopped, violating by this method the unity of his action. On the other hand, he keeps the unity of the time, which is limited to a few hours, and of the place, which is confined to the Capitoline hill.[47]

There is some appeal to the eye. We are shown the portico of the temple on the Capitoline with the statues of Pompey, Cato, and Scipio. Antony addresses the people from a tribune. In III, 8, "Le fond du théâtre s'ouvre; des licteurs apportent le corps de César couvert d'une robe sanglante; Antoine descend de la tribune et se jette à genoux auprès du corps."

The play is forcefully written, but it suffers from the inevitable comparison with Shakespeare's tragedy, or from comparison with Voltaire's *Mahomet,* in which a son also kills his father, but in which the author gave himself space enough to interest us in his characters. Voltaire spoke of it modestly in 1735 as "toute propre pour un collège," though he claimed that it was the tragedy in which he had "le plus travaillé la versification." [48]

After protesting against the unauthorized version and attacking Desfontaines for referring to it as if it were a genuine text, Voltaire published the play with a preface of his own, an *avertissement* by his friend, the abbé de Lamare, and the translation of a letter written by Algarotti in praise of the tragedy. When it was acted in 1743, Sarrazin played Caesar; Grandval, Brutus; Legrand, Antony; Paulin, Cassius.[49] It was given only eight times in that year, seven from Aug. 29 to Sept. 15 and on Nov. 21. Le Kain revived it in 1763, when it was acted five times.[50] The total number of performances at the Comédie Française was only forty-six, although it was acted there as recently as 1893. Its chief success was during the Revolution, when Gohier substituted a new ending, in which Antony and Dolabella are arrested and Brutus ends the play with a speech before the statue of Liberty.

[47] Edgar Allan Poe failed to understand that the action is located on the hill, not within the Capitol. He consequently held that Voltaire had no clear idea of where his action was taking place when he made Cassius say (II, 4), "courons au Capitole." Poe's error was pointed out by Percy G. Adams in *MLN,* LVII (1942), 273-5.
[48] Moland, XXXIII, 495; cf. p. 526, "elle n'est point faite pour le public."
[49] The troupe paid for fourteen "habits à la Romaine," ten helmets, thirteen wigs, and hired ten supernumeraries. Voltaire's share in the receipts was 382 fr.
[50] Thieriot indicates that Brizard and Le Kain distinguished themselves, probably as Caesar and Brutus, respectively, but that he was not pleased with Dubois, who played Antony; cf. *RHL,* XV (1908), 720.

La Harpe [51] admired the play greatly, though he thought it should have ended with Caesar's death. He noted the value of Antony's rôle as contrasting with Caesar's and typifying the Romans' turning from liberty to a dictatorship. He praised the simplicity of the subject, the well-knit intrigue, the scene of the conspiracy, the scene in which Brutus tells the other conspirators that he is Caesar's son, the two scenes between Caesar and Brutus, Cimber's *récit,* and the style of the play, which he considers " presque toujours sublime."

Lion praises the presentation of Caesar, his two interviews with Brutus, and the scene of the conspiracy. He finds that the play does not lack striking verses. But he criticizes severely the fact that Brutus leaves the decision of his problem to the other conspirators, his early disappearance from the third act, and the scenes of the orations, " un pur hors-d'œuvre." Voltaire, indeed, sought at the same time to compose a psychological tragedy in the French classical manner and to imitate the speeches that Shakespeare had put into the mouths of Antony and Brutus. His tragedy suffered the consequences of his attempt to graft Shakespeare upon Racine. In the history of Anglo-French literary relations it has this importance, that it is the first French play that would not have been written if Shakespeare had not lived. Whether it is the only tragedy by Voltaire of which this can be said depends on what debt he owed Shakespeare in the composition of his next tragedy.

It was shortly after the last performance of *Eriphyle* that Voltaire composed the most successful of his plays, ZAÏRE.[52] On May 29, 1732, he wrote that he had begun it. On June 25 he asserted that he had completed it in twenty-two days, a statement that he subsequently repeated, affirming that he made the plan in one day and, " l'imagination, échauffée par l'intérêt qui régnait dans ce plan, acheva la pièce en vingt-deux jours." [53] He declared that he took from history only " l'époque de la guerre de saint Louis: tout le reste est entièrement d'invention." [54] But he owed more to history than one would infer from this statement, in addition to what he owed to other dramatists.[55]

[51] *Op. cit.,* XI, 264-300.

[52] Rouen, Jore père et fils, et se vend à Paris, chez J.-B. Bauche, 1733, 8°. Dedicated to " M. Falkener, marchand anglais." For other editions cf. Bengesco, Moland, and Fontaine, Léger, Fréjafon et Couyba, *Zaïre tragédie de Voltaire,* Paris, Leroux, 1889. For eight Italian translations, one of which had eight editions, cf. Ferrari, *op. cit.* For Spanish translations cf. Ada M. Coe, *op. cit.,* p. 99. A German translation was published in 1740. A translation by Aaron Hill, with Mrs. Cibber as " Zara," was played in London in 1736. Lessing's criticism of the play is found in his *Hamburgische Dramaturgie.* Cf. also Lion, *op. cit.,* pp. 71-87.

[53] Moland, XXXIII, 270, 273, 283.

[54] Moland, XXXIII, 283.

[55] After Saladin's victories and death, Noradin, a Tartar, is supposed to have conquered Palestine and captured at Caesarea Lusignan, heir to the throne of Jeru-

He derived his background from Palestinian and French history, the
capture of Jerusalem by crusaders under French leadership, references
to Saladin, to Bovines, to Louis's victory over the English, to the crusade
that took him to Egypt, to various Frenchmen of distinction, but he
lengthened to twenty years Lusignan's brief captivity, invented Orosmane's
love of Zaïre, Nérestan's effort to ransom his comrades, Zaïre's reunion
with her father and brother, the quandary in which she finds herself, the
sultan's jealousy, his murder of Zaïre, and his suicide. Voltaire admitted

salem, his son, his daughter, and many French knights. Noradin has died and been
succeeded by his son, Orosmane, Lusignan has now been in prison for twenty years,
and his children have been enslaved and kept from knowing who their father is.
Three years before the play begins, Lusignan's son, Nérestan, has been allowed to go
to France on parole in the hope of ransoming the captives. After serving under
Saint Louis in his war with the English, he has returned to Jerusalem. Meanwhile
his sister, Zaïre, brought up as a Mohammedan, has fallen in love with Orosmane and
he with her. Their marriage is about to take place. Orosmane allows her unusual
freedom and promises that she will be his only wife. Nérestan brings enough money
to free Zaïre, her attendant, Fatime, and ten knights, but, as there is not enough
to pay for his own ransom, he proposes to return to captivity. Orosmane outdoes
him in generosity by bidding him keep his money, free a hundred knights, and depart
with them, but the sultan refuses to surrender Zaïre and Lusignan. In the interview
Orosmane notes that Nérestan looks at Zaïre, but he denies that he is jealous and
allows his fiancée to see the Christian. She greets Nérestan, with whom she has
passed her childhood, and Châtillon, a knight who will not accept freedom unless
Lusignan is liberated. The old man is allowed, at Zaïre's request, to come out of
prison and converse with her, with Nérestan, and with Châtillon. He identifies the
girl as his daughter, thanks to her mother's jeweled cross she wears; Nérestan as
his son because of a scar on his chest. Shocked to find that Zaïre is a Mohammedan,
he pleads with her until she promises to become a Christian, but he makes her agree
to keep their secret when she is led away by Orosmane's confidant, Corasmin. Subsequently Nérestan brings word that Lusignan is dying, that he longs for Zaïre's
conversion, and that a priest will come to baptize her. When Zaïre admits that she
loves Orosmane and is about to marry him, Nérestan opposes her plan and gets her
to promise to postpone her marriage until she has seen the priest. Zaïre, torn
between her love of the sultan and her loyalty to her father, begs Orosmane to delay
the ceremony and leaves in order to escape his anger. Orosmane consults Corasmin
and, though his confidant merely reports that Nérestan wept in Zaïre's presence,
decides to lock the doors of the seraglio. Zaïre wishes to tell Orosmane her secret,
but Fatime warns her that she may ruin Nérestan. Orosmane threatens to marry
someone else, then, convinced by Zaïre that she loves him, he agrees to postpone
their marriage for a day. At this point a letter addressed to Zaïre and found in
Nérestan's possession is brought to the sultan. It asks for an interview to which
Zaïre can come by a secret passage. Orosmane orders Corasmin to stab Zaïre, then
proposes to see her, then accepts his confidant's suggestion that she be allowed to
read the letter and her reaction observed. When Corasmin has left, Orosmane again
converses with Zaïre, but he interprets her confession of love as proof of her guilt.
He still hopes, however, that, though Nérestan loves her, she does not love him.
When the note is shown to Zaïre, she bids Fatime bring Nérestan to her. The slave
reports to Orosmane her reply. Corasmin is ordered to arrest Nérestan. When
Zaïre enters in the darkness and asks if the man she sees is Nérestan, Orosmane,
convinced that she is faithless, orders her to fall at his feet and, just behind the
scene, stabs her. When he shows her corpse to Nérestan, the latter exclaims, "Ah,
ma sœur!" and explains that his purpose in coming was to bring Zaïre news of
their father's death and to make sure of her conversion. Fatime reproaches Orosmane and tells him that Zaïre's love for him made her hesitate to become a Christian.
Overcome with remorse, Orosmane releases Nérestan and the other Christian captives,
orders that they be given money and taken to Joppa, swears that he adored Zaïre,
and kills himself.

Voltaire wrote a long analysis of the play, published in the *Mercure* of August,
1732, and reproduced in Moland, XXXIII, 282-9.

in his dedication that it was thanks to English usage that he had introduced into his tragedy the names of French kings and of old French families. It has been generally believed that he was referring to the series of plays that Shakespeare derived from English history. He says nothing about *Othello*.

The resemblance between the latter and *Zaïre* was soon noticed in England. In the prologue of Aaron Hill's *Zara,* published in 1735, it is said of Voltaire that

> From rack'd *Othello*'s Rage he rais'd his Style,
> And snatch'd the Brand, that lights this Tragic Pile.

In 1738 the abbé Le Blanc, while residing in England, went into greater detail: [56]

> Cette Piece pour le fonds n'est autre chose que celle de Shakespear dont je vous parle. *Orosmane* est *Othello* la vertueuse *Zaïre* est la sage *Desdemona* . . . Orosmane plus poli, mais non moins cruel se contente de poignarder *Zaïre*. Le Discours d'*Orosmane* après qu'il s'est tué lui même est presque tout imité de celui d'*Othello* qui est dans le même cas.

Hill and Le Blanc have been followed by many writers, notably by T. R. Lounsbury,[57] who seemed to think that Voltaire had written no play in which jealousy is an important motive before he came to England and failed to take into consideration what he may have owed to Racine. His arguments were effectively answered by E. J. Dubedout,[58] who believed that *Othello* had no influence whatsoever upon *Zaïre*. Now Voltaire did not need to imitate Shakespeare in order to devise a plot in which a man is led by jealousy to murder a woman he loves, for this theme had been dramatized in his own *Hérode et Mariamne* before he visited England. Nor is there any genuine resemblance between Iago and Corasmin, who strengthens his master's jealousy, but does not inspire it. To Lounsbury's contention that the letter was suggested by the handkerchief in *Othello,* Dubedout replied that it is much more reasonable to compare it with the letter in *Bajazet*. Nor is there anything in Shakespeare's tragedy that can account for the religious issue in *Zaïre,* the evocation of the crusades, the rôles of Lusignan and Nérestan. There are, moreover, French plays that must be taken into consideration before one can arrive at any conclusion.

Bajazet has been mentioned. There is also the rôle of Hermione in

---

[56] Monod-Cassidy, *op. cit.,* p. 289.
[57] *Shakespeare and Voltaire,* New York, 1902, pp. 78-9. On p. 80 he suggests that lines in the account of Lusignan's death and Orosmane's " j'étais aimé " were inspired by *King Lear*.
[58] *MP*, III (1906), 1-12.

Andromaque. There are the rôles of Nero and Narcisse in *Britannicus.* Still closer to *Zaïre* is Chateaubrun's *Mahomet Second,* where victorious Mohammedans are in conflict with defeated Christians, the daughter of a Christian prince is loved by her Mohammedan captor, her brother seeks to liberate her, and the monarch who loves her creates the situation that causes her death.[59] In view of these facts it is absurd to look upon *Zaïre* as merely a French adaptation of *Othello.* It is not even sure that Voltaire owed anything to this tragedy, but it is possible that he derived from it some details in his presentation of Zaïre's character and the struggle that takes place in the mind of his hero.

Voltaire's own account of his intention in composing his tragedy is the following: [60]

> La scène sera dans un lieu bien singulier: l'action se passera entre des Turcs et des chrétiens. Je peindrai leurs mœurs autant qu'il me sera possible, et je tâcherai de jeter dans cet ouvrage tout ce que la religion chrétienne semble avoir de plus pathétique et de plus intéressant, et tout ce que l'amour a de plus tendre et de plus cruel.

There had been a number of Turkish plays in France. In some of them, notably in Scudéry's *Illustre Bassa* and in Chateaubrun's tragedy just mentioned, both Turks and Christians had appeared. Moreover, the abbé d'Aubignac in his *Pucelle d'Orléans* and Ferrier in his *Anne de Bretagne* had taken their plots from medieval French history and had mentioned French names of distinction. Voltaire's originality lies in his emphasizing the conflict between adherents of the two religions during the period of the crusades, a subject familiar to readers of Tasso, but one that had not for many years been seen on the French stage. In treating it he revived interest in French history, for his tragedy, though not the first to introduce characters from this source, was the first to do so that made a deep impression upon the public and inspired in this respect a large number of imitators.

In contrasting the customs of Christians and Mohammedans, he stressed the freedom given by the former to women, the spirit of self-sacrifice said to characterize French knights, reverence for the cross, for Jerusalem, and for the water of baptism, while he attributed to Mohammedans the practice

---

[59] The fact that the brother and sister are suspected of being lovers may have been suggested by Giraldi Cinthio's *Hecatommithi,* 8th day, story 6. This was pointed out by A. H. Krappe in *MLR,* XX (1925), 305-9. He greatly exaggerated the importance to Voltaire of Cinthio's tale. His claim that Morf was in 1924 the first modern scholar to indicate striking differences between *Othello* and *Zaïre* is easily contradicted if one reads Fontaine (1889), Lion (1895), or Dubedout (1906). The name of Orosmane had been assigned by Scarron to the hero of his *Prince corsaire.*

[60] Moland, XXXIII, 270.

of polygamy, the insistence upon woman's obedience to man, the secrecy and voluptuousness of the carefully guarded seraglio, slavery, the proselytizing of Christian children, and worship in mosques. In praising the prowess of Christians, he appealed to national pride by references to victories won by Saint Louis and by Philippe Auguste (II, 3) :

> Je le suivis, seigneur, au bord de la Charente,
> Lorsque du fier Anglais la valeur menaçante,
> Cédant à nos efforts trop longtemps captivés,
> Satisfit en tombant aux lis qu'ils ont bravés. . . .
> Quand Philippe à Bovine enchaînait la victoire,
> Je combattais, seigneur, avec Montmorenci,
> Melun, d'Estaing, de Nesle, et ce fameux Couci.

At the same time he makes Zaïre refer (IV, 1) to the power and clemency of Saladin and has Châtillon describe at length the victory of Noradin (II, 1). He gives no evidence that Christians make better soldiers than Mohammedans, while he balances the fanaticism of Nérestan and Lusignan against that of Corasmin. Indeed, religion is, according to Zaïre, merely a matter of early environment (I, 1) :

> Je le vois trop: les soins qu'on prend de notre enfance
> Forment nos sentiments, nos mœurs, notre croyance.
> J'eusse été près du Gange esclave des faux dieux,
> Chrétienne dans Paris, musulmane en ces lieux.
> L'instruction fait tout: et la main de nos pères
> Grave en nos faibles cœurs ces premiers caractères.[61]

Nor does Zaïre believe that Christian training necessarily makes a man better. She says of Orosmane (II, 1) :

> Généreux, bienfaisant, juste, plein de vertus;
> S'il était né chrétien, que serait-il de plus?

It is inability to understand this liberal point of view that leads her family to make demands upon her that bring about her death. *Zaïre* is in this respect a tragedy of fanaticism, a predecessor of *Mahomet* and of many other writings in which Voltaire pleaded for tolerance.

This is not, however, the principal impression made by the work, which is more decidedly a tragedy of love and jealousy than it is a study of manners or a thesis play. The character that has the longest rôle is Orosmane, son of a Tartar, but inheriting traits from his Scythian ancestors.[62] He condemns polygamy as leading to the loss of manly virtues,

---

[61] This passage may well have been inspired by lines in Dryden's *Indian Emperour* that Voltaire copied into his *sottisier;* cf. T. W. Russell, *Voltaire, Dryden & Heroic Tragedy*, New York, Columbia University Press, 1946, p. 94.

[62] It may be on this account that Dufresne, when he played the rôle, wore furs, as shown by the *Registres.* The troupe had to provide also five " habits à la Turque."

centers his affections upon Zaïre, and gives her unusual freedom. He has distinguished himself in war, shows his generosity by granting Nérestan more than he asks for, his political sagacity by his decision in regard to Saint Louis and the Egyptians. The only flaw in his character is his haste in leaping to conclusions when his passions are stirred. In Act I [63] he denies that he is jealous, for "Quiconque est soupçonneux invite à le trahir," but, when Zaïre wishes to postpone their marriage and refers to the Christians, his latent jealousy flares up. It subsides when he is convinced that she loves him: "on m'aime, c'est assez" (IV, 3); but the letter renews his suspicions and inspires the test, though his love is still strong (IV, 7):

> Tu vois mon cœur, tu vois à quel excès je l'aime!
> Ma fureur est plus grande, et j'en tremble moi-même.
> J'ai honte des douleurs où je me suis plongé:
> Mais malheur aux ingrats qui m'auront outragé.

When he waits for her in the dark, he is in a highly emotional state, declares that the tears he sheds are forerunners of blood that will flow (V, 8), and has his dagger ready. Her mention of Nérestan's name is her final condemnation. When he learns her relationship to the man he had supposed to be her lover and discovers his ghastly error, he is as quick to punish himself as he had been to take her life.

Zaïre is not presented as a heroine of Corneille, or even of Racine. To Lanson she illustrates a type of heroine derived from Shakespeare, "douce, faible, séduisante, toute à l'amour, incapable d'effort héroïque." [64] She is caught between her love of Orosmane and the emotions aroused by the discovery that she is the daughter of a Christian who has for his religion suffered a long captivity. She seeks a solution by recalling the fact that Saladin's mother was a Christian and by arguing that we should not be held responsible for a religion thrust upon us in childhood. One may think that, in giving her this last reflection, Voltaire was allowing her to speak his own thoughts rather than hers, but they may also be regarded as inspired by the emotional conflict in her soul. She arrives at no conclusion, for she is murdered before she has an opportunity to accept or reject baptism, to marry Orosmane or renounce him. She is a victim of her lover's unwarranted jealousy and of her brother's blind fanaticism.

---

[63] Mlle Clairon noted the absence of love from Orosmane's first speech (I, 2) and thought Le Kain could have made up for it by his expression and by taking Zaïre's hand before he begins his instructions, but Mlle Dumesnil protested against the suggestion; cf. *Mémoires de Mlle Clairon*, Paris, 1822, pp. 313-5, and *Mémoires de Mlle Dumesnil*, Paris, 1823, pp. 169-75.

[64] *Esquisse d'une histoire de la tragédie française*, New York, 1920, p. 119. It is possible that Voltaire was imitating Desdemona, but he could have found an example of this type of heroine in Campistron's *Andronic*.

This brother is the most distinctly Voltairian creation in the play. He is the uncompromising crusader, oblivious to virtues found in the opposing camp. He has fought under Saint Louis, " Si grand par sa valeur, et plus grand par sa foi " (II, 3). He believes that God has made use of him (II, 1). He is willing to sacrifice himself in order to liberate others, but he boasts of his generosity, haughtily uses *tutoiement* in addressing Orosmane, and upbraids his sister for becoming a Mohammedan. When she proposes to turn Christian but to marry Orosmane, he is still more violent (III, 4):

> Opprobre malheureux du sang dont vous sortez,
> Vous demandez la mort, et vous la méritez.

And when his sister has been murdered as a result of his persuading her to postpone her marriage and to meet him at night, he has no blame for himself, but turns her death into an act of vengeance on the part of his God (V, 10):

> Hélas! elle offensait notre Dieu, notre loi;
> Et ce Dieu la punit d'avoir brûlé pour toi.

At the end of the play he is astonished to find himself pitying the enemy of his people and calls for divine guidance lest he may become tolerant.

Lusignan, on the contrary, is an appealing character, though he appears in only two scenes. He claims to have fought sixty years for the glory of God. In so doing he witnessed the destruction of Caesarea, lost his wife and two sons, and spent twenty years in prison, yet his faith is as strong as ever. When he first comes upon the stage, his eyes can hardly stand the light, but he rejoices upon recognizing Châtillon and soon succeeds in identifying his two remaining children. The discovery that Zaïre is not a Christian does not induce him, as it does Nérestan, to reproach her. He blames his imprisonment and pleads eloquently with her not to betray the God who has died for her (II, 3):

> Vois ces murs, vois ce temple envahi par tes maîtres;
> Tout annonce le Dieu qu'ont vengé tes ancêtres.
> Tourne les yeux, sa tombe est près de ce palais;
> C'est ici la montagne où, lavant nos forfaits,
> Il voulut expirer sous les coups de l'impie;
> C'est là que de sa tombe il rappela sa vie.

The other characters are largely confidants and messengers, but three of them are given more personality than one usually finds in such parts. Châtillon represents the knights captured by Moslems and awaiting their ransom; Fatime, though living in the seraglio, is a Christian who influences Zaïre; Corasmin is an ardent Mohammedan who disapproves of his master's liberality to "vils chrétiens," yet is not an Iago, for he does not plot to poison Orosmane's mind, nor does he falsify evidence. If Voltaire thought of Iago when he created Corasmin, he altered the character in order to put his chief emphasis upon Orosmane rather than upon his confidant.

The tragedy is classical in structure. The first act brings in all the elements of the plot, including a reference to Zaïre's cross and a first suggestion of Orosmane's jealousy. The second act is rendered striking by Lusignan's release from his dungeon and by the scene of double recognition. The interviews between Zaïre and Orosmane and the growth of his jealousy make Acts III and IV remarkable. In Act V there is intense suspense while Orosmane awaits Zaïre, and the act ends in murder and suicide. Like Racine, Voltaire sought to evoke the past by references to well-known localities and men. He indulged in long descriptive passages, introduced a number of intense scenes, and employed at times great simplicity in expression: "Zaïre, vous pleurez" (IV, 2); "Zaïre, vous m'aimez" (IV, 2); "Non, je n'en doute pas" (IV, 6); "Sa sœur? . . . J'étais aimé?" (V, 10). Such expressions and the rôles of Zaïre and Lusignan made the play rank with *Inès de Castro* as one of the two distinguished "tragédies de sentiment" that the century had produced.

The play met with great success, though at the first performance, Aug. 13, 1732, it came near being hissed.[65] It was acted ten times in August and September, twenty-one times from Nov. 12, 1732 to Jan. 11, 1733. Zaïre was played by la Gaussin, to whom Voltaire attributed his triumph; Orosmane, by Dufresne; Lusignan, by Sarrazin; Nérestan, by Grandval; Châtillon, by Legrand de Belleville.[66] In all of these productions except that of Jan. 11, Voltaire shared in the receipts. The amount paid him was 3754 fr., 12 s., a sum previously surpassed, so far as the records show, only by his own *Œdipe* and by *Inès de Castro.*

At the last performance before Easter in 1734 and in 1742, *Zaïre* was considered sufficiently religious to be substituted for *Polyeucte.* Subsequently Le Kain distinguished himself as Orosmane. Voltaire once played Lusignan at a private performance. In 1874 the two leading rôles were taken by Sarah Bernhardt and Mounet-Sully.[67] *Zaïre* became the most popular of Voltaire's tragedies at the Comédie Française, the only one to be acted there in the twentieth century. Between 1732 and 1936 it was given there 488 times, more frequently than *Rodogune* or *Bajazet.*

[65] Moland, I, 75, 359. Voltaire was so doubtful about the success of his play that he advised Dufresne to omit some of the lines if he found that the tragedy was not being well received.

[66] The *Mercure* and Moland, II, 556, X, 279-80. The *Registres* show that others who played were the younger La Thorillière, Du Breuil, Bercy, Dangeville le jeune, and la Jouvenot, who must have taken the part of Fatime.

[67] Moland, II, 535.

All Paris, however, did not have for *Zaïre* the eyes of Orosmane. Several parodies appeared, one of them entitled *Les Enfants trouvés ou le Sultan poli par l'amour*.[68] Nadal, in a *Lettre à Mme la comtesse de F.*, protested against Zaïre's opinion that religion is a matter of education, against the absence of the *merveilleux,* and the lack of preparation. He found Orosmane odious and the play lacking in verisimilitude.[69] The abbé Le Blanc [70] admitted the success of the play, but he declared that Voltaire had not done justice to French or to Oriental manners and religions.   J.-B. Rousseau [71] denied the charge his friends had made that Voltaire was trying to show that Saracens are " plus honnêtes " than Christians, but he accused him of dramatizing the impious doctrine that Grace has no power over the passions, a charge to which Voltaire replied by pointing to the failure of Rousseau's plays and the fact that *Zaïre* had been acted in religious establishments.

The play was criticized for the improbability of Zaïre's being allowed to keep her mother's cross from the time that she was first captured and of Nérestan's being identified by a scar on his chest. The plot was held to depend too much upon chance as, if Nérestan's letter had referred to Zaïre as " ma sœur," there would have been no catastrophe.[72] It may also have been noticed that if in V, 9 Zaïre had said, " O, mon frère, est-ce vous ? " instead of " Est-ce vous, Nérestan ? " she would not have been murdered. It is strange that Nérestan should return to Jerusalem only a few hours before the time appointed for his sister's marriage and that Lusignan, who dies before the play ends, should be released from prison in time to recognize his daughter. Voltaire must have been aware that his play was open to such criticism, for in the original text of his *Temple du goût* he called for more " vraisemblance à *Zaïre* " in a line that he ultimately suppressed.[73] He resented the criticism he received to the point of threatening to write no more plays,[74] certainly an idle threat.

Collé [75] considered it the most effective of Voltaire's plays when acted. He admired the heroine's love, but thought the hero's not sufficiently oriental. He claimed that the scene of double recognition is not properly

---

[68] Republished by Fontaine in the appendix of his edition of the play; cf. also Grannis, *op. cit.*, pp. 273-85.
[69] Cf. Fontaine's edition of *Zaïre*.
[70] Monod-Cassidy, *op. cit.*, pp. 160, 162.
[71] Moland, XXII, 73.
[72] There is none in the *Enfants trouvés*, the last scene of which begins as follows:
   C.:   Etes-vous là, ma sœur?
   D.: Sa sœur! Ah! j'allais faire une belle sotise!
     Cet éclaircissement m'épargne une méprise.
[73] Moland, VIII, 550, 588.
[74] First text of the dedication to Falkener.
[75] *Correspondance inédite*, 1864, pp. 421-44.

prepared and that Zaïre leaves the seraglio too readily. He would have preferred that Zaïre should become a Christian and admit the fact to Orosmane, but he realized that this would produce a different play. To Condorcet it was " la tragédie des cœurs tendres et des âmes pures." Jean-Jacques Rousseau called it a " Piece enchanteresse " and said of it that no other tragedy showed with greater charm the strength of love and beauty.[76]

La Harpe[77] hailed *Zaïre* as " la plus touchante de toutes les tragédies qui existent." He had known its text by heart since childhood. He praised the presentation of character and the structure. He defended the play against the charge of improbability and discovered only eight or ten verses that deserved to be omitted. " Tout me fait voir dans Zaïre," he concluded, " l'ouvrage le plus éminemment tragique que l'on ait jamais conçu . . . le plus grand triomphe d'un art qui a pour but principal d'émouvoir les hommes rassemblés."

To praise the play as highly as this one would have to be born in the eighteenth century, yet more recent critics have admired it in certain respects. Brunetière,[78] though he found it too romantic and held that some of the events were not well explained, considered it ingenious and moving, almost the first ancestor of plays dealing with national subjects. Lanson[79] looked upon Orosmane as an Othello weakened through the influence of Bajazet and noted that Voltaire sought to present characters as suffering from events due to chance rather than themselves preparing the action. However, he admitted the " tristesse touchante " of Zaïre's rôle and the lyric quality of Lusignan's verses. Lion's conclusion is[80] that " l'œuvre vit, claire, rapide, émouvante, bien qu'un peu romanesque, toute fraîche encore de sentiment et de poésie."

If one can pardon the fact that the style is less vigorous and picturesque than it might well have been if the play had been written a century later, and the use of melodramatic devices to rouse suspicion and produce recognition, one can find much pathos in the two leading rôles and in that of Lusignan, admirable simplicity in the plot, and a courageous effort to dwell upon the tragic effect of religious differences, a theme that is still far from being merely an historical survival.

The four tragedies studied in this chapter are those most likely to show English influence, for they were begun either in England or not long after Voltaire's return. He learned from the English, probably from certain of Shakespeare's plays, to make use of names from French history.

---

[76] " Lettre à d'Alembert," *Œuvres*, Geneva, 1782, XI, 257.
[77] *Op. cit.*, XI, 124-219.
[78] *Epoques du théâtre français*, Paris, 1896, pp. 255-81.
[79] *Esquisse*, pp. 119-20.
[80] *Op. cit.*, p. 86.

He imitated *Hamlet* when he showed a ghost upon the stage, first in *Eriphyle,* subsequently in *Sémiramis.* *La Mort de César* was suggested by *Julius Caesar,* and Antony's speech in Voltaire's play is derived from the corresponding discourse in Shakespeare's. It is also possible that Voltaire's interest in the spectacular, already displayed in *Œdipe* under the influence of *Athalie,* was developed by English example, so that he used more striking stage decoration in *Brutus, la Mort de César,* and *Eriphyle-Sémiramis* than he would have done if he had not visited England. On the other hand, it cannot be shown that Voltaire owed much of *Zaïre* to *Othello,* though some details in this tragedy may have been suggested by *Hamlet, Lear,* and Dryden's *Indian Emperour.* There are also details of *la Mort de César* and *Eriphyle* that may well have been suggested by Shakespeare. On the whole, however, the four plays, even *la Mort de César,* are written in accordance with the French dramatic tradition rather than the English. Whatever debt there was was amply repaid by Voltaire when he introduced Shakespeare to the general public of the continent. Even his bitter attacks upon him served to call attention to a genius that had been neglected there for over a century. It was in this way rather than in his borrowings from Shakespeare in his plays that Voltaire unintentionally contributed to the rise of Romanticism and the destruction of the system he most dearly cherished.

CHAPTER VII

TRAGEDY IN 1730-1734. PIRON, LA GRANGE-CHANCEL, LE FRANC DE POMPIGNAN

The scarcity of tragedies in the late twenties attracted, not only Voltaire, but La Grange-Chancel, Pellegrin, and four authors who had not previously composed this type of play. Twelve tragedies were offered to the actors by these seven authors, but one of them was withdrawn and is now lost. The three by Voltaire were discussed in the last chapter. Pellegrin's *Pélopée,* an altered version of a tragedy read in 1710, has been studied in my *Sunset.*[1] The others show, more than these four, a desire on their authors' part to enlarge the field of tragedy, for the scenes of some are laid in Sogdiana, Gaul, England, Sweden, and Zanzibar, while the incidents dramatized in three of the tragedies occurred as recently as the sixteenth century.

The sources are historians, ancient, medieval, and modern, Vergil, Metastasio, Boisrobert, Corneille, and other French dramatists. The treatment is thoroughly classical. Love plays an important part in all of them. Incest is feared in one, but there turns out to be no cause for alarm. There are several noteworthy scenes of recognition. Piron claims to have shown the evils of excessive ambition in his first tragedy. La Grange-Chancel sought to revive the religious tragedy, based on Christian martyrdom, and introduced a plea for tolerance. This play and Le Franc's *Didon* have an essential element of the supernatural. It is suggested in the latter that oracles may not speak the truth, but no such conclusion can be derived from the outcome of the tale. In *Callisthène,* on the other hand, an oracle is purchased. Elsewhere religious themes are avoided, notably by Tronchin in his *Marie Stuart.*

Most of the tragedies had only temporary success, but none of those acted was a complete failure, while two of them, *Gustave* and *Didon,* were often performed in the eighteenth century and were looked upon as good examples of work by dramatists inferior to Voltaire. Piron's *Gustave,* noteworthy for its theme from Scandinavian history, the use made of climate, and for several effective scenes, is, among these tragedies, the one that is most likely to give pleasure today. In order to complete the study of its author as a writer of tragedies, I have included in this chapter his last play, though it was acted in the next decade.

---

[1] Pp. 127-9. It was acted from July 18 to Aug. 29, 1733. The author's share was 941 fr., 18 s.

Alexis Piron [2] was born at Dijon on July 9, 1689, the son of a well-to-do citizen, celebrated locally for his noëls and other songs. Refusing to prepare for the church, young Piron studied law and was about to practise when the loss of his family's fortune obliged him to earn a living as a secretary. He gradually established himself in the literary world of Paris, where he counted among his friends the comte de Livry, Mme de Tessan, the marquis de Lassay, and the dramatist, Collé. His theatrical career began with *Arlequin Deucalion,* written in 1722 for the Foire. His *Métromanie* made him famous. In 1753 he was elected to the French Academy, but an indecent poem, written in his youth and shown to Louis XV, caused the king to prevent his occupying a *fauteuil.* Perhaps his making of Louis a censor of morals was the best of his jokes, but he may be remembered for others, especially for those at the expense of the Academy. "Voyez-vous," he said, "ils sont là quarante, qui ont de l'esprit comme quatre." And before his death on Jan. 21, 1773, he prepared for himself an epitaph:

> Ci gît Piron, qui ne fut rien
> Pas même académicien.

The first of his three tragedies was CALLISTHÈNE.[3] In a long preface that he published in 1758 Piron explained that he had sought to point out the evil effects of ambition and gave his source as Justin, Bk. XV, Chap. III. He must also have made use of Plutarch's *Life of Alexander.* From them he took the location of his action in Sogdiana, the characters of Alexander, Callisthène, Anaxarque, and Lysimaque, and the main events of his play, but he added a love interest by creating Léonide, sister of his hero.[4]

---

[2] Cf. the *Vie* published with Rigoley de Juvigny's edition of the *Œuvres complettes d'Alexis Piron,* Paris, Lambert, 1776.

[3] Paris, veuve Mergé, Le Gras, veuve Pissot, 1730, 8°. Dedicated to the "Duchesse douairière," that is, to Louise-Françoise de Bourbon, illegitimate daughter of Louis XIV. Republished, The Hague, Van Dole, 1738; Paris, Prault fils, 1738; Paris, Duchesne, 1758; Geneva, frères Cramer, 1761; in the edition of Rigoley de Juvigny just mentioned; and Paris, Guillot, 1928.

[4] After conquering Persia, Alexander decides to live like an Oriental monarch, to be called the son of Jupiter, and to continue his conquests indefinitely. The Spartan philosopher, Callisthène, who had followed Alexander because he saw in him the avenger of Greece, has been arrested for opposing his plans, but he is now liberated at the request of Lysimaque and in the hope that he may yield to the king's desires. Léonide reaches the camp, is well received by the queen, and assures Lysimaque of her love. Anaxarque, who had seen her at Sparta, also seeks to marry her, but he is rudely repelled by both Léonide and her brother. He flatters Alexander and seeks to proclaim him a god, while Callisthène still opposes the king's policies so firmly that Alexander decides to torture and mulilate him. When Lysimaque's friend, Cratérus, prepares a boat in which the Spartans may escape, Callisthène refuses to go. When he hears that Lysimaque has killed Anaxarque and will be thrown to a lion, he advises his sister to escape, but she declines to leave him. Lysimaque reports that he has strangled the lion and that Alexander, impressed by his courage, has restored him to favor. He brings a dagger with which they can all commit suicide and even

Alexander is represented as the victim of his conquests, preferring Persian luxury to Macedonian simplicity, desirous of conquering India and the rest of the world. Brooking no opposition, he turns against Callisthène, who had once saved his life. He even defends his conduct in purchasing from priests a favorable oracular pronouncement. But he is not wholly evil, for he secretly admires Callisthène and feels remorse when the sage commits suicide. His guilt is also diminished by the rôle of Anaxarque, who cleverly and unscrupulously panders to his vices.

Opposed to them are noble Lysimaque and the Spartans. It is not explained how this young man retains the friendship of both Alexander and Callisthène, nor are we prepared for his possession of enough physical strength to strangle a lion. Callisthène is represented as blunt, but he is not so crude in his speech as Plutarch makes him. Piron claims that he is somewhat guilty as he had sided with Alexander against the opinion of most Spartans. He is now in a tragic situation, as he sees that the avenger of Greece whom he had supported has become a tyrant. His sister is a woman of great beauty, whose " feu vertueux " does not allow " qu'on s'étende en frivoles discours." Though her rôle must have given little pleasure to an emotional actress, she is the only woman in the play. Piron was a brave man to begin a career in tragedy with so little to offer the feminine portion of the troupe.

The tragedy is well constructed, but it makes little appeal to the imagination. The rebellious youths in Alexander's army, the conquered Persians, and the wild inhabitants of Sogdiana are all kept off the stage, the characters we are allowed to see are too fixed in their resolutions for us to consider them dramatic, and the philosophic discussion of conquest is not properly presented. Piron admits that he found Callisthène so prolix that he was obliged to omit nearly a hundred of his verses. He claims that his play also suffered from an accident. When Callisthène took the dagger from Lysimaque,

> le manche, la poignée, la garde & la lame, tout se sépara de façon que l'Acteur reçut l'arme pièce à pièce, & fut obligé de tenir le tout du mieux qu'il put à pleine main.

Performances may have been rendered less effective by the facts that Piron withdrew the heroine's rôle after offering it to Adrienne Le Couvreur,[5] and that three actors, Sarrazin, Grandval, and la Balicourt had recently

---

starts to kill himself, but Callisthène seizes the weapon, bids them marry and live, and stabs himself just as Alexander enters. While he is dying, he urges the monarch to become again the noble warrior he had known. Alexander feels remorse and resolves to favor Lysimaque and his bride.

[5] Cf. *Revue des deux mondes*, XXXVII (1927), 360.

joined the troupe.[6] The tragedy was given only eight times, from Feb. 18 to March 6, 1730. Attendance at the first performance was excellent, with 1476 paid admissions, but it was tumultuous. Interest in the play quickly diminished until only 258 tickets were sold on March 6, although the tragedy had been acted at court on March 2. The author received 360 fr., 18 s. after the first performance, but the other seven productions raised the total to only 916 fr., 2 s. The play was not revived even after Piron had acquired a distinguished reputation.

Voltaire[7] referred to *Callisthène* with contempt. La Harpe[8] held that few subjects were worse selected or worse conceived. He objected to the presentation of only what was dishonorable in Alexander's career and of only what was admirable in that of Callisthène. In saying of the main theme that " il n'y en a pas de moins tragique " he was wrong, for, as many Europeans know today to their cost, there is tragedy in supporting for patriotic reasons a man who turns out to be a tyrant. It was not the career of Callisthène that was unsuited to tragedy, but Piron's method of treating it. La Harpe was on surer ground when he added that the Spartan attitude towards love was " fort peu théâtrale." Piron himself admitted that the dryness of his theme and the ineffective manner in which love was expressed displeased the audience. The brevity of his play's career must have convinced Piron that to succeed he must arouse the emotions of the spectators.

To do this he went to the other extreme. He again chose an historical theme, but, following the example set by La Motte in his main tragedy, he avoided an ancient subject. He became, indeed, more of a modern than the author of *Inès*, turning to the sixteenth century, as had done some fifty years before those who had dramatized the misfortunes of Essex and of Mary Queen of Scots. He is the first French dramatist to put on the stage an episode from Swedish history. This he did in GUSTAVE,[9] a tragedy first acted on Feb. 3, 1733.

Piron tells us that, with the exception of the love element, his plot

[6] The others who played, Montmény, Du Breuil, and the younger La Thorillière, were not actors of distinction.

[7] Moland, XXXIII, 326.

[8] *Op. cit.*, XIII, 173-5.

[9] Paris, Le Breton fils, 1733, 8°, and 1767. Dedicated to the comte de Lassay, to whom Piron sent a copy in his own hand. According to Brenner, there is a manuscript of the play in the Bibliothèque de Dijon. Republished, Utrecht, Néaulme, 1733; Brussels, Struckwart, 1733; Paris, Duchesne, 1758; Amsterdam, Markus et Arckstée, 1764; Paris, Lambert, 1776; as *Gustave Wasa*, Paris, Belin, Brunet, 1788; in *Répertoire Petitot*, 1803, 1817; in *Auteurs du second ordre*, 1808; in *Répertoires* of 1813, 1818, 1821, 1822; Paris, Belin, 1821; in *Chefs-d'œuvre dramatiques*, Paris, Didot aîné, 1824; Paris, Sanson, 1826; Paris, Guillot, 1928-31. It was translated into Dutch in 1761; into Italian in 1746. Another Italian translation, acted at Venice in 1772, was published in 1776, 1788, 1794, and 1798.

was drawn from Vertot's *Histoire des Révolutions de Suède.* He denies indignantly that he owed anything to the abbé Prévost, who had accused him of borrowing a scene from the *Mémoires d'un Homme de qualité.*[10] La Harpe,[11] while admitting that he followed history in certain respects, declared that " c'est l'intrigue d'Amasis sous d'autres noms." Now Virtot undoubtedly provided him with the location of the action in Stockholm, the characters of Christierne, Frédéric, and Gustave Wasa, as well as certain events: Christierne's usurpation, the reign of terror that followed, his imprisonment of Gustave's mother; Gustave's illegal capture, his escape, his wanderings in disguise in northern Sweden, his victories, his capture of Stockholm, his final triumph; and Frédéric's revolt against Christierne. The idea of dramatizing these facts may have sent him for guidance to La Grange-Chancel, whose *Amasis,* revived in 1731, tells the story of a usurper's overthrow by a young man whose mother he holds in his power. In both tragedies the young man pretends to the usurper that he has killed the person who is really himself, but the circumstances are less like those of *Amasis* than they are like those of *Electra* plays by Sophocles and Longepierre, where, as here, there has been no murder as there is in *Amasis.* There are, however, other resemblances to La Grange-Chancel's tragedy that cannot be dismissed in this way: the usurper and the hero are rivals in love, the hero's mother opposes the usurper and is threatened with death, the hero makes himself known and is arrested. It seems probable, then, that Piron did get suggestions from *Amasis,* but La Harpe greatly exaggerated his indebtedness.

As for Prévost, the abbé had accused Piron of imitating a scene described as follows:

La vieille dona Pastrino étoit assise près d'une fenêtre; dona Diana étoit à genoux à ses pieds, le sein découvert, et cette horrible femme lui tenoit la pointe d'un poignard appuyée sur la gorge. N'avancez pas, s'écria-t-elle en nous voyant; elle est morte si vous avancez.[12]

In *Gustave,* V, 2, we read:

> Christierne à ses pieds d'une main forcenée
> Tenant sur le tillac Léonor prosternée,
> Et de l'autre, déja haussant pour se venger
> Le fer étincelant tout prêt à l'égorger.

This is followed by the warning (V, 3):

> Ou rends moi la princesse, ou vois périr ta mère.

[10] Cf. Raynal, *Cor.*, I, 122.
[11] *Op. cit.*, XIII, 179.
[12] *Œuvres choisies de Prévost*, Paris, Leblanc, 1810, II, 57-8. Piron indicates that Prévost's accusation is found in " *le Pour & Contre,* vol. I, n° 6, p. 134."

No such scene is presented in Vertot's history,[13] though it is stated there that Christierne had threatened Gustave and others with death if Sténon did not agree to his terms, and that subsequently Gustave's mother was put into a sack and thrown into the sea.[14] Such threats had been common enough in French tragedies [15] and could have been invented by Piron from his knowledge of them and of Vertot, yet the spectacle of a woman lying on the ground while a weapon is raised over her and the threat made that she will be killed unless her friends yield to the demands of the person holding the weapon had not previously appeared on the French stage. Consequently it was natural that Prévost should suppose that he had inspired Piron's theme. Even if he did, however, most of the tragedy remains quite independent of his novel.

We may conclude that the play is mainly historical except for the love themes and the telescoping of events into the required twenty-four hours. Piron even made use of the fighting on the ice and its sudden cracking under the weight of the contestants, though he omitted reference to the unpatriotic Swedish clergy. He added the character of Adélaïde, supposed to be the daughter of Sténon, the administrator of Sweden who had died in battle with the Danes and had left a widow, active in the patriotic cause. Piron caused Adélaïde to be loved by the three chief men of the play and imagined that Gustave's mother disguised herself as her attendant. In working out his plot, he brought in, probably with the help of La Grange-Chancel and Prévost, unhistorical situations that added to the excitement. He also supplied a dream and contrived to produce several scenes of recognition.[16]

[13] According to Raynal (Cor., I, 122), when Piron met Prévost at the home of Mme de Tencin, he accused the novelist of borrowing the scene from Vertot, but Prévost replied that he had never read the book in question.

[14] Paris, frères Mame, 1808, pp. 82, 163.

[15] Cf. Andromaque, Commode, Camma, Amasis. Cf. also Mlle de Scudéry's Ibrahim, IV, 349 (edition of 1727), where Rustan holds Isabelle with one hand, his weapon with the other, and threatens to kill her if her lover does not yield.

[16] Christierne, King of Denmark and Norway, has invaded Sweden, captured Stockholm, and killed many of the nobles. His heir, Frédéric, has renounced the throne because of his desire for a tranquil life. He loves Adélaïde, daughter of Sténon, who had administered Sweden and died in battle. Adélaïde is a captive in Stockholm. Her supposed suivante, Léonor, is in reality the mother of Gustave Wasa. Her son had been unlawfully imprisoned by Christierne, had escaped, made his way to northern Sweden, worked in the mines, collected an army, and is now besieging Stockholm. As he loves Adélaïde, he disguises himself, enters the city, and asks for an interview with the king on the ground that he is bringing him the head of Gustave Wasa. Christierne informs his confidant, Rodolphe, that he has decided to marry Adélaïde and send Frédéric back to Copenhagen. Rodolphe warns him that a revolt may break out in Frédéric's favor. Adélaïde infers from Rodolphe's remarks that Gustave, whom she loves, is dead, but Léonor doubts it, as her own death has been reported and she has seen in a dream Gustave wearing royal purple with Christierne at his feet. In Act II Casimir, a Swedish nobleman who has pretended to support Christierne in order to overthrow him, prepares to avenge Gustave and urges Frédéric to seize the throne. When Gustave enters, Casimir draws, but

The large amount of preliminary material is well presented. Each act
has a startling or an emotional scene. There are four scenes of recognition.
In Act V suspense is effectively sustained. The revolt of the fleet has
been too carefully prepared for it to be considered a *deus ex machinâ*.
There is an unusual amount of local color in that the climate of Sweden
not only is described, but has a genuine part to play in the development
of the plot. Gustave had fled to a land (II, 3)

> Où le soleil n'échauffe et ne luit qu'à demi,
> Tombeau de la nature, effroyables rivages
> Que l'ours dispute encore à des hommes sauvages.

Adélaïde describes as follows the combat on the ice in the harbor of
Stockholm (V, 1):

> Sur ces bords dont l'hiver a glacé la surface
> Mes ravisseurs fuyoient, . . .
> Sur la glace long-temps l'avantage est égal; . . .
> Parmi des cris de rage et de mourantes voix
> Un bruit plus effrayant, plus sinistre cent fois,
> Sous nous, autour de nous, au loin se fait entendre;
> La glace en mille endroits, menace de se fendre,
> Se fend, s'ouvre, se brise, et s'épanche en glaçons
> Qui nagent sur un gouffre où nous disparaissons.

Unfortunately the author, bent on arranging striking situations, did
not portray his characters effectively. Gustave, as Petitot remarks, does
nothing in the play to deserve the reputation that is credited to him. He
makes a series of plans that fail. He does not dominate the action, but is

Gustave makes himself known, embraces him, and explains why he has come. Next
he tells Christierne that he has Gustave's head and shows him a note written in his
own hand that urges Adélaïde to obey the king. As a reward he asks that he may
see her. Christierne grants his request and prepares to marry Adélaïde next day.
In Act III Léonor denounces this proposed marriage, hears that her son's head is
to be displayed, in despair makes herself known, and is arrested. When Adélaïde
is alone, Gustave brings her the note. She reads it and then sees him at her feet.
After assurances of mutual love, he tells her where to met him and leaves. Frédéric
proposes that, in order to avoid marrying Christierne, Adélaïde join him on the
fleet, which is under his command. In Act IV Christierne, hearing that Frédéric is
preparing to leave, has him arrested. Rodolphe states that Gustave is alive and is
probably the man who had claimed to have his head, as this person has sought to
secure Léonor's freedom by bribery. Christierne has Léonor brought in, shows
Gustave to her, and orders him killed. Her protests reveal her son's identity. When
he is imprisoned, Adélaïde offers, if he is freed, to marry Frédéric. Christierne
replies that he will marry her himself. At this point he learns that Casimir has
led Gustave's army into the city, that Frédéric and Léonor have been taken to the
fleet, and that Gustave is fighting. In Act V we are told that the Swedes have
triumphed, that Adélaïde has made her escape thanks to the breaking of the ice
under the fighters, and that Christierne, who has reached the fleet, is threatening to
kill Léonor unless Adélaïde is given up. Gustave is willing to put himself in Christierne's power in order to save his mother, but she enters with the news that the
men of the fleet have revolted and replaced Christierne by Frédéric. Rodolphe has
been killed and his master is in chains. Gustave will marry Adélaïde and rule over
Sweden. He allows Christierne to live in order that he may suffer for his crimes.

saved by his friends. Frédéric is a more original creation. He has refused a throne in order to enjoy a life of ease, but he now realizes that his avoidance of duty has made possible the crimes of Christierne. We do not see enough of him, however, to appreciate his character. Christierne is a conventional villain. Adélaïde and Léonor are typical women in distress, who weep and refuse to be disloyal, but who do little to bring about their rescue or Gustave's.

The spectators were not influenced by such considerations. They received the play with enthusiasm.[17] It was acted twenty times in February, March, and April, four more in December. The author received 3038 fr., 12 s., more than three times what *Callisthène* had brought him. It remained in the repertory until 1791, with a total of 114 productions.[18] The abbé Le Blanc, who attended the first performance, declared that he had never witnessed such success and that, in comparison with *Gustave, Zaïre* was only whipped cream. He praised especially the last three acts and sent Bouhier an analysis of the tragedy. On March 17, however, he admitted that it was no longer attracting crowds, blamed the acting of la Gaussin, who played Adélaïde, and the excess of incidents.[19] The abbé Prévost asserted that there were enough of these to fill five volumes and accused Piron of writing many harsh or obscure verses.[20] La Harpe[21] admired the scenes in which Gustave is recognized by Adélaïde and in which Christierne's threat to kill Léonor is delivered to Gustave, accepting in the latter case Piron's claim that the situation came from Vertot. But he criticized the prosody severely and insisted that the play was full of *invraisemblances*: Gustave's risking himself alone in the royal palace, Christierne's failure to insist upon seeing the head, Léonor's admitting that she was Gustave's mother, and Adélaïde's escape from the crumbling ice. He declared that Gustave's claim to have the head in his possession is a " quolibet " unworthy of tragedy. He was disgusted with Christierne's declaration of love and found Frédéric neither heroic nor dramatic. On the other hand, he admitted that the " quolibet " roused the curiosity of the spectators and added that they, like Christierne, forgot about the head. He also gave the play credit for inspiring a scene in Voltaire's *Mérope,* which for him was high praise indeed. Voltaire[22] himself made no detailed criticism

---

[17] In spite of a cabal organized against the play by Voltaire, according to Mathieu Marais; cf. Lescure, *op. cit.*, IV, 465.

[18] The rôles of the women were taken by la Gaussin, la Balicourt, and la Jouvenot, who played, respectively, Adélaïde, Léonor, and Sophie. Dufresne played Gustave; Sarrazin, Christierne; Grandval, for whom a scarf was procured by the troupe, Frédéric; Legrand de Belleville, Casimir.

[19] Monod-Cassidy, *op. cit.*, pp. 167-72.

[20] Quoted by Reynal, *Cor.*, I, 122.

[21] *Op. cit.*, XIII, 179, XII, 36.

[22] Moland, XXXIII, 326.

of the tragedy, but he claimed, on the strength of what he heard about it, that it was "follement conduite et sottement écrite." He added that at its first performance it was put above *Athalie,* at its second beside *Callisthène.*

It is certainly true that much is left unexplained in the presentation of the characters and in the development of the intrigue. Yet the choice of a subject from Swedish history and the use made of climatic conditions show originality, while many of the scenes are effective if one does not restrain one's appreciation, as La Harpe did, by too great insistence upon probability.

Piron wrote only one more tragedy, Fernand Cortez ou Montézume.[23] It resembles his first two in subject and method. For a third time he selected a distinguished warrior as a leading character, introduced historical elements, but also imaginary characters in order to create love interests. In this last case love is so greatly emphasized that it becomes, as the author states in his preface, "la base même du sujet principal." In this respect it differs from *Callisthène,* but it resembles the earlier tragedy in the facts that only one woman is in the cast and that the warrior's ambition for further conquests is opposed by some of his followers.[24] In both cases the conquests continue, but our sympathies that had been with the followers in the play of 1730 are now with the conqueror.

Montezuma had already appeared in Dryden's *Indian Emperour* and in Ferrier's *Montézume.* With the English play Piron's has no connection except that in both, not only Montezuma, but an Indian high priest and Cortez take part. Whether Piron borrowed from Ferrier cannot be determined, as only two lines of *Montézume* have been preserved.[25] It may well be that the success of *Alzire* was alone enough to make him select a Spanish-American subject. He probably turned to Francisco López de Gomara's *Conquista de Méjico,* to which he refers in his preface and from which he could easily have obtained his historical information.[26]

He selected for his play the day of Montezuma's death in captivity and had him killed by his own people, but with a poisoned arrow instead of a

---

[23] Paris, Duchesne, 1757, 12°. Republished, Amsterdam, Markus et Arckstée, 1764; Paris, Lambert, 1776; Paris, Guillot, 1928-31. A Dutch translation appeared in 1764 and 1769; a Spanish translation of 1766, *Hernan Cortes,* was acted at Madrid in 1801 (cf. Ada M. Coe, *op. cit.,* p. 111).

[24] There is even a reference in *Fernand Cortez,* I, 4, to Alexander's ambitious crossing "De l'Hidaspe & du Gange."

[25] Cf. my *Sunset,* pp. 55-6.

[26] Such as the Spanish invasion of Mexico, the capture of Montezuma, the revolt against Cortez, the death of the Indian ruler at the hands of his own people, the opposition of Spaniards like Pánfilo de Narvaez to Cortez, the latter's refusal to leave Mexico, and his victory. Like López de Gomara, Piron in his preface assigns to Cortez 15 horses and 6 cannon for his attack upon the city of Mexico; cf. the *Biblioteca de autores españoles,* XXII, 325.

stone, showing thereby his preference for the nobler weapon. He made love the inspiration for Cortez's conquests, creating Elvire, whose hand is sought by both Montezuma and his conqueror. He invented the rôle of Elvire's father and devised a plot that treats of love and war in an exotic setting.[27]

The plot is even more unreal than that of *Gustave*. To have Cortez moved to conquest by love is romantic enough, but to have him attribute the conquest of Mexico to D. Pèdre because this Spaniard is Elvire's father, is, as La Harpe points out, utterly absurd. Nor is this foolish action in keeping with the character of Cortez as shown elsewhere in the play. Nor is D. Pèdre's change of heart consistent with his character. He has been represented as an extremely proud and jealous grandee who resents every act of kindness by which he benefits. He even plots to destroy the conqueror's work. His sudden recognition of his enemy's virtues seems introduced merely to give the play a happy ending.

Added to these faults in characterization are other departures from probability. D. Pèdre and his daughter, headed for Jamaica, are brought by shipwreck, capture by the Indians, and recapture by the Spaniards to Cortez's headquarters just at the proper moment, while Cortez fails to recognize the woman he loves until the time has come to produce an effective scene of recognition.

La Harpe [28] holds that Montezuma is too much of a coward to interest

---

[27] Cortez has invaded Mexico in order to win such fame that D. Pèdre, his father's enemy, will not refuse him the hand of his daughter, Elvire. He has entered the capital and captured Montezuma. From an interview between this prince and the high priest we learn that Montezuma sees hope in collaboration with the Spaniards, while the high priest would appeal to arms and sacrifice two captured Spaniards and 100 men of Tlascala, who are friendly to Cortez, but are in the power of his enemies. The hero rescues by force the men of Tlascala and the two Spaniards, who turn out to be D. Pèdre and Elvire. It seems that, named Governor of Jamaica, he had left Spain with his daughter and D. Sanche, to whom he wished to marry her, that they had been shipwrecked, D. Sanche had perished, and father and daughter had wandered in the wilds until they had been picked up by the Indians. Cortez fails to recognize them. As the thought of owing his life to Cortez is too much for his pride, D. Pèdre resolves to recover his dignity by marrying Elvire to Montezuma, who has fallen in love with her and desires to become a Christian. Cortez approves of the match as he does not know who the girl is. Elvire, who is kept away from other Spaniards by her father, tells Montezuma that she cannot marry him without the consent of the King of Spain, represented by Cortez. The Indian agrees to arrange the interview, but the high priest refuses to recognize him as monarch, opposes his marriage, demands the return of the Spaniards, and threatens to attack. For his insolence Cortez insists that he be present at Montezuma's marriage, but, when he recognizes Elvire, he orders that the affair be delayed. The high priest thinks the gods have influenced him, renounces allegiance to Montezuma, and departs. While the Indians are rejoicing over the selection of another monarch, Cortez assures Elvire of his love and suppresses an effort on the part of his men, led by D. Pèdre, to abandon the city. In the battle the Indians are defeated, but Montezuma is wounded by a poisoned arrow. Cortez offers to put D. Pèdre in command and asks for the hand of Elvire. D. Pèdre is conquered by the generosity of Cortez, but he cannot break his promise to Montezuma. As, however, the poison has done its work, the Indian dies and Cortez will marry Elvire.

[28] *Op. cit.*, XIII, 175-8.

the public, but our own experience with collaborators may make him seem a less improbable, though not a more admirable character. His sudden desire to marry Elvire is, however, another tribute to romance. The high priest, who contrasts with him sharply, gives the play most of its Mexican color. His presence enables Piron to emphasize the worship of strange gods, the use of arrows as weapons, and the practice of human sacrifice. This last custom is mentioned by Cortez's follower, Aguilar, who, in IV, 8, speaks of priests,

> Dont la vengeance voue à l'Idole insultée,
> De nos cœurs palpitans l'offrande ensanglantée,
> Et déja se dispose à l'horrible festin
> Où nos membres épars . . . Vous frémissez enfin.

This scene won the admiration of Collé,[29] who held that Cortez was "fièrement dessiné." La Harpe [30] admired in it the manner in which Cortez recovers the services of his men when they are about to desert him:

> Je reste seul! Eh bien, je serai seul. Partez.
> L'or fut l'unique objet pour qui vous soupirâtes!
> Vous me suivîtes moins en Guerriers qu'en Pirates! . . .
> Retournez en Espagne alors: & vantez-vous
> D'avoir abandonné votre Chef aux Barbares;
> Ce Chef à qui l'on dut des dépouilles si rares;
> Qui vous fit surmonter tant de périls divers;
> Qui, de son propre corps, vous a cent fois couverts;
> Qui veut même en partant vous en couvrir encore.
> Oui! Que ce dernier trait vous confonde & m'honore.
> Venez! C'est moi qui veille à votre embarquement,
> Et qui vous défendrai jusqu'au dernier moment.

Such eloquence was not enough to give the play a distinguished career. It was first acted on Jan. 8, 1744. The troupe provided diamonds for the high priest and fourteen wigs for actors and supernumeraries. Piron claims that there was enough confusion at the first performance to cause some of the actors to forget their lines and that the troupe had, without consulting him, omitted three or four hundred verses, rendering his text unintelligible. He may have been dissatisfied, too, with the actress who first took the part of heroine, for the *Registres* show that either la Connell or la Gaultier first interpreted the rôle, though it was played at the other performances by la Gaussin. Le Blanc [31] asserted that the tragedy would have fallen flat " dès

---

[29] *Correspondance*, 1864, pp. 464-6. Collé thought Piron had more genius than Voltaire, but was not sufficiently associated with aristocrats to acquire a brilliant style.

[30] *Op. cit.*, XIII, 178. He claimed that it was inspired by an episode in the life of Alexander the Great.

[31] Monod-Cassidy, *op. cit.*, p. 384. As the letter is dated Jan. 15, the day of the third performance, the abbé obviously misjudged the public.

11

la 1e Représentation sans une Harangue qu'on a été bien aise d'entendre deux fois & qu'on n'a pas voulu entendre trois." But this is certainly an exaggeration, for the play was given seven times, with a last performance on Jan. 25, and the receipts fell only once as low as 913 fr.[32] The reason why it was not played more often is probably one given by Piron, that the tragedy was being acted while rehearsals of Voltaire's *Mérope* were in progress and the actors were anxious to give their attention to what was to prove a far more remunerative tragedy.

In comparison with *Gustave,* however, the play must have seemed to its author bitterly disappointing. He regretted that Corneille had left the subject to be dramatized in a " temps de décadence " and declared that the tragedy's lack of success had caused him to abandon the theater. He added that people are no longer interested in works of the imagination and that libraries may soon limit themselves to four authors:

Ce seroient sans doute Molière, Corneille, Racine & La Fontaine . . . Corneille sera le Poëte des Hommes, Racine celui des Femmes, La Fontaine celui des Enfans, & Molière celui de tout le monde.

Piron's talents were best displayed in comedy and in epigrammes. Tragedy was a difficult undertaking for a man of his temperament. He showed, however, originality in selecting his subjects and from time to time invented thrilling situations and composed eloquent tirades. But he produced these with little regard for probability and failed to do justice to his characters, a fact that is especially obvious when he treats such distinguished warriors as Alexander the Great, Gustavus Vasa, and Cortez. He must be ranked far below Voltaire and Crébillon, even below La Motte, and, if we take into consideration the tragedies written before his exile, La Grange-Chancel. But his work in tragedy, taken as a whole, is superior to the production of others who began to write in the first half of Louis XV's reign.

At the age of twenty-six La Grange-Chancel had warned La Fosse, twenty-four years his senior, that

> Les Muses, tu le sais, sont de jeunes Deesses;
> Si l'on n'est de leur âge, on n'a point leurs caresses.[33]

When he was forty-two he had written to Voltaire:

> Et bientôt le dégoût, qu'inspire la vieillesse,
> Eloignera de moi les Nimphes de Permesse:

---

[32] Grandval and Sarrazin, who took part in the performances, probably played, respectively, Cortez and D. Pèdre. Piron's share in the receipts was 847 fr.

[33] *Œuvres*, Paris, 1758, V, 100. For the author cf. Otto Nietzelt, *La Grange-Chancel als Tragiker*, Leipzig, 1908, my *History*, Part IV, pp. 367-84, and my *Sunset*, pp. 37-51.

Aussi n'irai-je point offrir à leurs mépris
La honte d'une tête où soient les cheveux gris.[34]

Nevertheless he began to work on *Cassius et Victorinus* shortly afterwards and, when he returned from exile after the Regent's death, he prepared a "tragédie en machines" called *Orphée* for performance in honor of Louis XV's marriage. He asserts that his return to Holland was the cause of its not being acted on that occasion; the expense involved, the reason for its rejection by the actors two years later. At the same time they declined to play his *Pigmalion*.[35] On the other hand, his "comédie héroïque," *les Jeux olympiques ou le Prince malade,* was accepted by the Italians and acted by them on Nov. 12, 1729. Their presentation of this play may have influenced the actors of the Comédie Française in his favor. They revived his *Amasis* in 1731 and not long afterwards brought out two of his tragedies that had not previously been acted. By this time their author had passed the limit of fifty years to which he had referred when writing to La Fosse. His plays were obliged either to fail or to disprove his theory.

Both of them were novel for the period, yet reminiscent of the century in which their author had grown up. In one he attempted to revive tragicomedy without using the word. In the other he put on the stage of the Comédie Française the legend of a Christian martyr, something that no one else had done in the eighteenth century. The first to appear was ERIGONE,[36] acted on Dec. 17, 1731. La Grange-Chancel gives no hint as to its source, which Nietzelt was unable to discover, but its close resemblance to Boisrobert's *Cassandre* led me to point out [37] that the author imitated either this play or its Spanish source.[38] I would say now that he used the French play as a model rather than the Spanish. There is no evidence that he ever turned to Spanish literature, whereas he tells us himself that he owned many French plays, including some by Boisrobert. Moreover, when his play resembles that of Villegas, it also resembles Boisrobert's tragi-comedy, and his dénouement is closer to *Cassandre* than it is to *La Mentirosa Verdad*.[39]

---

[34] *Œuvres*, Paris, 1758, V, 215.

[35] He must, however, have tried again, for the play was read to the actors on July 29, 1727, according to the *Mercure* for August of that year. It is now lost except for 42 lines preserved in La Grange-Chancel's *Œuvres* of 1758, IV, 65-8. In the same volume (pp. 70-158) he published *Orphée* and stated that the subject had been suggested by Racine to Louis XIV at the time when Molière and Corneille proposed to write *Psyché*.

[36] Paris, veuve de Pierre Ribou et P.-J. Ribou fils, 1732, 12°. Approbation, Jan. 5, according to Beauchamps. Republished, Paris, veuve Ribou, 1734; Utrecht, Néaulme, 1734; and in the author's *Œuvres*, Paris, 1758.

[37] *History*, Part IV, p. 383. For *Cassandre* cf. the same work, Part III, pp. 138-41.

[38] *La Mentirosa Verdad*, by Villegas, a play analyzed by Tenner, *Fr. Le Metel de Boisrobert als Dramatiker*, Leipzig, 1907, pp. 111-4.

[39] The person who solves the mystery appears in the middle of the Spanish play,

La Grange-Chancel eliminated the subordinate plot found in *Cassandre* and transferred the action from modern or medieval Spain to ancient Greece. He made of Remond de Moncade a young King of Crete and in place of Don Bernard he put the hero's mother. He altered completely the names of the other characters, but he did not change in any important respect their natures or their adventures.[40]

The subject was a singular one to be selected for a tragedy. As the queen's threats against the man she loves will obviously not be carried out, and as we look in vain for a villain, no one is in any real danger. Androclide admits that he had felt some satisfaction at the thought that his daughter would reign, but his motive in declaring her queen was to weaken the power of the rebels and his continuing to keep up what he supposed to be a fraud was the fear that, if he said the queen was his daughter, he would be thought to be lying in order to make his own daughter queen. Erigone is unjust both to Attale and to Nérée, but she soon hastens to make amends. The other characters show no departure from admirable behavior. So much virtue deprives the play of variety in situation and

but at the end of both French plays. His withholding information is due in the *comedia* merely to a whim, but in both French plays to the fact that he has been imprisoned.

[40] The King of Epirus died while fighting against rebels. His grief-stricken wife died after giving birth prematurely to a daughter, Erigone. A minister, Androclide, fearing that this princess would not live, substituted for her his own daughter, Nérée. His wife, Ismène, in charge of the girls and of her son, Attale, made, without her husband's knowledge, a new exchange, so that Erigone grew up as Queen of Epirus, though Androclide thought she was his daughter. The King of Crete, called in to defeat the rebels, sought to keep Epirus for himself and carried off Ismène as a hostage. When he died, he left his throne to his son, Sténélus, whom Attale defeated and captured. The Cretan prince is now in love with Nérée and has ordered the release of Ismène, whose arrival is expected. The day has come for Erigone to select a husband. Androclide advises her to marry Sténélus, but Attale, who loves her, protests against her favoring a foreigner. As she returns his love, she takes his advice and proposes to marry him, but his father intervenes, tells him that Erigone is his sister, and advises him to leave the country. When the queen learns from Nérée that he is about to sail, she has him brought before her and asks the reason for his attempted departure, but his father warns him not to speak, she feels that he is flouting her love, and he is imprisoned. A letter found on him is brought to her. As Androclide refers in it to Attale's love for his sister, Erigone concludes that Nérée is guilty of an incestuous passion and threatens to punish her. When she again interviews Attale, he tells her that she is his sister. She realizes that she must give up the man she loves, restore the throne to the lawful queen, whom she believes to be Nérée, and enter Diana's temple. Sténélus wishes to marry Nérée at once and leave for Crete, but his fiancée insists upon remaining in Epirus till she has been cleared of the accusation the queen has brought against her. We hear that the people, the priests, and the Vestals wish Erigone to remain queen and object to her marrying the king of another country. At this moment Ismène arrives. She reports that she had approved of the first exchange of children, but that, when she found that the princess would live, she had made the second substitution, but had not told her husband for fear that his ambition might overcome his loyalty. Her captivity had subsequently prevented her from telling her secret. As no one now doubts that Erigone is the lawful queen and is not Attale's sister, she will marry him and Nérée will marry Sténélus.

of effects it might have achieved if Androclide had been presented as a second Amasis.

As the author does not take us into his confidence, the effect he seeks seems to have been one of surprise, yet there must have been few in his audience who failed to foresee that a happy solution would be found. The action does not begin until the third scene of Act II.[41] The only three scenes that are at all tense are those in which a revelation is made, first by Androclide to his son, then by Attale to Erigone, and finally by Ismène to the assembled company. La Grange-Chancel had apparently lost the skill he had displayed in *Amasis* and *Ino et Mélicerte*. The classical rules that he applied were quite pointless in a play of this nature.

What may be of more interest to the modern reader than the adventures of his hero and heroine is a passage that may well have been inspired by the punishment inflicted upon him by the duc d'Orléans for the *Philippiques*. He puts it into the mouth of Nérée (IV, 1):

> Aurois-je dû prévoir, excusez ce murmure,
> Que les amours des rois, quand nous les irritons,
> Fussent si différens de ceux que nous sentons,
> Et que de leurs bontés, la trompeuse apparence
> Portât à cet excès la soif de la vengeance!

The tragedy was acted eight times at Paris, Dec. 17, 1731, to Jan. 4, 1732, and once at Versailles, Dec. 20, 1731. The *Mercure* thought that it would have had a longer run if the author had been at Paris, so that he could have made a few alterations. Erigone was played by la Labatte; Nérée by la Gaussin; Attale, by Dufresne; Sténélus, by Grandval; Androclide, by Sarrazin. Attendance grew gradually smaller until the last two performances earned nothing for the actors. The author's share in the eight productions was only 660 fr., 8 s.

Voltaire [42] declared that there was not an acceptable line in the play, that five hundred of its verses were ridiculous, and that the work was "le comble de l'extravagance, de l'absurdité, et de la platitude." La Harpe [43] found it a "roman insipide et embrouillé"; Nietzelt, the worst of its author's tragedies. These criticisms are exaggerated, for the verses, though often dull, are not absurd, there is no difficulty in understanding the plot, and the work is not inferior to its author's first tragedy, or, perhaps, to his lost *Sophonisbe*. It is true, however, that it added nothing to his fame. Its interest lies chiefly in an aging author's attempt to revive a type of play that, even in his youth, had been considered antiquated.

[41] In this scene Erigone says to Androclide and to Attale, "prenez votre place," and consults them about the important decision she has to make. The resemblance to *Cinna* is obvious.

[42] Moland, XXXIII, 242. [43] *Op. cit.*, XIII, 151.

His other tragedy was also novel for its time since the last new play on the life of a Christian saint to be acted at the Comédie Française was Brueys's *Gabinie* of 1699. Moreover, while the time represented is that of the third century A. D., the location in Gaul is a step in the direction of putting national subjects on the tragic stage. In this respect CASSIUS ET VICTORINUS, MARTYRS,[44] is a forerunner of Voltaire's *Adélaïde du Guesclin.*

Beauchamps states that the tragedy was mentioned by La Grange-Chancel in a letter written at Genoa on May 10, 1722, addressed to a duchess, and published in a "recueil de ses œuvres mêlées," The Hague, Ch. le Vier, 1724, 8°. It may, then, have been composed before *Erigone,* though it was not acted until nearly a year later. The author gives his source as "Grégoire de Tours, chapitres 32 & 33. du premier Livre de ses Histoires françoises." He then translates the passage, which refers to the invasion of Gaul by the Germans in the time of "Valerian & Galien," and records that the invaders burned a town in Auvergne where there was a fine temple. "L'antiquité rapporte que Victorinus fut prêtre du susdit temple "[45] and that, while Victorinus was persecuting the Christians, he met Cassius, was converted by him, and joined him in martyrdom.

In treating this meager theme, La Grange-Chancel imitated *Polyeucte.* In both tragedies the cast includes a Christian, a heathen heroine and her father, who is converted in the course of the play, and a victorious young Roman who fell in love with the heroine before he became a distinguished warrior. In both the action takes place in a Roman province during the third century A. D. One cannot read the interview between father and daughter while they await the visit of the Roman without recalling the conversation between Félix and Pauline that precedes the arrival of Sévère. In the original text of La Grange's tragedy *stances* were assigned in Act IV to Victorinus after his conversion. They were omitted because the actors pointed out that "nous en avons dans la tragédie de Polyeucte."[46] The scene is laid, however, in Gaul instead of Armenia, the heroine is unmarried, the rôles of Félix and Polyeucte are combined, and Néarque becomes the father of Sévère.[47]

---

[44] Paris, veuve P. Ribou et P.-J. Ribou, 1733, 8°. Dedicated to the princesse de Conti, "première Douairière." The dedicatory ode is reproduced in the author's *Œuvres* of 1758, V, 114-8. The tragedy was republished in the third volume of this work. For a study of it cf. Nietzelt, *op. cit.,* pp. 46-50.

[45] The original reads "Nam refert antiquitas Victorinum servum fuisse ante dicti templi sacerdotis " (cf. Henri Omont, *Grégoire de Tours, Histoire des Francs, Livres I-VI,* Paris, 1886, p. 21). La Grange-Chancel adapted his translation to his play by making Victorinus the priest instead of the priest's slave.

[46] They were published by the author in the preface of his play; cf. edition of 1758, III, 142-4.

[47] Victorinus, a Gallic aristocrat and high priest of a temple at Clermont in Auvergne, has had as a slave a Christian named Licas, who by prayer has caused the death of a dragon just as the priest's daughter, Justine, was about to be

Profiting by his audience's ignorance of later Roman history, La Grange-Chancel adapted it to his needs, as he admits in an entertaining passage of his preface:

Les plaisanteries qu'on fit sur le nom de Valerian, lorsque le sieur de Riouperoux donna au public une tragédie qui portoit ce titre,[48] m'ont empêché de prononcer le nom de cet empereur. J'ai eu la même délicatesse pour le nom de Galien, à cause du célebre médecin qui l'a porté. Claudius qui leur succéda, m'a paru plus digne de paroître sur la scene.

He goes on to say that, as Claudius was of uncertain birth, he felt himself justified in making him the son of Cassius and in having him belong to the well-known Roman family of that name. Such "fraudes pieuses" are in keeping with the attribution of distinguished ancestry to Madeleine de Provence and to Saint Denis. But he went farther than this, for, according to Gregory, it was Victorinus, not Cassius, who was converted while persecuting Christians and, as I have pointed out, it was Victorinus, not Cassius, who was for a while a slave. Moreover, the introduction of love, the miraculous elements, and the theme of a son's condemning his father to death are not found in the passage quoted from Gregory.

devoured. The Christians are now being persecuted, Licas has disappeared, and Claudius, a Roman general who has driven the Germans out of Gaul, has been offered the title of Caesar and association with the Emperor Galienus. Justine fears that this new honor will make him forget his love for her and that he will disapprove of her father's mild attitude towards the Christians. Victorinus recalls the facts that Licas once gave him a sword, blessed by the blood of martyrs, that had saved his home from the Germans, and that Claudius believes his father, Cassius, to have been murdered by the Christians. When Claudius arrives, he assures Justine that his love is as strong as ever and that he will not agree to become emperor unless she will marry him. She refers him to her father. Claudius hopes that Victorinus can convert an old man named Licas, whom he had found among Christians holding a service in a cave. He has been impressed by Licas, but he threatens to put him to death if he remains a Christian. When he asks whether news of his father has reached Licas, the old man replies that Christians do not kill and that God will show Cassius to his son, but only if he puts him to death. When Victorinus offers to hide Licas, his help is refused. Licas tells him that he is Cassius and that he was miraculously converted, while persecuting Christians, by a storm and a divine voice. He has remained a slave in order to convert Victorinus and has sworn to reveal his identity to his son. He now invites Victorinus to die with him. The priest prays for guidance. When he and Licas approach the temple where Claudius is to marry Justine, other priests and the people demand the death of Licas, or, if he is protected, that of Victorinus, who is disarmed when he seeks to defend his friend with the sword that his former slave had given him. Claudius hesitates to put Licas to death till he learns that this sword had been his father's. As Licas will not tell how it came into his possession, Claudius concludes that he was involved in the murder of Cassius and condemns him to death. Licas expresses pleasure at the approach of marytrdom and predicts that Claudius will soon learn about his father's fate. Justine protests so strongly that she prevails upon Claudius to save Licas, but word is brought that Victorinus has declared himself a Christian, joined Licas on the scaffold, and been shot to death by arrows from the mob. Licas, brought before Claudius in a dying condition, tells him that he is his father, announces that he has learned by supernatural means of the emperor's death, and hopes that Claudius will become the emperor who will replace false gods by the God of the Christians. Claudius curses himself, laments the fact that his father has made of him a parricide, and leaves with the intention of saving Justine, who has attempted suicide, or of dying with her.

[48] Cf. my *History*, Part IV, p. 400.

The feminine element in the tragedy is distinctly minor. Justine and her confidant are the only women in it and could have been omitted without seriously affecting the plot, for some other reason than his desire to marry Justine could have been introduced to explain the presence of Claudius in Auvergne. The girl seeks to be loyal both to her father and to her lover, but her intervention accomplishes nothing. The three chief characters are Claudius, who persecutes Christians in order to avenge his father, Cassius, the Christian eager for martyrdom, and Victorinus, at first a benevolent pagan, then a Christian martyr. About the first two La Grange-Chancel writes:

J'ai rassemblé dans Claudius les qualités de roi, d'homme & de juge, qui, au rapport du grand Corneille, n'avoient pas encore été réunies dans un même personnage.[49] On m'a mandé que quelques critiques ont blâmé la dureté de Cassius envers son fils: mais ils ne connoissent pas le caractere des premiers chrétiens. Il n'y avoit point alors de dispense de vœux, & l'exemple de Jephté leur servoit de regle.

It seems, however, inconsistent with the character that he should have made such a vow and that, although he had labored as a slave in order to convert Victorinus, he should make no genuine attempt to convert his son. His zeal for martyrdom overcomes his paternal affection, just as in France when the play was acted monasticism was in many cases overcoming family ties, but La Grange-Chancel does not draw this parallel in defending his presentation of the man.

Victorinus is more dramatic than Cassius as we are shown the last wavering steps he takes in his progress from paganism to Christianity. The author puts into his mouth lines that must have recalled to the audience recent persecution of Protestants and show La Grange-Chancel as an enemy of fanaticism shortly after Voltaire had expressed similar ideas in *Zaïre*. The passage is found in I, 4:

Les chrétiens, dont les mœurs l'emportent sur les nôtres,
Sont aujourd'hui, Lépide, opprimés par les autres:
Car enfin, de tout tems chaque culte est jaloux
De vouloir que son Dieu soit le plus grand de tous;
Et peut-être leur joug, s'ils devenoient les maîtres,
Ne seroit pas moins dur que celui de nos prêtres.
Des deux extrémités choisissant le milieu,
J'y crois pouvoir fixer le culte du vrai Dieu;
Que le moyen pour nous le plus sûr de lui plaire,
Est d'être généreux, pitoyable, & sincere;
Et sans porter plus loin un esprit combattu,
Aimer tous les chemins qui vont à la vertu.

---

[49] Cf. *Examen de Clitandre* (Marty-Laveaux edition, I, 271-3). Corneille could name no king that acted in the three capacities, but he held that the governors in *Polyeucte* and *Théodore* could be thought to have done so. Strangely enough, he did not think of the king in Rotrou's *Venceslas*.

From this liberal position Victorinus is induced by the heroism of Cassius to put himself openly on the side of the persecuted Christians. At the end of Act III, when we last see him, he is on the verge of becoming a Christian, but he has not denounced the gods of the heathen. He originally did this in the *stances* of Act IV. When these were omitted, a gap was left in the account of his conversion. It is unfortunate that the author, after suppressing the *stances,* found no way of bringing so important a person into the last two acts of his play.

The tragedy has much of the supernatural, both pagan and Christian. Reference is made to portents of disaster seen in a heathen temple, to the conversion of Cassius by divine means, to his prophetic gift, to a miraculous sword, to a dragon, and to the *cri du sang* that Claudius fails to heed. There are scenes of recognition when Cassius reveals himself to Victorinus and to his son. These and the scenes between father and son (III, 3, IV, 6) are effective. The action moves rapidly in the later portion of the play, with suspense well sustained. Too much of it, however, is relegated to *récits,* the dialogue is often not sufficiently animated, and Cassius, as well as Victorinus, appears in only three acts.

The tragedy achieved a better record than its predecessor. It was acted eleven times, from Oct. 6, 1732, to Jan. 26, 1733. Legrand de Belleville played Victorinus and was provided with "diamants de Grand Prestre." Sarrazin played Cassius; Grandval, Claudius; Louise Baron, Justine. The troupe supplied two Roman costumes, two bouquets of plumes, and hired two "assistans à la Romaine." The author's share of the receipts was 659 fr., 18 s.

Fréron,[50] who detected heresy, perhaps, in the author's liberality, was quite unjust to the play. He declared that he knew no tragedy worse composed. He attributed to it "une fable dénuée de vraisemblance & de liaison, le sens commun à chaque instant blessé, des caractères manqués," and the misfortune to appear after *Polyeucte.* La Harpe [51] was less severe. He pronounced the tragedy "plus passable et mieux conduite" than *Erigone* and offered the suggestion that it was unsuccessful because in it Christianity was "trop mal entendu." He may have had in mind the unsympathetic attitude of Cassius towards his son.

This comment would have astonished La Grange-Chancel, for he had written to the princesse de Conti when he sent her a copy of his tragedy that he wished to consecrate his lyre to "vérités ineffables," and he undertook another religious play, a fact that is known through his sending an ode to the comtesse de Verteillac "en lui adressant la mort de Joas, tragédie

---

[50] *Année littéraire,* 1759, IV, 28-30.
[51] *Op. cit.,* XIII, 152.

tirée de la Ste Ecriture." [52]   In this poem he renounces the heroes of Rome and Athens for those of Israel:

> Parcourez ces héros, qui de Rome & d'Athenes
> Furent les plus beaux ornemens;
> Sont-ils à comparer à ces saints capitaines
> Qui commandoient aux élémens? . . .
> Dans ce même Joas, célebré par Racine,
> Et que je ranime après lui,
> Voyez d'un bras vengeur la justice divine
> Sur ceux qui perdent son appui.

His last tragedy must have been a sort of sequel to *Athalie*, in which Joad had foreseen the backsliding of his protégé. As the work is lost, it is impossible to say to what extent its author followed Racine in capturing the spirit of the Old Testament, but the fact that he wrote it shows how faithful he remained to his master's memory. Like Racine he had early turned to subjects treated by ancient historians and by Euripides and like him he composed late in life two tragedies of religious inspiration. Unfortunately the resemblance is only external, for neither as a dramatist nor as a poet can he be compared with the man who had given him the benefit of his long experience in dramatic composition.

Not long after La Grange-Chancel had located the action of a tragedy in Gaul, Piron had selected sixteenth-century Sweden and Voltaire medieval France for their tragedies, so that François Tronchin (1704-1798) must have thought himself quite free to dramatize a subject from modern English history. He was a member of a distinguished Protestant family of Geneva and became as conseiller a member of the city's governing body. He visited Paris, frequented the salon of Mme de Tencin, and knew Voltaire, Diderot, and Grimm. He practised law at Geneva, where he published in 1779-84 *Mes Récréations dramatiques,* which contains tragedies of his own as well as reworkings of older plays by well-known dramatists. His only tragedy acted at the Comédie Française is MARIE STUART, REINE D'ECOSSE,[53] first performed on May 3, 1734.

Henri Tronchin suggested that François published his play anonymously

---

[52] The ode was published in his *Œuvres* of 1758, V, 165-8. For the countess, who died in 1751, cf. the *Biographie générale.* La Grange-Chancel refers to her as one " à qui le sang me lie."

[53] Paris, Pierre Prault, 1734 and 1735, 8°. Approbation, signed by Danchet, Nov. 28, 1734. Republished, Utrecht, Néaulme, 1735, and in *Mes Récréations dramatiques.* For the author cf. Henri Tronchin, *le Conseiller François Tronchin et ses amis . . .,* Paris, Plon, 1895. For a study of the play cf. L. A. Hill, *The Tudors in French Drama,* Baltimore, Johns Hopkins Press, 1932, pp. 107-10, and Karl Kipka, *Maria Stuart im Drama der Weltliteratur,* Leipzig, 1907, pp. 236-49. The play has also been discussed by Louis Morel; cf. *RHL,* XVI (1909), 424. Ersch, probably because he misread Beauchamps, attributed the play to Le Franc de Pompignan and was followed by Quérard.

because of Calvinistic opposition to the stage. It may be that another motive was to keep the audience from attributing to his Protestantism his interpretation of Mary and Elizabeth. He declared in his *avertissement* that he had been shocked by the portrayal of the English queen in plays by Montchrestien, Regnault, and Boursault, and that he would have given her name to his tragedy if he could have found a subject in the history of her life that would have enabled him to concentrate upon her " cet intérêt capital qui fait l'essence & le succès de ce genre de poëme." The Essex episode might have done, but it had been treated too well by Thomas Corneille for him to attempt it. He goes on to say that, if he had assigned to Mary all her historical crimes, he would have alienated from her the sympathy of the audience, whereas, if he had freed her from all guilt, he would have made Elizabeth odious. He consequently sought to make Mary better than she was without making Elizabeth worse.[54]

His sources were both historical and dramatic. He could have found in Camden most of his characters, their names, and those of other persons mentioned ; [55] also an ample account of the conspiracy formed in 1586, its

[54] Elizabeth consults Cecil and Dudley, " comte de Leycestre," as to whether she should restore Mary to her throne or execute her. Cecil is for execution; Dudley suggests arresting Norfolck and making a treaty by which Mary will acknowledge Elizabeth as queen and prepare her son for succession to the English throne. Though Cecil warns that Mary will not respect the treaty, Elizabeth takes Dudley's advice and bids Cecil prepare the document. When Dudley has left, his love of Mary is revealed to Elizabeth by Cecil, who hopes to diminish his rival's influence and hasten Mary's end. Norfolck, admitted by Helton, who secretly favors Mary, tells the captive queen that, while Melvil surrounds the palace with his forces, Gray will enter with his followers and kill Elizabeth. Though Mary loves Norfolck and is eager to escape, she urges him to spare the queen's life. While Helton hides Norfolck, Dudley makes love to Mary, who rebuffs him. She thinks he is trying, in accordance with Elizabeth's orders, to implicate her in the plot. Elizabeth sends Dudley, who has won the confidence of Melvil, to discover Norfolck. When the hour has come for the conspirators to strike, Dudley tells Mary that Melvil will not help her and that Norfolck must be given up, but he promises her security if she will cease to hate him. She bids him leave her and assumes responsibility for any plot that Dudley may report to the queen. She bids Norfolck follow Helton and assures him that her rank will protect her. Elizabeth, believing an attempt was to have been made upon her life with Mary's approval, orders her to be tried, but hesitates to put her to death. In an interview with Mary, she accuses her of complicity in the murder of Darnley, of plotting to secure the English throne, and of taking part in the recent attempt upon her life. In reply Mary calls Elizabeth her subject and accuses her of inventing the charges. Elizabeth tells her that she must be tried. Mary has a moment of hope when she hears that Melvil has lost his life and that Norfolck is advancing on the palace with 600 men, but soon Norfolck enters, wounded, and reports that, though he has killed Dudley, his men have been disheartened by news of Mary's execution and have been defeated. Mary hopes that they will be reunited in death. She is taken out to be executed. Norfolck dies upon hearing that she is dead. The *Mercure* states that Elizabeth, at the first two performances, reappeared on the stage, resolved to revoke the sentence, but, as this was too much like her conduct in Thomas Corneille's *Essex*, she was obliged subsequently to refrain from so kindly an action.

[55] Helton, " l'un des principaux officiers de palais " may be for Hatton, Elizabeth's vice-chamberlain. Melvil is mentioned by Camden and Boursault, but as remaining faithful to Mary. Lord Grey and Patrick Grey are named by Camden, but as faithful to Elizabeth or opposed to Mary.

betrayal, its connection with Mary's trial, the interest taken in the affair by foreigners, her condemnation and execution in 1587. But to make Norfolck the leader of the plot and to have him attempt to rescue Mary on the day of her execution must have come from Boursault. The report that Mary was driven to England by a storm is found in Montchrestien and in Regnault. As all three of these dramatists are mentioned by Tronchin, it is not surprising to find resemblances between his work and theirs. He seems to have taken, too, a hint from Corneille's *Pompée*, for both tragedies open with an interview between a sovereign and advisers in regard to the fate of a distinguished refugee who is at their mercy.

Dr. Hill declares that for the first time Elizabeth is made the protagonist of a tragedy on the death of Mary Queen of Scots, but one may well question this assertion, as Mary has the longer rôle in this play and as the fact that Elizabeth dominates the action is also true of earlier tragedies on this subject. Both queens have a share in bringing about the result. Elizabeth is more prominent in the first act and the fourth, but she is less conspicuous than Mary in the second and does not appear in the third and fifth. I would say that the main interest shifts from Elizabeth to Mary, somewhat as it does in *Andromaque* from the title-rôle to that of Hermione. What is remarkable is that both queens are sympathetically presented.

Elizabeth is convinced that Mary has plotted against her. She is by no means sure that she did not approve of Darnley's murder. She has just heard that she was herself to be murdered with Mary's consent. She discovers that the man she loves, Dudley, is in love with Mary. Nevertheless she gives her rival the opportunity of saving her life and is even willing, early in the play, to restore her to the Scottish throne. She is by no means a heartless queen, but she will not allow her love to give her a master. She is a match for her ministers, whom she plays off against each other.

Mary is less intelligent and consequently more pathetic than she would otherwise have been. She insists that Norfolck must not take Elizabeth's life, though she believes the queen has usurped her throne and is now seeking an excuse for putting her to death. Her love for Norfolck diminishes her chances of coming to terms with Elizabeth. Tronchin does not discuss the question of Elizabeth's right to the throne, which Catholic extremists had denied on the ground that Henry VIII's first divorce was invalid. He may have supposed that the charge was too well known to require explanation. He makes Mary tragic by giving her an uncompromising and insolent attitude towards Elizabeth and Dudley, one that contributes to her condemnation.

In comparison with the queens, the other characters have very minor rôles. Cecil is a clever and vindictive politician; Dudley, a courtier, loved by one queen and hopelessly in love with another; Norfolck, an extreme partisan, willing to murder Elizabeth in order to put Mary on the throne; Helton, a traitor.

Tronchin does not bring up the religious question. He gives the impression that the English are turbulent and that Elizabeth has shown great skill in mastering them, but in other respects he pays little attention to the manners of the country. He avoids the spectacular and gives no description of Mary's execution. He writes simply, but he shows no art in his dialogue and tends to lengthen speeches unnecessarily and to employ monologues, of which there are practically four in the last act.

It was, perhaps, on this account that the play met with small success. According to a contract made with the actors,[56] the tragedy was to be given first on May 3, 1734, was to be acted until the receipts became too small, and was to be revived after the actors returned from Fontainebleau, the author then still sharing in the receipts. The troupe carried out the terms of this contract, performing the tragedy on May 3, 5, 8, 10, 12, 15, 17, then withdrawing it until Feb. 6, 1735, when it made its last appearance and earned a small sum for the author, who received in all only 325 fr., 4 s.

Tronchin had, however, the satisfaction of knowing that his tragedy was acted once at Fontainebleau, when Louis XV was present and the queen and other ladies were moved to tears.[57] But the abbé Le Blanc was not similarly impressed. On Dec. 28, 1733, he reported that the anonymous tragedy was said to be "fort intéressante," but, after it had been acted, he pronounced it a mediocre production that had failed to move the audience. He condemned most of the rôles and considered the play as a whole inferior to Boursault's tragedy on the same subject.[58] It gives, indeed, evidence of Tronchin's familiarity with history and fairness of temper rather than of his talent as a dramatist.

The next play to appear was composed by a person whose point of view was much more conservative, but whose work had far greater success with eighteenth-century Parisians. The author was Jean-Jacques Le Franc, marquis de Pompignan. He was born at Montauban on Aug. 10, 1709, received a classical education, and became a magistrate and man of letters. He won considerable reputation as a poet, attacked the *philosophes* when he was received into the Academy as the successor of Maupertuis, was

---

[56] This contract was reproduced by Henri Tronchin, *op. cit.*, pp. 388-9. The *Mercure* shows that la Dufresne had the title-rôle, that Elizabeth was played by la Balicourt; Norfolck, by Dufresne; Dudley, by Grandval; Cecil, by Sarrazin; Helton, by Legrand de Belleville.

[57] Henri Tronchin, *op. cit.*, p. 203.

[58] Monod-Cassidy, *op. cit.*, pp. 193, 207-8.

attacked in turn by Voltaire, retired to his château, and died in 1784. Besides composing poems and two plays, he translated Æschylus and the Psalms and wrote a *Voyage du Languedoc*. The only play that survived him is Didon,[59] acted on June 21, 1734.

His classical studies sent him to Vergil. He was not discouraged by the fact that four French tragedies on the subject of Dido and Æneas had already appeared, for those of Jodelle, Hardy, and Scudéry were forgotten by the public and the three acts of Montfleury's *Ambigu comique* devoted to the theme had also ceased to be acted. He was accused by Voltaire [60] of imitating Metastasio, from whose *Didone* he may have derived the importance given to Iarbe, his combat with the hero, and a reflection on the activities of the gods,[61] but he omitted Dido's sister, who has a rôle of some importance in the Italian work, he added Achate, and he had Æneas kill Iarbe, as Metastasio does not do. His main source is the fourth book of the *Æneid*, supplemented by information from the first.

In his preface Le Franc criticized Vergil for having Dido yield too readily to love and for making Æneas a faithless lover. He consequently altered his hero's character so that he is no longer superstitious and is honest in his relations with both the Trojans and Dido.[62] He tells us that, as his play had been originally composed far from Paris and without the help of friends, he was obliged to make some changes in his text. He added a scene to Act I, evidently the third, because Madherbal had not originally carried out his promise of urging the queen to accept Iarbe. He also added IV, 1, and, in order to emphasize Dido's approaching death, had reconstructed Act V. Other corrections were merely those "des vers foibles, des expressions négligées, des mots parasites, et des rimes peu exactes." These changes were approved by Venuti, who had translated the first form of the play. Unfortunately the actors had adopted only those found in the last act.

[59] Paris, Chaubert, 1734, 12°, 1746, 1753-4. There were two other editions in 1734. An Italian translation by Venuti appeared in the edition of 1746 and was republished in 1749 and 1788. The French text was republished: Paris, Le Mercier, 1756; Paris, Duchesne, 1757 (*Enée et Didon*); Paris, Nyon l'aîné, 1784; Paris, Belin, 1788; in the *Répertoire Petitot*, 1803, 1817; in *Auteurs du second ordre*, 1808; in *Répertoires* of 1813, 1818, 1821, 1822; by Touquet in 1821; in *Chefs-d'œuvre dramatiques*, Paris, Didot aîné, 1824. For the author cf. the notice in the Petitot edition. For a Spanish translation cf. *PMLA*, XLVI (1931), 371.

[60] Moland, X, 105.

[61] Cf. *Didone*, I, 17:

> Veramente non hanno
> Altra cura gli Dei, che' l tuo destino,

and *Didon*, III, 6:

> Les Dieux s'occupent-ils des amours des mortels?

[62] President Bouhier attacked him for criticizing Vergil's characterizations, but he was defended by the Accademia della Crusca, the abbé Desfontaines, and J.-B. Rousseau.

The play is built around Dido, who speaks more than a third of its verses.[63] She is primarily, as in Vergil, a "grande amoureuse," but she believes that empires are "dus à qui sait les fonder" (I, 2), she does not forget that it is her duty to protect Carthage, and she speaks haughtily to Iarbe when he is disrespectful. She recalls her obligations to her dead husband, emphasized by her seeing his ghost in a vision, but her love for Æneas overcomes them. She has not, however, been seduced. Her passion gives an actress a varied rôle of hope and dread, anger and pleading. In the last act, after execrating her lover and making her dire prediction, she ends her life with an expression of love:

> Toi, qui ne m'entends plus, adieu, mon cher Enée!
> Ne crains point ma colere . . . elle expire avec moi,
> Et mes derniers soupirs sont encore pour toi!

Le Franc's efforts to strengthen the character of his hero are seen in his restraining him from seducing Dido, in his prolonging his struggle between love and duty, and especially in his having him defeat the Africans and kill his rival. He feels for the queen both love and gratitude, but he has seen physical manifestations of divine power and received warnings from a priest and from Achate. The difficulty of his situation makes him realize how often rulers are unjustly criticized (IV, 3):

> Crois-moi, tant de héros, si souvent condamnés,
> D'un œil bien différent seroient examinés
> Si chacun des mortels connoissoit par lui-même
> Le pénible embarras qui suit le diadême;
> Ce combat éternel de nos propres desirs,
> Et le joug de la gloire, et l'amour des plaisirs.

With him contrast Achate, Madherbal, and Iarbe. The Trojan is quite

---

[63] In Act I, Iarbe, King of Numidia, tells his old friend Madherbal, the leader of Dido's army, that he fell in love with Dido when he saw her at Tyre and that, since she has founded Carthage, she has twice refused to marry him. Now he has come, disguised as his own ambassador, to renew his offer, but he fears that she prefers Æneas. Madherbal promises to speak to the queen in his behalf. Dido rejects Iarbe and bids Madherbal prepare for war. She admits to her attendants that she loves Æneas, who, in Act II, expresses to Achate his desire to marry Dido and the necessity of his leading his men to Italy. When the queen tells him that the time has come for them to marry and for him to defend Carthage, he hopes that his men will agree to her plans. The supposed ambassador now admits to Dido that he is Iarbe, is again rejected, and plans revenge. In Act III he leaves Carthage after warning Madherbal that he will destroy the city. Dido now learns from Æneas that the gods have ordered him to renounce his love and depart. She reproaches him and warns him of storms at sea. He is deeply impressed and promises to obey her, but in Act IV he learns that the sea is calm and is persuaded by Achate to believe that the gods wish him to leave. He is determined, however, first to save Dido from Iarbe. Act V takes place early next morning. Dido has been accused by her husband's ghost of betraying him. She learns that the Trojans have surprised and defeated the Africans and that Æneas has killed Iarbe, but her joy vanishes when she is told that Æneas and his men are now at sea. Dido expresses her indignation, predicts that her people will hate those of her fugitive lover, and stabs herself. As she dies, she says farewell to Æneas.

indifferent to Dido's demands and is confident that a great future awaits his people. It is he who recalls to Æneas Hector's words and convinces him that he must not abandon his followers for love of a woman. Madherbal is equally opposed to the queen's marrying Æneas and wishes the Trojans to leave, but " Je sais parler aux rois, mais non pas les trahir " (I, 1), so that, when his friend Iarbe attacks Carthage, he has no thought of disobeying Dido. The Numidian is moved entirely by a desire to possess the queen. When she rejects for the fourth time his offer of marriage, he resorts to force. He has none of a lover's wiles (II, 6) :

> Peu fait à l'art d'aimer, j'ignore ce langage
> Que pour surprendre un cœur l'amour met en usage.

It is unfortunate that we do not see him after the first scene of Act III.

Le Franc's conservative ideas are expressed, not only in Dido's approval of conquest and in the defense of kings, quoted above, but in sympathy for ministers of state, who are (IV, 1)

> Victimes de discours, de jugemens sinistres;
> Coupables, si l'on croit le peuple et le soldat,
> Des foiblesses du prince et des maux de l'état . . .
> Emplois trop enviés que la foudre environne! . . .
> Heureux qui voit de loin l'éclat de la couronne!

Though both Dido and Æneas, under the influence of their love, express at times credulity in regard to oracles (II, 2, III, 4, 6), the play has a large element of the supernatural. Both Æneas and Iarbe are descendants of Jupiter. The gods intervene directly to hasten the hero on his way. There are references to warnings from ghosts. The future greatness of Rome and the bitter quarrel between that city and Carthage are predicted.

The structure could have been improved. The exposition is made by the ancient device of bringing together two old friends who have much to tell each other and the audience. Iarbe and Æneas never meet. The last act is largely composed of *récits*. However, the action steadily progresses, Vergil's scanty material is well distributed throughout the play, and there are at least four rôles that could tempt good actors. These must have been taken by Dufresne, for whose costume the actors rented diamonds, by Sarrazin, who was provided by them with a helmet, by Grandval, and by la Dufresne, who played Dido.[64] The tragedy was given thirteen times,

---

[64] According to the *Registres*, the cast was composed of Dufresne, Legrand, Du Breuil, Sárrazin, Grandval, and the three actresses, Dufresne, Jouvenot, and Du Breuil. Of these last la Dufresne alone would have been given the heroine's rôle. The other women represented her two confidants. Dufresne must have played Æneas; Grandval, Iarbe; Sarrazin, Achate. Madherbal was probably played by Legrand de Belleville; Zama, by Du Breuil. The author's share in the receipts was 1521 fr., 18 s.

from June 21, 1734, until July 31, then on Aug. 17, four times in December, and twice in April of the following year. Attendance was good, but not to be compared with that attracted by *Zaïre* or *Gustave*. *Didon* remained in the repertory, however, longer than Piron's tragedy, lasting until 1818, with a total of 159 productions at the Comédie Française.

On July 20, 1734, the abbé Le Blanc [65] called it "très interessante & très Galante." He considered it an imitation of *Bérénice,* thought that it pleased women more than men, praised the structure, and, except that there were too many maxims, the verse. Fréron [66] admired the play, especially the character of Æneas, which he considered superior to that assigned to him by Vergil. But Voltaire [67] condemned Le Franc for his failure to employ "le mot propre," and La Harpe objected to some of his expressions and ideas.[68] Like Fréron he thought he had imitated *Bérénice.* Though Le Franc could not be compared to Vergil or Racine,

> il écrit avec assez de pureté, quelquefois avec élégance et noblesse. . . . Il y a des beautés dans les scènes entre Enée et Didon. La conduite de la pièce est sage et régulière: c'est un de ces ouvrages qui prouvent que la médiocrité peut être estimable.

The success of *Didon* encouraged Le Franc de Pompignan to write another tragedy. Now Voltaire had, according to his own report,[69] read to Dufresne in 1733 the first scenes of *Alzire,* and the following year Le Franc had written a play on the same plan, which had been read once to the assembled actors when Voltaire decided to have his own tragedy produced. He wrote to the players that they ought, in their interest as well as in that of justice, to put the original on the stage before they produced its imitation. His letter displays his usual cleverness and makes an amusing contrast with the opinions he had already expressed in regard to the author of *Didon*:

> Je ne doute pas que M. Lefranc, qui a au-dessus de moi des talents de l'esprit, et de l'imagination que donne la jeunesse, n'ait embelli son ouvrage par des ressources qui m'ont manqué; mais il arriverait que, si sa pièce était jouée la première, la mienne ne paraîtrait plus qu'une copie de la sienne; au lieu que, si sa tragédie n'est jouée qu'après, elle se soutiendra toujours par ses propres beautés. . . . Votre intérêt s'accorde, en cela, avec le plaisir du public, qui applaudira toujours à M. Lefranc, . . . et la justice exige que celui qui a inventé le sujet passe avant celui qui l'a embelli.

---

[65] Monod-Cassidy, *op. cit.,* p. 212.

[66] *Année littéraire,* 1754 (3), pp. 98-101; cf. 1759 (3), p. 352, where he calls the play "une des mieux faites & des mieux écrites depuis *Racine.*"

[67] Moland, X, 104-5.

[68] *Op. cit.,* XIII, 185-8. Petitot, in the *examen* of his edition, noted that Dido is presented both as a lover and as a queen, that Æneas is made more manly by his victory over Iarbe, but does not meet him on the stage, and that Madherbal is effective. He regrets that, though Le Franc imitated fine passages in Vergil's fourth book, he did not reproduce Dido's last words.

[69] Moland, XXXIII, 558, 575.

As the actors had heard Le Franc's play read only once, they insisted on a second reading. Irritated by their demand, he withdrew his tragedy after addressing to them this bitter protest:

> Je suis fort surpris, messieurs, que vous exigiez une seconde lecture d'une tragédie telle que *Zoraïde*. Si vous ne vous connaissez pas en mérite, je me connais en procédés, et je me souviendrai assez longtemps des vôtres pour ne pas m'occuper d'un théâtre où l'on distingue si peu les personnes et les talents.[70]

He claimed that he had shown his manuscript to Voltaire, who had derived from it the "plan" of *Alzire*. Raynal[71] seems to have believed him, for, after making this statement, he adds, "Il paraît que Voltaire ne s'est pas encore lavé de ce reproche." Whether he was the offended or the offender, Le Franc resented so deeply the preference given to *Alzire* that he never wrote another play for the Comédie Française.

Now what do we know about *Zoraïde*? According to the evidence supplied by men on both sides of the controversy, it resembled *Alzire*. From the way that both Voltaire and Le Franc expressed themselves it was inferred by Raynal and others that the scene of *Zoraïde* was laid in the New World, but this belief was refuted by Voltaire[72] in unmistakable language:

> Il n'est point question, dans *Zoraïde*, d'Américains. *Il s'agit* des Indes orientales conquises par les Portugais. . . . Il a transporté la scène *à Zanguebar*.

According to the abbé Le Blanc,[73] *Zoraïde* also resembled Cahusac's *Pharamond*, about which he wrote on Aug. 27, 1736, that it was nothing else than

> Zoraïde retournée & que l'opposition des Mœurs simples et innocentes des Gaulois & des Francs aux mœurs corrompües des Romains de ce tems la & à la molesse des Courtisans d'Honorius n'est autre chose que celle des Portugais & des Indiens.

Le Franc would seem to have described the conquest by the Portuguese of Zanzibar, which they held throughout most of the seventeenth century, and to have contrasted the manners of the Christian Portuguese with those of a decadent oriental court, whose inhabitants were called Indians by Le Blanc and were mistaken for American Indians by Raynal.

The hero of *Zoraïde* may have been named Marius. On Oct. 28, 1734, Le Blanc wrote that a new tragedy by Le Franc was to be given in the following winter season and that it would be his second. On Jan. 3, 1735,

---

[70] Cited by Voltaire; cf. Moland, III, 369, and X, 105.

[71] *Cor.*, I, 213.

[72] Moland, XXXII, 460. Cf., also, X, 105:

> . . . De Zoraïd; la scène est en Afrique.

[73] Monod-Cassidy, *op. cit.*, p. 248.

he called this new tragedy *Marius*. On Jan. 27, 1736, he spoke of the resemblance between *Pharamond* and *Marius,* but he put into the same paragraph the passage I have just quoted with its reference to *Pharamond* and *Zoraïde*. As it is most improbable that Le Franc offered the actors a third tragedy just as he was breaking off relations with them because of their proposing to postpone the performance of his second, I conclude that *Zoraïde* and *Marius* are the same play. Marius may well have been the Portuguese hero, Zoraïde the African heroine of a *Zoraïde et Marius*.[74]

The last tragedy of 1730-34 was written by Henry Richer, a lawyer born at Longueil in Normandy in 1685. His interest in the classics led him to translate Vergil's *Eclogues,* Æsop, some of Ovid's *Heroides,* and to publish a *Vie de Mécénas*. When he died in 1748, Raynal,[75] who considered his fables his best work, wrote of him, " Il a vécu sans biens parce qu'il est honnête homme, sans honneurs littéraires parce qu'il n'était pas cabaleur, presque sans réputation parce qu'il était modeste." His contributions to the theater were, like his other work, based upon ancient writers, a *Coriolan,* published in 1748, but not acted, and SABINUS ET EPONINE.[76]

Richer states in his preface that he utilized Tacitus, Plutarch, and Xiphilinus. He subsequently mentions Cassius Dio, Suetonius, the Younger Pliny, and Juvenal.[77] Most of his facts could have come from Books IV and V of Tacitus's *Historia* and from Plutarch's *Amatoriae narrationes,* XXV. There he could find that a rebellion broke out in Gaul while Vitellius and Vespasian were struggling for power; that Civilis was supported by Julius Sabinus, who claimed descent from Julius Caesar; that Sabinus, defeated by the Sequani, took refuge in cellars under one of his homes, burned the house, spread a report of his death, lived underground for nine years with his wife, Eponine, was finally captured and put to death by Vespasian.

Acting on the theory that a poet has the right to alter details, provided

---

[74] Cf. Monod-Cassidy, *op. cit.,* pp. 220, 223, 248, 484. She calls attention to an *Arisbe et Marius* mentioned in the *Anecdotes dramatiques* as a tragedy of 1735. In my review of her book (*MLN,* LI (1946), 339) I suggested that this title might designate *Zoraïde et Marius.* This now seems to me more likely to be true, as I have found the source of the statement made in the *Anecdotes dramatiques.* It is the *Mercure* for February, 1735 (p. 362), where I read: " La Tragédie nouvelle d'*Arisbe et Marius,* que les Comédiens François préparoient pour donner à la fin de ce mois, ne sera représentée que l'hyver prochain." This fits exactly with what we know of *Zoraïde,* partially accepted, postponed at Voltaire's request, and withdrawn by Le Franc. The scribe's error may be due to the fact that Arisbe is the heroine of Caux's *Marius.*

[75] *Cor.,* I, 148.

[76] Paris, Prault père, 1735, 8°. Approbation, Feb. 10, *privilège,* Feb. 20, according to Beauchamps. Republished, Utrecht, Néaulme, 1735. A Dutch translation appeared in 1738 and 1741; an Italian translation in 1758.

[77] He may have consulted the *Histoire de Julius Sabinus* that Secousse presented to the Academy of Inscriptions in 1725; cf. below, the study of Chabanon's *Eponine.*

he preserve the main characters and events as given in his sources, Richer represented the revolt as continuing when Sabinus emerged from his retreat and associated with him, not only Civilis, but Antonius Primus, Caecina Alienus, and Marcellus, although these three men opposed Vespasian independently of Sabinus. On his own authority he brought Vespasian and his sons to the banks of the Moselle, caused both sons to fall in love with Eponine, and had his heroine, while attempting to save her husband, betray him to the emperor. He laid on Domitian most of the blame for the execution of Sabinus. He adds that he altered the name of Martalius, assigned by Plutarch to one of Sabinus's freedmen,[78] and gave Domitian as a confidant the actor, Pâris.

He located his action in Gaul rather than in Rome in order to show the valor in battle of Sabinus and Titus,[79] and to keep his hero from appearing ignoble in his seeking to kill Vespasian. As he had noted the popularity of love, but not of conjugal love, he had Titus fall in love with the heroine and prevented her from talking much with her husband. He says nothing about Passerat's tragedy on the same subject, though, published in 1694, it may have given him certain suggestions.

As in Passerat's *Sabinus* [80] the hero joins Marcellus and Cécinna in a plot against Vespasian's life, Eponine is loved by a member of the imperial family, the conspiracy is betrayed, Sabinus fights with the emperor's men just before his capture, and Eponine, after her husband's death, stabs herself. If Richer imitated Passerat in these respects, his statement that to have Sabinus seek to kill Vespasian at Rome would be ignoble may have been made in criticism of the older play. Richer's bringing children on the stage may have been in imitation of *Inès de Castro*.

From the hero's point of view the tragedy is primarily patriotic. The scene is laid in Gaul, as had been the case in La Grange-Chancel's recent *Cassius et Victorinus*; in the north-eastern part of what is now France, as in Voltaire's still more recent *Adélaïde du Guesclin*. And the conquests of the Gauls are set forth (I, 3) :

> Je peignis d'Allia la célébre journée,
> Les Romains mis en fuite, & Rome abandonnée,
> Dans ses murs embrasés, son Sénat égorgé,
> Son Capitole altier par Brennus assiégé,[81]

---

[78] He changes the name to Albéric. The other freedman is called Sinorix, a name employed by Plutarch in his story of Camma.

[79] Cf. Æneas's fighting with Iarbe in the *Didon* of Le Franc de Pompignan, though no such contest is found in the *Æneid*.

[80] Cf. my *History*, Part IV, pp. 403-5. Voltaire states that his protégé, Linant, had thought of dramatizing the story of Sabinus, and that he had dissuaded him; cf. Moland, XXXIII, 369.

[81] In Book IV of Tacitus's *Historia* the Gauls are said to talk of Brennus's capture of Rome.

Nos généreux Guerriers ravageant l'Illyrie,
La Macédoine entiére à leurs loix asservie,
Byzance subjuguée, & nos fiers bataillons,
Aux rives de l'Euxin plantant leurs pavillons . . .[82]
Ces Peuples belliqueux, méprisant d'autres loix,
N'ont jamais respecté que les Dieux & leurs Rois.

There is praise, too, for Gallic women (III, 7):

Dans ce climat, Seigneur, fertile en grandes ames,
La molesse n'est pas le partage des femmes;
Et jalouses souvent du nom de leurs Epoux,
Leur bras s'est signalé par les plus nobles coups.

Sabinus is himself a desperate patriot, altogether a Gaul at heart, in spite of his descent from Julius Caesar.[83] It is love for his wife that causes him to be ineffective. He could have escaped after his defeat by the Sequani, if he had been willing to go alone. Fear of her tears prevented his telling her of his plot and thus caused the conspiracy to fail. With him love is almost as strong a force as patriotism. With her it is far stronger, leads her to reveal the plot without thought of the political consequences of her action, and to kill herself when she finds that she has occasioned her husband's death. In answer to the criticism that she would have consulted her husband before revealing the plot, Richer explained that she thought it was the work of his enemies and that there was no time for her to consult him. Moreover, she was no more imprudent than was Aga-

[82] Cf. Corneille, *Horace*, vv. 49, 50.
[83] Entering the Roman camp in disguise, Sabinus confers with Primus, who has helped place Vespasian on the throne, but who now finds him ungrateful. They count on the help of Civilis, who is advancing with Batavians through a forest, and on that of Marcellus and Cécinna. Sabinus goes to meet Civilis, while Primus is ordered by Domitian to look for Sabinus. Titus and Domitian have fallen in love with a beautiful woman seen in a temple. She is Sabinus's wife, Eponine, who learns from one of her husband's freedmen that Marcellus and Cécinna will admit the enemy into the camp and murder Vespasian and his sons. Since she looks upon Marcellus and Cécinna as enemies of Sabinus, she warns Vespasian, who thanks her and has the conspirators arrested. Titus tells her of his love and seeks to discover her identity. They hear that Primus has escaped to Civilis. In deep anxiety Eponine visits her husband's hiding-place and learns that he has taken up arms. When she offers a sacrifice, she sees evil omens. She next learns that Titus has won a victory, that Primus has been killed, that the Batavians are in flight, and that a distinguished warrior has been captured. Titus brings her his laurels, but she fears for her people. When he allows her to see the captive, she recognizes him as Sabinus, admits she has betrayed him, and reproaches him for concealing his plan. He explains that he feared her tears and asks her to stab him. She prefers to appeal to Titus, who would be merciful to the captive, but Domitian counsels severity. Vespasian, who has told us that Marcellus is dead, interviews Sabinus, but gets no information from him. Eponine informs Titus that the captive is her husband, and, when he has promised help, that he is Sabinus. Domitian declares that Civilis sues for terms. Vespasian confronts Sabinus with his children, who have been for the first time brought into the open air. By ordering them killed, he gets him to tell who he is. As he is leaving with Domitian to be executed, Eponine comes to plead for him. She and Titus win Vespasian over, but it is too late, for Domitian has hastened his execution. After asking Titus to protect her children, Eponine stabs herself.

memnon in the *Iphigénie* of Racine and its source in Euripides. He justifies her trust in Titus by her knowledge of his character, illustrated by his conduct in this play and by his sending Berenice home out of respect for law.

Vespasian hesitates between justice and mercy. He defends the conquest of Gaul on the ground that the Romans have put an end to constant civil strife among petty kings. He acts quickly when he hears of the conspiracy. His apparently heartless treatment of Sabinus is counterbalanced by the pardon he grants him. His sons contrast sharply. Titus is altogether generous and heroic, conquering his passion as well as the rebels. Domitian is jealous of his brother, treacherous, and cruel. The rejection of their love inspires magnanimity in one, a desire for revenge in the other. Richer tells us that he had devoted a scene at the end of Act II to Domitian's making love to Eponine, but that he omitted it, as persons of taste had advised him to do, since they considered his love odious.

The exposition is enlivened by the fact that it is given largely by two conspirators in the camp of their common enemy. The three scenes in which the heroine decides to reveal the plot, makes it known to the emperor, and confesses to her husband are effective, as are those in the last two acts between Vespasian and Sabinus. There is, however, little excuse for showing the hero and heroine together in only one scene (III, 7) apart from the two lines of V, 4. Nor do we see enough of Vespasian and Domitian, whose decisions bring about the dénouement. Eponine's betrayal of the conspiracy lacks preparation, and more might have been made of the silent children, brought for the first time from their life underground.

The *Mercure* of February, 1735, noted the author's fondness for epic style,[84] having in mind, I suppose, the third scene of Act I, from which verses were cited, above. The abbé Le Blanc wrote on July 20, 1734, that the play had been announced; on Oct. 28, that it was being rehearsed by the actors who were playing at Fontainebleau.[85] It was produced seven times, from Dec. 29, 1734, to Jan. 24, 1735. Dufresne and his wife had the title-rôles. Sarrazin played the emperor; Grandval, Titus; Legrand de Belleville, Domitian; La Thorillière, Primus; la Jouvenot, Elise. Diamonds were provided for Dufresne and the children, a Roman costume for La Thorillière, an "écharpe" for Legrand. The first performance attracted a large audience, so critical, however, that Le Blanc believed the play had fallen "comme un Bœuf." [86] But the author made a number of changes

---

[84] Cf. T. W. Russell, *Voltaire, Dryden and Heroic Tragedy*, New York, Columbia University Press, 1946, p. 124.

[85] Monod-Cassidy, *op. cit.*, pp. 213, 220.

[86] *Ibid.*, pp. 222-3.

before the second performance, that of Jan. 8, 1735. The audience was then much smaller, but, according to the *Mercure,* appreciative. In the opinion of Le Blanc, Richer " ne sait ni faire les vers ni arranger un sujet. Il a manqué les plus belles situations du monde." The *Mercure* is much less severe, but, on the whole, the public sided with Le Blanc.[87] The play is chiefly to be remembered as an early contribution towards capitalizing Gallic patriotism.

[87] The author earned 405 fr., 6 s., nearly half of which sum came from the first performance.

CHAPTER VIII

VOLTAIRE TRIUMPHS

Adélaïde, Alzire, Zulime, Mahomet, Mérope

Zaïre represents in many respects a turning point in Voltaire's career as a dramatist. His earlier tragedies, with the possible exception of fragmentary *Artémire*, had derived their plots from other plays, from history, or from legend. *Zaïre* was not entirely independent of such sources, but it was much more largely than they a work of the author's imagination. It was also one that employed French history for background, if not for plot and characters, and it was the first highly successful tragedy after *Polyeucte* to make of Christianity an important theme. It was also more deeply sentimental than Voltaire's earlier productions. In one or more of these respects it became a model for the five tragedies that followed next, those which, along with *Zaïre*, established Voltaire in the prevailing opinion of his century as the leading French author of tragedies after Corneille and Racine.

The first of them was ADÉLAÏDE DU GUESCLIN,[1] again a tragedy of love and jealousy with French history in the background and French names in the cast, but one that is more of a national tragedy than *Zaïre*, for the scene is laid in France instead of Palestine, and all of the characters are French. The time, as well as the place, is now nearer home, the fifteenth century rather than the thirteenth. Voltaire states [2] that his plot is derived from the history of Brittany. The Kehl editors explain that he is referring to an incident of 1387, when Bavalan, commanded by the Duke of Brittany to put Clisson to death, pretended to obey, noted the duke's remorse, and then informed him that he had failed to carry out his order. A similar incident had appeared in *Artaxare*, a tragedy in which a king orders a faithful follower to have his son executed, and this agent, though he is the prince's rival in love, spares the young man's life and renounces his claim on the girl. Here there is blood relationship between the person who gives the order and the proposed victim, and there is rivalry between the latter and the agent, so that the plot of *Artaxare* [3] is nearer to that of *Adélaïde*

---

[1] Though played in 1734, it was first published in 1765 (Paris, veuve Duchesne, 8°), and then thanks to Le Kain. For other editions cf. Bengesco and Moland. For three Italian translations, one of them in two editions, cf. Ferrari, *op. cit.* For a study of the tragedy, cf. Lion, *op. cit.*, pp. 89-97.

[2] Moland, XLII, 398.

[3] Cf., in Chap. II above, the discussion of *Artaxare*. Collé (*Journal*, 1807, II, 112) thought in 1755 that several situations and the dénouement came from an old

than is the historical incident, yet the resemblance is not sufficiently close to make it certain that one play inspired the other. Whether it did or not, the plot remains largely, like that of *Zaïre*, one invented by Voltaire.[4]

The tragedy is much simpler than *Artaxare*. Besides confidants and guards, it has only four characters. The most important, and by far the longest rôle is that of Vendôme, who is made intensely dramatic by his violent and unrequited love of Adélaïde, his jealousy that leads him to condemn his brother to death, his remorse over the order he has given, and his delight when he discovers that it has not been carried out. With his violence contrasts the calmness of Coucy, who gives an excellent illustration of feudal loyalty. He deplores his lord's alliance with the English, his

tragedy by Maréchal, but in 1761 (*Journal historique*, edited by Van Bever, 1911, p. 199) he stated that Acts IV and V came from Baro's *Parthénie*. Now in Maréchal's *Papyre*, as in *Parthénie*, a man in high position gives a death order that is not carried out, but in *Papyre* the order is revoked by the person who gives it, and in *Parthénie* there is no blood relationship. *Artaxare* is consequently closer to *Adélaïde* than either.

[4] Allied to the English against the Dauphin, son of Charles VI, Vendôme is defending Lille, besieged by French loyalists. He has rescued Adélaïde, niece of the great Du Guesclin, and has fallen in love with her, but she is already deeply attached to his brother, Nemours, who is in the hostile army. Coucy, though he disapproves of the alliance between his liege lord, Vendôme, and the English, remains loyal to him, even renouncing his love for Adélaïde and urging her to accept his master. This she declines to do. Nemours, captured by his brother, comes, wounded, upon the stage and is well received by Vendôme, but, when he learns that his brother loves Adélaïde and sees that she is in his power, he is overcome with emotion, his wound reopens, and he leaves the stage in a serious condition. Adélaïde rejects Vendôme's offer of marriage on the ground that he fights against his king, but he accuses her of loving another man, threatens to kill his rival, and suspects Coucy. The latter admits that he had once loved Adélaïde, but declares that he has urged her to accept Vendôme, who believes him and agrees to abandon the English if he can win the girl. Coucy tells him that he should do his duty without taking his marriage into consideration. [In the final version he wins him over and offers to report his decision to the French king.] Nemours and Adélaïde discover that each is faithful to the other. Vendôme declares that he has decided to support the King of France and invites Adélaïde to the altar, but she insists that an invincible obstacle still separates them. Vendôme begs Nemours to help him discover his rival and receives so unsatisfactory an answer that he declares he would suspect him if he had previously known Adélaïde. [In the final version Nemours admits that he is the rival, Vendôme has him arrested and entrusts him to Coucy, who releases him on his parole.] In Act IV Nemours admits that he is Vendôme's rival and is arrested, after he has taken Adélaïde as his wife, without the " pompe des autels." [In the final version Vendôme gives Adélaïde a last chance to marry him in order to save Nemours, who encourages her in her resistance and is imprisoned.] Vendôme bids Coucy put Nemours to death. Coucy promises to be faithful to him. Vendôme bids him fire " le canon des remparts " to announce his brother's death. He still offers to spare Nemours if Adélaïde will marry him, but she refuses, though, after he has gone, she decides to plead with him again [omitted in the final version]. In Act V we learn that Vendôme, distrusting Coucy, has sent a soldier to kill Nemours, but that, after a bitter struggle, he has decided to spare his brother. The noise of the cannon is heard. Adelaïde now agrees to marry Vendôme if he will spare Nemours and liberate him, but she is told that it is too late. Vendôme's remorse induces him to ask Adelaïde to kill him, but Coucy brings word that he has spared Nemours and that a corpse, reported to have been taken from the prison, was that of a soldier who had sought to stab Nemours. Vendôme joyfully greets his brother, surrenders Adélaïde to him, agrees to admit the French into Lille, and asks: " Es-tu content, Coucy ? "

subordination of military and political affairs to love, and his hostility to his brother, but he puts above everything else his loyalty to Vendôme except when he feels sure that the best way to aid him is to disobey him. It is his plan that triumphs at the end of the play with the brothers' reconciliation and the surrender of Lille to the French army.

The other characters are much less impressive. Adélaïde, whose rôle is about the length of Coucy's, is moved to resist Vendôme both by her love for Nemours and by her patriotism. Her only struggle is in bringing herself to accept Vendôme's offer in order to save his brother's life. It is unfortunate that the man she loves gives little evidence of force. Captured in battle, overcome by the sight of Adélaïde when he thinks she has deserted him, he is merely a pawn in the game that is played between his passionate brother and the imperturbable Coucy.

The play is a purely Aristotelian tragedy, with a protagonist that is not altogether evil, one whose passion leads him to give an order that would have produced tragic consequences if it had not been for Coucy's intervention, and with emphasis placed upon the recognition of Nemours, the discovery by Vendôme that he is his rival, and the striking change of fortune at the end of the play. There is, especially in the final form of the tragedy, marked progress in Vendôme's attitude towards his brother and in that of Adélaïde in regard to Vendôme. The scenes become more and more intense as the plot evolves. We should like, however, to know more about the circumstances that led Vendôme to become a collaborator. In the final version Voltaire made Coucy lay the responsibility on Charles VI (I, 1):

> Charles qui s'abandonne à d'indignes ministres
> Dans ce cruel parti tout l'a précipité,

but this is hardly sufficient explanation if we are to feel sympathy for Vendôme. Moreover, when the play was first given, Vendôme condemned his brother so quickly that Voltaire trembled for his fourth act. This error was corrected to a certain extent in the final version, but we should still like to know more about Vendôme's relations with the reigning family.

The play was undertaken as early as Jan. 27, 1733.[5] On June 10 the author was able to recite it. On Oct. 27 he sent a copy to Cideville.[6] It was first acted on Jan. 18, 1734, when Dufresne played Vendôme; la Gaussin, Adélaïde; Grandval, Nemours.[7] Admission was paid by 1470 persons. The audience disapproved of the use in a play of Du Guesclin's name, to the

---

[5] Lion, op. cit., p. 90.

[6] Moland, XXXIII, 388-9.

[7] The Registres show that other rôles were taken by Legrand de Belleville, who probably played Coucy, by La Thorillière, Du Breuil, and la Jouvenot, obviously Adélaïde's confidant.

firing of the cannon, to the criminal intent attributed without historical support to a prince of the blood, and to Vendôme's last words, " Es-tu content, Coucy," greeted by the parterre with the response, " couci-couci." [8]

The abbé Le Blanc [9] wrote on Feb. 4 that the tragedy had been " cruellement siflée " at this first performance and that Voltaire had subsequently rewritten the last three acts. He predicted that it would never be successful. However, the second performance, although less well attended, had already met with a better reception. It continued to be acted till Feb. 20. As this was the eleventh performance, the play can hardly be said to have failed,[10] yet in Voltaire's eyes it must have suffered by comparison with Zaïre. He withdrew it, refrained for many years from publishing it, and set about reworking it.

By the beginning of 1738 he had made many corrections.[11] On July 24, 1749, he declared that he was preparing a revised version, to be called the Duc de Foix.[12] He was then at Lunéville. The new version was completed at Potsdam and called Amélie ou le Duc de Foix, in honor, I suppose, of Frederick II's sister, Amelia. It was acted at Paris on Aug. 17, 1752, with Le Kain in the rôle of the duke,[13] la Gaussin in that of the heroine, Grandval in that of Lisois. The tragedy was played fifteen times in that year, until Dec. 16, and remained in the repertory until 1761, with a total of twenty-seven performances.[14]

Voltaire sought in this version to avoid what had occasioned criticism of Adélaïde. He kept the scene in France, but he selected for the time a period of French history less well known than that of Charles VI. Thierry III is King of France. The fact that he is dominated by Pépin d'Héristal makes the duc de Foix, in whose palace the scene is laid, ally himself with the Moors, who replace the English mentioned in Adélaïde. The heroine is called Amélie; Nemours, Vamir; Coucy, Lisois. Only the heroine's confidant retains her name. As the period is the eighth century, cannon could no longer be mentioned, nor the name of Vendôme employed. Lisois's name gave the parterre no opportunity for punning.

Voltaire made other changes. He did not allow the duke and the heroine to meet before the second act, or his brother to appear before the third. There is no suggestion that the brother may be dead, no show of blood when

---

[8] Moland, XXXIII, 410; Grimm, Cor., VI, 367-9.

[9] Monod-Cassidy, op. cit., p. 195.

[10] Voltaire's share in the receipts was 905 fr., 2 s.

[11] Moland, XXXIV, 376.

[12] Paris, Lambert, 1752, 8°; approbation, Dec. 6. For other editions cf. Bengesco and Moland. An Italian translation was published five times in 1774-1803. Cf. Moland, XLII, 398.

[13] Mémoires de Lekain, Paris, 1801, p. 25. Le Kain accepted the rôle after Grandval had refused it.

[14] Voltaire received 1796 fr., nearly twice what Adélaïde had earned for him.

he enters. His reputation for valor is enhanced by his surrendering of his own accord. His priestless marriage is omitted. The concluding lines are altered. What is of greater importance is the fact that Voltaire had the duke learn that his brother is his rival in Act III,[15] so that his decision to put him to death does not follow immediately upon this discovery. The brother is now present when the duke gives the heroine a chance to save him, so that it is the brother rather than the girl who refuses the duke's offer to marry her.

Voltaire preferred this new form of his tragedy and wrote in 1763 that the *Duc de Foix* was incomparably less " mauvais " than *Adélaïde*. It was mainly from *Le Duc de Foix* that he created *Le Duc d'Alençon ou les frères ennemis*,[16] a three-act tragedy written to be acted by the Prussian princes, but he retained from *Adélaïde* the names of Nemours, Coucy, and Dangeste, the time of the action, and the use of cannon. He made of Dangeste, who had been Nemours's confidant, Adélaïde's brother and gave some of her lines to him, others to Nemours, managing in this way to suppress the feminine rôles. The scene is now laid in " la ville de Lusignan en Poitou," in memory, perhaps, of the heroine's father in *Zaïre*. The majority of the verses are those found in the *Duc de Foix*, of which Voltaire omitted most of the second act and parts of the others.

Le Kain [17] refers to the *Duc d'Alençon* as having the same subject as *Adélaïde*, but one that had been " transporté dans un autre tems, et mis sous d'autres noms." The actor extracted from this tragedy and from the first version of *Adélaïde* the major portion of three acts and combined them with the last two acts of the *Duc de Foix*, adding a few verses from the second act of the *Duc d'Alençon*. Then, although the author refused his consent, he secured the approval of some of Voltaire's friends and produced the play on Sept. 9, 1765, at a time when de Belloy's *Siège de Calais* had shown that a tragedy representing the period of the Valois could succeed, even if it had a traitor as an important character. The production was applauded with " fureur sans égale." When the report reached Voltaire, he asked for the manuscript in order that he might correct it. When it left his hands, the tragedy was, except for a few slight changes, in its final form.

The original text of *Adélaïde* survived in the names of the characters, the time and place of the action, the sound of the cannon, the meeting of the duke and the heroine in the first act, her informal marriage to Nemours,

---

[15] This change may have been suggested by *Alzire;* cf., below, the discussion of that tragedy.

[16] First published in 1821. Voltaire also composed *Alamire*, a fourth version of *Adélaïde* with the scene laid in Spain. Wagnière had a manuscript copy, but the work was never published; cf. Moland, III, 79.

[17] *Mémoires de Lekain*, Paris, 1801, pp. 71-5; *Mémoires secrets*, II, 233.

and the phrase, " Es-tu content, Coucy ? " As in the *Duc de Foix*, more explanation is offered in regard to Vendôme's deserting to the English, it is in the third act that he identifies his rival in Nemours, and the latter is present when the duke's offer of marriage is rejected. The result is that the actions of Vendôme and Adélaïde are easier to understand, though Vendôme is given a new deed of brutality by his having Dangeste put to death.

The play was acted nine times, Sept. 9 to Oct. 6, and again on Nov. 2. Le Kain played Vendôme; la Dubois, Adélaïde; la d'Epinay, her confidant. The *Registres* show that Grandval, Molé, Dauberval, and Fromentin also acted. Grandval may have retained his old rôle of Nemours, but it is more likely that he surrendered it to Molé and took himself the part of Coucy. Twelve soldiers were hired as supernumeraries. Thieriot[18] reported the success of the play, though he regretted that la Clairon was not in the cast. Grimm[19] preferred it to the *Duc de Foix* and thought that, though it was " faiblement écrite," it had " un grand dessein et des beautés d'un ordre superieur." He found the hero admirable in Acts III and V. He said that, though la Dubois acted Adélaïde badly, the play succeeded at Fontaine-bleau in November, 1765. He mentioned a performance at Ferney in September, 1767, when La Harpe and his wife took the parts of Vendôme and Adélaïde. The tragedy remained in the repertory of the Comédie Française until 1846, with a total of 198 performances, or, if we add those of the *Duc de Foix*, 225.

Pride in his own acting may have helped create La Harpe's enthusiasm over the tragedy. He declared[20] that it contains one of the best examples of *péripétie* to be found on the stage and that Acts III, IV, and especially V put it, when performed, in the first rank of tragedies, though he admitted that, when read, it belongs in the second on account of its inferiority in style except where passion is expressed. He admired the rôles of Vendôme and Coucy, the portrayal of feudalism and anarchy as they existed in the period described, but he had certain reservations. Vendôme should have forced Nemours to identify himself as soon as he captured him, should have questioned him in regard to his motives for accompanying the attacking party, should have admitted to Adélaïde his intention of supporting the King of France as soon as she told him that his failure to do so prevented her marrying him. He thought it artificial to delay until Act III Vendôme's discovery of a rival in his brother. He held that the action languished at the beginning and at the end of this act, and he pointed out a number of defects in the verses.

---

[18] Cf. *RHL*, XVI (1909), 163.
[19] *Cor.*, VI, 367-9, 397, VII, 417.   [20] *Op. cit.*, XI, 219-57.

Lion [21] noted that the play was praised by président Hénault, was placed above *Zaïre* by the abbé Galiani, and was condemned by Geoffroy. He himself thought that Voltaire had lingered too long over the exposition and that the dramatist was unable to decide whether to make Adélaïde or Vendôme his leading character, " car Adélaïde conduit la première moitié du drame et Vendôme la seconde." This criticism seems to me unjust, for Vendôme dominates the action throughout the play, except in Act V, when his plan is happily thwarted by Coucy. It is between these two men and within Vendôme's soul that the action mainly takes place. In spite of the fact that Adélaïde gave her name to the play, her failure to appear in the *Duc d'Alençon* shows that Voltaire did not consider her presence on the stage essential. Lion was better advised when he offered the explanation that the dramatist's error lay in straining after emotional situations to the neglect of " ces peintures de sentiments qui sont l'honneur de *Zaïre*."

Voltaire began to write his next tragedy, ALZIRE OU LES AMÉRICAINS,[22] before *Adélaïde* was acted. There is considerable resemblance between the two plays. In each the scene is laid in a city governed by a nobleman who holds in his power a woman whom he loves, though she prefers a captive; hostile forces are defeated in a sortie; a prominent rôle is given to an older man who supports the governor, though he disapproves of his actions, and seeks to win for him the hand of the heroine. Except in regard to this marriage, the ideas of the older man prevail at the end of each play and help bring about a striking change of fortune. In each play, too, the heroine thinks for a while that her lover is dead. When they first meet, Alzire's emotions affect her as Nemours is affected by his. Compare *Adélaïde*, II, 3, and *Alzire*, III, 4:

> Nemours (entre les bras de son écuyer):
> Adélaïde . . . ô ciel! c'en est fait, je me meurs.
>
> Alzire (elle tombe entre les bras de sa confidente):
> Zamore! . . . Je succombe; à peine je respire.

In each tragedy the governor discovers that a captive is his rival,[23] condemns him to death, and at the end of the play changes his attitude towards him and allows him to marry the heroine. In each tragedy the action is delayed and, before it begins, a scene of recognition is effectively employed.

[21] *Op. cit.*, pp. 96-7.

[22] Paris, J. B. C. Bauche, 1736, 8°. Dedicated to Mme du Châtelet. For other editions cf. Bengesco, Moland, and *MLN*, XLIV (1929), 328, and XLVII, 236. For nine Italian translations, some of them reprinted several times, cf. Ferrari, *op. cit.*, pp. 13-24. German translations appeared in 1738, 1739, and 1741, the last of them by Frau Gottsched. A Spanish translation called *Elmira* was acted in 1788; cf. A. M. Coe, *op. cit.*, p. 82. For a study of the play cf. Lion, *op. cit.*, pp. 98-112.

[23] In the original version of *Adélaïde* the discovery is made in Act IV, but in *Alzire*, in the *Duc de Foix*, and in the final version of *Adélaïde* it occurs in Act III. As suggested above, the success of *Alzire* may have induced Voltaire to make this change.

But there are considerable differences between the two plays. In both love is predominant, but the part played by patriotism in one is taken by religion in the other. While both depart from the traditional Graeco-Roman subject, the scene of *Alzire* is laid, not in fifteenth-century France, but in sixteenth-century South America. The heroine, instead of the governor, has the longest rôle in the play, the rôle of the man she loves is lengthened, the governor's is greatly reduced. She is provided with two confidants instead of one and with a father who has no corresponding rôle in the earlier play. The changes enabled the author to profit by the appeal of sentiment, of ideas, and of the exotic, with the result that *Alzire* was much more warmly received than its predecessor and that the resemblance between the two plays has been usually overlooked.[24]

[24] Alvarez, former governor of Peru, has grown too old to continue in office and has turned over his duties to his son, Gusman, whom he advises to rule in accordance with Christian principles of mercy and forgiveness. Gusman is respectful to his father, but shows that he favors sterner measures in regard to the Indians. He agrees, however, to free the captives that are now in his power and asks his father to win for him in return the hand of Alzire, an Indian princess who, like Montèze, her father, has become a Christian. Montèze, who collaborates with the invaders, orders her to marry Gusman and soften the hearts of the Spaniards in their relations with her people. She answers that she loves Zamore, another Indian chieftain, and that the Spaniards have destroyed the empire of the " enfants du Soleil." She does not conceal her love from Gusman, but he feels that, as Zamore is dead, her affection for him is no obstacle to their marriage. In Act II Zamore and his followers, just released from prison, plan to attack the Spaniards with the help of Indians who are in a forest outside the city. Alvarez recognizes Zamore as the Indian who had once saved his life and allows him to see Montèze, who tells him that Alzire has not been enslaved, that he has himself been converted to Christianity, and that it is useless to resist the superior civilization of the Spaniards. When Montèze has left him, Zamore agrees to an attack on the city and expresses his desire to kill Gusman, who had destroyed his power and had tortured him nearly to death. When Act III begins, Alzire has married Gusman, but she continues to love Zamore. She learns that a battle has begun and that a captive desires to see her. When he enters, she recognizes Zamore, assures him of her love, and asks him to kill her for yielding to her father's demand that she should marry Gusman. Their conversation is interrupted by Alvarez, who presents Zamore to Gusman as one who has saved his life, but Zamore names himself and denounces Gusman, with the result that he is arrested. The governor goes to meet the attacking Indians, while Alvarez promises to help Alzire, but bids her remember that she is now married to his son. In Act IV we learn that the attacking Indians are dead or captured. Gusman yields to his father's request for delay in punishing Zamore, but reproves Alzire for her plea in his behalf, though he tells her not to believe him inflexible. Meanwhile one of Alzire's confidants has bribed the soldier in charge of Zamore, who invites the heroine to escape with him to the wilderness. This she refuses to do. Sent out with the soldier, he seizes his guard's sword and fatally wounds Gusman with it. Alzire is arrested as an accomplice. She learns in Act V that both she and Zamore have been condemned to death. Alvarez declares that they will be spared if Zamore will become a Christian, but, with Alzire's approval, he declines the offer. When Gusman is brought in, Zamore begs him to spare Alzire, but she asks for death. Gusman admits that he has led a cruel life and that his death is deserved. Then he declares that he will show Zamore the difference between their religions, pardons both captives, bids them marry, allows Zamore to rule again over his people, and asks Alvarez to protect them. Zamore is so deeply impressed that he begins to believe that Christianity is " la loi d'un Dieu même." Alzire repents of her errors. Gusman dies after asking Zamore to become a Christian. Alvarez sees in this ending the will of a " Dieu qui frappe et qui pardonne."

Voltaire had other sources than *Adélaïde*. For background he may well
have consulted Augustín de Zarate and Garcilaso de la Vega.[25] He tells
us that, in making so cruel a warrior as Gusman pardon, under religious
influence, his would-be assassin, he was imitating the action of François de
Guise when he forgave the Protestant who had made an attempt upon his
life.[26] Like Gusman, Guise was a "persécuteur en bonne santé, et pardon-
nant héroïquement quand il était en danger." He had said, "Ta religion
t'enseigne à m'assassiner, et la mienne à te pardonner," a remark that
becomes (V, 7):

> Des dieux que nous servons connais la différence :
> Les tiens t'ont commandé le meurtre et la vengeance :
> Et le mien, quand ton bras vient de m'assassiner,
> M'ordonne de te plaindre et de te pardonner.

These lines have also a remarkable resemblance to Rowe's *Tamerlane*
(1702), III, 5:

> Now learn the difference 'twixt thy Faith and mine:
> Thine bids thee lift thy dagger to my throat;
> Mine can forgive the wrong, and bid thee live.

La Place [27] pointed out this similarity when he translated Rowe's play, and
concluded that "deux grands hommes se rencontrent." It is quite possible,
however, that Voltaire combined in his verses his recollections of Rowe's
verses and of Guise's generous retort.

In selecting a subject from the history of the New World, Voltaire had
been preceded by Dryden in England and by Ferrier in France. As he
mentions both the *Indian Emperour* and *Montézume*,[28] it is possible that
he derived from either author the idea of laying his scene in America and
of making some of his characters Indians. As *Montézume* is lost, it is
impossible to say more about its relation to *Alzire*. Dr. T. W. Russell [29]
believed so strongly in the influence of Dryden upon Voltaire that he twice
called *Alzire* an adaptation of the *Indian Emperour*, but the plays differ
altogether in characters and plot. Heroic tragedies had been written in
France, not only before the time of Voltaire, but before that of Dryden.
Voltaire had introduced remarks about religion into his *Œdipe*, written in
all probability before he had ever read a line of Dryden. The mention of

---

[25] Cf. M. L. Perkins in *MLQ*, IV (1943), 433-6.
[26] Moland, XXXIII, 471.
[27] Cf. Lillian Cobb, *Pierre-Antoine de La Place*, Paris, Boccard, 1928, pp. 61-2.
[28] Cf. my *Sunset*, pp. 55-6. Voltaire quotes two lines from *Montézume*, but he may
have borrowed these, in somewhat altered form, from the frères Parfaict. For Le
Franc de Pompignan's claim that he inspired *Alzire*, cf. in the preceding chapter the
discussion of his *Zoraïde*.
[29] Cf. *Voltaire, Dryden & Heroic Tragedy*, New York, Columbia University Press,
1946, pp. 75, 80, 96-100, and my review of it in *MLN*, LXII (1947), 492-5.

torture may have been suggested by the English dramatist, but, if so, Voltaire made surprisingly little use of it. It is possible, of course, that some of the ideas in *Alzire* may have come from Dryden's play, but it is equally possible that they originated elsewhere. Certainly the tragedy is in no sense an adaptation of the *Indian Emperour*.

It has also been proposed [30] that Alvarez represents the merciful Las Casas, whose account of relations between Spaniards and Indians Voltaire may have used, as well as that of Garcilaso de la Vega. The ideas the tragedy presents are both in praise of Christianity and in condemnation of the manner in which many of its adherents practise it. In the rôle of Alvarez and in Gusman's remarks when he is about to die, Christianity is presented as a religion of kindness towards the weak, of brotherhood among men of different races, and of pardon for one's enemies. The true God is one who pardons (I, 1). But the Spaniards have caused " le nom de l'Europe et le nom catholique " to be abhorred (I, 1):

> Déserteurs de ces lois qu'il fallait enseigner,
> Nous égorgeons ce peuple au lieu de le gagner. . . .
> Fléaux du nouveau monde, injustes, vains, avares,
> Nous seuls en ces climats nous sommes les barbares.

The pagan Indians had spared Alvarez, whereas the Christian Spaniards had tortured Zamore. Forced conversion is approved by the Council, as it had been by Louis XIV in his treatment of Protestants, but it is eloquently rejected by Alzire, even at the risk of her lover's life and her own (V, 5):

> Mais renoncer aux dieux que l'on croit dans son cœur,
> C'est le crime d'un lâche, et non pas une erreur:
> C'est trahir à la fois, sous un masque hypocrite,
> Et le dieu qu'on préfère, et le Dieu que l'on quitte:
> C'est mentir au ciel même, à l'univers, à soi.

The religion that is recommended in *Alzire* is not one of priests and sacraments, of external observances, supported by force and tolerating cruelty towards the conquered, but one of sincere belief, typified by the life of Alvarez and by Gusman's last moments. It is not that of Montèze, who regards his newly acquired religion merely as an element in European culture, brought by certain Spaniards who have come (II, 4)

> Moins pour nous conquérir qu'afin de nous instruire;
> Qui nous ont apporté de nouvelles vertus,
> Des secrets immortels, et des arts inconnus,
> La science de l'homme, un grand exemple à suivre,
> Enfin l'art d'être heureux, de penser, et de vivre.

Voltaire comments upon these lines to the effect that Montèze loved his

---

[30] La Harpe, *op. cit.*, XI, 309.

religion and his daughter too well to give her to an " idolâtre qui ne pourrait la défendre," a practical consideration worthy of one who shows no indignation over the slaughter of his people, who forces his daughter to marry a man she does not love, and who keeps her in ignorance of the fact that her lover is alive, because he knows that knowledge of it may prevent her from acquiring a powerful husband. His daughter's conversion is no more profound. Influenced by her father, she thought she saw truth in Christianity. Its laws are offered by her as an argument against suicide, and she admits that it is her duty not to elope with Zamore, but it seems quite possible that she will revert to sun worship if her second husband fails to take Gusman's advice and turn Christian. That he may not be converted is shown by Voltaire's note on his last verses:

Ceux qui ont prétendu que c'est ici une conversion miraculeuse se sont trompés. Zamore est changé en ce qu'il s'attendrit pour son ennemi. Il commence à respecter le christianisme; une conversion subite serait ridicule en de telles circonstances.

In other words, his final attitude is that of Sévère rather than that of Félix, for *Alzire* does not admit the mystical inspiration of *Polyeucte*, though it is not hard to find some resemblance between the two tragedies.

Voltaire may well have been praised by eighteenth-century audiences for the " American " coloring he gave his tragedy. He laid his scene at " Los-Reyes, autrement Lima." Zamore and Montèze are sovereigns of parts of " Potoze." There are references to Peru, to Mexico, to the " mers de Magellan," to gold, to the heat of the climate, to the temples of the sun. The male Indians were to wear [31] an " habit à la romaine, le corselet orné d'un soleil, et des plumes pendant aux lambrequins; un petit casque garni de plumes." Alzire was to have a " jupe garnie de plumes par devant, une mante qui descende des épaules et qui traîne, la coiffure en cheveux, des poinçons de diamant dans les boucles." His Indians are described as brave, simple, ignorant of Spanish weapons, kindly except when their gods demand human blood upon their altars. They are children of Nature, without European arts and vices. To us, however, there is little difference between the Indian and the Spanish characters so far as their speech and manners are concerned. Alzire and her confidants would have felt quite at home in Madrid, as would Zamore if he could have escaped the Holy Inquisition.

Alvarez and Gusman, according to Voltaire, should be dressed alike, in old Spanish costumes, " la veste courte et serrée," their black cloaks lined with flame-colored satin, their stockings and plumes of the same vivid color. They represent two types of Spanish conquerors. Gusman believes that he can rule only by force, while Alvarez trusts the natives, wins their con-

[31] Cf. Moland, XL, 483.

fidence, and treats them with affection. Both would extend the Spanish empire and convert the Indians, but their methods are radically different until the approach of death wins over Gusman to his father's humanitarian principles. For this last event some preparation has been made by the respect he shows Alvarez and by his reminding Alzire in IV, 2 that he is not altogether fixed in his ideas.

There is a similar difference between the Indian leaders. Montèze believes in collaboration; Zamore in resistance. To Montèze resistance is hopeless, while surrender means a higher civilization and a nobler religion. Zamore is embittered by the treatment he and his people have received. For him the Spaniards are morally inferior to the Indians and are superior to them only in their equipment. Their cannon, their iron weapons, and their horses astonish, but cannot long prevail over the virtues of the Indians.

These four men influence Alzire in different ways. To Montèze she is obedient. She loves Zamore, bribes his guard for him, pleads when he is recaptured, supports him in his resistance to the pretense of conversion. She admires Alvarez, who has shown her how fine a Spaniard can be, but she has no liking for his son, whom she is induced to marry. It is only at the end of the play that she can say her soul is divided between Gusman and Zamore. Her most striking characteristic is her sincerity. When her confidant tells her that she will lose her honor if she is found alone with Zamore on her wedding night, she replies (IV, 3):

> Cet honneur étranger, parmi nous inconnu,
> N'est qu'un fantôme vain qu'on prend pour la vertu;
> C'est l'amour de la gloire, et non de la justice,
> La crainte du reproche, et non celle du vice.

The first act gives most of the exposition and prepares us for Alzire's marriage, but the fact that Zamore is living and his attitude towards the other characters are revealed only in the second act, which is enlivened by two scenes of recognition. The third act, which follows Alzire's marriage, shows her remorse, her encounter with Zamore, his recognition and arrest by Gusman. The action, previously limited to Alzire's decision to marry Gusman and Zamore's to attack the Spaniards, gets under way in this act. It becomes more intense in Act IV, where there are two changes of fortune, resulting from Zamore's escape and from his new arrest after he has stabbed Gusman. In Act V there is marked suspense until the knot is unexpectedly cut by Gusman's dramatic pardon of his rival and murderer.

According to Voltaire, he began *Alzire* in 1733 and read some of his scenes to Dufresne and Crébillon fils. He implies that the latter communicated the subject to Le Franc de Pompignan, who, as we have seen, composed a play of the same kind called *Zoraïde* and read it to the actors. When Voltaire discovered this, he insisted, in November, 1735, that his own tragedy should be performed before Le Franc's. The actors agreed, and the rival tragedy was withdrawn. Almost a year before, in December, 1734, Voltaire had sent his manuscript to d'Argental with the request that his name be kept secret.[32] Apparently he wished the religious views expressed in the play to be judged before it was known that they were his. On Jan. 4, 1735, he thanked d'Argental for advice and told him that " le sot père est actuellement délogé du quatrième acte," [33] that is, that he had removed Montèze from it. On Jan. 25, 1736, he wrote that *Alzire* had been acted at Cirey.[34]

Two days later it was produced at the Comédie Française, with la Gaussin as Alzire, Dufresne as Zamore, Sarrazin as Alvarez, Grandval as Gusman.[35] The *Mercure* and Desfontaines [36] testified to its great success, as did Father Brumoy [37] and the abbé Le Blanc.[38] It was acted twenty times at the Comédie Française in 1736, until March 14. Voltaire's share in the receipts was 3635 fr., almost as much as he had earned from *Zaïre*. In the same year it was twice played at court. It remained in the repertory until 1830, with a total of 328 performances that rank it fifth among Voltaire's plays.

Linant and Gresset wrote poems in its honor. Frederick the Great [39] praised it for contrasting the manners of savages with those of Europeans and for showing that Christianity, misunderstood and guided by false zeal, makes one more barbarous and cruel than does paganism. Le Blanc, though admitting that the tragedy deserved its success, thought it appealed more to the mind than the heart and asked Bouhier whether he considered that those were right who took it for a catechism. His correspondent replied that " l'ordonnance n'en plaira jamais aux connaisseurs, ni la morale aux gens sensés. On aperçoit trop son but en fait de religion." [40] He must have thought that Voltaire was less interested in defending the essentials of Christianity than he was in attacking those who failed to practise them. Father Brumoy went farther in his condemnation of the tragedy, in which he found " de l'amour sans intrigue, de l'esprit sans jugement, de la piété sans religion."

[32] Moland, XXXIII, 459.
[33] Moland, XXXIII, 471.
[34] Moland, XXIV, 16.
[35] Moland, III, 384, XXXIV, 24-5, 57. The *Registres* show that other rôles were taken by Legrand de Belleville, Fierville, and la Jouvenot, and that the actors provided wigs for Sarrazin, Fierville, and Legrand, an " écharpe " for Grandval, and a " fausse queue pour l'escharpe de la Jouvenot."
[36] Cf. Lion, *op. cit.*, p. 102.
[37] " L'on continue d'y courir," he wrote on Feb. 28; cf. *RHL*, XIII (1906), 129.
[38] Monod-Cassidy, *op. cit.*, p. 234.
[39] Moland, XXXIV, 104.
[40] Monod-Cassidy, *op. cit.*, pp. 241, 491.

In his dedication Voltaire stated that he had tried to paint the " grandeur d'âme qui fait le bien et qui pardonne le mal." In his *Discours préliminaire* he professed to have shown the superiority of the truly religious spirit over the virtues of nature and the vices of a Christian "mal instruit." He insisted that his writings had been inspired by desire for human happiness and horror over injustice and oppression. He then complained of those who attacked him [41] and insisted that he was never envious, even of Crébillon, who knew that he had inspired in him only emulation and friendship. When he subsequently redramatized several of the old author's subjects, he made emulation obvious enough, but hardly friendship.

In Beuchot's *avertissement* of *Alzire*, three parodies are mentioned: *Alzirette, les Sauvages*, and *la Fille obéissante*.[42] They are very slight productions, chiefly noteworthy for a criticism in *Les Sauvages* of the improbable devices by which Voltaire obtains his effects. The character substituted for Alvarez explains his silence in regard to his son's wedding in the lines:

> Mais aux coups de théâtre on doit un peu songer;
> On aime la surprise, il faut la ménager.

Similar criticism was made in greater detail in Clément's *De la tragédie*.[43] He found it strange that Zamore reached the capital without discovering that Gusman and Alvarez were there, that he should not have been recognized during his imprisonment, that he should not learn from Alvarez that Gusman is his son and is about to marry Alzire. He was also surprised that kindly Alvarez surrendered his governorship to his cruel son, that he had not freed the captives himself, that he favored Alzire's marriage to Gusman, and that the heroine did not make greater efforts to ascertain whether Zamore was living before she married Gusman. Collé [44] held that Gusman is jealous through pride rather than through love and that he resembles a

---

[41] In so doing he tells the story of a man who attacked his benefactor and defended himself by saying, "Il faut que je vive." The Kehl editors commented that the ingrate was Desfontaines; the benefactor, d'Argenson, who retorted, "Je n'en vois pas la nécessité." In his *Citations françaises* Guerlac gives this as the first occurrence of this familiar anecdote. The Kehl editors do not reveal their source, but, long before they wrote, the abbé Le Blanc, on April 24, 1739, had told the same story, with Desfontaines as the ingrate, d'Argenson as the benefactor. As his letter was unpublished until Mme Monod-Cassidy's edition appeared in 1941 (p. 331), it is unlikely that the Kehl editors had seen it. It consequently seems probable that the two accounts have their source in an incident that really occurred.

[42] *Alzirette* was published by Van Roosbroeck, New York, 1929. *Les Sauvages* is analyzed by V. B. Grannis, *op. cit.*, pp. 291-300. On p. 292 she concludes her analysis of Alzire with " The populace revolt in favor of Zamore and in the insurrection, he kills Gusman, who . . . unites Zamore and Alzire to reign happily in his stead." As a matter of fact, there is no such revolt, nor is there any suggestion that Zamore will be governor of Peru. The *Fille obéissante*, acted by marionettes, has survived in a form that is incomplete; cf. F. W. Lindsay, *op. cit.*, pp. 142-3.

[43] Quoted from the edition of 1784 by Van Roosbroeck, *Alzirette*, pp. 19-23.

[44] *Correspondance inédite*, 1864, pp. 445-64.

sultan rather than a Spaniard. He asks how Alzire can be alone in III, 1, thinks she appears indifferent to the destruction of her people, and regrets that she does not clear herself to Gusman at the end of the play. In other respects he admires the dénouement and predicts that the tragedy will remain forever in the repertory.

La Harpe,[45] too, pointed out unexplained situations. He could not understand why Zamore came to Los Reyes, why he failed to recognize Alvarez as soon as he saw him, why the soldier should bring him to the palace, why Gusman should leave his bride on their wedding night. He objected to the assumption that the Spaniards would spare Indians if they accepted Christianity,[46] and he would have preferred historical persons for the leading characters, but he added that, when the play was acted, such objections were overlooked. He considered *Alzire* the most original of Voltaire's tragedies, its third act " un chef-d'œuvre de tout point." He praised characters, situations, and verses, quoting a number of these as worthy of special mention, including those spoken by Alzire in her plea for Zamore (IV, 5):

> Grand Dieu, conduis Zamore au milieu des déserts.
> Ne serais-tu le Dieu que d'un autre univers?
> Les seuls Européans [*sic*] sont-ils nés pour te plaire?
> Es-tu tyran d'un monde, et de l'autre le père?
> Les vainqueurs, les vaincus, tous ces faibles humains,
> Sont tous également l'ouvrage de tes mains.

Such humanitarian words, daring enough when they were first spoken on the stage, the appealing characters of Alzire, Alvarez, and Zamore, and the series of striking situations made the audience overlook the lack of logic in the manner in which they were brought about. This is the opinion, not only of La Harpe, but of Geoffroy and of Lion, who ends his study of the play with the exclamation:

> Quoi de plus capable enfin de toucher les spectateurs, quels qu'ils fussent, que ces admirables scènes de la fin où les personnages, plus généreux et plus sympathiques les uns que les autres, rivalisent devant nous de grandeur d'âme et de simple éloquence!

Voltaire's next play is distinctly inferior to the three tragedies that he had recently written and to the two that were next to follow. Its existence illustrates the uneven flow of his inspiration. ZULIME [47] was begun in 1738.

---

[45] *Op. cit.*, XI, 300-40.

[46] Atahuallpa was induced to profess Christianity, not in order to save his life, but that he might be strangled rather than burned to death; cf. W. H. Prescott, *Conquest of Peru*, Philadelphia, 1874, I, 471-2.

[47] Published in 1761 by Grangé and by Duchesne without the author's consent. *Soleinne*, no. 1680, mentions an edition of Geneva, 1761. The first authentic edition appeared in Voltaire's *Œuvres*, 1763, with a dedicatory letter to la Clairon. For other editions cf. Bengesco and Moland. An Italian translation was published four times in 1776-98. Lion's study of the play is in his *op. cit.*, pp. 112-20.

On Jan. 7 of the next year he wrote to d'Argental that he was at work on this tragedy, which would show a father slain by a lover and a heroine abandoned by the slayer.[48] He received advice from d'Argental and la Quinault, made alterations, and wrote on Jan. 5, 1740, that he had completed two acts.[49] As he found that interest diminished after the heroine learned of her father's death, he changed the ending in such a way that he could claim on Feb. 4 that the ending remained uncertain till the end of the last scene.[50] By Feb. 16 he had selected the cast. Dufresne was to play Ramire; Sarrazin, Bénassar; la Dumesnil, Zulime; la Gaussin, Atide. On March 11 he expressed the desire that Legrand de Belleville should play Mohadir because his talents were well suited to giving the pathetic account of Bénassar's death.[51]

Acted first on June 8, 1740, the tragedy was not a success. It had only eight productions in that year,[52] all of which were poorly attended. Voltaire began to rewrite it, changing the names of the characters and sparing the father, whose death, he thought, had produced a double action and weakened interest in the lovers.[53] It was acted as *Zulime* at Sceaux in June, 1750; as *Fanime* at Lausanne in 1757, and at the Délices in September, 1760. On this last occasion parts were played by Voltaire's nieces and by Thibouville.[54] The next year, after the success of *Tancrède*, the actors of the Comédie Française revived *Zulime* and played it ten times in 1761-2, with la Clairon [55] and Le Kain in the rôles of Zulime and Ramire. It must have been the revival of the tragedy that suggested the printing of the unauthorized versions, though their texts present an earlier form of the play than that employed by the actors in 1761.[56] Voltaire made further alterations before he finally gave his consent to publication.[57]

---

[48] Moland, XXXV, 94.

[49] Moland, XXXV, 356.

[50] Moland, XXXV, 379-80.

[51] Moland, XXXV, 382-3, 395. The *Registres* indicate that these five actors took part in the play and that la Jouvenot played the confidant, Sérame. The *Mercure* agrees, adding that Du Breuil played Ménodore; Dubois, Osman.

[52] They took place on June 8, 9, 11, 13, 15, 18, 20, 25. Voltaire received from them only 493 fr.

[53] Moland, XXXV, 476-7.

[54] Cf. Moland, IV, 3, and *Cor.*, I, 436.

[55] Bachaumont (*Mémoires secrets*, I, 12) attributes to her alone whatever success the play may have had. For the cast cf. the *Mercure* of Jan., 1762.

[56] This is shown by a comparison of variants published by Moland with Grimm's account of the play as he had seen it acted. In the edition it is Atide who kills herself; in Grimm's account it is Zulime. Voltaire asserted that the printer was a pirate who had obtained the manuscript from a prompter and had altered two or three hundred verses; cf. Moland, XLI, 334, XLII, 27, *Cor.*, V, 13-8.

[57] The scene is laid in a "château de la province de Trémizène sur le bord de la mer d'Afrique." Bénassar, ruler of the province, owns Spanish slaves, including Ramire, whose father had been King of Valencia, and Atide, also of royal blood and secretly married to Ramire. When Turcomans had driven Bénassar from his possessions, his daughter, Zulime, had, with the slaves and certain guards, taken

He stated in his dedication that the subject came from Moorish history, but he pointed to no definite source. La Harpe [58] considered the tragedy purely a work of Voltaire's imagination and reproached him for not making use of history. He thought the time represented might be the tenth century, when the Moors were masters of Valencia, a province that Ramire hopes to liberate, but I fear that at this time neither Turks nor Turcomans could be found in what is now Morocco. It seems probable that history was employed only in the most general way, with little regard for dates, and that Voltaire's reference to it was an afterthought, like his claim that he had written the play in order to secure for a daughter better treatment from her father. The sources are dramatic rather than historical.

Voltaire admitted [59] on Jan. 7, 1739, that *Zulime* recalled *le Cid, Bajazet,* and Thomas Corneille's *Ariane*. On March 12 he added Roy's opera, *Callirhoé*. Just after *Zulime* was acted, Le Blanc [60] saw in it a mixture of *Ariane, Bajazet,* and *Inès de Castro*. On March 3, 1760, Voltaire compared his heroine to Dido.[61] It is quite possible that he had in mind some of these when he wrote his play. In its original form it resembled the *Cid,* when Ramire kills Bénassar and the heroine finds herself in the situation of Chimène. It resembles *Bajazet* in that the scenes of both plays are laid in a Mohammedan country and that the hero is loved by a powerful woman whom he is unwilling to anger and loves a princess named Atalide or Atide.

refuge in a fortress. Although Ramire had saved Bénassar's life and had defended his daughter, the Turks, after driving off the Turcomans, had asked for the head of the slave and Bénassar's council had agreed to sacrifice him, but Zulime had intervened and escaped with Ramire, Atide, and others to the seacoast, where ships await them. Zulime refuses a request that she return to her father, for she plans to marry Ramire and sail with him to Spain, but the slave, though he hesitates to break with Zulime, has no intention of deserting his wife. Bénassar's forces attack. Ramire goes to meet them. When there is a lull in the fighting, his confidant urges him to escape in a ship and leave Zulime behind, but he is unwilling to desert her. When she urges marriage, he tells her that he cannot have a Mohammedan wife, whereupon she agrees to become a Christian. Before he can give his answer, Bénassar makes his way into the fortress, reproaches his daughter, and begs her to return. When she insists upon following Ramire, he curses her and predicts her death. When he renews the attack, Ramire urges Zulime and Atide to board the ship, but Zulime again proposes that they marry. From his resistance and Atide's remarks she guesses their secret. She denounces Ramire and seeks her guards, but Atide calms her and persuades her to enter the boat. Bénassar returns and agrees that Ramire and Atide may escape if Zulime is surrendered. Ramire consents, but Bénassar discovers that his daughter has gone aboard, thinks that he has been deceived, leads his forces to the ship, and captures Ramire, who is condemned to death, but is pardoned by Bénassar when he is reminded that he has twice saved his life. When Bénassar offers him his daughter in marriage, Ramire replies that Atide is his wife. Zulime demands that her rival be punished. Atide admits that she has agreed to renounce Ramire if Zulime would save him and draws her dagger. Ramire prevents her suicide, but Zulime seizes the weapon, bids Ramire and Atide live happily together, and stabs herself.

[58] *Op. cit.,* XI, 342-3.
[59] Moland, XXXV, 94.
[60] Monod-Cassidy, *op. cit.,* p. 350.
[61] Moland, XL, 319-20.

It is also true that, as in *Callirhoé*, the hero marries the less powerful of the two women. The resemblances to *Ariane*, *Inès*, and the *Æneid* are much less striking.[62]

The complex origin of his characters seems to have prevented Voltaire from having a clear conception of them. Zulime is passionate enough to win our interest, but it is difficult to sympathize with her efforts to take Ramire from his wife, while her sudden respect for her father, which causes her to dismiss her soldiers, is not in keeping with her love for Ramire. Atide is ever ready to sacrifice herself, though she must know that to do so would bring no happiness to the man who loves her. Ramire is still less acceptable. He is exactly in the position of the Count de Gleichen, rescued by a Mohammedan princess who loves him and wishes to marry him, although he already has a wife. In his case the solution was polygamy with the pope's blessing, but, though this had seemed satisfactory to Alexandre Hardy, it would have given the play too bizarre a dénouement to suit Voltaire. He seems to have been as much perplexed as his hero in regard to the course of his action. Ramire never promises to marry Zulime, but he implies that he will do so if she will accompany him to Spain and become a Christian. He would have been more impressive if, as Grimm suggests, he had either been a scoundrel, scheming to make use of Zulime and then abandon her, or if he had been swept away by her passion at the expense of his wife. As it is, he wavers between sincerity and deception in love, as he does between fighting against kindly old Bénassar and protecting him, giving an impression of weakness that the author did not intend to produce.

That Voltaire had no clear conception of his plot is shown by the various forms it assumed. At first Ramire killed Bénassar in battle in order to save Atide, and Zulime committed suicide, so that interest was divided between the old man's fate and that of his daughter. Next Voltaire allowed him to live and sacrificed Atide, as Atalide, Inès, and Dido had been sacrificed. Then he spared Atide and had Zulime kill herself after she had dismissed Ramire and her rival. Finally, at the second performance in 1761, he kept Ramire and Atide on the stage and had Zulime die in their presence.[63]

Voltaire's changes were so extensive, especially in his last two acts, that the tragedy was announced in 1761 as practically new.[64] The abbé Le

---

[62] Moland notes similarities between individual verses of *Zulime* and of various plays, including *Bajazet* and *Inès de Castro*. Grimm (*Cor.*, V, 14) suggests that Ramire's offer to leave Atide as a hostage came from La Fosse's *Manlius*. Note, too, that Ramire alleges difference in religion as a reason for not marrying Zulime, who then agrees to change her religion, just as in *Adélaïde* the heroine gives Vendôme's disloyalty to the French cause as a reason for not marrying him, whereupon Vendôme agrees to renounce his support of the English.

[63] *Cor.*, V, 10.

[64] Moland, XXXV, 476-7, XXXIX, 143, XLI, 74-5, *Cor.*, V, 3.

Blanc,[65] who had attended in 1740 the second performance of the play, declared that it was written for the " Oisons des Premieres Loges," who, however, judged it the worst of Voltaire's tragedies, though derived from a dozen by other dramatists. Raynal's first acquaintance with the play was made in 1750, when he found it neither cold nor feebly written, but with some " embarras dans le sujet." [66]   Grimm [67] saw it acted by la Clairon and Le Kain. He admired the second act, but considered the first cold and noted that interest diminished after the second until, when Zulime appeared on the stage with a saber in her hand, the audience laughed. He declared that the audience hooted the dénouement. Zulime was the only character that could be endured. Atide inspired no interest. Ramire had the worst of rôles. The military situation was not clear. Though there was constant talk of taking ship, no one embarked. In short, the play was one of Voltaire's weakest productions as to style, structure, and verisimilitude. Grimm even held that la Clairon emphasized the play's defects by her deliberate diction.

Fréron [68] reviewed the unauthorized edition, condemned it utterly, and called it *Bajazet* warmed over. Bachaumont [69] made a damaging comparison between the latter tragedy and *Zulime*, calling the actions of Voltaire's characters absurd. In 1762 a parody emphasized the fact that the play interested the public little and the forlorn nature of Ramire's rôle. It ends with the lines:

> Du tems qui détruit tout, l'Autheur est la victime;
> Souvenez-vous de lui; mais oubliez Zulime.[70]

Condorcet [71] discovered novelty in Zulime's character and, in the *avertissement* of the play, admiration was expressed for the line (V, 3), " C'est à moi de mourir, puisque c'est toi qu'il aime," but La Harpe [72] denied that one could be interested in " cette espèce d'*imbroglio* tragique, ni même d'en démêler les ressorts." Zulime's situation is hopeless from the start. How can Ramire promise to restore Zulime to her father if she is in command? How can Zulime hasten to the ship while her beloved Ramire is with her father? Even the dénouement produces little effect, as Zulime has not won the interest of the audience. He concludes with an expression of

---

[65] Monod-Cassidy, *op. cit.*, pp. 349-50.
[66] *Cor.*, I, 436.
[67] *Cor.*, V, 3-18.
[68] *Année littéraire*, 1761 (7), p. 14.
[69] *Mémoires secrets*, I, 20-2.
[70] Cf. Grannis, *op. cit.*, pp. 301-4. The last line of *Zulime* is " Souvenez-vous de moi, mais oubliez mon crime."
[71] Moland, I, 216.
[72] *Op. cit.*, XI, 344-8.

surprise over the fact that *Zulime* was written shortly after *Alzire* and shortly before *Mahomet*.

It is quite possible, however, that the inferiority of *Zulime* may be explained by the fact that, while Voltaire was writing it, he was busy with one of his major productions, also begun in 1738, LE FANATISME OU MAHOMET LE PROPHÈTE.[73] It was his third Mohammedan play, but it differs from the others in that no Christians appear in it, and that religion, of little importance in *Zulime* and subordinated to love in *Zaïre*, here becomes dominant. Yet the play is in a sense an outgrowth of the latter tragedy, for the fanaticism of Nérestan had done much to bring about his sister's untimely death, even if Voltaire refers to *Mahomet* as if it were his first tragedy to attack superstition.[74] He declared [75] that his Séide found himself in a situation similar to that of the men who had been induced by fanaticism to murder Henri III and Henri IV, indicating that he was attacking any religion that conflicts with humanity and reason, while hoping that the censor and subsequently the pope would see in it only an exposé of Mohammedanism.

The tragedy is historical insofar as it is true that Mahomet was exiled from Mecca, returned to the holy city after a sojourn in Medina, inspired great devotion in his followers, and met with considerable opposition. Voltaire states that the Prophet " enleva la femme de Séide, l'un de ses disciples, et qu'il persécuta Abusofian, que je nomme Zopire." [76] Lion suggested that he drew his facts and his conception of Mahomet from Prideaux, whose *Life of Mahomet* had been translated into French in 1699. This may well be the case, but, if he did so, he made considerable changes, for Abusofian, after defeating Mahomet in battle and resisting for a long time, finally became his disciple, as he does not do in the play; Séide becomes Abusofian's son, brought up by the Prophet; and there are many additions: the rôle of Palmire, the negotiations with Zopire and the senate, the plot that results in Séide's murder of his father, and the cleverly devised miracle of the dénouement.

Voltaire's debts were not to history alone. Racine's Joad causes murder to be done in the name of religion and practises trickery in so doing, though, of course, he is presented as an inspired prophet, not as an impostor.[77]

---

[73] Brussels, 1742, 4°. It was in the edition of his *Œuvres*, Dresden, 1748, that first appeared the dedication to the pope. For other editions cf. Bengesco and Moland. For four Italian translations, one of them published eight times, cf. Ferrari, *op. cit.* For Lion's study of the play, cf. his *op. cit.*, pp. 125-48.

[74] Moland, XXXV, 331-2.

[75] Moland, XXXV, 331, XXXVI, 157.

[76] Moland, XXXV, 561.

[77] Voltaire subsequently wrote, " je crois que si un roi avait dans ses états un homme tel que Joad, il ferait fort bien de l'enfermer " (note on *Olympie*, III, 2).

Moland notes that the expression " saintement homicide " is borrowed from
Athalie.[78]   Palmire's imprecations (V, 2) are like those of Camille in
Horace.[79]   Moland pointed out that two verses of I, 4 are borrowed word
for word from *Eriphyle*, II, 1.[80]   Voltaire thanked d'Argental for the
admirable suggestion he had made in regard to Act V, that, perhaps, of the
" faux miracle." [81]   The editors of Kehl thought that Voltaire derived from
Lillo's *London Merchant* the scene in which Zopire forgives his murderer,
but, as Lion points out, the resemblance is not close enough to be convincing.[82]   The reunion of a father, near death, with a lost son and daughter
had already been dramatized by Voltaire in *Zaïre*.[83]   Despite all of these
repetitions or resemblances, the tragedy remains a highly original creation,
one of the most striking protests ever written against the evils of fanaticism
and yet, despite its moral content, a highly artistic creation.[84]

[78] In 1742 this expression occurs but once (IV, 4, which is IV, 3 in the authorized
edition). Voltaire subsequently introduced it into III, 7.

[79] Cf.
> Que cent peuples unis . . .
> Puissé-je de mes yeux . . .
> Voir ses maisons . . .

and

> Puissé-je de mes mains . . .
> Voir mourir . . .
> Que le monde . . .

Cf. also the use of " premier degré " in II, 5 and in *Cinna*, vv. 11, 12.

[80]
> Les mortels sont égaux: ce n'est point la naissance,
> C'est la seule vertu qui fait leur différence. (I, 4)

[81] Cf. Voltaire's letter of July 12, 1740 (Moland, XXXV, 482).

[82] This was admitted even by T. R. Lounsbury, who nevertheless follows Foote
(1747) in holding as proof that Voltaire imitated *Macbeth* the fact that Séide converses with Palmire both before and after the murder (cf. Lounsbury, *op. cit.*, pp.
121-4, 149). The characters and the motivation are so utterly different that the
suggestion can hardly be taken seriously.

[83] Noted by the abbé Le Blanc; cf. Monod-Cassidy, *op. cit.*, p. 378.

[84] Zopire, " sheik ou shérif de la Mecque," is bitterly opposed to Mahomet, who,
he thinks, has caused the death of his wife, his son, and his daughter. He has
killed Mahomet's son and captured Palmire, a girl in whom the Prophet is interested.
He refuses to come to terms with his enemy when Senator Phanor and the Prophet's
lieutenant, Omar, urge him to do so. He feels drawn to Palmire and is distressed
to learn that she considers Mahomet " l'envoyé du ciel, et son seul interprète." When
he rejects the offer of peace, Omar appeals to the senate. In Act II Séide, a young
Mohammedan, enters as a hostage. As he loves Palmire, he has chosen this means
of seeing her. Omar reports that Mahomet has been allowed to enter the city,
" l'olive à la main," and has already made a deep impression upon the people. He
soon appears, bids Séide rejoin his warriors, and warns Palmire against the sheik.
He then informs Omar that she and Séide are Zopire's children, carried off by
Hercide and brought up as Mohammedans without the knowledge that they are
brother and sister. Although the Prophet has encouraged their incestuous love, he
is now jealous of Séide and determined to add Palmire to his harem. He sends word
to his followers to besiege the city. A violent scene follows between him and Zopire.
Mahomet represents himself as a patriot, eager to lift Arabia above the " débris du
monde." Zopire considers him a brigand and an impostor. Mahomet threatens and
cajoles, then tells him that his children live and that, if Zopire will serve him, he
will free his son and marry his daughter. Zopire refuses. Mahomet resolves to be
pitiless. Omar warns that the truce expires next day, that half the senate has
condemned the Prophet, and that he may be assassinated. Mahomet remains calm,
declares that Zopire must die, and asks for an agent. Omar suggests Séide as

According to Prideaux,[85] Mahomet's " predominant Passions were *Ambition* and *Lust.*" He is similarly presented by Voltaire. He reveals his ambition to Zopire (II, 5) :

> Je suis ambitieux; tout homme l'est, sans doute;
> Mais jamais roi, pontife, ou chef, ou citoyen,
> Ne conçut un projet aussi grand que le mien.
> Chaque peuple à son tour a brillé sur la terre,
> Par les lois, par les arts, et surtout par la guerre;
> Le temps de l'Arabie est à la fin venu.

In the previous scene he had confided to Omar his other passion :

> L'amour seul me console; il est ma récompense,
> L'objet de mes travaux, l'idole que j'encense,
> Le dieu de Mahomet; et cette passion
> Est égale aux fureurs de mon ambition.

He is not, however, a sighing lover. He seeks to dominate Palmire, to receive from her unhesitating obedience. In return she may aspire to the honor of his couch. His desire for domination is shown even more strongly in the case of Séide, who regards him as almost divine. Omar has become his confidant and fellow-conspirator. Mahomet tries to win Zopire by

Zopire's murderer, and Mahomet welcomes the proposal. In Act III Séide confides in Palmire the fact that Omar would have him swear to die for Mahomet's law. The girl's suspicions are aroused. Mahomet warns her against her love for Séide and insists on obedience. Omar says it is time to carry off Palmire, to invade Mecca, and to punish Zopire. He has placed a weapon in Séide's hands and made preparations for his killing Zopire. Mahomet then fills the youth with religious ardor, promising that by this murder he will merit both Palmire and eternal life. When alone, Séide is troubled by the thought of killing the old man. Then Zopire offers him shelter and denounces those who shed blood. Séide resolves to break his promise of murder. Zopire, learning that Hercide would see him, agrees to meet him in the middle of the night before the altar of his gods. He wonders whether he will learn from Hercide that Palmire and Séide are his lost children. In Act IV Mahomet, after bringing back Séide to obedience and seeing to it that Omar prepares poison for the youth, decides to get rid of Hercide, who shows pity for Zopire. Séide again hesitates, consults Palmire, and is warned that doubt is blasphemy. The back of the stage opens and we see an altar, at which Zopire is praying to be reunited to his children. Séide draws his dagger, goes to the altar, and strikes Zopire. He is too deeply moved to strike again. The old man staggers forward. Word is brought him that Hercide, killed by Mahomet, had left word that Séide and Palmire are Zopire's children. They beg their father to kill them, but he embraces them and hopes that his death will cause the punishment of Mahomet. In Act V we hear that Zopire's death has been interpreted as an act of God, that Mahomet's army has come close to the city, and that Séide had been poisoned before he stabbed his father. Mahomet bids Palmire forget Séide and offers her a great career, but she denounces him as an impostor and a murderer. Omar reports that Séide, freed by the people, leads them against the Prophet, but the poison is taking effect. When Séide advances upon Mahomet with a dagger in his hand and Palmire calls for vengeance, the young man staggers and falls into the arms of his followers. Mahomet attributes his death to God and warns the people of the fate that awaits his enemies. Impressed, they retire. Palmire declares that Séide has been poisoned, denounces Mahomet, and stabs herself with her brother's dagger. The Prophet feels remorse and admits his trickery, but he begs Omar to conceal the fact that he is merely an erring mortal.

[85] Seventh edition, London, 1718, p. 80.

revealing to him his great design and offering him power and the hope of reunion with his children.   His relations with these four persons reveal his powerful personality, his zeal for conversion, and his hypocritical use of religion to further his ambition.   Voltaire, indeed, compared him to Tartuffe, and Gibbon protested against the manner in which he is presented, declaring that " some reverence is surely due to the fame of heroes and the religion of nations," [86] but he should have sympathized with Voltaire's major aim, which was not to write history, but to show the tragic consequences that may be produced if fanaticism is directed by an unscrupulous leader.

Mahomet, moreover, is not completely a villain.   La Harpe points out that he did not bring up Séide with the purpose of making him kill his father, as Crébillon had made Atrée bring up the son of Thyeste.   He is rather an opportunist in crime, accepting Omar's proposal that Séide be used against Zopire, quickly deciding upon the murder of Hercide, still more promptly making a miracle out of Séide's death.   At the end of the play he is even capable of remorse:

> Vainqueur et tout puissant, c'est moi qui suis puni.
> Il est donc des remords! ô fureur! ô justice!
> Mes forfaits dans mon cœur ont donc mis mon supplice.

Zopire, in contrast, might pass for an eighteenth-century deist, except that he worships the old gods of Arabia.   In the name of justice he resists Mahomet's efforts to bribe him, even when he offers to restore his children to him, though he shows his devotion to them when he embraces them after he has been mortally wounded by his son.   His own beliefs do not prevent him from recognizing virtue in persons professing another faith.   When Séide exclaims, " L'ennemi de mon dieu connaît donc la vertu!" he replies (III, 8):

> Tu la connais bien peu, puisque tu t'en étonnes.
> Mon fils, à quelle erreur, hélas! tu t'abandonnes!
> Ton esprit, fasciné par les lois d'un tyran,
> Pense que tout est crime hors d'être musulman.

Séide oscillates between these two men, between fanaticism and humanity. Youthful, brave, naïve, he is eager to fight for the Prophet's cause, but he is impressed by Zopire's highmindedness.   He swears to die for Mahomet's law, but he is troubled by the command that he must kill Zopire, until, threatened with the loss of his soul and of Palmire, he cries, " Je crois entendre Dieu; tu parles: j'obéis."   In the presence of Zopire he again hesitates, but he is overawed by Mahomet and prepares for the murder. Even then he might have renounced the undertaking, if Palmire had not

---

[86] *Decline and Fall*, Philadelphia, 1805, VI, 279. Gibbon had heard that a Turkish ambassador at Paris was scandalized by a performance of the play.

warned him that "le doute est un blasphème." When the deed is done,
he repents bitterly and seeks to avenge Zopire, but the poison is too far
advanced. His death serves only to promote the Prophet's fame. He is
more than anyone else the dupe of fanaticism. The deep impression created
by his rôle is shown by the fact that it contributed to the French language
the word *séide*, already employed as a common noun by Dorat [87] in 1774
and officially recognized by the Academy in 1878.

Palmire has a definite function in the tragedy. Her presence in Mecca
gives Séide a reason for offering himself as a hostage. Mahomet's love,
which makes him jealous of Séide, is an additional reason for his willingness
to use the young man as his agent in crime. The awe she feels for the
Prophet makes her help to overcome Séide's hesitation. Without her the
portrait of Mahomet would be less complete. This is true, too, of Omar,
no mere confidant, but destined to rule over Islam and already an active
agent in placing Mahomet at the head of the state. His attitude towards
the Prophet helps to account for the success of his hero, of whom he speaks
as follows (I, 4):

> Il est de ces esprits favorisés des cieux,
> Qui sont tout par eux-même,[88] et rien par leurs aïeux.
> Tel est l'homme, en un mot, que j'ai choisi pour maître;
> Lui seul dans l'univers a mérité de l'être.

These five characters produce a number of dramatic scenes. The first
act gives the exposition in conversations between Zopire, a senator, Palmire,
and Osman. Mahomet and Séide first appear in Act II. In the striking
fifth scene the Prophet reveals his plans to Zopire and tries in vain to
overcome his fundamental honesty and love of justice. J.-J. Rousseau, as
Moland notes, admired it greatly, declaring that he knew no scene in a
French play that shows more obviously the hand of a great master and in
which "le sacré caractere de la vertu l'emporte plus sensiblement sur l'élévation du génie." [89] Act III is especially devoted to Séide's hesitations and
to preparations for the murder. The fourth is the most impressive of the
acts, one of the best that Voltaire composed, combining to a remarkable
degree suspense, horror, and pity. After it the fifth may seem to produce
an anticlimax, but its brevity and the manner in which Mahomet creates
a miracle make it thoroughly effective.

The play has been criticized for lacking local color. It is true that
there is little to suggest seventh-century Arabia except proper names,
references to the Koran, to the angel of death, to the camels the Prophet

---

[87] Cf. below, the discussion of his *Adélaïde de Hongrie*.
[88] The lack of agreement in *eux-même* was severely criticized by the abbé Le Blanc;
cf. Monod-Cassidy, *op. cit.*, p. 378.
[89] "Lettre à d'Alembert" in Rousseau, *op. cit.*, XI, 211.

had driven in his youth, to burning sands and "rochers déserts." Certainly Palmire moves about the palace with great freedom, and there is little to differentiate Mecca from other cities. Yet, even if Voltaire had written a century later, it is doubtful whether he would have introduced into his play much more of the picturesque than he did, for he was seeking to dramatize the effect of superstition upon human action in a way that would give it extensive application. That he succeeded may be judged by Omar's account (I, 4) of his accepting Mahomet's leadership, if we compare his lines with what a Junker might have said in 1941 of his turning to Hitler:

> Je voulus le punir quand mon peu de lumière
> Méconnut ce grand homme entré dans la carrière:
> Mais enfin, quand j'ai vu que Mahomet est né
> Pour changer l'univers à ses pieds consterné;
> Quand mes yeux, éclairés du feu de son génie,
> Le virent s'élever dans sa course infinie;
> Eloquent, intrépide, admirable en tout lieu,
> Agir, parler, punir, ou pardonner en dieu;
> J'associai ma vie à ses travaux immenses:
> Des trônes, des autels en sont les récompenses.

Voltaire's intentions in writing this tragedy have been amply discussed. Lion has disposed of the arguments of those who imagined that he was seeking in Mahomet to represent Jesus Christ. It remains true, however, that he was attacking any religion that claimed a monopoly of virtue and sought by inhuman or untruthful methods to gain its ends. He put no representative of Christianity into his play, had no character mention it. Mahomet claims to bring a "culte épuré," nobler than the religions of Osiris, Zoroaster, Minos, and Numa, but he says nothing about Jews and Christians. However, those who knew Voltaire could easily infer that he had in mind examples of cruelty on the part of Catholics and Protestants. Nor did he hesitate to compose verses that could be applied to them:

> Sans la religion que Mahomet m'inspire,
> J'aurais eu des remords en accusant Zopire. (III, 1)
> Et la religion le remplit de fureur. (III, 5)
> Quiconque ose penser n'est pas né pour me croire. (III, 6)
> Que la religion est terrible est puissante! (IV, 3)
> Si le ciel veut un meurtre, est-ce à moi d'en juger? (IV, 4)

To have such lines declaimed at Paris may well have made Voltaire hesitate to offer his play to the actors, but, as Cardinal Fleury raised no objection to its performance, it was rehearsed at the Comédie Française before Feb. 5, 1741. This fact, overlooked by Moland and Lion, is indicated by Le Blanc: [90]

[90] Monod-Cassidy, *op. cit.*, p. 357.

Le Mahomet ne sera pas joüé cet hivert. M^r le Cardinal l'avoit permis; en un mot il n'y avoit rien ni contre la Rélligion, ni contre l'Etat, ni contre les bonnes mœurs. Il ne péchoit que contre le bon sens: les Comédiens qui l'ont répété une ou deux foix l'ont renvoyé à l'Autheur pour le corriger.

Then came La Noue's request that he might try out the play at Lille. As Voltaire gave his consent, the tragedy was acted there four times in the spring of 1741 and was well received despite the physical appearance of La Noue, who played Mahomet. Voltaire created considerable interest in his play by reading it at Paris, but Crébillon as censor refused his approbation. According to the Kehl editors, this decision was reached, not on religious grounds, but because the old dramatist saw in *Mahomet* a rival of his own *Atrée*. However, the tragedy was then referred to d'Alembert,[91] who gave his approval, with the result that the play was acted on Aug. 9, 1742.

According to Moland, Grandval played Mahomet; Sarrazin, Zopire; La Noue, Séide; la Gaussin, Palmire. There were 1205 tickets sold for this first performance; 1102 for the second, Aug. 11. On Aug. 12 the actors played *Tartuffe* as if to remind the public that a play once accused of attacking religion had become most popular. Next day there was a third performance of *Mahomet*, with 998 tickets sold. From the three Voltaire received 774 francs, more than he had earned from the first three productions of *Zaïre* or *Alzire*. Nevertheless there were so many protests that he then withdrew his play.[92]

It was published the same year, ostensibly at Brussels.[93] Voltaire referred to this edition and to a second in an *Avis au lecteur* published with an edition of Amsterdam, 1743. In 1745 he devised a clever method of confounding his pious critics. He sent a copy of the play to Pope Benedict XIV accompanied by a letter, a copy of his poem on the battle of Fontenoi, and a Latin couplet to adorn the pope's portrait. The pontiff, whose infallibility fell short of literary criticism, graciously accepted the gift, referred to " la sua bellissima tragedia di *Mahomet*," and hastened on to

---

[91] Collé (*Journal*, 1807, I, 435) tells the story differently: Voltaire read the tragedy to a cardinal, who went to sleep during the reading and, upon awaking, said it might be acted.

[92] For the four pamphlets concerned with *Mahomet* that appeared in 1742 cf. Moland, IV, 95. A parody by Favart called *l'Empirique*, in which Mahomet is replaced by a quack, was published by G. L. Van Roosbroeck in 1929; cf. also his article in *RHL*, XXXV (1928), 235-40, and Grannis, *op. cit.*, pp. 304-13.

[93] In a letter of Oct 20, 1742 (Moland, XXXVI, 171-2) Voltaire stated that this edition was printed at Paris, but with the name of Brussels. No printer is mentioned, and there is no approbation or *privilège*. There are printer's errors and mistakes in prosody, but the text is substantially as in later editions. Most of the variants are given by Moland. Note, however, that more scenes are indicated in Acts I and IV; that there is no reference to Hercide in III, 3; that his note is brought to Zopire before Séide has left the stage (III, 9); and that the presence of the people on the stage at the end of Act IV is indicated.

14

discuss pedantically the quantity of *hic* in Voltaire's Latin. He even sent the dramatist two gold medals.[94]

Finding his tragedy acceptable to so high an authority, Voltaire had it acted at his home by Le Kain and others [95] in June, 1750. The Comédie Française, too, unwilling to be more Catholic than Benedict XIV, played it on Sept. 30, 1751, with Le Kain in the rôle of Séide. The *Registres* show that the troupe provided diamonds, *babouches*, and an *écharpe* for Grandval, a turban for Dubois, coats for Grandval, Dubois, and Paulin, five Turkish costumes, six *vestes*, *écharpes*, and wigs. Grandval, Sarrazin, and la Gaussin must have kept their old rôles. Dubois probably played Omar; Paulin, the senator. Admission was paid by 1021 persons on Sept. 30. The play was acted eight times, until Oct. 16, with attendance that was somewhat better or almost as good. It was acted again on Nov. 27 and 29, Dec. 1 and 4. Voltaire's share in the receipts from the twelve productions was 1688 fr., making a total for the play of 2462 fr. It remained until 1852 in the repertory of the Comédie Française, where it was acted 273 times and ranked seventh in this respect among tragedies of the eighteenth century.

Voltaire himself spoke of it in September, 1739, as " ce que j'ai fait de moins mal." [96] Frederick the Great praised the structure and characters, declaring that the end of Act III and all of Act IV made him weep.[97] But the abbé Le Blanc was not of their opinion. On Aug. 13, 1742, he expressed his surprise that the police had allowed the play to be performed,[98] for politics fared in it no better than religion:

C'est le triomphe du Déisme ou plustôt du Fatalisme. Le caractere de Mahomet y est absolument manqué. Loin d'y paroitre cet habile imposteur qui veut qu'on le croye un Prophéte il avoüe de bonne foi qu'il est un Fourbe. Il n'inspire le Fanatisme qu'à une jeune Cervelle, qu'il veut sans raison entrainer dans le Parricide. Il y a plus le ton de la Garonne que le ton de Prophétie. . . . L'Horreur que le IV Acte peut inspirer est düe aux Imitations d'Atrée. Le Pretendu miracle qui fait le denoûment de la Piéce ne m'a paru que puéril. . . . Mais il faut avoüer aussi qu'il y a de grandes beautés beaucoup de force, beaucoup de hardiesse & des détails brillants.

Collé [99] admitted that there were more fine verses in this tragedy than

[94] M. Pierre Martino published in *RHL*, XXXV (1928), 563-7, an amusing letter written to the pope by a devout Frenchman, protesting against the presentation of these medals to " l'infame Athée Arrouët de Voltaire," quoting some of Voltaire's verses to establish his contention, and suggesting that he would himself like to receive two medals with the portrait of His Holiness, even if they were only of silver! For Martino's theory that the Jesuits favored *Mahomet* because they considered it anti-Jansenist, cf. his article in *Mémorial Henri Basset*, Paris, 1928.

[95] Cf. Raynal, *Cor.*, I, 436.

[96] Moland, XXXV, 324.

[97] On Sept. 9, 1739, he had objected to Voltaire's using *écraser* with *étincelles* and had proposed the substitution of *étouffer*, which Voltaire adopted; cf. *Mahomet*, I, 1, v. 14, and Moland, XXXV, 325, 400.

[98] Monod-Cassidy, *op. cit.*, pp. 377-8.

[99] *Journal*, 1807, I, 434-8, II, 113; *Correspondance inédite*, p. 236.

in any other by Voltaire, that it was an idea of genius to put on the stage a religious fanatic, and that it was also one to create the scene in which Zopire recognizes his children just after one of them has stabbed him. But he called the final miracle worthy of marionettes, Mahomet's love for Palmire trivial, and insisted that the Prophet's character is not shown in action. He was determined to carry out his theory that Voltaire was a poet rather than a dramatist, even at the expense of his own reputation as a critic.

La Harpe [100] called the play a *chef-d'œuvre*, a tragic *Tartuffe*. He knew nothing superior to its fourth act, but he objected to Mahomet's being in love, found that the poison worked too well, and thought that no proper explanation was given for the fact that Séide is allowed by Zopire to see Mahomet freely. Lion criticized Voltaire for not indicating where in Mecca the action takes place, although in the edition of 1742 the scene is said to be laid " dans le Temple des faux Dieux de Zopire." He found Omar's entrances poorly motivated and insisted that Hercide should have sought Séide rather than Zopire, but he admired greatly the fourth act and found striking tableaux in IV, 4 and in Act V.

The play has, of course, technical defects. La Harpe's point about the poison is especially well taken, for, if it had acted a little less quickly, Mahomet might have been killed; if a little more swiftly, there could have been no " faux miracle." Lovers of local color may object to Voltaire's lack of interest in it, though it has more than many eighteenth-century tragedies. But the play has five well-drawn characters, excellent scenes that are ably distributed among the acts, a lesson of tolerance that is clearly presented without loss of dramatic effect, a most appealing fourth act, and a striking dénouement. To write a tragedy dominated by a moral purpose that also has high esthetic value is no mean achievement. It deserves to rank with *Zaïre* as one of its author's two leading tragedies and at the same time is an important document in the struggle for religious freedom, the most daring play that had been acted in France since the time of *Tartuffe*.

Before *Mahomet* was performed, even before it was begun, Voltaire had started the composition of MÉROPE.[101] He says that the idea had occurred to him during the visit to Paris of Maffei in 1733, but, as he says nothing about it in his correspondence of that year and as the Italian dramatist was in Paris in 1736, Moland suggested that 1733 is an error for the later year. Voltaire probably completed the first form of the play in 1737, as by January, 1738, both la Quinault and Frederick the Great had read it. The

---

[100] *Op. cit.*, XI, 348-82.
[101] Paris, Prault fils, 1744, 8°. Dedicated to Scipio Maffei. For other editions see Bengesco and Moland. For Italian translations cf. Ferrari, *op. cit.* An English adaptation by Aaron Hill was acted in 1749; cf. Lounsbury, *op. cit.*, p. 152. The play has been studied by Lessing, *op. cit.*, and by Lion, *op. cit.*, pp. 149-69.

following month Voltaire wrote that *Mérope* was " prodigieusement corrigée et limée "; on May 2, that he had composed three new acts.[102]   His reconsideration of his work seems due to criticism from la Quinault.[103]   Now interested in *Mahomet*, he laid *Mérope* aside, but he returned to it after the other tragedy had been acted at Lille, so that it was finally played at the Comédie Française on Feb. 20, 1743.

During the six years that elapsed between conception and production Voltaire had ample opportunity to revise his play in accordance with earlier dramatizations of the theme.   No ancient tragedy on the subject has survived, though Aristotle refers to its most striking situation in his *Poetics* and Hyginus gives what may well be a résumé of a tragedy by Euripides that dramatizes the story.   In France the legend had been put on the stage by Gilbert, La Chapelle, La Grange-Chancel, and Longepierre before Maffei produced in 1713 a *Merope* that was translated into French in 1718 and inspired an English adaptation by George Jeffreys in 1731.   Voltaire was acquainted with all of these plays.   Let us see to what extent he utilized them.

His principal source was Maffei, from whose tragedy he derived his hero's name and the fact that the youth does not know who he is; the name of Euryclès, if it is a modification of Euriso; the background of political strife; Egisthe's reason for leaving his adopted father, the murder he commits, and its consequences; Mérope's interest in him and her desire, when she thinks he has murdered her son, that he should die by her own hand; and many circumstances of the catastrophe.   In short, he owed the Italian the original idea of dramatizing the ancient theme, certain names, seven scenes,[104] and suggestions for a number of others.

Certain elements in the tragedy may have come from other plays.   Like Gilbert's *Téléphonte*, *Mérope* begins with a conversation between the queen and an attendant and introduces the young hero in Act II.   In this play, in La Chapelle's *Téléphonte*, and in La Grange-Chancel's *Amasis* the hero's attention is called to the place where his father was murdered and the man who points it out is an old attendant who had rescued the boy while this murder was taking place.   As in La Chapelle's tragedy, the queen is indignant that a subject should wish to marry her, she makes the production of her son a condition when she agrees to marry the usurper, the latter gives permission for the young man to be interviewed by the queen and is called by him a tyrant.   In *Amasis*, too, the youth greets the usurper as a tyrant, while the view of tombs and the use of a sword for identification may have

---

[102] Moland, XXXIV, 420, 465.
[103] Moland, XXXIV, 374-7.
[104] II, 2, III, 2, 4, V, 5-8.

suggested to Voltaire the showing of Chresphonte's tomb and the substitution of armor for Maffei's ring.[105] Longepierre's *Electre* may have suggested to Voltaire the removal from his play of sexual love; [106] the similarity of a brief passage in his tragedy (IV, 9) and one in *Mérope*, III, 4, is striking:

> J'allois venger mon frere.—Vous l'alliez immoler; c'est Oreste.
> J'allais venger mon fils.—Vous alliez l'immoler . . . c'est Egisthe.

La Harpe [107] asserted that this last resemblance had been discovered by those who read everything, but he thought that the words were suggested independently to both dramatists. On the other hand, he held that the scene in which Mérope reveals to her enemy her son's identity was inspired by Piron's *Gustave*. Finally, Mérope's agreeing to marry the tyrant in order to save her son's life, but with the intention of killing herself at the altar, may well have been suggested by *Andromaque*.[108] These similarities show that Voltaire's originality was displayed, not in the materials that he used, but in his manner of putting them together. They also demonstrate the fact that his play was far from being merely an adaptation of Maffei's tragedy. There can be little doubt that in Voltaire's hands the ancient theme received its most effective dramatization.[109]

La Harpe and Lion have indicated the main differences between Voltaire's tragedy and Maffei's. In Voltaire's Mérope is still queen at the beginning, and Polyphonte is not proclaimed king until II, 3; the queen appears before the tyrant does, while Egisthe is first seen in Act II. Mérope does not know that Polyphonte has killed her husband and sons. Her maternal love and her fear for her son are much more developed than in Maffei's tragedy. It is she who questions the young stranger. The striking scene of Act IV in which Mérope identifies her son for the tyrant is not in the Italian tragedy, where, indeed, mother and son converse in only one scene. Voltaire avoids the second scene in which the queen attempts to kill her son before

---

[105] Such resemblances did not justify La Grange-Chancel in calling Voltaire's tragedy a copy of his own, as he did in a letter published in the *Journal étranger*, 1756 (4), pp. 234-8. The fact that the heroine is not married to the villain in *Amasis* and in Voltaire's play means nothing, as the same thing may be said of Maffei's and of La Chapelle's.

[106] Maffei has a pretense of love, not found in Longepierre's play or in Voltaire's. In the other tragedies love is an important element.

[107] *Op. cit.*, XII, 35-7.

[108] Voltaire transferred into *Mérope*, I, 3, at least nine verses from his *Eriphyle*, III, 5.

[109] The late Professor T. E. Oliver thought that Voltaire owed a good deal to Jeffreys, whose play the French dramatist ridiculed, but he failed to mention La Chapelle and Longepierre and he discovered no resemblances between Voltaire and Jeffries that cannot be explained by the existence of a common source except in the case of very minor details that could readily suggest themselves independently to two dramatists; cf. *The Merope of George Jeffreys as a Source of Voltaire's Mérope*, Urbana, Ill., 1927.

she discovers who he is, and he greatly reduces the number of conversations between unimportant persons. Apparently he thought at first of translating Maffei's play, but, as he worked on it, he became more and more conscious of its shortcomings, added more material from other authors who had treated the theme or from his own imagination, and finally produced a tragedy, the text of which is close to the Italian only in Act V and in scattered lines elsewhere.[110]

[110] Fifteen or sixteen years before the play begins, Polyphonte murdered Chresphonte, King of Messenia, and two of his three sons. The survivor, Egisthe, was carried to safety by Narbas, who brought him up as his son and kept his mother, Mérope, informed about his safety, but for four years all communications between them have ceased. Mérope is urged by her confidant, Isménie, to interest herself in the government, for, now that civil war is over, a ruler is to be chosen and there is danger that Polyphonte may be selected. Euryclès reports that he has sought in vain for Narbas, who may have hidden Egisthe to save him from Polyphonte's murderous agents, and that he fears the people will make their master king. Polyphonte proposes to Mérope that, as opinion is divided between them, they marry and share the throne. Mérope refuses indignantly and insists that her son must reign. Polyphonte replies that, even if he lives, he is inexperienced, whereas his own exploits in avenging Chresphonte and bringing peace to the state are well known, but she makes the restoration of her son a condition of her marriage. Fearing that, if Egisthe returns, he will be made king, Polyphonte has had Narbas' messengers arrested. His confidant, Erox, assures him that, if Narbas and Egisthe reappear, they will be killed by Polyphonte's agents. In Act II Mérope is troubled by the report that a poor young man has been arrested for murder. Fearing that her son has been killed, she has the man brought in and is told that he was praying for her in a temple of Hercules when two armed men threatened him with daggers, that he killed the younger and threw his body into a stream while the elder fled. Mérope is surprised to see in the youth resemblance to Chresphonte. She learns that he knows nothing of Narbas or Egisthe, and that, hearing of Mérope's misfortunes, he has desired to serve in her army. Mérope would aid him, for her own son may be wandering in a strange land and need assistance. She is told that the people have chosen Polyphonte to be their king, that they insist upon her marrying him, and that her son has been killed by the youth she wishes to protect. The proof of the murder lies in the fact that, to prevent identification, the murderer had thrown away armor that Narbas had taken with him when he left Messenia. Convinced, Mérope demands vengeance and agrees to marry Polyphonte, if he will allow her to kill the murderer. She tells her friends that, once vengeance has been secured, she will kill herself. In Act III Narbas laments over the disappearance of Egisthe and the fact that Polyphonte is king. He meets Isménie near the tomb of Chresphonte, learns from her that Egisthe has been murdered, that Mérope will kill the murderer beside the tomb and will then commit suicide. Narbas retires. Egisthe is led in, chained. Mérope, though moved by his reference to his mother, hardens her heart and is about to strike when Narbas intervenes and insists upon speaking to Mérope, but first persuades Euryclès to lead Egisthe away. He then tells Mérope she was on the point of killing her son. She faints, recovers, and is warned by Narbas not to reveal her son's identity. Euryclès returns to report that Polyphonte wishes to question the murderer, learns that it is Egisthe, and seeks to comfort Mérope with the thought that the prince will be protected by Polyphonte when he marries her, but Narbas protests against the marriage and informs the queen that Polyphonte has murdered Chresphonte and two of his sons. When the king comes to lead her to the altar, she asks to see the murderer again and rouses Polyphonte's suspicions. In Act IV he declares his intention of putting the murderer to death and of questioning the old man, said to be his father. The youth, brought before Mérope and Polyphonte, calls the king a tyrant. When Polyphonte orders his execution, Mérope throws herself between the young man and the soldiers, crying " il est mon fils ! " She pleads on her knees for his life, but Egisthe bids her rise and not to humiliate him. Polyphonte offers to adopt the youth, if Mérope will marry him, bids her decide whether Egisthe will live or die, and goes to wait for her in the temple. There he announces to the people that the marriage will take place. Mérope hopes

Voltaire boasted that in *Mérope* he had composed a tragedy without sexual love. Instead he emphasized maternal devotion, as Racine had done in *Andromaque,* but Racine's heroine is the widow of a man with whom she is still deeply in love, whereas Mérope is presented purely as a mother who forgets all thoughts of self in seeking her son's welfare. She is interested in the throne only for his sake. She will not avenge her husband, unless by so doing she furthers the interests of her son. When Voltaire was asked by Father Porée for sentimental scenes between mother and son, he replied that they would be insipid.[111] When they first meet, she does not know who he is. When they meet again, she is prepared to kill him as the murderer of her son. At their third meeting Polyphonte is present and her efforts are directed at saving the young man's life. At the fourth, he is filled with his determination to kill Polyphonte and has no opportunity to display affection. At the end of the play she is bending all her efforts towards establishing him on the throne. No presentation of a devoted mother could be less sentimental. Voltaire describes la Dumesnil's way of playing the rôle. When she intended to kill Egisthe, she advanced, " les yeux égarés, la voix entrecoupée, levant une main tremblante," and when she revealed his identity to Polyphonte, she crossed the stage, " les larmes dans les yeux, la pâleur sur le front, les sanglots à la bouche, les bras étendus." [112]

Her son is represented as brave and idealistic, modest and pious, with a boyish admiration for the queen in distress he has left home to aid. He has for Narbas filial devotion, for Polyphonte righteous indignation. He insists that he has killed only in self-defense, demands justice, but does not blame Mérope when she appears hostile. Upon hearing that he is the son of King Chresphonte, he feels lifted to a higher plane:

> Je me sens né des rois, je me sens votre fils. (IV, 2)
> Un nouveau sang m'anime, un nouveau jour m'éclaire. (V, 1)

He would have his mother do nothing unworthy of their rank. He speaks to her (V, 4) in brief, determined sentences:

to show her son in the temple and to appeal for support. In Act V Polyphonte returns to offer Egisthe his life and " grandeurs " if he will swear in the temple to do him homage. Egisthe asks for a sword and insults Polyphonte, who leaves him under the guard of Euryclès. Egisthe comes to a decision, questions his mother as to the positions taken by the guards, and escorts her to the temple. Cries are heard. Euryclès and Narbas fear that Mérope and her son have perished. The noise becomes louder. Isménie reports that, just as the marriage was about to take place, Egisthe seized an axe on the altar and killed Polyphonte and his confidant. Mérope then declared him to be her son. Her friends protected her from the soldiers. In the confusion that followed, Isménie escaped to the palace. Soon Mérope and Egisthe appear in triumph. The body of Polyphonte is seen at the back of the stage. Mérope calls on the people to recognize Egisthe as king. He is again identified by Narbas. Thunder is heard. Euryclès announces that calm has been restored in the city. Egisthe attributes his triumph to the gods and asks Narbas to be ever his father.

[111] Moland, XXXV, 116-7.   [112] Moland, XXIV, 220.

> Osez me suivre. . . .
> Voyez-vous en ces lieux le tombeau de mon père?
> Entendez-vous sa voix? Etes-vous reine et mère?
> Si vous l'êtes, venez.

He has already become a king.

Polyphonte is the villain of the tragedy, a murderer who seeks to win the throne by threats and bribery and to strengthen his position by marrying the widow of the king he has killed. He has no redeeming traits except the courage he has shown in war, yet Voltaire put into his mouth the most celebrated verse in the play (I, 3):

> Le premier qui fut roi fut un soldat heureux.

He even denies the principle of hereditary monarchy:

> Le droit de commander n'est plus un avantage
> Transmis par la nature, ainsi qu'un héritage;
> C'est le fruit des travaux et du sang répandu.

These verses probably escaped the censor because they were spoken by a villain and were opposed to the fundamental ideas of the play.

The most appealing of the other characters is old Narbas, a loyal adherent of monarchy, devoted to his ward and to the memory of the murdered king, wise in the manner in which he works for the queen without antagonizing Polyphonte and in the caution he displays in revealing the identity of Egisthe. The four main characters personify maternal love, virtuous youth, unscrupulous ambition, and benevolent old age. They lack complexity. None of them is tragic in the Aristotelian sense. They are less striking creations than the leading characters in *Zaïre* and *Mahomet*. The play owed its success less to them as individuals than to the series of dramatic scenes, carefully prepared and skillfully presented.[113] Voltaire's achievement can be judged by his criticism of Maffei.

In this he showed the same shrewdness that he had displayed in dedicating *Mahomet* to the pope. He invented a certain M. de La Lindelle and published in 1748 his sweeping criticism of Maffei's tragedy. His straw man condemned the queen for listening to the tyrant's marriage proposition, although she knew that he had killed her husband, a situation that Voltaire avoided by having his heroine discover Polyphonte's guilt late in the play. Maffei does not make it clear whom the young man has murdered, whereas Voltaire shows that it is an agent of Polyphonte. Moreover, in Maffei's tragedy the queen suspects without evidence that the young man is her son; her hesitation in attacking the supposed murderer of her son is poorly

---

[113] I, 3, II, 2, 5, III, 4, 5, IV, 2. It is true, however, as Lessing pointed out, that the delays of Polyphonte and Mérope in going to the altar are not well explained.

explained; the young man runs away from her, conveniently falls asleep, and is a second time in danger of being killed by her. All of these faults Voltaire avoided.

In his " Réponse à M. de La Lindelle " Voltaire accused his imaginary friend of being over critical, but he admitted that most of his charges were justified. He declared that he could not himself introduce a ring as Maffei had done, because of Boileau's criticism of Quinault's *Astrate,* but he supposed that one would not be objectionable in Italy. He softened his criticism by expressing admiration for the scene between the heroine and her son in Maffei's tragedy and the narration given in its last act, both of which he had imitated.

In his dedication, published four years earlier, he had praised the Italian for eliminating sexual love and for writing a simple and interesting tragedy, but he had objected to the ring, to the tyrant's pretending to love the queen, to the repetition of the scene in which the mother threatens her son, to the young man's falling asleep, to the naïveté of the dialogue, to the conversations between subordinate characters, and to Maffei's writing as a poet rather than as a dramatist. In short, he had explained why he was obliged to write a new *Mérope,* although he admitted that parts of the Italian tragedy were worth imitating.

When Voltaire's tragedy was acted, Feb. 20, 1743, la Dumesnil played Mérope; Grandval, Egisthe; Paulin, Polyphonte; Sarrazin, Narbas.[114] Admission was paid by 1182 persons at this performance, by 1313 at the second, three days later. The enthusiasm that greeted the play was so great that the audience called for the author. The play was given thirteen times before Easter, again on April 22 and 24, and from Feb. 3 to March 14, 1744. The receipts on one occasion rose to 4420 fr., and never fell below 1653 fr. The author's share was 6146 fr., 18 s., a sum unequaled by earlier tragedies for which we have records. The play remained in the repertory of the Comédie Française until 1869, when the total number of performances had reached 340. Only *Zaïre* and *Tancrède* surpassed it in this respect among tragedies of the eighteenth century.[115]

While Desfontaines and Lessing[116] criticized the play severely, La

---

[114] François Baron and Du Breuil played the male confidants. Isménie was acted in 1743 by la Lavoy, but in 1744 by the celebrated Clairon, who had joined the troupe in the interval. The troupe hired two " assistans à la Romaine," two mutes, and provided five wigs.

[115] For parodies cf. Grannis, *op. cit.,* pp. 313-22, and Lindsay, *op. cit.,* pp. 146-9.

[116] *Hamburgische Dramaturgie,* especially IX, 395-99, in the edition of Lessing's *Sämtliche Schriften,* Stuttgart, 1893. Moland and Lion have indicated the prejudice displayed by the German critic in attempting to show that Voltaire did little more than copy Maffei. An example that they do not refer to is found in Lessing's claim that Voltaire caused his hero to be attacked by two men instead of one merely to enhance the youth's dignity as son of a king, but it is obvious that the addition

Harpe [117] praised it extravagantly, showing in great detail its superiority over Maffei's tragedy, though not denying the imitation,[118] pointing out the steady progress in the action and in the interest it arouses, lauding characterization, style, situations, pronouncing the tragedy " sans contredit, ce que Voltaire a écrit de plus parfait . . . jamais il ne s'est plus approché de la pureté, de l'élégance et de l'harmonie de Racine."

Lion is far more favorable to the play than Lessing, but less enthusiastic than La Harpe. He shows that the tragedy is less simple than Voltaire supposed, for the action passes through three stages. In the first the question is whether Mérope will be reunited to her son; in the second, whether she will avenge his supposed murder; in the third, whether she will save him from the tyrant and place him on the throne. He admits some of the charges of *invraisemblance* brought by Voltaire himself, by La Harpe, or by Lessing, but he praises the presentation of Mérope, a creation worthy of " nos premiers poètes dramatiques," and of Egisthe, and attributes the warm reception the play received, not only to the characters, but to the structure, the rapid action, its " sensibilité," even a dash of anticlericalism [119] in what was essentially a monarchial production.

Mérope is less original than *Zaïre, Alzire,* or *Mahomet,* for it owed much to Maffei and other dramatists. It is less novel in its location and in its characters than these three tragedies. The absence of sexual love gives it less appeal to those primarily interested in that subject. But it has an excellent rôle for an actress no longer young, one which, played by la Dumesnil, must have done much to establish it in popular favor. This rôle, along with the careful structure and the fine quality of the style, makes it rank high among Voltaire's tragedies. Its production, following those of *Zaïre, Alzire,* and *Mahomet,* corresponds to that of *Polyeucte* after those of *le Cid, Horace,* and *Cinna,* and marks the climax of Voltaire's career as a dramatist, as they did that of Corneille. He wrote many more tragedies, inspired partly by his desire to outdo Crébillon, to promote the use of spectacle, or to further ideas that interested him, but he never renewed the achievement of these four tragedies, conceived shortly before or shortly after the middle of his life.

---

of the second man, older than his companion, is made in order to give Mérope more evidence that her son, whom she believed to be accompanied by Narbas, has been murdered.

[117] *Op. cit.,* XII, 1-57.

[118] Lion, *op. cit.,* p. 157, reports that La Harpe went so far as to claim that Voltaire owed Maffei nothing, but the critic had written (*op. cit.,* XII, 3) " on sait toutes les obligations qu'il eut à . . . Maffei."

[119]   Par l'or de ce tyran le grand-prêtre inspiré,
          A fait parler le dieu dans son temple adoré. (IV, 5)

CHAPTER IX

MORAND, LA CHAUSSÉE, AND OTHERS
1735 TO JANUARY, 1739

In the three and a half years that separate Richer's *Sabinus* from Deschamps's *Médus* nine tragedies appeared for the first time. Of these Voltaire's *Alzire*, greatly superior to the others, and Caux's posthumous *Lysimachus* have already been discussed. The remaining seven were composed by an author who had previously written two tragedies, by one well known for his comedies, and by three who began at this time to write for the Comédie Française. To familiar sources they added Herbelot's *Bibliothèque orientale* and Bayle's *Dictionnaire*. Their main themes were palace intrigues, but larger interests were suggested, though ineffectively dramatized, in Cahusac's *Pharamond* and in La Chaussée's *Maximien*. There are patriotic passages in these two plays and in Morand's *Childéric*, the first tragedy of the eighteenth century to put on the stage historical Franks.

Some attention was paid to exotic customs in Le Blanc's *Aben-Saïd* before *Alzire* was acted. The primitive virtues of Gauls and Franks are contrasted with the decadent culture of Rome in Cahusac's *Pharamond*. Elsewhere there is little to note in regard to manners. Nor do the claims to moral instruction made by Morand and Deschamps produce more than commonplace conclusions. A tirade against royal mistresses would have shown more daring a decade later.

The most effective characters are those of the emir in *Aben-Saïd*, of Fausta in *Maximien*, and of the title-rôle and Clovis in *Childéric*. These are the plays of the period, apart from *Alzire*, that have greatest interest for the modern reader. In their own day the first two were well received, at least during the first year of their existence. The others had only brief careers, one of them but a single production.

I have included in this chapter two plays that appeared later than 1739 in order to complete what I have to say about Morand and Cahusac. As one is lost and neither had a second performance, they have no significance elsewhere.

The abbé Jean-Bernard Le Blanc, born at Dijon in 1701, was the son of a man who combined in that city the functions of greffier and keeper of the jail. The classical education he received from the Jesuits and the protection of président Bouhier enabled him to seek a literary career at Paris, where he knew Piron, his fellow townsman; Prévost, Buffon, and Voltaire. He made himself known by a *Poème sur les gens de lettres de Bourgogne,* by his elegies, and by a *Discours* concerning this kind of poetry. He then tried the theater and made desperate, but unsuccessful efforts to become a member of the Academy. He visited England, published letters and reflexions on what he saw there, and translated tracts by Milton and Hume. He died in 1781.[1]

It may have been the success of *Zaïre* that turned his attention to the history of western Asia during the Middle Ages. In the preface of his tragedy he calls oriental history a new treasure for dramatists, one that relates at every page facts " dignes de la majesté du Cothurne." And Voltaire, graciously greeting him as a fellow explorer, wrote to him after *Alzire* had appeared: " Nous avons partagé les Indes entre nous; votre muse est au Mongol et la mienne au Perou." [2]

He tells us that the source of his ABEN-SAÏD, EMPEREUR DES MOGULS [3] is Herbelot's *Bibliothèque orientale* " à l'article d'Abou-Saïd." [4] He admits that he altered this name and others to please the delicacy of French ears, but he claims that the principal elements of his tragedy are historical:

L'amour de Sémire pour son Epoux; la passion du Sultan pour cette jeune Princesse; la Loi qui ordonne à tout Sujet de repudier sa femme lorsqu'il plaît au Sultan de l'épouser; la fermeté généreuse de l'Emir à s'opposer à l'éxécution d'une Loy si injuste; tous ces faits sont véritables.

He adds that he derived from the same source references to the vast conquests of " Genghiscan " and his successors, as well as to the power of the califs and its decay, but he fails to indicate that he altered his material considerably in order to make his characters appealing. The emperor did not renounce his love, as he makes him do. Hassan did repudiate his wife and send her to the imperial harem. The emir, who was by no means loyal to the emperor, was not mortally wounded in battle, but was beheaded as a traitor. While Le Blanc's Nasser represents the historical visir Sain, the dramatist seems to have invented Ilcan, as well as Hassan's return to court in disguise and minor details.[5]

[1] Cf. especially Hélène Monod-Cassidy, *op. cit.*
[2] *Ibid.,* p. 488.
[3] Paris, Prault fils, 1736, 8° and 1743. Dedicated to Condé's great-grandson, the comte de Clermont, about whose election to the Academy Le Blanc subsequently published a letter. Republished, Utrecht, Néaulme, 1736. A Dutch translation appeared at Amsterdam in 1738; an Italian translation at Bologna about 1740 and subsequently (cf. Ferrari, *op. cit.*, pp. 1, 2) ; and an English translation was undertaken (cf. Monod-Cassidy, *op. cit.*, p. 35). The play is analyzed by Mme Monod-Cassidy, *op. cit.*, pp. 33-4. She is mistaken in saying that the emperor gives his throne to Hassan.
[4] That is, Abousaid-Ben-Algiaptou: cf. *Bibliothèque orientale*, I, 59-70 in the edition of Paris, 1781.
[5] Aben-Saïd, descendant of Genghis Khan, is the youthful ruler of Persia. His sister, Roxane, is married to the emir, Timour, commander of the emperor's armies.

Some of the characters resemble those of *Britannicus*. In both plays an emperor who loves a young woman is urged by flatterers to take her for himself and to get rid of the man she loves, while a statesman and a feminine relative seek to keep him in the path of virtue. Aben-Saïd, who has the dominant and the longest rôle, is described as a youth who had lived the life of camps until Sémire attracted his attention. He applies in her case the law of his ancestors, but he wishes to win her affections too. He pleads and threatens, seeks the help of his sister and the emir, even orders Timour's arrest when he resists, but is so much impressed by his personality that he soon restores him to power. He wavers like Nero between the good and evil influences that are brought to bear on him, but, unlike his prototype, is finally induced to conquer his passion.

The character who does most to bring about this result is Timour, called by Herbelot Giouban. He is represented as victorious over Usbek and as conqueror of Korassan. He is a wise and energetic statesman, quick to perceive the evil designs of his chief opponent, loyal to the emperor, but unwilling to follow him in dishonor. As in Herbelot he is considered an " homme de bien, aimant la justice, & . . . grand zélateur de sa Religion." His tragic flaw lies in the facts that, without the emperor's permission, he returns from the front and that he seeks by force of arms to carry off his

---

This dignitary has married his daughter by an earlier marriage, Sémire, to a Mongol prince called Hassan, who is deeply devoted to her. Prince Ilcan, who aspires to replace Aben-Saïd on the throne, has praised Sémire's beauty to the emperor in the hope that he would fall in love with her, quarrel with Timour, and, in the confusion that might follow, make it possible for Ilcan to become emperor. The prince has an ally in Nasser, a visir whose father has been slain by Timour. Their conspiracy has progressed. Aben-Saïd has fallen in love with Sémire, Hassan has refused to give her up, and Nasser has been sent to arrest the recalcitrant husband in accordance with a decree of Genghis Khan that, if the monarch asks for a subject's wife, she must be repudiated by her husband. Nasser reports that he has killed Hassan and brought Sémire to Tauris, where the scene of the tragedy is laid. He has also aided Ilcan by rousing the religious feelings of those who keep their old gods and are dissatisfied with the emperor's Mohammedanism. But Aben-Saïd regrets the loss of Hassan, whom he thinks he could have bribed, and is distressed by Sémire's grief over her husband and hatred of himself. As he also fears that Timour may seek to avenge Hassan, he orders his arrest. Roxane, whom the emperor would placate, charges him with murder. After defeating the Tartars, Timour comes to court, throws down his sword, and gives himself up, but he refuses his consent to the emperor's marriage, though Aben-Saïd returns his sword and urges him to persuade his daughter to yield. Soon it is discovered that Hassan has not been killed, that he has reached the palace disguised as a soldier, and that he believes Ilcan to be his friend. Nasser is told to murder Hassan when he comes at night to carry off his wife, but Timour sees through Ilcan's plans and conceals soldiers about the palace to rescue the lovers. The result is that Hassan kills Nasser, but is arrested by Ilcan and ordered by the emperor to repudiate Sémire or perish. Timour and his daughter have almost won the emperor over when fighting breaks out and Ilcan is killed by Timour, who is mortally wounded. Aben-Saïd has learned at last that Ilcan has been his enemy and that Timour has saved his throne and his life. The emir admits that his death is deserved, though he has resorted to force only to save Sémire and her husband. Aben-Saïd is so deeply moved that he abolishes the law of Genghis Khan, allows Hassan to keep his wife, and appoints him emir in place of Timour.

daughter and her husband when there appears to be no other way to save them. For these acts of disobedience he pays by saving the emperor's life at the cost of his own.

Associated with him are brave, though somewhat naïve young Hassan and two women, differentiated by Sémire's violent expressions of grief and indignation [6] and by Roxane's restraint and greater maturity. Opposing them are Ilcan and his henchman, Nasser. Ilcan can pose as a devout Mohammedan when it seems desirable, or he can win the confidence of those who would throw off the Prophet's yoke. He pretends to work in the interests of the emperor and of Hassan in order to betray them both and to profit by their rivalry. He has recourse to assassination when milder methods fail.

The manners described differ from those of France chiefly in the references to the law that gave a sovereign power to take a subject's wife, in remarks about Mohammedanism and the ancient religion of the Mongols, and in the proper names, though some of these retain little Persian flavor. Aben-Saïd, it is true, differs little from Abousaïd. Hassan Ilkhain supplied Le Blanc with two names, one for Hassan, the other for Ilcan. Timour bears no resemblance to Giouban, but was a familiar substitute for Tamourlan. Sémire and Roxane, if more euphonious, lack the Persian quality of Satibeg and Bagdad Khatoun.

The play dramatizes a palace conspiracy that fails through a statesman's loyalty and presence of mind. The emperor's unhistorical conversion gives it a sentimental ending. The action is rapid and thoroughly unified. The novelty of the play lies in the choice of the subject rather than in the methods employed in its presentation.

Evidence in regard to its composition and production is supplied by Mme Monod-Cassidy.[7] On Oct. 31, 1733, Le Blanc confided in Bouhier that he was at work on a tragedy derived from d'Herbelot and that he had found it hard to give his characters names that would be both oriental and suited to the stage. He was still writing the following February, had reached the third act in March, and was giving the tragedy the "derniere main" in July, but he was revising verses at the end of October. In the last week of Lent, 1735, he read his play to the actors, although he claimed that Le Franc and others were intriguing against him and that Dufresne refused to play the rôle assigned him until an order from Louis XV made him accept it. As late as April 22 the author was hesitating between *Abou-Saïd* and *Abel Saïd* as his title. At last, on June 7, he writes that his play has received great applause, and on Jan. 11, 1736, he boasts that, when it was

---

[6] She addresses the emperor with *tu* and *toi* except in IV, 4, when, in accordance with her father's instructions, she is seeking to appease him.

[7] *Op. cit.*, pp. 185, 194-5, 198, 211, 219, 225-34.

given in the winter season, those who had been in the army were as much pleased as those who had seen it in June.[8]

It was acted twelve times, from June 6 to July 2, and five times, from Dec. 31, 1735, to Jan. 11, 1736. The troupe provided diamonds for Dufresne, who must have had the title-rôle, and eight "habits à la Turc" for the eight characters in the play. La Dufresne and la Balicourt probably represented, respectively, Sémire and Roxane; Sarrazin, Timour; Grandval, Hassan; Legrand de Belleville, Ilcan. Though the audiences were smaller in the winter than they had been in the summer, they continued to the end to be large enough to enable Le Blanc to share in the receipts. His earnings amounted to 983 fr., 16 s.

The tragedy was played at court and inspired a parody called the *Droit du Seigneur*. Mme Monod-Cassidy cites the praise the author received from the *Journal de Trévoux*, Prévost, and Desfontaines. Voltaire also complimented him. Le Blanc was so much gratified that he thanked Father Oudin for instructing him in honor, virtue, wisdom, and justice and thus enabling him to depict Timour as combating the lies of flatterers:

> C'est par la que dans cet Ouvrage
> Du Public j'obtiens le sufrage,
> Oudin, c'est par là que ma voix
> A frappé l'oreille des Rois.[9]

On Sept. 2, 1742, Le Blanc wrote that his play was being republished and that it would reappear on the stage the following winter, a prediction that was not fulfilled. He said that he had corrected certain verses in accordance with Bouhier's suggestions and had added passages, including one on fanaticism that was more prudently expressed than what Voltaire had written on this subject in *Mahomet* and the *Henriade*. He then quoted eight lines that might be understood, according to the reader's taste, as praise or blame of fanaticism:

> Haïs, persecutés pour la Foy de leurs Peres
> Ils attendent de vous la fin de leurs miseres,
> Et pour mettre en vos mains le sceptre des Sultans
> Ils vaincront glorieux, ou périront contents[.]
> Le Zele des Autels est toûjours redoutable,
> Il arme les ésprits d'un Courage indomtable,
> Et l'interet du Ciel animant chaque Etat,
> Fait du Soldat un Prêtre & du Prêtre un Soldat.[10]

---

[8] He notes that the lieutenant de police objected to the phrase, "les Loix ne sont Loix qu'autant qu'elles sont justes." He defends the dropping of an *s* at the rime from *reçoi*, *doi*, etc., but admits that he was wrong to rime *il* and *péril*. He declares that his tragedy is being translated into English and Italian.

[9] Monod-Cassidy, *op. cit.*, p. 235.

[10] *Ibid.*, pp. 379-80. On May 28 he wrote that the new edition had appeared.

A much more prolific dramatist than Le Blanc was born at Arles in the same year, 1701. This was Pierre de Morand, who, when a lawyer " au parlement d'Aix," took women's rôles in amateur performances of *Tartuffe* and *Phèdre*. He suffered from his mother-in-law, who deprived him of his wife, and avenged himself by putting her into a comedy. At Paris he was introduced into the circle of the duchesse du Maine, whom he helped to give plays at the Arsenal. About 1749-53 he was the Paris correspondent of Frederick the Great. The police reported that " quoique auteur de quelques pièces de théâtre," Morand " se pique d'une scrupuleuse délicatesse et d'une haute probité." Many anecdotes are told of his fiery disposition and of his sense of humor, which led him to dictate a will in the manner of Crispin of the *Légataire universel*. He died in 1757.[11]

He composed two comedies, a one-act tragedy called *Menzikof*,[12] acted at the Théâtre Italien, and three tragedies played at the Comédie Française. He addressed poems to the queen, to Cardinal Fleury, to Mme de Pompadour, and to la Dufresne, to whom he refers as playing Camille in *Horace* and the title-rôle in Crébillon's *Electre*. In a poem entitled the *Progrès de la Tragédie* he did homage especially to Corneille and Racine, but he mentioned also tragedies by Thomas Corneille, Campistron, Crébillon, La Fosse, Brueys, and La Grange-Chancel.[13] He referred, too, to women dramatists who had been seen to win laurels.[14]

After writing a prologue[15] for a troupe of amateurs allowed by the duchesse du Maine to play at the Arsenal on Feb. 21, 1734, he composed one for his PYRRHUS ET TÉGLIS, acted there six weeks later, on April 7. This prologue was recited by a Marquis and an Acteur in a scene, reminiscent of Molière, that asks indulgence for a " coup d'essai."[16] The production was successful enough to induce Morand to offer the tragedy to the actors of the Comédie Française, who gave it on Sept. 19, 1735, as TÉGLIS.[17]

[11] Cf. Paul d'Estrée, *RHL*, XVI (1909), 302-28.

[12] In this he portrayed Peter the Great, but the censor obliged him to change names and location in order to avoid international difficulties.

[13] *Stilicon, Andronic, Thyeste, Manlius, Gabinie, Oreste et Pilade.*

[14] In a note he mentions Mlle Bernard, Mlle Barbier, Mme de Gomez, and in his own day " les Du Boccages, les Graffignis." Cf. his *Théâtre*, II, 355-9.

[15] Spoken by Melpomene, Thalia, Apollo, Mercury, and Momus. The Muses argue about their relative merits until Apollo tells them that both are needed. Momus ridicules the idea of having amateurs play before the Goddess of the Arts, that is, the duchesse du Maine, but Apollo replies that, if she is pleased, all will be well.

[16] The Marquis seats himself in an armchair that is to be used in the tragedy and refuses to move. He declares that he has already visited the Opera, the Comédie Française, the Comédie Italienne, and that he proposes to go a little later to the Opéra Comique. He boasts of his ability to make a play succeed or fail. He likes plays derived from novels, filled with incidents and with heroes that do not sacrifice all for love. He leaves when the Acteur tells him that this tragedy follows history closely, that it is simple, natural, " vraisemblable," and that the hero has never appeared on the stage before. The Acteur then expresses the author's desire to please an illustrious princess.

[17] Paris, Pierre Ribou, 1735, 8°. Dedicated to the duchesse du Maine, who had

Morand states in his preface that he found his source in Bayle's *Dictionnaire*.[18] The article in question is derived chiefly from Justin, but it owes a few details to Athenaeus and a commentator upon Ovid. Morand learned from Bayle that Pyrrhus, King of Epirus, notorious for his invasion of Italy, had left a son named Alexander, who had married Olimpias and made her guardian of their sons, Pyrrhus and Ptolomée; that, become a widow and attacked by Ætolians, she turned for help to Demetrius, King of Macedonia, to whom she gave her daughter in marriage; that she poisoned a girl named Tigris, whom Pyrrhus loved; that Ptolomée succeeded Pyrrhus; and that the queen died soon after her two sons.

As Morand found the name Tigris ill suited to French tragedy, he changed it to Téglis. He made her the daughter of an ambitious minister, Sosthène. He not only kept the marriage of Demetrius to the daughter of Olimpias, but had the queen engage Pyrrhus to Antigone, daughter of Demetrius, and supposed that this princess and Ptolomée had fallen in love with each other. He gave to Olimpias the power to select the son that should succeed to the throne and had her cause Téglis to be abducted before the play begins. Although he does no violence to the sketchy information furnished by Bayle, most of his tragedy can hardly be called historical.

He declares that he sought to avoid having his play resemble *Rodogune* and *Inès de Castro*, but he succeeded only partially in doing so. Olimpias, like Cléopâtre, has the power to say which of her sons shall be king, and the princes, like their prototypes in *Rodogune*, are devoted to each other. Pyrrhus, like the hero of *Inès*, is a prince in love with a girl beneath him in rank; she is willing to subordinate her interests to his and is poisoned by a queen who wishes the prince to marry a princess to whom he has been promised. It seems probable that the unhistorical themes of the queen's power to choose and the princes' attachment to each other were suggested by *Rodogune*; the motivation for the poisoning of the heroine, by *Inès*. The place in which the scene is laid, Buthrotum, is that selected by Racine for *Andromaque*.[19]

offered the author suggestions. The approbation by Danchet of Oct. 3 refers to the applause the tragedy had received. Republished in the *Théâtre et Œuvres diverses de M. de Morand*, Paris, Jorry, 1751. Analyzed by Paul d'Estrée, *op. cit.*

[18] III, 2315 in the edition of Rotterdam, 1720.

[19] Antigone has come to Buthrotum to marry Pyrrhus, has discovered his love for Téglis, and has herself fallen in love with Ptolomée. Olimpias, suspecting her elder son's passion, has had Téglis carried off, but the ship has been wrecked and the girl is about to reappear. Olimpias offers the throne to Pyrrhus on condition he marry Antigone, and Ptolomée agrees to conquer his love for her, but Pyrrhus prefers Téglis and bids his mother choose another king. The queen urges him to reflect and proposes to marry Téglis to Ptolomée, a match that Sosthène pretends to favor, while he secretly rouses the people in the hope of making Pyrrhus reign with his daughter. Pyrrhus offers the throne to Ptolomée, who refuses it. Téglis begs her lover to reign without her and asks her father to send her away. Sosthène leads

Unfortunately the tragedy has neither the impressiveness of *Rodogune* nor the pathos of *Inès de Castro*. The central character, Olimpias, had at first enjoyed her power, but now, disgusted by courtiers, she is, unlike Cléopâtre in *Rodogune*, willing to give it up. She is supposed to be devoted to her sons, but she is determined that, if one becomes king, he shall not be ruled by love. This consideration and her fear of Sosthène make her seek to get rid of Téglis, first by abduction, then by marriage to Ptolomée, finally by murder. A milder method would have been to make Ptolomée king and allow Pyrrhus and Téglis to marry. Why she does not do this is attributed to her fear of Sosthène, but he would be no more powerful with his daughter married to Ptolomée and Pyrrhus reigning than with Téglis married to Pyrrhus and Ptolomée reigning. There is no law of primogeniture to force the queen to act as she does. Her function is merely to create situations. We are not allowed to see her at the end of the tragedy, or to learn what effect the death of the lovers has had upon her.

Morand avows a moral purpose in presenting as he does Pyrrhus, Sosthène, and Ptolomée. Pyrrhus illustrates the disastrous effect of love; Sosthène, that of ambition; while Ptolomée, who obeys his mother, controls his love, and refuses to fight his brother, is rewarded with the throne he has declined and with the princess he has been willing to give up. The demonstration is spoiled, however, by the queen, who poisons an innocent woman without being punished for it, and by Téglis, who dies though she subordinates her emotions to her ideal of honor (IV, 1):

> C'est à des cœurs communs, intéressés, sans foi,
> D'aimer sans nulle estime, & seulement pour soi;
> L'effort de la vertu, c'est de sçavoir soi-même,
> S'immoler à l'honneur de l'objet que l'on aime.

Except for Morand's failure to show how the dénouement affected the queen and the fact that little explanation is offered in regard to entrances and exits, the tragedy is constructed in accordance with classical regulations. There is a description of a storm at sea in II, 5; an account of battle in V, 4. The value of a faithful minister is set forth in III, 1. Less commonplace are the queen's remarks on the power of royal mistresses (I, 6):

> Mon esprit fut frapé des désordres affreux,
> Où se trouve plongé le malheureux Empire,
> Dont le Maître se livre à l'amour qui l'inspire.
> Il ne fait plus régner la justice & les loix;

---

rebels against the palace, but he is captured by Ptolomée. When Pyrrhus goes to his rescue, Ptolomée refuses to fight against him, the brothers embrace, and Ptolomée urges his mother to allow Pyrrhus to marry Téglis. It is now too late, for Olimpias has had the girl poisoned. When Pyrrhus sees her dying, he stabs himself and bids Ptolomée reign in his stead and protect Sosthène.

Son Idole en son cœur, en étouffe la voix ;
Elle règle l'Etat au gré de son caprice,
De son ambition, & de son avarice ;
Les emplois, les honneurs ne se dispensent plus
A la haute naissance, aux talens, aux vertus,
Ils sont en proye à ceux, qui peuvent satisfaire
A la cupidité de son cœur mercenaire ;
Et l'orgueilleuse enfin persécute à jamais
Tous ceux qui, méprisant son crédit, ses attraits,
Osent lui refuser un solemnel hommage,
Et lui ravir l'encens qu'elle veut en partage.

The censor raised no objection to these lines, recited when Louis XV was relatively faithful to his queen, but it is surprising that he tolerated them when the play was published in 1751, during the reign of la Pompadour.

The tragedy was acted eleven times at the Comédie Française. Olimpias was played by la Balicourt ; her elder son, by Grandval ; her younger, by Fleury ; Sosthène, by Sarrazin ; Téglis, by la Gaussin ; Antigone, by la Grandval. Legrand de Belleville appeared as Mitrane, captain of guards, and rôles of confidants were taken by la Jouvenot, la Du Boccage, and Du Breuil. The attendance was moderate, rewarding the author with only 439 fr., yet the spectators were responsive enough to enable the author and Danchet to say that the play was well received. Le Blanc thought little of it,[20] and Voltaire and La Harpe ignored it, but Paul d'Estrée found its action " bien conçue et fortement nouée." It seems to me that Morand introduced too many characters, with the result that the queen is unsatisfactorily motivated and that Antigone is insignificant, and that his effort to edify us diminishes the emotional effect of his situations.

In the preface of *Téglis* he promised that his next tragedy would show improvement. Selecting his subject from a field seldom cultivated, that of Frankish history, he composed CHILDÉRIC [21] while Cahusac was writing *Pharamond*. He states that the actors accepted his play first, though the rival Frankish tragedy was the first to be acted.[22]

Morand could have found the modicum of history he employed in Gregory of Tours or Mézeray, who tell of Childéric's exile in Thuringia, the fact that by Bazine he became the father of Clovis, and his return to power after the death of Ægidius or Gillon.[23] But these sources account for so little of the

---

[20] Cf. Monod-Cassidy, *op. cit.*, p. 261.

[21] Paris, Prault fils, 1737, 8°. Dedicated to the queen. *Privilège* for " Childéric, Teglis & autres Poësies," Feb. 1. Republished, Utrecht, Néaulme, 1737 ; in Morand's *Théâtre*, Paris, 1751 ; and in the *Fin du Répertoire*, Paris, veuve Dabo, 1824.

[22] Cf. Morand's note in his *Théâtre*, I, 107. The reason for the delay may be that, as the actors had given a tragedy by Morand, but not one by Cahusac, they preferred to risk the play of the untried poet in the summer, when receipts at best were small, rather than in winter. This would explain why *Pharamond* was given in August ; *Childéric*, in December.

[23] Morand changed Gillon to Gellon " pour éviter la mauvaise plaisanterie de

plot that imitation of Corneille's *Héraclius* was suggested.[24]   It is true that in both tragedies the heir to a throne has been brought up as the son of a usurper; the latter's son has lived with this prince since infancy; substitution has been made by a person loyal to a former ruler; and the identity of the prince is established by a letter written before her death by his mother; but there are also marked differences between the two plays.   In Morand's tragedy the usurper is dead, the lawful sovereign is no longer young, there is no danger of incest, there is rivalry in love between two princes, and the dénouement is brought about in part by an act of generosity on the part of a ruler that Corneille's Phocas would not have committed.   In one respect the story of substitution is nearer to La Grange-Chancel's recent *Erigone* than it is to *Héraclius*, for the person who makes one substitution does not learn until late in the play that there has been another.   There is, moreover, a patriotic element in *Childéric* that corresponds to nothing in *Héraclius* or *Erigone*.   Morand may have owed something to both plays, but his plot remains largely his own, a fact that some of his contemporaries, misled by the fame of Corneille, were unable to perceive.[25]

Gilles, Gillon," according to Philippe de Pretot's letter, published in Morand's *Théâtre*, I, 107.

[24] *Ibid.*, p. 99.   C. D. Brenner, *Histoire Nationale*, Berkeley, California, 1929, p. 227, cites a statement of 1757 to the same effect.

[25] Driven from his throne by Gellon, Childéric, King of the Franks, took refuge in Thuringia and was supposed to have died.   Gellon entrusted his two sons to Evagès, who substituted for the older boy Clovis, son of Childéric, and addressed a letter to the dethroned king enclosing one from the mother of Clovis that identified him.   But Evagès died before these letters were delivered, and Clodoade succeeded to his charge without knowing that one of the two boys was the son of Childéric.   He was ordered by Gellon to discover his predecessor's son and put him to death.   His investigations led to the discovery of Gellon's elder son, whom he mistook for Childéric's.   As, like Evagès, he was loyal to the former king, he substituted the boy he had found for Gellon's second son, who had just died, and showed the usurper Sigibert's body, which he had been careful to mutilate.   The result was that Clovis, son of Childéric, had grown up as Gellon's elder son, and that Sigibert was supposed to be the usurper's younger son, though he was really older than the one who had died.   Clodoade had pretended to be loyal to Gellon in order to make preparations for placing on the throne Sigibert, whom he believed to be the son of Childéric.   The action of the play begins some twenty years after Childéric had been exiled.   Clovis, who had succeeded his supposed father, is in love with Childéric's niece, Albizinde.   Though she loves him, she refuses to marry the son of a usurper and suggests that he renounce the throne in her favor.   When she rejects Sigibert for the same reason, this prince tells her that he is the son of Childéric.   He has just been told that he is by Clodoade and by Lisois, who gives him a sealed package containing the letters of Evagès and the queen.   When Sigibert reads these letters, he learns that he is the son of Gellon and that Clovis is the son of Childéric, but he keeps these facts secret in the hope of becoming king and of marrying Albizinde.   Clodoade now plans to have this princess agree to marry Clovis in order that he may be lured to the temple and murdered there.   At this point Childéric returns from exile and makes himself known to Albizinde, Clodoade, and Lisois.   These men tell Sigibert that they will murder Clovis, but that they will place Childéric on the throne.   When Sigibert is presented to his supposed father, he feels little emotion.   Meanwhile Albizinde cannot help warning Clovis about their marriage and in so doing admits that she loves him.   His suspicions aroused, Clovis secures a report about the conspiracy, revealed by Sigibert in the hope that Clovis

The plot is made complicated by the substitutions of children and by the ignorance of several characters in regard to the identity of others. However, if one can remember that Clovis, who believes that he is the son of Gellon, is really the son of Childéric, and that Sigibert, who for a while thinks he is Childéric's son, is really Gellon's, there is no difficulty in following the action. The spectators are made aware of the facts in the second scene of Act II, as soon as Sigibert discovers them. A hint that Childéric may be alive is given early in Act II, but he does not appear until III, 4, so that his return gives variety to the plot without introducing confusion while the identity of the two princes is being established.

The fact that he appears so late results in his having the shortest of the five major rôles in the play. He is presented as a man of majestic appearance, of great fortitude, and of keen perception. The two young princes are sharply contrasted. The virtues of Clovis are recognized even by those who would assassinate him. He has a high ideal of his duties as king, though he is willing to use torture in order to extract information from a captive. His abdication is inspired by his sense of justice, the pleading of Albizinde, and a mysterious feeling that he has for Childéric. His generosity is rewarded by his discovery that he has saved his father, by the power that is left to him, and by his success in love. Sigibert, on the other hand, is without a conscience. He is consumed with ambition and is so utterly incapable of understanding Clovis that he betrays the secret of his associates in the hope that it will induce this prince to put Childéric to death.

The longest rôle is that of Albizinde, who is torn between her love of Clovis and her devotion to the interests of the legitimate monarchy. When she interviews Clovis, she cannot bring herself to join in the plot that will mean his death, even if it restores Childéric to the throne. Like Chimène, she yields to love at the end, however much she has struggled. The scene in which she does so was admired by d'Estrée: [26]

> Alb.:   Vivez, Seigneur, vivez.
> Clovis: Eh, comment puis-je vivre?
>   A d'éternels tourmens, votre haine me livre.

---

would put Childéric to death, that the former king's friends would then revolt, and that he would himself succeed to the throne. Clovis orders military precautions to be taken and has a search made for the stranger who is supposed to have planned his murder. Brought before him, Childéric admits his identity and asks for death, but Clovis, influenced by Albizinde and impressed by the old king, abdicates in his favor. Meanwhile the conspirators are approaching the palace. When Childéric and Clovis meet them, their hostility turns into rejoicing except in the case of Sigibert, who attacks Clovis. When Childéric tries to separate them, Sigibert turns upon him and is killed by Clovis. Lisois produces the letters, Clovis is recognized as the son of Childéric, and his father bids him marry Albizinde and lead his armies to victory. When the tragedy was first acted, Childéric died of his wounds at the end of it.

[26] III, 12; cf. d'Estrée, op. cit., pp. 321-2.

Alb.:   Non, je ne vous hais pas.[27]
Clovis: Venez donc, sans trembler,
          Par un heureux hymen . . .
Alb.:   Non, c'est trop m'accabler!
          Ah! ne me parlez plus de cet hymen funeste!
          Plus vous montrez d'ardeur, & plus je le déteste.
          J'irois . . . moi . . . sans horreur, je ne puis y penser.
          Au nom de votre amour, cessez de m'en presser!
          Je m'égare . . . je cède à ma fureur extrême . . .
          Si mon cœur en frémit, c'est parce qu'il vous aime.
                                             (Elle sort.)

Unlike *Téglis, Childéric* has several scenes of recognition. Suspense is well sustained as the action oscillates in favor of Clovis, Sigibert, or Childéric. The supernatural is represented by the *cri du sang* when Clovis and his father meet. The patriotic element is conspicuous. The scene is laid in Tournai, almost in what is now France. The Gauls are called (I, 3) "neveux d'Hector." Clovis is urged by his father to conquer Romans, Goths, and Germans, then to establish his rule in " ces riches Climats où serpente la Seine," where a hundred kings, he hopes, will be the arbiters of war and peace,

> Le Refuge des Rois, la terreur des Tyrans,
> L'Amour d'un Peuple heureux par leurs soins bienfaisans.[28]

The play was acted seven times, from Dec. 19, 1736, to Jan. 9, 1737. The heroine's rôle was taken by la Gaussin; the hero's by Dufresne. It is probable that Sarrazin played Childéric; Grandval, Sigibert. The first five performances were well attended, but the last two were so poorly patronized that the actors were amply justified in playing it no longer.[29] They had not given it in accordance with the published text. The edition printed in Holland indicates that they did not read the letters of II, 2, and that they omitted V, 9. The scene in which Childéric greets Sigibert was not in the original version. The ending was distinctly different, for Sigibert, when the play was acted, killed Childéric and, while he was himself dying from a wound inflicted by Clovis, informed his rival that Childéric was his father.

Fréron[30] reported that a cabal operated against the tragedy and that,

---

[27] Cf. *le Cid,* III, 4, where under similar circumstances Chimène exclaims to Rodrigue, " Va je ne te hais point."

[28] V, 12, text of 1751. The earlier version mentions Gaul, but not the Seine, and ends the passage with

> La terreur & l'amour, & l'espoir des Mortels:
> Mais, pour mieux triompher, sois l'appui des Autels.

The elimination of *Autels* may be due to growing anticlericalism or to the author's realization of the fact that Childéric was not a Christian.

[29] The receipts for Jan. 7 were 329 fr.; 427 fr. for Jan. 9. It is consequently unnecessary to say with Mouhy (*Répertoire,* Paris, 1753, p. 24) that performances ceased because of Dufresne's illness. The author received from the play 890 fr., 10 s.

[30] Quoted by d'Estrée, *op. cit.,* p. 308.

when an actor arrived with a letter and tried to make his way among the spectators on the stage, a disguised monk cried, " place au facteur " and started a laugh that destroyed the effect of the scene. Similarly Philippe de Pretot [31] stated that the first audience was so tumultuous that the play could not be appreciated until subsequently.

This writer admits that the plot is complicated, but he finds it no more so than the plots of *Rodogune, Héraclius, Amasis,* and other successful tragedies. He praises the clarity with which the complex material is presented, the treatment of characters, and the noble simplicity of the diction. In witnessing a performance he felt " pitié, terreur, élévation de l'esprit, attendrissement du cœur." He answers critics who call it obscure, denies that Childéric's return is too daring, explains why the old king is recognized by only a few persons, and cites a few passages, one of which (V, 4) he compares with the " qu'il mourût " of *Horace*:

> Childéric: Jamais Usurpateur fit-il grace à son Roi?
> Suis leur noire maxime; achéve; hâte-toi:
> Du fils de mon Tyran que puis-je encore attendre?
> Clovis: Le Trône . . . il t'appartient: je suis prêt d'en descendre.

We learn from this letter that Morand was accused of borrowing from Crébillon's *Electre* Albizinde's hesitation in luring her lover to a temple where he is to be murdered.[32] Pretot admired the manner in which Sigibert is induced to tell Clovis who his father is and thought the reading of the queen's letter would not be effective. He said that Morand had wished to make the ending as happy as possible, but that the actors had insisted that Childéric should be mortally wounded while saving the life of Clovis. Morand added a note to the effect that in this new edition he had returned to his original idea of saving Childéric's life, as several persons of taste and even some of the actors had approved of his doing so.

Two critics differed with Pretot's estimate of the tragedy. The abbé Le Blanc parodied one of its lines in a couplet:

> Si sa Piéce est mauvaise si ses vers ennuïeux,
> Tenter est d'un Mortel, reussir est des Dieux.[33]

Voltaire placed it among the " barbaries de nos jours." [34] Fréron,[35] on the

---

[31] Cf. his letter published by Morand in the 1751 edition of *Childéric*.

[32] The heroine's hesitation resembles Electra's, but in Crébillon's tragedy it is the lover's father who is to be murdered.

[33] Letter of Dec. 29, 1736, quoted by Mme Monod-Cassidy, *op. cit.,* p. 261. The second line, with " des mortels " for " un Mortel," is found in *Childéric,* IV, 8.

[34] Letter of Sept. 4, 1767; cf. Moland, XLV, 366. Voltaire, who may not have read the play, referred to the " auteur de Childebrand," evidently a slip of his memory for *Childéric*, but Moland jumped to the conclusion that Morand had written a *Childebrand* and so stated in a note.

[35] *Année littéraire*, 1757 (6), p. 46.

other hand, called it the tragedy " la mieux combinée " since *Héraclius,* but he added that the public objected to its " peu de coloris." He subsequently declared that he preferred it to Mercier's *Childéric Premier* and insisted that it lacked neither situations nor interest. He thought in 1773 that, if revived, it would succeed.

Paul d'Estrée found the plot obscure, objected to the use of letters in the time of the Merovingians and to the fact that they are twice introduced. Although he admired the scene of the heroine's hesitation, he seems to have considered the tragedy inferior to *Téglis.* Its characters are, however, much more skillfully presented, its situations are more striking, and the dialogue is written with a firmer touch. If the reader is not frightened by the double substitution, there is much in the tragedy he may admire. It is unfortunate that a subject, novel in the time and place represented, should be dramatized in a play whose plot is hard to follow. Morand's reputation was not well enough established to withstand attacks on both counts. His tragedy soon ceased to appear in the repertory, though it is intrinsically superior to many of its time.

He next tried comedy and gave his work to the Théâtre Italien, but he returned to the Comédie Française in 1748 with MÉGARE,[36] first written as a *tragédie-ballet,* with a prologue, intermèdes, and entrées, for the Dauphin's marriage in 1747, but offered too late to be accepted.[37] In his preface he states that he followed chiefly Seneca's *Hercules furens,* but he also gives Brumoy's analysis of its source in Euripides. He found both ancient trage- dies more brutal than he liked and lacking in dramatic material and in unity. Consequently, although he followed Seneca for the main facts of the story [38] and occasionally for details,[39] he altered the material so exten- sively that most of its situations are not found in the ancient plays, but resemble rather situations in certain French tragedies.[40]

---

[36] Paris, S. Jorry, 1748, 8°, and in Morand's *Théâtre,* Paris, Jorry, 1751.
[37] *Ibid.,* III, 126-7.
[38] Hercules's visit to Hades, his love of Mégare, his return as an avenger, his murder of Lycus and of Mégare, his madness; Mégare's refusal to marry Lycus; the latter's exile, his causing the death of Mégare's brothers, his usurpation of the throne, his threats; the introduction of Theseus.
[39] " C'est à Sénèque que je dois les principaux détails de ma Piéce, & beaucoup de pensées que j'ai traduites ou imitées. J'en ai même retranché plusieurs que j'avois insérées dans mes fureurs d'Hercule " (*Théâtre,* II, 204). He refers especially to accounts of the hero's labors, to disasters associated with Thebes, and to passages in his last scene, when Hercules loses his mind.
[40] Créon, King of Thebes, had engaged his daughter, Mégare, to Hercules and had befriended Lycus, who, exiled while Hercules was away, had headed a revolt, caused the death in battle of Créon's sons, imprisoned the king, and usurped the throne. He now demands Mégare in marriage. Released from his chains, Créon longs for the return of Hercules, said to be detained in Hades, reproaches Lycus for his crimes, and refuses to give him his daughter. Lycus sends him back to prison and asks Mégare to marry him. She refuses, declaring that she loves Hercules, but Lycus obtains her consent by threatening to kill her father. She is prevented by

As in the original version of his own *Childéric,* the villain, in danger of death, derives a feeling of satisfaction from giving his enemy information that horrifies him. Mégare's agreeing to marry Lycus in order to save her father and planning to kill herself resembles the heroine's conduct in *Andromaque.* The return of Hercules and his discovery that the woman he loves is married are not unlike his situation in La Grange-Chancel's *Alceste.* Créon, who replaces Seneca's Amphitryon, is freed from prison somewhat as Lusignan had been recently freed in *Zaïre.* Hercules goes mad after accidentally killing Mégare, as Orestes does in Crébillon's *Electre* after he has accidentally killed his mother.

The tragedy is divided into two parts. Acts I and II lead up to the heroine's marriage to a man she hates, while the remaining acts are filled with her efforts to save her husband's life, his new conspiracy, its failure, and the madness of Hercules, which is the result, not the cause of Mégare's death. This arrangement does not destroy the unity of the action, since the possibility of Hercules's return is indicated early in the tragedy, but it makes Mégare the principal character. In presenting her Morand was satisfying a desire to depict love in opposition " tantôt avec les devoirs qu'exigent les liens du sang & la tendresse filiale, & tantôt avec ceux du lien conjugal." But in doing so, he reduces self-sacrifice to an absurdity. One may admire Mégare for marrying a man she loathes in order to save her father's life, but one cannot reconcile with rational behavior her effort to save and rejoin Lycus, who had killed her brothers, imprisoned and threatened to kill her father, and forced her to marry him. The author was seeking to create an impossibly heroic character on the theory that virtues " poussées à l'excès ne déparent pas le théâtre." Even after his play had failed, he defended his conception against those who insisted that, as Mégare's marriage was " nul & cassable suivant toutes les loix divines & humaines, elle avoit tort d'en vouloir défendre la validité " and that all she said and did was " ni naturel, ni vraisemblable."

Hercules and Créon are almost as impossibly generous in their attitude towards Lycus, who remains to the end utterly evil. Such presentation of his characters rendered ineffective Morand's improvements in regard to Seneca's text. He omitted Juno, substituted dialogue for long descriptive

---

Créon from committing suicide. Hercules enters, rejoicing in his victory, but Lycus, captured and condemned to death, reveals the fact that he has married Mégare, who feels bound by her marriage to save Lycus. She prevails upon Lycus to leave the decision to Créon, who offers to pardon Lycus if he will divorce his daughter. When this offer is refused, Lycus is imprisoned, but Mégare has him released and offers to join him when he reaches a place of safety. Lycus heads a new conspiracy. In the fighting that follows, Hercules kills Lycus after trying to spare him and accidentally kills Mégare. When he learns of her death, he loses his mind, raves, and falls unconscious.

speeches, constructed the scenes more logically, sought to substitute pity for horror. In his preface he defends his reference to Hercules's visit to Hades, though, as he admits, Racine had presented it in *Phèdre* only as a rumor and though La Grange-Chancel had omitted it in his *Alceste*, as Boissy had done in his *Admète et Alceste*. He excuses an anachronistic reference to Œdipus on the ground that Seneca had employed it.[41] He concludes by attacking his critics, accusing them of knowing neither ancient tragedies nor the rules of drama. To them the names, Alcide, Hercule, Lycus, and Créon, seem ridiculous, while some " qui se piquent de littérature " even ask if Mégare is the name of a city!

The tragedy was acted only once, on Oct. 19, 1748. The title-rôle was assigned to la Clairon, who wore diamonds. Ribou played Hercules; La Noue, Créon; Paulin, Lycus. Confidants' rôles were taken by Dubois, Bonneval, and la Connell. The actors provided mantles and helmets for Dubois and La Noue, shoes for Ribou, and four " habits à la Romaine." Over a thousand people paid admission, and the author received 196 francs, but Collé declares [42] that the tragedy was " sifflée et baffouée " and that at the end the parterre called on the only character still capable of speech to list the dead and wounded. Even la Clairon's acting did not induce her colleagues to give the play a second trial.

With the failure of this tragedy ended Morand's career at the Comédie Française. Raynal [43] said that " il fait un métier qu'il n'entend pas." Le Blanc [44] considered him a " médiocre." Voltaire and La Harpe would certainly have ranked him as low as that, but Frederick the Great admired his work enough to make him his correspondent at Paris, and Fréron,[45] though he found him awkward in society, insisted that he had " l'esprit juste & des idées saines & profondes sur le Théâtre." He considered him among the best dramatists of the second class. Even in our century Paul d'Estrée found some kind things to say about him.

He knew the stage as an amateur actor, was able to win the protection of several important persons, was familiar with ancient tragedies and with those of various Frenchmen. He showed a desire to select novel themes.

---

[41] He admits that in II, 4, he counts *voyent* as one syllable, in accordance with pronunciation and by analogy to *ayent* and *soyent*. " Cette régle nouvelle ne sera pas inutile aux Versificateurs."

[42] *Journal*, 1807, I, 13-4.

[43] *Cor.*, II, 46. Subsequently Grimm (*Cor.*, VI, 16) reported that at the end of the performance of *Mégare* Morand climbed upon the stage and harangued the parterre with so much emotion that he hurled his hat into the midst of it. He added that he continued to write tragedies, but had them neither acted nor published. Among them was said to be the outline of a play on Cromwell that was utilized after Morand's death by Maillet Du Clairon. This tragedy is discussed below.

[44] Monod-Cassidy, *op. cit.*, p. 320.

[45] *Année littéraire*, 1757 (6), p. 51.

He was the first author of the eighteenth century to have a tragedy accepted that put on the stage in French surroundings characters from French history, the first to turn to the recent history of Russia. When he went to the ancients for a plot, he selected a theme that had not been dramatized, or one that he altered so decidedly that he made it largely an original creation. But he had little ability as a stylist and his presentation of character was marred by his desire to preach. In the preface of *Mégare* he wrote:

C'est peu lorsqu'on fait une Piéce de Théâtre d'arranger son sujet suivant les régles de l'art, il faut encore avoir en vuë quelque moralité frappante digne de plaire & d'instruire.

Otherwise one pleased only "des cœurs corrompus." These last, however, seem to have been in the majority. They were not sufficiently impressed by Morand's presentation of heroic virtues to pardon the complexity of *Childéric* or the abnormal psychology of *Téglis* and *Mégare*.

The Franks who had inspired Morand to do his best work for the Comédie Française attracted about the same time Louis de Cahusac, who belonged to a noble family of Montauban and became secretary to the comte de Clermont. His name appears as that of a censor in April, 1750. According to Grimm, his character made him odious and unhappy and he became a "fou enragé." He died on June 22, 1759. He wrote a treatise on the history of dancing; an opera for which Rameau composed the music; *Zénéide*, a comedy first acted in 1743; a *comédie-ballet*; and two tragedies.[46]

We have seen that his PHARAMOND,[47] though acted four months before *Childéric*, was accepted by the actors at a later date. There is no evidence that he knew the rival tragedy. He may have been influenced by *Cassius et Victorinus* or *Sabinus* to lay his scene in Gaul. He did not venture beyond the reign of Honorius and he admitted a Roman to his cast,[48] but he related his action to his own times by imagining that the mythical Pharamond united Franks and Gauls into a people that were to be the French.[49]

---

[46] Cf. the *Biographie générale* and *Cor.*, IV, 161.

[47] Paris, Prault fils, 1736, 8°. Approbation, signed by La Serre, Sept. 27. Dedicated to the comte de S. Florentin.

[48] Brenner, *loc. cit.*, says that "la plupart de ses personnages sont Romains," but the fact is that, besides "suites" of Romans, Franks, and Gauls, the cast is composed of one Roman, one Frank, and four Gauls.

[49] Vindorix, a Gaul of noble birth, had been captured in his native town, Tournai, by Stilico and taken with his son and daughter to Rome, where he became a gladiator and met his son in the arena. When they embraced, a tiger was loosed upon them. The young man threw himself in front of his father and was killed. Maxime, a Roman general and praetor of the Belgae, persuaded the emperor to free Vindorix, who retired to Germany and prevailed upon Pharamond, whom he believed to be descended from Francus, to invade Gaul and drive out the Romans. They have now reached Rheims, where Pharamond has fallen in love with a captive, Arminie, who refuses to marry him because she loves Maxime. Gauls, led by Ambiomer, and Franks complain that Pharamond is lingering at the knees of a slave while Maxime is advancing at the head of a Roman army. Vindorix discovers that Arminie is his

The play has some relation to history in its reference to Honorius, Stilico, the Franks, and the Gauls, but doubt had already been cast upon the existence of Pharamond. His engagement to the daughter of Gondebaut was probably suggested by Clovis's marriage to a Burgundian princess. The story of his rivalry with a Roman for the hand of a Gaul is not even symbolic, as he failed in his courtship, whereas it was the Franks rather than the Romans who were merged with the Gauls.

Vindorix has the leading rôle, that of a wise and virtuous minister who labors for what he conceives to be best for his people, union with the Franks and liberation from the Romans. Pharamond is a victorious young warrior, restive under the obligation to subordinate love to political considerations. Arminie and Maxime are typical lovers. There are no villains and only one confidant, Segeste, a Gaul attached to Vindorix.

The play is based upon a series of improbable encounters: the meeting of father and son in the arena, that of father and daughter when she is a captive, that of the lovers after a battle. The resulting scenes of recognition, as well as several lengthy *récits*, may have been well received, but Pharamond's sudden change of heart, devised to give the tragedy a happy ending, could hardly have met with approval. What is most novel in the play is its primitivism and patriotism, both of which appear when Pharamond contrasts the fading glory of Rome, corrupted by culture, with the success of the unsophisticated Franks (III, 1):

> Des Romains d'aujourd'hui tu flattes le portrait,
> Et ces Arts dangereux dont tu vantes l'attrait,
> Ont corrompu leurs mœurs, énervé leur courage;
> C'est un fléau pour eux, plûtôt qu'un avantage; . . .
> Et devant leur raison qu'un faux brillant égare,
> L'honneur est étranger, & la candeur barbare;

---

daughter, but he conceals their relationship as he wishes Pharamond to marry the daughter of Gondebaut, King of the Burgundians. He is shocked to learn that his daughter loves a Roman until she tells him that her lover is Maxime. Pharamond now defeats the Romans, abolishes slavery in Gaul, frees his prisoners, including Maxime, and allows this general to return to Rome. He offers to make Arminie queen, but she resists and assures Maxime of her love, though she opposes his plan of collecting an army in order to take her from the Franks. Vindorix approves of their marriage, bids Maxime leave, and sends off his daughter with other captives. He makes Maxime promise to protect her when they meet and seems to consider that he has married them. While Pharamond is receiving the Burgundian emissaries, Arminie escapes, but she is brought back and Ambiomer, suspected of helping her, is imprisoned. Pharamond decides to risk the anger of Gondebaut and calls upon Arminie to marry him, but she tells him she already has a husband. Pharamond threatens to destroy his rival and offers to grant any request the person who discovers him may make. Maxime gets Pharamond to swear to keep this promise, declares that he is the man in question, and asks that Arminie be set free. Pharamond is about to have him executed when Vindorix takes the blame upon himself, asserts that he has married them, and gives as one of his reasons for doing so his desire to keep Pharamond from breaking his treaty with the Burgundians. Pharamond conquers his love, frees Ambiomer, promotes Vindorix, and allows the marriage of Arminie and Maxime to stand.

Nous sommes trop heureux, Soldats qu'elle a nourris,
De mériter ce titre & d'avoir leur mépris:
Ils sont dignes du notre; & l'amour de la gloire,
Du côté des Français passe avec la victoire.

In the following scene Vindorix asks that the wise simplicity of old Gaul be made to flourish again, and Pharamond promises to restore it,

Telle que le Français [the Frank] la conserve encor pure,
Et telle qu'il la tient des mains de la nature.
Sa justice est son bras; sa loi, la probité,
Sa réplique, le fer; son bien, la liberté.

Lines that recall Corneille's *Attila* predict that new conquerors

Sur les débris de Rome élevent leur grandeur.
Livrez-vous à la joye, heureux peuples de France,
Son Regne va finir, & le votre commence.[50]

The play has verses for kings, ministers, and heroes:

Qui fait un peuple seul des Francs & des Gaulois,
Et chasse les Tyrans, pour établir les Rois. (II, 3)
Un Ministre éclairé, prudent & vertueux,
Est du ciel pour les Rois la faveur la plus chere. (V, 7)
L'heroisme parfait a seul de si beaux droits,
Et par là le grand homme est au-dessus des Rois. (III, 8)

The tragedy was first acted on Aug. 14, 1736. Le Blanc [51] wrote on Aug. 27 that it contained some fine verses, but that a school boy could write a better play so far as " la conduite, la liaison des scenes, l'interêt, le Pathetique " were concerned. He thought that " Causat " had merely loaned his name to the real author, who in the opinion of some was Le Franc de Pompignan. As nothing has been discovered to support this suggestion, it may well be dismissed.

Pharamond was acted eleven times, from August 14 till September 20, and again on Dec. 1. Dufresne, Grandval, Sarrazin, Legrand de Belleville, and la Balicourt took, respectively, the rôles of Pharamond, Maxime, Vindorix, Ambiomer, and Arminie. The audiences were so small that, after September 17, the author ceased to share in the receipts. He earned only 341 fr., 18 s. Nevertheless the play was well enough known to inspire a parody called *les Gaulois*.[52]

Cahusac, moreover, thought well enough of his tragedy to try fortune again, this time with a medieval theme and one derived, like Tronchin's

[50] III, 1. Cf. *Attila*, vv. 141-2:
Un grand destin commence, un grand destin s'achève:
L'empire est prêt à choir, et la France s'élève.
[51] Cf. Monod-Cassidy, *op. cit.*, p. 248.
[52] *Ibid.*, p. 250.

Marie Stuart, from English history. His COMTE DE WARWICK must have
been tentatively accepted by the actors before May 23, 1739, for on that day
Le Blanc [53] stated that the condition of the text was such that it had to be
withdrawn " à la veille de la Représentation." Two and a half years later,
on Nov. 28, 1742, it was produced, but the performance was not completed.[54]
A contributing factor in its failure may have been that the line, " Trans-
portons l'Angleterre au milieu de la France," caused a man in the parterre
to call out, " Place à l'Angleterre." [55] The play was never published. When
La Harpe brought out one with the same title, he referred to Cahusac's
tragedy and said that it was no longer in existence unless a manuscript copy
of it had been preserved by the police or by the actors. One of 1742, in five
acts and in verse, was owned by de Soleinne.[56] I am informed by Dr.
Brenner that one is said to be in the possession of the Comédie Française,
but that in 1946 it could not be located.

Much better known than Cahusac, Morand, or Le Blanc is Pierre-Claude
Nivelle de la Chaussée,[57] whose bourgeois family was sufficiently prosperous
for him to choose the career of a writer. He is celebrated as the father of
the *comédie larmoyante,* but he did not neglect tragedy altogether. Following the example of Voltaire, who had selected for his first tragedy a subject
dramatized by Pierre Corneille, La Chaussée chose one put on the stage by
Thomas Corneille. His MAXIMIEN [58] was played without mention of his
name on Feb. 28, 1738. A month later he wrote to the abbé Le Blanc that
the tragedy had been attributed to all "nos illustres du temps dont vous
estes du nombre et enfin elle m'est restée." [59] He had at first thought of
calling it *Fausta,* perhaps in the hope of concealing his source, but he finally
decided to reproduce the title of Thomas Corneille's *Maximian,* a tragedy
well enough remembered by a contemporary for him to write, " Et de
Thomas Corneille apprends à conspirer." The advice was quite unnecessary
for this is just what he had done.

" Il n'a pas regardé l'histoire," wrote Lanson, " mais l'œuvre de son de-
vancier . . . la tragédie commence au troisième acte de Thomas Corneille." [60]

[53] *Ibid.,* p. 334.

[54] Grandval and la Gaussin probably took leading parts in it. The author's share
in the receipts was 254 fr.

[55] *Cor.,* V, 405.

[56] Cf. *Soleinne,* no. 1787.

[57] Cf. G. Lanson, *Nivelle de la Chaussée et la comédie larmoyante,* Paris, Hachette,
1903. La Chaussée was born at Paris in 1691 or 1692, was elected to the Academy in
1736, and died in 1754.

[58] Paris, Le Breton, 1738, 12°; approbation of March 19, signed by Danchet, who
refers to the public's just applause. Republished twice at The Hague in the same
year, in editions of the author's plays, and in the *Suite du Répertoire,* Paris, veuve
Dabo, 1822. For a study of the tragedy cf. Lanson, *op. cit.,* pp. 102-10.

[59] Monod-Cassidy, *op. cit.,* p. 512.

[60] *Op. cit.,* p. 107. For Thomas Corneille's play cf. my *History,* Part III, pp. 442-3.

True, except that he introduced from history a Christian element not found in his predecessor's tragedy and that he made use of material placed by Thomas Corneille before his third act.[61] He suppressed Constance and Licinius and substituted for Sévère a Christian, Aurèle, who has a similar, but less important rôle as he has conquered his love for the empress and appears in only two acts. Martian, who conspires in the earlier tragedy with Maximian, is called Albin. Fausta is now represented as loving her husband. The plot is simplified, and the dénouement is brought about in a different way from that employed in his model. However, the main characters and the plot owe a great deal to the seventeenth-century tragedy.[62]

The play has only one rôle of importance for a woman, as one of the confidants does not speak and the other is merely a foil for her mistress. Lanson notes that a woman who has to choose between her father and her husband may be temporarily interesting, but that this conflict does not furnish enough material for a major rôle in a play if the woman remains as inactive as Fausta. It is true that she accomplishes little, but she is by no means inactive. The pathos of her situation increases as she struggles to save her husband from himself. When she learns of the conspiracy, she tries to warn him without denouncing her father. She appeals in vain to Maximian, then persuades Constantine to put Aurèle in charge of the palace, activities that serve as evidence against her when she is accused of conspiring. Nothing she can say will convince the emperor of her innocence, and she feels sure that, if he discredits her, he will lose his life (IV, 5):

[61] Cf. I, 4, and II, 6, of Thomas Corneille's *Maximian*.

[62] Influenced by Diocletian, Maximian had abdicated, but, subsequently desiring to reign again, had given his daughter, Fausta, to Constantine and now, seeing that his son-in-law is disinclined to make way for him, has decided to have him murdered. He has plotted with Albin, whom Constantine trusts, and with Aurèle, a general and former lover of Fausta. This general has pretended to join the conspiracy in order to reveal Maximian's plans to Fausta, who, when he tells her about them, hesitates to betray her father, but persuades her husband to put Aurèle at the head of the palace guard. Albin suspects Aurèle, reports to Constantine that he has arrested two pagans who were seeking to murder him, gets permission to torture them, and tells the emperor they have admitted that Aurèle is their leader. He also suggests that Fausta is in the plot and rouses Constantine's jealousy. Maximian pleads for his daughter and she pleads for him. Albin reports that Aurèle has been killed while attempting to escape and produces a letter, written in his hand to Fausta, that tells of a plot to kill Constantine. The empress asks for Maurice, Aurèle's former " gouverneur," but she is told that he is in hiding. She receives word from him, however, that certain Christian guards have informed him of the plot, but she fears the rescuers will not arrive in time. Albin makes it possible for Maximian to enter Constantine's room at night in order to murder him. A guard brings Fausta a cup of poison with an order from Constantine to drink it. Maximian snatches it from her and tells her that he now reigns as Constantine is dead. Fausta reproaches him bitterly, but, just as Maximian is offering to divide his power with Albin, Constantine enters, explains that the man Maximian had killed was a guilty slave, and that Maurice and the Christian guards deceived Maximian and revealed the plot. He condemns his father-in-law and Albin to death, but, when Fausta begs for her father's life, he pardons him and even offers to share the empire with him. Maximian, however, believing that a colleague is a " Maître importun," stabs himself, leaving his daughter reunited to her husband.

> Ils me justifieront, en vous perçant le sein.
> Ce n'est qu'en expirant sous le fer assassin,
> Que tout s'éclaircira dans votre ame jalouse.

We see her again in the last act, desperately trying to save Constantine, only to be condemned by him to drink poison, which she is about to do when she is rescued. The rôle is about twice as long as that of Thomas Corneille's empress. "Je fais tomber tout le fort sur Fausta," wrote La Chaussée to Sablier.[63] The rôle is by no means that of a woman who "ne sait que se plaindre," as Lanson would have us believe, but that of one whose actions make her situation steadily worse and increase the pathos of the rôle. It was probably this part, well acted, that gave the tragedy its success.

For the other characters are distinctly inferior. Maximian is a feeble figure, eaten up by ambition, but so deeply troubled by fear for his daughter that he has at one point to be forcibly detained by Albin in his apartment. It is not he, but Albin who conducts the plot, suspects Aurèle, puts him out of the way, and almost succeeds in murdering the emperor. But he is not clever enough to discover Maurice's counter-plot, which saves the emperor and brings about Albin's execution and Maximian's suicide. Constantine, who accepts suggestions from friends and conspirators with an equal lack of discernment, is so weak a monarch that it is hard to understand how he conquered his rivals and the Germans, or how he won the love of Fausta. Aurèle disappears too soon for us to know much about him.

La Chaussée seems to have wished to depict the struggle between Christians and pagans after the new cult had been made the official religion of Rome. Constantine, Fausta, Aurèle, and Maurice are Christians, as Albin pretends to be in order to win the emperor's confidence, while Maximian has remained a pagan. It is the Christian guards who foil the plot. Christians are discussed by the conspirators in II, 1:

> Albin: Vous ne connoissez pas cette Secte insensée,
>   Qui s'accroît chaque jour sous le nom de Chrétiens.
> Maximian: Que je les hais!
> Albin: Aurele est un de leurs soutiens.
>   Si-tôt qu'on a reçu les eaux de leur baptême,
>   Il semble qu'on devienne ennemi de soi-même;
>   Ils exercent sur eux les plus grandes rigueurs;
>   Ils se font des devoirs, des vertus & des mœurs,
>   Qui ne furent jamais que de tristes chimeres;
>   Ils n'ont d'autres plaisirs que des douleurs ameres;
>   Ils ne desirent plus que des biens à venir,
>   Que l'esprit ne sçauroit prévoir, ni définir.

Unfortunately La Chaussée failed to bring out the conflict between the

---

[63] Quoted by Lanson, *op. cit.*, p. 108.

two religions. His Christians do not act differently from the friends of Constantine in Thomas Corneille's tragedy, into which the religious question is not introduced. The references to them may, however, have helped the play by recalling *Polyeucte* and *Zaïre*, just as the tragedy may have attracted patriots by its location in Marseilles and the couplet (II, 4):

> Je n'attendois pas moins de ces braves Guerriers,
> Dont la Gaule est toujours une source féconde.

Such references, the rôle of Fausta, interpreted by la Gaussin, the simple and unified structure, and the suspense of the last act may account for the play's great, if temporary success. It was acted eleven times, from Feb. 28 to March 22,[64] then, after the Easter recess and accompanied by Pont de Vesle's *Fat puni*,[65] nine times, April 14 to May 3. It is probable that Dufresne played Constantine; Sarrazin, Maximian; Grandval, Aurèle. The receipts never fell below 1100 francs,[66] and the author's share in them was 3500 fr., 18 s., more than Voltaire had received from *Hérode et Mariamne*, not much less than had been earned for him by *Zaïre* and *Alzire*.

Maximien was acted three times at court and was parodied twice.[67] Le Blanc[68] paid it an unintended compliment when he wrote on April 19, 1738:

Je vous dis mais en confidence que son Albin ressemble comme deux gouttes d'eau à un certain Iago de Shakespear qui est un maître Scélérat.

This suggests that La Chaussée had learned English, though Le Blanc writes in the same letter that his friend had expressed a strong desire to do so, implying that he had not yet begun his study of the language. Perhaps his own English was insufficient for him to realize the difference between Albin and Iago.

The *Mercure*[69] praised the verse, though the writer would have preferred a more elevated style. Maximian was thought to be too much influenced by paternal affection. It should have been made clearer that his suicide was due to his unwillingness to share the empire with Constantine. The latter is criticized for condemning Fausta to death too readily and for his willingness to entrust to Maximian a portion of his power.

[64] "Le Théâtre retentit de *Maximien*," wrote Father Brumoy on March 11; cf. *RHL*, XIII (1906), 153.
[65] Although this was a new play, its author seems to have had no share in the receipts, for he received nothing on May 5 and 7 when it was given with the *Comte d'Essex* and *Phèdre*.
[66] In spite of this fact, the author received nothing when his play was revived on Feb. 4, 1739, perhaps because the receipts were then only 736 fr., 10 s.
[67] Lanson, *op. cit.*, pp. 102-5.
[68] Monod-Cassidy, *op. cit.*, pp. 301, 298. Voltaire, who must have been unaware of the impression made by the tragedy, wrote on March 28, 1738, that it had had the fate of all plays that were too " intriguées "; cf. Moland, XXXIV, 445.
[69] April, 1737, p. 758.

16

La Chaussée was sufficiently gratified to write a second tragedy, *Palmire, reine d'Assyrie*, which was read to the actors of the Comédie Française on Dec. 2, 1739. They accepted it and agreed to play it upon the reopening of the theater after Easter, 1740,[70] though Le Blanc[71] reported on Jan. 13 of that year that they had at first rejected it. They seem to have returned to this position, for it is not recorded in the *Registres*[72] as ever having been acted. Soleinne[73] owned an autograph copy, now at the Bibliothèque Nationale, which Lanson identified as written in La Chaussée's hand. To judge from his analysis,[74] it is an imbroglio, based on mistaken identity and danger of incest, that justifies the actors in not playing it and La Chaussée in his renunciation of tragedy.

A similar fate befell the ARTAXERCE of Deschamps,[75] who had begun his career with a *Caton d'Utique* that had made for him in 1714 a certain reputation. Three years later his *Antiochus et Cléopâtre* had been much less successful. The *Mercure* of September, 1721, declares that the actors had accepted his "Artaxerxes" and were to play it the following year after La Motte's *Romulus*. They did not do so, however, until fourteen years later. When it was produced on Dec. 19, 1735, the actors provided three "habits de Turc," diamonds for Sarrazin's costume and for Grandval's, "écharpes" for Sarrazin, Dufresne, and Legrand de Belleville. Except that these actors took part in it, little is known about the play. The attendance was large enough to give the author 155 fr., 14 s., but, as the text has disappeared, the play has been even more completely forgotten than La Chaussée's *Palmire*.

Its failure did not discourage its author, but it may have induced him to keep his name from the public when he brought out his next play, entitled MÉDUS.[76] The actors had merely announced that they were going to give *Médus*, but on the day of its first performance, they had "affiché Phédre & Hippolite, & sous main l'on avoit répandu que l'on jouroit la Piece nouvelle." Le Blanc, who provides this information,[77] was himself accused of writing the tragedy. He was sure that it was not by Voltaire, La Chaussée, Piron, or La Grange-Chancel, and concluded that it was the work of a new author or of a mediocre writer like "Morand, Richer, Deschamps &c."

The author states in his preface that he derived his tragedy from the

[70] Lanson, *op. cit.*, p. 110.
[71] Monod-Cassidy, *op. cit.*, p. 345.
[72] Though these are incomplete for 1740 before Easter, they are complete for the period after Easter.
[73] Cf. *Soleinne*, no. 3076. No name of author is mentioned there.
[74] *Op. cit.*, pp. 303-7.
[75] Cf. my *Sunset*, pp. 140-3.
[76] Paris, Prault fils, 1739, 8°. Approbation by Crébillon, Feb. 3.
[77] Monod-Cassidy, *op. cit.*, pp. 319-20.

twenty-seventh of Hyginus's Fables. He indicates as his chief alterations of the legend the introduction of Idalide to satisfy French demand for a love interest, and of Démarate, in order that he might lie to save his master's life and thus keep the hero from pretending that he is the son of Créon. Deschamps declares that he was accused of plagiarism by those who were unfamiliar with Hyginus, although the ancient tale was his only source. He may have had in mind the abbé Le Blanc, who had heard gossip by Dec. 26, 1738, before *Médus* was acted, to the effect that it was a reworking of *Amasis* and other plays and that the subject was the same as that which Voltaire was to make into *Mérope*. After the tragedy appeared, Le Blanc called it a "Rapsodie de toutes les autres Tragédies & surtout de l'Amasis de La Grange & de l'Oreste & Pilade du même Autheur." [78]

Strangely enough, he said nothing about La Grange-Chancel's opera, *Médus*,[79] which has the same subject as Deschamps's play. However, a comparison of the latter with Hyginus, with the opera, and with the three tragedies he was accused of imitating, justifies Deschamps, except that it is possible that he derived from *Oreste et Pilade*, its source in Euripides, or the opera the idea of human sacrifice, which is not in Hyginus, and from the opera, in which Médus loves the daughter of Persès, the idea of having him love the king's niece.[80] On the other hand, the abbé was probably correct in pointing to a well-known line in Corneille's *Médée* as the source of a verse in Deschamps's tragedy [81] and he could have added that, when the heroine, required to marry a king or see her lover perish, decides to marry and commit suicide, she is acting much as does the heroine of *Andromaque*. Such borrowings, however, do not support Le Blanc's contention that the tragedy is merely a "Rapsodie de toutes les autres." [82]

---

[78] Monod-Cassidy, *op. cit.*, pp. 316-7, 320.

[79] Produced in 1701. The text is found in the author's *Œuvres*, 1758, III, 85-136.

[80] In *Médus*, as in *Amasis*, *Mérope*, and the opera, but also in Hyginus, a usurper seeks to kill the heir to the throne; the prince and his mother, after she has been on the point of killing him, triumph; and the usurper dies. Human sacrifice is not in Hyginus, but it is demanded in the opera and has been practised by Medea for some time in *Médus*, as in *Oreste et Pilade* and its source.

[81] Le Blanc misquotes Corneille as follows:

          Contre tant d'ennemis que vous reste-t-il?
Médée: Moi.

He declares that a similar question is put to the adventuress in *Médus* and that she replies, "L'Audace." The reference is to *Médus*, V, 7:

          Qui peut de ses fureurs vous garantir?
Médée: L'audace.

He might also have quoted from III, 7:

          Que dis-je? & qu'ai-je à craindre? Il me reste Médée.

[82] Persès, "Roi d'Iberie, de Colchide & d'Arménie," has killed his two brothers, Ætes, father of Medea, and Alodétès, father of Idalide, and taken possession of their kingdoms. As he has been warned by an oracle that Medea's son, Médus, may

In portraying Medea, Deschamps rejected the help of magic and "la machine, qui ne m'ont jamais paru convenir à la Tragédie." He tried to substitute for these devices Medea's "courage & son génie," making her "implacable, dissimulée, artificieuse, occupée de sa vengeance." She is also sacrilegious, inventing oracles to support her own interests, and a murderess. She has no inner struggle, never wavering in her desire to kill Persès, but she alters her methods to fit the circumstances and sees her fortunes undergo a remarkable series of changes. She had triumphed at Athens, but she had been driven out of the city. She is delighted to meet Démarate, but is almost in despair when she hears that her son is dead. She tries to kill the prisoner, but discovers in time that he is her son. At the end of the play she hears of victory, then of defeat, is in danger of death, then sees her son triumph and her enemy kill himself. Her rôle, when played by la Dumesnil, must have been effective.

Idalide, too, has a rôle of considerable variety, as she is given love scenes with Médus, scenes in which she resists Persès, pleads with him, decides to sacrifice herself, and finally finds happiness. This rôle was assigned to la Gaussin. Médus was played by Dufresne, who had only to act the young hero and the ardent lover. Sarrazin, as Persès, had the villain's rôle, that of one tortured by his belief that Médus will bring destruction upon him and by his inability to identify his enemy.

The author distributes the material of his exposition over several scenes,

---

cause his death, he is anxious to take the young man's life. Now Medea has arrived in his dominions, has established herself as priestess of Diana, and has won such influence over Persès that she has been able to sacrifice to the goddess his adherents and to prepare her father's for revolt. Exiled Médus has organized a military expedition with his former "gouverneur," Démarate, and has sailed to Persès's land, but he has been shipwrecked and washed ashore. He is protected by his cousin, Idalide, who had fallen in love with him when she had been a refugee in Egypt. Démarate meets Medea, tells her that her son has been drowned, but that the Greeks from the other ships are safe in a neighboring harbor. Medea bids him bring them to the palace and promises an uprising. Before Démarate leaves, Idalide brings Médus to him and admits that she loves him. Persès insists upon knowing who the strangers are. To save Médus, Démarate declares that the young man is Iphiclès, son of the Créon whom Medea had murdered. He says that he has come for vengeance, but, not finding Medea, would return to Greece. As Medea, whose identity is unknown to Persès, declares Démarate worthy of confidence, he is allowed to depart, but Persès has Médus arrested, since he is jealous of Idalide's interest in him. He then tells her that, unless she marries him, he will put the prisoner to death. Idalide decides to marry Persès, secure the safety of Médus, and kill herself. Unwilling to accept her sacrifice, Médus admits to Persès that he is his rival and is sent back to prison. Persès informs Medea that his prisoner is Iphiclès or Médus. Believing that he is Iphiclès and fearing that he will tell who she is, she resolves to stab him, but, when she meets him, she recognizes him as her son. The Greeks attack. Persès goes to meet them, leaving Medea in command of the palace. She frees Médus and sends him into the battle. Persès comes to tell us that he has captured Démarate and to accuse Medea of treachery, but, before he can put them to death, Médus makes himself master of the palace. Medea gloats over Persès, telling who she and her son are. He kills himself. Medea is avenged. Médus will reign with Idalide over their ancestral dominions.

makes much use of suspense, contrives scenes of recognition, and seems to have counted especially on the one in which Medea starts to kill a supposed enemy and discovers him to be her son, one that may well have been suggested by the Merope tradition, as well as by a brief phrase in Hyginus. He writes in his preface:

Quoi de plus propre à remuer le cœur & à l'attacher, qu'une mere qui par les soins qu'elle prend d'assouvir sa vengeance & de garentir sa vie, se précipite elle-même dans le péril d'immoler son propre fils, & tombe avec lui dans les plus grands dangers?

The tragedy was first acted on Jan. 12, 1739. The actors who played the four leading rôles have been indicated. Legrand de Belleville played Démarate. It was acted eight times, until Jan. 31, with satisfactory receipts, but was then withdrawn in order that other plays might be given.[83]

Le Blanc [84] found the tragedy poorly constructed, lacking invention and interest. He reported that when Deschamps, imitating Corneille's *Médée*, made Medea reply " L'audace," [85] the audience, instead of trembling, laughed. Deschamps himself admits that his plot was considered too complex. The charge of plagiarism indicates that certain scenes lacked novelty, while others may have fallen short of the expectations of those who looked for evidence of magic power in the rôle of Medea since Corneille and Longepierre had shown it in their tragedies in which she appears.

Deschamps's defense of his play in his preface shows that he was criticized for having Persès arrest Médus when he believes him to be Iphiclès, for having Persès return to the palace before the battle is over, and for having him commit suicide. His explanations indicate that he was more interested in creating effective scenes than in the manner in which they were produced. He claims that he thought the view of a guilty man led to kill himself would be striking and would fulfill the aim of tragedy, which is to " corriger les mœurs," but he admits that the scene of Persès's death lost some of its effectiveness through the crowding of spectators upon the stage:

Il devoit y avoir de grands intervales entre Persès & Médus, & il n'a pas été possible aux Acteurs d'y observer les distances nécessaires, à cause du grand nombre de spectateurs qui étoient debout sur le Théâtre.

---

[83] Deschamps's statement to this effect is supported by the *Registres*, which show that the smallest amount received was 753 fr. The author's share in the receipts from eight productions was 966 fr.

[84] Monod-Cassidy, *loc. cit.*

[85] Cf. above, note 81.

CHAPTER X

LA NOUE, GRESSET, LANDOIS, AND OTHERS

Feb., 1739 to Jan., 1744

In these five years twelve tragedies were acted for the first time at the Comédie Française. The most famous of them are Voltaire's *Mahomet* and *Mérope*, which, as well as his *Mort de César* and *Zulime*, Piron's *Fernand Cortez*, and Cahusac's lost *Comte de Warwick*, have already been discussed. The other six tragedies were written by an actor and by five men who had not previously shown interest in the stage. It is worth noting that only a third of the twelve plays have ancient subjects. Even more remarkable than the fact that Arabian, Mexican, and medieval English history is now dramatized is the adventure of Landois in writing a tragedy of contemporary life in France.

Among the plays that have not been previously discussed the most meritorious is *Mahomet Second*, but there are scenes in *Edouard III* and in *Silvie* that are by no means devoid of interest. The most striking characters are those of the protagonist and the Aga in the first of these tragedies, those of Worcester and Arondel in the second. Some attention is paid to manners in La Noue's tragedy, to stage decoration in *Silvie*, and there are anticlerical verses in *Thélamire*, but the new authors showed less interest than Voltaire in these matters. Their work is especially to be remembered for departures from classical regulation in regard to the proprieties and to form.

La Noue was bold enough to select a subject that calls for the hero's murder of the heroine, but he kept the actual killing off the stage. Gresset went farther and allowed the spectators to witness a murder. It would have been still more daring to show on the stage the assassination of a person with whom we sympathize, but this point in brutality had not yet been reached even by Landois, who showed his independence in other ways. He composed the first French " tragédie bourgeoise " and at the same time startled his audience by writing it in prose and by making of it a play in one act and a prologue. The reaction of the audience shows that the classical system was in no immediate danger, but the fact that *Edouard III* and *Silvie* were acted indicates that cracks in the seventeenth-century edifice were beginning to appear.

I include in this chapter tragedies by Thibouville and Boistel that were

246

composed at a later date, in order to complete my study of these minor dramatists.

The first eighteenth-century professional actor to write a tragedy was Jean Sauvé, called La Noue.[1] Quite naturally he selected for dramatization a subject that had already inspired a tragedy, one in which he may have played, Chateaubrun's *Mahomet Second*.[2] He probably drew his data from this play, using the same title, MAHOMET SECOND,[3] its main characters, Mahomet and Irène, and some of its incidents and references. As in the earlier tragedy Mahomet has loved Irène for two years and proposes to marry her, she meets a near relative whom she has supposed to be dead, thus creating an effective scene of recognition, the army starts to revolt, Irène begs to be allowed to leave, and there are references to the conquest of Caraman, to Scanderbeg and the Hungarians, to Mahomet's planning to capture Rhodes and to invade Italy.

On the other hand, there are marked differences between the two tragedies. Mahomet looms much larger in La Noue's play, his character is more carefully explained, Irène is in love with him, it is her father, not her disguised brother, that she meets in the palace, the plot is engineered by discontented Turks rather than by a Greek, and Irène, instead of committing suicide, is killed by her imperial lover. In this last incident and in the plea of the Aga, which is much more striking than the confidant's protest in Chateaubrun's play, La Noue follows the old tradition, found in Boaistuau (1559), that Mahomet II had killed his Greek mistress after an eloquent plea made by an elderly servant.[4]

La Noue tells us in his preface that his purpose was to dramatize a simple subject with one dominant character, to set forth " le développement du cœur de Mahomet, le péril & la mort d'Irene." [5] He consequently placed

---

[1] For an account of him see above, Chap. I.

[2] Cf. my *Sunset*, pp. 138-40. It is improbable that La Noue knew Claude Basset's lost tragedy on the same subject, for which cf. my *History*, Part III, p. 167.

[3] Paris, Prault fils, 1739, 8°. The approbation by Crébillon of May 13 refers to the pleasure the play has given. It was republished, The Hague, Van Dôle, 1739; in the author's *Œuvres de théâtre*, Paris, Duchesne, 1765; by Petitot in 1803; in the *Auteurs du second ordre*, 1808; and in the *Répertoires* of 1813, 1817, 1818, 1821, and 1822. Dutch translations appeared in 1740 and 1763; an Italian translation in 1750.

[4] Cf. C. D. Rouillard, *The Turk in French History, Thought, and Literature (1520-1660)*, Paris, Boivin, n. d., pp. 522-4.

[5] Mahomet II, after sacking Constantinople, has for love of a Greek slave, Irène, adopted a kindly attitude towards its inhabitants. The Grand Visir stirs up the army by reporting that the sultan is sacrificing to love his fame as a warrior and is seeking aid from the conquered Greeks by freeing Théodore, a prince who is Irène's father. The Visir informs Théodore that Mahomet is seducing his daughter and proposes that he stab the sultan. When Mahomet announces his intention of marrying Irène, the Visir urges the Mufti to appeal to the religious prejudices of the troops. Irène, who hopes to do for her people what Esther did for hers, meets Théodore and reassures him in regard to her virtue. When he first hears that marriage is proposed, his patriotism obliges him to consent, but, when he learns that this marriage is causing a rebellion, he writes to warn Irène of the danger

Mahomet in the center of the stage. He presented him as a Turkish conqueror, trained by the Aga of the Janissaries, proud of his ancestors' progress from Scythia to Belgrade, desirous of further conquests, yet influenced by his love for Irène. There is a marked conflict between his barbarous instincts and the thoughts that paternal government is better than war and that love inspires virtue. The former prevail in the end, as is shown by his murdering the woman he loves, but his motives are quite complex, for his love combines with the urge of absolutism to make him react violently against the rebels in his army, while the joy of the conflict, though undertaken partly in defense of Irène, rouses him to rid himself of a woman who might be an obstacle to his conquests. His is a deeply emotional character, that of a Turk in contact with European civilization, capable of generous conduct, but still dominated by the traditions of his people.

The other characters are divided into two groups, Turkish and Greek. The Grand Visir resents the fact that he has been obliged to put his son to death, longs for revenge, and intrigues with both Turks and Greeks. His brother, the Aga, has nothing of the politician about him. Proud of Turkish achievements, he is altogether opposed to revolt and is willing to die as punishment for his men when they turn against the sultan, but he disapproves of Mahomet's marriage, wishes him to continue his victorious march to the west, and does not hesitate to tell him so. The Mufti is a tool in the Visir's hands. Tadill is merely a confidant, but he supports the arguments of the Aga.

The Greeks are represented as having little hope of regaining their freedom, but two of them are as brave as their conquerors. Irène loves the sultan and is anxious to help her people, but, when she sees that her existence is a menace to both, she is quite willing to die. Mahomet's dagger saves her from the unchristian act of suicide. Her father is equally ready to sacrifice himself, but he would protect his people by marrying his daughter to the sultan. La Noue admits that his presentation of this character justified "un reproche de foiblesse et d'indécision," but he claimed that he

she is in. When she shows his note to the sultan, he declares that he will marry her in the camp, but he is deeply impressed by the Aga of the Janissaries, who begs him to conquer his love and lead his army to Rome. Nevertheless he bids the Aga tell the soldiers that the marriage will take place. The rebellion, led by the Visir and the Mufti, breaks out, but Mahomet shows himself to the soldiers and kills many of them, including the Visir. He cannot, however, prevent the massacre of Christians or suppress the demand that Irène be put to death. The shedding of blood has roused Mahomet's ardor for conquest. He proposes to attack Rhodes and Albania. The Aga encourages him and offers to kill Irène, who admits to the sultan that she loves him, but frees him from his promise to marry her. The sultan weeps, but he lifts his dagger as if to stab her. She asks why he hesitates, promises forgiveness, and stops him when he attempts suicide. He offers to crown her, then bids her leave him. Théodore, mortally wounded, begs him to save her, for she has gone out to rescue the Greeks. She impresses the rebellious soldiers, but Mahomet himself stabs her, crying, " je l'immole à ma gloire! "

wanted to keep Théodore from attracting to himself interest that should be taken in Mahomet and Irène. He consequently made of him a practical statesman rather than one who would make no compromise with the enemy of his people.

In Act I La Noue gives too much prominence to the Visir, who subsequently disappears except in two scenes of Act III. The action is unnecessarily hurried in the last scenes of the play. The author fails, as Petitot indicates, to prepare us sufficiently for Mahomet's murder of Irène. La Noue writes:

> Aux premieres Représentations, on me fit un crime de l'action de Mahomet; on auroit souhaité, ou que j'eusse fait sauver Irene, ou du moins qu'un autre l'eût immolée; et je me souviendrai toujours de l'effet terrible que produisit ce vers décisif:
>
> Frémissez, c'est la main du cruel Mahomet.

Subsequently, however, he was reproached for not having Mahomet stab Irène when the audience saw him raise his dagger. To this criticism he replied that he preferred not to wound "les mœurs et les regles," for he feared that his example might make of the stage an "arene sanglante, une école d'inhumanité." He might have added that, if the heroine had been killed at that moment, the preparation for the event would have been even less satisfactory than it is at present.

Petitot calls the scene between the Aga and Mahomet (III, 6) one of the most beautiful ever written. It begins in Turkish style:

> L'Aga, *prosterné aux pieds de Mahomet:*
> 　　Ton esclave à genoux, pénétré de douleur,
> 　　Osera-t-il parler?
> Mahomet:　　　　　　　Parle.
> L'Aga, *se relevant:*　　　　Frémis d'horreur.
> 　　Tes soldats révoltés menacent ta puissance:
> 　　Je suis leur chef, je viens m'offrir à ta vengeance;
> 　　Frappe, mais n'étends point ta colere sur eux:
> 　　Ils veulent t'arracher à des liens honteux.

Though Mahomet threatens him with death if he seeks to thwart his love, the Aga repeats the words of the Janissaries, points out the weakness of western nations, and urges him to take advantage of it instead of limiting his efforts to the conquest of a woman. Throwing himself at the sultan's knees, he cries:

> 　　Tu rougis! . . . Ah! rends-moi mon auguste empereur!
> 　　Que la gloire t'éveille! elle parle à ton cœur; . . .
> 　　Tu l'entends, Mahomet, et ton trouble t'accuse.
> 　　Sous tes coups maintenant puissé-je être immolé!
> 　　J'ai le prix de ma mort, la gloire t'a parlé.

Striking, too, is the scene between the Aga and the Grand Visir (III, 8) in which their political views are brought into sharp conflict. The Visir insists that he is the eye, the voice, and the arm of the sultan, whom he must force to do what will promote the monarch's happiness and the good of the Turks. The Aga replies that, as he is only a soldier, he has supposed that the Visir owed the sultan greater loyalty than did anyone else:

> Souviens-toi qu'un sultan par le ciel couronné
> Peut être condamnable, et non pas condamné.
> Si sur toi, sur les tiens tombe son injustice,
> S'il entraîne l'état au bord du précipice,
> S'il immole sa gloire à de lâches amours,
> S'il ternit en un jour l'éclat de tant de jours,
> Pleure; mais obéis: c'est là ton seul partage.

When Petitot refers to La Noue's use of " coloris local," he doubtless has in mind the rôle of the Aga, who prostrates himself at the sultan's feet and accords him absolute power, but who dares to offer him advice; that of the wily Visir, who represents a different element in the Turkish hierarchy; the introduction of conflicting religions; and the barbarous element in the character of the protagonist. There is little local color in the vocabulary. In the simplicity of the plot, the analysis of motive, and the concentration upon the main figure the play is thoroughly classical.

It was quite successful; " extraordinairement," according to Collé.[6] Acted first on Feb. 23, 1739, it was played nine times before the Easter recess, at the opening of the theater after that vacation, six [7] times subsequently in 1739, seven times in 1745, and five times in 1788-9.

Dufresne played Mahomet; la Gaussin, Irène; la Jouvenot, her confidant, Zamis; Grandval, the Aga; Sarrazin, Théodore; Fierville, the Mufti; Legrand de Belleville, the Visir; La Thorillière, Du Breuil, and young Dangeville, confidants. The author's share in the receipts from the first nine productions was 2359 fr. If we had the complete record, we should probably find that he earned from the play over 3000 fr.

On March 4, 1739, the abbé Le Blanc [8] wrote that the tragedy was winning great and deserved success:

Il est rempli de Beautés & de vers heureux; & surement gagnera encor à la Lecture. La catastrophe est cruelle & révoltante mais, c'est le sujet: Du moins on ne dira pas que ce sont des François à qui l'Autheur a donné des Turbans.

He praises as new the scene of the lifted dagger, but he prefers the second act. He thinks that English kings are marvelously depicted in IV, 3:

---

[6] *Journal*, 1807, II, 132.
[7] As the *Registres* from Easter, 1739, to Easter, 1740, are lost, Joannidès took this number from Mouhy.
[8] Monod-Cassidy, *op. cit.*, pp. 325-6.

Tu n'es plus sous ces rois tremblants, subordonnés,
D'un peuple impérieux esclaves couronnés,
Monarques dépendans, asservis sur le trône,
Que sous le nom de lois l'impuissance environne,
Fantômes du pouvoir, dont le bras impuissant
Courbe au gré de l'audace un sceptre obéissant.

Le Blanc's enthusiasm did not last. On April 24 he wrote [9] that the work, well received during Lent, had not "ressuscité" at Easter and was "mort et enterré." He added that the Comédie Italienne had given a wretched parody of it.[10] On May 23, after the tragedy was printed, he was surprised to find in it a great number of errors.[11]

After Voltaire had received his copy, he addressed to La Noue a letter [12] in which he observed that there were in the tragedy "vers de génie" surrounded by others that could stand polishing. He praised the author for putting into Mahomet's mouth more daring expressions than Racine had assigned to Bajazet. He liked especially the Aga's rôle and the scene of the lifted dagger. These made him accept the story as artistically true, though, as a student of history, he felt obliged to say that the insurrection of the Janissaries and the murder of Irène were Christian inventions, reported by the monk "Bandelli" and repeated by a score of other writers.

La Harpe [13] praised the presentation of Mahomet and that of the Aga. He thought that the revival of the tragedy had been prevented by the horror of the dénouement, which, unlike Voltaire, he believed to be historically justified. Though he found the style unequal and incorrect, a mixture of force and declamation, he held that the play had "de la couleur tragique" and that, if acted again, it would succeed.

With the exception of Voltaire's plays, and Piron's *Gustave*, it is the most praiseworthy tragedy that had appeared in France for a decade. Its success must have helped secure for its author admission to the troupe of the Comédie Française and may well have encouraged the actors to accept another Turkish play, produced before the end of the year.

This was BAJAZET PREMIER,[14] published as the work of le chevalier de P***, an initial that caused it to be attributed to Pellegrin, though, as Paul Lacroix remarks,[15] the preface presents it as the first attempt of a youthful author. As Pellegrin had been writing for over thirty years, it seems much

---

[9] *Ibid.*, p. 331.
[10] Cf. *ibid.*, p. 520, where Mme Monod-Cassidy indicates that the parody in question is Favart's *Moulinet premier*, acted on March 15, 1739.
[11] *Ibid.*, p. 333.
[12] Moland, XXXV, 236-41.
[13] *Op. cit.*, XIII, 188-90.
[14] Paris, Prault fils, 1739, 8°. Approbation of Aug. 18 signed by Crébillon.
[15] *Soleinne*, no. 1819. It was attributed to Pellegrin by the *Bib. du th. fr.*, but Léris, La Porte, and the *Almanach des Spectacles* assigned it to Pacarony.

more probable that the attribution to Pacarony is correct. The author
writes:

J'étois fort jeune, & je ne connoissois encore les ouvrages de Théâtre que par la
lecture, lorsque me trouvant presque seul à la campagne, il me prit envie d'essaïer
quelques Scénes pour me désennuier. Le Roman de Madame de Villedieu, intitulé
Astérie ou Tamerlan, m'offrit le sujet.[16]

In this novel Astérie, daughter of Bajazet, is loved by Andronic, son of
the Greek emperor, Emmanuel, and by two sons of Tamerlane, the younger
of whom she prefers to her other lovers. Tamerlane favors the older son and
asks the younger to speak to Astérie in his behalf, but it turns out that the
older prince is really the son of Odmar, Tamerlane's crafty adviser, who
kills him while believing that he is taking the life of his monarch's son.
The lovers are then united. Bajazet has died in a paroxysm of rage.

From this tale Pacarony may well have derived the location of his tragedy
at Samarcand, the idea of putting on the stage Tamerlane, Bajazet, Astérie,
and her young lover, as well as the names of Odmar, Axala, and Emmanuel,
but his work owes much less to this romance than it does to Pradon's *Tamerlan ou la Mort de Bajazet*,[17] a tragedy of 1675 that had been acted as recently
as 1725. In this work, which may owe something to the novel as well as
to history, Tamerlane, Bajazet, Andronic, and Astérie appear, but Andronic
is now the successful, Tamerlane himself the unsuccessful lover of Astérie.
In these respects, as well as in other matters,[18] Pradon's tragedy is nearer
Pacarony's than the novel is.

We must accept the author's statement that his subject was suggested to
him by the novel, but he certainly dramatized it under the influence of
Pradon's tragedy. He produced a simpler play by reducing references to
the historical background and by omitting the theme of Tamerlane's engagement to Princess Araxide and his effort to have Andronic marry her. He
rearranged, too, the order of the scenes and produced a melancholy ending
by causing the deaths of Andronic and Astérie, as well as that of Bajazet,
which is found in both of his sources.[19]

[16] Published originally in 1667, this novel appeared in the works of Mme de Ville-
dieu, but also in those of Mlle de La Roche-Guilhem, who seems to have been its
author. In a reduced form it was republished in the *Bibliothèque universelle des
romans*, April, 1780, II, 51-134.

[17] Cf. my *History*, Part IV, pp. 163-5.

[18] In each play there are seven characters besides guards. Four of them, including
Astérie's confidant, Zaïde (called Xaire in the novel), have the same names. In both
tragedies Andronic had fallen in love with Astérie at Burse (Pruze); Tamerlane
asks Andronic to propose that Bajazet give his daughter in marriage to his conqueror; a plan is made for Bajazet's escape; Bajazet taunts Tamerlane with his
low birth and commits suicide at the end of the play. There is little verbal similarity, but ideas expressed in the plays at times resemble one another closely. III, 5,
for instance, ends as does III, 3 in Pradon's play, with Tamerlane's asking why
Andronic is interested in the prisoners, Andronic's replying that it is a question of
Tamerlane's honor, and the Tartar's assuring him that he can do without his advice.

[19] Tamerlane has captured Bajazet and his daughter, Astérie, whom he desires to

The author makes no distinction among the manners of Tartars, Turks, and Greeks. He neglects the interesting historical material he might have employed. The characters are not properly presented. Tamerlane, the only important person who survives at the end of the tragedy, has a villain's rôle, yet his genius is discounted because of his humble birth, and his generous offer is rejected with insults by persons with whom we are supposed to sympathize. Bajazet's haughtiness, his daughter's pride, and the ineffectiveness of Andronic, who plans to cut his way from Samarcand to Constantinople, unite to deprive them of whatever interest we might have taken in their fate. Though constructed in accordance with classical requirements and without disguise and recognition, the tragedy is inferior even to the play by Pradon that Pacarony imitated.

He declares that a cabal began to work against his tragedy before anyone had seen it acted. At the first performance the public was irritated by the abruptness with which Bajazet decided to commit suicide. The text as then spoken was (V, 6):

> Astérie: J'ose encor l'espérer. Dis-moi si je m'abuse.
> Tamerlan: Oui, j'accorde sa grace.
> Bajazet *se frapant d'un poignard qu'il tenoit caché*:
> Et moi, je la refuse.

As this couplet "souleva le Parterre," Pacarony sent Sarrazin next day four verses and two half verses to be inserted between *sa grace* and *Et moi*. These were spoken at later performances, but not at the second, for Fontenelle said he was unable to understand what had excited the audience.

Some of the critics objected to the perfunctory manner in which love is presented. They asked why, when Astérie realizes that she ought not to have doubted her lover's fidelity, she was not given with him "une de ces Scénes tendres, délicates, intéressantes, & filées avec cet art enchanteur que nos Tragiques modernes sçavent si bien emploïer." They reminded the author that love alone causes much weeping and that all French tragedies

marry. Andronic, son of the Greek emperor, had called in Tamerlane to save his country from Bajazet and had helped in the Turk's defeat, but, like his ally, he is in love with Astérie. Bajazet meets with disdain Tamerlane's offer of friendship and refuses to accept him as a son-in-law when Odmar and Andronic are sent to arrange the match. Andronic assembles his men to help the captives to escape, but first he asks Tamerlane to allow him to escort them to Greece. He shows such ardor that the Tartar suspects his motives and has him watched. Tamerlane offers to restore his throne to Bajazet if he will allow him to marry Astérie, but the princess tells him his proposition is an outrage, though she knows her refusal may mean her father's death. Bajazet asks Andronic to look after Astérie, discovers that they are in love, and gives his consent to their marriage, but Andronic's plan is discovered, he is killed by Tamerlane in the fight that follows, and Bajazet, who had joined in the fray, is recaptured. When he is brought before Tamerlane, Astérie tells them that she has taken poison. Tamerlane is so deeply moved that he offers to pardon Bajazet, who refuses to be his debtor and stabs himself. Tamerlane mourns over them and regrets that he is no better than a tyrant.

owe it their success.   But Pacarony preferred to follow "Nature" and to
allow Astérie to go no farther than to say "L'Ami de Bajazet ne sçauroit
me déplaire" (III, 2).   He was gratified to note that in the "secondes
Loges" there were some young persons who were moved by family misfortunes.   Apparently, however, lovers were so decidedly in the majority
that he judged it wise to interrupt the production of his play after the fifth
performance.

The first was on Aug. 6, 1739.   Legrand represented Tamerlane in a
manner that would have been to the author's satisfaction if the actor had
been in the habit of taking this kind of rôle.   Sarrazin played Bajazet;
Grandval, Andronic; the younger La Thorillière, Odmar.   The author
thought that the acting of la Dumesnil as Astérie could not have been
surpassed.   The confidants, Zaïde and Arcas, were played by la Jouvenot
and Fierville.

This was not the only failure in the summer of 1739.   A month before
Bajazet Premier appeared, an anonymous tragedy, THÉLAMIRE,[20] had been
given but four times.   The author claimed that he had essential reasons
for withdrawing his play and keeping his name from the public.   He admits
that in doing so he allowed suspicion to rest on certain persons, but these
considered the matter of so little consequence that they allowed him to
continue to conceal his name.   It seems probable that Voltaire and his
friends were the persons in question, for a number of the lines omitted from
the first edition present kings, gods, and priests in an unfavorable light.
Mouhy seems to have Voltaire in mind when he states that the tragedy was
attributed to an "homme d'esprit fort connu."

As for the authorship, eighteenth-century writers list the play as anonymous,[21] or attribute it to the marquis de Thibouville.[22]   Paul Lacroix [23]
at first assigned it to the marquis, but he subsequently cited Mouhy as
attributing it to Denise Lebrun.   He may have had in mind Mouhy's
Journal, a most unreliable production.   He was followed by the cataloguers
of the Bibliothèque Nationale and by Joannidès, although they admit that
Thibouville was often considered the author.   More reliable evidence is
furnished by a letter of Voltaire's niece, Mme Denis, who wrote on March 6,
1759, that Thibouville had sent her uncle and herself a copy of his tragedy.[24]

---

[20] Paris, Le Breton, 1739, 8°. Approbation, signed by Crébillon, July 24. Republished, The Hague, Gibert, 1740; and, according to *Soleinne*, no. 3121, in a collection
published by Prault fils, 1740-43. Fifty lines, omitted in the first edition, were
restored in that of The Hague. The first performance was on July 6. Dufresne had
the title-rôle. The heroine was played by la Gaussin; Amintas, by Sarrazin.
[21] Mouhy, *Tablettes*, 1752; Léris, 1763; *Bib. du th. fr.*, 1768.
[22] La Porte et Chamfort, 1775-6; Mouhy, *Abrégé*, 1780.
[23] *Soleinne*, nos. 1813 and 3121.
[24] Moland, XL, 56.

She does not give its title, but she refers to its " lourde chute," which could not have been said of a play that had not been acted, and Thibouville's second tragedy was not played till the latter part of 1759. She mentions, too, a queen, a prince, and a minister, the only important rôles in *Thélamire*. I consequently conclude that Moland is correct in stating that this is the tragedy by Thibouville [25] to which Mme Denis refers.

The source is unknown. The fact that the scene is laid at Syracuse has no significance, for any other place in a pagan world would have done as well. The subject recalls Thomas Corneille's *Stilicon* in that it is centered upon a minister's criminal and abortive efforts to put his son on the throne, and Pierre Corneille's *Héraclius* in that an exchange of children and fear of incest are important themes.[26] The most striking character is the clever and unscrupulous minister who boasts of his loyalty and devotion to duty. The young king and the princess, deeply in love and with a high sense of honor, are unable to cope with him before Thélamire meets him in battle. His son might have made a fourth character of some importance, but he does not appear on the stage.

The author showed little imagination in the devices he employed, twice introducing letters left by deceased parents. It is not clear why Thélamire should choose Athis, rather than some other nobleman, as a husband for Elismène, or why he should hasten her marriage except to preserve the unity of time. There is, however, a certain pathos in the situation of the lovers, which Mme Denis, to whom incest was no great crime, failed to appreciate. She writes:

L'intérêt est absolument manqué. Je n'ai rien lu de si froid en voulant toujours être chaud, surtout les trois premiers actes. Le grand malheur, c'est qu'on ignore le motif qui fait agir et la reine, et le prince, et le ministre; que l'amour principal ne suit nullement la marche du cœur; que le sujet est vide, et la pièce trop longue.

---

[25] Henri-Lambert d'Herbigny, marquis de Thibouville, was born at Paris in 1710, had an inglorious career both as a soldier and as a writer, and died in 1784. His chief title to fame is that he was one of Voltaire's correspondents. Besides *Thélamire*, he composed an unpublished tragedy called *Namir* and two *comédies-proverbes*. Cf. the *Biographie générale* and Moland.

[26] As the King of Syracuse had only one child, a daughter, he exchanged her for the son of Cydnus, Thélamire, who is now on the throne. A minister, Amintas, schemes to make Athis, his own son, king. To do this he advises Thélamire to marry a princess rather than Elismène, daughter of the late king, but supposed to be of lesser birth. He also bribes a priest to frighten Elismène by warning her that, if she marries the king, he will die. Though she loves Thélamire, she refuses to marry him. He thinks he may have a rival, hears that Amintas wishes her to marry Athis, and questions him, only to be told that he himself and Elismène are brother and sister. To prove it, Amintas produces a letter written by the dead king and stating that Elismène is his daughter. The lovers are horrified and think of permanent separation as they cannot overcome their feeling for each other. To put a barrier between them, Thélamire marries her to Athis, whereupon Amintas declares that she is the lawful queen and leads a troop against Thélamire, but he is defeated and killed. His son frees Elismène from her matrimonial vows, but it is too late. Elismène has taken poison. She dies after she has restored to Thélamire the title of king.

As a matter of fact, the motives of the three leading characters—love, fear of incest, ambition—are carefully indicated, and the play is no longer than most tragedies of the time, but it is true that the dialogue lacks variety and that, if the tragedy had been reduced to three acts, it would have been improved. What Voltaire's niece ought to have appreciated is the criticism of tyranny and religious fanaticism contained in the fifty censored lines. These, which may have been written in imitation of Voltaire's *Œdipe*, are marked with square brackets in the 1740 edition. Some of them deserve quotation:

> Je veux croire qu'un feu qu'ils [les dieux] allument en nous,
> Ne sçauroit devenir l'objet de leur couroux.   (I, 2)
> Ne t'en étonne point; même au pied de l'Autel
> Il est souvent aisé de séduire un mortel,
> La faveur où je suis a corrompu nos Prêtres:
> Les Dieux, comme les Rois, sont servis par des traîtres.   (I, 3)
> Et vous, Dieux tout-puissans, mais souvent inhumains.   (II, 1)
> La Foiblesse des Rois ne peut être cachée.   (IV, 3)
> Je voix de sa vertu rougir les Dieux jaloux.   (IV, 3)
> Nos sentimens, enfin, dépendent-ils de nous?   (IV, 4)
> Nous sçavons nous punir de la faute des Dieux.   (IV, 5)

Thibouville's second tragedy, NAMIR,[27] was attributed to him by Collé,[28] the *Almanach des Spectacles*,[29] and Grimm.[30] Its one performance, which took place on Nov. 12, 1759, was interrupted in the fourth act. As it was not published, information about its plot is limited to what is told us by Fréron,[31] who apparently had the complete manuscript before him, and by Collé, who was acquainted only with the part of the play that he had seen acted.[32]

Fréron [33] is mistaken in asserting that the subject is that of La Chapelle's

---

[27] The *Almanach des Spectacles*, which had at first recorded it as *Namir*, listed it in 1767 and subsequently as " *Ramir*, Trag. 1759." Quérard followed suit, giving it as " *Ramir*, 1759, 12°," with the implication that it had been published. *Soleinne*, no. 1812, merely quoted Quérard. In this way a new tragedy, born of a misprint, was added to the repertory!

[28] *Op. cit.*, II, 304-7.

[29] 1760, p. 110.

[30] *Cor.*, IV, 156.

[31] *Année littéraire*, 1759 (7), pp. 284-8.

[32] The Zégris have conquered the Abencérages, the last of whom, young Namir, has been saved by Zulmar, minister of Zaïde, Queen of Grenada, a Zégri. As Zulmar hopes to win the throne with the help of Namir, he has persuaded the queen to allow the young prince to live. At the request of the soldiers she even puts him at the head of her army. When she interviews him, she falls in love with him, but he has lost his heart to Léonide, daughter of Alphonse, King of Andalusia, a princess he captured when he defeated her father. He rejects the queen's offer of marriage. Alphonse's envoy proposes that Namir marry Léonide. When this princess appears, Namir makes love to her and falls at her feet. The queen surprises them in this situation, but she nobly decides to conquer her love. Zulmar arranges the marriage of Namir and Léonide, but he bribes the "Iman" to poison the nuptial cup. Namir falls dead. Zulmar, arrested, confesses, adds that he intended to poison the queen also, and stabs himself. Zaïde is left to mourn.

[33] *Loc. cit.*

Zaïde, about which he apparently knew nothing except its title. Nor could Thibouville have derived from the *Zaïde* of Mme de La Fayette more than the queen's name and the well-known hostility of the two Moorish families. The plot has some resemblance to the author's earlier tragedy, for in each a minister schemes to win a throne, bribes an ecclesiastic, causes the death by poison of a princess, and dies at the end of the play. The hostility of the Zégris and Abencérages had been introduced into Quinault's *Généreuse Ingratitude*; the poisoning of a nuptial cup into Thomas Corneille's *Camma*. One may conclude from what is known of the play that, though no definite source has been discovered, the devices employed were far from being novel.

Fréron held that the tragedy lacked action and that love was not presented with the proper intensity. Collé was much more severe, calling it a " ramas de situations les plus communes et les moins touchantes." It seems that the audience, disgusted by the fact that Léonide did not appear till the beginning of Act IV, greeted her entrance with hoots. When she said, in reply to Namir's proposal of marriage, " Prince, n'abusez pas de l'état où je suis," the remark was at once applied to the play itself. Laughter thus excited was increased by Zaïde's interruption of the love scene. So great was the disturbance that Le Kain, who was playing Namir, advanced to the edge of the stage and announced the comedy that was to follow. He was heartily applauded by the spectators, willing to remain in ignorance of the fatal cup and the villain's suicide.

The only other information we have about the tragedy is that Mlle Hus played Léonide; Mlle Clairon, Zaïde; and that the author received 199 fr., 18 s., 9 d. With its failure the career of the marquis as a dramatist ended about in the manner of his military exploits.

Two plays of 1740-41 are greatly superior to the tragedies of Pacarony and Thibouville. Each of them is a forerunner of important changes in French usage. The first of them is EDOUARD III [34] by Jean-Baptiste-Louis Gresset, known chiefly for his satirical poem, *Vert-Vert*, and for his comedy, *le Méchant*. In the *avertissement* of his tragedy he declares that there is nothing historical about it except Edward's love for the Countess of Salisbury, her heroic resistance, and the renewal of Edward I's claim upon the Scottish throne, but he makes no mention of sources in earlier plays.

[34] Paris, Prault père, 1740, 8°. Approbation, signed by Crébillon, Feb. 26. Republished, The Hague, Gibert, 1740; without place or date; and Paris, Belin, 1788. A Dutch translation was published at Amsterdam in 1760 and 1761; Italian translations, at Venice in 1743 and at Lucca in 1757. *Eduardo, Rey de Inglaterra*, played in 1815, is probably a Spanish translation of this tragedy; cf. Ada M. Coe, *op. cit.*, pp. 80-1. Gresset was born at Amiens in 1709, was elected to the Academy in 1748, although Mme de Pompadour was then supporting the candidacy of the abbé Le Blanc, and died in 1777.

Now La Calprenède had dramatized in his *Edouard*,[35] written a century before, the love of Edward III and the Countess of Salisbury. In both plays the three chief characters are the king, the countess, and her father; Edward is unmarried; the countess is a widow who, though she loves the king, rejects his proposals and wins the approval of her father; a plot is formed against the countess and her father; the king offers to spare the accused if he can have his way with the countess; the falseness of the accusation is revealed and the plotters are punished. It seems probable that Gresset received suggestions from this play, but he changed the story considerably, substituting new conspirators, having the king seek marriage instead of seduction, altering the names of father and daughter, and causing the heroine's death.[36]

Some of his changes may have been suggested by *Andromaque*, in which a princess is at the court of her royal fiancé, whom she loves, and discovers that he prefers another woman; the king threatens the woman he loves with the death of a near relative if she refuses to marry him; and the rejected princess has recourse to murder and suicide. It is also possible, as La Harpe suggests, that the poisoning of Eugénie by a princess, jealous of her power over the hero, may have been an imitation of *Inès de Castro*.

[35] Cf. my *History*, Part II, pp. 254-7. La Calprenède's source in Bandello is less close to Gresset's tragedy than is the earlier French play.

[36] Edward wishes to marry Eugénie, the widowed Countess of Salisbury, but her father, " Duc de Worcestre " and a minister, opposes the match on the grounds that the king is already engaged to Alzonde, heir to the throne of Scotland, and that, if he marries this princess, the Scots will be peacefully united to the English. Now Alzonde, after taking refuge in Norway, where she has known an English nobleman, Arondel, has taken ship for Scotland, been captured by the English, and is now, under the name of Aglaé, at the court in London. There she intrigues with Wolfax, captain of the palace guard. As she sees that Edward prefers Eugénie, she seeks, not only to regain her throne in Scotland, but to rouse the English against their king. She is anxious to go to Scotland and avoid Arondel, who has returned from Norway. Though Eugénie also loves Edward, she promises her father obedience and rejects the king's offer of marriage, a refusal that prejudices Edward against Worcester, who, accused of treason by Wolfax, is arrested. Edward asks Aglaé (Alzonde) to assure Eugénie of his love and to tell her that she will, by marrying him, save her father. Alzonde, instead of complying with this request, advises her rival to escape from court. Wolfax keeps Eugénie from her father, who is tried by jealous judges and condemned to death. Arondel, who has returned from Norway to inform Worcester of Alzonde's intrigues, is allowed by Wolfax to interview his old friend, while the captain listens from a hiding-place. Arondel urges Worcester to escape and, when he refuses, offers him a dagger, which the statesman declines as he considers suicide the act of a coward. He asks Arondel to look after Eugénie and to show Edward a paper, received just before his arrest, that reveals the dealings of Wolfax and Alzonde with the king's enemies. When Wolfax hears it mentioned, he interrupts the conversation and orders the arrest of Arondel, who promptly kills him with the dagger he had offered Worcester. Edward gives Eugénie a last chance to save her father, but she still refuses to marry him. He then interviews Arondel, who shows him the paper. Edward thanks him and liberates Worcester, who asks that Aglaé be punished for her part in the conspiracy. When she enters, she is identified as Alzonde by Arondel. She realizes that she will be condemned, but predicts that Edward will suffer more than she. The king soon learns that she has poisoned her rival. Alzonde stabs herself to death behind the scenes. Eugénie comes on the stage to die, but first tells Edward that she loves him.

A poem that Gresset published with his tragedy shows that he considered Worcester his principal character:

> J'Avois à peindre un Sage, heureux, digne de l'être,
> L'oracle de la Probité,
> Le Pere des Sujets, le Conseil de son Maître,
> L'Honneur de la Patrie & de l'Humanité.

He did not paint him as happy, for he suffers from the intrigues of courtiers, is imprisoned, condemned to death, and sees his daughter die, but in other respects the author's intention was carried out. Worcester is "Blanchi dans la droiture & la fidélité" (II, 2). He speaks as boldly to his sovereign as the Aga speaks to his in *Mahomet Second,* and he recalls the fate of Edward's father as the Aga recalls the prowess of Mahomet's predecessors, but, while the Aga calls to battle, Worcester works for peace, sacrificing the interests of his own family in order that Edward may keep his word and do the will of "l'Etat assemblé." He rejects suicide as "le destin d'un lâche" and expresses his firm belief in immortality.

Arondel is equally incorruptible, but he has a different opinion about suicide and about his duty to his country. A great lord, descended from kings, he finds his independence suppressed at the English court and seeks more primitive conditions at the Norwegian, but he returns to his country when he uncovers a plot and acts boldly and promptly when he stabs Wolfax. Like Worcester he believes in immortality (IV, 7):

> Dans cette nuit d'erreurs la vie est un sommeil,
> La mort conduit au jour, & j'aspire au réveil.

These two men and Eugénie, who sacrifices her love and the chance of becoming queen to her patriotic and filial duty, are opposed by haughty and boastful Alzonde and by hypocritical Wolfax, both of whom are devoid of moral sense and are resolved to betray each other as soon as their common purpose is accomplished. Between the two parties is Edward, deeply in love, yet willing to threaten the Countess with her father's death, longing for conquest in Scotland and across the sea, contemptuous of civilian authority (I, 6):

> Quelle est donc la Patrie? Et le brave Soldat,
> Le Vainqueur, le Héros, ne sont-ils point l'Etat?
> Quoi! d'obscurs Sénateurs, que l'orgueil seul inspire,
> Sous le titre imposant de zèle pour l'Empire,
> Croiront-ils à leur gré, du sein de leur repos,
> Permettre ou retarder la course des Héros? . . .
> Je n'examine point ce que doit applaudir
> Un Peuple audacieux, mais fait pour obéïr.

We hear that he is a hero, but in the play he is deceived by Wolfax and

Alzonde, fails to appreciate Worcester, and gives no evidence of statesman-
ship. One could hardly imagine that he was one of England's distinguished
rulers.

The only approach to local color lies in the remarks that in Scotland one
is never a " tranquille esclave " and that the English, a people of heroes,
are not satisfied to accept the limits assigned them by nature, have the
ideal " D'un Peuple toujours libre, & d'un Roi citoyen," and, if this is not
respected, murmur today and are avenged tomorrow.[37]

There are several peculiarities about the plot. How can Alzonde linger
at the English court without being recognized? How does she manage to
poison Eugénie while little more than a hundred lines are being recited?
Why does the discovery of her identity convince her that she must die?
How is it that crafty Wolfax allows an incriminating document to fall into
Worcester's hands? Why are Arondel and Worcester not searched when
they are arrested?

Still more unusual in a classical tragedy than this lack of explanation is
the scene in which murder is committed before the eyes of the spectators.
The author asserts that it is a " spectacle offert en France pour la premiere
fois." He says that he defends it, not by the example of the English stage,
but by Corneille's interpretation [38] of Horace's maxim:

> La maxime de ne point ensanglanter la Scène, ne doit s'entendre que des actions
> hors de la Justice ou de l'humanité: Médée égorgeant publiquement ses Enfans,
> révolteroit la Nature, & ne produiroit que de l'horreur; mais la mort d'un scelérat,
> en offrant avec terreur le châtiment du crime, satisfait le Spectateur.

As a step towards the usage of Romantic tragedy, Gresset's scene is
worth quoting: [39]

> Wolfax: Holà, Gardes, à moi! Saisissez-les tous deux.
> Arondel (*frappant Wolfax du poignard qu'il tenoit encore*) :
>   Voilà ton dernier crime; expire, malheureux.
>   (*Il jette le poignard.*)
> (*Aux Gardes*) Faites votre devoir; je suis prêt à vous suivre;
>   Vous vivrez, cher Worcestre, ou je cesse de vivre.
>   (*On l'emmene.*)

This scene is said to have been applauded, but it did not bring the
tragedy much success. Acted first on Jan. 22, 1740, it is thought to have

---

[37] I, 4, 6.

[38] Gresset cites Corneille's *Discours*. The passage to which he refers is found in
the Marty-Laveaux edition, I, 78. Brenner (*op. cit.*, p. 229) must have read Gresset
hurriedly, for he writes that he justifies his scene by citing " l'assassinat par Médée
de ses propres enfants sur la scène grecque."

[39] IV, 8.

been played only nine times.[40] Le Blanc,[41] writing at the end of the month, implies that there were even fewer performances:

> C'est avec quelques beaux vers une aussi mauvaise Tragédie que j'en aïe encor vu de ma vie. Aussi malgré les Chaunes & les Picquigny qui la protégent, la Piéce est tombé [sic] & ils ont beau dire que c'est un chef d'œuvre[;] personne ne veut l'aller voir.

Raynal,[42] however, expressed a very different opinion, finding in the play the boldness and sublimity of Corneille as well as the grace and sweetness of Racine, though he admitted that the action languishes, that some of the situations are peculiar, that verisimilitude is not always respected, and that the style is too sententious.

When Gresset sent Voltaire a copy of his tragedy, he received a letter of thanks, dated March 28, that praised the murder scene. A few days later Voltaire found in the play an English manner that did not displease him, but on April 25 he described it as "une déclamation vide d'intérêt." [43] La Harpe [44] went into greater detail. The tragedy is a "roman, sans vraisemblance, sans intérêt, sans aucune entente du théâtre." Alzonde would have been recognized, Edward is a dupe, the love theme is cold, Worcester is a "moraliste dissertateur." He admires the murder scene, but he considers it placed too near the end of the play. He admits that some passages are well written and that the style has "noblesse," but he finds it "sec & glacé" and attributes whatever success the tragedy had to French interest in England. That he read the play carelessly is shown by his failure to understand why Worcester refused to allow his daughter to marry the king and by his asserting that a "traité sur le suicide . . . remplit la principale scène du quatrième acte," though it really takes up scarcely a fourth of it.

He overlooked the historical importance of the tragedy in that it is the first of its century to allow murder to be committed on the stage and the first in which an English theme is derived from other than Tudor history. In this last respect it is a forerunner of La Harpe's own *Comte de Warwick* and of de Belloy's *Siège de Calais* and *Pierre le Cruel*, in which Edward III or the Black Prince appears. The play deserved, too, less censure than it received from him, from Voltaire, and from Le Blanc. Worcester, Arondel,

---

[40] So states Mouhy, *Tablettes*, p. 80. Joannidès follows him, as the *Registres* for the months of 1740 that preceded Easter are lost. The *Mercure* for March and April, 1740, states that the tragedy was acted at court on March 3. It shows that Grandval played Edward; Dufresne, Arondel; Sarrazin, Worcester; Legrand, Wolfax; la Dumesnil, Alzonde; la Gaussin, Eugénie.

[41] Monod-Cassidy, *op. cit.*, p. 348.

[42] *Cor.*, I, 116-7.

[43] Moland, XXXV, 402-6, 409, 423.

[44] *Op. cit.*, X, 303.

and Wolfax are effective characters, the second act and the fourth are striking, and the style, though often over sententious, is superior to that of many tragedies of its day. The chief fault lies in the character and function of Alzonde, whose irritating and declamatory rôle gives an impression of melodrama and interferes with the effect that would have been produced without her by Arondel and Worcester.

The second of these plays is still more revolutionary in character, introducing methods that were to be adopted after a considerable interval by many dramatists. The production in question is SILVIE,[45] " en Prose et en un acte," by an obscure author, Paul Landois, who corresponded with Diderot and contributed to the *Encyclopédie*.[46] The *Biographie générale* hails him as the inventor of the " genre bâtard " developed by La Chaussée, Diderot, and Beaumarchais. Gaiffe [47] declares that Diderot's whole dramatic theory is found in *Silvie*, a play mentioned by Diderot himself as a model.[48] Lanson [49] admits that Diderot considered Landois a precursor, but he claims that *Silvie* might never have been written if it had not been for certain productions of La Chaussée. The latter, however, had composed no tragedy in prose. But Landois did not invent the prose tragedy. It had been attempted in the middle of the seventeenth century, long abandoned, then revived by La Motte, who had defended it in theory and had written an *Œdipe* in prose. As for the reduction to a single act, a few tragedies of this kind were written in the seventeenth century, but they always formed part of a longer play. One example had been supplied as recently as 1729 by Dumas d'Aigueberre in his *Trois Spectacles*, where one of the acts is a miniature tragedy. What one may say of Landois is that he was the first writer of his century to persuade the actors of the Comédie Française to attempt a tragedy in prose, to accept a tragedy in one act that was not associated with plays in other *genres*, and that he was the first author to select for a tragedy middle-class characters engaged in the occupations of middle-class life. While La Chaussée was making comedy approach tragedy, Landois was bringing tragedy closer to comedy. One may well ask whether he was inspired by the example of such English plays as Lillo's *London Merchant*, though this play was not translated into French until 1748, but there is no evidence on which such a conclusion can be based.

To make his tragedy palatable, Landois wrote a dramatic prologue, as

---

[45] Paris, Prault fils, 1742, 8°. In *Soleinne*, no. 1855, it is listed as a " Tragédie (bourgeoise)." The latter word is found, not in the printed title, but in the prologue and in the *Registres*.
[46] *Œuvres complètes de Diderot*, Assézat edition, VII, 119, and XIX, 432-8.
[47] *Etude sur le Drame en France au XVIIIe siècle*, Paris, Colin, 1910, pp. 33-4.
[48] *Op. cit.*, VII, 119.
[49] *Nivelle de La Chaussée*, Paris, 1903, p. 276.

Palaprat had done for the *Grondeur*. It consists of three prose scenes spoken by the Autheur and the Commandeur, who favor the enterprise, the Marquis, who keeps an open mind, the empty-headed Chevalier and stupid Mr Grosset, who oppose all novelties. It is pointed out that a tragedy in one act and in prose cannot succeed, and the author is criticized because his characters speak only of their own affairs, calling things by their names,[50] and talking of drinking, eating, clothes, and furniture instead of uttering moral commonplaces and " rodomontades heroïques." The play is said to be unlike the usual tragedy in which, according to Mr Grosset,

> Vous voyez un Héros s'avancer gravement du fond du Théatre; de l'autre côté, une Princesse qui pleure. On est tout d'un coup ému. Vous entendez qu'il lui adresse la parole avec poids & mesure; & la Princesse lui répond de même des choses, dont je ne me souviens plus. . . . Et puis, viennent ces maximes, ces rêves, ces beaux traits de morale, ces portraits. . . . C'est presque toujours de même. Oh! vous avez beau dire, votre Prose ne dit point les choses comme cela.

The Autheur would not banish heroes, but he would select characters whose lives have some relation to those of the spectators. He expresses the hope that one may find for the tragic stage " parmi les gens de qualité, les Personnages comiques les plus ridicules," but no such character appears in the one-act play that is introduced by this prologue.

" Cette piece est tirée du Roman des Illustres Françoises," [51] one written by Robert Challes and published in 1713 and in 1722. It was reprinted in reduced form in the *Bibliothèque universelle des romans* for April, 1776, Vol. II. In this novel Des Francs, Des Ronais, and others relate anecdotes. Des Francs tells of his marriage to Silvie, of her committing adultery, retiring to a convent, and dying. Des Francs learns that his rival, Gallouin, had bewitched a collar belonging to Silvie in such a way that she had become unfaithful to her husband and that, when the collar was removed, she had been horrified by her conduct. Gallouin had drugged the servants to prevent their interfering with his plans. For a while Des Francs had shut up his wife in a wretched room, had deprived her of her jewels, and had given her a miserable costume.

Landois omitted the use of magic, administered the drug to Silvie instead of her servants, prevented adultery, caused the would-be ravisher to die rather than the heroine, and gave the play a happy ending.[52] He followed

---

[50] " Le matin n'est point le blond Phœbus qui va sur son char lumineux fournir sa brillante carriere; c'est tout uniment le matin." It is true, of course, that the *style noble* was employed in eighteenth-century tragedy, but not to this extent. Landois seems in this instance to be thinking of tragedies written under Senecan influence in the sixteenth century and the early seventeenth. Théophile, though he used similar conceits himself, had protested against this particular use of mythology (cf. my article in *MP*, XXI (1923), 1-6), and Scarron had satirized it at the beginning of his *Roman comique*.

[51] *Bib. du th. fr.*, III, 193. Cf. Mouhy, *Tablettes*.

[52] Des Francs prepares a room for Silvie and informs Des Ronais that, coming

French classical usage in that he had a small cast, emphasized the emotions of his leading characters rather than events, preserved the unities, employed preparation and suspense, admitted no comic element, and reached the solution only at the end of the tragedy. On the other hand, he not only wrote in prose and limited himself to a single act, but he took his subject from a novel of contemporary French life. His three important characters are bourgeois. There are, as he states, references to food, to clothes, and to the furnishings of a room. The events are those that could readily occur in the society in which the author lived.

The chief emphasis is laid on Des Francs, who is torn between his love for his wife and his desire to have revenge for her supposed adultery. His motivation is that of Voltaire's Herod or Orosmane except that he has no one to urge him to vengeance. He is agitated and intense while he makes plans for torture or death that he cannot carry out:

Des Francs: Tu vas perir . . . Silvie.
Silvie: Tu crois que je vis pour un autre, & semble frémir du coup?
Des Francs: Tien, épargne m'en l'horreur.
Silvie: Ah donne.
Des Francs: Silvie . . . Non, s'il te sert, que ce soit pour percer le cœur d'un desesperé. Hé bien oui, je t'adore. . . . Que ce sincere aveu que te fait mon cœur, ranime la cruauté du tien. Il est encore des degrez pour sa barbarie. Tu ne m'as pas dit que tu l'aimes, . . . il te trouvoit belle?

There is less variety in the heroine's rôle, that of a faithful and bewildered wife who would not live without her husband's love. Des Ronais serves chiefly in the exposition and in the dénouement, which he brings about by reporting Galouïn's confession, received by him as a result of Des Francs's asking him to seek the villain's confidence.

The setting, praised by Diderot,[53] is of special interest as it serves to

---

unexpectedly to his country house the night before, he had found his wife with Galouïn, who had fled when he drew his hunting knife. Des Ronais is surprised since Galouïn had left the house with him after they had supped there on the previous evening. Des Francs replies that he discovered Galouïn's coat with compromising letters in the pockets, that he questioned the maid, and that he found his wife pretending to be asleep. He had removed her collar as proof of his visit. Des Ronais is not convinced of Silvie's guilt, wishes to see her, but is sent away by his host. A servant reports that it is hard to awaken her mistress. Presently she appears, says she is still sleepy, and asks why her husband seems sad. He takes her jewels and asks for her collar, then declares that he has it and condemns her to live in this cheerless room and in the garments of a beggar. She cannot understand his attitude until he shows her Galouïn's coat and accuses her of adultery. She insists that she is innocent, that she dislikes Galouïn, and that she has received him only because her husband has asked her to do so. He bids her choose between poison and his knife, but, when she asks for the quickest form of death, he admits that he loves her and starts to commit suicide. She proposes that they die together. Des Ronais enters with the information that Galouïn has died of a wound he received from Des Francs and that, before his death, he confessed that he had bribed Silvie's maid to drug her mistress and that only the return of Des Francs had prevented him from accomplishing his purpose. Des Francs asks pardon of Silvie and is forgiven.
   [53] Loc. cit. The actors set aside 500 fr. to pay for it.

emphasize the husband's cruelty. At the end of the play it has a symbolic meaning. The stage represents a room with bare walls and a table on which are placed a light, a pitcher, and a loaf of bread. One sees, too, " un habit d'homme & une mauvaise robbe de femme." A mirror is brought in so that Silvie may see her expression and feel horror over her crime. An armchair appears as in many tragedies. There is a container for poison that may not have been unfamiliar to the audience, but a hunting knife is substituted for the usual dagger or sword. When peace is made and Des Francs calls attention to " l'horreur de ce lieu," Des Ronais's reply, " Sortons-en," would have been enough for a more modern audience, but Landois felt obliged to add, " oublions ce qui s'y est passé. Puissiez-vous l'un & l'autre ne vous en jamais souvenir." Despite traces such as this of older usage, it must be admitted that Landois made in this little play a greater effort to renovate tragedy than Voltaire or any of his contemporaries had attempted.

Silvie had the fate of reforms for which the public is not ready. It was played only twice, Aug. 17 and 19, 1741.[54] On Sept. 15 Le Blanc[55] wrote about

une Tragédie Bourgeoise en Prose & en un acte, dont il ne faut parler que comme de ces Monstres qui paroissent de tems en tems, & dont le succès a répondu au ridicule de l'entreprise.

Eight years later Collé[56] was willing to consider acceptable a tragedy like " Desfrans et Silvie," provided it contained no jests or comic scenes. But, while the play may have influenced Diderot and other authors of *drames*, it was overlooked by such critics as Voltaire and La Harpe as well as by many who have followed them.

Much less revolutionary was Jean-Baptiste Robert Boistel d'Welles, a " Trésorier de France de la Généralité d'Amiens," whose chief claim to originality lies in the fact that, after having his first tragedy performed, he waited twenty-one years before the second and last appeared on the stage. A somewhat longer interval might have separated them if the actors had been more ready to receive his ANTOINE ET CLÉOPÂTRE,[57] of which the abbé Le Blanc wrote[58] that they had rejected a

---

[54] It was given the first time with two new plays in one act, *le Bal de Passy* and *la Belle Orgueilleuse*; the second time, with the latter and an older one-act play, *le Fat puni*. As I find mentioned in the *Registres* "parts d'auteurs," I conclude that each of the three authors of new plays received a share in the receipts, and that Landois earned from the first forty-two francs; from the second, twenty-nine. Grandval and la Gaussin, who acted on both days, may well have had in *Silvie* the rôles of husband and wife.

[55] Monod-Cassidy, *op. cit.*, pp. 366-7.

[56] *Journal*, 1807, I, 62.

[57] Paris, Prault père, 1741, 8°. Approbation, signed by Crébillon, March 4. Dedicated to Mgr. Orry, " Controlleur General des Finances." Republished in the author's *Œuvres*, Amiens, Caron fils, 1782, 8°.

[58] Monod-Cassidy, *op. cit.*, p. 356.

Cléopatre que j'ai entendüe. Je ne crois pas qu'ils ayent grand tort & a quelques vers près qui sont beaux, je ne pense pas qu'elle vaille celle de La Chapelle. La Piece est d'un jeune Picard nommé Boitel.

This was written on Jan. 4, 1741, but the tragedy was accepted later in the year and was acted on Nov. 6, when it was both applauded and hissed.[59] Le Blanc claimed that the author had borrowed "plusieurs traits" from La Chapelle's *Cléopâtre* and from "Antoine & Cléopatre Tragédie du Poëte Anglois Dryden." But Plutarch's *Antony* is the author's main source, though he may have received a few suggestions from La Chapelle.[60] As for Dryden's *All for Love*, the play to which Le Blanc refers, there is no evidence that Boistel had seen it, for the similarities that Le Blanc may have had in mind can be better explained by Boistel's imitation of Plutarch and La Chapelle.

Boistel's chief innovations are found in the introduction of Antony's son by Octavia, the selection of Herod as a minor character, the confrontation of Antony and Octavius, the fact that Cleopatra dies before her lover, and the choice of the place represented. Egyptian tombs, already seen in La Grange-Chancel's *Amasis*, must have made an impressive setting, emphasized by the fact that the two principal characters apostrophize them. As they are supposed to lie between the two camps, they readily serve for the meeting of the rival leaders while retaining their historical function of supplying shelter for the last moments of the hero and heroine.[61]

---

[59] *Ibid.*, pp. 371-3.

[60] The introduction of Octavia's son and his efforts to persuade Antony to return to his mother may have been suggested by Octavia's rôle in the earlier tragedy. The fifth act resembles La Chapelle's fourth. In both Antony, disarmed, enters with a group of Romans, asks about Cleopatra, is told of her death, and exclaims, "Cléopâtre n'est plus." In both Eros, requested by Antony to kill him, asks his master to turn away his face and then commits suicide. For Eros Dryden substitutes Ventidius.

[61] Julius, son of Antony by Octavia, has come to Egypt to represent his mother and is advised by Herod to allow Eros to select the proper moment for him to make his plea. Antony, moved by the threats of his soldiers, has agreed to discuss with Octavius terms of peace. He has selected the tombs of Egyptian kings as the place of meeting. He learns that Cleopatra has come there to die, but that her love for him induces her to live. When he meets Octavius, he urges him to restore Roman liberty, but is assured that Rome needs a strong ruler, or two strong rulers. They are about to divide the territory under Roman domination when Octavius insists that Antony must give up Cleopatra. As Antony refuses to do so, the conference breaks up. When Cleopatra hears about it, she offers to surrender to the Roman senate, but Antony prepares for battle. He agrees to see the supposed son of Ventidius, who pleads for Octavia, makes himself known as Antony's son, and persuades his father to see Octavius again. When, however, Cleopatra proposes to go away in her boats, Antony refuses to be separated from her and repudiates Octavia upon her brother's arrival. He declares that Cleopatra is his wife and threatens to make the senate kneel before her. When the news of this declaration reaches Antony's soldiers, many desert to Octavius. Herod proposes to Antony to put Cleopatra to death and is dismissed from his service. Cleopatra hears that Antony has fought with some success, but that his son has been killed by his side and his army has gone over to Octavius. She then enters the tombs to die. Told of her death, Antony calls her name, gets no reply, and asks Eros to kill him. Eros kills himself. Antony seizes the sword his attendant has dropped and commits suicide.

Antony is described by Herod as " Voluptueux outré, guerrier infatigable . . . , toujours plus grand que sage " (I, 1). His love of Cleopatra prevents his coming to terms with Octavius, causes him to repudiate Octavia, and makes him lose his soldiers. Only paternal affection causes him to waver momentarily in his devotion to the queen. We are told of his prowess in battle, but, when he speaks, he gives us little impression of daring. Octavius is called (I, 1) " souple, adroit " and is said to be

> Plus grand homme d'Etat, que héros dans la guerre.

Brought together in II, 2, the leaders begin, as Corneille might have had them do, a discussion concerning the relative merits of freedom and dictatorial government:

> Ant.: Rendons Rome à ses droits; rendons-lui sa puissance;
> Le consul au Sénat, au peuple le tribun,
> La liberté par tout, & la vie à chacun.
> Oct.: Seigneur, vous vous trompez sur l'intérêt de Rome;
> Au dessus de sa tête elle a besoin d'un homme. . . .
> Pour s'assûrer la paix, Rome demande un maître.

But soon Antony proposes that Rome and her possessions be divided between them, and the political argument degenerates into a personal one, as to whether or not Antony will give up Cleopatra.

To the queen is assigned her reputation for beauty and for power over Antony, but we hear nothing of her relations with other men. She is presented as a self-sacrificing person, ready to give herself up to the Roman senate, to go into exile, or to kill herself in order not to endanger Antony. No attempt is made to reconcile her noble conduct with her flight from Actium, though Antony's defeat there is mentioned. The only other feminine rôle is that of Iras, a confidant. Eros is given importance as an adviser to Julius and as, up to his heroic death, a faithful attendant upon Antony. Herod is, as Le Blanc remarks, totally useless. He keeps his reputation for cruelty when he proposes to put Cleopatra to death, an offer that induces Antony to call him the " Barbare & détestable époux de Mariamne " (IV, 6). Julius is presented as young and naïve, anxious to defend his mother, but admiring Cleopatra's courage in spite of himself.[62]

Le Blanc [63] admitted that there are fine passages in the play and that the author had a turn for verse, but he held that he had not learned how to construct a tragedy, that " il a manqué absolument la reconnoissance du Pere & du Fils," and that Act IV " se passe en discours quand il est ques-

---

[62] When he says to her (IV, 3), " Reine, que de vertus ma surprise contemple," Boistel may be imitating *Pompée*, v. 1072, " O ciel! que de vertus vous me faites haïr! " Le Blanc calls him Fulvius, which may have been his name when the tragedy was acted, though his mother is Octavia, not Fulvia.

[63] Monod-Cassidy, *op. cit.*, pp. 356, 370-2.

tion d'agir." This last criticism could have been made also about the third act, and attention might well have been called to the fact that the exposition is assigned chiefly to minor characters.

Le Blanc found the acting unsatisfactory except that of Sarrazin, who played Herod.[64] Boistel stated in his dedication that he would not have published his tragedy except for the " succès flatteur d'une seconde représentation." Like his hero, he was misled by this momentary success, for his play had but six productions, November 6 to 18. In 1750 Collé[65] remembered it as a feeble tragedy, badly constructed and uninteresting, but he admired the scene between Antony and Octavius and, as he thought that the verse predicted a poet, he was surprised that Boistel had not composed a second tragedy.

He had to wait twelve more years before Boistel did what he had expected him to do and produced Irène ou l'Innocence reconnue.[66] This tragedy is concerned with events that are supposed to take place while a Comnenus was on the throne of Constantinople. Bachaumont[67] thought the time that of Charlemagne; Grimm,[68] that of Alexis Comnenus. It seems more probable that the emperor of the tragedy was Manuel Comnenus, whose first queen came from western Europe and took the name of Irene. It is quite possible, however, that Boistel had no historical persons in mind, merely such characteristic names as Comnenus, Constantine, Irene, and Courtenay.

The plot and the sub-title suggest a relationship with Cériziers's novel, *Innocence reconnuë en la personne de S. Geneviève de Brabant,* or with one of several plays derived from it.[69] We meet again the falsely accused wife who escapes the death to which she has been condemned for supposed adultery, her living long in a cave, her meeting her husband, her vindication, and the punishment of the man who has slandered her for fear that she would reveal his efforts to seduce her. Boistel also employed the familiar story of children exchanged by a statesman in order that he might put his son on the throne, one found in La Chazette's *Dom Ramir* and approximately in Thibouville's *Thélamire.* The statesman's murdering his son when he seeks to kill another youth recalls a situation in La Grange-

[64] The title-rôles were taken by Grandval and la Gaussin. The actors set aside 754 fr. for the expenses of the productions. The author's share in the receipts was 401 fr.

[65] *Journal,* 1807, I, 206-7.

[66] Published in the author's *Œuvres,* Amiens, J. B. Caron fils, 1782, 8°. The author was at work on it as early as 1758, for in that year the *Almanach des Spectacles* declares that he " travaille à la Tragédie d'Irene."

[67] *Mémoires secrets,* XVI, 163.

[68] *Cor.,* V, 186.

[69] Cf. my *History,* Part III, p. 420, Part IV, p. 282. Collé, *Journal historique* (edition Van Bever, Paris, 1911), pp. 342-5, declares that the " fond est le même que celuy d'Adèle," that is, La Place's *Adèle de Ponthieu,* but there is too little resemblance between the two tragedies for one to be regarded as the source of the other.

Chancel's *Ino et Mélicerte*. The setting on an island before the mouth of a cave used as a residence may have been suggested by Chateaubrun's *Philoctète*, acted in 1755, or by its source in Sophocles. It consequently appears that Boistel displayed little originality despite the fact that he paid slight attention to history[70]

The characters and devices are those of a fairy-tale: an injured and innocent queen, a monstrous prime-minister, an erring and penitent emperor, and his noble son; striking resemblances between fathers and their offspring; a storm of mysterious origin, the *cri du sang*, a happy ending when virtue, though it has appeared to be powerless, triumphs over the rulers of an empire. Maternal devotion, desire for revenge, and ambition are the mainsprings of action. Sexual love counts little, for we never see the girl to whom Constantin is devoted, Irène shows little affection for Comnène, and the emperor is moved by remorse at the end of the play rather than love of his maltreated wife.

Irène is not a patient Griselda. She resents the treatment she has received and longs for vengeance. The impressiveness of her bearing and the keenness of her insight have not been diminished by fifteen years of residence in a cave! The emperor is described as " soupçonneux, crédule, autant qu'impétueux." For many years he has been a tool in the hands of

---

[70] Irène, a princess descended from Hugues Capet, has married Comnène, Emperor of Constantinople. More than fifteen years before the play begins, the prime-minister, Vodemar, after attempting in vain to seduce the empress, accused her of adultery with Courtenay, whose murder, interpreted as suicide, caused her husband to condemn her to death. Vodemar, instead of killing her, allowed her to live in a cave on an island. He substituted his son, Thémir, for her son, Constantin, and brought up the latter as his own. Both young men now love Almérie, who prefers Constantin. The girl is sent away in a boat. Constantin pursues her in another. About the same time Comnène, accompanied by Vodemar, sets sail for Albania, where he is to find a second bride. A storm brings all these persons to Irène's island, though Thémir and Almérie do not appear on the stage. When Irène meets Constantin, she is so strongly drawn to him that she makes herself known, tells her story, and asks him to avenge her, but he replies that Vodemar is his father and cannot have betrayed her. Comnène and Vodemar soon meet Constantin and Irène, who covers her face with a veil. Comnène offers her shelter in Constantinople, seeks to learn her name, objects to her mentioning his former wife, and concludes that she is Almérie. When she hears that Thémir has been rescued, she reveals her identity to Comnène and Vodemar, declaring that she will be protected by her son, but, when she meets Thémir, she is horrified by his resemblance to Vodemar. As she notes, too, that Constantin resembles Comnène, she concludes that the two had been exchanged in infancy. Constantin finds her evidence insufficient. Vodemar tries to placate her by saying that he has obtained her pardon for seeking to murder Comnène and marry Courtenay. She denies that she is guilty and accuses Vodemar of murdering Courtenay and slandering her. She appeals to Comnène and tells him of the boys' exchange. Comnène, insisting on an investigation, makes an appointment with Irène. Vodemar plans to murder him when he visits her cave, but, in the darkness, he mistakes Thémir for the emperor and kills him. He then accuses Constantin of the crime and orders his arrest, but Comnène rescues the prince and shows Vodemar the corpse of his son. In despair Vodemar confesses that he has accused Irène falsely and substituted his son for the prince. He attempts to kill himself, but the emperor intervenes and turns him over to the guards. Comnène will remarry Irène, whom he has divorced.

his prime-minister. He recognizes his error only when the evidence is overwhelming. Vodemar is a villain, whose slight feeling of remorse does not affect his actions. He slanders or murders anyone who opposes his ambition. The fourth character, Constantin, is ineffective in his efforts to help Irène or to rescue his supposed father. He is in the unusual position of a young lover whose beloved we never see.

The action begins in the early morning and ends during the night that follows. It takes place before the entrance to Irène's cavern. An apparent break in linking (V, 2-3) may be explained by what d'Aubignac called *liaison de temps*, for both Vodemar, who leaves the stage, and Irène, who enters, await the visit of Constantin at an appointed time. The author makes use of the supernatural when it is suggested that the storm is sent by God to give the heroine an opportunity to clear herself. He twice introduces recognition: first when Irène reveals her identity to her son; then, more effectively, when she removes her veil in the presence of Comnène and Vodemar, who have mistaken her for Almérie (III, 3):

> Vodemar: De vous seule haï, ce Prince qui vous aime
> Renaît: Tremblez.
> Irene: Méchant, à qui crois-tu parler?
> La main qui te poursuit, se plaît à t'aveugler.
> A mes bouillans transports mon cœur suffit à peine.
> Thémir! Ah, frémissez, reconnoissez Irène.
> (Elle leve son voile.)

These scenes of recognition, the use of suspense late in the play when Vodemar leads us to suspect that he has killed the emperor, sympathy for virtue oppressed and ultimately triumphant, and the unusual nature of the setting may have prevented the complete failure of the tragedy, but they could not long induce the audience to overlook the extraordinary rôle played by chance, the lack of logic in the actions of Irène and Vodemar, and the lack of action in Acts II and IV. Collé, who attended the first performance on Nov. 6, 1762, declares [71] that the first three acts, especially the third, were applauded, but that the last two were "huez." When the second performance was being announced, the actor was not allowed to finish his speech, yet, when it was next given, the play was "portée aux nues," and the author, called for by the audience, came on the stage supported by two actors and almost fainting from delight. It seems unlikely that Collé was among those who applauded, for he considered the events lacking in verisimilitude, the characters forced or foolish, and the style extremely feeble.

Bachaumont [72] notes the absurdity of assembling on a wild island the

[71] *Op. cit.*, pp. 342-5.   [72] *Mémoires secrets*, XVI, 163-4.

chief members of the Byzantine court. He calls the play a " roman mal tissu," but he admits that skill is shown in the first three acts. He attributes the success of the second performance to intrigues and to the acting of la Clairon rather than to the fact that some changes had been made in the text after the play first appeared.

The tragedy may, indeed, have been acted more brilliantly than it deserved. Grimm [73] implies as much when he speaks of la Clairon, who took the rôle of Irène. She was supported by Le Kain as Comnène, Brizard as Vodemar, Molé as Constantin, and la Préville as a confidant, Faustine. But Grimm was not blinded by the acting to the defects of the tragedy. He denounced the author for lack of verisimilitude and common sense, for poor taste, for lack of action, and for platitudes. Though he admitted that certain " vers de sentiment " were applauded, he insisted that the play was more puerile even than de Belloy's *Zelmire* and predicted that it would not last long after the third performance. As a matter of fact, it was acted seven times, Nov. 6 to 20. With it ended the author's brief career as a dramatist. He had succeeded neither in so familiar a subject as that of Antony and Cleopatra nor in so peculiar a theme as that of Irène's rehabilitation. A total of thirteen productions was all that his tragedies received, probably all that they deserved.

[73] *Cor.*, V, 185-7.

CHAPTER XI

TRAGEDIES OF 1745-1749. LINANT, LA PLACE, MAUGER, MME DU BOCCAGE

Twelve new tragedies were acted at the Comédie Française for the first time in this, as in the preceding period of five years. One of them, Morand's *Mégare*, has already been discussed. Four, composed by Marmontel, Crébillon, and Voltaire, will be taken up in the next two chapters. The group shows a conservative reaction in regard to subjects and to form. Except for two tragedies written under English influence and Linant's *Vanda*, all the subjects are ancient, while experiments in presentation appear only in the emphasis laid upon spectacle in Voltaire's *Sémiramis*, in the picturesque setting of La Place's *Venise sauvée*, and in the facts that the latter author once violated the rule for the linking of scenes and allowed, like Gresset, a murder to take place on the stage.

Similar violations of classical usage are allowed in two tragedies acted after the period was over, but included here in order to complete the study of their authors. Mauger, in his *Cosroës* of 1752, exhibits three different scenes, though the localities represented are close together, and La Place, in his *Adèle de Ponthieu* of 1757 allows a villain to be murdered on the stage.

The period is one in which Voltaire began to compose tragedies that were intended to overshadow those with similar subjects by Crébillon, in which the first adaptations of English plays were acted at the Comédie Française, and in which Marmontel began his career as a dramatist. The other new authors were a woman and two disciples of Voltaire, an abbé and a " garde du corps." None of their plays was as successful as those of Voltaire, Crébillon, and Marmontel, but only one of their tragedies played in 1745-9 was, like Morand's *Mégare*, a complete failure. I will discuss the authors in the order in which they began to contribute to the repertory of the Comédie Française.

Voltaire's protégé, Michel Linant,[1] was born at Louviers, or possibly at Rouen, about 1708. His mother is thought to have kept a provincial inn. He became an abbé, was recommended to Voltaire by Cideville and Formont, and, despite his ecclesiastical connections, was soon his disciple. Voltaire referred to him as " le joufflu abbé de Linant, au teint fleuri et au cœur aimable, . . . de minois rond, de croupe rebondie." He praised his judgment, his wit, and his talent, but also noted his stammering and his poor

[1] Cf. Moland, especially Vols. XXXIII-XXXV.

eyesight. He found him lacking in social experience, lazy, conceited, spell-
ing poorly, writing illegibly, and with too little Latin to become a satisfactory
teacher. Nevertheless he secured for him a position as the preceptor of
Mme du Châtelet's son, but not for long. Dismissed, the abbé retired to
Paris, where Voltaire loaned him money through the publisher, Prault fils,
and introduced him to the actress, Mlle Quinault.

Linant wrote a preface to the *Henriade* and published an edition of Voltaire's works. In 1733 he thought of composing a tragedy on Sabinus, a
task that Richer was to accomplish not long afterwards, but Voltaire dissuaded him and proposed instead an Egyptian subject to be dramatized as
Ramessès. After several years he had completed only four acts. He won,
however, three of the Academy's prizes for poetry and, after Voltaire ceased
to be in touch with him, completed two tragedies that were acted at the
Comédie Française. They met with so little success that Voltaire could
say of him after his death in 1749, " les sifflets et la faim l'avaient fait périr."

His first tragedy may have been a revised version of *Ramessès*, as it is
Egyptian in setting and in most of its characters. It is called ALZAÏDE.[2]
The source of the plot is unknown.[3] Linant had learned the classical
requirements of a simple subject, a moral conflict, and a unified plot, but
he had not learned how to portray character, to devise effective scenes, or
compose striking verses. The heroine has been married against her will to a
man who does not love her, yet, when she fails to do what he asks and kill
the man she loves, she feels such remorse after her husband's defeat that
she commits suicide. Zaraès is equally unconvincing. He conspires with

---

[2] Paris, Jacques Clousier, 1746, 8°. Crébillon, who signed the approbation on Jan.
7, thought the public would be pleased to see the play in print. The tragedy is
preceded by an ode to the " Prince de Galles," announcing that " Londre attend son
Héros, l'Ecosse en fait son Maître," but failing to foresee the disaster that awaited
Charles-Edward at Colloden.

[3] In the time of Busiris, King of Egypt, Arabia had revolted. An Egyptian prince,
outraged by the king's cruelty, had given his daughter, Alzaïde, to Zaraès, son of
the Arabian rebel, and had promised to join him in an attack on Busiris. When
Zaraès became king, he invaded Egypt, but he was defeated by Aménophis, nephew
and successor of Busiris. Both Zaraès and his follower, Iphis, were captured and
imprisoned. Alzaïde, who, unknown to her husband, loved Aménophis before her
marriage, has been called to the aid of Zaraès. She persuades Aménophis to spare
him, although he knows that Zaraès has taken advantage of the freedom granted
him to plot against the King of Egypt and to bring in soldiers from Syria. The
people attack the prisoners and kill Iphis, mistaking him for Zaraès, who succeeds
in reaching Alzaïde. He tells her that he has won over enough Egyptian officers
to start a revolution, gives her a dagger, and asks her to stab Aménophis with it.
Surprised while she is saying to herself that she cannot kill the man she loves, she
drops the dagger and rouses the suspicions of Aménophis. He has Zaraès arrested
and recalls the army that he had sent to meet forces that Zaraès had made him
believe to be advancing from Syria. He questions the captive, mistaking him for
Iphis, shows that he loves Alzaïde, but allows her to depart with him. Zaraès
rejoins his comrades and starts the revolt, but he is defeated and fatally wounded.
He blames Alzaïde for destroying his chance of success by dropping the dagger and
declares that he will punish her by dying in her presence, but she, overcome by
remorse, stabs herself and dies before he does.

18

great cleverness, yet he is so blind to his wife's love of his enemy that he entrusts her with secrets of vital importance to his undertaking. Aménophis, too, though supposed to be an able ruler, yields readily to suggestions both from his officers and from the wife of his enemy.

Egyptian coloring is limited to the names, Memphis and Aménophis, and references to Arabia and Syria as neighboring lands. Nor does the structure redeem the treatment of character and manners. After the exposition and an interview between the heroine and Aménophis, the action begins in the third act with the escape of Zaraès and the incident of the dagger. The use of an overheard monologue is worthy of a farce. The only scenes to win respect are in Act IV, when Zaraès, mistaken for Iphis, defends his policy and regains his freedom. The last act contains reports about actions that take place elsewhere and an abrupt and illogical dénouement.

The *Mercure* for January, 1746, praises the first three acts, but condemns the last two. It is surprising to learn that the tragedy was acted seven times, from Dec. 13, 1745, to Jan. 3, 1746, and that the receipts fell only once below 1000 francs. The credit may belong to la Clairon, who played the heroine.[4] The record was enough to induce the author to make another attempt, but with the dramatization of a more modern and more complex subject.

The story of Vanda, Queen of Poland, had been told in a school play of 1639, in the *Sigismond* of Gillet de la Tessonerie about 1646, and by Jobert in *Balde Reine des Sarmates* about 1650,[5] but there seems to have been no relation between these plays and Linant's VANDA REINE DE POLOGNE,[6] except that the queen's name occurs in two of them and that Poland is the country in which all of them are located. Linant's queen sacrifices herself, not to her gods, but to love. The action occurs at a time when Danes and Hungarians might be supposed to take an interest in the succession to the Polish throne. The source is unknown, unless *Zaïre* suggested the husband's jealousy of his wife's brother.[7]

[4] Her confidant was la Connell. Grandval and Legrand de Belleville probably had the two most important rôles for men. The author earned 813 fr.

[5] Cf. my *History*, Part II, pp. 639-41, 706-9.

[6] Paris, Cailleau, 1751, 8°. Approbation signed by Cahusac, April 16, 1750. *Soleinne*, no. 1864, gives a duodecimo edition of the same place and year, published by Jacques Clousier, who had printed the author's other tragedy.

[7] Prémislas, "Palatin de Sandomir," was promised by the King of Denmark that, if he became a king, he could marry his daughter, Ulrie. As no crown was offered, the king withdrew his promise and proposed a marriage between Ulrie and the King of Poland. To avoid this calamity, Ulrie married Prémislas secretly and fled to Poland with him. There she met her brother, Frédéric, who, driven by rebels from Denmark, has taken the name of Volomir and is supposed to be a Czech. When her husband saw her fall into the arms of the supposed Volomir, he sought to kill her, but her brother placed her under the protection of Vanda, now Queen of Poland. Frédéric, who hopes to marry Vanda, warns his sister that to make known his identity may cost him his life. But the queen loves Prémislas and consults him as

Queen Vanda is autocratic and amorous, eager to have Prémislas obtain a divorce until she is made sure that he loves Ulrie, when suicide becomes her only resource. Ulrie is a devoted and intelligent wife with a highly unfeminine ability to keep a secret. Her brother is a clever politician, who admits that he has bought up a majority of the Polish senate and does not hesitate to endanger his sister's life by insisting that she conceal his identity. Prémislas, who has freed his country of its enemies and endeavored to fight against its queen, is presented chiefly as an extremely ardent and jealous lover.

The plot is constructed with a view to maintaining suspense, but with the result that the situations seem by no means unavoidable, for all Ulrie has to do is to tell Prémislas that Frédéric is her brother. She is kept from doing this until the last scene of the play. Strange, too, is the account of the meeting between the Polish and Hungarian armies, about to fight when Vanda appears and makes such an impression by her beauty that peace is declared and Tabor, the Hungarian leader, commits suicide because the queen refuses to marry him. Yet her charms attract neither Prémislas, whom she would like to marry, nor Frédéric, whose courtship is inspired purely by political considerations.

Apart from the names of Prémislas and Bolestky and the fact that the monarchy is presented as elective, there is no attempt to reproduce Polish manners and customs. The Poles are differentiated from eighteenth-century Frenchmen chiefly by the fact that divorce is legal in " ces heureux climats," as the abbé Linant makes Volomir declare.

The tragedy was acted on May 17, 1747, by the distinguished actresses, la Clairon, who played Vanda, and la Gaussin, who took the rôle of Ulrie; also by Grandval as Prémislas, Rosély as Frédéric, Dubois as Bolestky, and la Lavoy as a confidant, Hernice. It was played subsequently only four times, until May 27. The *avertissement* published with Cailleau's edition states that performances were " assez considérables," [8] but that Linant

---

to whom she should marry. He advises her to be king, herself. He meets Ulrie, who assures him that she has not betrayed him, asks him to keep her secret, and is about to tell him that Volomir is Frédéric, her brother, when she is hurried off to prison. Prémislas wishes to enter the senate chamber in order to kill Volomir, but he is prevented from doing so and is threatened by the senators. Vanda tells him that the only safe place for him is the throne, that he should divorce Ulrie and become king, but the sight of his wife makes him reject the throne and the love of Vanda. The queen puts him in charge of her forces, but he is defeated by those of the senate under Volomir and is besieged in a fort. To save him Vanda agrees to surrender Ulrie to Volomir. When Prémislas hears of this, he sends a captain, Bolestky, to stab Ulrie, but the captain hesitates and is driven off by Volomir, who is about to come to blows with Prémislas when Vanda enters and Ulrie begs her to save " mon epoux & mon frere." Prémislas asks his wife to pardon his jealous conduct. Volomir, who resumes his former name, will reign in Denmark, as the rebels have been subdued. Vanda, in despair over the loss of Prémislas, stabs herself.

[8] At the first performance 827 persons paid admission; subsequently, between 322

withdrew the play in order to correct the text and was about to have it acted again when he died.

These two plays constitute Linant's only claim to consideration as a dramatist. His editor assures us that, among Voltaire's disciples, he was not the one who derived least profit from the master's instructions. As he was an abbé, it would have been hard for him to follow Voltaire in his anticlericalism, nor was he able to reproduce his style. *Zaïre* may have given him a taste for unhistorical plots, as well as for the emphasis he placed in his second tragedy upon jealousy, but Voltaire, whose correspondence gives no evidence that he had seen the tragedies when they were submitted to the actors, cannot be held responsible for their lack of logic or the shortcomings of their characters. One may accept Raynal's verdict [9] in regard to the second tragedy as applying to both, that Linant wrote correctly and understood " passablement " the stage, but that " il n'avait point de coloris, il pensait peu, et manquait de cette chaleur qui fait les poëtes."

Voltaire had another disciple, one who belonged to Linant's generation, but who developed a field that the latter had neglected, though their common guide had shown some interest in it, the field of English drama. It had inspired La Fosse's *Manlius Capitolinus* in 1698, perhaps had influenced Belin's *Mustapha et Zéangir* in 1705. Voltaire's borrowings from it were discussed five chapters back. No work by any of these authors can be called an adaptation of an English play. The first person to make one that was acted at the Comédie Française is La Place.[10]

Born at Calais on March 1, 1707, he was sent, as the son of a Protestant and converted to Catholicism, to be schooled by English Jesuits at Saint-Omer, where he learned to speak the language of his teachers. He became a lawyer, was married in 1733, and addressed a poem to Voltaire in which he referred to himself as his disciple. Established at Paris, he brought out in 1745 a translation of Mrs. Behn's *Oronoko*. In the same year and the four that followed he published eight volumes, entitled *le Théâtre anglois*, that contained translations of ten plays by Shakespeare,[11] of Ben Jonson's *Catiline*, of Otway's *Venice Preserved*, and of plays by Dryden, Rowe, Congreve, and others.[12] Not satisfied with a public of readers, he made for the

---

and 410. The author received 325 fr., considerably less than his first tragedy had earned for him.

[9] *Cor.*, I, 488.

[10] For this author cf. Lillian Cobb, *Pierre-Antoine de La Place, sa vie et son œuvre (1707-93)*, Paris, Boccard, 1928.

[11] *Othello, Richard III, Henry VI, Hamlet, Macbeth, Julius Caesar, Antony and Cleopatra, Cymbeline, Timon, Merry Wives.*

[12] For a complete list cf. Lillian Cobb, *op. cit.*, pp. 53, 211. The bibliography of his other works, including his translation of *Tom Jones*, is given on pp. 203-9.

Comédie Française an adaptation of Otway's play which proved to be the most popular of his contributions to the stage.[13]

The text of his VENISE SAUVÉE[14] is less close to the English than the translation that La Place published later in the same year of *Venice Preserved*, but little originality is shown in the alterations, inspired chiefly by French dramatic regulations in regard to unity and propriety. As the time in Otway's play does not exceed twenty-four hours, La Place found nothing to change in this respect. He selected as his place " le Cours du Rialto " with the " Palais du Sénat dans l'enfoncement." By this choice he was able to show both the conspirators and their enemy, Priuli, but, as he wished to include the senate, he violated *liaison* at the beginning of IV, 2, when " L'intérieur du Théatre s'ouvre. On voit le Doge de Venise, avec Priuli, & quelques Sénateurs." Elsewhere he avoided Otway's sudden shifts of scene. He eliminated the comic theme of Antonio and Aquilina and the final scene in which ghosts appear. Miss Cobb suggests that his having his heroine die before her husband, though illogical, served to concentrate attention at the end of the play upon the two chief characters.

He omitted, not only what is comic in Otway, but what is indecent or trivial, references to religion, and the sight of the scaffold and the wheel. He made other changes in order to produce greater concentration. His attitude towards violence is peculiar. He leaves out the blow that Pedre gives to Jaffier, though he might have excused it by the example of the *Cid* and though he shows on the stage Jaffier's merciful killing of Pedre, as well as his suicide. His is the first tragedy after Gresset's *Edouard III* to make a French audience witness a murder, again one of which the spectators must have approved.

Miss Cobb suggests that, in having the Venetian senate annul Jaffier's marriage, La Place was imitating *Manlius Capitolinus*. Unfortunately for this suggestion, nothing of the kind happens in La Fosse's tragedy, where the heroine's father proposes that her husband should seek a divorce, but he makes no effort to intervene when his son-in-law rejects the proposal. Miss Cobb would have been correct if she had pointed out that in *Venise sauvée*, as in *Manlius*, the father had promised his daughter to another man before she acquired a husband, an addition that gives Priuli better motivation than Otway allows him. A reference to Spanish help in the conspiracy,

---

[13] In addition to the plays mentioned below he wrote two comedies, *l'Epouse à la mode*, acted once in 1760, and *le Veuvage trompeur*, acted four times in 1777; also a tragedy, *Polixène*, published in 1783, but never acted.
[14] Paris, J. Clousier, 1747, 8° and 12°. Approbation, signed by Crébillon, Jan. 11. Republished, Paris, Jorry, 1747, 1758, and 1772; Marseilles, Mossy, 1769; Paris, veuve Duchesne, 1772, 1777; and in the author's *Théâtre*, Paris, Barrois l'aîné, 1782-3. Miss Cobb mentions an edition of 1750. A Dutch translation was published at Utrecht in 1755.

omitted by Otway, was probably derived from Saint-Réal's *Conjuration des Espagnols*, which had been a source for both Otway and La Fosse. There are few other changes except those required when English blank verse is turned into French alexandrines.[15]

La Place's mild improvements were made at the expense of the vigor, passion, and picturesqueness of Otway's play, but it is doubtful whether a faithful translation would have been as successful. It was first performed on Dec. 5, 1746. Jaffier was played by La Noue; Pedre, by Grandval; Priuli, by Sarrazin; Renault, by Legrand; the doge, by Paulin; Belvidéra, by la Gaussin.[16] Rosély introduced the play by a speech in which he declared that, while French tragedy, based on nature, reason, and the proprieties, was the only one that could make live again the taste of Athens and of Rome, authors had also turned to plays of other nations, such as the English, whose theater is " peut-être trop peu connu en France," but can be enjoyed there if it is made more decent and more " vraisemblable."

The play was acted fifteen times, till Jan. 14, 1747, and four times, April 19 to 26, 1749. It was also produced three times in 1751 and twice in 1783. The author's share, received in 1747, in 1749, and in 1751, amounted to 2616 fr. Yet it won no such success as did *Manlius Capitolinus*, which owed much to Otway, but was far less close to *Venice Preserved* than was La Place's tragedy. The difference was that La Fosse had felt free to write a French classical play of his own, while La Place had sacrificed too much of the original without compensating for it by contributing such characteristically French qualities as analysis of motive and unity of impression. To La Place's compatriots, most of whom were unfamiliar with English drama, the play must have seemed, not a naturalized *Venice Preserved*, but an inferior *Manlius Capitolinus*.[17]

---

[15] Jaffier had rescued Belvidéra from the sea, had fallen in love with her, and, as her father, Senator Priuli, had promised her to another man, had eloped with her and married her. Even the fact that she has borne him a son fails to soften the heart of Priuli, who receives Jaffier rudely and has the senate annul his marriage and deprive him of his property. Driven to desperation, Jaffier joins a conspiracy headed by Renault, in which is engaged his devoted friend, Pedre. In order to allay Renault's suspicions, Jaffier puts his wife in his charge as a hostage, but Renault's attempt to seduce her and her husband's manner and appearance make Belvidéra question Jaffier, who, despite the oath he has taken, reveals to her the conspiracy. They inform the doge and the senate on condition that all involved in the plot be pardoned. The conspirators, when arrested, refuse to ask forgiveness and are condemned to death. Belvidéra persuades her father to seek a revision of the sentence, but his appeal is rejected. Jaffier says farewell to his wife, who kills herself. He joins Pedre on his way to the scaffold, learns that the other conspirators have perished, and, in order to save his friend from an ignominious fate, stabs him mortally. He then commits suicide.

[16] Four supernumeraries were employed as conspirators. The troupe provided for the performances 15 wigs.

[17] When he published his play, La Place printed a preface in which he claimed that *Venice Preserved* had been written in 1672-3, instead of nine years later. He then drew the erroneous conclusion that Otway made no use of Saint-Réal, whose

Voltaire [18] is supposed to refer to *Venise sauvée* when he mentions horrible copies of English drama that mistake the stage for a scaffold. Collé,[19] though he considered the tragedy inferior to *Manlius*, wrote in 1764 that it was the only English tragedy that had succeeded in France. La Harpe [20] attributed its temporary success to French interest in things English and to the fact that *Manlius* had not been acted for a long time.[21] He said that, when Le Kain revived La Fosse's tragedy, one felt that *Venise sauvée* was not worth one of its scenes. When La Place's tragedy was revived in 1783, Grimm [22] reported that it failed, though some beauty was found in Acts I and IV. The tolling of the bell that signaled the conspirator's death was received with laughter and jeers, and the dénouement was ineffective despite the play's last line, which he admired:

> Embrassons-nous . . . meurs libre . . . & sois vengé d'un traître.

He considered the work superfluous for actors who had in their repertory *Manlius*, a tragedy that he regarded as more dramatic, constructed with greater regularity, and superior in characterization. He found in it force, " élan," and " verve tragique " that were lacking in *Venise sauvée*.

The initial success of the tragedy induced the author to give it a successor, which he entitled JEANNE D'ANGLETERRE.[23] As he had in 1747 translated Rowe's *Tamerlane*, it is not surprising that he undertook an imitation of his *Lady Jane Grey*. He was obliged to make considerable changes, for so anti-Catholic a tragedy as Rowe's could not have been acted at Paris in 1748. He omitted all references to the difference in religion between Jane and her cousin, Mary Tudor, except in an inconspicuous remark (I, 2) to the effect that Spain and Rome would object to Jane's becoming queen. An offer of pardon, made in both plays, is conditioned in Rowe's upon the lovers' giving up their religion; in La Place's upon the young hero's revealing his father's whereabouts. The evil bishop of the English play disappears from the French.

La Place eliminated five other characters: the Duke and Duchess of Suffolk, the Earl of Sussex, Sir John Gates, and the lieutenant of the Tower. Out of Pembroke, who is a young man in Rowe's play, he made two char-

---

work appeared in 1674. He also referred to his literal translation of Otway that was to be published later in the year.

[18] Moland, III, 254.
[19] *Journal*, 1807, III, 127.
[20] *Op. cit.*, XVI, 349-51.
[21] An error, for *Manlius* had been played nine times in 1744.
[22] *Cor.*, XIII, 320-1.
[23] The MS. is at the Bibliothèque Nationale, f. fr. 25, 475 (T. II); a copy on film, at The Johns Hopkins University. Miss Cobb (*op. cit.*, p. 121), thinking that the play existed only in a scenario at the Comédie Française, made no study of it. Léris declared that it was translated from English, but he did not mention the author or the title of the original.

acters, Pembroke himself and his son Derby,[24] giving to one the name, to the other the age and personality of his model. The rôle that the father plays is not, however, a new creation, for it resembles that of Bishop Gardiner in the older production.

The English tragedy begins just before the death of Edward VI; the French, just after it. Reference is made in both to this young king's leaving his crown to Jane and to Henry VIII's excluding his daughters from the succession. In both Jane protests against becoming queen, but finally gives her consent. In both the news of Edward's death is for a while kept secret. The Tower is the scene of three acts in Rowe's play, of all five in the French. In both Northumberland leaves London, Guilford's rival quarrels with him, turns against him, is captured by him, is spared, and then secures from Mary a pardon for him and Jane. Both plays end just after the execution of Jane and Guilford, but, for Rowe's final scene, in which Pembroke preaches to the bishop, La Place substitutes a dramatic dialogue between Derby and his father:

> Derby: Pour moy!
> Pembroke: Ouy, pour toi seul! . . . ce fut pour toy mon fils,
>   Que je devins coupable.
> Derby: Eh bien, je t'en punis. *il se tuë.*
> Pembroke: Ciel! lorsque sur ma tête éclate la justice,
>   Pouvois-tu me choisir un plus affreux suplice.

La Place made other changes. Jane and Guilford appear on the stage in his first scene, though in the English play the young lover enters in the later part of the first act; the heroine, only in the second. In Rowe the lovers marry; in La Place they do not. The French author adds Northumberland's letter and makes no mention of his death. He gives more importance to Pembroke than Rowe does to the bishop, having him suggest that Northumberland poisoned King Edward and making him seek to marry his son either to Jane or to Mary. He develops the rôle of Derby and has him commit suicide. He adds Guilford's thought of suicide, Jane's intervention, and, perhaps under the influence of *Polyeucte,* his bequeathing Jane to his rival. He distributed his material more evenly among his acts, but, hampered by his efforts to avoid religious controversy, he supplies a much less satisfactory description of the political background. One is left with the impression that Pembroke's intrigues were of greater importance in ending Jane's career than were British ideas of legitimate succession to the throne.[25]

---

[24] This name may have been suggested by La Calprenède's *Jeanne Reyne d'Angleterre,* in which he is the nobleman who informs the heroine of her condemnation; cf. my *History,* Part II, p. 176. No son of the historical Pembroke had this name.

[25] The "Comte de Guilfort" tells Jeanne of Edward's death and declares that the

Jane is presented as deeply devoted to Guilford, brave, and inspired by a high sense of duty, which makes us wonder why she agrees to become queen. In this respect her motivation is less satisfactory than in Rowe, who makes her a martyr to the Protestant cause. La Place, moreover, fails to refer to her learning. Guilford is Jane's lover and Derby's friend. No explanation is given of his supporting so heartily his father's schemes. Derby is more dramatic than either, torn between his love of Jane and his deep friendship for Guilford. His unreasonable anger over Jane's engagement and his indignation at Northumberland's lack of confidence in him are utilized by his father to make him support Mary. He shows his rashness by entering the Tower with insufficient forces, his nobility by his efforts to save his rival and by his suicide when he fails.

Contrasting with these young people are the two fathers, Northumberland and Pembroke, each seeking to make of his son a queen's consort, each suspicious of the other and striving to dominate England. Northumberland's character is not presented in enough detail. He is not seen after the third act, nor is there any indication of his fate. Pembroke becomes, on the contrary, one of the leading characters. He is a scheming hypocrite, willing to marry his son to either Mary or Jane, gaining his ends by bribery and misrepresentation, corrupting his son, betraying Jane, and finally, like the protagonist in Thomas Corneille's *Stilicon*, having all his hopes destroyed by Derby's suicide.

Mary does not appear on the stage, but one gets the impression that she is easily influenced and hardly a person to excite much enthusiasm. How-

---

king has left her his throne. Her stepfather, the duc de Northumberland, will report the death to the people only when she has been invited by the " Pairs au Conseil " to succeed. Jeanne protests that, though Henry VIII had excluded his daughters, now that he is dead their claim to the throne is justified. Guilfort replies that, if she refuses to reign, civil war will break out. When Northumberland, Pembroc, and his son Derby also urge her to become queen, she finally agrees. But Pembroc plays a double game, informing Mary of Edward's death, while pretending to favor her rival. Mary assembles an army. Derby, told by his father that Jeanne loves Guilfort, questions them, learns of their engagement, threatens Guilfort, and persuades Jeanne to delay her marriage. When Pembroc shows him a paper in which Northumberland threatens to arrest the youth if he shows any signs of deserting Jeanne, Derby becomes so angry that he joins his father in supporting Mary. We hear that courtiers and citizens are deserting Jeanne. To raise troops Northumberland leaves for the north of England. Derby seeks with a few soldiers to capture Jeanne, but he is trapped. As Guilfort rescues him, their former friendship is renewed. Pembroc bribes his way into the Tower, sends Derby to Mary, and hopes that she will marry his son. He pretends affection for Guilfort in the hope of discovering where Northumberland is, but fails in the attempt. Jeanne prevents Guilfort from killing himself by convincing him that her death will follow his. Derby promises to free the lovers at night and persuades Mary to pardon them, but Pembroc has them put to death after Guilfort has refused to tell where his father is and Jeanne has declined to marry Derby. Before going to his death, Guilfort hopes that his rival may win Jeanne. When both have been executed in Derby's presence, the young nobleman rushes in with drawn sword, bitterly reproaches Pembroc, and, to punish him, commits suicide.

ever, as she is undoubtedly the heir to the throne, it must have been difficult
for a French audience to sympathize with persons who were plotting to set
aside her claims. The main conflict is between Mary and Northumberland,
but we are allowed to see nothing of one and too little of the other. The
emphasis is placed on minor figures in this historical drama and the main
forces that decided the question are unsatisfactorily presented. This may
explain the failure of the play, though La Place preferred to attribute it to
the "sourdes menées d'usage pour croiser un succès qu'on croyait avoir
intérêt à prévenir." [26]

The tragedy was acted only once, May 8, 1748.[27] Nearly thirty years
later, in 1777, La Place again presented the play to the actors, calling it
Jeanne Gray. They accepted it, but the absence of Brizard, who was to
take the part of Pembroke or Northumberland, delayed its presentation.
On March 5, 1781, La Place refused to read the tragedy a second time to
the actors and complained of their indifference in regard to his productions.
As they made no further effort to consider the play, La Place published it
in 1781. In so doing he claimed that his plan was entirely new,[28] but his
memory must have failed him, for plot and characters [29] differ only in minor
details from those of *Jeanne d'Angleterre*. Chiefly worthy of note is a
change in the decoration. When Pembroke offers Jane a choice between
marrying Derby and execution, a curtain is raised to show on one side a
throne, on the other a scaffold.[30] No such scenic attraction had been offered
the audience in 1748.

For some years after the failure of this tragedy La Place confined his
literary efforts to translations, then he produced another play,[31] this time
apparently without an English source. His ADÈLE DE PONTHIEU [32] has,

---

[26] Quoted by Miss Cobb, *op. cit.*, p. 129. La Place here gives to *succès* its present
meaning, as he does in IV, 1 of the play, where Derby refuses to applaud a "honteux
succés."

[27] Joannidès and the *Registres* give May 8; the manuscript, May 3. The heroine
was played by la Gaussin. It is probable that the other rôles were taken by Sarrazin, Grandval, La Noue, and Paulin. La Place received 258 fr.

[28] Cf. Miss Cobb, *op. cit.*, pp. 129-30. On the other hand, the *Mémoires secrets*
(XX, 10) quotes him as saying that *Jeanne d'Angleterre* had been "refondue" to
make the new tragedy.

[29] Cf. with my analysis of the earlier play that given of the later by Miss Alfreda
Hill in her *Tudors in French Drama*, Baltimore, Johns Hopkins Press, 1932, pp. 59-60.

[30] Miss Cobb notes that in the final scene Derby seizes his father's dagger in order
to kill himself with it. In *Jeanne d'Angleterre* he uses his own sword. Tastes may
be divided as to which is the more spectacular piece of stage business.

[31] Collé (*Journal*, II, 148) stated in January, 1757, that the play had been shown
to him three years before.

[32] Paris, S. Jorry, 1758, 12° and 8°. Approbation by Crébillon, Nov. 13, 1757.
Republished, The Hague, 1759; Paris, Jorry, 1772, and Ruault, 1777; in the author's
Théâtre, Paris, veuve Duchesne, 1772, and Paris, Barrois l'aîné, 1783. A Dutch
translation was published in 1762; an Italian, in 1776 and 1788. The play is analyzed by Miss Cobb, *op. cit.*, p. 122. She notes the resemblance to *Zaïre* and cites
the remarks of several contemporaries of the author in regard to his tragedy.

however, some resemblance to *Zaïre*. In both tragedies, the scene is laid at Jerusalem in the time of Saint Louis, distinguished French families are mentioned, and a well-meaning Mohammedan who has defeated Christians loves a French woman who has been a slave, and he holds relatives of hers in his power. Moreover, the character of the visir is not unlike that of the emir in Le Blanc's *Aben-Saïd,* and Saurin and Collé pointed out the resemblance between the dénouement and that of the former's *Aménophis.* But for most of the plot none of these authors is responsible. It is far more complex than theirs or than either of the tragedies he had previously composed for the stage.[33]

The only feminine rôle in the play, that of Adèle, would have pleased Mlle de Scudéry, for, in spite of arson, abduction, shipwreck, and nearly ten years of slavery, she preserves her beauty, her loyalty to Renaud, and her attraction for him, for Raymond, and for the young sultan. Despite her apparent gentleness, she does not hesitate to use her dagger upon the villain at the proper moment. Her husband and her father are crusaders ready to sacrifice their lives rather than to urge Lusignan to make peace with the infidels. They are differentiated by the fact that Renaud's confidence in his wife is quickly restored, whereas Roger keeps his doubts up to the last scene of the tragedy. Contrasting with them is the renegade, Raymond, who abducts the heroine, betrays the crusaders, and is false even to his allies.

---

[33] Adèle de Ponthieu is loved by Renaud de Bourbon, nephew of Saint Louis, and by Raymond de Montalban. She has married Renaud, but in his absence has fled from a burning house and has been forced by Raymond to enter a ship and cross the sea. After a shipwreck on the coast of Cyprus, she has been captured by the Sultan of Babylon, has been made a slave, and has suffered from his wife's persecutions. Meledin, the sultan's son, loves her, but his stepmother interferes with his plans and after his father's death Adèle, now called Sophie, has disappeared. Meanwhile Raymond has written a note claiming that her departure with him has been voluntary, so that her husband and her father, Roger, believe her guilty of adultery. These two noblemen are captured when Meledin seizes Jerusalem. At the beginning of the play they appear in chains and are offered freedom if they will persuade Lusignan, who holds Sion, to make peace. This they refuse to do. The visir, Omarzis, has signed a treaty agreeing to the marriage of Meledin and an Egyptian princess, but the young prince prefers Adèle, whom he discovers after she has been hidden by Omarzis. She gives his engagement as a pretext for not marrying him. Raymond, who has turned Mohammedan and holds Joppa, suggests that Renaud and Roger be put to death, but Meledin still hopes they will accept his terms. Omarzis arranges for Adèle to escape with Roger. She recognizes him as her father and discovers that he believes her guilty. Warned by Raymond, Meledin interrupts their conversation and detains Roger. Raymond incites a revolt among the Christians and uses it as an argument for putting Roger and Renaud to death. He accuses them of killing Adèle, Renaud's wife, and in this way makes known to Meledin that she is married. The sultan allows her to meet her husband and convince him of her innocence. She recognizes Raymond and accuses him to Renaud, who denounces him as a traitor. Perceiving that they have seen through his pretense of friendship, Raymond threatens to kill Renaud, but, to save her husband, Adèle gives their enemy a fatal wound. In order to make Meledin suffer, Raymond informs him that Adèle has always loved Renaud. Upon hearing this confession, Roger begs his daughter's pardon for his suspicions. Raymond dies. Meledin frees the captives and presents Adèle to her husband.

The two Mohammedans are favorably presented. The visir helps suppress an insurrection, is kind to Adèle, and insists that his sovereign must respect the treaty with Egypt. Meledin is essentially a warrior, but he is deeply influenced by love and pity. He can be quite ferocious, but he admires the valor of his opponents and is prompt to make amends. In the end he conquers his passion and promotes the happiness of his rival. To him is given an interesting criticism of the crusades. He resents the original invasion of Palestine and fails to understand how crusaders can still consider it inspired by God, since it has led to two centuries of suffering for Christians as well as for Mohammedans.

The play has too many prominent characters and enough material to make a novel. It required a more skillful hand than that of La Place to be impressive. He indulges in several scenes of recognition and allows his heroine to murder a man before the eyes of the audience. Apart from the use of names there is little local color. Religion is not stressed. The sultan can both compliment and condemn his enemies. His praise of Saint Louis must have pleased the audience (II, 3):

> Indomptable Guerrier, Monarque vertueux,
> Qui trahi par le sort, & captif en ces lieux,
> Toujours Roi, toujours Grand dans son malheur extrême,
> Jadis a fait trembler jusqu'à mon Pere même:
> C'est Louis, en un mot!

But he condemns the First Crusade (I, 4):

> Lorsque Bouillon, jadis, couronnant ses exploits,
> Sur ces murs subjugués, fit arborer la Croix;
> Rappelez-vous, Chrétiens, quels excès, quel carnage,
> De vos pieux Guerriers ont signalé la rage!
> Par le fer & le feu nos Temples saccagés;
> Vingt mille Musulmans, en un jour égorgés; . . .

According to Collé, the play was submitted to the actors in September, 1756. They wished to reject it, but the author appealed to the duc de Richelieu, who ordered them to produce it.[34] This they did on April 28, 1757, with la Clairon playing Adèle. It was acted fourteen times, ending its career on December 30.[35] The audiences were fairly large, the receipts on only one occasion fell below 1000 fr., and the author received 1943 fr., 3 s. It would seem that the duke knew the public better than the actors. Shortly after the first performance the *Journal Encyclopédique* [36] ana-

---

[34] Cf. Miss Cobb, *op. cit.*, pp. 121, 123.

[35] Collé (*op. cit.*, II, 179) states that the illness of la Clairon caused La Place to withdraw his play after May 30. He also indicates that on one occasion the receipts rose to 4200 fr., but the *Registres* show that 3211 fr. was the largest amount paid at any performance of the play.

[36] XII (May, 1757), 115-22.

lyzed the tragedy in detail and concluded that, while Raymond's character was too base, the sultan's too weak, and the plot too romantic, yet there were some fine situations, the two scenes of recognition were well introduced and very touching, and the heroine's character was interesting and well sustained. The *Mercure* of June, 1757, admired the scene in which the heroine's innocence is established. Collé admitted that *Adèle* was applauded, but he condemned structure, characterization, and style, pointing out resemblances to *Zaïre* and *Mahomet II*, as well as to *Aménophis*. Grimm [37] could find in the play "ni fonds, ni caractère, ni style." Voltaire knew so little about it that he was obliged to ask Saurin, " Est-ce qu'il y a une *Adèle* ? " [38]

Long communion with Shakespeare and acquaintance with Voltaire could not make a genuine dramatist out of La Place. In composing his plays that were acted he either followed Otway closely except for certain omissions, or imitated Rowe, or, in his most nearly original tragedy, became wildly romantic without having the resources of imagination and style that might have kept his play long in the repertory. His importance is limited to the facts that he was the first Frenchman who can be called a translator of Shakespeare and that he rendered accessible to other playwrights minor English dramatists like Rowe and Thomson.

Little is known of Mauger except that he was born at Paris about 1707, became a " garde du corps," wrote a poem about his fellow guardsmen, one on the *Art de plaire*, a comedy, and three tragedies, only two of which were published. The first of these was AMESTRIS,[39] in which he put Xerxes on the stage, as Du Ryer, Crébillon, and others had done before him. His source is Book IX of Herodotus, in which it is related that, after his defeat in Greece, the king returned to Susa, fell in love with the wife of his brother, Masistes, and, to win her, gave his brother's daughter to his own son, Darius. He then transferred his affections to the younger woman, who became his mistress, whereupon his wife, Amestris, discovering the intrigue, had Masistes's wife mutilated, as she blamed her for her daughter's conduct. Masistes then set out with his children for Bactria, of which province he was governor. He intended to revolt, but his brother sent forces after them and put them to death. Apparently the king's mistress perished with the rest.

Mauger retained Xerxes, Amestris, Masistes, and his daughter, whom he called Egéside, but he made no mention of Darius and kept Masistes's wife

[37] *Cor.*, III, 375.

[38] Moland, XXXIX, 562.

[39] Paris, veuve Delormel et fils, 1748, 8°. Approbation, signed by Crébillon, Nov. 23, 1747. There is a copy at the Arsenal, Th. N. 639. The tragedy is not mentioned by Goldstein in his *Darius, Xerxes und Artaxerxes im Drama der neueren Literaturen*, Leipzig, 1912.

behind the scenes. The horrible tale of mutilation disappears. Amestris merely consents to the arrest of her sister-in-law, who is murdered by the people. Egéside does not become the king's mistress. Xerxes now desires to marry her after divorcing and exiling Amestris. Mauger lays his chief emphasis upon Masistes, who becomes the king's brother-in-law and a much more distinguished warrior than he is reported to have been. He now has to choose between his sister's marital rights and his daughter's ambition. The solution he reaches by killing Egéside and himself is Mauger's invention. By his changes he softened to a certain extent the conduct of the two leading women, removed horror from the tale, and centered his plot round a moral problem, giving unity to the scattered material he derived from Herodotus.[40]

Maziste is described as an elderly warrior who believes that his sister's cause is just. His tragic flaw lies in the fact that he has allowed his wife to keep their daughter at court, where her ambition to reign at all costs has been developed. He shows no emotion over his wife's death and kills his daughter in order to prevent her from dethroning his sister. His strength of character contrasts with the weakness of the king, dominated by his love for Egéside, but seeking to gain his ends by diplomacy rather than by force. Egéside is a cold and beautiful princess, ruled by ambition and employing against her father the power she has over the king. The sympathy that might be felt for Amestris is diminished by her seeking to kill her rival

---

[40] The scene is laid at Ecbatana not long after the expedition against the Greeks, to whom Xerxes is willing to grant peace as he thinks of nothing but his love for Egéside, niece of Queen Amestris and daughter of Maziste, Governor of Bactriana. Xerxes proposes to bribe Maziste by making him king of this district, to divorce and exile Amestris, and to marry Egéside, who, anxious to reign, increases the king's desire by refusing to say that she loves him. But Amestris will not accept divorce without a struggle and prefers death to exile. In Act II Maziste returns to court after conquering Macedonia, Bactriana, and Egypt. He suspects the offer of a kingdom and promises to help his sister, who once saved his life by breaking up a court conspiracy. When Xerxes makes him the offer, he declines it, giving as a pretext his advanced age. When the king insists, he agrees to consider the offer. In Act III a stormy scene between aunt and niece is followed by one in which Maziste bids his daughter renounce Xerxes and retire from court. He then tells the king that to marry the daughter he must destroy the father. Xerxes orders his arrest. In Act IV Amestris agrees to the arrest of Zarès, Egéside's mother, and begs Xerxes not to divorce her. Egéside reports that her mother has been killed, accuses Amestris, and obtains from Xerxes a promise that she will be avenged and made queen. Act V begins with an interview between Maziste and his daughter. The old man declares that his sister is innocent and that his wife deserved her fate. He insists that his daughter leave the court with him, but she refuses to go. Word is brought that Xerxes is waiting at the altar to marry Egéside, who leaves in spite of her father's order. Amestris informs us that her popularity with her subjects has caused them to kill Zarès, that she fears she will herself be put to death, and that she hopes first to destroy her rival. Xerxes again orders the arrest of Maziste, but he learns that, prevented by superior forces from carrying off his daughter, he has plunged a dagger into her breast. Maziste has then stabbed himself. When soldiers bring him in, he blames Xerxes for his love of Egéside and hopes that he will be reunited to Amestris. Filled with remorse, the king seeks to kill himself, but he is prevented by Amestris from doing so.

and consenting to the arrest of her sister-in-law. Except for the passion of Xerxes for Egéside, love is absent from the tragedy.

The most dramatic scenes are II, 4, in which Maziste declines to be bribed; III, 1, 3, 4, in which Egéside meets the queen, then her father, and Maziste gives Xerxes his final answer; and V, 1, in which Maziste attempts for the last time to make his daughter obey him. The tragedy is constructed in the main to accord with classical principles. It is devoid of local color. The author fails to explain why the first order to arrest Maziste is not carried out, to what extent Amestris is to blame for the death of her sister-in-law, or what the future has in store for the king and Amestris.

The play was first acted on July 3, 1747. Sarrazin played Maziste; Grandval, Xerxes; la Dumesnil, Amestris; la Gaultier, Egéside. Legrand, la Lavoy, and la Connell represented the three confidants. It was given nine times in July and twice in December. The author earned 783 fr. Raynal [41] acknowledged its success, though he had little to say in its praise:

Le style de cet ouvrage est naturel, mais faible; le sentiment vrai, mais usé; les situations amenées, mais un peu froides. On peut louer cet ouvrage d'être bien filé, on y doit blâmer les caractères, qui sont tous misérables.

For his second tragedy, acted on Jan. 10, 1748, Mauger selected a more familiar theme, that of Coriolanus. When he published CORIOLAN,[42] he added a long preface in which he upheld the classical principles laid down, as he says, by Aristotle and his commentators, Horace, Boileau, and Pierre Corneille. The last of these is called the " génie le plus élevé que la nature ait peut-être jamais formé." He quotes La Bruyère and refers to *Cinna*, *Phèdre*, *Britannicus*, *Iphigénie*, *Electre*, and *Œdipe*, probably meaning by the last two the tragedies of Crébillon and Voltaire. He mentions *Timocrate* and *Judith* as plays that won great, but only temporary success. He maintains that good taste has existed since the time of the Greeks and that it may be acquired by a careful study of great Greek, Latin, and French writers. He holds that one cannot admire at the same time Corneille and Hardy, J.-B. Rousseau and Ronsard. Drama is in the first rank of literary productions. In great plays " l'ordre, la vraisemblance, la pureté du stile sont joints à la force ou à délicatesse du sentiment." The unities, *liaison*, and the preparation of events are essential. Those who dislike the unity of place should turn to the opera; those who want to describe many events, to the epic. In tragedy style should be elevated; vice should not be opposed to virtue, but vice to vice and virtue to virtue in the manner illustrated by Corneille. Certain minor departures from the rules are allowed the

[41] *Cor.*, I, 72-3. The *Mercure* for June, 1747, also spoke of it as successful.
[42] Amsterdam, Zacharie Chatelain, 1751, 8°, " et se trouve à Paris, chez Ganeau."

great, such, for instance, as Rodrigue's twice visiting the home of Chimène after he has killed her father, but the ordinary dramatist should not be so daring.

Such principles he tried to follow in composing *Coriolan*. He selected a well-known subject from Roman history, one that had been dramatized in France by Hardy, whom he disparages in his preface, by Chapoton, Chevreau, Abeille, and Chaligny. There is no evidence that he imitated any of these authors or Shakespeare. Instead he went directly to Livy and Plutarch, giving to his hero's mother and wife Livy's names, though most of his predecessors had preferred Plutarch's, yet keeping the latter's Valeria.[43] His respect for the unity of place induced him to lay his scene in the Volscian camp before Rome and to cause the death of Coriolanus to take place there. He prepared carefully for this event by showing the jealousy that his hero had excited among the Volscians. He invented a truce accorded the Romans by Coriolanus, his fighting against the Volscians after he had yielded to his mother's plea, and, after he had saved Rome, his surrender to Tullus.[44]

Little attention is paid to the political background, to the eternal struggle between patricians and plebeians. No voice is raised to defend the latter. It is admitted that Coriolanus has been badly treated, but in his mother's eyes he is not justified in turning against his country. Though he is angry with the Romans, now united against him, he does not wish to destroy the city, but he realizes that, if he does not do so, he will betray the Volscians

[43] As Dionysius of Halicarnassus gives Livy's names to the two leading women and also mentions Valeria, his work may be the source, or Mauger may have known the story through some later history of Rome. The names he gives the three women are those used by Chaligny also.

[44] Rome seems about to fall. Tullus, leader of the Volscians, puts Coriolanus in supreme command despite the misgivings of his lieutenants, Junius and Icilius. Coriolanus, who has rejected the proposals of Roman ambassadors and priests, expresses to his confidant his hatred of Rome, especially of the tribunes, and his belief that, when Rome has fallen, he will be put to death by the Volscians. His mother, Véturie, brings his wife, Volumnie, and a Roman lady, Valérie, into the camp, but returns to the city for her grandchildren. Valérie urges Volumnie to influence her husband, but Volumnie fears for his life. She begs him, however, to save his mother, herself, and their children. Coriolanus is sufficiently moved to declare a truce and to agree to raise the siege if Rome will give up her conquests and pay tribute to the Volscians. Véturie now returns alone, as she has not been allowed to bring her grandchildren. She declares that the terms are unacceptable, but that the senate is willing to negotiate. She interviews Tullus, who leaves the decision to Coriolanus, but he denounces Rome. While they are in the midst of their conference, they hear that the Romans have broken the truce and are attacking. Coriolanus defeats them. Junius and Icilius think it is dangerous to leave him in command, but a third officer, Ceson, praises him and Tullus urges all to obey him. Coriolanus is about to attack the city when his mother begs him to kill her with a dagger she offers him. He is so profoundly affected that he promises to save Rome, though it will cost him his life. To keep this promise he joins the Romans, defeats the Volscians, and kills Icilius. Then he gives himself up. His mother and wife refuse to leave him. Tullus is willing to consider his offer of alliance with Rome, but Junius gives him a fatal blow. Dying, he returns to the stage and bids his mother and his wife escape in order to avenge him.

who have befriended him. He offers terms, which the Romans do not accept.
He defeats them when they break the truce. But his mother is too much
for him. He solves his problem by defeating the Volscians, saving the city,
and then, to make amends, giving himself up. He is a melancholy warrior
who sees from the beginning of the play that his own situation is hopeless,
whether Rome is destroyed or saved.

His mother has the patriotism that ancient writers attribute to her, but
she is more violent in the reproof she administers to her son, more firmly
convinced of Rome's ultimate destiny. The hero's wife has a more feminine
rôle. She hesitates between her city and her husband. She is willing to
sacrifice her life, but she never forgets her husband's danger. She is given
a definite function as she obtains the truce, though she leaves to her mother-
in-law the greater honor of inducing Coriolanus to renounce his hostility
to Rome. The author manages to keep both women on the stage in the
last scene of his play, but in so doing he leaves us uncertain as to whether
they succeeded in returning to the city.

The Volscians are represented by Tullus, who conquers his jealousy of
Coriolanus and, even after he has joined the Romans, is willing to leave
his fate to the army; by Ceson, who supports Coriolanus; and by Junius
and Icilius, jealous of his power, anxious to have him deposed from his
high position, ready to charge him with treachery and to bring about his
death.

Most of the play consists of arguments carried on by the Volscians among
themselves or with Coriolanus, or by Coriolanus with his wife and his
mother. The actions to which the discussions lead—the Romans' attack
in violation of the truce, their defeat, Coriolanus's fighting on their side
against the Volscians, and his death—all take place behind the scenes. The
only situation calculated to stir one's blood is in IV, 4, when Véturie enters,
dagger in hand, bids her son kill her with it, and sees him fall at her feet:

> Qui peut te retenir; frappe . . . Tu t'attendris?
> C'en est fait. . . . Dieux puissans! je retrouve mon fils.
>
> C.: Oui! vous le retróuvez; la voix de la nature,
> De ma haine pour Rome etouffe le murmure.
>
> V.: Ainsi Rome est sauvée!
>
> C.:   Oui vous avez vaincu,
> Mais, vous n'en doutez point, votre fils est perdu.

It is difficult, however, to understand why Coriolanus is won over by
the display of a dagger when he has resisted, not only his wife's plea, but
the arguments advanced by his mother at their first meeting. The obvious
scène à faire is thus rendered less impressive than it should have been, while

19

the ending is brought about by a jealous individual rather than as the inevitable result of the tragic hero's actions.

The play was given only five times, Jan. 10 to 20. The hero's mother was played by la Dumesnil; his wife by la Gaussin; Valérie by la Lavoy. It is probable that Sarrazin played Tullus.[45] The troupe provided two "habits à la Romaine" and a helmet for Sarrazin. The author received 505 francs, about two-thirds as much as he had earned from *Amestris*.

Raynal [46] thought that Véturie was a poor imitation of Emilie in *Cinna* and of Cornélie in *la Mort de Pompée*. He considered the first two acts tiresome, the fifth wretched, but he admired the fourth, especially on account of the resemblance he detected between Coriolanus and the Maréchal de Saxe. "On y voit la jalousie relever l'éclat du mérite de Coriolan." However, the play was, on the whole, merely "un assemblage mal dirigé d'amplifications de collége, relevées par quelques maximes détachées de politique."

Mauger's third tragedy may have been his best, though it was the least successful, but it is hard to be sure of it since it survives only in an incomplete manuscript of which many lines have been stricken out, perhaps by the censor, and some inserted in a different hand. The title, COSROËS,[47] suggests that the author had in mind Rotrou's tragedy of the same name, which may well have been a partial source of Mauger's tragedy. The later play tells how the king came to his throne; the earlier how he lost his power.

It is quite likely that he read in d'Herbelot's *Bibliothèque orientale* the accounts of Hormizdas, Buzurge, Baharam, and Khosroes Parviz.[48] According to this work, Hormizdas was instructed in his youth by the sage, Buzurge, reigned over Persia, warred against the Turks, and put many Persian noblemen to death. His general, Baharam, who resembled a "chat sauvage," defeated a large Turkish army, but was slandered by a courtier, who induced Hormizdas to send him feminine utensils for spinning. Outraged, he secured the support of his army, proclaimed as king Prince Khosroes Parviz, who had been exiled, and defeated Hormizdas, whose eyes were put out by the insurgents. Khosroes Parviz came to an understanding with his father and became king officially twelve years later.

Nothing is said by d'Herbelot about a second wife of Hormizdas or about

---

[45] Other members of the cast were Legrand de Belleville, Dubois, Bonneval, Paulin, and Rosély.

[46] *Cor.*, I, 133-4.

[47] Rondel MSS 317 at the Arsenal. A copy on film is at The Johns Hopkins University. The first three acts are complete. A page is missing from the fourth. Many lines in Act V are deleted, and the manuscript breaks off before what was originally the end of the fourth scene. In the *Bib. du th. fr.*, III, 197, the title is given as *Cosroés roy des Perses*.

[48] II, 91-3, and III, 222-7, 476, in the edition of Paris, 1783.

her son. For them Mauger must have turned to Rotrou's play, where he found that a King of Persia was persuaded by his second wife to put her son on the throne at the expense of her stepson, whom she sought to poison, and that the queen was killed in a revolt. Mauger, like Rotrou, laid considerable emphasis on this second wife. He called her son Ormuz, probably because Hormizdas is also called by d'Herbelot Hormouz or Hormuz. He altered d'Herbelot's four important names to Hormisdas, Cosroës, Busurge, and Varame. He had Busurge save the heir to the throne by substituting another child in his place and by pretending that he was dead, possibly in imitation of *Héraclius*. He kept the prince in ignorance of his identity till near the end of the play, made of a slave's robe the insulting gift that the general receives, added the defeat of the Persians by the Romans, the incident of the note brought by a slave, the imprisonment of Busurge and Vindoës, the attempt of Phanor upon the lives of the king and queen, and minor incidents.[49]

[49] Hormisdas, King of Persia, had a son, Cosroës, by his first wife. After her death he married Apamis, who bore him Ormuz and twice attempted to poison Cosroës. Busurge, the prime-minister, witnessed her attempts, pretended that Cosroës was dead, and brought him up as Vindoës, who was supposed to be the son of the king's sister. The queen, fearing Busurge's knowledge of her evil intentions, had him imprisoned for ten years. When her son was about twenty, she persuaded the king to give him equal authority in the army with Varame, a celebrated warrior. The result was that the Persians were defeated by the Romans, but the queen and the king's confidant, Phanor, laid the blame on Varame, accusing him of betraying Ormuz because he was unwilling to share with him credit for a victory. In order further to strengthen her son's position the queen has prevailed upon the king to share his rule with Ormuz and to proclaim him king next day. Vindoës warns her that this will bring disaster, for the people hold Ormuz responsible for the defeat. There is already a report, which Vindoës does not credit, that Cosroës lives. She resents the advice and asks Phanor to watch Vindoës and put an end to his career. Hormisdas assures her that he will punish Varame and, whether Cosroës lives or not, will make Ormuz king. In Act II Varame, after recalling the fate of Busurge and criticizing the king's government, urges Vindoës to take over the royal power and save the country, but Vindoës refuses to violate the laws, fearing that a rebellion will substitute twenty tyrants for one. Hormisdas enters, sends Vindoës out, accuses Varame of the defeat and, when the general replies that Ormuz was responsible for it, deprives him of his command. When Varame has left, he has him presented with the robe of a Roman slave. Vindoës returns to protest and to warn the king that such an act will not be forgiven. Phanor reports that Varame has, with the people's help, fought his way out of the city and that the mob is calling Vindoës to the throne. Hormisdas has Vindoës imprisoned and goes to make sure of the army's loyalty. In Act III, just as Apamis believes she has finally triumphed, she receives a note, written to the king by Busurge and entrusted to a slave. It urges him to spare Vindoës, for he is Cosroës, as all Persia will know next day. Apamis keeps the note, orders the slave killed, and tells Phanor that Vindoës must die before dawn. Her agent replies that only by the king's order can he enter the tower. She bids him incite the people to demand that Vindoës rule, so that Hormisdas will fear him and have him executed. When the king reports that he has been well received by the army, she urges him to do away with Vindoës, but he prefers to humiliate him by having him present when Ormuz is crowned, until he learns from Hydaspe, captain of his guard, that Varame is besieging the city. He then orders the execution of Vindoës and, as Hydaspe protests, he deprives him of his office and entrusts the execution to Phanor. In Act IV the scene shifts to the tower where Busurge awaits the slave's return. Hydaspe, surprised to find him alive, tells him that the rebels have captured the city, which is in flames, have broken open some of the dungeons,

The king claims to have been a warrior of distinction, but he is now completely dominated by his wife and by Phanor. He retains his pride and his duplicity even when he has fled from his palace into the prison. There is no question of his sanity, as there is in Rotrou's play. The queen resembles her prototype in the latter tragedy. No measure is too evil if it will result in the triumph of her son. She poisons the king's mind, slanders Busurge, Vindoës, and Varame, seeks to put to death anyone who may endanger her plans, even the poor slave whose only crime is to carry a note containing an important secret. Her agent, Phanor, resembles her in his slanderous and criminal activities, but he adds to these disloyalty, turning against the royal pair as soon as he sees that the rebels are winning, causing the queen's death and seeking to kill the king. The young prince, Ormuz, is, according to Varame, brave, but utterly incompetent.

The group is opposed by three important characters. Busurge's wisdom guided the king for twenty years. His ten years of imprisonment have by no means embittered him. He pardons Hormisdas, but he advises him to rule no longer. Varame, described by the queen as an " orgueilleux emporté," is a victorious general who sees further triumphs prevented by court intrigue. He resents bitterly the humiliation that is inflicted upon him and never forgives the king, so far as can be determined. He is much less impressed by the idea that kings are sacred than is Vindoës, who, though

have killed the queen, betrayed by Phanor, and are besieging the palace. Busurge begs Hydaspe to discover what has happened to Vindoës and to bring him word. After he has gone, Hormisdas, disguised, enters by a secret passage and meets Busurge, who, thinking him a victim of tyranny, tries to comfort him. Hormisdas recognizes him and makes himself known. Busurge forgives him, but tells him that his only hope is to abdicate and to recognize Cosroës and his right to the throne. When the old man has left by the secret passage, Hormisdas remembers that his grandfather, though imprisoned, returned to power. He thinks it will be wise to recognize Cosroës and to cause trouble between him and Vindoës. Hydaspe and Vindoës enter and mistake the king for Busurge, but he throws off the mantle that conceals his fine clothes and threatens them. Hydaspe says he is powerless, but Vindoës pities him and declares that he has himself taken over the government only because the death of Hormisdas has been reported. He promises to save the king's life. Hormisdas disdains his pity, but asks to be present in the palace when Busurge makes an important announcement. In Act V we are in the throne room of the palace. Varame declares that he has rescued Vindoës and has put him in the place of the dead king. Busurge objects to revolution and gets the grandees to swear they will give the throne to Cosroës. Vindoës reports that he was bringing Hormisdas to the palace when Phanor and his followers seized the king and asked for his death, but that he killed Phanor and placed Hormisdas in the temple of the sun. Busurge announces that Cosroës lives. Vindoës declares that Cosroës will reign. He asks Varame to pardon Hormisdas, but the general refuses and adds that, if he were to do so, the people would not consent.

Here the manuscript breaks off. Vindoës must have been publicly identified as Cosroës. He may have succeeded at once to the throne, or, as in the *Bibliothèque orientale*, he may have allowed his father to continue to be at least the nominal sovereign, while he shared the rule as Ormuz was to have done. The younger prince was probably killed in battle, as Varame refers to two victories he has won. It is also possible that Hormisdas committed suicide, as the defeated king does in Rotrou's tragedy, or was killed by the people, or by Varame, but this last suggestion is improbable, as it would leave unsolved the question of the regicide's punishment.

admired by Varame, does his best to warn Hormisdas and is unwilling to dethrone him. He accepts power only because he thinks the king is dead and knows that Ormuz is unfit to rule. When he hears that Cosroës is alive, he is ready to turn over to him the crown. The scene in which he discovers that he is himself Cosroës is unfortunately lost.

The manners described are those attributed to the Persians before they accepted Mohammedanism. They worship the sun, war with Turks and with Romans, that is, with armies of the Eastern Empire. They are monarchists, whose laws uphold the right of the oldest son to succeed his father. Garments are given as a reward for victory. Slavery is allowed. Near the luxurious court is a prison where men may be placed in dungeons and kept there for many years without knowing what charges have been brought against them.

The exposition takes up the first act and the first two scenes of the second. It is not complete until III, 2, when we first learn that Vindoës is Cosroës. The action begins with the interview between the king and Varame (II, 3), a striking scene, but the unpardonable insult, the presentation of the slave's robe, is unfortunately kept behind the scenes. We do not see the queen after the third act, or Busurge before the fourth and most impressive act, with the contrast it offers between the wise and forgiving minister and the overbearing, foolish, and discredited king. The final act has been so badly mutilated that it is difficult to tell to what extent it was effective. Apparently the public revelation of the elder prince's identity was reserved for the last scene of the play.

Mauger had objected to violations of the unity of place and had respected the regulation strictly in his first two tragedies, but here he gives us three distinct settings: the usual palace room, the prison, and the hall in which the throne is placed and the grandees assemble around it. He sought to avoid criticism by placing the prison close to the palace from which its towers can be seen and with which it is connected by a secret passage. He gives the following directions:

Le théâtre représente le palais d'hormisdas, orné de tout le luxe asiatique, sur les cotés on apperçoit les tours d'une prison d'Etat, suivant l'usage existant parmi les despotes orientaux (Act I). Le théâtre représente une prison qui a été [*corrected to* qui n'a pas été] forcée par les rebelles. Busurge sort d'un cachot placé sur le coté droit de la prison (Act IV). Le théâtre représente le palais dans tout son lustre. au milieu le trône reste vacant. tout autour sont des siéges pour les Grands. Sur les cotés sont des soldats armées . . . le peuple est debout dans l'enfoncement (Act V).

This appeal to the eye, the fourth act, and the portrayal of the leading male characters should have made the play more popular than Mauger's earlier tragedies, but this was not the case. *Cosroës* was acted only on April 20, 1752. There was a large attendance, 1123 persons paying admission.[50] The actors had set aside 400 francs for the expenses of the production and had provided four "habits à la grec" and a "Rozette p^r Mr Paulin," but their efforts were unavailing. It is not known whether they were hissed off the stage, or whether the punishment inflicted upon Hormisdas, however richly deserved, was considered dangerous as an example. Whatever the cause of the failure, it is regrettable, as Mauger, who had shown considerable improvement in his methods, seems to have been discouraged by it from further effort.

A "garde du corps," he was interested in plots that concerned palace intrigues and the fate of distinguished warriors. Maziste, Coriolanus, and Varame are presented as conquerors who oppose the authority of their governments with disastrous consequences to themselves except, probably, in the case of Varame. To them are opposed intriguing courtiers or jealous officers and misguided sovereigns. His most original creation is Cosroës, a prince who, in spite of his efforts to the contrary, replaces his father on the throne, or at least renders him powerless. With the exception of those in *Coriolan*, his important women have few admirable qualities. Sexual love, apart from that of husband and wife, appears only in the infatuation of Xerxes for a woman who shows him no affection. The women in his first play are prominent, but not appealing; in his second they are essential to the plot, but his emphasis is placed on Coriolanus rather than on them; in the third they are only the criminal queen of the first three acts and her confidant. Perhaps Mauger's profession kept him from preparing rôles that would have been more pleasing to the influential women of the troupe, and they avenged themselves by causing his contributions to the repertory to be forgotten.

But they gave no greater fame to a dramatist of their sex, one of the few who lived in the middle of the eighteenth century. Marie-Anne Le Page was born at Rouen in 1710, was married to Fiquet du Boccage, a man of means, and died in 1802. She gained considerable notoriety in her day as a literary figure, composing a *Colombiade* in ten cantos, translating Pope, imitating *Paradise Lost*, and becoming a member of several academies. She knew Voltaire, who called her "la Sapho de Normandie,"[51] and Fontenelle, who observed when he gave the official approbation to the publication of her one tragedy, LES AMAZONES:[52]

[50] The author's share in the receipts was 232 fr.

[51] Moland, XXXVI, 466. For her life cf. Grace Gill-Mark, *Une femme de lettres au XVIIIe siècle, Anne-Marie Du Boccage*, Paris, 1927.

[52] Paris, Mérigot, 1749, 8°. Approbation by Fontenelle, Aug. 10. An Italian translation by Luisa-Bergalli Gozzi, published at Venice in 1756, was reviewed with

j'ai crû que le public verroit avec beaucoup de plaisir les Amazones Guerrieres, si bien représentées par une illustre Amazone du Parnasse.

This remark might lead one to expect a feminist tract, but Mme Du Boccage, far from exalting Amazonian customs, dramatized the triumph of those who adopted a normal way of life. She must have read in Plutarch's *Life of Theseus* that the Athenian hero lured to his boat Antiope, Queen of the Amazons, and carried her off, an act that led to an attack upon Athens by her abandoned subjects. She also could have found there that one of his comrades in another amorous adventure was named Idas. But she constructed a plot that was largely her own, dramatizing the events that led up to the marriage of Theseus and Antiope.

To Theseus is accorded his traditional prowess in war and love. It is he who upholds the usual relations between the sexes, speaks to women as an Athenian gentleman is supposed to do in romantic novels, but overcomes the "sexe foible" when the Amazons meet him in battle. Idas has the rôle of a confidant. There are three kinds of Amazons, one who adheres to her tribal traditions and two who yield to love, with happy consequences for one, suicide for the other.[53]

It is only in the soul of Orithie that a struggle takes place. As queen and priestess she feels that she should be a model Amazon, but her love for Theseus is too strong to be resisted. She orders him to be sacrificed only when she is sure that she cannot win him. Her jealousy of Antiope is strengthened by the facts that she has brought up the girl and has expected her soon to share with her the government of the tribe. But Antiope is a sport in her species. Though she goes to war like other

extensive extracts in the *Journal étranger* of February, 1757, pp. 132-41. The tragedy is briefly analyzed by Mlle Gill-Mark, *op. cit.*, p. 156.

[53] Theseus, King of Athens, has led a band into a country where Scyths and Amazons are at war. Joining the Scyths, he becomes separated from his comrades, falls in love with Antiope when she loses her helmet, and slays two Scyths who are about to kill her. In pursuing her he is captured by Amazons and taken to "Thémiscyre sur les bords du Thermodon," where the scene of the tragedy is laid. Ménalippe, who commands the army of Amazons, urges Queen Orithie to sacrifice Theseus to Mars, but, as the queen, like Antiope, loves the Athenian, she gives him and Idas the freedom of her palace, insists upon consulting an oracle, and confides in Antiope that she will spare Theseus if he loves her. She shows Theseus that she is interested in him and asks Antiope to discover whether her affection is returned, but, when Theseus tells Antiope that he loves her, she cannot resist making known her feeling for him, though she warns him that his life is in danger. Gélon, King of the Scyths, now offers to make peace if he may marry Antiope, but his proposal, though approved by Orithie, is rejected by Antiope. Meanwhile Idas, disguised as an Amazon, slips away and rejoins the Greeks, who rescue Theseus after Orithie, learning from him that he loves her rival, has sent him to be sacrificed. In the fighting that follows Ménalippe kills Idas, mistaking him for Theseus, and reports a victory, but Theseus rallies his men, captures the city, and demands the hand of Antiope, who agrees to marry him. Orithie, overcome by jealousy and realizing that her love has violated the laws of her people, stabs herself and dies after she has left the government to Ménalippe, who threatens to join the Scyths in an attack on Athens and ultimately to rule the world.

Amazons, she quickly falls in love and ends by deserting her people for a foreign hero. Ménalippe, who never wavers in her loyalty to tradition and wields effectively her two-edged axe, despises love, relates with gusto the Amazons' murder of their husbands, and describes her people as follows (II, 5):

> Dès notre tendre Enfance on nous destine aux armes;
> Nos yeux farouches, durs, & stériles de larmes
> Ignorent l'art flateur inventé pour charmer;
> Nous inspirons l'effroi, non le désir d'aimer.
> Nos mains de nos attraits négligeant la parure
> S'occupent sur le fer à forger notre armure.
> Loin de régler nos pas sur des sons cadencés,
> A la course, à la lutte, on les trouve exercés.
> Les Centaures de nous apprirent à conduire
> Les coursiers indomptés, que notre Art sçut réduire.
> La hâche à deux tranchans secondant nos fureurs,
> Des traits de l'ennemi rend nos efforts vainqueurs. . . .
> Si nous nous soumettons aux loix de la nature,
> Ce n'est que pour regner dans la race future,
> Et repeupler ces champs de femmes dont le bras
> Soit libre, généreux, & terrible aux combats.

It is in vain for Theseus to protest against human sacrifice or to point out that, while women rule elsewhere by their charms, the Amazons banish pleasure, tenderness, and the union of hearts. She insists that liberty is the sovereign blessing and that the Athenian will be sacrificed if she has anything to say about it.

According to classical standards the play is well constructed, but it has few dramatic moments and retains the flavor of romances à la Scudéry. Collé [54] states that the actors accepted it only on condition that it should be played in summer and that the author's share in the receipts should be ceded to them. He says that it was well attended when first played, on July 24, 1749, and on the two Saturdays that followed, but on the other days the attendance was so small that the actors wished to stop with the eighth. They were prevailed upon, however, by the author and her husband to continue until they had produced the play eleven times. He attributes whatever success it had to the acting of la Dumesnil. [55]

---

[54] *Journal*, 1807, I, 102-5, 110.

[55] Most of these statements are confirmed by the *Registres*. Of the first nine performances those at which the largest number of spectators paid admission were on July 24, 26, and Aug. 2. The tenth and eleventh were well attended because a new afterpiece was acted with *les Amazones*. Mme Du Boccage did not share in the receipts. The cast is remarkable for the fact that it contained more women than men. At the first performance la Dumesnil, la Clairon, and la Gaussin all played. The *Mercure* for Sept., 1749, p. 201, shows that la Dumesnil played Orithie. It is probable that la Clairon played Ménalippe; la Gaussin, Antiope. According to the *Registres*, they played at the other performances, except that at the second la La Motte was substituted for la Gaussin. Grandval probably represented Theseus; Paulin, the ambassador.

Collé accused Mme Du Boccage of borrowing from *le Comte d'Essex*, *Bajazet, Ariane,* and Crébillon's *Sémiramis.* In these, as in *les Amazones,* two women are in love with the same man, in three of them the more powerful woman is disappointed in love, while in the fourth, *Ariane,* Theseus is the man in question, but such resemblances are of too general a nature to prove imitation. Collé expressed supreme contempt for *les Amazones,* finding in the tragedy no characters and no "vers de marque."

The abbé Trublet,[56] who attended the first performance, reported that the parterre was respectful, but that, with the exception of la Dumesnil, who acted divinely, all the actors, even la Gaussin, played badly. He found the tragedy cold except in the fourth act. A cause of the indifferent acting was the fact that la Clairon disliked her rôle and laughed at the play to her colleagues.

Voltaire [57] wrote that Mme Du Boccage regarded her tragedy as a failure and "prenait la chose fort au cœur," so much so, indeed, that she never wrote another. Nor was one by any other woman acted at the Comédie Française in the twenty-five years that remained of Louis XV's reign.

[56] Cf. J. Jacquart, *la Correspondance de l'abbé Trublet,* Paris, 1926, pp. 8, 9.
[57] Moland, XXXVII, 36.

CHAPTER XII

MARMONTEL AND SAURIN

1748-1767

Of all the authors who began to bring out tragedies in the reign of Louis XV only two, Voltaire and La Motte, had composed more than three of them that were acted at the Comédie Française when two new dramatists began their careers. One was the son of peasants; the other grew up among men of letters. Both were friends of Voltaire and other " philosophes " and both became members of the French Academy. One composed his acted plays in five years; the other, his in twenty-eight. One was conservative in his selection of subjects and in his methods of dramatizing them; the other daring. Each acquired considerable reputation in the eighteenth century, but Marmontel is now chiefly remembered for his non-dramatic writings; Saurin, as one who followed La Place in making adaptations of English plays.

That tragedy had become a stepping-stone to social success at Paris is better illustrated by the career of Marmontel even than by that of Voltaire, who began higher up in the scale and possessed genius that the younger author could not claim. The son of a poor tailor with a large family, Jean-François Marmontel [1] was born in a village of Limousin on July 11, 1723. He was taught by a local priest, then by Jesuits at the collège de Mauriac and at Clermont. After his father's death he was obliged to aid in the support of his family. He came near becoming a Jesuit and for a while called himself an abbé, but his turn for writing triumphed over the call of the church. As verses he sent to the Jeux floraux at Toulouse failed to win a prize, he appealed to Voltaire, who encouraged him, invited him to Paris, where he arrived late in 1745, and advised him to write a comedy. " Hélas! monsieur, comment ferais-je des portraits? " replied Marmontel, " je ne connais pas les visages." Voltaire smiled and said, " Eh bien! faites des tragédies." [2]

While supporting himself by teaching, Marmontel took Voltaire's advice. He studied tragedies by Corneille, Racine, Voltaire, and other dramatists and frequently went to the theater. The result was the production of five tragedies, acted in 1748-53. They won for him useful friends and public

---

[1] Cf. especially Marmontel's *Mémoires* and S. Lenel, *Un Homme de lettres au XVIIIe siècle*, Paris, Hachette, 1902.
[2] *Mémoires*, I, 113 in the edition of Paris, Costes, 1819.

recognition, but they finally convinced him that his talents could be employed to greater advantage elsewhere, so that he composed the works that gave him his chief title to fame, his *Contes moraux*, including *Bélisaire*, his *Incas*, and his *Mémoires*.[3] While preceptor in the home of Mme Harenc, he completed in 1747 the first draft of his DENYS LE TYRAN.[4] When he read it to the actors, they obliged him to rewrite the fourth act in three days. By giving the heroine's rôle to la Clairon, he helped the production, but offended la Gaussin. Sarrazin must have played Dion or the elder Dionysius; Grandval, the younger. Other rôles were taken by Legrand de Belleville, Dangeville the younger, and Ribou. The tragedy was acted sixteen times, from Feb. 5 to March 30, the last day plays were performed before Easter, so that it had the honor of replacing *Polyeucte* on that day. At each of the first three productions the parterre was so enthusiastic that Marmontel was obliged to appear on the stage.[5] At the sixth performance 1,347 persons paid admission. The play reappeared six times, from Nov. 25 to Dec. 6, 1748, and on May 21 and 24, 1749. The author's share in the receipts was 3529 fr., almost as much as Voltaire had received from *Alzire*. It was thought for a while that Marmontel might be the young man who would carry on the work of Voltaire and Crébillon.

His success was achieved by no stroke of genius, but by careful imitation of leading French dramatists. He laid his scene in ancient Syracuse and introduced three well-known historical characters, but he invented his plot and the heroic rôle he assigned to la Clairon. His method was not unlike that of Corneille in *Héraclius*, where all that is historical is the rulers' order of succession. Knowing that Dionysius was followed as ruler by his son, who was driven out by Dion, Marmontel put all three men into his play in order to make it seem historical, and for the same reason borrowed the name of Damoclès and the reference to the suspended sword. Dion's character, his influence with the younger Dionysius, and his praise of Gelon probably came from Plutarch's *Life of Dion*. The heroine's name may have been suggested by the same biography, though there she is the daughter of

[3] Mme de Pompadour secured for him a position as secretary of the buildings at Versailles. He contributed to the *Encyclopédie*, edited the *Mercure*, was elected to the Academy in 1763, and was made royal historiographer in 1772. He married in 1777 and became the father of five sons. Denounced by Marat, he escaped the guillotine by leaving Paris, but he took some part in political life through his election to the Conseil des Anciens. He died on Dec. 31, 1799.

[4] Paris, Prault, 1748, 8°, and S. Jorry, 1749, 12°. Dedicated in verse to Voltaire. Two other editions appeared in the same year. Republished at The Hague in 1749 and 1752; in the author's *Œuvres*, Paris, Née de la Rochelle, 1787; Paris, Verdière, 1818-20; Paris, Costes, 1819; Paris, Belin, 1819. A Dutch translation was published at Amsterdam in 1759; an Italian translation, at Florence in 1767.

[5] According to Marmontel (*Mémoires*, I, 140), this was the second play to bring such an honor upon its author. The first was Voltaire's *Mérope*.

the elder Dionysius and the wife of Dion, whereas in the tragedy she is the patriot's daughter.

On the other hand, the main incidents are not historical. The rivalry of an authoritative father and a respectful son had been made familiar by Racine's *Mithridate*. The dénouement resembles that of Thomas Corneille's *Camma*, in which the heroine marries a man she hates, poisons the nuptial cup, and kills both the tyrant and herself. Nor did Marmontel fail to echo lines from distinguished tragedies:

> . . . A mes yeux avec soin fardent la verité.[6]
> Au milieu de son peuple il marchoit sans alarmes.[7]
> La honte suit le crime.[8]
> Qu'on me mène à la mort.[9]

The simple plot [10] is presented with due regard for clarity, unity, and propriety. The interest is centered on four characters: an evil ruler, his well-meaning son, a patriotic and influential citizen, and the latter's heroic daughter. The tyrant is described as successful in war and astute in politics, but as caring little for his people, many of whom he has executed and to whose desire for peace he turns a deaf ear. He has no affection for his son or for Dion, both of whom he suspects. His motive for marrying Arétie is purely political. It is made clear that he lives in dread of assassination,

---

[6] I, 5; cf. *Britannicus*, I, 2, " D'un soldat qui sait mal farder la vérité."

[7] I, 5; cf. Voltaire, *Œdipe*, IV, 1, " Au milieu des sujets . . . il marchait sans défense."

[8] IV, 3; cf. Thomas Corneille, *Essex*, IV, 3, " Le crime fait la honte."

[9] IV, 3; cf. *Polyeucte*, IV, 4, " Qu'on me mène à la mort."

[10] Hated by his people, Denys, Tyrant of Syracuse, holds his power by employing mercenaries. He is extremely suspicious, feels that a sword is hanging over his head, even orders his confidant, Damoclès, to watch his son, though he has put the prince in charge of forces destined to attack Epirus. This young man loves Arétie, daughter of Dion, a statesman who has the confidence of the people, but the tyrant proposes to strengthen his government by marrying her himself. Although she loves the son, she is willing to marry the father if by doing so she can make of him a merciful ruler. As the leaders of the people are irritated by the tyrant's plan of warring upon the Carthaginians, Dion prepares them for revolt. Arétie urges her lover to accept the throne as his father is soon to be deprived of it. Denys tests his son by having Arétie offer him the throne. When he answers that, since his father orders him to become king, he will obey, he is arrested. On his way to execution he informs his father than an insurrection is about to break out, but he refuses, even under the threat of death, to name the leaders of it. The king sends for Dion, holds his daughter as a hostage, and bids him assemble the leading citizens. He offers to allow Arétie to marry his son, if she will get his secret from him. The lovers are given an opportunity to escape, but young Denys refuses to take advantage of it and threatens to kill Arétie if an attack is made upon the palace. The tyrant now agrees that, if Arétie will marry him, he will spare his son and Dion. The latter tells his daughter that there will be no revolt, as the people are unwilling to endanger her life, but she takes matters into her own hands, agrees to marry the tyrant, meets him at the altar, slips into the nuptial cup poison that she has carried for her own protection, and dies almost as soon as she touches the cup to her lips. Denys orders his son's execution, but Dion delays it, so that the tyrant dies of the poison before his command can be obeyed. The son, though his father has just lifted a dagger over him, is overwhelmed with grief.

but the picturesque possibilities presented by the familiar account of the
sword are reduced to a brief reference in the opening monologue:

> Je me sens poursuivi par le courroux céleste;
> Et du sang que je verse un vengeur assidu
> Me montre, sur ma tête, un glaive suspendu.

The prince is an inexperienced youth, eager for distinction in war, but
dominated by his father, at whose command he gives up the woman he loves,
even threatens to kill her if by doing so he can save his father, and mourns
over the tyrant even though his last act is an attempt to take the young
man's life. Dion is said to have gained great influence over the prince,
as well as over most of the population, but we are given little evidence of it.
As he does not carry out the revolt he has planned, his chief merit lies in
the boldness with which he speaks to the tyrant, but he would have remained
quite ineffective except for his daughter, who at the cost of her life saves
her lover, her father, and the state.

The most dramatic scenes are III, 4, when Dionysius the younger falls
into his father's trap and is suddenly arrested; IV, 3, when he tells his
father that there is a plot against him, but refuses to reveal the names of
the conspirators; and V, 6, when Arétie resolves to sacrifice herself:

> Le désir de la gloire aiguillonne mon ame.
> Un dieu remplit mon cœur, il l'élève, il l'enflamme,
> Que je me sens de force en cet heureux instant!

These scenes and the acting of la Clairon probably caused the enthusiasm
with which the tragedy was at first greeted. When the charm of novelty
was lost, the actors did not think it wise to revive it, but Marmontel had a
different explanation. He claimed [11] that his first tragedies ceased to be
performed because one of his actors killed another and fled from Paris,[12]
and because a new actor,[13] " qui depuis a été si sublime," became his enemy
on account of his article on declamation in the *Encyclopédie* and constantly
opposed la Clairon's desire to bring back his tragedies to the stage.

The *Mercure* for February, 1748, praised *Denys* highly, noting with
approval that comparatively slight emphasis was placed on love, but Fréron
held that its characters and situations resembled those of many other
tragedies. Marmontel replied and drew from his critic a second attack.
So strained did their relations become that on Nov. 15, 1749, they were
seen to leave the theater together and to draw their swords, but they were

---

[11] V, 298 in the Belin edition of his *Œuvres*.
[12] Ribou and Rosély; cf. above, Chap. I. As the murder did not take place till
December, 1750, nineteen months after *Denys* was acted for the last time, the explanation hardly applies to that tragedy.
[13] Le Kain.

separated before blood was shed. Raynal [14] found the play well written, with dramatic situations, sustained characters, "morceaux vraiment épiques," and steadily increasing interest. The only objection he raised was to the length of the reflexions assigned to the tyrant in the first act. "Jamais," he wrote, "aucun auteur depuis Voltaire n'a débuté aussi glorieusement."

Collé [15] was less enthusiastic. The verses were acceptable, though somewhat declamatory, there were some new situations, there were praiseworthy elements in Acts III and IV, but the tragedy lacked warmth, owing to the length of the exposition and the presence in Act V of unnecessary and uninteresting characters. He noted the resemblance of the dénouement to that of *Camma*. The abbé de La Porte [16] condemned the tragedy and wrote a parody of it called *Denys le Pédant*. La Harpe [17] had little good to say of it. He held that the subject is less bizarre than those of Marmontel's other tragedies, but that the rivalry of father and son, commonplace at best, produces in this tragedy no result. He condemned the conspiracy because we are not told what measures are taken to bring it about; the character of the prince as unhistorical; that of Arétie because she believes too readily she can reform the tyrant, agrees too quickly to marry him, and reveals the conspiracy to her lover without realizing that his duty to his father will oblige him to tell him about it. He considered it absurd to have the father lift his dagger over his son and die before he could stab him.[18] He found the prosody "pénible et froide," the dialogue full of commonplaces.

Marmontel soon had ready a second tragedy, ARISTOMÈNE.[19] Again the plot is fictitious, though there are historical elements: the leading character, the civil strife in Messenia, and the conflict with Sparta. Raynal [20] asserted that the subject came from the history of Corsica, with the substitution of Greek names to give a more imposing air, and that the two main situations, the hero's having to choose between his son's life and his wife's and his threatening to kill the boy in order to control the army, were drawn, "à ce qu'on m'a dit, de l'opéra de *Rhadamiste et Zénobie*, de l'abbé Metastasio."

---

[14] *Cor.*, I, 134-6. Subsequently (II, 327) it was admitted that some persons found the tragedy "trop égale, trop arrangée."

[15] *Op. cit.*, I, 26-7.

[16] Cf. Lenel, *op. cit.*, pp. 102-4.

[17] *Op. cit.*, XIV, 380-95.

[18] This last criticism had already been made in a *Lettre à Mlle Clairon*, as indicated by Lenel, *op. cit.*, p. 104. The situation is not, however, very different from that at the end of *Mahomet*, when Séide dies of poison just as he is seeking to kill the protagonist. Voltaire's play may, indeed, have suggested the situation to Marmontel.

[19] Paris, S. Jorry, 1750, 8° and 12°. Republished in the four editions of the author's *Œuvres*. A Dutch translation was published at Amsterdam in 1755 and 1763; an Italian translation, at Florence in 1767.

[20] *Cor.*, I, 297-300. The same statement about Corsica is made in the *Mercure* for December, 1749, p. 188.

He was misinformed about Metastasio, for in his *Zenobia* there is no boy,
no army, no comparable situation. Raynal's informant may have thought
of Metastasio's *Artaserse*, in which a person is threatened with death, but
there are too many similar situations in other plays to make this resemblance
significant. As for the history of Corsica, Raynal and the writer in the
Mercure were probably thinking of Sampietro, who in the sixteenth century
opposed Genoa with the same hatred and energy that Aristomène displays
in the war with Sparta, and whose wife appealed to the enemy in somewhat
the same fashion as does the wife in the play, but, as Sampietro's wife did
not go to Genoa and was not forgiven by her husband, there is too little
resemblance between this historical incident and the tragedy to justify the
conclusion that it was a source.

The story is again one of exalted heroism, but the leading figure is now
a man,[21] one who is a match for the Spartans in war, skillful in diplomacy,
devoted to his family and his soldiers, but who is unable to perceive the
evil intentions of the hostile senators. His wife is equally ready to sacrifice
herself, but only for her husband and her son. She is without patriotism
and does not understand how her husband can love a city when its governing
body turns against him. The boy, who appears in several scenes and is given
twenty lines to recite, is shown merely as an obedient child. The Spartan
envoy has a pleasing rôle, but one that gives no conception of his city's
overbearing attitude towards Messenia. Arcire and Théonis are contrasted
sharply. One is the hero's devoted follower, who defends his family,
opposes surrender, and brings about the dénouement by violent action; while

[21] By his prowess and by the alliances he has formed with other Greek cities
Aristomène has saved Messenia from conquest by Sparta. He is greatly admired
by young Alcire and by other senators, but he is hated by many of their colleagues,
including Dracon and old Théonis, who would surrender to Sparta, both to avoid
war and to curb the power of Aristomène. When the latter returns to the city,
he is told that his wife, Léonide, and his only son, Leuxis, a boy of twelve, have
fallen into Spartan hands. A note from his wife reveals the fact that she and
Leuxis will be put to death if Messenia does not surrender, but Aristomène refuses
to give up the city. Euribate, the Spartan envoy, tells him that his wife and son
appeared before the kings and that Léonide said, " Menacez-nous; qu'il tremble;
et Messène est soumise." Though shocked by such treachery, Aristomène agrees to
see his wife, sent home by the Spartans. She explains that she has been moved by
her love for her husband, whom some of the senators have proposed to deliver to
Sparta in order to secure better terms. Aristomène admits that he still loves her,
but he allows her and his son to be judged by the senators, who condemn them to
death. Though he knows that he can overcome the senators by leading the army
against them, he refuses to do so. Théonis adds to his anguish by persuading his
colleagues to agree to execute only one member of Aristomène's family and to
allow him to say whether his wife or his son should be spared. Before a decision
is reached, Arcire and Euribate take the matter to the army, which advances upon
the city, but Aristomène appears upon the walls with his son and threatens to kill
him if the soldiers do not retire. When they submit, the senate praises his action
and agrees to release Léonide and Leuxis provided the leaders of the army are
punished. Aristomène is again unable to reply, but Arcire intervenes, kills Théonis
and Dracon, and induces the rest of the senators to pardon the hero's family and
comrades and to proclaim him " l'appui, le défenseur, le vengeur de l'Etat."

the other is a wily old man, fearful of losing power, plotting against Aristomène, and torturing him by the difficult choices he leaves to his decision.

There is no sexual love in the play except that of man and wife. There
is only one rôle for a woman. The struggle is a political one, between
selfish senators, willing to rule under a foreign conqueror, and an able
patriot, who has faith in democracy and struggles to maintain the freedom
of his people. Théonis expresses the thought of many Quislings and Pé-
tainistes (I, 1):

> Au nom de Sparte, au moins, ce sénat redouté,
> Sur un peuple asservi régnait avec empire.
> La liberté renaît; notre pouvoir expire;
> Nous rentrons dans la foule; et je vois le moment
> Où dans la solitude et dans l'abaissement,
> Avilis, dégradés du rang de nos ancêtres,
> Nous aurons à gémir d'avoir changé de maîtres.

Aristomène, on the contrary, continues to believe in the people even when
they turn against him (II, 1):

> Pardonnons à des cœurs trop long-temps abattus.
> La liberté, Léarque, est mère des vertus.
> Son ouvrage commence; attendons qu'il s'achève,
> Ce n'est pas en un jour qu'un grand peuple s'élève.

He offers economic considerations to show the senators that Sparta is by
no means invincible (I, 2):

> Du commerce & des arts la richesse est le fruit:
> Le commerce & les arts sont bannis loin de Sparte.
> Comme des corrupteurs Lycurgue les écarte;
> Et par là de la guerre il détruit l'aliment.
> Osez donc résister à l'effort d'un moment.

Marmontel's chief intention, however, seems to have been to throw into
relief a series of difficult moral situations: will a wife sacrifice the state in
order to save her husband? will she seek to die in place of her son? will
the boy offer to lose his life for his mother? will a hero sacrifice his family
to the state? will he allow senators to condemn his family when he can
prevent their doing so? will he save his wife and son when they are condemned? if he has to choose between them, which will it be? or, if he has
to decide between them and his comrades, what will he do? Some of these
problems are readily solved, but for others no solution is reached. We see
Aristomène in debate rather than in action. The one situation in which
he does more than talk takes place behind the scenes. It is not he, but a
minor character that brings about the dénouement.

Nevertheless the tragedy was well received. It was first acted on April

30, 1749, when Voltaire, in a box with Marmontel, witnessed the performance. Arcire was played by Rosély; Léonide, by Mlle Clairon.[22] The author was again called to the stage. Soon afterwards he was invited by Mme de Tencin to read his tragedy in the presence of Montesquieu, Fontenelle, Marivaux, and Helvétius. The play was acted six times, until May 12, then, according to the *Mercure* for June, 1749, performances were interrupted by the sudden and serious illness of a young actor who had an important rôle, probably Rosély. They were not resumed until December, when the tragedy was acted eleven times, from the first to the thirty-first. It might have had a longer run if Marmontel had not had a new play ready for 1950.

Critics were less favorable than the public. One who remained anonymous [23] attributed the early success of *Aristomène* to the acting of la Clairon. Collé [24] held that the plot was " mal imaginée et encore plus mal conduite," and that the verses, though superior to those of *Denys le Tyran*, still " sentent trop la poésie." Raynal,[25] though he witnessed the great applause that greeted the actors at the first performance, showed no enthusiasm, condemned the hero as half wise, half foolish, more an orator than an actor, and declared that the " gens de l'art " protested against the play's success. He explained that the absurdity of the play was rendered endurable by the author's " pensées neuves, sans être forcées, sentencieuses sans être froides," and that each time a peculiar event offended the audience, " quelques vers éclatants " restored the author to favor. The *Mercure* praised the style, but held that Marmontel did not explain clearly why the hero considered the destruction of his family necessary to the safety of the state. La Harpe [26] called the tragedy a masterpiece of folly, for Léonide's treachery is absurd, Aristomène does not reproach her sufficiently, the senate fails to answer his criticism, and it condemns to death a child of twelve. He found many " mauvais vers." He explained the temporary success of the tragedy by " le prestige d'une fausse grandeur," which easily blinds the multitude, and supported his judgment by referring to the profound oblivion into which the play had fallen before it was recalled to public attention by its appearance in the author's *Œuvres*.

For his third tragedy Marmontel selected a much more familiar subject, one that had been dramatized in France at least seven times before he wrote.

---

[22] Legrand de Belleville, who was provided with diamonds, probably had the title-rôle. Grandval, Paulin, Dubois, François Baron, Bonneval, and Dangeville the younger also played. The boy's rôle may have been taken by la Gaultier. The author's share of the receipts was 2862 fr.

[23] Cf. Lenel, *op. cit.*, pp. 104-5.

[24] *Op. cit.*, I, 84-7.

[25] *Cor.*, I, 297-300.

[26] *Op. cit.*, XIV, 395-413.

20

Moreover, Shakespeare's *Antony and Cleopatra* had been translated by La Place in 1746; Dryden's *All for Love*, by Prévost in 1735. Though the principal source of his CLÉOPÂTRE [27] is Plutarch's *Life of Antony*, Marmontel was probably influenced by three of these nine tragedies. The introduction of Ventidius as Antony's friend and critic may well have been suggested by Dryden, for Plutarch does not bring him to Egypt. The idea of having a conference between Antony and Octavius, in which Antony urges that they restore Roman liberty, Octavius emphasizes the need for a strong ruler, and they propose to divide between them all Roman territory, had been dramatized by Boistel about nine years before Marmontel's tragedy appeared. The rôle of Octavia in the final version of *Cléopâtre* was probably inspired by La Chapelle's *Cléopâtre* of 1681.

In the edition of 1784 Marmontel referred to Plutarch and evidently considered him his chief guide, but he sought to ennoble his two leading characters by making Cleopatra more ready to sacrifice her own interests and by emphasizing Antony's military achievements and his somewhat belated desire for the liberty of Rome.[28] His deserting his wife and children, his part in the proscriptions, his neglect of his affairs are mentioned, but greater emphasis is placed upon his love for Cleopatra and his unwillingness to desert her. The queen is equally devoted and self-sacrificing. She receives her rival graciously, listens to the arguments of Ventidius, who represents the virtues of an older Roman society, and blames herself for the flight from Actium. Still more magnanimous is Octavia, who seems

---

[27] Paris, S. Jorry, 1750, 12°. Republished, Paris, Moutard, 1784, and in four editions of the author's *Œuvres*.

[28] After their defeat at Actium, Antony and Cleopatra have retired to Alexandria. Ventidius describes the decay of virtue at Rome, the need for Antony to save the state from cruel and wily Octavius, and the opportunity that is offered him if he will renounce Cleopatra. The queen is so much impressed that, to save her lover, she is willing to give up her throne, but Antony refuses to abandon her. Octavia, sent by her brother and well received by Cleopatra, begs Antony to accept Octavius's terms and live for their children, but her husband consents only to interview Octavius. The latter enters in Act III, receives from his sister an encouraging report about Cleopatra, tells the queen that he will pardon Antony, but that he will not forget the duty the latter owes his wife. He then meets his opponent, who proposes that both submit to the senate. Octavius replies that Rome needs a master and offers Antony the position that Pompey would have had under Caesar. Antony prefers to divide the world or to fight. They agree to settle their discussion at Rome, but, when Antony learns that Cleopatra is to lose her children and all the benefits conferred upon her by Caesar, and when Octavius refuses to rescind the decree, he takes up arms and is promptly defeated. Meanwhile Cleopatra has provided herself with a vase containing asps and proposes that she and Antony die together. Ventidius gives Antony a chance to escape in a ship to Syria, where three legions will join him, but, as Cleopatra is refused passage, he declines to go. The queen hears that Octavius intends to attach her to his triumphal chariot. Knowing that Antony will not escape while she is alive, she bids her attendant tell him that she is dead and conceals herself in the royal tombs. Antony reproaches Octavius for causing the queen's death. When he sees her dying from the serpent's poison, he seizes the sword of Eros and kills himself. Octavius comments, " Grands dieux! qu'une faiblesse a détruit de vertus! "

to bear Cleopatra no ill will and does her best to reconcile her husband and her brother. The only character with whom we are not supposed to sympathize is Octavius, described as substituting art for courage, a scheming politician who admits that he has bought up the Roman senate and that, if he loses control of affairs, he will be put to death. As he is not sure of his army's loyalty, he prefers to get Antony into his power by peaceful measures. He wishes to get possession of Cleopatra in order that she may march in his triumph.

The first three acts deal with negotiations designed to bring about a peaceful settlement of Roman affairs. In Act IV Antony is defeated, Cleopatra prepares to commit suicide, and Marmontel makes his chief contribution to the story by devising a method of escape for his hero. The failure of the plan is reported in Act V, which is chiefly concerned with the double suicide. The plot is simple, constructed in accordance with classical principles except that two rooms are represented, one in the first three acts, the other in the last two, and that there is a break in *liaison* (V, 1-2) that might easily have been avoided. A modest attempt at the spectacular is made with the help of Egyptian priests in the opening scene, of the vase, and originally of a serpent.

Marmontel would have written a more effective tragedy if he had followed Plutarch more closely and not attempted to idealize the famous lovers. He originally included Cesarion in his cast, but, realizing that to introduce Cleopatra's illegitimate son did not help to redeem her character, he substituted Octavia. He made a number of other changes to meet objections that had been raised. He admits in his *Mémoires* [29] that the tragedy in its first form was carelessly written. He then states that he had originally shown the asp. His friend Vaucanson had made for the scene an automatic serpent which, when Cleopatra pressed it to her bosom, imitated almost as in reality the movement of a living snake. As the surprise excited by the invention rendered the tragic scene ineffective, he had substituted a less mechanized dénouement. Grimm [30] tells the story differently. According to him, the asp hissed as it struck, and Piron cried from the parterre, " je suis de l'avis de l'aspic." The tragic effect was lost less by surprise than by laughter.

This first performance was on May 20, 1750. The play was given eleven times, till June 13, less often than Marmontel's two earlier tragedies. [31]

---

[29] I, 194.

[30] *Cor.*, XIV, 72.

[31] Cleopatra was played by la Clairon; Antony and Ventidius, probably by Grandval and Sarrazin, respectively. Other members of the cast were Dubois, the younger Dangeville, François Baron, Bonneval, Rosély, Ribou, la Grandval, la Lavoy, and la Beauménard. The author's share in the receipts was 1078 fr.

After much revision it was acted in 1784. According to the author, the first three acts were then well received, but not the last two, though after further revisions the whole play was applauded on two occasions; by that time, however, the audiences were so small that he thought it wise to withdraw it.

Collé's criticism [32] is concerned with the play as it was performed in 1750. Crébillon, who obviously had not read Shakespeare, had told him it was impossible to make an acceptable tragedy out of the subject. Collé felt that Marmontel had followed history too closely except in the case of Octavius, whom he had debased. He protested against the presence of Cesarion, the advice he gives to Antony, and the idea of proposing him as the future ruler of Rome. He noted that Acts I and II lack action; that the interview between Antony and Octavius is " ratée " despite the imitation of *Sertorius*; that Cleopatra should not flirt with Octavius; and that the remarks of Ventidius render Antony "plus petit et plus fade." The only situation for which he expresses admiration is one that was subsequently omitted, one in which Eros, induced by Cleopatra to make an attempt upon the life of Octavius, is disarmed by Antony. The verse seemed to him bombastic, but better than in the author's earlier tragedies. When he saw the performance of May 30, he noted improvements, especially in the removal of Cesarion from the scene between Antony and Octavius, but he still considered the subject suitable only for opera.

In May, 1750, Voltaire [33] had written to la Clairon predicting a successful performance, but at the end of the month Baculard d'Arnaud informed him that, as he expected, the tragedy had been hissed, for the author lacked warmth and tact. On June 1 Raynal [34] declared that order was lacking in the plan, interest in the situations, vivacity in the dialogue, dignity in the characters, decency in the manners, and naturalness in the verse. " La pièce fut presque huée depuis le commencement jusqu'à la fin." If there was less protest at the second and third performances, it was because la Clairon's lover, M. de Villegagnon, sent to the theater a large number of musketeers.

When the play had attained its final form, a writer in the *Mémoires secrets* [35] found much beauty in it, but pointed out that the introduction of Octavia had the unfortunate effect of making Antony appear in a still worse light. La Harpe agreed,[36] writing that she is as much out of place as Cesarion and that she is too magnanimous. He considered it absurd of Antony to propose that he and Octavius should surrender their power. He held that Marmontel showed his ignorance of Roman history and gave his

[32] *Op. cit.*, I, 201-15.
[33] Moland, XXXVII, 125, 129.
[34] *Cor.*, I, 428-9.

[35] XXVII, 15-7.
[36] *Op. cit.*, XIV, 413-39.

own thoughts to his characters. He admitted that Marmontel had improved his style, but he found verses that he could praise only in the description of Rome's decay and in Cleopatra's final message to her lover (V, 1):

> . . . Il le croira sans peine: il sait que je l'adore.
> Mais c'est peu pour mon cœur. Ajoute, ajoute encore
> Qu'il n'a jamais bien su, qu'il ne saura jamais
> Avec quelle tendresse & combien je l'aimois.
> (*Elle prend le vase où sont cachés les aspics sous les fleurs.*)
> Et toi, mon seul appui, ma dernière défense,
> Viens: c'est toi que j'oppose à l'injure, à l'offense.
> Si je vis, c'est à toi de me fortifier:
> Si je meurs, c'est à toi de me justifier.

Marmontel's fourth tragedy has not only an ancient subject, but one that had been dramatized by Euripides. He tells us that he undertook it because he wanted a more pathetic subject than that of Antony and Cleopatra, that is, I suppose, one in which the sufferers would be more deserving of our sympathy. He found such a subject in the *Children of Hercules*, but he thought it necessary to give his tragedy, which he entitled LES HÉRA-CLIDES,[37] greater unity than the Greek play has and to provide it with a love intrigue. He acted as de Brie and Danchet had done before him, but his changes are so much in keeping with French usage that they give no evidence of his imitating the tragedies of these authors on the same subject. Nor do the facts that, like de Brie, he eliminated the miraculous rejuvenation of Iolaus and kept Eurystheus off the stage. He went directly to Euripides, borrowing the general theme of the suppliants' rescue by Athenian kindness and valor and by the willingness of a daughter of Hercules to sacrifice herself. He retained the characters of Demophon, Iolaus, and Kopreus, changed Makaria's name to Olympie, and for Hercules's mother substituted his wife, Dejaneira, an alteration that allowed him to add remorse to the older woman's subjects of sorrow. He added Sténélus, his love for Olympie, hers for him, and the herald's effort to deceive Iolas. The dénouement, with its Voltairian suggestion, is entirely different from that of the Greek tragedy.[38]

[37] Paris, S. Jorry, 1753, 12°. Republished in four editions of the author's *Œuvres* and in the *Répertoire* of the veuve Dabo, Paris, 1822.

[38] Déjanire, widow of Hercules, her daughter, Olympie, and others of her children have reached Athens under the guidance of Iolas and have take refuge in the temple of Jupiter. They have fled from Euristhée, King of Argos, who claims them as his subjects and wishes to put them to death. Protection is offered by Sténélus, then by his father, Démophon, King of Athens. Under threat of war, Coprée demands that the refugees be delivered to his master, Euristhée, whose forces are on the Athenian frontier. When Coprée is alone with Iolas, he invites him to return to Argos with the women in order to incite a revolt there, but Iolas accuses him of treachery. Démophon now consents to the marriage of Olympie and Sténélus, provided the young man will prove himself worthy by defeating Euristhée. Sténélus takes command of the army, but before attacking awaits his father's signal, one

The subject is pathetic and heroic. The character of old Déjanire, who condemns herself for her husband's last sufferings and death, her plea for her children, her daughter's willingness to be sacrificed, the fidelity of Iolas, the kindliness of Démophon, who has to think of his subjects as well as of the refugees, the valor of young Sténélus, and the sight of the silent children are all appealing, while Coprée is artful enough to enhance the suppliants' danger. But the love scenes are perfunctory, the fourth act does not make the action progress, and the dénouement has the effect of a *deus ex machinâ*, as it is brought about by negotiations of which we have been told nothing and with the help of a slave whose acquaintance we make in the last scene of the play. The only preparation for this dénouement is given in lines spoken by Déjanire, who has had no opportunity to learn anything about Coprée's undertaking:

> Eh, quoi! si dans leur temple un fourbe assez farouche
> Prête son ame au dieu que fait parler sa bouche,
> Est-ce à vous d'écouter son horrible fureur?   (IV, 3)

This suggestion of anticlericalism finds an echo in verses assigned at the end of the play to Démophon, who abandons the character that Euripides had given him to become an eighteenth-century "philosophe":

> Peuple, enfin vous voyez par quel art odieux,
> En trompant les humains on outrage les Dieux.
> Jusqu'au pied des autels redoutons l'imposture,
> Et pour premier oracle écoutons la nature.

Marmontel gave in this tragedy a more varied spectacle than he had previously attempted. In Act I the stage represents the vestibule of a temple, whose doors open in II, 3 to show the children of Hercules. A crowd comes to witness the sight. In Act III we see the vestibule of Démophon's palace, which remains the place of the action during the rest of the tragedy.

It was first acted on May 24, 1752. Déjanire was played by la Dumesnil; Olympie, by la Clairon.[39] Marmontel expected great success, as there had

that Démophon hesitates to give, for an oracle has predicted that Athens will be victorious only if a high-born virgin is sacrificed on the altar of Ceres. Told of this by Iolas, Olympie agrees to be the victim and refuses the king's offer to send her away on a ship with her family. Déjanire would die in her stead, but she cannot claim to be a virgin. Olympie says farewell to Sténélus without revealing her intention and goes in a chariot to a temple at Eleusis. Déjanire faints when she hears the signal for battle, as she takes it to mean that her daughter has perished. News is brought that the Argives have been defeated and Euristhée killed, then Sténélus, Olympie, and a slave enter. The slave had told Sténélus that Coprée had bribed the priest of Ceres and that they had invented the oracular pronouncement. Sténélus had reached the altar in time to rescue Olympie and to cause the priest to kill himself. He had taken her to the army, had called on his men to fight for her, and had given the signal that Déjanire had misinterpreted. Démophon warns his people to beware of deception practised in the name of the gods.

[39] Other rôles were taken by Grandval, who probably represented the young hero,

been much weeping at rehearsals. The first act went off well, but before the second la Dumesnil, who liked the support of wine, drank a goblet full which her servant had failed to dilute, with the result that during the rest of the performance she was intoxicated.[40] At subsequent productions she tried to atone for the harm she had done, but it was too late. The play was acted only eleven times.

Marmontel was chagrined by what he considered the failure of his play, especially as La Poplinière, his wealthy patron, had arranged an entertainment at his country home to honor its success. He held, however, that the pathos of the tragedy would have made up for the fact that it was the most weakly written of his productions, if it had not been for the hostility of la Gaussin, of Voltaire's enemies, of the group that met at the Café Procope, and for the report that he was attempting to rival Racine's *Iphigénie*. The two tragedies were contrasted in an anonymous *Lettre de M. Racine fils à M. M****.[41] Déjanire was called in it "bavarde, criailleuse"; Sténélus, "timide, indécis"; Olympie, "une fille du grand monde, qui a reçu une éducation mâle." Accepting the condemnation of his play, though he considered it unjust, Marmontel did not attempt to revive it, as he did in the case of *Cléopâtre*.

Strangely enough La Harpe,[42] who had criticized Marmontel's earlier tragedies severely, declared that *les Héraclides* did honor to its author. He admired even the introduction of love and the dénouement. He praised the structure, the presentation of characters, and the style, which showed few errors of importance and many fine verses.

The last tragedy that Marmontel produced at the Comédie Française was EGYPTUS, acted on Feb. 5, 1753. It was so complete a failure that it was not acted a second time and was never published. What is known about it comes from the *Registres*, the *Almanach des Spectacles*,[43] which sketches the plot, and the author's *Mémoires*.[44] The first of these sources shows that la Dumesnil and probably Le Kain played in it, that the actors provided diamonds for Legrand de Belleville, who may well have taken the part of the usurper, that they also supplied an "aulne de gaze" and

---

Sarrazin, Dubois, the younger Dangeville, François Baron, Bonneval, and Paulin. The author received 1048 fr.

[40] Marmontel, *Mémoires*, I, 198.

[41] Quoted by Lenel, *op. cit.*, p. 106.

[42] *Op. cit.*, XIV, 445-52.

[43] 1754, p. 194. When Egyptus, heir to the throne of Egypt, was about to be assassinated by rebels, a minister took him out of the kingdom and brought him up without telling him who he was. The minister's wife, pretending that her own son was Egyptus, made him king. The heir to the throne served the usurper well, but the minister returned and identified Egyptus, who succeeded to the throne "après un long combat de politesse entre lui & le faux Roi."

[44] I, 203-5.

eighteen " aulnes de Ruban couleur de Roze," and that Marmontel's share in the receipts was 274 fr. The author tells us that Mme de Pompadour had encouraged him to write a new tragedy and that he had sought a subject that would be quite novel, invented by himself. Nevertheless the theme that he selected bears a curious resemblance to Mauger's *Cosroës*, which had failed the year before. In each tragedy a prince is rescued by a minister, is brought up without knowing who he is, and acts as a loyal subject until he is identified by the minister and succeeds to the throne. The absence of love makes the two plots closer to each other than they are to the *Sémiramis* of Crébillon or of Voltaire, tragedies that have similar elements. However, without seeing the text of *Egyptus* and the complete text of *Cosroës*, one cannot say whether definite influence was exerted upon Marmontel, but there is enough evidence for us to conclude that his claim to novelty was not justified.

He tells us that the exposition in which the funeral of Sesostris was represented had " une majesté imposante," that the characters contrasted well with one another, and that the intrigue was so well devised that no one could foresee the solution. He states that there was no love in the tragedy and that its action was " toute politique et morale." Mme de Pompadour gave it her approbation. The actors liked " la beauté des mœurs dont j'avais décoré les derniers actes." However, when the play was produced, the weakness of these acts became apparent. " Des combats de générosité et de vertu n'avaient rien de tragique. Le public s'ennuya de n'être point ému, et ma pièce tomba." According to Fréron,[45] the work was " sifflé."

Subsequently Marmontel rewrote Rotrou's *Venceslas*, but Le Kain preferred the original version. He tried his hand at bringing up to date the text of other seventeenth-century tragedies and composed, in 1783, *Numitor*, but he abandoned the idea of having this tragedy acted. His contribution to the tragic repertory of the Comédie Française is consequently limited to the years 1748-53. Whatever may be said of its value, it established him in the literary and social life of Paris. When this was accomplished, the composition of tragedies was abandoned or became merely an occasional diversion. He must have realized how much he owed to Voltaire's support and to la Clairon's acting. His careful imitation of earlier writers seemed at first to mark him as a promising dramatist, but his second tragedy was acted less frequently than his first, his third and fourth than his second, while his fifth was an utter failure. He remained faithful to ancient themes while others were seeking greater variety in the material they selected for dramatization. He reduced the importance of love, except in *Cléopâtre*, and

---

[45] *Année littéraire*, 1760 (4), p. 4.

omitted it entirely in *Egyptus.* He sought to replace it by heroism and magnanimity, but he ceased to be convincing as he strained for his effects. He lacked dramatic imagination and the ability to express himself in striking verse. He learned that it was necessary even in tragedy to "connaître les visages."

While Marmontel composed by the time he was thirty his five tragedies that were acted, his older contemporary, Bernard Joseph Saurin, did not bring out his first tragedy until he was forty-four and was over seventy when the last of them appeared. Yet his early advantages would have made one look for a more precocious career. His father, a mathematician and member of the Academy of Sciences, won celebrity by the part he took against J.-B. Rousseau in the affair of the sonnets. Born in 1706, Bernard Joseph grew up among his father's learned and literary friends, became a lawyer and secretary to the duc d'Orléans, was on friendly terms with Voltaire and Collé, and received a pension from Helvétius. In 1761 his verse won him a seat in the French Academy. He died on Nov. 17, 1781.[46] Mlle Clairon [47] said of him that "ses mœurs étaient pures, son commerce doux, gai, sûr; sa conduite et sa probité le rendaient cher à ses amis, et recommendable à tout le monde."

In the preface of his *Spartacus* he divides tragedies into three kinds: *terribles, grandes,* and *pathétiques.* He illustrated each variety with a tragedy of his own composition. To the first category belongs AMÉNOPHIS.[48] Voltaire,[49] who thought in 1750 that it was by Linant, held that "c'est l'Artaxerce de Metastasio," and Raynal [50] subsequently expressed the same opinion, but Collé,[51] who knew the play before it was acted, had pointed out in 1749 that the source is *Carmante,* a "petit roman de Madame de Villedieu."

From this novel [52] Saurin derived the love of the hero and heroine, the false report of his death, her marriage to the usurper of his throne, the help received by the hero from a faithful retainer, the murder of the usurper by a nobleman who seeks the throne and has promised to marry an ambitious princess, the discovery of the body by the hero, who is charged with murder, his arrest, the confession of the ambitious princess, motivated by the fact

[46] Cf. Petitot, *Répertoire,* 1803, Vol. IV.
[47] *Mémoires de Mlle Clairon,* Paris, 1822, p. 331.
[48] Paris, Prault fils, 1758, 8°. Approbation, signed by Trublet, June 9. The title-page misdated the first performance 1752, misleading the *Mercure* of January, 1760, in which the play is analyzed at length.
[49] Moland, XXXVII, 205. Voltaire's mistake must have been due to the fact that the scene of Linant's *Alzaïde* is laid in Memphis and that an important character in it is called Aménophis.
[50] *Cor.,* I, 492.
[51] *Op. cit.,* I, 117.
[52] Cf. *Œuvres de Madame de Ville-Dieu,* Paris, 1741, Vol. III.

that her accomplice has jilted her, the death of the murderer, the poisoning
of the ambitious princess, and the marriage of the hero and heroine.   The
change of scene to Memphis and the names, Apriès, Amasis, and Aménophis,
were probably inspired by the *Grand Cyrus*.   It is unnecessary to suppose
that Saurin also imitated Metastasio's *Artaserse*, as Voltaire suggested, for
the resemblances are of too general a nature to establish a source.   Voltaire
was probably misled by the false acusation of murder, but the situation in
question is closer to one in *Carmante* than to the corresponding scene in
Artaserse.[53]

Saurin eliminated a great deal of the rambling novel, altered relationships to a certain extent, and added situations, notably those in which the
hero prevents the heroine's suicide and in which she kills Sosis.   He also
added the high priest and the anticlericalism expressed in his accepting a
bribe to condemn an innocent prince to death, for " Le pouvoir est leur
Dieu, l'intérêt est leur loi " (III, 5).   He assigned to this priest a theory
worthy of the Jacobins.   The scepter is a trust:

> Si celui qui n'en est que le dépositaire
> En fait des maux publics l'instrument arbitraire:
> Né pour les maintenir, s'il viole les loix,
> Le peuple devient libre & rentre en tous ses droits,
> Telle est du trône, ici, la loi fondamentale.   (IV, 6)

---

[53] Amasis has killed Apriès and succeeded him as King of Egypt.   Aménophis,
son of Apriès, has grown up at the court of Menès, King of Hécatompyle, and has
won the love of his host's daughter, Arthésis.   Amasis has defeated Menès, captured
him, and left Aménophis so severely wounded that he is supposed to be dead.
Arthésis has led an army against Amasis, only to be captured.   When the play
begins, she has most unwillingly agreed to marry Amasis in order to free her father
and to save her city from destruction.   Nephté, an aristocratic woman who has been
engaged to Amasis, now plans to kill him, to put his brother, Sosis, on the throne,
and to marry this prince.   Aménophis, rescued from the field of battle and restored
to health, arrives just after the marriage of Arthésis.   He is told of this event by
Ramessès, a loyal follower of Apriès and his son, but one who has gained the confidence of Amasis.   When Arthésis is about to kill herself, Aménophis snatches away
her dagger and makes sure that she still loves him, but he finds that she is opposed
to his killing her husband.   Just after he has left her, she learns that Amasis has
been murdered.   Sosis tells Ramessès that the assassin has been arrested and must
be judged by the widowed queen.   He plans to have the murderer implicate Nephté
so that she may be put to death, leaving him free to marry Arthésis.   He bids
Ramessès arrest Nephté's brother, captain of the palace guard.   When the supposed
murderer is brought before Arthésis, she sees that it is Aménophis, who insists that
he is innocent.   He says that he saw the flash of a dagger in the dark, heard the
king cry out, went to his aid, and was arrested.   Arthésis believes him, but the
priests of Isis, bribed by Sosis, condemn him to death.   Sosis offers to save him in
return for the hand of the queen, but she declines to marry him.   A scaffold is
erected, but it is surrounded by an angry mob, incited by Ramessès, who is ordered
by Sosis to kill the condemned prince while he is still in prison.   Nephté, poisoned
by Sosis while drinking from a cup in an engagement ceremony, has strength enough
to tell Arthésis that she and Sosis are guilty of murdering Amasis.   Aménophis,
freed by Ramessès, enters with his friends.   Sosis threatens to stab Arthésis if they
attack him, but the queen, who has a dagger of her own, strikes him dead with it.
Aménophis will reign and will marry Arthésis.

It is true that the priest's argument is refuted, but there are other verses to which no objection is offered in the text of the play:

> Du Prince on fit un homme & de l'homme un Héros.[54]
> Quand par un crime heureux un sceptre est acheté,
> Qui monte sur le trône y trouve son refuge:
> Il n'est plus de forfait quand il n'est plus de juge.[55]

The characters are villains or persons capable of great loyalty and devotion. Amasis, murderer and usurper, does not appear on the stage, but his ambitious and criminal nature is represented by his brother, Sosis, and by Nephté, who intrigues to become queen, plans a murder, and gets her revenge when she is poisoned by her accomplice. On the side of justice are Ramessès, the faithful and resourceful official, clever enough to inspire trust in those he hates; heroic Aménophis; and Arthésis, who sacrifices her happiness to save her father, defends the husband she has been forced to marry, and is quick with her dagger to frustrate the forces of evil.

Egyptian coloring consists in the choice of Memphis for the location of the action, several proper names, the fact that Amasis is having a pyramid erected that will be consecrated " à son néant," and the introduction of the priests of Isis, two of whom, like two of the judges in *Inès de Castro*, refrain from speaking.

Saurin filled his tragedy with violence and proposals of violence. Before the action begins, Apriès has been murdered, his son desperately wounded. In the course of the play several murders are projected, Amasis is killed behind the scenes, the heroine threatens suicide, Nephté is poisoned, a dagger is raised upon a queen, and we witness the killing of the villain (V, 8):

> Sosie: Je sais qu'il faut périr, mais ma victime est prête,
>   Tout son sang va couler, regne à ce prix . . .
> Aménophis: Arrête;
>   En ce moment, grands Dieux! qui me secourra?
> Arthésis *frappant Sosis*:   Moi.

The author claimed that this sudden change of fortune, effected by the heroine's killing the man who threatens her, was imitated by Lemierre in the last act of *Hypermnestre* and resembled closely a situation in La Place's *Adèle de Ponthieu*, though he admitted that the latter author was not necessarily his debtor.[56] His tragedy was composed before Sept. 10, 1749,

---

[54] I, 1. Collé (*op. cit.*, I, 301-4) quotes this line and a number of others that were stricken out by Crébillon as censor. However, most of them were recited by the actors in spite of this prohibition.

[55] I, 4. The copy of *Aménophis* at the University of Michigan shows a marginal comment written in faded ink and probably dating from the Second Empire: " exemple, Napoléon III."

[56] As a matter of fact, the situation is closer to one in *Adèle* than to one in *Hypermnestre*, where the heroine does not kill the man who puts her life in danger.

when Collé presented it to Grandval. At the time he feared competition with Linant, who had influence with la Clairon and a tragedy ready to be acted.[57] Collé admired the subject and the structure, but he found the verses weak, no warmth or vigor in the dialogue. He reported at the end of the month [58] that the actors had refused to play it, but that Saurin, though hurt by their decision, asked him to take his manuscript to Mme de Tencin and get her to use her influence with d'Argental and the maréchal de Richelieu. The result of these negotiations was that the tragedy was acted on Nov. 12, 1750. Mlle Clairon played Arthésis; Le Kain, Aménophis; Ribou, soon to be a murderer himself, Sosis; la Gaultier, Nephté.[59]

Collé asserts [60] that, with the exception of la Clairon, all the actors played badly. Saurin had, moreover, spoiled the structure in such a way that the chief situation lost much of the effect it should have had. Even the author admitted that his play failed, though he claimed that passages in all the acts were applauded. He was advised by Marivaux and Helvétius not to withdraw the tragedy, but Collé and la Clairon persuaded him to do so. He continued to alter his text, but, by the time he was ready to submit it again to the actors, several tragedies that resembled it had appeared, so that he decided against a second attempt.

Fréron [61] considered commonplace the themes of an assassinated usurper and the restoration of a prince to his throne, as well as tirades against priests, though he admitted that these last were always applauded by the multitude. His main objection was to the style, which he considered incorrect and not sufficiently noble for tragedy. Marmontel replied, defending Saurin's style, and Fréron again condemned it. Raynal [62] thought the tragedy " mal conduite et mal écrite." He noted that it failed despite the adroit efforts of a cabal and the skill shown by Saurin in introducing the " démêlés du clergé et de la cour." Voltaire [63] also noted the manner in which priests are presented. After mentioning the " beaux vers " of the tragedy, he wrote:

Les prêtres d'Isis n'ont pas beau jeu avec vous; l'archevêque de Memphis vous lâchera un mandement, et les jésuites de Tanis vous demanderont une rétraction.

Petitot,[64] on the other hand, defended priests, claiming that they had

[57] Collé, op. cit., I, 117-8. The reference must be to Linant's Vanda, in which la Clairon had a leading rôle. As we have seen, Linant was trying to have it revived just before his death in 1749.
[58] Ibid., I, 122-3.
[59] Saurin's share in the receipts was 182 fr.
[60] Op. cit., I, 299-301.
[61] Année littéraire, 1759 (7), pp. 308-18; 1760 (4), pp. 3-7.
[62] Cor., I, 492.
[63] Moland, XXXIX, 562.
[64] Répertoire, 1803, IV, 194-5.

never murdered kings. He then avenged them by criticizing Saurin for his portrayal of character and for his verse, which he called laborious, harsh, and incorrect.

Saurin may have meditated upon the criticism he received and concluded that it was wise to soften attacks upon priests, to select history rather than a novel as his source, and to spend more time upon his style. At any rate he waited over nine years before producing another tragedy. Then he had his SPARTACUS[65] acted, a play that shows the influence of Corneille and of internationalist ideas. He desired to depict a hero " humain et vertueux," a Marcus Aurelius or a Titus, rather than a Caesar. For this purpose he made the somewhat singular choice of Spartacus, whom Racine had called " un esclave, un vil gladiateur." To avoid such condemnation he represented him, not as a Thracian of humble birth, but as the son of a German prince, Ariovistus, King of the Suevi, and supposed that he had been captured in infancy with his heroic mother, who had instilled in him hatred of the Romans and a desire to promote universal freedom and brotherhood.

He had probably read in Plutarch's *Life of Crassus* the account of Spartacus, his revolt, his victories, and his death in battle, as well as the difficulties he had in controlling his followers, many of whom were Gauls. He had also learned from Plutarch that Spartacus was not only brave and spirited, but a man of understanding and kindliness. This was enough, he thought, to justify his giving his hero a dream of general freedom, once the Romans should be overcome; his attributing the defeat to a love affair and the treachery of an ally; and his inventing episodes that would illustrate the valor of Spartacus, his hatred of Rome, his devotion to his mother, his mercy for his captives, his willingness to subordinate to the general welfare his pride and his love. La Harpe suggests that he owed the account of his fight as a gladiator to La Calprenède's *Cléopâtre* and the incident of his apologizing to a subordinate to a story told of Henri IV and a Swiss captain. The final incident of the dagger with which the heroine stabs herself before passing it to the man she loves resembles closely the account of Arria and Petus related by Tacitus and the Younger Pliny and already employed in a tragedy by Mlle Barbier.

The tragedy is built around Spartacus.[66] We learn of his royal birth,

---

[65] Paris, Prault petit-fils, 1760, 12°. Dedicated to Helvétius. Republished, Paris, veuve Duchesne, 1769 and 1783; Paris, Belin, 1788; Paris, Fages, 1801; Paris, Vente, 1818; Paris, Barba, 1818; in Petitot's *Répertoire*, 1803 and 1817; in *Auteurs du second ordre*, 1808; in the author's *Œuvres choisies*, Paris, Didot, 1812; in the *Répertoires* of 1813, 1818, 1824, 1825; and by Touquet in 1821. An Italian translation was published at Venice in 1804.

[66] Noricus, a Gaul, has been offered freedom for his people if he will desert Spartacus, but, though jealous of his ally, he has a deeper hatred of the Romans, who have killed his son. Spartacus learns that his mother, captured by the Romans, has stabbed herself upon hearing that they have threatened to kill her unless her

the heroic and humanitarian principles taught him by his mother, his manly beauty when he appeared in the amphitheater and, after being forced to kill his opponent, warned the Romans that he would have revenge for the treatment he has received (II, 1) :

> Des flots de sang romain pourront seuls effacer
> La tache de celui que je viens de verser.

He swears to avenge his mother's death and has an opportunity to do so, but he discovers that the captured daughter of Crassus is the woman he loves (II, 3) :

> Quoi! ma mere n'est plus! quoi! son sang fume encore;
> Et vous êtes Romaine, et mon cœur vous adore!

We see him win over his followers by baring his breast to their blows. He expresses to Messala his contempt for Rome and defends his men against the charge of cruelty:

> Eh! que sont en effet quelques cités détruites,
> Quelques champs ravagés, si j'atteins à mon but,
> Si du monde opprimé leur perte est le salut,
> Et si des nations par mon bras affranchies
> Les biens, les libertés, les honneurs et les vies
> Ne sont plus le jouet de ces brigands titrés,
> De tous ces proconsuls à qui vous les livrez.[67]

---

son surrenders. She has sent him the dagger with a demand for vengeance. He swears on the weapon that he will be avenged and immediately learns that Emilie, daughter by a secret marriage of Crassus, the consul, has been captured. She had been attracted to Spartacus when he had triumphed as a gladiator, had reproached the Romans for making him, though the son of a king, fight in the arena, and had been rescued by him when he captured Tarentum. She now admits to him that she returns his love, but army chieftains demand that she be put to death in order to avenge the mother of Spartacus and the son of Noricus. Spartacus, however, threatens to resign his command if Roman cruelty is imitated, warns of the dissensions that will follow if he does so, and gets them to obey him. Messala, sent by Crassus, offers to ransom Emilie, but Spartacus frees her without accepting compensation. When Noricus twice fails to take a hill, Spartacus calls him a coward, captures the hill, and completes the encirclement of Crassus. Then, in the presence of his men, he apologizes to Noricus and admits that his success may have been due to the Gaul's earlier efforts. Noricus is apparently won over, but the insult continues to rankle. Crassus now offers the senate's terms: citizenship for Spartacus's men, a place in the senate for their leader, knighthood for his second in command, but Spartacus refuses to enter into the corrupt Roman government and even declines Crassus's offer of his daughter's hand. He is confident of victory and, when the consul has retired, orders the attack, but he is delayed by Emilie, who has returned to his camp to urge him to save her father and to reform Rome. When he refuses, she draws a dagger and threatens to kill herself, but at this moment Spartacus hears that Noricus has deserted him and has enabled the Romans to gain the upper hand. He rushes out, rallies his troops three times, and kills Noricus, but, unable to withdraw his sword from the body of the Gaul, he is overpowered and brought back into his tent. When he asks Emilie for poison or a weapon, she draws her dagger, stabs herself, and presents it to him, so that he is able to follow her example.

[67] III, 3. Substitute Gauleiter for proconsul and you have here an explanation of the damage done to Caen and Saint-Lô in 1944 by liberating armies.

In his debate with Crassus, Spartacus accounts for his unwillingness to accept a compromise (IV, 3):

> Du tems des Scipions j'aurois pu accepter;
> Rome étoit digne alors qu'on s'en fît adopter: . . .
> Aujourd'hui qu'en son sein les richesses versées
> Usurpent tout l'éclat des vertus éclipsées,
> Que l'orgueil, l'avarice ont infecté vos cœurs,
> Et que, de l'univers avides oppresseurs,
> Vous en avez conquis les trésors et les vices,
> Que m'offrez-vous, sinon d'être un de vos complices?

He resists even the offer of Emilie's hand, reproducing an argument employed in *le Cid*:

> Pour être digne d'elle il y faut renoncer,
> Et ne point immoler, en m'unissant à Rome,
> La liberté du monde à l'intérêt d'un homme:
> Je n'acheterai point mon bonheur à ce prix. (IV, 3)

This heroic humanitarian and internationalist overshadows the other characters in the play. Emilie's rôle is not sufficiently emotional to justify her suicide at the end of it. We are supposed to look upon her as a patriotic woman in love with an enemy of her country, but her love is too restrained to be impressive and her political ideas are not in keeping with her decision to kill herself (V, 5):

> Il faut, pour en bannir les malheurs et la guerre,
> Qu'un seul peuple commande et tienne les vaincus
> Soumis par sa puissance, heureux par ses vertus.
> Les Romains sont ce peuple: en grands hommes féconde,
> Bienfaitrice à la fois et maîtresse du monde,
> Si Rome sous ses lois a su tout asservir,
> C'est pour tout rendre heureux.

The other leading characters are Crassus and Noricus. The Roman consul, whose rôle might have been advantageously combined, as it originally was, with that of Messala, his envoy, conducts himself with dignity both in defeat and in victory. The avarice for which he was noted is not mentioned. If he is willing to marry his daughter to Spartacus, it is not through fear, but because he believes that such a marriage will save Rome from defeat. Noricus, whose rôle is essential since the dénouement is brought about by his treachery, is insufficiently presented. He is prominent enough in Act I and in the first scene of Act III, but elsewhere he appears only in three scenes, one with a confidant, one a monologue, and one in which he does not speak. The emotional states through which he passes from hatred of Rome to betrayal of her enemy called for more extensive and more dramatic treatment.

The first two acts are largely devoted to the exposition, but they are enlivened by the account of the hero's mother's suicide and by Emilie's impressions of Spartacus as a gladiator. The action begins in Act III with Spartacus's refusal to sacrifice Emilie or to keep her in captivity. The events enacted or described in Act IV develop Noricus's hostility to the hero and destroy all hope of a compromise between Spartacus and the senate. In Act V the treachery of the Gaul and the delay imposed upon the hero make possible the victory of Crassus and the suicide of the lovers.

The verses are forcefully written in the classical manner. The anti-clericalism of *Aménophis* finds only a slight echo in the remark of Spartacus (IV, 3) that at Rome "on fit parler les dieux" to convince the people of the city's destiny. Elsewhere the author attacks the longing for universal conquest, cruelty in war, selfishness and disloyalty among leaders, rather than the baleful influence of priests. Saurin imitated Corneille, but the older dramatist would have made out a better case for Rome than that presented by Crassus, Messala, and Emilie.

The tragedy was acted on Feb. 20, 1760. Le Kain played Spartacus; la Clairon, Emilie; Brizard, Crassus; Bellecour, Noricus. Collé[68] heard that the actors did not know their lines, with the exception of la Clairon, who came near fainting in the fifth act; that the musketeers, who had a quarrel with the actors, hissed; and that Fréron directed a cabal against the play. The first performance was consequently pronounced a failure, but before the second Saurin had placated the musketeers and had removed from his text some objectionable features. Collé still thought that Le Kain, Brizard, and Bellecour acted badly, but he reported that Acts I, II, and III were applauded with fury, Act V still more so, and that the silence that greeted Act IV could be explained by its lack of action. The play was given nine times, until April 26. In 1769 Saurin sought to have it revived, offering Le Kain his "part d'auteur" as an inducement,[69] but it was not acted again until after they were both dead. In 1783-1818 it was given nineteen times.

Collé admired the presentation of Spartacus, but he thought that love was out of place in the tragedy and that Crassus was not heroic enough to be a Roman. He considered Noricus an imitation of Perpenna in *Sertorius*, but less well connected with the plot. He put the style infinitely above anything the author had previously written.

Grimm,[70] who attended the first performance with Diderot, was quick to criticize the play. He pointed out the violence done to history, the failure

---

[68] *Op. cit.*, II, 324-9.

[69] *Mémoires de Lekain*, Paris, 1801, pp. 320-1. The share he had received was 958 fr., 15 s., 7 d.

[70] *Cor.*, IV, 188-96, 227-30.

to attach some of the episodes to the main action, and the manner in which love scenes are injected into acts that should be devoted to other matters. He appreciated the references to the hero's mother, but he thought that she should have been the chief character, a feminine Regulus, visiting her son's camp to forbid his acceptance of Roman terms and returning to captivity. He would have had the dagger with which she kills herself shown at the end of the fourth act instead of in the first.

On April 15 Grimm wrote that the actors had given the play at the reopening of their theater after the Easter recess and that, as the visit of Crassus to the slave camp had been criticized, Saurin had substituted Messala for the consul in what had been his first appearance in the play. He then quoted the reflections of Diderot in regard to the tragedy, that the facts are " décousus, la versification est d'une dureté barbaresque, pas un son musical, peu d'idées, jamais de tableaux qu'ébauchés." Diderot held that the preparation is insufficient, that the emotional expressions are rhetorical, and that the hero's mother should not have died so early in the play. However, he admired the second and third scenes of Act IV and the dénouement, but he thought that the tragedy should be rewritten, the characters given more color, for " dans le genre de Corneille il faut être Corneille, et point au-dessous." [71]

Saurin sought, when he wrote his preface, to defend his play against such critics as Grimm and Diderot. It is there that he refers to three kinds of tragedy, putting *Spartacus* among the " grandes," that is, among those concerned with great interests of state that rouse admiration and fear.[72] This type of play, he admits, makes less impression on his contemporaries than the " pathétiques," but he insists that the success of *Spartacus* indicates that spectators can still enjoy the portrayal of actions that are noble and virtuous. He denies that he presents Roman manners falsely, for he is describing the time of Crassus, not that of the Scipios.[73] He defends his

[71] Tourneux calls attention to a different, but no more complimentary account of the play given by Diderot in a letter of July 1. It is published in the Assézat et Tourneux edition, Paris, 1876, XVIII, 436-7. Diderot found the audience not sufficiently moved and detected in the dénouement a borrowing from the story of Arria and Petus. He said that the events are unconnected, that the hero's mother dies too soon, and that Emilie is too calm in the hostile camp, is sent away too quickly, and violates the proprieties by her return. He admired the scene in which Spartacus asks pardon of Noricus and the one in which the consul offers terms to the former gladiator. He is unjust in claiming that Spartacus is not made sufficiently unhappy, although Saurin makes him lose his mother and the girl he loves and commit suicide, and that Crassus should not allow his daughter to visit her lover's camp, although in doing so Crassus, who is presented as a patriot, is trying desperately to save the Roman army. It is surprising to find in Diderot such respect for the *bienséances*.
[72] Others in this group are *Nicomède, Athalie, Sertorius*, the tragedy that *Spartacus* is most likely to recall, and Voltaire's *Brutus*. Examples he gives of " terribles " are *Rodogune, Mahomet, Sémiramis, Atrée et Thyeste*; of " pathétiques," *Inès de Castro, Zaïre*, and most of Racine's tragedies.
[73] To emphasize this point he reproduces eight lines on the effect of luxury and civil strife that had been omitted when his tragedy was acted.

presentation of the consul and the fact that he gives Spartacus royal birth. If his protagonist had been merely a gladiator, he would not have had enough education to make his noble sentiments possible. Saurin means his ideas about human brotherhood, which, he thinks, could not have been acquired by a Thracian peasant, but might have been instilled in her son by the queen of a German tribe! He is, however, somewhat doubtful about the soundness of his own explanation and adds that, if one removes twenty verses from the play, the aristocracy of the gladiator will disappear.

It was not this argument, but the criticism of Roman imperialism and of Roman cruelty as shown in war and in gladiatorial shows that appealed to Voltaire,[74] who asserted that Saurin had avenged humanity in his tragedy, " remplie de traits dignes du grand Corneille." He would rather have composed a hundred verses of it than all that had been written since the time of Racine. In his opinion the rôle of Spartacus is superior to that of Sertorius. Fréron,[75] on the other hand, condemned the structure, the devices employed, the characters, the manners, and the style. Nor did La Harpe agree with Voltaire.[76] For him the tragedy was untrue to history and too philosophical. He found the love scenes cold and the rôle of Crassus, despite Saurin's defense, abject.

The criticisms that the tragedy received were to a certain extent justified. The play is awkwardly constructed. The preparation for the leading scenes is inadequate, love should either have been omitted or been more effectively presented, and the hero is too much given to boasting of his virtues. Nevertheless, it is a much more memorable production than many of its day, it contains striking situations, and Saurin deserves credit for seeking to revive the Cornelian type of drama with its emphasis upon political ideas. It made, moreover, a contribution to the humanitarian and internationalist movement of the eighteenth century, and it secured for its author a position among the leading dramatists of his day.

He had not as yet written a tragedy belonging to the group that he called pathetic. To do this he turned to an English play, the *Tancred and Sigismunda* of James Thomson, author of *The Seasons*. Thomson had derived his plot from a story in *Gil Blas* [77] called " le Mariage de vengeance." He had altered the names and some of the circumstances, but on the whole he had followed Lesage rather closely. In 1761 Thomson's play had been translated by La Place into French prose for the *Mercure*. When he pub-

---

[74] Moland, VII, 243, XLVI, 306.
[75] *Année littéraire*, 1760 (4), pp. 145-66.
[76] La Harpe speaks of Messala as the son of Crassus and accuses Saurin of an anachronism in making his hero the son of Ariovistus, although in the play Messala is merely the consul's envoy and the father of Spartacus is not supposed to be the Ariovistus whom Julius Caesar defeated. Cf. La Harpe, *op. cit.*, XIII, 218-29.
[77] Book IV, Chap. IV.

lished it subsequently, he stated in his preface that *Tancred and Sigismunda* was the source of Saurin's tragedy.[78] It is probable that the French dramatist followed La Place's version rather than the English text.

BLANCHE ET GUISCARD [79] is not, as has been asserted, a translation of Thomson's play, but an adaptation with other changes than those required to turn English blank verse into French alexandrines. Saurin omitted the last scenes of Acts I, III, V, and almost completely rearranged the contents of Act II. He had his third act take place at Belmont, though in the English play this act, like Acts I and II, seems to describe incidents that occur at Palermo. He added the threat that Constance might marry the Roi des Romains and omitted the proposal that the heroine should retire to a convent, as well as other details.

That Saurin knew Lesage is shown by his following him in calling the heroine Blanche, whereas Thomson had preferred Sigismunda; also by a reference to Roger not found in Thomson's play. The hero's name must have been taken from the history of the Normans, as it is given him neither by Lesage nor by Thomson. Even when an idea comes from the English author, Saurin's expression of it may be more effective, as in the following instance:

> . . . Gone to that awful State
> Where kings the crown wear only of their virtues. (I, 2)

> . . . il est passé dans ce monde terrible
> Où des foibles humains le juge incorruptible
> Voit frémir à ses pieds nos maîtres abattus,
> Sans garde, et protégés de leurs seules vertus. (I, 2)

The plot,[80] however, closely resembles Thomson's. The subject of love

---

[78] Cf. Miss Cobb, *op. cit.*, pp. 126 and 206. The preface appeared in 1772. The numbers of the *Mercure* containing the translation are those of January and February, 1761.

[79] Paris, S. Jorry, 1764, 12°. Republished, The Hague, 1764; Paris, veuve Duchesne, 1772 and 1783; Paris, Belin, 1788; in Petitot's *Répertoire*, 1803 and 1817; in *Auteurs du second ordre*, 1808; and in the *Répertoires* of 1813, 1818, 1821, 1825. Italian translations were published at Venice in 1778 and in 1798.

[80] Guillaume le Cruel had put to death his older brother, Mainfroi, had reigned for two years, and had left the throne of Sicily to his son, who is dying when the play begins. Mainfroi's son, the dying king's first cousin, has been brought up as the comte de Guiscard on the estate of Siffredi, the chancellor. His identity is known only to the king and to Siffredi, whose daughter, Blanche, has promised to marry him. When the king dies, his will makes known the fact that Guiscard is to succeed him, but only on condition that he marry Constance, daughter of Guillaume le Cruel. If he refuses to do so, the princess will marry the Roi des Romains, who will in that case rule over Sicily. Fearing that there will be a civil war unless Guiscard marries Constance, Siffredi tells the prince that he is the heir to the throne and that the marriage must take place as directed in the will. Guiscard refuses and gives Blanche a blank with his signature, expecting her father to write in both her name and the promise of marriage. Siffredi, however, writes the name of Constance and in the presence of both women shows the document to the senate. Guiscard's supposed decision is applauded, but he adjourns the meeting of the senate and swears to Siffredi that he will remain faithful to Blanche. The chancellor

and death in the charmed environment of Sicily under Norman rule was one to stir the imagination of a Romanticist, but it also permitted classical treatment with the small cast it required and the moral problems that the leading characters have to face. Old Siffredi, presented as a wise statesman who loves both his daughter and the prince he has brought up, has the problem of choosing between their happiness and what he believes to be the good of the state. He solves it by hurrying his daughter into marriage with a man she does not love and by stooping to what is the moral equivalent of forgery. Osmont is not a villain, but one who deludes himself with the idea that he can win Blanche's affections after he marries her and who avenges himself when he discovers what he considers to be her treachery. The chief emphasis is laid upon the lovers, upon Guiscard, who, though desiring to be faithful to both the state and Blanche, allows himself to be tricked, then revolts against the consequences of his thoughtlessness; and upon the heroine, a victim partly of pique, partly of obedience to her father, one who seeks to remain faithful to the husband that has been thrust upon her despite the demands of the prince she loves. Mlle Clairon knew no rôle that she preferred to play:

En jouant Blanche, je restais toujours moi: . . . c'est à la nature seule qu'il faut demander les nuances de la candeur, la teinte fraîche des premières sensations d'une jeunesse pure, la touchante et noble simplicité qui n'émane que de l'âme.[81]

Saurin was bold enough to violate the unity of place, shifting the scene from Palermo to Belmont. The respect shown by both Thomson and himself for the unity of time crowded too many events into less than twenty-four hours and violated Catholic practice [82] by the assumption that a marriage could be arranged and celebrated within a few hours. The action is unified, but too much of it takes place behind the scenes. The meeting

removes his daughter to his estate, Belmont, a few miles from Palermo, and there marries her to Count Osmont, constable of the realm. Blanche yields because she believes that Guiscard has deserted her and because she fears that her refusal may cause her father's death. Her attendant brings her a letter from Guiscard assuring her of his fidelity. Soon he appears, only to learn that she is married. Their interview is interrupted by Osmont, who is accused of deception and arrested by Guiscard. Siffredi persuades the latter to allow Osmont to be released at dawn, but the warden permits him to leave during the night. Osmont hastens to Palermo, starts a movement to give the throne to Constance, returns to Belmont, and places his friends around the house with the intention of abducting Blanche. Meanwhile Guiscard enters by a secret passage, urges her to follow him, and, when she refuses, draws his sword and threatens to kill himself. She begs him rather to kill her. He falls at her feet. Osmont discovers them, attacks Guiscard, and is wounded, but, before he dies, he strikes Blanche with his sword. She lives long enough to beg Guiscard to spare her father and to ask Siffredi to console Guiscard, who tries to kill himself, but who is disarmed.

[81] *Mémoires*, Paris, 1822, pp. 330-1. Her rival, Mlle Dumesnil, retorted sourly in her own *Mémoires* (Paris, 1823, pp. 186-90) that la Clairon was not at all suited by nature to this rôle.

[82] Nothing is said, moreover, about the dispensation required for the marriage of Guiscard and Constance, his first cousin.

of the senate would have been effective. Saurin should have shown, as Thomson did, the scene between the hero and heroine when he presents her with the paper and his signature. This omission has the unfortunate result that Blanche and Guiscard meet on the stage for the first time in the third scene of Act IV. They are together, indeed, only in three scenes of this act and in three of the fifth, too few for a play in which their love is the main concern.

The tragedy supplies a date in regard to the *bienséances*. Murder on the stage had been seen in tragedies by Gresset, by La Place, and by Saurin himself, but each time it was one of which the audience approved. The fatal wounding of Osmont is not very different, especially as it seemed for a moment that it might result in the lovers' happiness, but the murder of Blanche before our eyes exemplifies the kind of violence against which Corneille had protested, the killing on the stage of a person with whom we sympathize. In this case English influence was helping to abolish a cherished classical principle.

But Saurin did not follow Thomson in his insistence upon pointing a moral. At the end of his play the Englishman has Siffredi address directly to the spectators verses advising them not to imitate him in doing evil that good may come of it, whereas Saurin merely slips a brief comment to this effect into the end of Siffredi's monologue at the beginning of Act V. Unfortunately neither author was equipped with a sufficiently rich vocabulary or a sufficiently vivid style to do justice to the subject.

Saurin read the first act of his tragedy at a public meeting of the French Academy on Aug. 25, 1762. According to Bachaumont,[83] his declamatory reading was greeted with laughter and hoots, but this reception did not deter the actors from giving the play on Sept. 26, 1763, when Le Kain played Guiscard; la Clairon, Blanche; Bellecour, Osmont; Brizard, Siffredi.[84] The actors had gone to the " cabinet des estampes " to learn what kind of costume was worn in Sicily at the time represented, but, finding it not sufficiently picturesque, they had modernized it. Bachaumont thought that la Clairon did not play as well as usual, though she was said to have taken lessons from Garrick in regard to her rôle, but that Bellecour showed great dexterity in stabbing Blanche while he was lying on the floor. He regretted the omission of Constance, considered the tragedy vicious in its characters and its texture, and was shocked by the author's putting in his first act a scene of recognition.

[83] *Mémoires secrets*, I, 119, 277-82.
[84] Cf. *ibid.*; Grimm in *Cor.*, V, 395-9; and *Mémoires de Lekain*, Paris, 1801, p. 57. Mlle Clairon (*Mémoires*, p. 331) indicates that Molé took one of the chief rôles, but she must have been thinking of the fourth performance, Jan. 23, 1764, when the *Mercure* indicates that Molé played Osmont. The journalist thought that he

Grimm reported that Garrick attended the first performance and that the English in the audience said that the play held their interest much less than Thomson's, in which "Blanche est couchée lorsque Guiscard entre dans son appartement pendant la nuit," but this method of presentation must have been invented by the English actors, for the text of *Tancred and Sigismunda* says nothing about it. Grimm was himself sufficiently pleased with the subject to declare that the tragedy might have been the best of French plays if Saurin had had the genius of Racine and the warmth and passion of Voltaire. Unfortunately the author had "ni force, ni vérité, ni sentiment, ni logique, ni pathétique. Son style est en général plat, et sa pièce mal écrite." Yet he admired a few verses and held that the play was damaged by the acting. He blamed especially la Clairon's method of emphasizing almost every syllable, so that the weakness of the verses became apparent.

Le Kain considered two of the scenes in which he played very dramatic, one with Siffredi in Act II, the other with Blanche in Act IV. Mlle Clairon expected brilliant success for the play, but she was disappointed. She was told that love, purity, and duty were out of date. Collé [85] reported that the first performance had a cold reception, but that public response was better at the second, still better at the third. By Jan. 23 the last two acts had been improved, but the play still lacked warmth and probability. He objected to the author's representing as a tragic error a hasty action on the part of the heroine. Voltaire [86] heard from Mme Du Deffand that the tragedy "tombait à plat." La Harpe [87] admired Acts I-III, but he condemned the others because Osmont is unjustly arrested and because we are not moved by his death. Unlike Voltaire, he referred to the success of the play, which he attributed to the sympathy excited by the heroine in the earlier acts. Though he did not care for Saurin's style, he cited several verses as effective.

Petitot praised the exposition, free from long narrations, and the love scenes, but he considered it illogical for intelligent and highminded Siffredi to allow the hero and heroine to grow up together and for him to employ the "blanc-seing"; also for virtuous Blanche to read Guiscard's note after her marriage. He also criticized Saurin for crowding the events. A more modern critic would lay less stress upon apparent inconsistencies in conduct, but he would not give the author much credit for a play that owes so much to an English tragedy and its source in Lesage. The actors did not count

and Le Kain should have exchanged rôles, a suggestion that brought an indignant reply from Le Kain.

[85] *Op. cit.*, III, 58-9, 79.
[86] Moland, XLII, 584, letter of Sept. 30.
[87] *Op. cit.*, XIII, 229-32.

much upon its popularity. They played it nine times, from Sept. 26, 1763, to Feb. 4, 1764, then occasionally down to 1786, but only eighteen times in all at the Comédie Française.[88] According to Petitot, it had a warmer reception in the provinces than at Paris.

The pathos of this tragedy, the fact that it had its source in an English play, and growing French interest in "drames" probably induced Saurin to adopt Diderot's suggestion that he make an adaptation of Edward Moore's *Gamester,* a sentimental and moralistic middle-class tragedy, acted at London in 1753. Diderot had himself translated it into French somewhat freely, but his work was not published till long after his death, as a more faithful translation by Bruté de Loirelle had been printed in 1762. He is said, however, to have shown his manuscript to his friend Saurin.[89]

The latter entitled his play BÉVERLEI, "tragédie bourgeoise imitée de l'anglois." [90] In his dedication he referred to the tears shed over his tragedy and the appreciation of the spectators, who, he thought, wanted to encourage the new *genre,* inferior to the heroic play, but having beauties of its own:

La tragédie bourgeoise est un champ nouveau qui, cultivé par des mains plus habiles que les miennes, pourroit fournir quelques moissons heureuses: je dis quelques moissons, car ce genre se trouve resserré entre deux écueils presque inévitables, la basse scélératesse et le romanesque outré. . . . On s'est trop hâté de poser les bornes de l'art. Est-ce une tragédie, est-ce une comédie que *le Philosophe sans le savoir?* je n'en sais rien; mais je sais que c'est un drame très beau et très original.

Saurin kept most of Moore's characters and situations, but Bates and Dawson no longer appear on the stage. Instead of inheriting from an uncle, the protagonist receives a large sum of money from Cadix. The plan to murder Lewson is left out. The villain is killed by one of his henchmen. Act IV is made more spectacular by the arrival of the gambler's wife with a lantern and by the fact that the gambler's arrest is acted, not merely related. The most striking addition is that of the gambler's child, Tomi, suggested by Prévost's novel, *Clèveland,* as Grimm points out.[91] On the whole, Saurin added to the horror of Moore's play and to its spectacular

[88] On Nov. 15, 1768, it was given at the home of the duc de Duras to entertain the King of Denmark. Though la Clairon had left the troupe, she then took the part of Blanche.

[89] Cf. Gaiffe, *op. cit.,* pp. 53-4. He states that Diderot's manuscript was published in 1819. It is reproduced in the Assézat et Tourneux edition, VII (1875), 413-525.

[90] Paris, veuve Duchesne, 1768, 8°. Dedicated to the duc d'Orléans. Republished, Geneva, Pellet, 1768; Paris, Belin, 1788; in Petitot's *Répertoire,* 1804; in *Auteurs du second ordre,* 1810; in Saurin's *Œuvres choisies,* Paris, Didot, 1812; by Touquet in 1821; and in the *Répertoires* of 1823, 1824, and 1825. A Spanish translation was acted in 1801; cf. Ada M. Coe, *op. cit.,* p. 28.

[91] Cf. *Cor.,* VIII, 79. He does not indicate where in this four-volume novel the passage occurs. It is found in Book VI (*Œuvres choisies de Prévost,* Paris, 1810, V, 441-3). Saurin kept one of the two boys in *Clèveland,* altered his name from Thoms to Tomi, and made some changes in the situation, but he reproduced the main facts: the father's resolve to free the boy from the woes of life, the child's terror, the appeal to paternal affection, and the abandonment of the projected murder.

elements. He kept the first act much as it is in the original, but he made distinct omissions, additions, and alterations in the other acts and at times changed the order of the scenes.[92]

Béverlei, who is said to possess much charm, though the rôle does not show it, is presented as in the English play. His hopeless love of the game blinds him to his wife's affection, his duty to his son, and his financial obligations to his sister. The only solution of his problem seems to be suicide. Reformation, though Saurin ultimately offered it, would have been unconvincing. His wife's infatuation leads her to excuse his conduct and give him her last resources, whatever effect her action may have upon her child. Unlike her, Henriette is intelligent and helpful, quite deserving Leuson, her admirable and energetic lover. The villain, Stukéli, personifies

---

[92] Béverlei's passion for gambling and the treachery of Stukéli have reduced his family to poverty. Most of the furniture has been sold, but his wife still has her diamonds and there is hope of money from an investment at Cadix. His wife is distressed by her husband's conduct, but she finds an excuse for everything he does. His sister, Henriette, reproaches him, but she postpones her marriage to Leuson in order to help her sister-in-law and her nephew, Tomi. When the play begins, it is 8:30 A. M., but Béverlei has not come home. Jarvis, who has been dismissed after many years of service, offers to work for his former master without pay. He is sent to bring him home from "chez Vilson." Tomi is told to kiss his father when he sees him. Stukéli hints that Béverlei's wife may have cause for jealousy. He admits in a monologue that before her marriage she had disdained his love, boasts that he has now ruined his rival, and hopes to win his wife. Leuson accuses him of using illegal methods to get Béverlei's money and tells Henriette that he hopes soon to have definite proof of it. In Act II the scene changes from Béverlei's parlor to a street near his house, where we see him, remorseful and showing the effects of having gambled all night. Jarvis begs him to return to his wife. Stukéli, claiming that he has been ruined by his loans to Béverlei, fears that he will be imprisoned unless his friend rescues him by selling his wife's diamonds. Béverlei, who admits that he has just lost his sister's fortune, at first refuses, but he soon yields. When Henriette asks him for her securities, he puts her off. A letter is brought from Stukéli announcing his intention of leaving the country. Béverlei, who thinks he has ruined his friend, threatens to go with him till his wife gives him her diamonds on condition he will gamble no more. In Act III Stukéli informs us that the diamonds have gone as well as money Béverlei has borrowed. He pretends to Béverlei's wife that her husband has given the diamonds to his mistress. She dismisses him, but she is deeply affected by the interview. Leuson persuades Henriette to marry him next day, then tells her that her fortune has been lost. Bates, Stukéli's comrade, has given him this information and has promised more. Béverlei announces that he has given up gambling and has received from Cadix 300,000 francs, a sum that will pay his debts and enable him to lead a peaceful life, but Stukéli, though advising him to avoid the gambling establishment, soon has him there. Act IV takes place at night. Béverlei has lost everything and quarrels with Leuson, whose calmness alone prevents a duel. Béverlei thinks of suicide, but Jarvis deprives him of his sword. He refuses to go home and lies down in the street. There his wife finds him by the light of a lantern and the police arrest him. Act V takes place in the debtors' prison. Tomi sleeps in an armchair. Jarvis deplores his master's condition. He is sent to bring Leuson. When Béverlei is alone, he takes poison. Believing life to be misery, he lifts his dagger to stab Tomi, but the boy awakes and begs for mercy. Béverlei throws away the dagger, and his wife comforts the boy. Leuson brings word that Stukéli has been killed by another gambler, that certain securities, entrusted to him by Béverlei, have been recovered, and that Béverlei is now free. All would have been well, but for the poison. Béverlei admits that he has taken it, holds himself up as a warning to his son, takes his wife's hand, and dies. Grimm (Cor., IX, 226) wrote on Jan. 1, 1771, that Saurin had composed a happy ending for the play, with the suicide prevented and a satisfactory amount of money rescued. This ending might be substituted if the actors so desired.

the "basse scélératesse" to which Saurin refers in his dedication. His cleverness in handling Béverlei produces the best part of the dialogue. The unselfish old servant and the child are added in order to move us to tears.

The theme is not purely one of gambling, for Béverlei is never allowed to win, and he is a victim, not of chance, but of crooks. The moral is not necessarily that gambling should be avoided, but that one should not gamble with dishonest men. Béverlei is consequently much less the typical gambler than is the protagonist of Regnard's *Joueur*. The author's departure from classical standards is shown here rather than in the tone, which is never comic, but it appears also in the selection for a tragedy of bourgeois characters, in the author's attitude in regard to the unities, and in the verse.[93]

Though the events take place within twenty-four hours, and though fewer places are represented than in *The Gamester*, there are three distinct localities in London shown: Béverlei's parlor, the street, and the prison; while Stukéli's death, caused by outside intervention, violates the unity of action. The "vers libres" in which the tragedy is written are composed mainly of alexandrines and of 8-syllable lines, but there are also verses of ten syllables. The rime scheme is varied, but there seems to be little connection between the sprightly form and the gloomy thoughts and emotions that are expressed. The play would have profited if Saurin had employed prose or the alexandrine couplet.

Yet the sentimental appeal of the play and the novelty of the subject, if not that of the form, brought considerable success. On June 21, 1767, the tragedy was acted by lords and ladies on the stage of the duc d'Orléans at Villers-Cotterets.[94] On Dec. 15 Bachaumont[95] refers to a performance at the home of the duc de Noailles at Saint-Germain. On May 7, 1768, the play was given at the Comédie Française, where the first run was interrupted after thirteen productions by the death of Queen Maria Leczinska. Molé played Béverlei; la Doligny, his wife; la Préville, Henriette; Préville, Stukéli; Bellecour, Leuson; Brizard, Jarvis. Grimm declares that a deep impression was produced when Béverlei took poison and when he threatened his son, and that Stukéli was received throughout the play with hoots that did credit to the realistic acting and to the morality of the audience. The play was acted also on Nov. 16 and 27, making for the year fifteen performances, at only one of which did the spectators who paid admission number less than a thousand. The actors proposed to give it at Fontaine-

---

[93] Perhaps, too, in the description of conjugal bliss (II, 1). Gaiffe (*op. cit.*, p. 484) declares that the *Journal de Trévoux* would not have pardoned the passage if it had not been taken from Moore.

[94] Cf. Grimm in *Cor.*, VII, 364-5, VIII, 74-83, and Collé, *op. cit.*, III, 315-7, 379-81. The latter states that the play was at first called *le Joueur*.

[95] *Mémoires secrets*, III, 270.

bleau, but Louis XV preferred to witness a less melancholy production.[96] It was performed seven times in 1769, April 4 to 22, and, because it was, according to the *Registres*, asked for by " des personnes de Distinction," twice in February, 1770. It remained in the repertory until 1819. Its seventy-five productions at the Comédie Française make it the one of Saurin's tragedies that was most frequently given there.

Collé thought his friend had improved upon the English original, but he did not consider gambling a proper subject for tragedy. At so realistic a spectacle, one does not weep, " on étouffe." Grimm held that there are many unnecessary comings and goings in the early acts, that the intrigue is weak, the tragedy arid. He disliked the form of verse employed. Béverlei was not made sufficiently attractive. His moral disintegration would have been more interesting than the poison and the dagger of the last act. His wife should not have been so foolish as to leave in his hands the money from Spain, nor should Jarvis, whom Grimm considers the most touching character in the play, have given his money to his master when he knew he would lose it.[97]

Diderot, according to Grimm, suggested to Saurin that he should make Stukéli a passionate lover, who, when repelled by Mme Béverlei, would throw at her feet the portfolio containing her husband's money and then be killed in a duel with Leuson. Grimm adds that all Saurin derived from this advice was Stukéli's hope of winning Mme Béverlei, with whom in Moore's play he is not in love, but this statement is incorrect, for in *The Gamester*, I, 2, Stukely says, " I love his wife. . . . If jealousy should weaken her affections, want may corrupt her virtue." Saurin merely reproduced what he found in the English play. There is no evidence that in this matter he received any assistance from Diderot.[98]

Bachaumont [99] thought the play deserved the great success it achieved. He admired the simplicity of the subject, the rapidity of the action, the portrayal of the gambler and his wife. He stated that originally Béverlei threatened his child twice and horrified the audience to such an extent that he subsequently lifted his dagger over him only once and immediately " s'attendrit tout-à-coup, l'embrasse, & c." On Jan. 13, 1768, Voltaire [100] asked Saurin for a copy of the play. He thanked him on July 1 and said

[96] Cf. Gaiffe, *op. cit.*, p. 128.

[97] He does not actually give him his money, but he comes near doing so in II, 2, and again in IV, 7. The text may have been different when Grimm saw the play acted.

[98] Grimm also tells the story of a neurotic Englishman, sent by his physician to Paris in order that he might recover from despondency. When he went to the theater, he saw *Béverlei*, concluded that life was worth no more at Paris than at London, and hanged himself.

[99] *Mémoires secrets*, IV, 27-9.

[100] Moland, XLV, 489, XLVI, 71.

that he had been moved for a whole hour while he read it. He was surprised that Mme Béverlei had received money from Cadix, for he had recently lost there 20,000 écus. Only Voltaire could discover a joke while reading Saurin's tragedy.

La Harpe [101] was remarkably gracious about the play, possibly because he disliked Diderot. He found *Béverlei* better planned and written than *le Père de famille* and held that it presented a striking and truthful picture of the effects produced by gambling. He thought it strange, however, that Mme Béverlei should sell her furniture before her diamonds, he was disgusted by Stukéli, and he was sure that Saurin went too far in having Béverlei start to kill his boy. Such an act weakens the moral lesson, for gambling does not produce such inhumanity. He concluded that, while the play cannot be compared with Regnard's *Joueur*, it does its author credit.

Petitot also contrasted the play unfavorably with the *Joueur*. He thought that its success indicated the decay of French society, for the seventeenth century would have reserved its pity for men of moral stamina, whereas in the eighteenth men were " plus avides de grands événements que difficiles sur les causes qui les produisent." However, he republished the tragedy, praised the plot, admired Henriette and Leuson, and admitted that the child appealed to the audience. His objections concerned the three chief characters. Béverlei had been too good a husband and father to become a gambler and threaten his child. His wife might have endured poverty, but not the disorder indicated by the stage direction of Act I, which calls for a " salon mal meublé, et dont les murs sont presque nus, avec des restes de dorure." [102] Stukéli's love for her is unconvincing in France, though there may be persons in England who like this " scélérat froid."

With this play Saurin's contributions to tragedy end. He sought variety in subject-matter, location, and appeal, borrowing from French novelists, ancient historians, and English dramatists, laying his scenes in Egypt, ancient Italy, medieval Sicily, and London, writing of court intrigue, servile rebellion, and middle-class life, seeking to excite admiration, terror, and pity. He did not hesitate to use novel methods, admitting on the stage the murder of a woman with whom we sympathize, violating the unity of place, writing in free verse as well as in alexandrine couplets. He succeeded in producing effective scenes, but his methods of bringing them about and his style were not sufficiently satisfying to keep his plays long before the public. He may be ranked ahead of Marmontel, but after Voltaire and Crébillon, even after de Belloy and Lemierre.

---

[101] *Op. cit.*, XIII, 403-5.

[102] Yet Becque was to use this type of furnishing in the last act of *les Corbeaux* when he sought to indicate respectability reduced to poverty.